Expositions on the Book of Psalms: Psalms I - LXXII

St. Augustine of Hippo

Edited by
Paul A. Böer, Sr.

Veritatis Splendor Publications

et cognoscetis veritatem et veritas liberabit vos

AD MAJOREM DEI GLORIAM

St. Augustine of Hippo

A SELECT LIBRARY

OF THE

NICENE AND POST-NICENE FATHERS

OF

THE CHRISTIAN CHURCH.

EDITED BY

PHILIP SCHAFF, D.D., LL.D.,

PROFESSOR IN THE UNION THEOLOGICAL SEMINARY, NEW YORK.

IN CONNECTION WITH A NUMBER OF PATRISTIC SCHOLARS OF EUROPE AND

AMERICA.

VOLUME VIII

ST. AUGUSTIN:

EXPOSITIONS ON THE BOOK OF PSALMS

TRANSLATED, WITH NOTES AND INDICES

Augustine's *Expositions of the Psalms* are the longest of his works and the richest in spiritual doctrine; they form the only complete treatise on the Psalms in Patristic literature. They do not present a historical-philological interpretation, but rather a theological-spiritual one based on the doctrine of the *Christus totus:* the Psalms resound with the voice of Christ, of the church, and of the individual faithful. The content treats all the important themes of Christian doctrine and includes philosophy, theology, spiritual doctrine, and mysticism. Augustine has particularly developed the themes of the mystical body, of the two cities, and of the ascent of the soul to God for which the lyric tone of the Psalms provide the wings.

The composition of this work extended over a period of time from 392 (1-32) until 416 or, according to some, up until 422 for Psalm 118. The work can be divided into two classes: expositions which were dictated and expositions which were preached. The dictated expositions can be further subdivided into three groups: brief exegetical notes (Psalms 1-31, with a few exceptions), longer expositions (67, 71, 77 and others) and homilies intended to be read to the people. All the rest are sermons delivered before the people in various cities, mostly Carthage. The text on which the commentary is based is a Latin translation of the Septuagint revised by Augustine himself.

CONTENTS

PSALMS 1-41: THE 1ST BOOK OF THE PSALMS

PSALM I.

1. "Blessed is the man that hath not gone away in the counsel of the ungodly" (ver. 1). This is to be understood of our Lord Jesus Christ, the Lord Man. "Blessed is the man that hath not gone away in the counsel of the ungodly," as "the man of earth did," who consented to his wife deceived by the serpent, to the transgressing the commandment of God. "Nor stood in the way of sinners." For He came indeed in the way of sinners, by being born as sinners are; but He "stood" not therein, for that the enticements of the world held Him not. And hath not sat in the seat of pestilence." He willed not an earthly kingdom, with pride, which is well taken for "the seat of pestilence;" for that there is hardly any one who is free from the love of rule, and craves not human glory. For a "pestilence" is disease widely spread, and involving all or nearly all. Yet "the seat of pestilence" may be more appropriately understood of hurtful doctrine; "whose word spreadeth as a canker." The order too of the words must be considered: "went away, stood, sat." For he "went away," when he drew back from God. He "stood," when he took pleasure in sin. He "sat," when, confirmed in his pride, he could not go back, unless set free by Him, who neither "hath gone away in the counsel of the ungodly, nor stood in the way of sinners, nor sat in the seat of pestilence.

2. "But his delight is in the law of the Lord, and in His law will he meditate by day and by night (ver. 2). The law is not made for a righteous man," 4 says the Apostle. But it is one thing to be in the law, another under the law. Whoso is in the law, acteth according to the law; whoso is under the law, is acted upon according to the law: the one therefore is free, the other a slave. Again, the law, which is written and imposed upon the servant, is one thing; the law, which is mentally discerned by him who needeth not its "letter," is another thing. "He will meditate by day and by night," is to be understood either as without ceasing; or "by day" in joy," by night" in tribulations. For it is said, "Abraham saw my day, and was glad:" and of tribulation it is said, "my reins also have instructed me, even unto the night."

3. "And he shall be like a tree planted hard by the running streams of waters" (ver. 3); that is either Very "Wisdom," which vouchsafed to assume man's nature for our salvation; that as man He might be "the tree planted hard by the running streams of waters;" for in this sense can that too be taken which is said in another Psalm, "the river of God is full of water." Or by the Holy Ghost, of whom it is said, "He shall baptize you in the Holy Ghost;" and again, "If any man thirst, let

him come unto Me, and drink;" and again, "If thou knewest the gift of God, and who it is that asketh water of thee, thou wouldest have asked of Him, and He would have given thee living water, of which whoso drinketh shall never thirst, but it shall be made in him a well of water springing up into everlasting life." Or, "by the running streams of waters" may be by the sins of the people, because first the waters are called "peoples" in the Apocalypse; and again, by "running stream" is not unreasonably understood "fall," which hath relation to sin. That "tree" then, that is, our Lord, from the running streams of water, that is, from the sinful people's drawing them by the way into the roots of His discipline, will "bring forth fruit," that is, will establish Churches; "in His season," that is, after He hath been glorified by His Resurrection and Ascension into heaven. For then, by the sending of the Holy Ghost to the Apostles, and by the confirming of their faith in Him, and their mission to the world, He made the Churches to "bring forth fruit." "His leaf also shall not fall," that is, His Word shall not be in vain. For, "all flesh is grass, and the glory of man as the flower of grass; the grass withereth, and the flower falleth, but the word of the Lord abideth for ever. And whatsoever He doeth shall prosper" that is, whatsoever that tree shall bear; which all must be taken of fruit and leaves, that is, deeds and words.

4. "The ungodly are not so," they are not so, "but are like the dust which the wind casteth forth from the face of the earth" (ver. 4). "The earth" is here to be taken as that stedfastness in God, with a view to which it is said, "The Lord is the portion of mine inheritance, yea, I have a goodly heritage." With a view to this it is said, "Wait on the Lord and keep His ways, and He shall exalt thee to inherit the earth." With a view to this it is said, "Blessed are the meek, for they shall inherit the earth." A comparison too is derived hence, for as this visible earth supports and contains the outer man, so that earth invisible the inner man. "From the face of" which "earth the wind casteth forth the ungodly," that is, pride, in that it puffeth him up. On his guard against which he, who was inebriated by the richness of the house of the Lord, and drunken of the torrent stream of its pleasures, saith, "Let not the foot of pride come against me." From this earth pride cast forth him who said, "I will place my seat in the north, and I will be like the Most High." From the face of the earth it cast forth him also who, after that he had consented and tasted of the forbidden tree that he might be as God, hid himself from the Face of God. That his earth has reference to the inner man, and that man is cast forth thence by pride, may be particularly seen in that which is written, "Why is earth and ashes proud? Because, in his life, he cast forth his bowels." For, whence he hath been cast forth, he is not unreasonably said to have cast forth himself.

5. "Therefore the ungodly rise not in the judgment" (ver. 5): "therefore," namely, because "as dust they are cast forth from the face of the earth." And well did he say that this should be taken away from them, which in their pride they court, namely, that they may judge; so that this same idea is more clearly expressed in the following sentence, "nor sinners in the counsel of the righteous." For it is usual for what goes before, to be thus repeated more clearly. So that by "sinners" should be understood the "ungodly;" what is before "in the judgment," should be here "in the counsel of the righteous." Or if indeed the ungodly are one thing, and sinners another, so that although every ungodly man is a sinner, yet every sinner is not ungodly; "The ungodly rise not in the judgment," that is, they shall rise indeed, but not that they should be judged, for they are already appointed to most certain punishment. But "sinners" do not rise "in counsel of the just" that is that the may, judge, but peradventure that they may be judged; so as of these it were said, "The fire shall try every man's work of what sort it is. If any man's work abide, he shall receive a reward. If any man's work shall be burned, he shall then suffer loss: but he himself shall be saved; yet so as by fire."

6. "For the Lord knoweth the way of the righteous" (ver. 6). As it is said, medicine knows health, but knows not disease, and yet disease is recognised by the art of medicine. In like manner can it be said that "the Lord knoweth the way of the righteous," but the way of the ungodly He knoweth not. Not that the Lord is ignorant of anything, and yet He says to sinners, "I never knew you." "But the way of the ungodly shall perish;" is the same as if it were said, the way of the ungodly the Lord knoweth not. But it is expressed more plainly that this should be not to be known of the Lord, namely, to "perish;" and this to be known of the Lord, namely, to "abide;" so as that to be should appertain to the knowledge of God, but to His not knowing not to be. For the Lord saith, "I AM that I AM," and, "I AM hath sent me."

PSALM II.

1. "Why do the heathen rage, and the people meditate vain things?" (ver. 1). "The kings of the earth have stood up, and the rulers taken counsel together, against the Lord, and against His Christ" (ver. 2). It is said, "why?" as if it were said, in vain. For what they wished, namely, Christ's destruction, they accomplished not; for this is spoken of our Lord's persecutors, of whom also mention is made in the Acts of the Apostles.

2. "Let us break their bonds asunder, and cast away their yoke from us" (ver. 3). Although it admits of another acceptation, yet is it more fitly understood as in the person of those who are said to "meditate vain things." So that "let us break their bonds asunder, and cast away their yoke from us," may be, let us do our endeavour, that the Christian religion do not bind us, nor be imposed upon us.

3. "He that dwelleth in the heavens shall laugh them to scorn, and the Lord shall have them in derision" (ver. 4). The sentence is repeated; for "He who dwelleth in the heavens," is afterwards put, "the Lord;" and for "shall laugh them to scorn," is afterwards put, "shall have them in derision." Nothing of this however must be taken in a carnal sort, as if God either laugheth with cheek, or derideth with nostril; but it is to be understood of that power which He giveth to His saints, that they seeing things to come, namely, that the Name and rule of Christ is to pervade posterity and possess all nations, should understand that those men "meditate a vain thing." For this power whereby these things are foreknown is God's "laughter" and "derision." "He that dwelleth in the heavens shall laugh them to scorn." If by "heavens" we understand holy souls, by these God, as foreknowing what is to come, will "laugh them to scorn, and have them in derision."

4. "Then He shall speak unto them in His wrath, and vex them in His sore displeasure" (ver. 5). For showing more clearly how He will "speak unto them," he added, He will "vex them;" so that "in His wrath," is, "in His sore displeasure." But by the "wrath and sore displeasure" of the Lord God must not be understood any mental perturbation; but the might whereby He most justly avengeth, by the subjection of all creation to His service. For that is to be observed and remembered which is written in the Wisdom of Solomon, "But Thou, Lord of power, judgest with tranquillity, and with great favour orderest us." The "wrath" of God then is an emotion which is produced in the soul which knoweth the law of God, when it sees this same law transgressed by the sinner. For by this emotion of righteous souls many things are avenged. Although the "wrath" of God can be well

understood of that darkening of the mind, which overtakes those who transgress the law of God.

5. "Yet am I set by Him as King upon Sion, His holy hill, preaching His decree" (ver. 6). This is clearly spoken in the Person of the very Lord our Saviour Christ. But if Sion signify, as some interpret, beholding, we must not understand it of anything rather than of the Church, where daily is the desire raised of beholding the bright glory of God, according to that of the Apostle, "but we with open face beholding the glory of the Lord." Therefore the meaning of this is, Yet I am set by Him as King over His holy Church; which for its eminence and stability He calleth a mountain. "Yet I am set by Him as King." I, that is, whose "bands" they were meditating "to break asunder," and whose "yoke" to "cast away." "Preaching His decree." Who doth not see the meaning of this, seeing it is daily practised?

6. "The Lord hath said unto me, Thou art My Son, to-day have I begotten Thee" (ver. 7)., Although that day may also seem to be prophetically spoken of, on which Jesus Christ was born according to the flesh; and in eternity there is nothing past as if it had ceased to be, nor future as if it were not yet, but present only, since whatever is eternal, always is; yet as "today" intimates presentiality, a divine interpretation is given to that expression, "To-day have I begotten Thee," whereby the uncorrupt and Catholic faith proclaims the eternal generation of the power and Wisdom of God, who is the Only-begotten Son.

7. "Ask of Me, and I shall give Thee the nations for Thine inheritance" (ver. 8). This has at once a temporal sense with reference to the Manhood which He took on Himself, who offered up Himself as a Sacrifice in the stead of all sacrifices, who also maketh intercession for us; so that the words, "ask of Me," may be referred to all this temporal dispensation, which has been instituted for mankind, namely, that the "nations" should be joined to the Name of Christ, and so be redeemed from death, and possessed by God. "I shall give Thee the nations for Thine inheritance," which so possess them for their salvation, and to bear unto Thee spiritual fruit. "And the uttermost parts of the earth for Thy possession." The same repeated, "The uttermost parts of the earth," is put for "the nations;" but more clearly, that we might understand all the nations. And "Thy possession" stands for "Thine inheritance."

8. "Thou shalt rule them with a rod of iron," with inflexible justice, and "Thou shall break them like a potter's vessel" (ver. 9); hat is, "Thou shalt break" in them earthly lusts, and the filthy doings of the old man, and whatsoever hath been

derived and inured from the sinful clay. "And now understand, ye kings" (ver. 10). "And now;" that is, being now renewed, your covering of clay worn out, that is, the carnal vessels of error which belong to your past life, "now understand," ye who now are "kings;" that is, able now to govern all that is servile and brutish in you, able now too to fight, not as "they who beat the air, but chastening your bodies, and bringing them into subjection." "Be instructed, all ye who judge the earth." This again is a repetition; "Be instructed" is instead of "understand; and" ye who judge the earth instead of ye kings. For He signifies the spiritual by "those who judge the earth." For whatsoever we judge, is below us; and whatsoever is below the spiritual man, is with good reason called "the earth;" because it is defiled with earthly corruption.

9. "Serve the Lord with fear;" lest what is said, "Ye kings and judges of the earth," turn into pride: "And rejoice with trembling" (ver. 11). Very excellently is "rejoice" added, lest "serve the Lord with fear" should seem to tend to misery. But again, lest this same rejoicing should run on to unrestrained inconsiderateness, there is added "with trembling," that it might avail for a warning, and for the careful guarding of holiness. It can also be taken thus, "And now ye kings understand;" that is, And now that I am set as King, be ye not sad, kings of the earth, as if your excellency were taken from you, but rather "understand and be instructed." For it is expedient for you, that ye should be under Him, by whom understanding and instruction are given you. And this is expedient for you, that ye lord it not with rashness, but that ye "serve the Lord" of all "with fear," and "rejoice" in bliss most sure and most pure, with all caution and carefulness, lest ye fall therefrom into pride.

10. "Lay hold of discipline, lest at any time the Lord be angry, and ye perish from the righteous way" (ver. 12). This is the same as, "understand," and, "be instructed." For to understand and be instructed, this is to lay hold of discipline. Still in that it is said, "lay hold of," it is plainly enough intimated that there is some protection and defence against all things which might do hurt unless with so great carefulness it be laid hold of. "Lest at any time the Lord be angry," is expressed with a doubt, not as regards the vision of the prophet to whom it is certain, but as regards those who are warned; for they, to whom it is not openly revealed, are wont to think with doubt of the anger of God. This then they ought to say to themselves, let us "lay hold of discipline, lest at any time the Lord be angry, and we perish from the righteous way." Now, how "the Lord be angry" is to be taken, has been said above. And "ye perish from the righteous way." This is a great punishment, and dreaded by those who have had any perception of the sweetness

of righteousness; for he who perisheth from the way of righteousness, in much misery will wander through the ways of unrighteousness.

11. "When His anger shall be shortly kindled, blessed are all they who put their trust in Him;" that is, when the vengeance shall come which is prepared for the ungodly and for sinners, not only will it not light on those "who put their trust in" the Lord, but it will even avail for the foundation and exaltation of a kingdom for them. For he said not, "When His anger shall be shortly kindled," safe "are all they who put their trust in Him," as though they should have this only thereby, to be exempt from punishment; but he said, "blessed ;" in which there is the sum and accumulation of all good things. Now the meaning of "shortly" I suppose to be this, that it will be something sudden, whilst sinners will deem it far off and long to Come,

PSALM III.

A PSALM OF DAVID, WHEN HE FLED FROM THE FACE OF ABESSALON HIS SON.

1. The words, "I slept, and took rest; and rose, for the Lord will take me up," lead us to believe that this Psalm is to be understood as in the Person of Christ; for they sound more applicable to the Passion and Resurrection of our Lord, than to that history in which David's flight is described from the face of his rebellious son. And, since it is written of Christ's disciples, "The sons of the bridegroom fast not as long as the bridegroom is with them;" it is no wonder if by his undutiful son be here meant that undutiful disciple who betrayed Him. From whose face although it may be understood historically that He fled, when on his departure He withdrew with the rest to the mountain; yet in a spiritual sense, when the Son of God, that is the Power and Wisdom of God, abandoned the mind of Judas; when the Devil wholly occupied him; as it is written, "The Devil entered into his heart," may it be well understood that Christ fled from his face; not that Christ gave place to the Devil, but that on Christ's departure the Devil took possession. Which departure, I suppose, is called a flight in this Psalm, because of its quickness; which is indicated also by the word of our Lord, saying, "That thou doest, do quickly." So even in common conversation we say of anything that does not come to mind, it has fled from me; and of a man of much learning we say, nothing flies from him. Wherefore truth fled from the mind of Judas, when it ceased to enlighten him. But Absalom, as some interpret, in the Latin tongue signifies, Patris pax, a father's peace. And it may seem strange, whether in the history of the kings, when Absalom carried on war against his father; or in the history of the New Testament, when Judas was, the betrayer of our Lord; how "father's peace" can be understood. But both in the former place they who read carefully, see that David in that war was at peace with his son, who even with sore grief lamented his death, saying, "O Absalom, my son, would God I had died for thee!" And in the history of the New Testament by that so great and so wonderful forbearance of our Lord; in that He bore so long with him as if good, when He was not ignorant of his thoughts; in that He admitted him to the Supper in which He committed and delivered to His disciples the figure of His Body and Blood; finally, in that He received the kiss of peace at the very time of His betrayal; it is easily understood how Christ showed peace to. His betrayer, although he was laid waste by the intestine war of so abominable a device. And therefore is Absalom called "father's peace," because his father had the peace, which he had not.

2. "O Lord, how are they multiplied that trouble me!" (ver. 1). So multiplied indeed were they, that one even from the number of His disciples was not wanting, who was added to the number of His persecutors. "Many rise up against me; many say unto my soul, There is no salvation for him in his God" (ver. 2). It is clear that if they had had any idea that He would rise again, assuredly they would not have slain Him. To this end are those speeches, "Let Him come down from the cross, if He be the Son of God;" and again, "He saved others, Himself He cannot save." Therefore, neither would Judas have betrayed Him, if he had not been of the number of those who despised Christ, saying, "There is no salvation for Him in His God."

3. "But Thou, O Lord, art my taker." It is said to God in the nature of man, for the taking of man is, the Word made Flesh. "My glory." Even He calls God his glory, whom the Word of God so took, that God became one with Him. Let the proud learn, who unwillingly hear, when it is said to them, "For what hast thou that thou didst not receive? Now if thou didst receive it, why dost thou glory as if thou hadst not received it?" " And the lifter up of my head" (ver. 3). I think that this should be here taken of the human mind, which is not unreasonably called the head of the soul; which so inhered in, and in a sort coalesced with, the supereminent excellency of the Word taking man, that it was not laid aside by so great humiliation of the Passion.

4. "With my voice have I cried unto the Lord" (ver. 4); that is, not with the voice of the body, which is drawn out with the sound of the reverberation of the air; but with the voice of the heart, which to men speaks not, but with God sounds as a cry. By this voice Susanna was heard; and with this voice the Lord Himself commanded that prayer should be made in closets, that is, in the recesses of the heart noiselessly. Nor would one easily say that prayer is not made with this voice, if no sound of words is uttered from the body; since even when in silence we pray within the heart, if thoughts interpose alien from the mind of one praying, it cannot yet be said, "With my voice have I cried unto the Lord." Nor is this rightly said, save when the soul alone, taking to itself nothing of the flesh, and nothing of the aims of the flesh, in prayer, speaks to God, where He only hears. But even this is called a cry by reason of the strength of its intention. "And He heard me out of His holy mountain." We have the Lord Himself called a mountain by the Prophet, as it is written, "The stone that was cut out without hands grew to the size of a mountain." But this cannot be taken of His Person, unless peradventure He would speak thus, out of myself, as of His holy mountain He heard me, when He dwelt in me, that is, in this very mountain. But it is more plain and unembarrassed, if we understand that God out of His justice heard. For it was just that He should raise

again from the dead the Innocent who was slain, and to whom evil had been recompensed for good, and that He should render to the persecutor a meet reward, who repaid Him evil for good. For we read, "Thy justice is as the mountains of God."

5. "I slept, and took rest" (ver. 5). It may be not unsuitably remarked, that it is expressly said," I," to signify that of His own Will He underwent death, according to that, "Therefore doth My Father love Me, because I lay down My life, that I might take it again. No man taketh it from Me; I have power to lay it down, and I have power to take it again." Therefore, saith He, you have not taken Me as though against My will, and slain Me; but "I slept, and took rest; and rose, for the Lord will take me up." Scripture contains numberless instances of sleep being put for death; as the Apostle says, "I would not have you to be ignorant, brethren, concerning them which are asleep." Nor need we make any question why it is added, "took rest," seeing that it has already been said, "I slept." Repetitions of this kind are usual in Scripture, as we have pointed out many in the second Psalm. But some copies have, "I slept, and was cast into a deep sleep." And different copies express it differently, according to the possible renderings of the Greek words, egw` de` ekokoimh'thhn kai` hu'pnwsa. Unless perhaps sleeping may be taken of one dying, but sleep of one dead: so that sleeping may be the transition into sleep, as awakening is the transition into wakefulness. Let us not deem these repetitions in the sacred writings empty ornaments of speech. "I slept, and took rest," is therefore well understood as "I gave Myself up to My Passion, and death ensued." "And I rose, for the Lord will take Me up." This is the more to be remarked, how that in one sentence the Psalmist has used a verb of past and future time. For he has said, both "I rose," which is the past, and "will take Me up," which is the future; seeing that assuredly the rising again could not be without that taking up. But in prophecy the future is well joined to the past, whereby both are signified. Since things which are prophesied of as yet to come in reference to time are future; but in reference to the knowledge of those who prophesy they are already to be viewed as done. Verbs of the present tense are also mixed in, which shall be treated of in their proper place when they occur.

6. "I will not fear the thousands of people that surround me" (ver. 6). It is written in the Gospels how great a multitude stood around Him as He was suffering, and on the cross. "Arise, O Lord, save me, O my God" (ver. 7). It is not said to God, "Arise," as if asleep or lying down, but it is usual in holy Scripture to attribute to God what He doeth in us; not indeed universally, but where it can be done suitably; as when He is said to speak, when by His gift Prophets speak, and Apostles, or whatsoever messengers of the truth. Hence that text, "Would you

have proof of Christ, who speaketh in me?" For he doth not say, of Christ, by whose enlightening or order I speak; but he attributes at once the speaking itself to Him, by whose gift he spake.

7. "Since Thou hast smitten all who oppose me without a cause." It is not to be pointed as if it were one sentence, "Arise, O Lord, save me, O my God; since Thou hast smitten all who oppose me without a cause." For He did not therefore save Him, because He smote His enemies; but rather He being saved, He smote them. Therefore it belongs to what follows, so that the sense is this; "Since Thou hast smitten all who oppose me without a cause, Thou hast broken the teeth of the sinners;" that is, thereby hast Thou broken the teeth of the sinners, since Thou hast smitten all who oppose me. It is forsooth the punishment of the opposers, whereby. their teeth have been broken, that is, the words of sinners rending with their cursing the Son of God, brought to nought, as it were to dust; so that we may understand "teeth" thus, as words of cursing. Of which teeth the Apostle speaks, "If ye bite one another, take heed that ye be not consumed one of another." The teeth of sinners can also be taken as the chiefs of sinners; by whose authority each one is cut off from the fellowship of godly livers, and as it were incorporated with evil livers. To these teeth are opposed the Church's teeth, by whose authority believers are cut off from the error of the Gentiles and divers opinions, and are translated into that fellowship which is the body of Christ. With these teeth Peter was told to eat the animals when they bad been killed, that is, by killing in the Gentiles what they were, and changing them into what he was himself. Of these teeth too of the Church it is said, "Thy teeth are as a flock of shorn sheep, coming up from the bath, whereof every one beareth twins, and there is not one barren among them." These are they who prescribe rightly, and as they prescribe, live; who do what is written, "Let your works shine before men, that they may bless your Father which is in heaven." For moved by their authority, they believe God who speaketh and worketh through these men; and separated from the world, to which they were once conformed, they pass over into the members of the Church. And rightly therefore are they, through whom such things are done, called teeth like to shorn sheep; for they have laid aside the burdens of earthly cares, and coming up from the bath, from the washing away of the filth of the world by the Sacrament of Baptism, every one beareth twins. For they fulfil the two commandments, of which it is said, "On these two commandments hang all the Law and the Prophets;" loving God with all their heart, and with all their soul, and with all their mind, and their neighbour as themselves. "There is not one barren among them," for much fruit they render unto God. According to this sense then it is to be thus understood, "Thou hast broken the teeth of the sinners," that is, Thou hast brought the chiefs of the sinners to nought, by smiting all who oppose Me

without a cause. For the chiefs according to the Gospel history persecuted Him, whilst the lower people honoured Him.

8. "Salvation is of the Lord; and upon Thy people be Thy blessing" (ver. 8). In one sentence the Psalmist has enjoined men what to believe, and has prayed for believers. For when it is said, "Salvation is of the Lord," the words are addressed to men. Nor does it follow, "And upon Thy people" be" Thy blessing," in such wise as that the whole is spoken to men, but there is a change into prayer addressed to God Himself, for the very people to whom it was said, "Salvation is of the Lord." What else r then doth he say but this? Let no man presume on himself, seeing that it is of the Lord to save from the death of sin; for, "Wretched man that I am, who shall deliver me from the body of this death? The grace of God through Jesus Christ our Lord." But do Thou, O Lord, bless Thy people, who look for salvation from Thee.

9. This Psalm can be taken as in the Person of Christ another way; which is that whole Christ should speak? I mean by whole, with His body, of which He is the Head, according to the Apostle, who says, "Ye are the body of Christ, and the members." He therefore is the Head of this body; wherefore in another place be saith, "But doing the truth in love, we may increase in Him in all things, who is the Head, Christ, from whom the whole body is joined together and compacted. In the Prophet then at once, the Church, and her Head (the Church rounded amidst the storms of persecution throughout the whole world, which we know already to have come to pass), speaks, "O Lord, how are they multiplied that trouble me! many rise up against me;" wishing to exterminate the Christian name. "Many say unto my soul, There is no salvation for him in his God." For they would not otherwise hope that they could destroy the Church, branching out so very far and wide, unless they believed that God had no care thereof. "But Thou, O Lord, art my taker;" in Christ of course. For into that flesh s the Church too hath been taken by the Word," who was made flesh, and dwelt in us;" for that "In heavenly places hath He made us to sit together with Him." When the Head goes before, the other members will follow; for, "Who shall separate us from the love of Christ?" Justly then does the Church say, "Thou art my taker. My glory;" for she doth not attribute her excellency to herself, seeing that she knoweth by whose grace and mercy she is what she is. "And the lifter up of my head," of Him, namely, who, "the First-born from the dead," ascended up into heaven. "With my voice have I cried unto the Lord, and He heard me out of His holy mountain." This is the prayer of all the Saints, the odour of sweetness, which ascends up in the sight of the Lord. For now the Church is heard out of this mountain, which is also her head; or, out of that justice of God, by which both His elect are set free, and their persecutors punished.

Let the people of God also say, "I slept, and took rest; and rose, for the Lord will take me up; "that they may be joined, and cleave to their Head? For to this people is it said, "Awake thou that sleepest, and arise from the dead, and Christ shall lay hold on thee." Since they are taken out of sinners, of whom it is said generally," But they that sleep, sleep in the night." Let them say moreover, "I will not fear the thousands of people that surround me;" of the heathen verily that compass me about to extinguish everywhere, if they could, the Christian name. But how should they be feared, when by the blood of the martyrs in Christ, as by oil, the ardour of love is inflamed? "Arise, O Lord, save me, O my God." The body can address this to its own Head. For at His rising the body was saved; who "ascended up on high, led captivity captive, gave gifts unto men." For this is said by the Prophet, in the secret purpose of God, until that ripe harvest ,s which is spoken of in the Gospel, whose salvation is in His Resurrection, who vouchsafed to die for us, shed out our Lord to the earth. "Since Thou hast smitten all who oppose me without a cause, Thou hast broken the teeth of the sinners." Now while the Church hath rule, the enemies of the Christian name are smitten with confusion; and, whether their curses or their chiefs, brought to nought. Believe then, O man, that "salvation is of the Lord: and," Thou, O Lord, may "Thy blessing" be "upon Thy people."

10. Each one too of us may say, when a multitude of vices and lusts leads the resisting mind in the law of sin, "O Lord, how are they multiplied that trouble me! many rise up against me." And, since despair of recovery generally creeps in through the accumulation of vices, as though these same vices were mocking the soul, or even as though the Devil and his angels through their poisonous suggestions were at work to make us despair, it is said with great truth, "Many say unto my soul, There is no salvation for him in his God. But Thou, O Lord, art my taker." For this is our hope, that He hath vouchsafed to take the nature of man in Christ. "My glory;" according to that rule, that no one should ascribe ought to himself. "And the lifter up of my head;" either of Him, who is the Head of us all, or of the spirit of each several one of us, which is the head of the soul and body. For "the head of the woman is the man, and the head of the man is Christ." But the mind is lifted up, when it can be said already, "With the mind I serve the law of God;" that the rest of man may be reduced to peaceable submission, when in the resurrection of the flesh "death is swallowed up in victory." With my voice I have cried unto the Lord;" with that most inward and intensive voice. "And He heard me out of His holy mountain;" Him, through whom He hath succoured us, through whose mediation He heareth us. "I slept, and took rest; and rose, for the Lord will take me up." Who of the faithful is not able to say this, when he calls to mind the death of his sins, and the gift of regeneration? "I will not fear the thousands of people that surround me." Besides those which the Church universally hath borne and beareth, each one also hath temptations, by which, when compassed about, he

may speak these words, "Arise, O Lord; save me, O my God:" that is, make me to arise. "Since Thou hast smitten all who oppose me without a cause:" it is well in God's determinate a purpose said of the Devil and his angels; who rage not only against the whole body of Christ, but also against each one in particular. "Thou hast broken the teeth of the sinners." Each man hath those that revile him, he hath too the prime authors of vice, who strive to cut him off from the body of Christ. But "salvation is of the Lord." Pride is to be guarded against, and we must say, "My soul cleaved after Thee." "And upon Thy people" be "Thy blessing:" that is, upon each one of us.

PSALM IV.

TO THE END, A PSALM SONG TO DAVID.

1. "Christ is the end of the law for righteousness to every one that believeth." For this "end" signifies perfection, not consumption. Now it may be a question, whether every Song be a Psalm, or rather every Psalm a Song; whether there are some Songs which cannot be called Psalms, and some Psalms which cannot be called Songs. But the Scripture must be attended to, if haply "Song" do not denote a joyful theme. But those are called Psalms which are sung to the Psaltery; which the history as a high mystery declares the Prophet David to have used. Of which matter this is not the place to discourse; for it requires prolonged inquiry, and much discussion. Now meanwhile we must look either for the words of the Lord Man s after the Resurrection, or of man in the Church believing and hoping on Him.

2. "When I called, the God of my righteousness heard me" (ver. 1). When I called, God heard me, the Psalmist says, of whom is my righteousness. "In tribulation Thou hast enlarged me." Thou hast led me from the straits of sadness into the broad ways of joy. For, "tribulation and straitness is on every soul of man that doeth evil." But he who says, "We rejoice in tribulations, knowing that tribulation worketh patience;" up to that where he says, "Because the love of God is shed abroad in our hearts by the Holy Ghost, which is given unto us;" he hath no straits of heart, they be heaped on him outwardly by them that persecute him. Now the change of person, for that from the third person, where he says, "He heard," he passes at once to the second, where he says, "Thou hast enlarged me;" if it be not done for the sake of variety and grace, it is strange why the Psalmist should first wish to declare to men that he had been heard, and afterwards address Him who heard him. Unless perchance, when he had declared how he was heard, in this very enlargement of heart he preferred to speak with God; that he might even in this way show what it is to be enlarged in heart, that is, to have God already shed abroad in the heart, with whom he might hold converse interiorly. Which is rightly understood as spoken in the person of him who, believing on Christ, has been enlightened; but in that of the very Lord Man, whom the Wisdom of God took, I do not see how this can be suitable. For He was never deserted by It. But as His very prayer against trouble is a sign rather of our infirmity, so also of that sudden enlargement of heart the same Lord may speak for His faithful ones, whom He has personated also when He said, "I was an hungered, and ye gave Me no meat; I was thirsty, and ye gave Me no drink," and so forth. Wherefore here also He can say, "Thou hast enlarged me," for one of the least of His, holding converse with God,

22

whose "love" he has "shed abroad in his heart by the Holy Ghost, which is given unto us." "Have mercy upon me and hear my prayer." Why does he again ask, when already he declared that he had been heard and enlarged? It is for our sakes, of whom it is said, "But if we hope for that we see not, we wait in patience;" or is it, that in him who has believed that which is begun may be perfected?

3. "O ye sons of men, how long heavy in heart" (ver. 2). Let your error, says he, have lasted at least up to the coming of the Son of God; why then any longer are ye heavy in heart? When will ye make an end of crafty wiles, if now when the truth is present ye make it not? "Why do ye love vanity, and seek a lie?" Why would ye be blessed by the lowest things? Truth alone, from which all things are true, maketh blessed. For, "vanity is of deceivers, and all is vanity." "What profit hath a man of all his labour, wherewith he laboureth under the sun?" Why then are ye held back by the love of things temporal? Why follow ye after the last things, as though the first, which is vanity and a lie? For you would have them abide with you, which all pass away, as doth a shadow.

4. "And know ye that the Lord hath magnified his Holy One" (ver. 3). Whom but Him, whom He raised up from below, and placed in heaven at His right hand? Therefore doth he chide mankind, that they would turn at length from the love of this world to Him. But if the addition of the conjunction (for he says, "and know ye") is to any a difficulty, he may easily observe in Scripture that this manner of speech is usual in that language, in which the Prophets spoke. For you often find this beginning, "And" the Lord said unto him, "And" the word of the Lord came to him. Which joining by a conjunction, when no sentence has gone before, to which the following one may be annexed, peradventure admirably conveys to us, that the utterance of the truth in words is connected with that vision which goes on in the heart. Although in this place it may be said, that the former sentence, "Why do ye love vanity, and seek a lie?" is as if it were written, Do not love vanity, and seek a lie. And being thus read, it follows in the most direct construction, "and know ye that the Lord hath magnified His Holy One." But the interposition of the Diapsalma forbids our joining this sentence with the preceding one. For whether this be a Hebrew word, as some would have it, which means, so be it; or a Greek word, which marks a pause in the psalmody (so as that Psalma should be what is sung in psalmody, but Diapsalma an interval of silence in the psalmody; that as the coupling of voices in singing is called Sympsalma, so their separation Diapsalma, where a certain pause of interrupted continuity is marked): whether I say it be the former, or the latter, or something else, this at least is probable, that the sense cannot rightly be continued and joined, where the Diapsalma intervenes.

5. "The Lord will hear me, when I cry unto Him." I believe that we are here warned, that with great earnestness of heart, that is, with an inward and incorporeal cry, we should implore help of God. For as we must give thanks for enlightenment in this life, so must we pray for rest after this life. Wherefore in the person, either of the faithful preacher of the Gospel, or of our Lord Himself, it may be taken, as if it were written, the Lord will hear you, when you cry unto Him.

6. "Be ye angry, and sin not" (ver. 4) For the thought occurred, Who is worthy to be heard? or how shall the sinner not cry in vain unto the Lord? Therefore, "Be ye angry," saith he, "and sin not." Which may be taken two ways: either, even if ye be angry, do not sin; that is, even if there arise an emotion in the soul, which now by reason of the punishment of sin is not in our power, at least let not the reason and the mind, which is after God regenerated within, that with the mind we should serve the law of God, although with the flesh we as yet serve the law of sin? consent thereunto; or, repent ye, that is, be ye angry with yourselves for your past sins, and henceforth cease to sin. "What you say in your hearts:" there is understood, "say ye:" so that the complete sentence is, "What ye say in your hearts, that say ye;" that is, be ye not the people of whom it is said, "with their lips they honour Me, but their heart is far from Me. In your chambers be ye pricked." This is what has been expressed already "in heart." For this is the chamber, of which our Lord warns us, that we should pray within, with closed doors. But, "be ye pricked," refers either to the pain of repentance, that the soul in punishment should prick itself, that it be not condemned and tormented in God's judgment; or, to arousing, that we should awake to behold the light of Christ, as if pricks were made use of. But some say that not, "be ye pricked," but, "be ye opened," is the better reading; because in the Greek Psalter it is katanu'ghte, which refers to that enlargement of the heart, in order that the shedding abroad of love by the Holy Ghost may be received.

7. "Offer the sacrifice of righteousness, and hope in the Lord" (ver. 5). He says the same in another Psalm, "the sacrifice for God is a troubled spirit." Wherefore that this is the sacrifice of righteousness which is offered through repentance it is not unreasonably here understood. For what more righteous, than that each one should be angry with his own sins, rather than those of others, and that in self-punishment he should sacrifice himself unto God? Or are righteous works after repentance the sacrifice of righteousness? For the interposition of Diapsalma not unreasonably perhaps intimates even a transition from the old life to the new life: that on the old man being destroyed or weakened by repentance, the sacrifice of righteousness, according to the regeneration of the new man, may be offered to God; when the soul now cleansed offers and places itself on the altar of faith, to be encompassed

by heavenly fire, that is, by the Holy Ghost. So that this may be the meaning, "Offer the sacrifice of righteousness, and hope in the Lord;" that is, live uprightly, and hope for the gift of the Holy Ghost, that the truth, in which you have believed, may shine upon you.

8. But yet, "hope in the Lord," is as yet expressed without explanation. Now what is hoped for, but good things? But since each one would obtain from God that good, which he loves; and they are not easy to be found who love interior goods, that is, which belong to the inward man, which alone should be loved, but the rest are to be used for necessity, not to be enjoyed for pleasure; excellently did he subjoin, when he had said, "hope in the Lord" (ver. 6), "Many say, Who showeth us good things?" This is the speech, and this the daily inquiry of all the foolish and unrighteous; whether of those who long for the peace and quiet of a worldly life, and from the frowardness of mankind find it not; who even in their blindness dare to find fault with the order of events, when involved in their own deservings they deem the times worse than these which are past: or, of those who doubt and despair of that future life, which is promised us; who are often saying, Who knows if it's true? or, who ever came from below, to tell us this? Very exquisitely then, and briefly, he shows (to those, that is, who have interior sight), what good things are to be sought; answering their question, who say, "Who showeth us good things?" "The light of Thy countenance," saith he, "is stamped on us, O Lord." This light is the whole and true good of man, which is seen not with the eye, but with the mind. But he says, "stamped on us," as a penny is stamped with the king's image. For man was made after the image and likeness of God, which he defaced by sin: therefore it is his true and eternal good, if by a new birth he be stamped. And I believe this to be the bearing of that which some understand skilfully; I mean, what the Lord said on seeing Caesar's tribute money, "Render to Caesar the things that are Caesar's; and to God the things that are God's." As if He had said, In like manner as Caesar exacts from you the impression of his image, so also does God: that as the tribute money is rendered to him, so should the soul to God, illumined and stamped with the light of His countenance. (Ver. 7.)"Thou hast put gladness into my heart." Gladness then is not to be sought without by them, who, being still heavy in heart, "love vanity, and seek a lie;" but within, where the light of God's countenance is stamped. For Christ dwelleth in the inner man, as the Apostle says; for to Him doth it appertain to see truth, since He hath said, "I am the truth." And again, when He spake in the Apostle, saying, "Would you receive a proof of Christ, who speaketh in me?" He spake not of course from without to him, but in his very heart, that is, in that chamber where we are to pray.

9. But men (who doubtless are many) who follow after things temporal, know not to say aught else, than, "Who showeth us good things?" when the true and certain good within their very selves they cannot see. Of these accordingly is most justly said, what he adds next: "From the time of His corn, of wine, and oil, they have been multiplied." For the addition of His, is not superfluous. For the corn is God's: inasmuch as He is "the living bread which came down from heaven." The wine too is God's: for, "they shall be inebriated," he says, "with the fatness of thine house." The oil too is God's: of which it is said, "Thou hast fattened my head with oil." But those many, who say, "Who showeth us good things?" and who see not that the kingdom of heaven is within them: these, "from the time of His corn, of wine, and oil, are multiplied." For multiplication does not always betoken plentifulness, and not, generally, scantiness: when the soul, given up to temporal pleasures, burns ever with desire, and cannot be satisfied; and, distracted with manifold and anxious thought, is not permitted to see the simple good. Such is the soul of which it is said, "For the corruptible body presseth down the soul, and the earthly tabernacle weigheth down the mind that museth on many things." A soul like this, by the departure and succession of temporal goods, that is, "from the time of His corn, wine, and oil," filled with numberless idle fancies, is so multiplied, that it cannot do that which is commanded, "Think on the Lord in goodness, and in simplicity of heart seek Him." For this multiplicity is strongly opposed to that simplicity. And therefore leaving these, who are many, multiplied, that is, by the desire of things temporal, and who say, "Who showeth us good things?" which are to be sought not with the eyes without, but with simplicity of heart within, the faithful man rejoices and says, "In peace, together, I will sleep, and take rest" (ver. 8). For such men justly hope for all manner of estrangement of mind from things mortal, and forgetfulness of this world's miseries; which is beautifully and prophetically signified under the name of sleep and rest, where the most perfect peace cannot be interrupted by any tumult. But this is not had now in this life, but is to be hoped for after this life. This even the words themselves, which are in the future tense, show us. For it is not said, either, I have slept, and taken rest; or, I do sleep, and take rest; but, "I will sleep, and take rest." Then shall "this corruptible put on incorruption, and this mortal shall put on immortality; then shall death be swallowed up in victory." Hence it is said, "But if we hope for that we see not, we wait in patience."

10. Wherefore, consistently with this, he adds the last words, and says, "Since Thou, O Lord, in singleness hast made me dwell in hope." Here he does not say, wilt make; but, "hast made." In whom then this hope now is, there will be assuredly that which is hoped for. And well does he say, "in singleness." For this may refer in opposition to those many, who being multiplied from the time of His corn, of wine, and oil, say, "Who showeth us good things?" For this multiplicity

perishes, and singleness is observed among the saints: of whom it is said in the Acts of the Apostles, "and of the multitude of them that believed, there was one soul, and one heart." In singleness, then, and simplicity, removed, that is, from the multitude and crowd of things, that are born and die, we ought to be lovers of eternity, and unity, if we desire to cleave to the one God and our Lord.

PSALM V.

1. The title of the Psalm is, "For her who receiveth the inheritance." The Church then is signified, who receiveth for her inheritance eternal life through our Lord Jesus Christ; that she may possess God Himself, in cleaving to whom she may be blessed, according to that, "Blessed are the meek, for they shall possess the earth." What earth, but that of which it is said, "Thou art my hope, my portion in the land of the living"? And again more clearly, "The Lord is the portion of mine inheritance and of my cup." And conversely the word Church is said to be God's inheritance according to that, "Ask of Me, and I shall give thee the heathen for thine inheritance." Therefore is God said to be our inheritance, because He feedeth and sustaineth us: and we are said to be God's inheritance, because He ordereth and ruleth us. Wherefore it is the voice of the Church in this Psalm called to her inheritance, that she too may herself become the inheritance of the Lord.

2. "Hear my words, O Lord" (ver. 1). Being called she calleth upon the Lord; that the same Lord being her helper, she may pass through the wickedness of this world, and attain unto Him. "Understand my cry." The Psalmist well shows what this cry is; how from within, from the chamber of the heart, without the body's utterance, it reaches unto God: for the bodily voice is heard, but the spiritual is understood. Although this too may be God's hearing, not with carnal ear, but in the omnipresence of His Majesty.

3. "Attend Thou to the voice of my supplication;" that is, to that voice, which he maketh request that God would understand: of which what the nature is, he hath already intimated, when he said, "Understand my cry. Attend Thou to the voice of my supplication, my King, and my God" (ver. 2). Although both the Son is God, and the Father God, and the Father and the Son together One God; and if asked of the Holy Ghost, we must give no other answer than that He is God; and when the Father, and the Son, and the Holy Ghost are mentioned together, we must understand nothing else, than One God; nevertheless Scripture is wont to give the appellation of King to the Son. According then to that which is said, "By Me man cometh to the Father," rightly is it first, "my King;" and then, "my God." And yet has not the Psalmist said, Attend Ye; but, "Attend Thou." For the Catholic faith preaches not two or three Gods, but the Very Trinity, One God. Not that the same Trinity can be together, now the Father, now the Son, now the Holy Ghost, as Sabellius believed: but that the Father must be none but the Father, and the Son none but the Son, and the Holy Ghost none but the Holy Ghost, and this Trinity but One God. Hence when the Apostle had said, "Of whom are all things, by whom are all things, in whom are all things," he is believed to have conveyed an

intimation of the Very Trinity; and yet he did not add, to Them be glory; but, "to Him be glory."

4. "Because I will pray unto Thee (ver. 3). O Lord, in the morning Thou wilt hear my voice." What does that, which he said above, "Hear Thou," mean, as if he desired to be heard immediately? But now he saith," in the morning Thou wilt hear;" not, hear Thou: and, "I will pray unto Thee;" not, I do pray unto Thee: and, as follows, "in the morning I will stand by Thee, and will see;" not, I do stand by Thee, and do see. Unless perhaps his former prayer marks the invocation itself: but being in darkness amidst the storms of this world, he perceives that he does not see what he desires, and yet does not cease to hope," For hope that is seen, is not hope." Nevertheless, he understands why he does not see, because the night is not yet past, that is, the darkness which our sins have merited. He says therefore, "Because I will pray unto Thee, O Lord;" that is, because Thou art so mighty to whom I shall make my prayer, "in the morning Thou wilt hear my voice." Thou art not He, he says, that can be seen by those, from whose eyes the night of sins is not yet withdrawn: when the night then of my error is past, and the darkness gone, which by my sins I have brought upon myself, then "Thou wilt hear my voice." Why then did he say above not, "Thou wilt hear," but "hear Thou"? Is it that after the Church cried out, "hear Thou," and was not heard, she perceived what must needs pass away to enable her to be heard? Or is it that she was heard above, but doth not yet understand that she was heard, because she doth not yet see by whom she hath been heard; and what she now says, "In the morning Thou wilt hear," she would have thus taken, In the morning I shall understand that I have been heard? Such is that expression, "Arise, O Lord," that is, make me arise. But this latter is taken of Christ's resurrection: but at all events that Scripture, "The Lord your God proveth you, that He may know whether ye love Him, cannot be taken in any other sense, than, that ye by Him may know, and that it may be made evident to yourselves, what progress ye have made in His love.

5. "In the morning I will stand by Thee, and will see" (ver. 3). What is, "I will stand," but "I will not lie down"? Now what else is, to lie down, but to take rest on the earth, which is a seeking happiness in earthly pleasures? "I will stand by," he says, "and will see." We must not then cleave to things earthly, if we would see God, who is beheld by a clean heart. "For Thou art not a God who hast pleasure in iniquity. The malignant man shall not dwell near Thee, nor shall the unrighteous abide before Thine eyes. Thou hast hated all that work iniquity, Thou wilt destroy all that speak a lie. The man of blood, and the crafty man, the Lord will abominate" (vers. 4-6). Iniquity, malignity, lying, homicide, craft, and all the like, are the night of which we speak: on the passing away of which, the morning

dawns, that God may be seen. He has unfolded the reason, then, why he will stand by in the morning, and see: "For," he says, "Thou art not a God who hast pleasure in iniquity." For if He were a God who had pleasure in iniquity, He could be seen even by the iniquitous, so that He would not be seen in the morning, that is, when the night of iniquity is over.

6. "The malignant man shall not dwell near Thee:" that is, he shall not so see, as to cleave to Thee. Hence follows, "Nor shall the unrighteous abide before Thine eyes." For their eyes, that is, their mind is beaten back by the light of truth, because of the darkness of their sins; by the habitual practice of which they are not able to sustain the brightness of right understanding. Therefore even they who see sometimes, that is, who understand the truth, are yet still unrighteous, they abide not therein through love of those things, which turn away from the truth. For they carry about with them their night, that is, not only the habit, but even the love, of sinning. But if this night shall pass away, that is, if they shall cease to sin, and this love and habit thereof be put to flight, the morning dawns, so that they not only understand, but also cleave to the truth.

7. "Thou hast hated all that work iniquity." God's hatred may be understood from that form of expression, by which every sinner hates the truth. For it seems that she too hates those, whom she suffers not to abide in her. Now they do not abide, who cannot bear the truth. "Thou wilt destroy all that speak a lie." For this is the opposite to truth. But lest any one should suppose that any substance or nature is opposite to truth, let him understand that "a lie" has relation to that which is not, not to that which is. For if that which is be spoken, truth is spoken: but if that which is not be spoken, it is a lie. Therefore saith he, "Thou wilt destroy all that speak a lie;" because drawing back from that which is, they turn aside to that which is not. Many lies indeed seem to be for some one's safety or advantage, spoken not in malice, but in kindness: such was that of those midwives in Exodus, who gave a false report to Pharaoh, to the end that the infants of the children of Israel might not be slain. But even these are praised not for the fact, but for the disposition shown; since those who only lie in this way, will attain in time to a freedom from all lying. For in those that are perfect, not even these lies are found. For to these it is said, "Let there be in your mouth, yea, yea; nay, nay; whatsoever is more, is of evil." Nor is it without reason written in another place, "The mouth that lieth slayeth the soul:" lest any should imagine that the perfect and spiritual man ought to lie for this temporal life, in the death of which no soul is slain, neither his own, nor another's. But since it is one thing to lie, another to conceal the truth (if indeed it be one thing to say what is false, another not to say what is true), if haply one does not wish to give a man up even to this visible death, he

should be prepared to conceal what is true, not to say what is false; so that he may neither give him up, nor yet lie, lest he slay his own soul for another's body. But if he cannot yet do this, let him at all events admit only lies of such necessity, that he may attain to be freed even from these, if they alone remain, and receive the strength of the Holy Ghost, whereby he may despise all that must be suffered for the truth's sake. In fine, there are two kinds of lies, in which there is no great fault, and yet they are not without fault, either when we are in jest, or when we lie that we may do good. That first kind, in jest, is for this reason not very hurtful, because there is no deception. For he to whom it is said knows that it is said for the sake of the jest. But the second kind is for this reason the more inoffensive, because it carries with it some kindly intention. And to say truth, that which has no duplicity, cannot even be called a lie. As if, for example, a sword be intrusted to any one, and he promises to return it, when he who intrusted it to him shall demand it: if he chance to require his sword when in a fit of madness, it is clear it must not be returned then, lest he kill either himself or others, until soundness of mind be restored to him. Here then is no duplicity, because he, to whom the sword was intrusted, when he promised that he would return it at the other's demand, did not imagine that he could require it when in a fit of madness. But even the Lord concealed the truth, when He said to the disciples, not yet strong enough, "I have many things to say unto you, but ye cannot bear them now:" and the Apostle Paul when he said, "I could not speak unto you as unto spiritual, but as unto carnal." Whence it is clear that it is not blamable, sometimes not to speak what is trite. But to say what is false is not found to have been allowed to the perfect.

8. "The man of blood, and the crafty man, the Lord will abominate." What he said above, "Thou hast hated all that work iniquity, Thou wilt destroy all that speak a lie," may well seem to be repeated here: so that one may refer "the man of blood" to "the worker of iniquity," and "the crafty man" to; the "lie." For it is craft, when one thing is done, another pretended. He used an apt word too, when he said, "will abominate." For the disinherited are usually called: abominated. Now this Psalm is, "for her who receiveth the inheritance;" and she adds the exulting joy of her hope, in saying, "But I, in the multitude of Thy mercy, will enter into Thine house" (vet. 7). "In the multitude of mercy:" perhaps he means in the multitude of perfected and blessed men, of whom that city shall consist, of which the Church is now in travail, and is bearing few by few. Now that many men regenerated and perfected, are rightly called the multitude of God's mercy, who can deny; when it is most truly said, "What is man that Thou art mindful of him, or the son of man that Thou visitest him? I will enter into Thine house:" as a stone into a building, I suppose, is the meaning. For what else is the house of God than the Temple of God, of which it is said, "for the temple of God is holy, which temple ye are"? Of

which building He is the cornerstone, whom the Power and Wisdom of God coeternal with the Father assumed.

9. "I will worship at Thy holy temple, in Thy fear." "At the temple," we understand as, "near" the temple. For he does not say, I will worship "in" Thy holy temple; but, "I will worship at Thy holy temple." It must be understood too to be spoken not of perfection, but of progress toward perfection: so that the words, "I will enter into Thine house," should signify perfection. But that this may come to a happy issue, "I will" first, he says, "worship at Thy holy temple." And perhaps on this account he added, "in Thy fear;" which is a great defence to those that are advancing toward salvation. But when any one shall have arrived there, in him comes to pass that which is written, "perfect love casteth out fear." For they do not fear Him who is now their friend, to whom it is said, "henceforth I will not call you servants, but friends," when they have been brought through to that which was promised.

10. "O Lord, lead me forth in Thy justice because of mine enemies" (ver. 8). He has here sufficiently plainly declared that he is on his onward road, that is, in progress toward perfection, not yet in perfection itself, when he desires eagerly that he may be led forth. But, "in Thy justice," not in that which seems so to men. For to return evil for evil seems justice: but it is not His justice of whom it is said, "He maketh His sun to rise on the good and on the evil:" for even when God punishes sinners, He does not inflict His evil on them, but leaves them to their own evil. "Behold," the Psalmist says, "he travailed with injustice, he hath conceived toil, and brought forth iniquity: he hath opened a ditch, and digged it, and hath fallen into the pit which he wrought: his pains shall be turned on his own head, and his iniquity shall descend on his own pate." When then God punishes, He punishes as a judge those that transgress the law, not by bringing evil upon them from Himself, but driving them on to that which they have chosen, to fill up the sum of their misery. But man, when he returns evil for evil, does it with an evil will: and on this account is himself first evil, when he would punish evil.

11. "Direct in Thy sight my way." Nothing is clearer, than that he here sets forth that time, in which he is journeying onward. For this is a way which is traversed not in any regions of the earth, but in the affections of the heart. "In Thy sight," he says, "direct my way:" that is, where no man sees; who are not to be trusted in their praise or blame. For they can in no wise judge of another man's conscience, wherein the way toward God is traversed. Hence it is added, "for truth is not in their mouth" (ver. 9). To whose judgment of course then there is no trusting, and therefore must we fly within to conscience, and the sight of God. "Their heart is

vain." How then can truth be in their mouth, whose heart is deceived by sin, and the punishment of sin? Whence men are called back by that voice, "Wherefore do ye love vanity, and seek a lie?"

12. "Their throat is an open sepulchre." It may be referred to signify gluttony, for the sake of which men very often lie by flattery. And admirably has he said, "an open sepulchre:" for this gluttony is ever gaping with open mouth, not as sepulchres, which, on the reception of corpses, are closed up. This also may be understood hereby, that with lying and blind flattery men draw to themselves those whom they entice to sin; and as it were devour them, when they turn them to their own way of living. And when this happens to them, since by sin they die, those by whom they are led along, are rightly called open sepulchres: for themselves too are in a manner lifeless, being destitute of the life of truth; and they take in to themselves dead men, whom having slain by lying words and a vain heart, they turn unto themselves. "With their own tongues they dealt craftily:" that is, with evil tongues. For this seems to be signified, when he says "their own." For the evil have evil tongues, that is, they speak evil, when they speak craftily. To whom the Lord saith, "How can ye, being evil, speak good things?"

13. "Judge them, O God: let them fall from their own thoughts" (ver. 10). It is a prophecy, not a curse. For he does not wish that it should come to pass; but he perceives what will come to pass. For this happens to them, not because he appears to have wished for it, but because they are such as to deserve that it should happen. For so also what he says after wards, "Let all that hope in Thee rejoice," he says by way of prophecy; since he perceives that they will rejoice. Likewise is it said prophetically, "Stir up Thy strength, and come:" for he saw that He would come. Although the words, "Let them fall from their own thoughts," may be taken thus also, that it may rather be believed to be a wish for their good by the Psalmist, whilst they fall from their evil thoughts, that is, that they may no more think evil. But what follows, "drive them out," forbids this interpretation. For it can in no wise be taken in a favourable sense, that one is driven out by God. Wherefore it is understood to be said prophetically, and not of ill will; when this is said, which must necessarily happen to such as chose to persevere in those sins, which have been mentioned. "Let them," therefore, "fall from their own thoughts," is, let them fall by their self-accusing thoughts, "their own conscience also bearing witness," as the Apostle says, "and their thoughts accusing or excusing, in the revelation of the just judgment of God."

14. "According to the multitude of their ungodlinesses drive them out:" that is, drive them out far away. For this is "according to the multitude of their

ungodlinesses," that they should be driven out far away. The ungodly then are driven out from that inheritance, which is possessed by knowing and seeing God: as diseased eyes are driven out from the shining of the light, when what is gladness to others is pain to them. Therefore these shall not stand in the morning, and see. And that expression is as great a punishment, as that which is said, "But for me it is good to cleave to the Lord," is a great reward. To this punishment is opposed, "Enter thou into the joy of Thy Lord;" for similar to this expulsion is, "Cast him into outer darkness."

15. "Since they have embittered Thee, O Lord: I am," saith He, "the Bread which came down from heaven;" again, "Labour for the meat which wasteth not;" again, "Taste and see that the Lord is sweet." But to sinners the bread of truth is bitter. Whence they hate the mouth of him that speaketh the truth. These then have embittered God, who by sin have fallen into such a state of sickliness, that the food of truth, in which healthy souls delight, as if it were bitter as gall, they cannot bear.

16. "And let all rejoice that hope in Thee;" those of course to whose taste the Lord is sweet. "They will exult for evermore, and Thou wilt dwell in them" (ver. 11). This will be the exultation for evermore, when the just become the Temple of God, and He, their Indweller, will be their joy. "And all that love Thy name shall glory in Thee:" as when what they love is present for them to enjoy. And well is it said, "in Thee," as if in possession of the inheritance, of which the title of the Psalm speaks: when they too are His inheritance, which is intimated by, "Thou wilt dwell in them." From which good they are kept back, whom God, according to the multitude of their ungodlinesses, driveth out.

17. "For Thou wilt bless the just man" (ver. 12). This is blessing, to glory in God, and to be inhabited by God. Such sanctification is given to the just. But that they may be justified, a calling goes before: which is not of merit, but of the grace of God. "For all have sinned, and want the glory of God." "For whom He called, them He also justified; and whom He, justified, them He also glorified." Since then calling is not of our merit, but of the goodness and mercy of God, he went on to say, "O Lord, as with the shield of Thy good will Thou hast crowned us." For God's good will goes before our good will, to call sinners to repentance. And these are the arms whereby the enemy is overcome, against whom it is said, "Who will bring accusation against God's elect?" Again, "if God be for us, who can be against us? Who spared not His Only Son, but delivered Him up for us all." "For if, when we were enemies, Christ died for us; much more being reconciled shall we be saved from wrath through Him." This is that unconquerable shield, whereby

the enemy is driven back, when he suggests despair of our salvation through the multitude of tribulaions and temptations.

18. The whole contents of the Psalm, then, are a prayer that she may be heard, from the words, "hear my words, O Lord," unto, "my King, and my God." Then follows a view of those things which hinder the sight of God, that is, a knowledge that she s is heard, from the words, "because I shall pray unto Thee, O Lord, in the morning Thou wilt hear my voice," unto, "the man of blood and the crafty man the Lord will abominate." Thirdly, she hopes that she, who is to be the house of God, even now begins to draw near to Him in fear, before that perfection which casteth out fear, from the words, "but I in the multitude of Thy mercy," unto, "I will worship at Thy holy temple in Thy fear." Fourthly, as she is progressing and advancing amongst those very things which she feels to hinder her, she prays that she may be assisted within, where no man seeth, lest she be turned aside by evil tongues, for the words, "O Lord, lead me forth in Thy justice because of my enemies," unto, "with their tongues they dealt craftily." Fifthly, is a prophecy of what punishment awaits the ungodly, when the just man shall scarcely be saved; and of what reward the just shall obtain, who, when they were called, came, and bore all things manfully, till they were brought to the end, from the words, "judge them, O God," unto the end of the Psalm.

PSALM VI.

TO THE END, IN THE HYMNS OF THE EIGHTH, A PSALM TO DAVID.

1. "Of the eighth," seems here obscure. For the rest of this title is more clear. Now it has seemed to some to intimate the day of judgment, that is, the time of the coming of our Lord, when He will come to judge the quick and dead. Which coming, it is believed, is to be, after reckoning the years from Adam, seven thousand years: so as that seven thousand years should pass as seven days, and afterwards that time arrive as it were the eighth day. But since it has been said by the Lord, "It is not yours to know the times, which the Father hath put m His own power:" and, "But of the day and that hour knoweth no man, no, neither angel, nor Power, neither the Son, but the Father alone:" and again, that which is written, "that the day of the Lord cometh as a thief," shows clearly enough that no man should arrogate to himself the knowledge of that time, by any computation of years. For if that day is to come after seven thousand years, every man could learn its advent by reckoning the years. What comes then of the Son's even not knowing this? Which of course is said with this meaning, that men do not learn this by the Son, not that He by Himself doth not know it: according to that form of speech, "the Lord your God trieth you that He may know;" that is, that He may make you know: and, "arise, O Lord;" that is, make us arise. When therefore the Son is thus said not to know this day; not because He knoweth it not, but because He causeth those to know it not, for whom it is not expedient to know it, that is, He doth not show it to them; what does that strange presumption mean, which, by a reckoning up of years, expects the day of the Lord as most certain after seven thousand years?

2. Be we then willingly ignorant of that which the Lord would not have us know: and let us inquire what this title, "of the eighth," means. The day of judgment may indeed, even without any rash computation of years, be understood by the eighth, for that immediately after the end of this world, life eternal being attained, the souls of the righteous will not then be subject unto times: and, since all times have their revolution in a repetition of those seven days, that per-adventure is called the eighth day, which will not have this variety. There is another reason, which may be here not unreasonably accepted, why the judgment should be called the eighth, because it will take place after two generations, one relating to the body, the other to the soul, For from Adam unto Moses the human race lived of the body, that is, according to the flesh: which is called the outward and the old man, and to which the Old Testament was given, that it might prefigure the spiritual things to come by operations, albeit religious, yet carnal. Through this entire season, when men

36

lived according to the body, "death reigned," as the Apostle saith, "even over those that had not sinned." Now it reigned "after the similitude of Adam's transgression," as the same Apostle saith; for it must be taken of the period up to Moses, up to which time the works of the law, that is, those sacraments of carnal observance, held even those bound, for the sake of a certain mystery, who were subject to the One God. But from the coming of the Lord, from whom there was a transition from the circumcision of the flesh to the circumcision of the heart, the call was made, that man should live according to the soul, that is, according to the inner man, who is also called the "new man" by reason of the new birth and the renewing of spiritual conversation. Now it is plain that the number four has relation to the body, from the four well known elements of which it consists, and the four qualities of dry, humid, warm, cold. Hence too it is administered by four seasons, spring, summer, autumn, winter. All this is very well known. For of the number four relating to the body we have treated elsewhere somewhat subtilly, but obscurely: which must be avoided in this discourse, which we would have accommodated to the unlearned. But that the number three has relation to the mind may be understood from this, that we are commanded to love God after a threefold manner, with the whole heart, with the whole soul, with the whole mind: of each of which severally we must treat, not in the Psalms, but in the Gospels: for the present, for proof of the relation of the number three to the mind, I think what has been said enough. Those numbers then of the body which have relation to the old man and the Old Testament, being past and gone, the numbers too of the soul, which have relation to the new man and the New Testament, being past and gone, a septenary so to say being passed; because everything is done in time, four having been distributed to the body, three to the mind; the eighth will come, the day of judgment: which assigning to deserts their due, will transfer at once the saint, not to temporal works, but to eternal life; but will condemn the ungodly to eternal punishment.

3. In fear of which comdemnation the Church prays in this Psalm, and says," Reprove me not, O Lord, in Thine anger" (ver. 1). The Apostle too mentions the anger of the judgment; "Thou treasurest up unto thyself," he says, "anger against the day of the anger of the just judgment of God." In which he would not be reproved, whosoever longs to be healed in this life. "Nor in Thy rage chasten me." "Chasten," seems rather too mild a word; for it availeth toward amendment. For for him who is reproved, that is, accused, it is to be feared lest his end be condemnation. But since "rage" seems to be more than "anger," it may be a difficulty, why that which is milder, namely, chastening, is joined to that which is more severe, namely, rage. But I suppose that one and the same thing is signified by the two words. For in the Greek thumo`s, which is in the first verse, means the same as orgh`, which is in the second verse. But when the Latins themselves too

wished to use two distinct words, they looked out for what was akin to "anger," and "rage" was used. Hence copies vary. For in some "anger" is found first, and then "rage:" in others, for "rage," "indignation" or "choler" is used. But whatever the reading, it is an emotion of the soul urging to the infliction of punishment. Yet this emotion must not be attributed to God, as if to a soul, of whom it is said, "but Thou, O Lord of power, judgest with tranquillity." Now that which is tranquil, is not disturbed. Disturbance then does not attach to God as judge: but what is done by His ministers, in that it is done by His laws, is called His anger. In which anger, the soul, which now prays, would not only not be reproved, but not even chastened, that is, amended or instructed. For in the Greek it is, paideu'sh(i)s, that is, instruct. Now in the day of judgment all are "reproved" that hold not the foundation, which is Christ. But they are amended, that is, purged, who "upon this foundation build wood, hay, stubble. For they shall suffer loss, but shall be saved, as by fire." What then does he pray, who would not be either reproved or amended in the anger of the Lord? what else but that he may be healed? For where sound health is, neither death is to be dreaded, nor the physician's hand with caustics or the knife.

4. He proceeds accordingly to say, "Pity me, O Lord, for I am weak: heal me, O Lord, for my bones are troubled" (ver. 2), that is, the support of my soul, or strength: for this is the meaning of "bones." The soul therefore says, that her strength is troubled, when she speaks of bones. For it is not to be supposed, that the soul has bones, such as we see in the body. Wherefore, what follows tends to explain it," and my soul is troubled exceedingly" (ver. 3), lest because he mentioned bones, they should be understood as of the body. "And Thou, O Lord, how long?" Who does not see represented here a soul struggling with her diseases; but long kept back by the physician, that she may be convinced what evils she has plunged herself into through sin? For what is easily healed, is not much avoided: but from the difficulty of the healing, there will be the more careful keeping of recovered health. God then, to whom it is said, "And Thou, O Lord, how long?" must not be deemed as if cruel: but as a kind convincer of the soul, what evil she hath procured for herself. For this soul does not yet pray so perfectly, as that it can be said to her, "Whilst thou art yet speaking I will say, Behold, here I am." That she may at the same time also come to know, if they who do turn meet with so great difficulty, how great punishment is prepared for the ungodly, who will not turn to God: as it is written in another place, "If the righteous scarcely be saved, where shall the sinner and ungodly appear?"

5. "Turn, O Lord, and deliver my soul" (ver. 4). Turning herself she prays that God too would turn to her: as it is said, "Turn ye unto Me, and I will turn unto you,

saith the Lord." Or is it to be understood according to that way of speaking, "Turn, O Lord," that is make me turn, since the soul in this her turning feels difficulty and toil? For our perfected turning findeth God ready, as says the Prophet, "We shall find Him ready as the dawn." Since it was not His absence who is everywhere present, but our turning away that made us lose Him; "He was in this world," it is said, "and the world was made by Him, and the world knew Him not." If, then, He was in this world, and the world knew Him not, our impurity doth not endure the sight of Him. But whilst we are turning ourselves, that is, by changing our old life are fashioning our spirit; we feel it hard and toilsome to be wrested back from the darkness of earthly lusts, to the serene and quiet and tranquillity of the divine light. And in such difficulty we say, "Turn, O Lord," that is, help us, that that turning may be perfected in us, which findeth Thee ready, and offering Thyself for the fruition of them that love Thee. And hence after he said, "Turn, O Lord," he added, "and deliver my soul:" cleaving as it were to the entanglements of this world, and suffering, in the very act of turning, from the thorns, as it were, of rending and tearing desires. "Make me whole," he says, "for Thy pity's sake." He knows that it is not of his own merits that he is healed: for to him sinning, and transgressing a given command, was just condemnation due. Heal me therefore, he says, not for my merit's sake, but for Thy pity's sake.

6. "For in death there is no one that is mindful of Thee" (ver. 5). He knows too that now is the time for turning unto God: for when this life shall have passed away, there remaineth but a retribution of our deserts. "But in hell who shall confess to Thee?" That rich man, of whom the Lord speaks, who saw Lazarus in rest, but bewailed himself in torments, confessed in hell, yea so as to wish even to have his brethren warned, that they might keep themselves from sin, because of the punishment which is not believed to be in hell. Although therefore to no purpose, yet he confessed that those torments had deservedly lighted upon him; since he even wished his brethren to be instructed, lest they should fall into the same. What then is, "But in hell who will confess to Thee?" Is hell to be understood as that place, whither the ungodly will be cast down after the judgment, when by reason of that deeper darkness they will no more see any light of God, to whom they may confess aught? For as yet that rich man by raising his eyes, although a vast gulf lay between, could still see Lazarus established in rest: by comparing himself with whom, he was driven to a confession of his own deserts. It may be understood also, as if the Psalmist calls sin, that is committed in contempt of God's law, death: so as that we should give the name of death to the sting of death, because it procures death. "For the sting of death is sin." In which death this is to be unmindful of God, to despise His law and commandments: so that by hell the Psalmist would mean that blindness of soul which overtakes and enwraps the sinner, that is, the dying. "As they did not think good," the Apostle says, "to retain

God in "their" knowledge, God gave them over to a reprobate mind." From this death, and this hell, the soul earnestly prays that she may be kept safe, whilst she strives to turn to God, and feels her difficulties.

7. Wherefore he goes on to say, "I have laboured in my groaning." And as if this availed but little, he adds, "I will wash each night my couch" (ver. 6). That is here called a couch, where the sick and weak soul rests, that is, in bodily gratification and in every worldly pleasure. Which pleasure, whoso endeavours to withdraw himself from it, washes with tears. For he sees that he already condemns carnal lusts; and yet his weakness is held by the pleasure, and willingly lies down therein, from whence none but the soul that is made whole can rise. As for what he says, "each night," he would perhaps have it taken thus: that he who, ready in spirit, perceives some light of truth, and yet, through weakness of the flesh, rests sometime in the pleasure of this world, is compelled to suffer as it were days and nights in an alternation of feeling: as when he says, "With the mind I serve the law of God," he feels as it were day; again when he says, "but with the flesh the law of sin," he declines into night: until all night passeth away, and that one day comes, of which it is said, "In the morning I will stand by Thee, and will see." For then he will stand, but now he lies down, when he is on his couch; which he will wash each night, that with so great abundance of tears he may obtain the most assured remedy from the mercy of God. "I will drench my bed with tears." It is a repetition. For when he says, "with tears," he shows with what meaning he said above, "I will wash." For we take "bed" here to be the same as "couch" above. Although, "I will drench," is something more than, "I will wash:" since anything may be washed superficially, but drenching penetrates to the more inward parts; which here signifies weeping to the very bottom of the heart. Now the variety of tenses which he uses; the past, when he said, "I have laboured in my groaning;" and the future, when he said, "I will wash each night my couch;" the future again, "I will drench my bed with tears;" this shows what every man ought to say to himself, when he labours in groaning to no purpose. As if he should say, It hath not profited when I have done this, therefore I will do the other.

8. "Mine eye is disordered by anger" (ver. 7): is it by his own, or God's anger, in which he maketh petition that he might not be reproved, or chastened? But if anger in that place intimate the day of judgment, how can it be understood now? Is it a beginning of it, that men here suffer pains and torments, and above all the loss of the understanding of the truth; as I have already quoted that which is said, "God gave them over to a reprobate mind"? For such is the blindness of the mind. Whosoever is given over thereunto, is shut out from the interior light of God: but not wholly as yet, whilst he is in this life. For there is "outer darkness," which is

understood to belong rather to the day of judgment; that he should rather be wholly without God, whosoever whilst there is time refuses correction. Now to be wholly without God, what else is it, but to be in extreme blindness? If indeed God "dwell in inaccessible light," whereinto they enter, to whom it is said, "Enter thou into the joy of thy Lord." It is then the beginning of this anger, which in this life every sinner suffers. In fear therefore of the day of judgment, he is in trial and grief; lest he be brought to that, the disastrous commencement of which he experiences now. And therefore he did not say, mine eye is extinguished, but, "mine eye is disordered by anger." But if he mean that his eye is disordered by his own anger, there is no wonder either in this. For hence perhaps it is said, "Let not the sun go down upon your wrath;" because the mind, which, from her own disorder, is not permitted to see God, supposes that the inner sun, that is, the wisdom of God, suffers as it were a setting in her.

9. "I have grown old in all mine enemies." He had only spoken of anger (if it were yet of his own anger that he spoke): but thinking on his other vices, he found that he was entrenched by them all. Which vices, as they belong to the old life and the old man, which we must put off, that we may put on the new man, it is well said, "I have grown old." But "in all mine enemies," he means, either amidst these vices, or amidst men who will not be converted to God. For these, even if they know them not, even if they bear with them, even if they use the same tables and houses and cities, with no strife arising between them, and in frequent converse together with seeming concord: notwithstanding, by the contrariety of their aims, they are enemies to those who turn unto God. For seeing that the one love and desire this world, the others wish to be freed from this world, who sees not that the first are enemies to the last? For if they can, they draw the others into punishment with them. And it is a great grace, to be conversant daily with their words, and not to depart from the way of God's commandments. For often the mind which is striving to go on to God-ward, being rudely handled in the very road, is alarmed; and generally fulfils not its good intent, lest it should offend those with whom it lives, who love and follow after other perishable and transient goods. From such every one that is whole is separated, not in space, but in soul. For the body is contained in space, but the soul's space is her affection.

10. Wherefore after the labour, and groaning, and very frequent showers of tears, since that cannot be ineffectual, which is asked so earnestly of Him, who is the Fountain of all mercies, and it is most truly said, "the Lord is nigh unto them that are of a broken heart:" after difficulties so great, the pious soul, by which we may also understand the Church, intimating that she has been heard, see what she adds: "Depart from me, all ye that work iniquity; for the Lord hath heard the voice of my

weeping" (ver. 8). It is either spoken prophetically, since they will depart, that is, the ungodly will be separated from the righteous, when the day of judgment arrives, or, for this time present. For although both are equally found in the same assemblies, yet on the open floor the wheat is already separated from the chaff, though it be hid among the chaff. They can therefore be associated together, but cannot be carried away by the wind together.

11. "For the Lord hath heard the voice of my weeping; The Lord hath heard my supplication; the Lord hath received my prayer" (ver. 9). The frequent repetition of the same sentiments shows not, so to say, the necessities of the narrator, but the warm feeling of his joy. For they that rejoice are wont so to speak, as that it is not enough for them to declare once for all the object of their joy. This is the fruit of that groaning in which there is labour, and those tears with which the couch is washed, and-bed drenched: for, "he that sows in tears, shall reap in joy:" and, "blessed are they that mourn, for they shall be comforted."

12. "Let all mine enemies be ashamed and vexed" (ver. 10). He said above, "depart from me all ye:" which can take place, as it has been explained, even in this life: but as to what he says, "let them be ashamed and vexed," I do not see how it can happen, save on that day when the rewards of the righteous and the punishments of the sinners shall be made manifest. For at present so far are the ungodly from being ashamed, that they do not cease to insult us. And for the most part their mockings are of such avail, that they make the weak to be ashamed of the name of Christ. Hence it is said, "Whosoever shall be ashamed of Me before men, of him will I be ashamed before My Father." But now whosoever would fulfil those sublime commands, to disperse, to give to the poor, that his righteousness may endure for ever; and selling all his earthly goods, and spending them on the needy, would follow Christ, saying, "We brought nothing into this world, and truly we can carry nothing out; having food and raiment, let us be therewith content;" incurs the profane raillery of those men, and by those who will not be made whole, is called mad; and often to avoid being so called by desperate men, he fears to do, and puts off that, which the most faithful and powerful of all physicians hath ordered. It is not then at present that these can be ashamed, by whom we have to wish that we be not made ashamed, and so be either called back from our proposed journey, or hindered, or delayed. But the time will come when they shall be ashamed, saying as it is written, "These are they whom we had sometimes in derision, and a parable of reproach: we fools counted their life madness, and their end to be without honour: how are they numbered among the children of God, and their lot is among the saints? Therefore have we erred from the way of truth, and the light of rightousness hath not shined into us, nor the sun risen upon us: we

have been filled with the way of wickedness and destruction, and have walked through rugged deserts, but the way of the Lord we have not known. What hath pride profited us, or what hath the vaunting of riches brought us? All those things are passed away like a shadow."

13. But as to what he says, "Let them be turned and confounded," who would not judge it to be a most righteous punishment, that they should have a turning unto confusion, who would not have one unto salvation? After this he added, "exceeding quickly." For when the day of judgment shall have begun to be no longer looked for, when they shall have said, "Peace, then shall sudden destruction come upon them." Now whensoever it come, that comes very quickly, of whose coming we give up all expectation; and nothing makes the length of this life be felt but the hope of living. For nothing seems more quick, than all that has already passed in it. When then the day of judgment shall come, then will sinners feel how that all the life which passeth away is not long. Nor will that any way possibly seem to them to have come tardily, which shall have come without their desiring, or rather without their believing. Although it can too be taken in this place thus, that inasmuch as God has heard, so to say, her groans, and her long and frequent tears, she may be understood to be freed from her sins, and to have tamed every disordered impulse of carnal affection: as she saith, "Depart from me, all ye that work iniquity, for the Lord hath heard the voice of my weeping:" and when she has had this happy issue, it is no marvel if she be already so perfect as to pray for her enemies. The words then, "Let all mine enemies be ashamed, and vexed," may have this meaning; that they should repent of their sins, which cannot be effected without confusion and vexation. There is then nothing to hinder us from taking what follows too in this sense, "let them be turned and ashamed," that is, let them be turned to God, and be ashamed that they sometime gloried in the former darkness of their sins; as the Apostle says, "For what glory had ye sometime in those things of which ye are now ashamed?" But as to what he added, "exceeding quickly," it must be referred either to the warm affection of her wish, or to the power of Christ; who converteth to the faith of the Gospel in such quick time the nations, which in their idols' cause did persecute the Church.

PSALM VII.

A PSALM TO DAVID HIMSELF, WHICH HE SUNG TO THE LORD, FOR THE WORDS OF CHUSI, SON OF JEMINI.

1. Now the story which gave occasion to this prophecy may be easily recognised in the second book of Kings. For there Chusi, the friend of king David, went over to the side of Abessalon, his son, who was carrying on war against his father, for the purpose of discovering and reporting the designs which he was taking against his father, at the instigation of Achitophel, who had revolted from David's friendship, and was instructing by his counsel, to the best of his power, the son against the father. But since it is not the story itself which is to be the subject of consideration in this Psalm, from which the prophet hath taken a veil of mysteries, if we have passed over to Christ, let the veil be taken away. And first let us inquire into the signification of the very names, what it means. For there have not been wanting interpreters, who investigating these same words, not carnally according to the letter, but spiritually, declare to us that Chusi should be interpreted silence; and Gemini, right- handed; Achitophel, brother's ruin. Among which interpretations, Judas, that traitor, again meets us, that Abessalon should bear his image, according to that interpretation of it as a father's peace; in that his father was full of thoughts of peace toward him: although he in his guile had war in his heart, as was treated of in the third Psalm. Now as we find in the Gospels that the disciples of our Lord Jesus Christ are called sons, so in the same Gospels we find they are called brethren also. For the Lord on the resurrection saith, "Go and say to My brethren." And the Apostle calls Him "the first begotten among many brethren." The ruin then of that disciple, who betrayed Him, is rightly understood to be a brother's ruin, which we said is the interpretation of Achitophel. Now as to Chusi, from the interpretation of silence, it is rightly understood that our Lord contended against that guile in silence, that is, in that most deep secret, whereby "blindness happened in part to Israel," when they were persecuting the Lord, that the fulness of the Gentiles might enter in, and "so all Israel might be saved." When the Apostle came to this profound secret and deep silence, he exclaimed, as if struck with a kind of awe of its very depth, "O the depth of the riches of the wisdom and knowledge of God! how unsearchable are His judgments, and His ways past finding out! For who hath known the wind of the Lord, or who hath been His counsellor?" Thus that great silence he does not so much discover by explanation, as he sets forth its greatness in admiration. In this silence the Lord, hiding the sacrament of His adorable passion, turns the brother's voluntary ruin, that is, His betrayer's impious wickedness, into the order of His mercy and providence: that what he with perverse mind wrought for one Man's destruction,

He might by providential overruling dispose for all men's salvation. The perfect soul then, which is already worthy to know the secret of God, sings a Psalm unto the Lord, she sings" for the words of Chusi," because she has attained to know the words of that silence: for among unbelievers and persecutors there is that silence and secret. But among His own, to whom it is said," Now I call you no more servants; for the servant knoweth not what his lord doeth; but I have called you friends, for all things that I have heard of My Father I have made known unto you: among His friends, I say, there is not the silence, but the words of the silence, that is, the meaning of that silence set forth and manifested. Which silence, that is, Chusi, is called the son of Gemini, that is, righthanded. For what was done for the Saints was not to be hidden from them. And yet He saith," Let not the left hand know what the right hand doeth." The perfect soul then, to which that secret has been made known, sings in prophecy "for the words of Chusi," that is, for the knowledge of that same secret. Which secret God at her fight hand, that is, favourable and propitious unto her, has wrought. Wherefore this silence is called the Son of the right hand, which is, "Chusi, the son of Gemini."

2. "O Lord my God, in Thee have I hoped: save me from all them that persecute me, and deliver me" (ver. 1). As one to whom, already perfected, all the war and enmity of vice being overcome, there remaineth no enemy but the envious devil, he says, "Save me from all them that persecute me, and deliver me (ver. 2): lest at any time he tear my soul as a lion." The Apostle says, "Your adversary the devil, as a roaring lion, walketh about, seeking whom he may devour.' Therefore when the Psalmist said in the plural number, "Save me from all them that persecute me:" he afterwards introduced the singular, saying, "lest at any time he tear my soul as a lion." For he does not say, lest at any time they tear: he knew what enemy and violent adversary of the perfect soul remained. "Whilst there be none to redeem, nor to save:" that is, lest he tear me, whilst Thou redeemest not, nor savest. For, if God redeem not, nor save, he tears.

3. And that it might be clear that the already perfect soul, which is to be on her guard against the most insidious snares of the devil only, says this, see what follows. "O Lord my God, if I have done this" (ver. 3). What is it that he calls "this"? Since he does not mention the sin by name, are we to understand sin generally? If this sense displease us, we may take that to be meant which follows: as if we had asked, what is this that you say, "this"? He answers, "If there be iniquity in my hands." Now then it is clear that it is said of all sin," If I have repaid them that recompense me evil" (ver. 4). Which none can say with truth, but the perfect. For so the Lord says, "Be ye perfect, as your Father which is in heaven; who maketh His sun to rise upon the good and the evil, and raineth on the just and

the unjust." He then who repayeth not them that recompense evil, is perfect. When therefore the perfect soul prays "for the words of Chusi, the son of Jemini," that is, for the knowledge of that secret and silence, which the Lord, favourable to us and merciful, wrought for our salvation, so as to endure, and with all patience bear, the guiles of this betrayer: as if He should say to this perfect soul, explaining the design of this secret, For thee ungodly and a sinner, that thine iniquities might be washed away by My blood-shedding, in great silence and great patience I bore with My betrayer; wilt not thou imitate me, that thou too mayest not repay evil for evil? Considering then, and understanding what the Lord has done for him, and by His example going on to perfection, the Psalmist says, "If I have repaid them that recompense me evil:" that is, if I have not done what Thou hast taught me by Thy example: "may I therefore fall by mine enemies empty." And he says well, not, If I have repaid them that do me evil; but, who "recompense." For who so recompenseth, had received somewhat already. Now it is an instance of greater patience, not even to repay him evil, who after receiving benefits returns evil for good, than if without receiving any previous benefit he had had a mind to injure. If therefore he says, "I have repaid them that recompense me evil:" that is, If I have not imitated Thee in that silence, that is, in Thy patience, which Thou hast wrought for me, "may I fall by mine enemies empty." For he is an empty boaster, who, being himself a man, desires to avenge himself on a man; and whilst he openly seeks to overcome a man, is secretly himself overcome by the devil, rendered empty by vain and proud joy, because he could not, as it were, be conquered. The Psalmist knows then where a greater victory may be obtained, and where "the Father which seeth in secret will reward." Lest then he repay them that recompense evil, he overcomes his anger rather than another man, being instructed too by those writings, wherein it is written, "Better is he that overcometh his anger, than he that taketh a city." "If I have repaid them that recompense me evil, may I therefore fall by my enemies empty." He seems to swear by way of execration, which is the heaviest kind of oath, as when one says, If I have done so and so, may I suffer so and so. But swearing in a swearer's mouth is one thing, in a prophet's meaning another. For here he mentions what will really befall men who repay them that recompense evil; not what, as by an oath, he would imprecate on himself or any other.

4. "Let the enemy" therefore "persecute my soul and take it" (ver. 5). By again naming the enemy in the singular number, he more and more clearly points out him whom he spoke of above as a lion. For he persecutes the soul, and if he has deceived it, will take it. For the limit of men's rage is the destruction of the body; but the soul, after this visible death, they cannot keep in their power: whereas whatever souls the devil shall have taken by his persecutions, he will keep. "And let him tread my life upon the earth:" that is, by treading let him make my life

earth, that is to say, his food. For he is not only called a lion, but a serpent too, to whom it was said, "Earth shalt thou eat." And to the sinner was it said, "Earth thou art, and into earth shalt thou go." "And let him bring down my glory to the dust." This is that dust which "the wind casteth forth from the face of the earth," to wit, vain and silly boasting of the proud, puffed up, not of solid weight, as a cloud of dust carried away by the wind. Justly then has he here spoken of the glory, which he would not have brought down to dust. For he would have it solidly established in conscience before God, where there is no boasting. "He that glorieth," saith the Apostle, "let him glory in the Lord." This solidity is brought down to the dust if one through pride despising the secrecy of conscience, where God only proves a man, desires to glory before men. Hence comes what the Psalmist elsewhere says, "God shall bruise the bones of them that please men." Now he that has well learnt or experienced the steps in overcoming vices, knows that this vice of empty glory is either alone, or more than all, to be shunned by the perfect. For that by which the soul first fell, she overcomes the last. "For the beginning of all sin is pride:" and again, "The beginning of man's pride is to depart from God."

5. "Arise, O Lord, in Thine anger" (ver. 6). Why yet does he, who we say is perfect, incite God to anger? Must we not see, whether he rather be not perfect, who, when he was being stoned, said, "O Lord, lay not this sin to their charge"? Or does the Psalmist pray thus not against men, but against the devil and his angels, whose possession sinners and the ungodly are? He then does not pray against him in wrath, but in mercy, whosoever prays that that possession may be taken from him by that Lord "who justifieth the ungodly." For when the ungodly is justified, from ungodly he is made just, and from being the possession of the devil he passes into the temple of God. And since it is a punishment that a possession, in which one longs to have rule, should be taken away from him: this punishment, that he should cease to possess those whom he now possesses, the Psalmist calls the anger of God against the devil. "Arise, O Lord; in Thine anger." "Arise" (he has used it as "appear"), in words, that is, human and obscure; as though God sleeps, when He is unrecognised and hidden in His secret workings. "Be exalted in the borders of mine enemies." He means by borders the possession itself, in which he wishes that God should be exalted, that is, be honoured and glorified, rather than the devil, while the ungodly are justified and praise God. "And arise, O Lord my God, in the commandment that Thou hast given:" that is, since Thou hast enjoined humility, appear in humility; and first fulfil what Thou hast enjoined; that men by Thy example overcoming pride may not be possessed of the devil, who against Thy commandments advised to pride, saying, "Eat, and your eyes shall be opened, and ye shall be as gods."

6. "And the congregation of the people shall surround Thee." This may be understood two ways. For the congregation of the people can be taken, either of them that believe, or of them that persecute, both of which took place in the same humiliation of our Lord: in contempt of which the multitude of them that persecute surrounded Him; concerning which it is said, "Why have the heathen raged, and the people meditated vain things?" But of them that believe through His humiliation the multitude so surrounded Him, that it could be said with the greatest truth, "blindness in part is happened unto Israel, that the fulness of the Gentiles might come in:" and again, "Ask of me, and I will give Thee the Gentiles for Thine inheritance, and the boundaries of the earth for Thy possession." "And for their sakes return Thou on high:" that is, for the sake of this congregation return Thou on high: which He is understood to have done by His resurrection and ascension into heaven. For being thus glorified He gave the Holy Ghost, which before His exaltation could not be given, as it is written in the Gospel, "for the Holy Ghost was not yet given, because that Jesus was not yet glorified." Having then returned on high for the sake of the congregation of the people, He sent the Holy Ghost: by whom the preachers of the Gospel being filled, filled the whole world with Churches.

7. It can be taken also in this sense: "Arise, O Lord, in Thine anger, and be exalted in the borders of mine enemies:" that is, arise in Thine anger, and let not mine enemies understand Thee; so that to "be exalted," should be this, become high, that Thou mayest not be understood; which has reference to the silence spoken of above. For it is of this exaltation thus said in another Psalm, "And He ascended upon Cherubim, and flew:" and, "He made darkness His secret place." In which exaltation, or concealment, when for their sins' desert they shall not understand Thee, who shall crucify Thee, "the congregation" of believers "shall surround Thee." For in His very humiliation He was exalted, that is, was not understood. So that, "And arise, O Lord my God, in the commandment that Thou hast given:" may have reference to this, that is, when Thou showest Thyself, be high or deep that mine enemies may not understand Thee. Now sinners are the enemies of the just man, and the ungodly of the godly man. "And the congregation of the people shall surround Thee:" that is, by this very circumstance, that those who crucify Thee understand Thee not, the Gentiles shall believe on Thee, and so "shall the congregation of the people surround Thee." But what follows, if this be the true meaning, has in it more pain, that it begins already to be perceived, than joy that it is understood. For it follows, "and for their sakes return Thou on high," that is, and for the sake of this congregation of the human race, wherewith the Churches are crowded, return Thou on high, that is, again cease to be understood. What then is, "and for their sakes," but that this congregation too will offend Thee, so that Thou mayest most truly foretell and say, "Thinkest Thou when the Son of man shall

come, He will find faith on the earth?" Again, of the false prophets, who are understood to be heretics, He says, Because of their iniquity the love of many shall wax cold." Since then even in the Churches, that is, in that congregation of peoples and nations, where the Christian name has most widely spread, there shall be so great abundance of sinners, which is already, in great measure, perceived; is not that famine of the word here predicted, which has been threatened by another prophet also? Is it not too for this congregation's sake, who, by their sins, are estranging from themselves that light of truth, that God returns on high, that is, so that faith, pure and cleansed from the corruption of all perverse opinions, is held and received, either not at all, or by the very few of whom it was said, "Blessed is he that shall endure to the end, the same shall be saved"? Not without cause then is it said, "and for the sake of this" congregation "return Thou on high:" that is, again withdraw into the depth of Thy secrecy, even for the sake of this congregation of the peoples, that hath Thy name, and doeth not Thy deeds.

8. But whether the former exposition of this place, or this last be the more suitable, without prejudice to any one better, or equal, or as good, it follows very consistently, "the Lord judgeth the people." For whether He returned on high, when, after the resurrection, He ascended into heaven, well does it follow, "The Lord judgeth the people: "for that He will come from thence to judge the quick and the dead. Or whether He return on high, when the understanding of the truth leaves sinful Christians, for that of His coming it has been said, "Thinkest thou the Son of Man on His coming will find faith on the earth?" "The Lord" then "judgeth the people." What Lord, but Jesus Christ? "For the Father judgeth no man, but hath committed all judgment unto the Son." Wherefore this soul which prayeth perfectly, see how she fears not the day of judgment, and with a truly secure longing says in her prayer, "Thy kingdom come: judge me," she says, "O Lord, according to my righteousness." In the former Psalm a weak one was entreating, imploring rather the mercy of God, than mentioning any desert of his own: since the Son of God came "to call sinners to repentance.Therefore he had there said," Save me, O Lord, for Thy mercy's sake;" that is, not for my desert's sake. But now, since being called he hath held and kept the commandments which he received, he is bold to say, "Judge me, O Lord, according to my righteousness, and according to my harmlessness, that is upon me." This is true harmlessness, which harms not even an enemy. Accordingly, well does he require to be judged according to his harmlessness, who could say with truth, "If I have repaid them that recompense me evil." As for what he added, "that is upon me," it can refer not only to harmlessness, but can be understood also with reference to righteousness; that the sense should be this, Judge me, O Lord, according to my righteousness, and according to my harmlessness, which righteousness and harmlessness is upon me. By which addition he shows that this very thing, that the soul is righteous and

harmless, she has not by herself, but by God who giveth brightness and light. For of this he says in another Psalm, "Thou, O Lord, wilt light my candle." And of John it is said, that "he was not the light, but bore witness of the light." "He was a burning and shining candle." That light then, whence souls, as candles, are kindled, shines forth not with borrowed, but with original, brightness, which light is truth itself. It is then so said, "According to my righteousness, and according to my harmlessness, that is upon me," as if a burning and shining candle should say, Judge me according to the flame which is upon me, that is, not that wherewith I am myself, but that whereby I shine enkindled of thee.

9. "But let the wickedness of sinners be consummated" (ver. 9). He says, "be consummated," be completed, according to that in the Apocalypse, "Let the righteous become more righteous, and let the filthy be filthy still." For the wickedness of those men appears consummate, who crucified the Son of God; but greater is theirs who will not live uprightly, and hate the precepts of truth, for whom the Son of God was crucified. "Let the wickedness of sinners," then he says, "be consummated," that is, arrive at the height of wickedness, that just judgment may be able to come at once. But since it is not only said, "Let the filthy be filthy still;" but it is said also, "Let the righteous become more righteous;" he joins on the words, "And Thou shalt direct the righteous, O God, who searcheth the hearts and reins." How then can the righteous be directed but in secret? when even by means of those things which, in the commencement of the Christian ages, when as yet the saints were oppressed by the persecution of the men of this world, appeared marvellous to men, now that the Christian name has begun to be in such high dignity, hypocrisy, that is pretence, has increased; of those, I mean, who by the Christian profession had rather please men than God. How then is the righteous man directed in so great confusion of pretence, save whilst God searcheth the hearts and reins; seeing all men's thoughts, which are meant by the word heart; and their delights, which are understood by the word reins? For the delight in things temporal and earthly is rightly ascribed to the reins; for that it is both the lower part of man, and that region where the pleasure of carnal generation dwells, through which man's nature is transferred into this life of care, and deceiving joy, by the succession of the race. God then, searching our heart, and perceiving that it is there where our treasure is, that is, in heaven; searching also the reins, and perceiving that we do not assent to flesh and blood, but delight ourselves in the Lord, directs the righteous man in his inward conscience before Him, where no man seeth, but He alone who perceiveth what each man thinketh, and what delighteth each. For delight is the end of care; because to this end does each man strive by care and thought, that he may attain to his delight. He therefore seeth our cares, who searcheth the heart. He seeth too the ends of cares, that is delights, who narrowly searcheth the reins; that when He shall find that our cares incline neither

to the lust of the flesh, nor to the lust of the eyes, nor to the pride of life, all which pass away as a shadow, but that they are raised upward to the joys of things eternal, which are spoilt by no change, He may direct the righteous, even He, the God who searcheth the hearts and reins. For our works, which we do in deeds and words, may be known unto men; but with what mind they are done, and to what end we would attain by means of them, He alone knoweth, the God who searcheth the hearts and reins.

10. "My righteous help is from the Lord, who maketh whole the upright in heart" (ver. 10). The offices of medicine are twofold, on the curing infirmity, the other the preserving health. According to the first it was said in the preceding Psalm, "Have mercy on me, O Lord, for I am weak;" according to the second it is said in this Psalm, "If there be iniquity in my hands, if I have repaid them that recompense me evil, may I therefore fall by my enemies empty." For there the weak prays that he may be delivered, here one already whole that he may not change for the worse. According to the one it is there said, "Make me whole for Thy mercy's sake;" according to this other it is here said," Judge me, O Lord, according to my righteousness." For there he asks for a remedy to escape from disease; but here for protection from falling into disease. According to the former it is said, "Make me whole, O Lord, according to Thy mercy:" according to the latter it is said, "My righteous help is from the Lord, who maketh whole the upright in heart." Both the one and the other maketh men whole; but the former removes them from sickness into health, the latter preserves them in this health. Therefore there the help is merciful, because the sinner hath no desert, who as yet longeth to be justified, "believing on Him who justifieth the ungodly;" but here the help is righteous, because it is given to one already righteous. Let the sinner then who said, "I am weak," say in the first place, "Make me whole, O Lord, for Thy mercy's sake;" and here let the righteous man, who said, "If I have repaid them that recompense me evil," say, "My righteous help is from the Lord, who maketh whole the upright in heart." For if he sets forth the medicine, by which we may be healed when weak, how much more that by which we may be kept in health. For if "while we were yet sinners, Christ died for us, how much more being now justified shall we be kept whole from wrath through Him."

11. "My righteous help is from the Lord, who maketh whole the upright in heart." God, who searcheth the hearts and reins, directeth the righteous; but with righteous help maketh He whole the upright in heart. He doth not as He searcheth the hearts and reins, so make whole the upright in heart and reins; for the thoughts are both bad in a depraved heart, and good in an upright heart; but delights which are not good belong to the reins, for they are more low and earthly; but those that are good

not to the reins, but to the heart itself. Wherefore men cannot be so called upright in reins, as they are called upright in heart, since where the thought is, there at once the delight is too; which cannot be, unless when things divine and eternal are thought of. "Thou hast given," he says, "joy in my heart," when he had said, "The light of Thy countenance has been stamped on us, O Lord." For although the phantoms of things temporal, which the mind falsely pictures to itself, when tossed by vain and mortal hope, to vain imagination oftentimes bring a delirious and maddened joy; yet this delight must be attributed not to the heart, but to the reins; for all these imaginations have been drawn from lower, that is, earthly and carnal things. Hence it comes, that God, who searcheth he hearts and reins, and perceiveth in the heart upright thoughts, in the reins no delights, affordeth righteous help to the upright in heart, where heavenly delights are coupled with clean thoughts. And therefore when in another Psalm he had said, "Moreover even to-night my reins have chided me;" he went on to say as touching help, "I foresaw the Lord alway in my sight, for He is on my right hand, that I should not be moved." Where he shows that he suffered suggestions only from the reins, not delights as well; for he had suffered these, then he would of course be moved. But he said, "The Lord is on my right hand, that I should not be moved;" and then he adds, "Wherefore was my heart delighted;" that the reins should have been able to chide, not delight him. The delight accordingly was produced not in the reins, but there, where against the chiding of the reins God was foreseen to be on the right hand, that is, in the heart.

12. "God the righteous judge, strong (in endurance) and long- suffering" (yet. 11). What God is judge, but the Lord, who judgeth the people? He is righteous; who "shall render to every man according to his works." He is strong (in endurance); who, being most powerful, for our salvation bore even with ungodly persecutors. He is long-suffering; who did not immediately, after His resurrection, hurry away to punishment, even those that persecuted Him, but bore with them, that they might at length turn from that ungodliness to salvation: and still He beareth with them, reserving the last penalty for the last judgment, and up to this present time inviting sinners to repentance. "Not bringing in anger every day." Perhaps "bringing in anger" is a more significant expression than being angry (and so we find it in the Greek copies); that the anger, whereby He punisheth, should not be in Him, but in the minds of those ministers who obey the commandments of truth through whom orders are given even to the lower ministries, who are called angels of wrath, to punish sin: whom even now the punishment of men delights not for justice' sake, in which they have no pleasure, but for malice' sake. God then doth not "bring in anger every day," that is, He doth not collect His ministers for vengeance every day. For now the patience of God inviteth to repentance: but in the last time, when men "through their hardness and impenitent heart shall have

treasured up for themselves anger in the day of anger, and revelation of the righteous judgment of God, then He will brandish His sword." 13. "Unless ye be converted," He says, "He will brandish His sword" (ver. 12). The Lord Man Himself may be taken to be God's double-edged sword, that is, His spear, which at His first coming He will not brandish, but hideth as it were in the sheath of humiliation: but He will brandish it, when at the second coming to judge the quick and dead, in the manifest splendour of His glory, He shall flash light on His righteous ones, and terror on the ungodly. For in other copies, instead of," He shall brandish His sword," it has been written, "He shall make bright His spear:" by which word I think the last coming of the Lord's glory most appropriately signified: seeing that is understood of His person, which another Psalm has, "Deliver, O Lord, my soul from the ungodly, Thy spear from the enemies of Thine hand. He hath bent His bow, and made it ready." The tenses of the words must not be altogether overlooked, how he has spoken of "the sword" in the future, "He will brandish;" of "the bow" in the past, "He hath bent:" and these words of the past tense follow after.

14. "And in it He hath prepared the instruments of death: He hath wrought His arrows for the burning" (ver. 13). That bow then I would readily take to be the Holy Scripture, in which by the strength of the New Testament, as by a sort of string, the hardness of the Old has been bent and subdued. From thence the Apostles are sent forth like arrows, or divine preachings are shot. Which arrows "He has wrought for the burning," arrows, that is, whereby being stricken they might be inflamed with heavenly love. For by what other arrows was she stricken, who saith, "Bring me into the house of wine, place me among perfumes, crowd me among honey, for I have been wounded with love"? By what other arrows is he kindled, who, desirous of returning to God, and coming back from wandering, asketh for help against crafty tongues, and to whom it is said, "What shall be given thee, or what added to thee against the crafty tongue? Sharp arrows of the mighty, with devastating coals:" that is, coals, whereby, when thou art stricken and set on fire, thou mayest burn with so great love of the kingdom of heaven, as to despise the tongues of all that resist thee, and would recall thee from thy purpose, and to deride their persecutions, saying, "Who shall separate me from the love of Christ? shall tribulation, or distress, or persecution, or famine, or nakedness, or peril, or sword? For I am persuaded," he says, "that neither death, nor life, nor angel, nor principality, nor things present, not things to come, nor power, nor height, nor depth, nor other creature, shall be able to separate me from the love of God, which is in Christ Jesus our Lord." Thus for the burning hath He wrought His arrows. For in the Greek copies it is found thus, "He hath wrought His arrows for the burning." But most of the Latin copies have "burning arrows." But whether the arrows

themselves burn, or make others burn, which of course they cannot do unless they burn themselves, the sense is complete.

15. But since he has said that the Lord has prepared not arrows only, but "instruments of death" too, in the bow, it may be asked, what are "instruments of death"? Are they, peradventure, heretics? For they too, out of the same bow, that is, out of the same Scriptures, light upon souls not to be inflamed with love but destroyed with poison: which does not happen but after their deserts: wherefore even this dispensation is to be assigned to the Divine Providence, not that it makes men sinners, but that it orders them after they have sinned. For through sin reaching them with an ill purpose, they are forced to understand them ill, that this should be itself the punishment of sin: by whose death, nevertheless, the sons of the Catholic Church are, as it were by certain thorns, so to say, aroused from slumber, and make progress toward the understanding of the holy Scriptures. "For there must be also heresies, that they which are approved," he says, "may be made manifest among you:" that is, among men, seeing they are manifest to God. Or has He haply ordained the same arrows to be at once instruments of death for the destruction of unbelievers, and wrought them burning, or for the burning, for the exercising of the faithful? For that is not false that the Apostle says, "To the one we are the savour of life unto life, to the other the savour of death unto death; and who is sufficient for these things?" It is no wonder then if the same Apostles be both instruments of death in those from whom they suffered persecution, and fiery arrows to inflame the hearts of believers.

16. Now after this dispensation righteous judgment will come: of which the Psalmist so speaks, as that we may understand that each man's punishment is wrought out of his own sin, and his iniquity turned into vengeance: that we may not suppose that that tranquillity and ineffable light of God brings forth from Itself the means of punishing sin; but that it so ordereth sins, that what have been delights to man in sinning, should be instruments to the Lord avenging. "Behold," he says, "he hath travailed with injustice." Now what had he conceived, that he should travail with injustice? "He hath conceived," he says, "toil." Hence then comes that, "In toil shall thou eat thy bread." Hence too that, "Come unto Me all ye that toil and are heavy laden; for My yoke is easy, and My burden light." For toil will never cease, except one love that which cannot be taken away against his will. For when those things are loved which we can lose against our wilt, we must needs toil for them most miserably; and to obtain them, amid the straitnesses of earthly cares, whilst each desires to snatch them for himself, and to be beforehand with another, or to wrest it from him, must scheme injustice. Duly then, and quite in order, hath he travailed with injustice, who has conceived toil. Now he bringeth

forth what, save that with which he hath travailed, although he has not travailed with that which he conceived? For that is not born, which is not conceived; but seed is conceived, that which is formed from the seed is born. Toil is then the seed of iniquity, but sin the conception of toil, that is, that first sin, to "depart from God." He then hath travailed with injustice, who hath conceived toil. "And he hath brought forth iniquity." "Iniquity" is the same as "injustice:" he hath brought forth then that with which he travailed. What follows next?

17. "He hath opened a ditch, and digged it" (ver. 15). To open a ditch is, in earthly matters, that is, as it were in the earth, to prepare deceit, that another fall therein, whom the unrighteous man wishes to deceive. Now this ditch is opened when consent is given to the evil suggestion of earthly lusts: but it is digged when after consent we press on to actual work of deceit. But how can it be, that iniquity should rather hurt the righteous man against whom it proceeds, than the unrighteous heart whence it proceeds? Accordingly, the stealer of money, for instance, while he desires to inflict painful harm upon another, is himself maimed by the wound of avarice. Now who, even out of his right mind, sees not how great is the difference between these men, when one suffers the loss of money, the other of innocence? "He will fall" then "into the pit which he hath made." As it is said in another Psalm, "The Lord is known in executing judgments; the sinner is caught in the works of his own hands."

18. "His toil shall be turned on his head, and his iniquity shall descend on his pate "(ver. 16). For he had no mind to escape sin: but was brought under sin as a slave, so to say, as the Lord saith, "Whosoever sinneth is a slave." His iniquity then will be upon him, when he is subject to his iniquity; for he could not say to the Lord, what the innocent and upright say, "My glory, and the lifter up of my head." He then will be in such wise below, as that his iniquity may be above, and descend on him; for that it weigheth him down and burdens him, and suffers him not to fly back to the rest of the saints. This occurs, when in an ill regulated man reason is a slave, and lust hath dominion.

19. "I will confess to the Lord according to His justice" (ver. 17). This is not the sinner's confession: for he says this, who said above most truly, "If there be iniquity in my hands:" but it is a confession of God's justice, in which we speak thus, Verily, O Lord, Thou art just, in that Thou both so protectest the just, that Thou enlightenest them by Thyself; and so orderest sinners, that they be punished not by Thine, but by their own malice. This confession so praises the Lord, that the blasphemies of the ungodly can avail nothing, who, willing to excuse their evil deeds, are unwilling to attribute to their own fault that they sin, that is, are

unwilling to attribute their fault to their fault. Accordingly they find either fortune or fate to accuse, or the devil, to whom He who made us hath willed that it should be in our power to refuse consent: or they bring in another nature, which is not of God: wretched waverers, and erring, rather than confessing to God, that He should pardon them. For it is not fit that any be pardoned, except he says, I have sinned. He, then, that sees the deserts of souls so ordered by God, that while each has his own given him, the fair beauty of the universe is in no part violated, in all things praises God: and this is not the confession of sinners, but of the righteous. For it is not the sinner's confession when the Lord says, "I confess to Thee, O Lord of heaven and earth, because Thou hast hid these things from the wise, and revealed them to babes." Likewise in Ecclesiasticus it is said, "Confess to the Lord in all His works: and in confession ye shall say this, All the works of the Lord are exceeding good." Which can be seen in this Psalm, if any one with a pious mind, by the Lord's help, distinguish between the rewards of the righteous and the penalties of the sinners, how that in these two the whole creation, which God made and rules, is adorned with a beauty wondrous and known to few. Thus then he says, "I will confess to the Lord according to His justice," as one who saw that darkness was not made by God, but ordered nevertheless. For God said, "Let light be made, and light was made." He did not say, Let darkness be made, and darkness was made: and yet He ordered it. And therefore it is said, "God divided between the light, and the darkness: and God called the light day, and the darkness He called night." This is the distinction, He made the one and ordered it: but the other He made not, but yet He ordered this too. But now that sins are signified by darkness, so is it seen in the Prophet, who says, "And thy darkness shall be as the noon day:" and in the Apostle, who says, "He that hateth his brother is in darkness:" and above all that text, "Let us cast off the works of darkness, and let us put on the armour of light." Not that there is any nature of darkness. For all nature, in so far as it is nature, is compelled to be. Now being belongs to light: not-being to darkness. He then that leaves Him by whom he was made, and inclines to that whence he was made, that is, to nothing, is in this sin endarkened: and yet he does not utterly perish, but he is ordered among the lowest things. Therefore after the Psalmist said, "I will confess unto the Lord:" that we might not understand it of confession of sins, he adds lastly, "And I will sing to the name of the Lord most high." Now singing has relation to joy, but repentance of sins to sadness.

20. This Psalm can also be taken in the person of the Lord Man: if only that which is there spoken in humiliation be referred to our weakness, which He bore.

PSALM VIII.

TO THE END, FOR THE WINE-PRESSES, A PSALM OF DAVID HIMSELF.

1. He seems to say nothing of wine-presses in the text of the Psalm of which this is the title. By which it appears, that one and the same thing is often signified in Scripture by many and various similitudes. We may then take wine-presses to be Churches, on the same principle by which we understand also by a threshing-floor the Church. For whether in the threshing-floor, or in the wine-press, there is nothing else done but the clearing the produce of its covering; which is necessary, both for its first growth and increase, and arrival at the maturity either of the harvest or the vintage. Of these coverings or supporters then; that is, of chaff, on the threshing-floor, the corn; and of husks, in the presses, the wine is stripped: as in the Churches, from the multitude of worldly men, which is collected together with the good, for whose birth and adapting to the divine word that multitude was necessary, this is effected, that by spiritual love they be separated through the operation of God's ministers. For now so it is that the good are, for a time, separated from the bad, not in space, but in affection: although they have converse together in the Churches, as far as respects bodily presence. But another time will come, the corn will be stored up apart in the granaries, and the wine in the cellars. "The wheat," saith he, "He will lay up in garners; but the chaff He will burn with fire unquenchable." The same thing may be thus understood in another similitude: the wine He will lay up in cellars, but the husks He will cast forth to cattle: so that by the bellies of the cattle we may be allowed by way of similitude to understand the pains of hell.

2. There is another interpretation concerning the wine-presses, yet still keeping to the meaning of Churches. For even the Divine Word may be understood by the grape: for the Lord even has been called a Cluster of grapes; which they that were sent before by the people of Israel brought from the land of promise hanging on a staff, crucified as it were. Accordingly, when the Divine Word maketh use of, by the necessity of declaring Himself, the sound of the voice, whereby to convey Himself to the ears of the hearers; in the same sound of the voice, as it were in husks, knowledge, like the wine, is enclosed: and so this grape comes into the ears, as into the pressing machines of the wine-pressers. For there the separation is made, that the sound may reach as far as the ear; but knowledge be received in the memory of those that hear, as it were in a sort of vat; whence it passes into discipline of the conversation and habit of mind, as from the vat into the cellar: where if it do not through negligence grow sour, it will acquire soundness by age. For it grew sour among the Jews, and this sour vinegar they gave the Lord to

drink. For that wine, which from the produce of the vine of the New Testament the Lord is to drink with His saints in the kingdom of His Father, must needs be most sweet and most sound.

3. "Wine-presses" are also usually taken for martyrdoms, as if when they who have confessed the name of Christ have been trodden down by the blows of persecution, their mortal remains as husks remained on earth, but their souls flowed forth into the rest of a heavenly habitation. Nor yet by this interpretation do we depart from the fruitfulness of the Churches. It is sung then, "for the wine-presses," for the Church's establishment; when our Lord after His resurrection ascended into heaven. For then He sent the Holy Ghost: by whom the disciples being fulfilled preached with confidence the Word of God, that Churches might be collected.

4. Accordingly it is said," O Lord, our Lord, how admirable is Thy Name in all the earth!" (ver. 1). I ask, how is His Name wonderful in all the earth? The answer is, "For Thy glory has been raised above the heavens." So that the meaning is this, O Lord, who art our Lord, how do all that inhabit the earth admire Thee! for Thy glory hath been raised from earthly humiliation above the heavens. For hence it appeared who Thou wast that descendedst, when it was by some seen, and by the rest believed, whither it was that Thou ascendedst.

5. "Out of the mouth of babes and sucklings Thou hast made perfect praise, because of Thine enemies" (ver. 2). I cannot take babes and sucklings to be any other than those to whom the Apostle says, "As unto babes in Christ I have given you milk to drink, not meat." Who were meant by those who went before the Lord praising Him, of whom the Lord Himself used this testimony, when He answered the Jews who bade Him rebuke them," Have ye not read, out of the mouth of babes and sucklings Thou hast made perfect praise?" Now with good reason He says not, Thou hast made, but," Thou hast made perfect praise." For there are in the Churches also those who now no more drink milk, but eat meat: whom the same Apostle points out, saying, "We speak wisdom among them that are perfect;" but not by those only are the Churches perfected; for if there were only these, little consideration would be had of the human race. But consideration is had, when they too, who are not as yet capable of the knowledge of things spiritual and eternal, are nourished by the faith of the temporal history, which for our salvation after the Patriarchs and Prophets was administered by the most excellent Power and Wisdom of God, even in the Sacrament of the assumed Manhood, in which there is salvation for every one that believeth; to the end that moved by Its authority each one may obey Its precepts, whereby being purified and "rooted and

grounded in love," he may be able to run with Saints, no more now a child in milk, but a young man in meat, "to comprehend the breadth, the length, the height, and depth, to know also the surpassing knowledge of the love of Christ."

6. "Out of the mouth of babes and sucklings Thou hast made perfect praise, because of Thine enemies." By enemies to this dispensation, which has been wrought through Jesus Christ and Him crucified, we ought generally to understand all who forbid belief in things unknown, and promise certain knowledge: as all heretics do, and they who in the superstition of the Gentiles are called philosophers. Not that the promise of knowledge is to be blamed; but because they deem the most healthful and necessary step of faith is to be neglected, by which we must needs ascend to something certain, which nothing but that which is eternal can be. Hence it appears that they do not possess even this knowledge, which in contempt of faith they promise; seeing that they know not so useful and necessary a step thereof. "Out of the mouth," then "of babes and sucklings Thou hast made perfect praise," Thou, our Lord, declaring first by the Apostle, "Except ye believe, ye shall not understand;" and saying by His own mouth," Blessed are they that have not seen, and shall believe." "Because of the enemies: "against whom too that is said, "I confess to Thee, O Lord of heaven and earth, because Thou hast hid these things from the wise, and revealed them unto babes." "From the wise," he saith, not the really wise, but those who deem themselves such. "That Thou mayest destroy the enemy and the defender." Whom but the heretic? For he is both an enemy and a defender, who when he would assault the Christian faith, seems to defend it. Although the philosophers too of this world may be well taken as the enemies and defenders: forasmuch as the Son of God is the Power and Wisdom of God by which every one is enlightened who is made wise by the truth: of which they profess themselves to be lovers, whence too their name of philosophers; and therefore they seem to defend it, while they are its enemies, since they cease not to recommend noxious superstitions, that the elements of this world should be worshipped and revered.

7. "For I shall see Thy heavens, the works of Thy fingers" (ver. 3). We read that the law was written with the finger of God, and given through Moses, His holy servant: by which finger of God many understand the Holy Ghost. Wherefore if, by the fingers of God, we are right in understanding these same ministers filled with the Holy Ghost, by reason of this same Spirit which worketh in them, since by them all holy Scripture has been completed for us; we understand consistently with this, that, in this place, the books of both Testaments are called "the heavens." Now it is said too of Moses himself, by the magicians of king Pharaoh, when they were conquered by him, "This is the finger of God." And what is written," The

heavens shall be rolled up as a book." Although it be said of this aethereal heaven, yet naturally, according to the same image, the heavens of books are named by allegory. "For I shall see," he says, "the heavens, the works of Thy fingers:" that is, I shall discern and understand the Scriptures, which Thou, by the operation of the Holy Ghost, hast written by Thy ministers.

8. Accordingly the heavens named above also may be interpreted as the same books, where he says, "For Thy glory hath been raised above the heavens:" so that the complete meaning should be this, "For Thy glory hath been raised above the heavens;" for Thy glory hath exceeded the declarations of all the Scriptures: "Out of the mouth of babes and sucklings Thou hast made perfect praise," that they should begin by belief in the Scriptures, who would arrive at the knowledge of Thy glory: which hath been raised above the Scriptures, in that it passeth by and transcends the announcements of all words and languages. Therefore hath God lowered the Scriptures even to the capacity of babes and sucklings, as it is sung in another Psalm, "And He lowered the heaven, and came down:" and this did He because of the enemies, who through pride of talkativeness, being enemies of the cross of Christ, even when they do speak some truth, still cannot profit babes and sucklings. So is the enemy and defender destroyed, who, whether he seem to defend wisdom, or even the name of Christ, still, from the step of this faith, assaults that truth, which he so readily makes promise of. Whereby too he is convicted of not possessing it; since by assaulting the step thereof, namely faith, he knows not how one should mount up thereto. Hence then is the rash and blind promiser of truth, who is the enemy and defender, destroyed, when the heavens, the works of God's fingers, are seen, that is, when the Scriptures, brought down even to the slowness of babes, are understood; and by means of the lowness of the faith of the history, which was transacted in time, they raise them, well nurtured and strengthened, unto the grand height of the understanding of things eternal, up to those things which they establish. For these heavens, that is, these books, are the works of God's fingers; for by the operation of the Holy Ghost in the Saints they were completed. For they that have regarded their own glory rather than man's salvation, have spoken without the Holy Ghost, in whom are the bowel: of the mercy of God.

9. "For I shall see the heavens, the works of Thy fingers, the moon and the stars, which Thou hast ordained." The moon and stars are ordained in the heavens; since both the Church universal, to signify which the moon is often put, and Churches in the several places particularly, which I imagine to be intimated by the name of stars, are established in the same Scriptures, which we believe to be expressed by the word heavens. But why the moon justly signifies the Church, will be more

seasonably considered in another Psalm, where it is said, "The sinners have bent their bow, that they may shoot in the obscure moon the upright in heart."

10. "What is man, that Thou art mindful of him? or the son of man, that Thou visitest him?" (ver. 4). It may be asked, what distinction there is between man and son of man. For if there were none, it would not be expressed thus," man, or son of man," disjunctively. For if it were written thus, "What is man, that Thou art mindful of him, and son of man, that Thou visitest him?" it might appear to be a repetition of the word "man." But now when the expression is, "man or son of-man," a distinction is more clearly intimated. This is certainly to be remembered, that every son of man is a man; although every man cannot be taken to be a son of man. Adam, for instance, was a man, but not a son of man. Wherefore we may from hence consider and distinguish what is the difference in this place between man and son of man; namely, that they who bear the image of the earthy man, who is not a son of man, should be signified by the name of men; but that they who bear the image of the heavenly Man should be rather called sons of men; for the former again is called the old man and the latter the new; but the new is born of the old, since spiritual regeneration is begun by a change of an earthy, and worldly life; and therefore the latter is called son of man. "Man" then in this place is earthy, but "son of man" heavenly; and the former is far removed from God, but the latter present with God; and therefore is He mindful of the former, as in far distance from Him; but the latter He visiteth, with whom being present He enlighteneth him with His countenance. For "salvation is far from sinners;" and, "The light of Thy countenance hath been stamped upon us, O Lord." So in another Psalm he saith, that men in conjunction with beasts are made whole together with these beasts, not by any present inward illumination, but by the multiplication of the mercy of God, whereby His goodness reacheth even to the lowest things; for the wholeness of carnal men is carnal, as of the beasts; but separating the sons of men from those whom being men he joined with cattle, he proclaims that they are made blessed, after a far more exalted method, by the enlightening of the truth itself, and by a certain inundation of the fountain of life. For he speaketh thus: "Men and beasts Thou wilt make whole, O Lord, as Thy mercy hath been multiplied, O God. But the sons of men shall put their trust in the covering of Thy wings. They shall be inebriated with the richness of Thine house, and of the torrent of Thy pleasures Thou shall make them drink. For with Thee is the fountain of life, and in Thy light shall we see light. Extend Thy mercy to them that know Thee." Through the multiplication of mercy then He is mindful of man, as of beasts; for that multiplied mercy reacheth even to them that are afar off; but He visiteth the son of man, over whom, placed under the covering of His wings, He extendeth mercy, and in His light giveth light, and maketh him drink of His pleasures, and inebriateth him with the richness of His house, to forget the sorrows

and the wanderings of his former conversation. This son of man, that is, the new man, the repentance of the old man begets with pain and tears. He, though new, is nevertheless called yet carnal, whilst he is fed with milk; "I would not speak unto you as unto spiritual, but as unto carnal," says the Apostle. And to show that they were already regenerate, he says, "As unto babes in Christ, I have given you milk to drink, not meat." And when he relapses, as often happens, to the old life, he hears in reproof that he is a man; "Are ye not men," he says, "and walk as men?"

11. Therefore was the son of man first visited in the person of the very Lord Man, born of the Virgin Mary. Of whom, by reason of the very weakness of the flesh, which the Wisdom of God vouchsafed to bear, and the humiliation of the Passion, it is justly said, "Thou hast lowered Him a little lower than the Angels" (ver. 5). But that glorifying is added, in which He rose and ascended up into heaven; "With glory," he says, "and with honour hast Thou crowned Him; and hast set Him over the works of Thine hands" (ver. 6). Since even Angels are the works of God's hands, even over Angels we understand the Only-begotten Son to have been set; whom we hear and believe, by the humiliation of the carnal generation and passion, to have been lowered a little lower than the Angels.

12. "Thou hast put," he says, "all things in subjection under His feet." When he says, "all things," he excepts nothing. And that he might not be allowed to understand it otherwise, the Apostle enjoins it to be believed thus, when he says, "He being excepted which put all things under Him." And to the Hebrews he uses this very testimony from this Psalm, when he would have it to be understood that all things are in such sort put under our Lord Jesus Christ, as that nothing should be excepted. And yet he does not seem, as it were, to subjoin any great thing, when he says, "All sheep and oxen, yea, moreover, the beasts of the field, birds of the air, and the fish of the sea, which walk through the paths of the sea" (ver. 7). For, leaving the heavenly excellencies and powers, and all the hosts of Angels, leaving even man himself, he seems to have put under Him the beasts merely; unless by sheep and oxen we understand holy souls, either yielding the fruit of innocence, or even working that the earth may bear fruit, that is, that earthly men may be regenerated unto spiritual richness. By these holy souls then we ought to understand not those of men only, but of all Angels too, if we would gather from hence that all things are put under our Lord Jesus Christ. For there will be no creature that will not be put under Him, under whom the pre-eminent spirits, that I may so speak, are put. But whence shall we prove that sheep can be interpreted even, not of men, but of the blessed spirits of the angelical creatures on high? May we from the Lord's saying that He had left ninety and nine sheep in the mountains, that is, in the higher regions, and had come down for one? For if we take the one

lost sheep to be the human soul in Adam, since Eve even was made out of his side, for the spiritual handling and consideration of all which things this is not the time, it remains that, by the ninety and nine left in the mountains, spirits not human, but angelical, should be meant. For as regards the oxen, this sentence is easily despatched; since men themselves are for no other reason called oxen, but because by preaching the Gospel of the word of God they imitate Angels, as where it is said, "Thou shalt not muzzle the ox that treadeth out the corn." How much more easily then do we take the Angels themselves, the messengers of truth, to be oxen, when Evangelists by the participation of their title are called oxen? "Thou hast put under" therefore, he says, "all sheep and oxen," that is, all the holy spiritual creation; in which we include that of holy men, who are in the Church, in those wine-presses to wit, which are intimated under the other similitude of the moon and stars.

13. "Yea moreover," saith he, "the beasts of the field." The addition of "moreover" is by no means idle. First, because by beasts of the plain may be understood both sheep and oxen: so that, if goats are the beasts of rocky and mountainous regions, sheep may be well taken to be the beasts of the field. Accordingly had it been written even thus, "all sheep and oxen and beasts of the field;" it might be reasonably asked what beasts of the plain meant, since even sheep and oxen could be taken as such. But the addition of "moreover" besides, obliges us, beyond question, to recognise some difference or another. But under this word, "moreover," not only "beasts of the field," but also "birds of the air, and fish of the sea, which walk through the paths of the sea" (ver. 8), are to be taken in. What is then this distinction? Call to mind the "wine-presses," holding husks and wine; and the threshing-floor, containing chaff and corn; and the nets, in which were enclosed good fish and bad; and the ark of Noah, in which were both unclean and clean animals: and you will see that the Churches for a while, now in this time, unto the last time of judgment, contain not only sheep and oxen, that is, holy laymen and holy ministers, but "moreover beasts of the field, birds of the air, and birds of the sea, that walk through the paths of the sea." For the beasts of the field were very fitly understood, as men rejoicing in the pleasure of the flesh where they mount up to nothing high, nothing laborious. For the field is also "the broad way, that leadeth to destruction:" and in a field is Abel slain. Wherefore there is cause to fear, test one coming down from the mountains of God's righteousness ("for thy righteousness," he says, "is as the mountains of God") making choice of the broad and easy paths of carnal pleasure, be slain by the devil. See now too "the birds of heaven," the proud, of whom it is said, "They have set their mouth against the heaven." See how they are carried on high by the wind, "who say, We will magnify our tongue, our lips are our own, who is our Lord?" Behold too the fish of the sea, that is, the curious; who walk through the paths of the sea, that is, search

in the deep after the temporal things of this world: which, like: paths in the sea, vanish and perish, as quickly as the water comes together again after it has given room, in their passage, to ships, or to whatsoever walketh or swimmeth. For he said not merely, who walk the paths of the sea; but "walk through," he said; showing the very determined earnestness of those who seek after vain and fleeting things. Now these three kinds of vice, namely, the pleasure of the flesh, and pride, and curiosity, include all sins. And they appear to me to be enumerated by the Apostle John, when he says, "Love not the world; for all that is in the world is the lust of the flesh, and the lust of the eyes, and the pride of life." For through the eyes especially prevails curiosity. To what the rest indeed belong is clear. And that temptation of the Lord Man was threefold: by food, that is, by the lust of the flesh, where it is suggested, "command these stones that they be made bread:" by vain boasting, where, when stationed on a mountain, all the kingdoms of this earth are shown Him, and promised if He would worship: by curiosity, where, from the pinnacle of the temple, He is advised to cast Himself down, for the sake of trying whether He would be borne up by Angels. And accordingly after that the enemy could prevail with Him by none of these temptations, this is said of him, "When the devil had ended all his temptation." With a reference then to the meaning of the wine- presses, not only the wine, but the husks too are put under His feet; to wit, not only sheep and oxen, that is, the holy souls of believers, either in the laity, or in the ministry; but moreover both beasts of pleasure, and birds of pride, and fish of curiosity. All which classes of sinners we see mingled now in the Churches with the good and holy. May He work then in His Churches, and separate the wine from the husks: let us give heed, that we be wine, and sheep or oxen; not husks, or beasts of the field, or birds of heaven, or fish of the sea, which walk through the paths of the sea. Not that these names can be understood and explained in this way only, but the explanation of them must be according to the place where they are found. For elsewhere they have other meanings. And this rule must be kept to in every allegory, that what is expressed by the similitude should be considered agreeably to the meaning of the particular place: for this is the manner of the Lord's and the Apostles' teaching. Let us repeat then the last verse, which is also put at the beginning of the Psalm, and let us praise God, saying, "0 Lord our Lord, how wonderful is Thy name in all the earth!" For fitly, after the matter of the discourse, is the return made to the heading, whither all that discourse must be referred.

PSALM IX.

1. The inscription of this Psalm is, "To the end for the hidden things of the Son, a Psalm of David himself." As to the hidden things of the Son there may be a question: but since he has not added whose, the very only-begotten Son of God should be understood. For where a Psalm has been inscribed of the son of David, "When," he says, "he fled from the face of Absalom his son;" although his name even was mentioned, and therefore there could be no obscurity as to whom it was spoken of: yet it is not merely said, from the face of son Absalom; but "his" is added. But here both because "his" is not added, and much is said of the Gentiles, it cannot properly be taken of Absalom. For the war which that abandoned one waged with his father, no way relates to the Gentiles, since there the people of Israel only were divided against themselves. This Psalm is then sung for the hidden things of the only-begotten Son of God. For the Lord Himself too, when, without addition, He uses the word Son, would have Himself, the Only-begotten to be understood; as where He says, "If the Son shall make you free, then shall ye be free indeed." For He said not, the Son of God; but in saying merely, Son, He gives us to understand whose Son it is. Which form of expression nothing admits of, save His excellency of whom we so speak, that, though we name Him not, He can be understood. For so we say, it rains, clears up, thunders, and such like expressions; and we do not add who does it all; for that the excellency of the doer spontaneously presents itself to all men's minds, and does not want words. What then are the hidden things of the Son? By which expression we must first understand that there are some things of the Son manifest, from which those are distinguished which are called hidden. Wherefore since we believe two advents of the Lord, one past, which the Jews understood not: the other future, which we both hope for; and since the one which the Jews understood not, profited the Gentiles; "For the hidden things of the Son" is not unsuitably understood to be spoken of this advent, in which "blindness in part is happened to Israel, that the fulness of the Gentiles might come in."

For notice of two judgments is conveyed to us throughout the Scriptures, if any one will give heed to them, one hidden, the other manifest. The hidden one is passing now, of which the Apostle Peter says, "The time is come that judgment should begin from the house of the Lord." The hidden judgment accordingly is the pain, by which now each man is either exercised to purification, or warned to conversion, or if he despise the calling and discipline of God, is blinded unto damnation. But the manifest judgment is that in which the Lord, at His coming, will judge the quick and the dead, all men confessing that it is He by whom both rewards shall be assigned to the good, and punishments to the evil. But then that confession will avail, not to the remedy of evils, but to the accumulation of damnation. Of these two judgments, the one hidden, the other manifest, the Lord seems to me to have spoken, where He says, "Whoso believeth on Me hath passed from death unto life, and shall not come into judgment; into the manifest judgment, that is. For that which passes from death unto life by means of some affliction, whereby "He scourgeth every son whom He receiveth,"is the hidden judgment. "But whoso believeth not," saith He, "hath been judged already:" that is, by this hidden judgment hath been already prepared for that manifest one. These two judgments we read of also in Wisdom, whence it is written, "Therefore unto them, as to children without the use of reason, Thou didst give a judgment to mock them; But they that have not been corrected by this judgment have felt a judgment worthy of God." Whoso then are not corrected by this hidden judgment of God, shall most worthily be punished by that manifest one. ...

2. "I will confess unto Thee, O Lord, with my whole heart" (ver. 1). He doth not, with a whole heart, confess unto God, who doubteth of His Providence in any particular: but he who sees already the hidden things of the wisdom of God, how great is Iris invisible reward, who saith, "We rejoice in tribulations;" and how all torments, which are inflicted on the body, are either for the exercising of those that are converted to God, or for warning that they be converted, or for just preparation of the obdurate unto their last damnation: and so now all things are referred to the governance of Divine Providence, which fools think done as it were by chance and at random, and without any Divine ordering. "I will tell all Thy marvels." He tells all God's marvels, who sees them performed not only openly on the body, but invisibly indeed too in the soul, but far more sublimely and excellently. For men earthly, and led wholly by the eye, marvel more that the dead Lazarus rose again in the body, than that Paul the persecutor rose again in soul. But since the visible miracle calleth the soul to the light, but the invisible enlighteneth the soul that comes when called, he tells all God's marvels, who, by believing the visible, passes on to the understanding of the invisible.

3. "I will be glad and exult in Thee" (ver. 2). Not any more in this world, not in pleasure of bodily dalliance, not in relish of palate and tongue, not in sweetness of perfumes, not in joyousness of passing sounds, not in the variously coloured forms of figure, not in vanities of men's praise, not in wedlock and perishable offspring, not in superfluity of temporal wealth, not in this world's getting, whether it extend over place and space, or be prolonged in time's succession: but, "I will be glad and exult in Thee," namely, in the hidden things of the Son, where "the light of Thy countenance hath been stamped on us, O Lord:" for, "Thou wilt hide them," saith he, "in the hiding place of Thy countenance." He then will be glad and exult in

Thee, who tells all Thy marvels. And He will tell all Thy marvels (since it is now spoken of prophetically), "who came not to do His own will, but the will of Him who sent Him."

4. For now the Person of the Lord begins to appear speaking in this Psalm. For it follows, "I will sing to Thy Name, O Most High, in turning mine enemy behind." His enemy then, where was he turned back? Was it when it was said to him, "Get thee behind, Satan"? For then he who by tempting desired to put himself before, was turned behind, by failing in deceiving Him who was tempted, and by availing nothing against Him. For earthly men are behind: but the heavenly man is preferred before, although he came after. For "the first man is of the earth, earthy: the second Man is from heaven, heavenly." But from this stock he came by whom it was said, "He who cometh after me is preferred before me." And the Apostle forgets "those things that are behind, and reaches forth unto those things that are before." The enemy, therefore, was turned behind, after that he could not deceive the heavenly Man being tempted; and he turned himself to earthy men, where he can have dominion....For in truth the devil is turned behind, even in the persecution of the righteous, and he, much more to their advantage, is a persecutor, than if he went before as a leader and a prince. We midst sing then to the Name of the Most High in turning the enemy behind: since we ought to choose rather to fly from him as a persecutor, than to follow him as a leader. For we have whither we may fly and hide ourselves in the hidden things of the Son; seeing that "the Lord hath been made a refuge for us."

5. "They will be weakened, and perish from Thy face" (ver. 3). Who will be weakened and perish, but the unrighteous and ungodly? "They will be weakened," while they shall avail nothing; "and they shall perish," because the ungodly will not be; "from the face" of God, that is, from the knowledge of God, as he perished who said," But now I live not, but Christ liveth in me." But why will the ungodly "be weakened and perish from thy face ?" "Because," he saith, "Thou hast made my judgment, and my cause:" that is, the judgment in which I seemed to be judged, Thou hast made mine; and the cause in which men condemned me just and innocent, Thou hast made mine. For such things served Him for our deliverance: as sailors too call the wind theirs, which they take advantage of for prosperous sailing.

6. "Thou satest on the throne Who judgest equity" (ver. 4). Whether the Son say this to the Father, who said also, "Thou couldest have no power against Me, except it were given thee from above," referring this very thing, that the Judge of men was judged for men's advantage, to the Father's equity and His own hidden things:

or whether man say to God, "Thou satest on the throne Who judgest equity," giving the name of God's throne to his soul, so that his body may peradventure be the earth, which is called God's "footstool: " for "God was in Christ, reconciling the world unto Himself:" or whether the soul of the Church, perfect now and without spot and wrinkle, worthy, that is, of the hidden things of the Son, in that "the King hath brought her into His chamber," say to her spouse, "Thou satest upon the throne Who judgest equity," in that Thou hast risen from the dead, and ascended up into heaven, and sittest at the right hand of the Father: whichsoever, I say, of those opinions, whereunto this verse may be referred, is preferred, it transgresses not the rule of faith.

7. "Thou hast rebuked the heathen, and the ungodly hath perished" (ver. 5). We take this to be more suitably said to the Lord Jesus Christ, than said by Him. For who else hath rebuked the heathen, and the ungodly perished, save He, who after that He ascended up into heaven, sent the Holy Ghost, that, filled by Him, the Apostles should preach the word of God with boldness, and freely reprove men's sins? At which rebuke the ungodly perished; because the ungodly was justified and was made godly. "Thou hast effaced their name for the world, and for the world's world. The name of the ungodly hath been effaced. For they are not called ungodly who believe in the true God. Now their name is effaced "for the world," that is, as long as the course of the temporal world endures. "And for the world's world." What is "the world's world," but that whose image and shadow, as it were, this world possesses? For the change of seasons succeeding one another, whilst the moon is on the wane, and again on the increase, whilst the sun each year returns to his quarter, whilst spring, or summer, or autumn, or winter passes away only to return, is m some sort an imitation of eternity. But this world's world is that which abides in immutable eternity. As a verse in the mind, and a verse in the voice, the former is understood, the latter heard; and the former fashions the latter; and hence the former works in art and abides, the latter sounds in the air and passes away. So the fashion of this changeable world is defined by that world unchangeable which is called the world's world. And hence the one abides in the art, that is, in the Wisdom and Power of God: but the other is made to pass in the governance of creation. If after all it be not a repetition, so that after it was said "for the world," lest it should be understood of this world that passeth away, it were added "for the world's world." For in the Greek copies it is thus, eis to`n aiw^na, kai` eis to`n aiw^na tou^ aiw^nos. Which the Latins have for the most rendered, not, "for the world, and for the world's world;" but, "for ever, and for the world's world," that in the words "for the world's world," the, words "for ever," should be explained. "The name," then, "of the ungodly Thou hast effaced for ever," for from henceforth the ungodly shall never be. And if their name be not prolonged unto this world, much less unto the world's world."

8. "The swords of the enemy have failed at the end" (ver. 6). Not enemies in the plural, but this enemy in the singular. Now what enemy's swords have failed but the devil's? Now these are understood to be divers erroneous opinions, whereby as with swords he destroys souls, In overcoming these swords, and in bringing them to failure, that sword is employed, of which it is said in the seventh Psalm, "If ye be not converted, He will brandish His sword." And peradventure this is the end, against which the swords of the enemy fail; since up to it they are of some avail. Now it worketh secretly, but in the last judgment it will be brandished openly. By it the cities are destroyed. For so it follows, "The swords of the enemy have failed at the end: and Thou hast destroyed the cities." Cities indeed wherein the devil rules, where crafty and deceitful counsels hold, as it were, the place of a court, on which supremacy attend as officers and ministers the services of all the members, the eyes for curiosity, the ears for lasciviousness, or for whatsoever else is gladly listened to that bears on evil, the hands for rapine or any other violence or pollution soever, and all the other members after this manner serving the tyrannical supremacy, that is, perverse counsels. Of this city the commonalty, as it were, are all soft affections and disturbing emotions of the mind, stirring up daily seditions in a man. So then where a king, where a court, where ministers, where commonalty are found, there is a city. Now again would such things be in bad cities, unless they were first in individual men, who are, as it were, the elements and seeds of cities. These cities He destroys, when on the prince being shut out thence, of whom it was said, "The prince of this world" has been "cast out," these kingdoms are wasted by the word of truth, evil counsels are laid to sleep, vile affections tamed, the ministries of the members and senses taken captive, and transferred to the service of righteousness and good works: that as the Apostle says, "Sin should no more reign in" our "mortal body," and so forth. Then is the soul at peace, and the man is disposed to receive rest and blessedness. "Their memorial has perished with uproar:" with the uproar, that is, of the ungodly. But it is said, "with uproar," either because when ungodliness is overturned, there is uproar made: for none passeth to the highest place, where there is the deepest silence, but he who with much uproar shall first have warred with his own vices: or "with uproar," is said, that the memory of the ungodly should perish in the perishing even of the very uproar, in which ungodliness riots.

9. "And the Lord abideth for ever" (ver. 7). "Wherefore" then "have the heathen raged, and the people imagined vain things against the Lord, and against His anointed:" for" the Lord abideth for ever. He hath prepared His seat in judgment, and He shall judge the world in equity." He prepared His seat when He was judged. For by that patience Man purchased heaven, and God in Man profited believers. And this is the Son's hidden judgment. But seeing He is also to come openly and in the sight of all to judge the quick arid the dead, He hath prepared

His seat in the hidden judgment: and He shall also openly "judge the world in equity:" that is, He shall distribute gifts proportioned to desert, setting the sheep on His right hand, and the goats on His left. "He shall judge the people with justice "(ver. 8). This is the same as was said above, "He shall judge the world in equity." Not as men judge who see not the heart, by whom very often worse men are acquitted than are condemned: but "in equity" and "with justice "shall the Lord judge, "conscience bearing witness, and thoughts accusing, or else excusing."

10. "And the Lord hath become a refuge to the poor" (ver. 9). Whatsoever be the persecutions of that enemy, who hath been turned behind, what harm shall he do to them whose refuge the Lord hath become? But this will be, if in this world, in which that one has an office of power, they shall choose to be poor, by loving nothing which either here leaves a man while he lives and loves, or is left by him when he dies. For to such a poor man hath the Lord become a refuge, "an Helper in due season, in tribulation." Lo, He maketh poor, for "He scourgeth every son whom He receiveth." For what "an Helper in due season "is, he explained by adding "in tribulation." For the soul is not turned to God, save when it is turned away from this world: nor is it more seasonably turned away from this world, except toils and pains be mingled with its trifling and hurtful and destructive pleasures.

11. "And let them who know Thy Name, hope in Thee" (ver. 10), when they shall have ceased hoping in wealth, and in the other enticements of this world. For the soul indeed that seeketh where to fix her hope, when she is torn away from this world, the knowledge of God's Name seasonably receives. For the mere Name of God hath now been published everywhere: but the knowledge of the name is, when He is known whose name it is. For the name is not a name for its own sake, but for that which it signifies. Now it has been said, "The Lord is His Name." Wherefore whoso willingly submits himself to God as His servant, hath known this name. "And let them who know Thy Name hope in Thee" (ver. 10), Again, the Lord saith to Moses, "I am That I am; and Thou shalt say to the children of Israel, I AM, hath sent me." "Let them" then "who know Thy Name, hope in Thee;" that they may not hope in those things which flow by in time's quick revolution, having nothing but" will be" and "has been." For what in them is future, when it arrives, straightway becomes the past; it is awaited with eagerness, it is lost with pain. But in the nature of God nothing will be, as if it were not yet; or hath been, as if it were no longer: but there is only that which is, and this is eternity. Let them cease then to hope in and love things temporal, and let them apply themselves to hope eternal, who know His name who said, "I am That I am;" and of whom it was said, "I AM hath sent me." "For Thou hast not forsaken them that seek Thee, O Lord." Whoso

seek Him, seek no more things transient and perishable; "For no man can serve two masters."

12. "Sing to the Lord, who dwelleth in Sion" (ver. 11), is said to them, whom the Lord forsakes not as they seek Him. He dwelleth in Sion, which is interpreted watching, and which beareth the likeness Of the Church that now is; as Jerusalem beareth the likeness of the Church that is to come, that is, the city of Saints already enjoying life angelical; for Jerusalem is by interpretation the vision of peace. Now watching goes before vision, as this Church goes before that one which is promised, the city immortal and eternal. But in time it goes before, not in dignity: because more honourable is that whither we are striving to arrive, than what we practise, that we may attain to arrive; now we practise watching, that we may arrive at vision. But again this same Church which now is, unless the Lord inhabit her, the most earnest watching might run into any sort of error. And to this Church it was said, "For the temple of God is holy, which temple ye are:" again," that Christ may dwell in the inner man in your hearts by faith." It is enjoined us then, that we sing to the Lord who dwelleth in Sion, that with one accord we praise the Lord, the Inhabitant of the Church. "Show forth His wonders among the heathen." It has both been done, and will not cease to be done.

13. "For requiring their blood He hath remembered" (ver. 12). As if they, who were sent to preach the Gospel, should make answer to that injunction which has been mentioned, "Show forth His wonders among the heathen," and should say, "O Lord, who hath believed our report?" and again, "For Thy sake we are killed all the day long ;" the Psalmist suitably goes on to say, That Christians not without great reward of eternity will die in persecution, "for requiring their blood He hath remembered." But why did he choose to say, "their blood"? Was it, as if one of imperfect knowledge and less faith should ask, How will they "show them forth," seeing that the infidelity of the heathen will rage against them; and he should be answered, "For requiring their blood He hath remembered," that is, the last judgment will come, in which both the glory of the slain and the punishment of the slayers shall be made manifest? But let no one suppose "He hath remembered" to be so used, as though forgetfulness can attach to God; but since the judgment will be after a long interval, it is used in accordance with the feeling of weak men, who think God hath forgotten, because He doth not act so speedily as they wish. To such is said what follows also, "He hath not forgotten the cry of the poor:" that is, He hath not, as you suppose, forgotten. As if they should on hearing," He hath remembered," say, Then He had forgotten; No, "He hath not forgotten," says the Psalmist, "the cry of the poor."

14. But I ask, what is that cry of the poor, which God forgetteth not? Is it that cry, the words whereof are these, "Pity me, O Lord, see my humiliation at the hands of my enemies "? (ver. 13). Why then did he not say, Pity "us" O Lord, see our humiliation at the hands of "our" enemies, as if many poor were crying; but as if one, Pity "me," O Lord? Is it because One intercedeth for the Saints, "who" first "for our sakes became poor, though He was rich;" and it is He who saith, "Who exaltest me from the gates of death (ver. 14), that I may declare all Thy praises in the gates of the daughter of Sion"? For man is exalted in Him, not that Man only which He beareth, which is the Head of the Church; but whichsoever one of us also is among the other members, and is exalted from all depraved desires; which are the gates of death, for that through them is the road to death. But the joy in the fruition is at once death itself, when one gains what he hath in abandoned wilfulness coveted: for "coveting is the root of all evil: " and therefore is the gate of death, for "the widow that liveth in pleasures is dead." At which pleasures we arrive through desires as it were through the gates of death. But all highest purposes are the gates of the daughter of Sion, through which we come to the vision of peace in the Holy Church.... Or haply are the gates of death the bodily senses and eyes, which were opened when the man tasted of the forbidden tree, ... and are the gates of the daughter of Sion the sacraments and beginnings of faith, which are opened to them that knock, that they may arrive at the hidden things of the Son?...

15. Then follows, "I will exult for Thy salvation:' that is, with blessedness shall I be holden by Thy salvation, which is our Lord Jesus Christ, the Power and Wisdom of God. Therefore says the Church, which is here in affliction and is saved by hope, as long as the hidden judgment of the Son is, in hope she says," I will exult for Thy salvation:" for now she is worn down either by the roar of violence around her, or by the errors of the heathen. "The heathen are fixed in the corruption, which they made" (ver.

15). Consider ye how punishment is reserved for the sinner, out of his own works; and how they that have wished to persecute the Church, have been fixed in that corruption, which they thought to inflict. For they were desiring to kill the body, whilst they themselves were dying in soul. "In that snare which they hid, has their foot been taken." The hidden snare is crafty devising. The foot of the soul is well understood to be its love: which, when depraved, is called coveting or lust; but when upright, love or charity.... And the Apostle says, "That being rooted and grounded in love, ye may be able to take in." The foot then of sinners, that is, their love, is taken in the snare, which they hide: for when delight shall have followed on to deceitful dealing, when God shall have delivered them over to the lust of their heart; that delight at once binds them, that they dare not tear away their love thence and apply it to profitable objects; for when they shall make the attempt, they will be pained in heart, as if desiring to free their foot from a fetter: and giving way trader this pain they refuse to withdraw from pernicious delights. "In the snare" then "which they have hid," that is, in deceitful counsel, "their foot hath been taken," that is, their love, which through deceit attains to that vain joy whereby pain is purchased.

16. "The Lord is known executing judgments" (ver. 16). These are God's judgments. Not from that tranquillity of His blessedness, nor from the secret places of wisdom, wherein blessed souls are received, is the sword, or fire, or wild beast, or any such thing brought forth, whereby sinners maybe tormented: but how are they tormented, and how does the Lord do judgment? "In the works," he says, "of his own hands hath the sinner been caught."

17. Here is interposed, "The song of the diapsalma" (ver. 16): as it were the hidden joy, as far as we can imagine, of the separation which is now made, not in place, but in the affections of the heart, between sinners and the righteous, as of the corn from the chaff, as yet on the floor. And then follows, "Let the sinners be turned into hell" (ver. 17): that is, let them be given into their own hands, when they are spared, and let them be ensnared in deadly delight. "All the nations that forget God." Because "when they did not think good to retain God in their knowledge, God gave them over to a reprobate mind."

18. "For there shall not be forgetfulness of the poor man to the end" (ver. 18); who now seems to be in forgetfulness, when sinners are thought to flourish in this world's happiness, and the righteous to be in travail: but "the patience," saith He, "of the poor shall not perish for ever." Wherefore there is need of patience now to bear with the evil, who are already separated in will, till they be also separated at the last judgment.

19. "Arise, O Lord, let not man prevail" (ver. 19). The future judgment is prayed for: but before it come, "Let the heathen," saith he, "be judged in Thy sight:" that is, in secret; which is called in God's sight, with the knowledge of a few holy and righteous ones. "Place a lawgiver over them, O Lord." (ver. 20). He seems to me to point out Antichrist: of whom the Apostle says, "When the man of sin shall be revealed." "Let the heathen know that they are men." That they who will be set free by the Son of God, and belong to the Son of Man, and be sons of men, that is, new men, may serve man, that is, the old man the sinner, "for that they are men."

20. And because it is believed that he is to arrive at so great a pitch of empty glory, and he will be permitted to do so great things, both against all men and against the Saints of God, that then some weak ones shall indeed think that God cares not for human affairs, the Psalmist interposing a diapsalma, adds as it were the voice of men groaning and asking why judgment is deferred.

PSALM X.

"Why, O Lord," saith he, "hast Thou withdrawn afar off?" (ver. 1). Then he who thus inquired, as if all on a sudden he understood, or as if he asked, though he knew, that he might teach, adds, "Thou despisest in due seasons, in tribulations:" that is, Thou despisest seasonably, and causest tribulations to inflame men's minds with longing for Thy coming. For that fountain of life is sweeter to them that have much thirst. Therefore he hints the reason of the delay, saying, "Whilst the ungodly vaunteth himself, the poor man is inflamed" (ver. 2). Wondrous it is and true with what earnestness of good hope the little ones are inflamed unto an upright living by comparison with sinners. In which mystery it comes to pass, that even heresies are permitted to exist; not that heretics themselves wish this, but because Divine Providence worketh this result from their sins, which both maketh and ordaineth the light; but ordereth only the darkness, that by comparison therewith the light may be more pleasant, as by comparison with heretics the discovery of truth is more sweet. For so, by this comparison, the approved, who are known to God, are made manifest among men.

1. "They are taken in their thoughts, which they think:" that is, their evil thoughts become chains to them. But how become they chains? "For the sinner is praised," saith he, "in the desires of his soul" (ver. 3). The tongues of flatterers bind souls in sin. For there is pleasure in doing those things, in which not only is no reprover feared, but even an approver heard. "And he that does unrighteous deeds is blessed." Hence "are they taken in their thoughts, which they think."

2. "The sinner hath angered the Lord" (ver. 4). Let no one congratulate the man that prospers in his way, to whose sins no avenger is nigh, and an approver is by. This is the greater anger of the Lord. For the sinner hath angered the Lord, that he should suffer these things, that is, should not suffer the scourging of correction. "The sinner hath angered the Lord: according to the multitude of His anger He will not search it out." Great is His anger, when He searcheth not out, when He as it were forgetteth and marketh not sin, and by fraud and wickedness man attains to riches and honours: which will especially be the case in that Antichrist, who will seem to man blessed to that degree, that he will even be thought God. But how great this anger of God is, we are taught by what follows.

3. "God is not in his sight, his ways are polluted in all time" (ver. 5). He that knows what in the soul gives joy and gladness, knows how great an ill it is to be abandoned by the light of truth: since a great ill do men reckon the blindness of

their bodily eyes, whereby this light is withdrawn. How great then the punishment he endures, who through the prosperous issue of his sins is brought to that pass, that God is not in his sight, and that his ways are polluted in all time, that is, his thoughts and counsels are unclean! "Thy judgments are taken away from his face." For the mind conscious of evil, whilst it seems to itself to suffer no punishment, believes that God cloth not judge, and so are God's judgments taken away from its face; while this very thing is great condemnation. "And he shall have dominion over all his enemies." For so is it delivered, that he will overcome all kings, and alone obtain the kingdom; since too according to the Apostle, who preaches concerning him, "He shall sit in the temple of God, exalting himself above all that is worshipped and that is called God."

4. And seeing that being delivered over to the lust of his own heart, and predestinated to extreme condemnation, he is to come, by wicked arts, to that vain and empty height and rule; therefore it follows, "For he hath said in his heart, I shall not move from generation to generation without evil" (ver. 6): that is, my fame and my name will not pass from this generation to the generation of posterity, unless by evil arts I acquire so lofty a principality, that posterity cannot be silent concerning it. For a mind abandoned and void of good arts, and estranged from the light of righteousness, by bad arts devises a passage for itself to a fame so lasting, as is celebrated even in posterity. And they that cannot be known for good, desire that men should speak of them even for ill, provided that their name spread far and wide. And this I think is here meant, "I shall not move from generation to generation without evil." There is too another interpretation, if a mind vain and full of error supposes that it cannot come from the mortal generation to the generation of eternity, but by bad arts: which indeed was also reported of Simon, when he thought that he would gain heaven by wicked arts, and pass from the human generation to the generation divine by magic. Where then is the wonder, if that man of sin too, who is to fill up all the wickedness and ungodliness, which all false prophets have begun, and to do such" great signs; that, if it were possible, he should deceive the very elect," shall say in his heart, "I shall not move from generation to generation without evil"?

5. "Whose mouth is full of cursing and bitterness and deceit" (ver. 7). For it is a great curse to seek heaven by such abominable arts, and to get together such earnings for acquiring the eternal seat. But of this cursing his mouth is full. For this desire shall not take effect, but within his mouth only will avail to destroy him, who dared promise himself such things with bitterness and deceit, that is, with anger and insidiousness, whereby he is to bring over the multitude to his side. "Under his tongue is toil and grief." Nothing is more toilsome than

unrighteousness and ungodliness: upon which toil follows grief; for that the toil is not only without fruit, but even unto destruction. Which toil and grief refer to that which he hath said in his heart, "I shall not be moved from generation to generation without evil." And therefore, "under his tongue," not on his tongue, because he will devise these things in silence, and to men will speak other things, that he may appear good and just, and a son of God.

6. "He lieth in ambush with the rich" (ver. 8). What rich, but those whom he will load with this world's gifts? And he is therefore said to lie in ambush with them, because he will display their false happiness to deceive men; who, when with a perverted will they desire to be such as they, and seek not the good things eternal, will fall into his snares. "That in the dark he may kill the innocent." "In the dark," I suppose, is said, where it is not easily understood what should be sought, or what avoided. Now to kill the innocent, is of an innocent to make one guilty.

7. "His eyes look against the poor," for he is chiefly to persecute the righteous, of whom it is said, "Blessed are the poor in spirit, for theirs is the kingdom of heaven" (ver. 9). "He lieth in wait in a secret place, as a lion in his den." By a lion in a den, he means one in whom both violence and deceit will work. For the first persecution of the Church was violent, when by proscriptions, by torments, by murders, the Christians were compelled to sacrifice: another persecution is crafty, which is now conducted by heretics of any kind and false brethren: there remains a third, which is to come by Antichrist, than which there is nothing more perilous; for it will be at once violent and crafty. Violence he will exert in empire, craft in miracles. To the violence, the word "lion" refers; to craft, the words "in his den." And these are again repeated with a change of order. "He lieth in wait," he says, "that he may catch the poor;" this hath reference to craft: but what follows, "To catch the poor whilst he draweth him," is put to the score of violence. For "draweth" means, he bringeth him to himself by violence, by whatever tortures he can.

8. Again, the two which follow are the same "In his snare he will humble him," is craft (ver. 10). "He shall decline and fall, whilst he shall have domination over the poor," is violence. For a "snare" naturally points to "lying in wait:" but domination most openly conveys the idea of terror. And well does he say, "He will humble him in his snare." For when he shall begin to do those signs, the more wonderful they shall appear to men, the more those Saints that shall be then will be despised, and, as it were, set at nought: he, whom they shall resist by righteousness and innocence, shall seem to overcome by the marvels that he does. But "he shall decline and fall, whilst he shall have domination over the poor;" that is, whilst he

shall inflict whatsoever punishments he will upon the servants of God that resist him.

9. But how shall he decline, and fall? "For he hath said in his heart, God hath forgotten; He turneth away His face, that He see not unto the end" (ver. 11). This is declining, and the most wretched fall, while the mind of a man prospers as it were in its iniquities, and thinks that it is spared; when it is being blinded, and kept for an extreme and timely vengeance: of which the Psalmist now speaks: "Arise, O Lord God, let Thine hand be exalted" (ver. 12): that is, let Thy power be made manifest. Now he had said above, "Arise, O Lord, let not man prevail, let the heathen be judged in Thy sight:" that is, in secret, where God alone seeth. This comes to pass when the ungodly have arrived at what seems great happiness to men: over whom is placed a lawgiver, such as they had deserved to have, of whom it is said," Place a lawgiver over them, O Lord, let the heathen know that they are men." But now after that hidden punishment and vengeance it is said, "Arise, O Lord God, let Thine hand be exalted;" not of course in secret, but now in glory most manifest. "That Thou forget not the poor unto the end ;" that is, as the ungodly think, who say, "God hath forgotten, He turneth away His face, that He should not see unto the end." Now they deny that God seeth unto the end, who say that He careth not for things human and earthly, for the earth is as it were the end of things; in that it is the last element, in which men labour in most orderly sort, but they cannot see the order of their labours, which specially belongs to the hidden things of the Son. The Church then labouring in such times, like a ship in great waves and tempests, awaketh the Lord as if He were sleeping, that He should command the winds, and calm should be restored. He says therefore, "Arise, O Lord God, let Thine hand be exalted, that Thou forget not the poor unto the end."

10. Accordingly understanding now the manifest judgment, and in exultation at it, they say, "Wherefore hath the ungodly angered God?" (ver. 13); that is, what hath it profiled him to do so great evil? "For he said in his heart, He will not require it." Then follows, "For Thou seest toil and considerest anger, to deliver them into Thine hands" (ver. 14). This sentence looks for distinct explanation, wherein if there shall be error it becomes obscure. For thus has the ungodly said in his heart, God will not require it, as though God regarded toil and anger, to deliver them into His hands; that is, as though He feared toil and anger, and for this reason would spare them, lest their punishment be too burdensome to Him, or lest He should be disturbed by the storm of anger: as men generally act, excusing themselves of vengeance, to avoid toil or anger.

11. "The poor hath been left unto Thee." For therefore is he poor, that is, hath despised all the temporal goods of this world, that Thou only mayest be his hope. "Thou wilt be a helper to the orphan," that is, to him to whom his father this world, by whom he was born after the flesh, dies, and who can already say, "The world hath been crucified unto me, and I unto the world." For of such orphans God becomes the Father. The Lord teaches us in truth that His disciples do become orphans, to whom He saith, "Call no man father on earth." Of which He first Himself gave an example in saying," Who is my mother, and who my brethren?" Whence some most mischievous heretics 3 would assert that He had no mother; and they do not see that it follows from this, if they pay attention to these words, that neither had His disciples fathers. For as He said, "Who is my mother?" so He taught them, when He said, "Call no man your father on earth."

12. "Break the arm of the sinner and of the malicious" (ver. 15); of him, namely, of whom it was said above, "He shall have dominion over all his enemies." He called his power then, his arm; to which Christ's power is opposed, of which it is said, "Arise, O Lord God, let Thine hand be exalted. His fault shall be required, and he shall not be found because of it;" that is he shall be judged for his sins, and himself shall perish because of his sin. After this, what wonder if there follow, "The Lord shall reign for ever and world without end; ye heathen shall perish out of His earth"? (ver. 16). He uses heathen for sinners and ungodly.

13. "The Lord hath heard the longing of the poor"(ver. 17): that longing wherewith they were burning, when in the straits and tribulations of this world they desired the day of the Lord. "Thine ear hath heard the preparation of their heart." This is the preparation of the heart, of which it is sung in another Psalm, "My heart is prepared, O God, my heart is prepared:" of which the Apostle says, "But if we hope for what we see not, we do with patience wait for it." Now, by the ear of God, we ought, according to a general rule of interpretation, to understand not a bodily member, but the power whereby He heareth; and so (not to repeat this often) by whatever members of His are mentioned, which in us are visible and bodily, must be understood powers of operation. For we must not suppose it anything bodily, in that the Lord God hears not the sound of the voice, but the preparation of the heart.

14. "To judge for the orphan and the humble" (ver. 18): that is, not for him who is conformed to this world, nor for the proud. For it is one thing to judge the orphan, another to judge for the orphan. He judges the orphan even, who condemns him; but he judges for the orphan, who delivers sentence for him. "That man add not further to magnify himself upon earth." For they are men, of whom it was said,

"Place a lawgiver over them, O Lord: let the heathen know that they are men." But he too, who in this same passage is understood to be placed over them, will be man, of whom it is now said, "That man add not further to magnify himself upon earth:" namely, when the Son of Man shall come to judge for the orphan, who hath put off from himself the old man, and thus, as it were, buried his father.

15. After the hidden things then of the Son, of which, in this Psalm, many things have been said, will come the manifest things of the Son, of which a little has been now said at the end of the same Psalm. But the title is given from the former, which here occupy the larger portion. Indeed, the very day of the Lord's advent may be rightly numbered among the hidden things of the Son, although the very presence of the Lord itself will be manifest. For of that day it is said, that no man knoweth it, neither angels, nor powers, nor the Son of man. What then so hidden, as that which is said to be hidden even to the Judge Himself, not as regards knowledge, but disclosure? But concerning the hidden things of the Son, even if any one would not wish to understand the Son of God, but of David himself, to whose name the whole Psalter is attributed, for the Psalms we know are called the Psalms of David, let him give ear to those words in which it is said to the Lord, "Have mercy on us, O Son of David:" and so even in this manner let him understand the same Lord Christ, concerning whose hidden things is the inscription of this Psalm. For so likewise is it said by the Angel: "God shall give unto Him the throne of His father David." Nor to this understanding of it is the sentence opposed in which the same Lord asks of the Jews," If Christ be the Son of David, how then doth he in spirit call Him Lord, saying, The Lord said unto my Lord, Sit Thou on my right hand, until I put Thine enemies under Thy feet." For it was said to the unskilled, who although they looked for Christ's coming, yet expected Him as man, not as the Power and Wisdom of God. He teacheth then, in that place, the most true and pure faith, that He is both the Lord of king David, in that He is the Word in the beginning, God with God, by which all things were made; and Son, in that He was made to him of the seed of David according to the flesh. For He doth not say, Christ is not David's Son, but if ye already hold that He is his Son, learn how He is his Lord: and do not hold in respect of Christ that He is the Son of Man, for so is He David's Son; and leave out that He is the Son of God, for so is He David's Lord.

PSALM XI.

TO THE END, A PSALM OF DAVID HIMSELF.

1. This title does not require a fresh consideration: for the meaning of, "to the end," has already been sufficiently handled. Let us then look to the text itself of the Psalm, which to me appears to be sung against the heretics, who, by rehearsing and exaggerating the sins of many in the Church, as if either all or the majority among themselves were righteous, strive to turn and snatch us away from the breasts of the one True Mother Church: affirming that Christ is with them, and warning us as if with piety and earnestness, that by passing over to them we may go over to Christ, whom they falsely declare they have. Now it is known that in prophecy Christ, among the many names in which notice of Him is conveyed in allegory, is also called a mountain. We must accordingly answer these people, and say, "I trust in the Lord: how say ye to my soul, Remove into the mountains as a sparrow?" (ver. 1). I keep to one mountain wherein I trust, how say ye that I should pass over to you, as if there were many Christs? Or if through pride you say that you are mountains, I had indeed need to be a sparrow winged with the powers and commandments of God: but these very things hinder my flying to these mountains, and placing my trust in proud men. I have a house where I may rest, in that I trust in the Lord. For even "the sparrow hath found her a house," and, "The Lord hath become a refuge to the poor." Let us say then with all confidence, lest while we seek Christ among heretics we lose Him, "In the Lord I trust: how say ye to my soul, Remove into the mountains as a sparrow?"

2. "For, lo, sinners have bent the bow, they have prepared their arrows in the quiver, that they may in the obscure moon shoot at the upright in heart" (ver. 2). These be the terrors of those who threaten us as touching sinners, that we may pass over to them as the righteous. "Lo," they say, "the sinners have bent the bow:" the Scriptures, I suppose, by carnal interpretation of which they emit envenomed sentences from them. "They have prepared their arrows in the quiver:" the same words, that is, which they will shoot out on the authority of Scripture, they have prepared in the secret place of the heart. "That they may in the obscure moon shoot at the upright in heart:" that when they see, from the Church's light being obscured by the multitude of the unlearned and the carnal, that they cannot be convicted, they may corrupt good manners by evil communications. But against all these terrors we must say, "In the Lord I trust."

3. Now I remember that I promised to consider in this Psalm with what suitableness the moon signifies the Church. There are two probable opinions concerning the moon: but of these which is the true, I suppose it either impossible or very difficult for a man to decide. For when we ask whence the moon has her light, some say that it is her own, but that of her globe half is bright, and half dark: and when she revolves in her own orbit, that part wherein she is bright gradually turns towards the earth, so as that it may be seen by us; and that therefore at first her appearance is as if she were horned. ...According to this opinion the moon in allegory signifies the Church, because in its spiritual part the Church is bright, but in its carnal part is dark: and sometimes the spiritual part is seen by good works, but sometimes it lies hid in the conscience, and is known to God alone, since in the body alone is it seen by men. ... But according to the other opinion also the moon is understood to be the Church, because she has no light of her own, but is lighted by the only-begotten Son of God, who in many places of holy Scripture is allegorically called the Sun. Whom certain heretics being ignorant of, and not able to discern Him, endeavour to turn away the minds of the simple to this corporeal and visible sun, which is the common light of the flesh of men and flies, and some they do pervert, who as long as they cannot behold with the mind the inner light of truth, will not be content with the simple Catholic faith; which is the only safety to babes, and by which milk alone they can arrive in assured strength at the firm support of more solid food. Whichever then of these two opinions be the true, the moon in allegory is fitly understood as the Church. Or if in such difficulties as these, troublesome rather than edifying, there be either no satisfaction or no leisure to exercise the mind, or if the mind itself be not capable of it, it is sufficient to regard the moon with ordinary eyes, and not to seek out obscure causes, but with all men to perceive her increasings and fulnesses and wanings; and if she wanes to the end that she may be renewed, even to this rude multitude she sets forth the image of the Church, in which the resurrection of the dead is believed.

4. Next we must enquire, what in this Psalm is meant by "the obscure moon," in which sinners have prepared to shoot at the upright in heart? For not in one way only may the moon be said to be obscure: for when her monthly course is finished, and when her brightness is interrupted by a cloud, and when she is eclipsed at the full, the moon may be called obscure. It may then be understood first of the persecutors of the Martyrs, for that they wished in the obscure moon to shoot at the upright in heart; whether it be yet in the time of the Church's youth, because she had not yet shone forth in greatness on the earth, and conquered the darkness of heathen superstitions; or by the tongues of blasphemers and such as defame the Christian name, when the earth was as it were beclouded, the moon, that is, the Church, could not be clearly seen; or when by the slaughter of the Martyrs themselves and so great effusion of blood, as by that eclipse and obscuration,

wherein the moon seems to exhibit a bloody face, the weak were deterred from the Christian name; in which terror sinners shot out words crafty and sacrilegious to pervert even the upright in heart. And secondly, it can be understood of these sinners, whom the Church contains, because at that time, taking the opportunity of this moon's obscurity, they committed many crimes, which are now tauntingly objected to us by the heretics, whereas their founders are said to have been guilty of them. But howsoever that be which was done in the obscure moon, now that the Catholic name is spread and celebrated throughout the whole world, what concern of mine is it to be disturbed by things unknown? For "in the Lord I trust;" nor do I listen to them that say to my soul, "Remove into the mountains as a sparrow. For, lo, sinners have bent the bow, that they may in the obscure moon shoot at the upright in heart." Or if the moon seem even now obscure to them, because they would make it uncertain which is the Catholic Church, and they strive to convict her by the sins of those many carnal men whom she contains; what concern is this to him, who says in truth, "In the Lord I trust"? By which word every one shows that he is himself wheat, and endures the chaff with patience unto the time of winnowing.

5. "In the Lord," therefore, "I trust." Let them fear who trust in man, and cannot deny that they are of man's party, by whose grey hairs they swear; and when in conversation it is demanded of them, of what communion they are, unless they say that they are of his party, they cannot be recognised. ...Or perhaps you will say that it is written, "Ye shall know them by their works"? I see indeed marvellous works the daily violences of the Circumcelliones, with the bishops and presbyters for their leaders, flying about in every direction, and calling their terrible clubs "Israels;" which men now living daily see and feel. But for the times of Macarius, respecting which they raise an invidious cry, most men have not seen them, and no one sees them now: and any Catholic who saw them could say, if he wished to be a servant of God, "In the Lord I trust."...

6. Let the Catholic soul then say, "In the Lord I trust; how say ye to my soul, Remove into the mountains as a sparrow? For, lo, the sinners have bent the bow, they have prepared their arrows in the quiver, that they may in the obscure moon shoot at the upright in heart:" and from them let her turn her speech to the Lord and say, "For they have destroyed what Thou hast perfected" (ver. 3). And this let her say not against these only, but against all heretics. For they have all, as far as in them lies, destroyed the praise which God hath perfected out of the mouth of babes and sucklings, when they disturb the little ones with vain and I scrupulous questions, and suffer them not to be nourished with the milk of faith. As if then it were said to this soul, why do they say to you, "Remove into the mountains as a

sparrow;" why do they frighten you with sinners, who "have bent the bow, to shoot in the obscure moon at the upright in heart"? She answers, Therefore it is they frighten me, "because they have destroyed what Thou hast perfected." Where but in their conventicles, where they nourish not with milk, but kill with poison the babes and ignorant of the interior light. "But what hath the Just done?" If Macarius, if Caecilianus, offend you, what hath Christ done to you, who said, "My peace I give unto you, My peace I leave with you;" which ye with your abominable dissensions have violated? What hath Christ done to you? who with such exceeding patience endured His betrayer, as to give to him, as to the other Apostles, the first Eucharist consecrated with His own hands, and blessed with His own mouth. What hath Christ done to you? who sent this same betrayer, whom He called a devil, who before betraying the Lord could not show good faith even to the Lord's purse, with the other disciples to preach the kingdom of heaven; that He might show that the gifts of God come to those that with faith receive them, though he, through whom they receive them, be such as Judas was.

7. "The Lord is in His holy temple" (ver. 4), yea in such wise as the Apostle saith, "For the temple of God is holy, which" temple "ye are." "Now if any man shall violate the temple of God, him shall God destroy." He violateth the temple of God, who violateth unity: for he "holdeth not the head, from which the whole body fitly joined together and compacted by that which every joint supplieth according to the working after the measure of every part maketh increase of the body to the edifying of itself in love." The Lord is in this His holy temple; which consisteth of His many members, fulfilling each his own separate duties, by love built up into one building. Which temple he violateth, who for the sake of his own pre-eminence separateth himself from the Catholic society. "The Lord is in His holy temple; the Lord, His seat is in heaven." If you take heaven to be the just man, as you take the earth to be the sinner, to whom it was said, "Earth thou art, and unto earth shalt thou go;" the words, "The Lord is in His holy temple" you will understand to be repeated, whilst it is said, "The Lord, His seat is in heaven."

8. "His eyes look upon the poor." His to Whom the poor man hath been left, and Who hath been made a refuge to the poor. And therefore all the seditions and tumults within these nets, until they be drawn to shore, concerning which heretics upbraid us to their own ruin and our correction, are caused by those men, who will not be Christ's poor. But do they turn away God's eyes from such as would be so? "For His eyes look upon the poor." Is it to be feared lest, in the crowd of the rich, He may not be able to see the few poor, whom He brings up in safe keeping in the bosom of the Catholic Church? "His eyelids question the sons of men." Here by that rule I would wish to take "the sons of men" of those that from old men have

been regenerated by faith. For these, by certain obscure passages of Scripture, as it were the closed eyes of God, are exercised that they may seek: and again, by certain clear passages, as it were the open eyes of God, are enlightened that they may rejoice. And this frequent closing and opening in the holy Books are as it were the eyelids of God; which question, that is, which try the "sons of men;" who are neither wearied with the obscurity of the matter, but exercised; nor puffed up by knowledge, but confirmed.

9. "The Lord questioneth the righteous and ungodly" (ver. 5). Why then do we fear lest the ungodly should be any hurt to us, if so be they do with insincere heart share the sacraments with us, seeing that He "questioneth the righteous and the ungodly." "But whoso loveth iniquity, hateth his own soul:" that is, not him who believeth God, and putteth not his hope in man, but only his own soul doth the lover of iniquity hurt.

10. "He shall rain snares upon the sinners" (ver. 6). If by clouds are understood prophets generally, whether good or bad, who are also called false prophets: false prophets are so ordered by the Lord God, that by them He may rain snares upon sinners. For no one, but the sinner, falls into a following of them, whether by way of preparation for the last punishment, if he shall choose to persevere in sin; or to dissuade from pride, if in time he shall come to seek God with a more sincere intent. But if by clouds are understood good and true prophets only; by these too it is clear that God raineth snares upon sinners, although by them He watereth also the godly unto fruitfulness. "To some," saith the Apostle, "we are the savour of life unto life; to some the savour of death unto death." For not prophets only, but all who with the word of God water souls, may be called clouds. Who when they are understood amiss, God raineth snares upon sinners; but when they are understood aright, He maketh the hearts of the godly and believing fruitful. As, for instance, the passage, "and they two shall be in one flesh," if one interpret it with an eye to lust, He raineth a snare upon the sinner. But if you understand it, as he who says, "But I speak concerning Christ and the Church," He raineth a shower on the fertile soil. Now both are effected by the same cloud, that is, holy Scripture. Again the Lord says, "Not that which goeth into your mouth defileth you, but that which cometh out." The sinner hears this, and makes ready his palate for gluttony: the righteous hears it, and is guarded against the superstitious distinction in meats. Here then also out of the same cloud of Scripture, according to the several desert of each, upon the sinner the rain of snares, upon the righteous the rain of fruitfulness, is poured.

11. "Fire and brimstone and the blast of the tempest is the portion of their cup." This is their punishment and end, by whom the name of God is blaspbemed; that first they should be wasted by the fire of their own lusts, then by the ill savour of their evil deeds cast off from the company of the blessed, at last carried away and overwhelmed suffer penalties unspeakable. For this is the portion of their cup: as of the righteous, "Thy cup inebriating how excellent is it! for they shall be inebriated with the richness of Thine house." Now I suppose a cup is mentioned for this reason, that we should not suppose that anything is done by God's providence, even in the very punishments of sinners, beyond moderation and measure. And therefore as if he were giving a reason why this should be, he added, "For the Lord is righteous, and hath loved righteousnesses" (ver. 7). The plural not without meaning, but only because he speaks of men, is as that righteousnesses be understood to be used for righteous men. For in many righteous men there seem, so to say, to be righteousnesses, whereas there is one only righteousness of God whereof they all participate. Like as when one face looks upon many mirrors, what in it is one only, is by those many mirrors reflected manifoldly. Wherefore he recurs to the singular, saying, "His face hath seen equity." Perhaps, "His face hath seen equity," is as if it were said, Equity hath been seen in His face, that is, in knowledge of Him. For God's face is the power by which He is made known to them that are worthy. Or at least, "His face hath seen equity," because He doth not allow Himself to be known by the evil, but by the good; and this is equity.

12. But if any one would understand the moon of the synagogue, let him refer the Psalm to the Lord's passion, and of the Jews say, "For they have destroyed what Thou hast perfected; and of the Lord Himself, "But what hath the Just done?" whom they accused as the destroyer of the Law: whose precepts, by their corrupt living, and by despising them, and by setting up their own, they had destroyed, so that the Lord Himself may speak as Man, as He is wont, saying, "In the Lord I trust; how say ye to my soul, Remove into the mountains as a sparrow?" by reason, that is, of the fear of those who desire to apprehend and crucify Him. Since the interpretation is not unreasonable of sinners wishing to "shoot at the upright in heart," that is, those who believed in Christ, "in the obscure moon," that is, the Synagogue filled with sinners. To this too the words, "The Lord is in His holy temple; the Lord, His seat is in heaven," are suitable; that is, the Word in Man, s or the very Son of Man who is in heaven. "His eyes look upon the poor;" either on t Him whom He assumed as God, or for whom He suffered as Man. "His eyelids question the sons of men." The closing and opening of the d eyes, which is probably meant by the word eyelids, we may take to be His death and resurrection, whereby He tried the sons of men His disciples, terrified at His passion, and gladdened by the resurrection. "The Lord questioneth the righteous and ungodly," even now from out of Heaven governing the Church. "But whoso loveth iniquity,

hateth his own soul." Why it is so, what follows teaches us. For "He shall rain snares upon the sinners:" which is to be taken according to the exposition above given, and so on with all the rest to the end of the Psalm.

PSALM XII.

TO THE END, FOR THE EIGHTH, A PSALM OF DAVID.

1. It has been said on the sixth Psalm, that "the eighth" may be taken as the day of judgment. "For the eighth" may also be taken "for the eternal age;" for that after the time present, which is a cycle of seven days, it shall be given to the Saints.

2. "Save me, O Lord, for the holy hath failed;" that is, is not found: as we speak when we say, Corn fails, or, Money fails. "For the truths have been minished from among the sons of men" (ver. 1). The truth is one, whereby holy souls are enlightened: but forasmuch as there are many souls, there may be said in them to be many truths: as in mirrors there are seen many reflections from one face.

3. "He hath talked vanity each man to his neighbour" (ver. 2). By neighbour we must understand every man: for that there is no one with whom we should work evil; "and the love of our neighbour worketh no evil." "Deceitful lips, with a heart and a heart they have spoken evil things." The repetition, "with a heart and a heart," signifies a double heart.

4. "May the Lord destroy all deceitful lips" (ver. 3). He says "all," that no one may suppose himself excepted: as the Apostle says, "Upon every soul of man that doeth evil, of the Jew first, and of the Greek." "The tongue speaking great things:" the proud tongue.

5. "Who have said, We will magnify our tongue, our lips are our own, who is Lord over us?" (ver. 4). Proud hypocrites are meant, putting confidence in their speech to deceive men, and not submitting themselves to God.

6. "Because of the wretchedness of the needy and the sighing of the poor, now I will arise, saith the Lord" (ver. 5). For so the Lord Himself in the Gospel pitied His people, because they had no ruler, when they could well obey. Whence too it is said in the Gospel, "The harvest is plenteous, but the labourers are few." But this must be taken as spoken in the person of God the Father, who, because of the needy and the poor, that is, who in need and poverty were lacking spiritual good things, vouchsafed to send His own Son. From thence begins His sermon on the mount to Matthew, where He says, "Blessed are the poor in spirit: for theirs is the

kingdom of heaven." "I will place in salvation." He does not say what He would place: but, "in salvation," must be understood as, in Christ; according to that, "For mine eyes have seen Thy salvation." And hence He is understood to have placed in Him what appertains to the taking away the wretchedness of the needy, and the comforting the sighing of the poor. "I will deal confidently in Him:" according to that in the Gospel, "For He taught them as one having authority, and not as their scribes."

7. "The words of the Lord" are "pure words" (ver. 6). This is in the person of the Prophet himself, "The words of the Lord" are "pure words." He says "pure," without the alloy of pretence. For many preach the truth impurely; for they sell it for the bribe of the advantages of this life. Of such the Apostle says, that they declared Christ not purely. "Silver tried by the fire for the earth." These words of the Lord by means of tribulations approved to sinners. "Purified seven times:" by the fear of God, by godliness, by knowledge, by might, by counsel, by understanding, by wisdom. For seven steps also of beatitude there are, which the Lord goes over, according to Matthew, in the same sermon which He spake on the Mount, "Blessed" are "the poor in spirit, blessed the meek, blessed they that mourn, blessed they which do hunger and thirst after righteousness, blessed the merciful, blessed the pure in heart, blessed the peacemakers." Of which seven sentences, it may be observed how all that long sermon was spoken. For the eighth where it is said, "Blessed" are "they which suffer persecution for righteousness' sake," denotes the fire itself, whereby the silver is proved seven times. And at the termination of this sermon it is said, "For He taught them as one having authority, and not as their scribes." Which refers to that which is said in this Psalm, "I deal confidently in Him."

8. "Thou, O Lord, shalt preserve us, and keep us from this generation to eternity" (ver. 7): here as needy and poor, there as wealthy and rich.

9. "The ungodly walk in a circle round about" (ver. 8): that is, in the desire of things temporal, which revolves as a wheel in a repeated circle of seven days; and therefore they do not arrive at the eighth, that is, at eternity, for which this Psalm is entitled. So too it is said by Solomon, "For the wise king is the winnower of the ungodly, and he bringeth on them the wheel of the wicked.—After Thine height Thou hast multiplied the sons of men." For there is in temporal things too a multiplication, which turns away from the unity of God. Hence "the corruptible body weigheth down the soul, and the earthy tabernacle presseth down the mind that museth upon many things." But the righteous are multiplied "after the height of God," when "they shall go from strength to strength."13

PSALM XIII.

UNTO THE END, A PSALM OF DAVID.

1. "For Christ is the end of the law to every one that believeth." "How long, O Lord, wilt Thou forget me unto the end?" (ver. 1) that is, put me off as to spiritually understanding Christ, who is the Wisdom of God, and the true end of all the aim of the soul. "How long dost Thou turn away Thy face from me?" As God doth not forget, so neither doth He turn His face away: but Scripture speaks after our manner. Now God is said to turn away His face, when He doth not give to the soul, which as yet hath not the pure eye of the mind, the knowledge of Himself.

2. "How long shall I place counsel in my soul?" (ver. 2). There is no need of counsel but in adversity. Therefore "How long shall I place counsel in my soul?" is as if it were said,

How long shall I be in adversity? Or at least it is an answer, so that the meaning is this, So long, O Lord, wilt Thou forget me to the end, and so long turn away Thy face from me, until I shall place counsel in mine own soul: so that except a man place counsel in his own soul to work mercy perfectly, God will not direct him to the end, nor give him that full knowledge of Himself, which is "face to face." "Sorrow in my heart through the day?" How long shall I have, is understood. And "through the day" signifies continuance, so that day is taken for time: from which as each one longs to be free, he has sorrow in his heart, making entreaty to rise to things eternal, and not endure man's day.

3. "How long shall mine enemy be exalted over me?" either the devil, or carnal habit.

4. "Look on me, and hear me, O Lord my God" (ver. 3). "Look on me," refers to what was said, "How long" dost "Thou turn away Thy face from me." "Hear," refers to what was said," How long wilt Thou forget me to the end? Lighten mine eyes, that I sleep not in death." The eyes of the heart must be understood, that they be not closed by the pleasurable eclipse of sin.

5. "Lest at any time mine enemy say, I have prevailed against him" (ver. 4). The devil's mockery is to be feared. "They that trouble me will exult, if I be moved;"

the devil and his angels; who exulted not over that righteous man, Job, when they troubled him; because he was not moved, that is, did not draw back from the stedfastness of his faith.

6. "But I have hoped in Thy mercy" (ver. 5). Because this very thing, that a man be not moved, and that he abide fixed in the Lord, he should not attribute to self: lest when he glories that he hath not been moved, he be moved by this very pride. "My heart shall exult in Thy salvation;" in Christ, in the Wisdom of God. "I will sing to the Lord who hath given me good things;" spiritual good things, not belonging to man's day. "And I will chant to the name of the Lord most high" (ver. 6); that is, I give thanks with joy, and in most due order employ my body, which is the song of the spiritual soul. But if any distinction is to be marked here, "I will sing" with the heart, "I will chant" with my works; "to the Lord," that which He alone seeth, but "to the name of the Lord," that which is known among men, which is serviceable not for Him, but for us.

PSALM XIV.

TO THE END, A PSALM OF DAVID HIMSELF.

1. What "to the end" means, must not be too often repeated. "For Christ is the end of the law for righteousness to every one that believeth;" as the Apostle saith. We believe on Him, when we begin to enter on the good road: we shall see Him, when we shall get to the end. And therefore is He the end.

2. "The fool hath said in his heart, There is no God" (ver. 1). For not even have certain sacrilegious and abominable philosophers, who entertain perverse and false notions of God, dared to say, "There is no God." Therefore it is, hath said "in his heart;" for that no one dares to say it, even if he has dared to think it. "They are corrupt, and become abominable in their affections:" that is, whilst they love this world and love not God; these are the affections which corrupt the soul, and so blind it, that the fool can even say, "in his heart, There is no God. For as they did not like to retain God in their knowledge, God gave them over to a reprobate mind." "There is none that doeth goodness, no not up to one." "Up to one," can be understood either with that one, so that no man be understood: or besides one, that the Lord Christ may be excepted. As we say, This field is up to the sea; we do not of course reckon the sea together with the field. And this is the better interpretation, so that none be understood to have done goodness up to Christ; for that no man can do goodness, except He shall have shown it. And that is true; for until a man know the one God, he cannot do goodness.

3. "The Lord from heaven looked out upon the sons of men, to see if there be one understanding, or seeking after God" (ver. 2). It may be interpreted, upon the Jews; as he may have given them the more honourable name of the sons of men, by reason of their worship of the One God, in comparison with the Gentiles; of whom I suppose it was said above, "The fool hath said in his heart, There is no God," etc. Now the Lord looks out, that He may see, by His holy souls: which is the meaning of, "from heaven." For by Himself nothing is hid from Him.

4. "All have gone out of the way, they have together become useless:" that is, the Jews have become as the Gentiles, who were spoken of above. "There is none that doeth good, no not up to one" (ver. 3), must be interpreted as above. "Their throat is an open sepulchre." Either the voracity of the ever open palate is signified: or allegorically those who slay, and as it were devour those they have slain, into

whom they instil the disorder of their own conversation. Like to which with the contrary meaning is that which was said to Peter, "Kill and eat; "a that he should convert the Gentiles to his own faith and good conversation. "With their tongues they have dealt craftily." Flattery is the companion of the greedy and of all bad men. "The poison of asps is under their lips." By "poison," he means deceit; and "of asps," because they will not hear the precepts of the law, as asps "will not hear the voice of the charmer;" which is said more clearly in another Psalm. "Whose mouth is full of cursing and bitterness:" this is, "the poison of asps." "Their feet are Swift to shed blood." He here shows forth the habit of ill doing. "Destruction and unhappiness" are "in their ways." For all the ways of evil men are full of toil and misery. Hence the Lord cries out, "Come unto Me, all ye that labour and are heavy laden, and I will refresh you. Take My yoke upon you, and learn of Me, for I am meek and lowly in heart. For My yoke is easy and My burden light." "And the way of peace have they not known:" that way, namely, which the Lord, as I said, mentions, in the easy yoke and light burden. "There is no fear of God before their eyes." These do not say, "There is no God;" but yet they do not fear God.

5. "Shall not all, who work iniquity, know?" (ver. 4). He threatens the judgment. "Who devour My people as the food of bread:" that is, daily. For the food of bread is daily food. Now they devour the people, who serve their own ends out of them, not referring their ministry to the glory of God, and the salvation of those over whom they are.

6. "They have not called upon the Lord." For he doth not really call upon Him, who longs for such things as are displeasing to Him. "There they trembled for fear, where no fear was" (ver. 5): that is, for the loss of things temporal. For they said, "If we let Him thus alone, all men will believe on Him; and the Romans will come, and take away both our place and nation." They feared to lose an earthly kingdom, where no fear was; and they lost the kingdom of heaven, which they ought to have feared. And this must be understood of all temporal goods, the loss of which when men fear, they come not to things eternal.

7. "For God is in the just generation." It refers to what went before, so that the sense is, "shall not all they that work iniquity know that the Lord is in the just generation;" that is, He is not in them who love the world. For it is unjust to leave the Maker of the worlds, and "serve the creature more than the Creator." Ye have shamed the counsel of the poor, for the Lord is his hope" (ver. 6): that is, ye have despised the humble coining of the Son of God, because ye saw not in Him the pomp of the world: that they, whom he was calling, should put their hope in God alone, not in the things that pass away.

8. "Who will give salvation to Israel out of Sion?" (ver. 7). Who but He whose humiliation ye have despised? is understood. For He will come in glory to the judgment of the quick and the dead, and the kingdom of the just: that, forasmuch as in that humble coming "blindness hath happened in part unto Israel, that the fulness of the Gentiles might enter in," in that other should happen what follows, "and so all Israel should be saved." For the Apostle too takes that testimony of Isaiah, where it is said, "There shall come out of Sion He who shall turn away ungodliness from Jacob:" for the Jews, as it is here, "Who shall give salvation to Israel out of Sion?" "When the Lord shall turn away the captivity of His people, Jacob shall rejoice, and Israel shall be glad." It is a repetition, as is usual: for I suppose, "Israel shall be glad," is the same as, "Jacob shall rejoice."

PSALM XV.

A PSALM OF DAVID HIMSELF.

1. Touching this title there is no question. "0 Lord who shall sojourn in Thy tabernacle?" (ver. 1). Although tabernacle be sometimes used even for an everlasting habitation: yet when tabernacle is taken in its proper meaning, it is a thing of war. Hence soldiers are called tent-fellows, as having their tents together. This sense is assisted by the words, "Who shall sojourn?" For we war with the devil for a time, and then we need a tabernacle wherein we may refresh ourselves. Which specially points out the faith of the temporal Dispensation, which was wrought for us in time through the Incarnation of the Lord. "And who shall rest in Thy holy mountain?" Here perhaps he signifies at once the eternal habitation itself, that we should understand by "mountain" the supereminence of the love of Christ in life eternal.

2. "He who walketh without stain, and worketh righteousness" (ver. 2). Here he has laid down the proposition; in what follows he sets it forth in detail.

3. "Who speaketh the truth in his heart." For some have truth on their lips, and not in their heart. As if one should deceitfully point out a road, knowing that there were robbers there, and should say, If you go this way, you will be safe from robbers; and it should turn out that in fact there were no robbers found there: he has spoken the truth, but not in his heart. For he supposed it to be otherwise, and spoke the truth in ignorance. Therefore it is not enough to speak the truth, unless it be so also in heart. "Who hath practised no deceit in his tongue" (vet. 3). Deceit is practised with the tongue, when one thing is professed with the mouth, another concealed in the breast. "Nor tone evil to his neighhour." It is well known that by "neighbour," every man should be understood. "And hath not entertained slander against his neighbour," that is, hath not readily or rashly given credence to an accuser.

4. "The malicious one hath been brought to nought in his sight" (ver. 4). This is perfection, that the malicious one have no force against a man; and that this be "in his sight;" that is, that he know most surely that the malicious is not, save when the mind turns itself away from the eternal and immutable form of her own Creator to the form of the creature, which was made out of nothing. "But those that fear the Lord, He glorifieth:" the Lord Himself, that is. Now "the fear of the Lord is the

beginning of wisdom." As then the things above belong to the perfect, so what he is now going to say belongs to beginners.

5. "Who sweareth unto his neighbour, and deceiveth him not." "Who hath not given his money upon usury, and hath not taken rewards against the innocent" (ver. 5). These are no great things: but he who is not able to do even this, much less able is he to speak the truth in his heart, and to practise no deceit in his tongue, but as the truth is in the heart, so to profess and have it in his mouth, "yea, yea; nay, nay;" and to do no evil to his neighbour, that is, to any man; and to entertain no slander against his neighbour: all which are the virtues of the perfect, in whose sight the malicious one hath been brought to nought. Yet he concludes even these lesser things thus, "Whoso doeth these things shall not be moved for ever:" that is, he shall attain unto those greater things, wherein is great and unshaken stability. For even the very tenses are, perhaps not without cause, so varied, as that in the conclusion above the past tense should be used, but in this the future. For there it was said, "The malicious one hath been brought to nought in his sight:"but here, "shall not be moved for ever."

PSALM XVI.

THE INSCRIPTION OF THE TITLE, OF DAVID HIMSELF.

1. Our King in this Psalm speaks in the character of the human nature He assumed, of whom the royal tle at the time of His passion was eminently set forth.

2. Now He saith as follows; "Preserve me, O Lord, for in Thee have I hoped" (ver. 1): "I have said to the Lord, Thou art my God, for Thou requirest not my goods" (ver. 2): for with my goods Thou dost not look to be made blessed.

3. "To the saints who are on His earth" (ver. 3): to the saints who have placed their hope in the laud of the living, the citizens of the heavenly Jerusalem, whose spiritual conversation is, by the anchor of hope, fixed in that country, which is rightly called God's earth; although as yet in this earth too they be conversant in the flesh. "He hath wonderfully fulfilled all My wishes in them." To those saints then He hath wonderfully fulfilled all My wishes in their advancement, whereby they have perceived, how both the humanity of My divinity hath profited them that I might die, and the divinity of the humanity that I might rise again.

4. "Their infirmities have been multiplied" (ver. 4): their infirmities have been multiplied not for their destruction, but that they might long for the Physician. "Afterwards they made haste." Accordingly after infirmities multiplied they made haste, that they might be healed. "I will not gather together their assemblies by blood." For their assemblies shall not be carnal, nor will I gather them together as one propitiated by the blood of cattle. "Nor will I be mindful of their names within My lips." But by a spiritual change what they have been shall be forgotten; nor by Me shall they be any more called either sinners, or enemies, or men; but righteous, and My brethren, and sons of God through My peace.

5. "The Lord is the portion of Mine inheritance, and of My cup" (ver. 5). For together with Me they shall possess the inheritance, the Lord Himself. Let others choose for themselves portions, earthly and temporal, to enjoy: the portion of the Saints is the Lord eternal. Let others drink of deadly pleasures, the portion of My cup is the Lord. In that I say, "Mine," I include the Church: for where the Head is, there is the body also. For into the inheritance will I gather together their assemblies, and by the inebriation of the cup I will forget their old names. "Thou

art He who will restore to Me My inheritance:" that to these too, whom I free, may be known "the glory wherein I was with Thee before the world was made." For Thou wilt not restore to Me that which I never lost, but Thou wilt restore to these, who have lost it, the knowledge of that glory: in whom because I am, Thou wilt restore to Me.

6. "The lines have fallen to me in glorious places" (ver. 6). The boundaries of my possession have fallen in Thy glory as it were by lot, like as God is the possession of the Priests and Levites. "For Mine inheritance is glorious to Me." "For Mine inheritance is glorious," not to all, but to them that see; in whom because I am, "it is to Me."

7. "I will bless the Lord, who hath given Me understanding" (ver. 7): whereby this inheritance may be seen and possessed. "Yea moreover too even unto night my reins have chastened Me." Yea besides understanding, even unto death, My inferior part, the assumption of flesh, hath instructed Me, that I might experience the darkness of mortality, which that understanding hath not.

8. "I foresaw the Lord in My sight always" (ver. 8). But coming into things that pass away, I removed not Mine eye from Him who abideth ever, foreseeing this, that to Him I should return after passing through the things temporal. "For He is on My right hand, that I should not be moved." For He favoureth Me, that I should abide fixedly in Him.

9. "Wherefore My heart was glad, and My tongue exulted" (ver. 9). Wherefore both in My thoughts is gladness, and in my words exultation. "Moreover too My flesh shall rest in hope." Moreover too My flesh shall not fail unto destruction, but shall sleep in hope of the resurrection.

10. "For Thou wilt not leave My soul in hell" (ver. 10). For Thou wilt neither give My soul for a possession to those parts below. "Neither wilt Thou grant Thine Holy One to see corruption." Neither wilt Thou suffer that sanctified body, whereby others are to be also sanctified, to see corruption. "Thou hast made known to Me the paths of life" (ver. 11). Thou hast made known through Me the paths of humiliation, that men might return to life, from whence they fell through pride; in whom because I am, "Thou hast made known to Me." "Thou wilt fill Me with joy with Thy countenance." Thou wilt fill them with joy, that they should seek nothing further, when they shall see Thee "face to face;" in whom because I

am, "Thou wilt fill Me." "Pleasure is at Thy right hand even to the end." Pleasure is in Thy favour and mercy in this life's journey, leading on even to the end of the glory of Thy countenance.

PSALM XVII.

A PRAYER OF DAVID HIMSELF.

1. This prayer must be assigned to the Person of the Lord, with the addition of the Church, which is His body.

2. "Hear My righteousness, O God, consider My supplication" (ver. 1). "Hearken unto My prayer, not in deceitful lips:" not going forth to Thee in deceitful lips. "Let My judgment from Thy countenance go forth" (ver. 2). From the enlightening of the knowledge of Thee, let Me judge truth. Or at least, let My judgment go forth, not in deceitful lips, from Thy countenance, that is, that I may not in judging utter aught else than I understand in Thee. "Let Mine eyes see equity:" the eyes, of course, of the heart.

3. "Thou hast proved and visited Mine heart in the night season" (ver. 3). For this Mine heart hath been proved by the visitation of tribulation. "Thou hast examined Me by fire, and iniquity hath not been found in Me." Now not night only, in that it is wont to disturb, but fire also, in that it burns, is this tribulation to be called; whereby when I was examined I was found righteous.

4. "That My mouth may not speak the works of men" (ver. 4). That nothing may proceed out of My mouth, but what relates to Thy glory and praise; not to the works of men, which they do beside Thy will. "Because of the words of Thy lips." Because of the words of Thy peace, or of Thy prophets. "I have kept hard ways." I have kept the toilsome ways of human mortality and suffering.

5. "To perfect My steps in Thy paths" (ver. 5). That the love of the Church might be perfected in the strait ways, whereby she arrives at Thy rest. "That My footsteps be not moved." That the signs of My way, which, like footsteps, have been imprinted on the Sacraments and Apostolical writings, be not moved, that they may mark them who would follow Me. Or at least, that I may still abide fixedly in eternity, after that I have accomplished the hard ways, and have finished My steps in the straits of Thy paths.

6. "I have cried out, for Thou hast heard Me, O God" (ver. 6). With a free and strong effort have I directed My prayers unto Thee: for that I might have this

power, Thou hast heard Me when praying more weakly. "Incline Thine ear to Me, and hear My words." Let not Thy hearing forsake My humiliation.

7. "Make Thy mercies marvellous" (ver. 7). Let not Thy mercies be disesteemed, lest they be loved too little.

8. "Who savest them that hope in Thee from such as resist Thy right hand:" from such as resist the favour, whereby Thou favourest Me. "Keep Me, O Lord, as the apple of Thine eye" (ver. 8): which seems very little and minute: yet by it is the sight of the eye directed, whereby the light is distinguished from the darkness; as by Christ's humanity, the divinity of the Judgment s distinguishing between the righteous and sinners. "In the covering of Thy wings protect Me." In the defence of Thy love and mercy protect Me. "From the face of the ungodly who have troubled Me" (ver. 9).

9. "Mine enemies have compassed about My soul;" "they have shut up their own fat" (ver.10). They have been covered with their own gross joy, after that their desire hath been satiated with wickedness. "Their mouth hath spoken pride." And therefore their mouth spoke pride, in saying, "Hail, King of the Jews," and other like words.

10. "Casting Me forth they have now compassed Me about" (ver. 11). Casting Me forth outside the city, they have now compassed Me about on the Cross. "Their eyes they have determined to turn down on the earth." The bent of their heart they have determined to turn down on these earthly things: deeming Him, who was slain, to endure a mighty evil, and themselves, that slew Him, none.

11. "As a lion ready for prey, have they taken Me" (ver. 12). They have taken Me, like that adversary who "walketh about, seeking whom he may devour." "And as a lion's whelp dwelling in secret places." And as his whelp, the people to whom it was said, "Ye are of your father the devil:" meditating on the snares, whereby they might circumvent and destroy the just One.

12. "Arise, O Lord, prevent them, and cast them down" (ver. 13). Arise, O Lord, Thou whom they suppose to be asleep, and regardless of men's iniquities; be they blinded before by their own malice, that vengeance may prevent their deed; and so cast them down.

13. "Deliver My soul from the ungodly." Deliver My soul, by restoring Me after the death, which the ungodly have inflicted on Me. "Thy weapon: from the enemies of Thine hand" (ver. 14). For My soul is Thy weapon, which Thy hand, that is, Thy eternal Power, hath taken to subdue thereby the kingdoms of iniquity, and divide the righteous from the ungodly. This weapon then "deliver from the enemies of Thine hand" that is of Thy Power that is from Mine enemies. "Destroy them, O Lord, from off the earth, scatter them in their life." O Lord, destroy them from off the earth, which they inhabit, scatter them throughout the world in this life, which only they think their life, who despair of life eternal. "And by Thy hidden things their belly hath been filled." Now not only this visible punishment shall overtake them, but also their memory hath been filled with sins, which as darkness are hidden from the light of Thy truth, that they should forget God. "They have been filled with swine's flesh." They have been filled with uncleanness, treading under foot the pearls of God's words. "And they have left the rest to their babes:" crying out, "This sin be upon us and upon our children."

14. "But I shall appear in Thy righteousness in Thy sight" (ver. 15). But I, Who have not appeared to them that, with their filthy and darkened heart, cannot see the light of wisdom, "I shall appear in Thy righteousness in Thy sight."

I shall be satiated, when Thy glory shall be manifested." And when they have been satiated with their uncleanness, that they could not know Me, I shall be satiated, when Thy glory shall be manifested, in them that know Me. In that verse indeed where it is said, "filled with swine's flesh," some copies have, "filled with children:" for from the ambiguity of the Greek a double interpretation has resulted. Now by "children" we understand works; and as by good children, good works, so by evil, evil.

PSALM XVIII.

TO THE END, FOR THE SERVANT OF THE LORD, DAVID HIMSELF.

1. That is, for the strong of hand, Christ in His Manhood. "The words of this song which he spoke to the Lord on the day when the Lord delivered him out of the hands of his enemies, and of the hand of Saul; and he said, On the day when the Lord delivered him out of the hands of his enemies and of the hand of Saul:" namely, the king of the Jews, whom they had demanded for themselves. For as "David" is said to be by interpretation, strong of hand; so "Saul" is said to be demanding. Now it is well known, how that People demanded for themselves a king, and received him for their king, not according to the will of God, but according to their own will.

2. Christ, then, and the Church, that is, whole Christ, the Head and the Body, saith here, "I will love Thee, O Lord, My strength" (ver. 1). I will love Thee, O Lord, by whom I am strong.

3. "O Lord, My stay, and My refuge, and My deliverer" (ver. 2). O Lord, who hast stayed Me, because I sought refuge with Thee: and I sought refuge, because Thou hast delivered Me. "My God is My helper; and I will hope in Him." My God, who hast first afforded me the help of Thy call, that I might be able to hope in Thee. "My defender, and the horn of My salvation, and My redeemer." My defender, because I have not leant upon Myself, lifting up as it were the horn of pride against Thee; but have found Thee a horn indeed, that is, the sure height of salvation: and that I might find it, Thou redeemedst Me.

4. "With praise will I call upon the Lord, and I shall be safe from Mine enemies" (ver. 3). Seeking not My own but the Lord's glory, I will call upon Him, and there shall be no means whereby the errors of ungodliness can hurt Me.

5. "The pains of death," that is, of the flesh, have "compassed Me about. And the overflowings of ungodliness have troubled Me" (ver. 4). Ungodly troublesstirred up for a time, like torrents of rain which will soon subside, have come on to trouble Me.

6. "The pains of hell compassed Me about" (ver. 5). Among those that compassed Me about to destroy Me, were pains of envy, which work death, and lead on to the hell of sin. "The snares of death prevented Me." They prevented Me, so that they wished to hurt Me first, which shall afterwards be recompensed unto them. Now they seize unto destruction such men as they have evilly persuaded by the boast of righteousness: in the name but not in the reality of which they glory against the Gentiles.

7. "And in Mine oppression I called upon the Lord, and cried unto My God. And He heard My voice from His holy temple" (ver. 6). He heard from My heart, wherein He dwelleth, My voice. "And My cry in His sight entered into His ears;" and My cry, which I utter, not in the ears of men, but inwardly before Him Himself, "entered into His ears."

8. "And the earth was moved and trembled" (ver. 7). When the Son of Man was thus glorified, sinners were moved and trembled. "And the foundations of the mountains were troubled." And the hopes of the proud, which were in this life, were troubled. "And were moved, for God was wroth with them." That is, that the hope of temporal goods might have now no more establishment in the hearts of men.

9. "There went up smoke in His wrath" (ver. 8). The tearful supplication of penitents went up, when they came to know God's threatenings against the ungodly. "And fire burneth from His face." And the ardour of love after repentance burns by the knowledge of Him. "Coals were kindled from Him." They, who were already dead, abandoned by the fire of good desire and the light of righteousness, and who remained in coldness and darkness, re-enkindled and enlightened, have come to life again.

10. "And He bowed the heaven, and came down" (ver. 9). And He humbled the just One, that He might descend to men's infirmity. "And darkness under His feet." And the ungodly, who savour of things earthly, in the darkness of their own malice, knew not Him: for the earth under His feet is as it were His footstool.

11. "And He mounted above the cherubim, and did fly" (ver. 10). And He was exalted above the fulness of knowledge, that no man should come to Him but by love: for "love is the fulfilling of the law." And full soon He showed to His lovers that He is incomprehensible, lest they should suppose that He is comprehended by

corporeal imaginations. "He flew above the wings of the winds." But that swiftness, whereby He showed Himself to be incomprehensible, is above the powers of souls, whereon as upon wings they raise themselves from earthly fears into the air of liberty.

12. "And hath made darkness His hiding place" (ver. 11). And hath settled the obscurity of the Sacraments, and the hidden hope in the heart of believers, where He may lie hid, and not abandon them. In this darkness too, wherein "we yet walk by faith, and not by sight," as long as "we hope for what we see not, and with patience wait for it." Round about Him is His tabernacle." Yet they that believe Him turn to Him and encircle Him; for that He is in the midst of them, since He is equally the friend of all, in whom as in a tabernacle He at this time dwells. "Dark water in clouds of air." Nor let any one on this account, if he understand the Scripture, imagine that he is already in that light, which will be when we shall have come out of faith into sight: for in the prophets and in all the preachers of the word of God there is obscure teaching.

13. "In respect of the brightness in His sight" (ver. 12): in comparison with the brightness, which is in the sight of His manifestation. "His clouds have passed over." The preachers of His word are not now bounded by the confines of Judaea, but have passed over to the Gentiles. "Hail and coals of fire." Reproofs are figured, whereby, as by hail, the hard hearts are bruised: but if a cultivated and genial soil, that is, a godly mind, receive them, the hail's hardness dissolves into water, that is, the terror of the lightning-charged, and as it were frozen, reproof dissolves into satisfying doctrine; and hearts kindled by the fire of love revive. All these things in His clouds have passed over to the Gentiles.

14. "And the Lord hath thundered from heaven" (ver. 13). And in confidence of the Gospel the Lord hath sounded forth from the heart of the just One. "And the Highest gave His voice;" that we might entertain it, and in the depth of human things, might hear things heavenly.

15. "And He sent out His arrows, and scattered them" (ver. 14). And He sent out Evangelists traversing straight paths on the wings of strength, not in their own power, but His by whom they were sent. And "He scattered them," to whom they were sent, that to some of them they should be "the savour of life unto life, to others the savour of death unto death." "And He multiplied lightnings, and troubled them." And He multiplied miracles, and troubled them.

16. "And the fountains of water were seen. And the fountains of water springing up into everlasting life," which were made in the preachers, were seen. "And the foundations of the round world were revealed" (ver. 15). And the Prophets, who were not understood, and upon whom was to be built the world of believers in the Lord, were revealed. "At Thy chiding, O Lord:" crying out, "The kingdom of God is come nigh unto you." "At the blasting of the breath of Thy displeasure;" saying, "Except ye repent, ye shall all likewise perish."

17. "He hath sent down from on high, and hath fetched Me (ver. 16): by calling out of the Gentiles for an inheritance "a glorious Church, not having spot, or wrinkle." "He hath taken Me out of the multitude of waters." He hath taken Me out of the multitude of peoples.

18. "He hath delivered Me from My strongest enemies" (ver. 17). He hath delivered Me from Mine enemies, who prevailed to the afflicting and overturning of this temporal life of Mine. "And from them which hate Me; for they are too strong for Me:" as long as I am under them knowing not God.

19. "They have prevented Me in the day of My affliction" (ver. 18). They have first injured Me, in the time when I am bearing a mortal and toilsome body. "And the Lord hath become My stay." And since the stay of earthly pleasure was disturbed and torn up by the bitterness of misery, the Lord hath become My stay.

20. "And hath brought Me forth into a broad place" (ver. 19). And since I was enduring the straits of the flesh, He brought Me forth into the spiritual breadth of faith. "He hath delivered Me, because He desired Me." Before that I desired Him, He delivered Me from My most powerful enemies (who were envious of Me when I once desired Him), and from them that hated Me, because I do desire Him.

21. "And the Lord shall reward Me according to My righteousness" (vet. 20). And the Lord shall reward Me according to the righteousness of My good will, who first showed mercy, before that I had the good will. "And according to the cleanness of My hands He will recompense Me." And according to the cleanness of My deeds He will recompense Me, who hath given Me to do well by bringing Me forth into the broad place of faith.

22. "Because I have kept the ways of the Lord" (ver. 21). That the breadth of good works, that are by faith, and the long-suffering of perseverance should follow after.

23. "Nor have I walked impiously apart from My God." "For all His judgments are in My sight" (ver. 22). "For" with persevering contemplation I weigh "all His judgments," that is, the rewards of the righteous, and the punishments of the ungodly, and the scourges of such as are to be chastened, and the trials of such as are to be proved. "And I have not cast out His righteousness from Me:" as they do that faint under their burden of them, and return to their own vomit.

24. "And I shall be undefiled with Him, and I shall keep Myself from Mine iniquity" (ver. 23).

25. "And the Lord shall reward Me according to My righteousness (ver. 24). Accordingly not only for the breadth of faith, which worketh by love; but also for the length of perseverance, will the Lord reward Me according to My righteousness. "And according to the cleanness of My hands in the sight of His eyes." Not as men see, but "in the sight of His eyes." For "the things that are seen are temporal; but the things that are not seen are eternal:" whereto the height of hope appertains.

26. "With the holy Thou shalt be holy" (ver. 25). There is a hidden depth also, wherein Thou art known to be holy with the holy, for that Thou makest holy. "And with the harmless Thou shalt be harmless." For Thou harmest no man, but each one is bound by the bands of his own sins.

27. "And with the chosen Thou shalt be chosen." (ver. 26). And by him whom Thou choosest, Thou art chosen. "And with the froward Thou shalt be froward." And with the froward Thou seemest froward: for they say, "The way of the Lord is not right: " and their way is not right.

28. "For Thou wilt make whole the humble people" (ver. 27). Now this seems froward to the froward, that Thou wilt make them whole that confess their sins. "And Thou wilt humble the eyes of the proud." But them that are "ignorant of God's righteousness, and seek to establish their own," Thou wilt humble.

29. "For thou wilt light My candle, O Lord" (ver. 28). For our light is not from ourselves; but "Thou wilt light my candle, O Lord. O my God, Thou wilt enlighten my darkness." For we through our sins are darkness; but "Thou, O my God, wilt enlighten my darkness."

30. "For by Thee shall I be delivered from temptation" (ver. 29). For not by myself, but by Thee, shall I be delivered from temptation. "And in my God shall I leap over the wall." And not in myself, but in my God shall I leap over the wall, which sin has raised between men and the heavenly Jerusalem.

31. "My God, His way is undefiled "(ver. 30). My God cometh not unto men, except they shall have purified the way of faith, whereby He may come to them; for that" His way is undefiled." "The words of the Lord have been proved by fire." The words of the Lord are tried by the fire of tribulation. "He is the Protector of them that hope in Him." And all that hope not in themselves, but in Him, are not consumed by that same tribulation. For hope followeth faith.

32. "For who is God, but the Lord?" (ver. 31) whom we serve. "And who God, but our God?" And who is God, but the Lord? whom after good service we sons shall possess as the hoped-for inheritance.

33. "God, who hath girded me with strength" (ver. 32). God, who hath girded me that I might be strong, lest the loosely flowing folds of desire hinder my deeds and steps. "And hath made my way undefiled." And hath made the way of love, whereby I may come to Him, undefiled, as the way of faith is undefiled, whereby He comes to me.

34. "Who hath made my feet perfect like harts' feet" (ver. 33). Who hath made my love perfect to surmount the thorny and dark entanglements of this world. "And will set me up on high." And will fix my aim on the heavenly habitation, that "I may be filled with all the fulness of God."

35. "Who teacheth my hands for battle" (ver. 34). Who teacheth me to work for the overthrow of mine enemies, who strive to shut the kingdom of heaven against us. "And Thou hast made mine arms as a bow of steel." And Thou hast made my earnest striving after good works unwearied.

36. "And Thou hast given me the defence of my salvation, and Thy right hand hath held me up" (ver. 35). And the favour of Thy grace hath held me up. "And Thy discipline hath directed me to the end." And Thy correction, not suffering me to wander from the way, hath directed me that whatsoever I do, I refer to that end, whereby I may cleave to Thee. "And this Thy discipline, it shall teach me." And that same correction of Thine shall teach me to attain to that, whereunto it hath directed me.

37. "Thou hast enlarged my steps under me" (ver. 36). Nor shall the straits of the flesh hinder me; for Thou hast enlarged my love, working in gladness even with these mortal things and members which are under me. "And my footsteps have not been weakened." And either my goings, or the marks which I have imprinted for the imitation of those that follow, have not been weakened.

38. "I will follow up mine enemies, and seize them" (ver. 37). I will follow up my carnal affections, and will not be seized by them, but will seize them, so that they may be consumed. "And I will not turn, till they fail." And from this purpose I will not turn myself to rest, till they fail who make a tumult about me.

39. "I will break them, and they shall not be able to stand" (ver. 38): and they shall not hold out against me. "They shall fall under my feet." When they are cast down, I will place before me the loves whereby I walk for evermore.

40. "And Thou hast girded me with strength to the war" (ver. 39). And the loose desires of my flesh hast Thou bound up with strength, that in such a fight I may not be encumbered. "Thou hast supplanted under me them that rose up against me." Thou hast caused them to be deceived, who followed upon me, that they should be brought under me, who desired to be over me.

41. "And thou hast given mine enemies the back to me" (ver. 40). And thou hast turned mine enemies, and hast made them to be a back to me, that is, to follow me. "And Thou hast destroyed them that hate me." But such other of them as have persisted in hatred, Thou hast destroyed.

42. "They have cried out, and there was none to save them" (ver. 41). For who can save them, whom Thou wouldest not save? "To the Lord, and He did not hear

them." Nor did they cry out to any chance one, but to the Lord: and He did not judge them worthy of being heard, who depart not from their wickedness.

43. "And I will beat them as small as dust before the face of the wind" (ver. 42). And I will beat them small; for dry they are, receiving not the shower of God's mercy; that borne aloft and puffed up with pride they may be hurried along from firm and unshaken hope, and as it were from the earth's solidity and stability. "As the clay of the streets I will destroy them." In their wanton and loose course along the broad ways of perdition, which many walk, will I destroy them.

44. "Thou wilt deliver Me from the contradictions of the people" (ver. 43). Thou wilt deliver Me from the contradictions of them who said, "If we send Him away, all the world will go after Him."

45. "Thou shall make Me the head of the Gentiles. A people whom I have not known have served Me." The people of the Gentiles, whom in bodily presence I have not visited, have served Me. "At the hearing of the ear they have obeyed Me" (ver. 44). They have not seen Me with the eye: but, receiving my preachers, at the hearing of the ear they have obeyed Me.

46. "The strange children have lied unto Me." Children, not to be called Mine, but rather strange children, to whom it is rightly said, "Ye are of your father the devil," have lied unto Me. "The strange children have waxen old" (ver. 45). The strange children, to whom for their renovation I brought the new Testament, have remained in the old man. "And they have halted from their own paths." And like those that are weak in one foot, for holding the old they have rejected the new Testament, they have become halt, even in their old Law, rather following their own traditions, than God's. For they brought frivolous charges of unwashen hands, because such were the paths, which themselves had made and worn by long use, in wandering from the ways of God's commands.

47. "The Lord liveth, and blessed be my God." "But to be carnally minded is death:" for "the Lord liveth, and blessed be my God. And let the God of my salvation be exalted" (ver. 46). And let me not think after an earthly fashion of the God of my salvation; nor look from Him for this earthly salvation, but that on high.

48. "O God, who givest Me vengeance, and subduest the people under Me" (ver. 47). O God, who avengest Me by subduing the people under Me. "My Deliverer from My angry enemies:" the Jews crying out, "Crucify Him, Crucify Him."

49. "From them that rise up against Me Thou wilt exalt Me" (ver. 48). From the Jews that rise up against Me in My passion, Thou wilt exalt Me in My resurrection. "From the unjust man Thou wilt deliver Me." From their unjust rule Thou wilt deliver Me.

50. "For this cause will I confess to Thee among the Gentiles, O Lord" (ver. 49). For this cause shall the Gentiles confess to Thee through Me, O Lord. "And I will sing unto Thy Name." And Thou shall be more widely known by My good deeds.

51. "Magnifying the salvation of His King" (ver. 50). God, who magnifieth, so as to make wonderful, the salvation, which His Son giveth to believers. "And showing mercy to His Christ: "God, who showeth mercy to His Christ: "To David and to His seed for evermore:" to the Deliverer Himself strong of hand, who hath overcome this world; and to them whom, as believers in the Gospel, He hath begotten for evermore. What things soever are spoken in this Psalm which cannot apply to the Lord Himself personally, that is to the Head of the Church, must be referred to the Church. For whole Christ speaks here, in whom are all His members.

PSALM XIX.

TO THE END, A PSALM OF DAVID HIMSELF.

1. It is a well-known title; nor does the Lord Jesus Christ say what follows, but it is said of Him.

2. "The heavens tell out the glory of God" (ver. 1). The righteous Evangelists, in whom, as in the heavens, God dwelleth, set forth the glory of our Lord Jesus Christ, or the glory wherewith the Son glorified the Father upon earth. "And the firmament showeth forth the works of His hands." And the firmament showeth forth the deeds of the Lord's power, that now made heaven by the assurance of the Holy Ghost, which before was earth by fear.

3. "Day unto day uttereth word" (ver. 2). To the spiritual the Spirit giveth out the fulness of the unchangeable Wisdom of God, the Word which in the beginning is God with God. "And night unto night announceth knowledge." And to the fleshly, as to those afar off, the mortality of the flesh, by conveying faith, announceth future knowledge.

4. "There is no speech nor language, in which their voices are not heard" (ver. 3). In which the voices of the Evangelists have not been heard, seeing that the Gospel was preached in every tongue.

5. "Their sound is gone out into all the earth, and their words to the ends of the world" (ver. 4).

6. "In the sun hath He set His tabernacle." Now that He might war against the powers of temporal error, the Lord, being about to send not peace but a sword on earth, in time, or in manifestation, set so to say His military dwelling, that is, the dispensation of His incarnation. "And He as a bridegroom coming forth out of His chamber" (ver. 5). And He, coming forth out of the Virgin's womb, where God was united to man's nature as a bridegroom to a bride. "Rejoiced as a giant to run His way." Rejoiced as One exceeding strong, and surpassing all other men in power incomparable, not to inhabit, but to run His way. For, "He stood not in the way of sinners. "

112

7. "His going forth is from the highest heaven" (ver. 6). From the Father is His going forth, not that in time, but from everlasting, whereby He was born of the Father. "And His meeting is even to the height of heaven." And in the fulness of the Godhead He meets even to an equality with the Father. "And there is none that may hide himself from His heat." But whereas, "the Word was even made flesh, and dwelt in us," assuming our mortality, He permitted no man to excuse himself from the shadow of death; for the heat of the Word penetrated even it.

8. "The law of the Lord is undefiled, converting souls" (ver. 7). The law of the Lord, therefore, is Himself who came to fulfil the law, not to destroy it; an undefiled law, "Who did no sin, neither was guile found in His mouth," not oppressing souls with the yoke of bondage, but converting them to imitate Him in liberty. "The testimony of the Lord is sure, giving wisdom to babes." "The testimony of the Lord is sure;" for, "no man knoweth the Father save the Son, and he to whomsoever the Son will reveal Him," which things have been hidden from the wise and revealed to babes; for, "God resisteth the proud, but giveth grace to the humble." 8)

9. "The statutes of the Lord are right, rejoicing the heart" (ver. 8). All the statutes of the Lord are right in Him who taught not what He did not; that they who should imitate Him might rejoice in heart, in those things which they should do freely with love, not slavishly with fear. "The commandment of the Lord is lucid, enlightening the eyes." "The commandment of the Lord is lucid," with no veil of carnal observances, enlightening the sight of the inner man.

10. "The fear of the Lord is chaste, enduring for ever" (ver. 9). "The fear of the Lord;" not that distressing fear under the law, dreading exceedingly the withdrawal of temporal goods, by the love of which the soul commits fornication; but that chaste fear wherewith the Church, the more ardently she loves her Spouse, the more carefully does she take heed of offending Him, and therefore, "perfect love casteth" not "out" this" fear," but it endureth for ever.

11. "The judgments of the Lord are true, justified together." The judgments of Him, who "judgeth no man, but hath committed all judgment unto the Son," are justified in truth unchangeably. For neither in His threatenings nor His promises doth God deceive any man, nor can any withdraw either from the ungodly His punishment, or from the godly His reward. "To be desired more than gold, and much precious stone" (ver. 10). Whether it be "gold and stone itself much," or "much precious," or "much to be desired;" still, the judgments of God are to be

desired more than the pomp of this world; by desire of which it is brought to pass that the judgments of God are not desired, but feared, or despised, or not believed. But if any be himself gold and precious stone, that he may not be consumed by fire, but received into the treasury of God, more than himself does he desire the judgments of God, whose will he preferreth to his own. "And sweeter than honey and the honey comb." And whether one be even now honey, who, disenthralled already from the chains of this life, is awaiting the day when he may come up to God's feast; or whether he be yet as the honey comb, wrapped about with this life as it were with wax, not mixed and become one with it, but filling it, needing some pressure of God's hand, not oppressing but expressing it, whereby from life temporal it may be strained out into life eternal: to such an one the judgments of God are sweeter than he himself is to himself, for that they are "sweeter than honey and the honey comb."

12. "For Thy servant keepeth them "(ver. 11). For to him who keepeth them not the day of the Lord is bitter. "In keeping them there is great reward." Not in any external benefit, but in the thing itself, that God's judgments are kept, is there great reward; great because one rejoiceth therein.

13. "Who understandeth sins?" (ver. But what sort of sweetness can there be in sins, where there is no understanding? For who can understand sins, which close the very eye, to which truth is pleasant, to which the judgments of God are desirable and sweet? yea, as darkness closes the eye, so do sins the mind, and suffer it not to see either the light, or itself.

14. "Cleanse me, O Lord, from my secret faults." From the lusts which lie hid in me, cleanse me, O Lord. "And from the" faults "of others preserve Thy servant" (ver. 13). Let me not be led astray by others. For he is not a prey to the faults of others, who is cleansed from his own. Preserve therefore from the lusts of others, not the proud man, and him who would be his own master, but, Thy servant. "If they get not the dominion over me, then shall I be undefiled." If neither my own secret sins, nor those of others, get the dominion over me, then shall I be undefiled. For there is no third source of sin, but one's own secret sin, by which the devil fell, and another's sin, by which man is seduced, so as by consenting to make it his own. "And I shall be cleansed from the great offence." What but pride? for there is none greater than apostasy from God, which is "the beginning of the pride of man." And he shall indeed be undefiled, who is free from this offence also; for tiffs is the last to them who are returning to God, which was the first as they departed from Him.

15. "And the words of my mouth shall be pleasing, and the meditation of my heart is always in Thy sight" (ver. 14). The meditation of my heart is not after the vain glory of pleasing men, for now there is pride no more, but in Thy sight alway, who regardest a pure conscience "O Lord, my Helper, and my Redeemer" (ver. 15). O Lord, my Helper, in my approach to Thee; for Thou art my Redeemer, that I might set out unto Thee: lest any attributing to his own wisdom his conversion to Thee, or to his own strength his attaining to Thee, should be rather driven back by Thee, who resistest the proud; for he is not cleansed from the great offence, nor pleasing in Thy sight, who redeemest us that we may be converted, and helpest us that we may attain unto Thee.

PSALM XX.

TO THE END, A PSALM OF DAVID.

1. This is a well-known title; and it is not Christ who speaks; but the prophet speaks to Christ, under the form of wishing, foretelling things to come.

2. "The Lord hear Thee in the day of trouble" (ver. 1). The Lord hear Thee in the day in which Thou saidst, "Father glorify Thy Son." "The name of the God of Jacob protect Thee." For to Thee belongeth the younger people. Since "the eider shall serve the younger."

3. "Send Thee help from the Holy, and from Sion defend Thee" (ver. 2). Making for Thee a sanctified Body, the Church, from watching safe, which waiteth when Thou shalt come from the wedding.

4. "Be mindful of all Thy sacrifice" (ver. 3). Make us mindful of all Thy injuries and despiteful treatment, which Thou hast borne for us. "And be Thy whole burnt offering made fat." And turn the cross, whereon Thou wast wholly offered up to God, into the joy of the resurrection.

5. "Diapsalma. The Lord render to Thee according to Thine Heart" (ver. 4). The Lord render to Thee, not according to their heart, who thought by persecution they could destroy Thee; but according to Thine Heart, wherein Thou knewest what profit Thy passion would have. "And fulfil all Thy counsel." "And fulfil all Thy counsel," not only that whereby Thou didst lay down Thy life for Thy friends, that the corrupted grain might rise again to more abundance; but that also whereby "blindness in part hath happened unto Israel, that the fulness of the Gentiles might enter in, and so an Israel might be saved."

6. "We will exult in Thy salvation" (ver. 5). We will exult in that death will in no wise hurt Thee; for so Thou wilt also show that it cannot hurt us either. "And in the name of the Lord our God will we be magnified." And the confession of Thy name shall not only not destroy us, but shall even magnify us.

7. "The Lord fulfil all Thy petitions." The Lord fulfil not only the petitions which Thou madest on earth, but those also whereby Thou intercedest for us in heaven. "Now have I known that the Lord hath saved his Christ" (ver. 6). Now hath it been shown to me in prophecy, that the Lord will raise up His Christ again. "He will hear Him from His holy heaven." He will hear Him not from earth only, where He prayed to be glorified; but from heaven also, where interceding for us at the Right Hand of the Father, He hath from thence shed abroad the Holy Spirit on them that believe on Him. "In strength is the safety of His right hand." Our strength is in the safety of His favour, when even out of tribulation He giveth help, that "when we are weak, then we may be strong." "For vain is "that "safety of man," which comes not of His right hand but of His left: for thereby are they lifted up to great pride, whosoever in their sins have secured a temporal safety.

8. "Some in chariots, and some in horses" (ver. 7). Some are drawn away by the ever moving succession of temporal goods; and some are preferred to proud honours, and in them exult: "But we will exult in the name of the Lord our God." But we, fixing our hope on things eternal, and not seeking our own glory, will exult in the name of the Lord our God.

9. "They have been bound, and fallen" (ver. 8). And therefore were they bound by the lust of temporal things, fearing to spare the Lord, lest they should lose their place by "the Romans:" and rushing violently on the stone of offence and rock of stumbling, they fell from the heavenly hope: to whom the blindness in part of Israel hath happened, being ignorant of God's righteousness, and wishing to establish their own. "But we are risen, and stand upright." But we, that the Gentile people might enter in, out of the stones raised up as children to Abraham, who followed not after righteousness, have attained to it, and are risen; and not by our own strength, but being justified by faith, we stand upright.

10. "O Lord, save the King:" that He, who in His Passion hath shown us an example of conflict, should also offer up our sacrifices, the Priest raised from the dead, and established in heaven. "And hear us in the day when we shall call on Thee" (ver. 9). And as He now offereth for us, "hear us in the day when we shall call on Thee."

PSALM XXI.

TO THE END, A PSALM OF DAVID HIMSELF.

1. The title is a familiar one; the Psalm is of Christ.

2. "O Lord, the King shall rejoice in Thy strength" (ver. 1). O Lord, in Thy strength, whereby the Word was made flesh, the Man Christ Jesus shall rejoice. "And shall exult exceedingly in Thy salvation." And in that, whereby Thou quckenest all things, shall exult exceedingly.

3. "Thou hast given Him the desire of His soul" (vet. 2). He desired to eat the Passover, and to lay down His life when He would, and again when He would to take it; and Thou hast given it to Him. "And hast not deprived Him of the good pleasure of His lips." "My peace," saith He, "I leave with you:" and it was done.

4. "For Thou hast presented Him with the blessings of sweetness" (ver. 3). Because He had first quaffed the blessing of Thy sweetness, the gall of our sins did not hurt Him. "Diapsalma. Thou hast set a crown of precious stone on His Head." At the beginning of His discoursing precious stones were brought, and compassed Him about; His disciples, from whom the commencement of His preaching should be made.

5. "He asked life; and Thou gavest Him:" He asked a resurrection, saying, "Father, glorify Thy Son;" and Thou gavest it Him, "Length of days for ever and ever" (ver. 4). The prolonged ages of this world which the Church was to have, and after them an eternity, world without end.

6. "His glory is great in Thy salvation" (ver. 5). Great indeed is His glory in the salvation, whereby Thou hast raised Him up again. "Glory and great honour shalt Thou lay upon Him." But Thou shalt yet add unto Him glory and great honour, when Thou shall place Him in heaven at Thy right hand.

7. "For Thou shalt give Him blessing for ever and ever." This is the blessing which Thou shalt give Him for ever and ever: "Thou shall make Him glad in joy together

with Thy countenance" (ver. 6). According to His manhood, Thou shall make Him glad together with Thy countenance, which He lifted up to Thee.

8. "For the King hopeth in the Lord." For the King is not proud, but humble in heart, he hopeth in the Lord. "And in the mercy of the Most Highest He shall not be moved" (ver. 7). And in the mercy of the Most Highest His obedience even unto the death of the Cross shall not disturb His humility.

9. "Let Thy hand be found by all Thine enemies." Be Thy power, O King, when Thou comest to judgment, found by all Thine enemies; who in Thy humiliation discerned it not. "Let Thy right hand find out all that hate Thee" (ver. 8). Let the glory, wherein Thou reignest at the right hand of the Father, find out for punishment in the day of judgment all that hate Thee; for that now they have not found it.

10. "Thou shalt make them like a fiery oven:" Thou shalt make them on fire within, by the consciousness of their ungodliness: "In the time of Thy countenance:" in the time of Thy manifestation. "The Lord shall trouble them in His wrath, and the fire shall devour them" (ver. 9). And then, being troubled by the vengeance of the Lord, after the accusation of their conscience, they shall be given up to eternal fire, to be devoured.

11. "Their fruit shalt Thou destroy cut of the earth." Their fruit, because it is earthly, shalt Thou destroy out of the earth. "And their seed from the sons of men" (ver. 10). And their works; or, whomsoever they have seduced, Thou shalt not reckon among the sons of men, whom Thou hast called into the everlasting inheritance.

12. "Because they turned evils against Thee." Now this punishment shall be recompensed to them, because the evils which they supposed to hang over them by Thy reign, they turned against Thee to Thy death. "They imagined a device, which they were not able to establish" (ver. 11). They imagined a device, saying, "It is expedient that one die for all:" which they were not able to establish, not knowing what they said.

13. "For Thou shalt set them low." For Thou shalt rank them among those from whom in degradation and contempt Thou wilt turn away. "In Thy leavings Thou

shalt make ready their countenance" (ver. 12). And in these things that Thou leavest, that is, in the desires of an earthly kingdom, Thou shalt make ready their shamelessness for Thy passion.

14. "Be Thou exalted, O Lord, in Thy strength" (ver. 13). Be Thou, Lord, whom in humiliation they did not discern, exalted in Thy strength, which they thought weakness. "We will sing and praise Thy power." In heart and in deed we will celebrate and make known Thy marvels.

PSALM XXII.

TO THE END, FOR THE TAKING UP OF THE MORNING, A PSALM OF DAVID.

1. "To the end," for His own resurrection, the Lord Jesus Christ Himself speaketh. For in the morning on the first day of the week was His resurrection, whereby He was taken up, into eternal life, "Over whom death shall have no more dominion." Now what follows is spoken in the person of The Crucified. For from the head of this Psalm are the words, which He cried out, whilst hanging on the Cross, sustaining also the person of the old man, whose mortality He bare. For our old man was nailed together with Him to the Cross.

2. "O God, my God, look upon me, why hast Thou forsaken me far from my salvation?" (ver. 1). Far removed from my salvation: for" salvation is far from sinners." "The words of my sins." For these are not the words of righteousness, but of my sins. For it is the old man nailed to the Cross that speaks, ignorant even of the reason why God hath forsaken him: or else it may be thus, The words of my sins are far from my salvation.

3. "My God, I will cry unto Thee in the daytime, and Thou wilt not hear (ver. 2). My God, I will cry unto Thee in the prosperous circumstances of this life, that they be not changed; and Thou wilt not hear, because I shall cry unto Thee in the words of my sins. "And in the night-season, and not to my folly." And so in the adversities of this life will I cry to Thee for prosperity; and in like manner Thou wilt not hear. And this Thou doest not to my folly, but rather that I may have wisdom to know what Thou wouldest have me cry for, not with the words of sins out of longing for life temporal, but with the words of turning to Thee for life eternal.

4. "But Thou dwellest in the holy place, O Thou praise of Israel" (ver. 3). But Thou dwellest in the holy place, and therefore wilt not hear the unclean words of sins. The "praise" of him that seeth Thee; not of him who hath sought his own praise in tasting of the forbidden fruit, that on the opening of his bodily eyes he should endeavour to hide himself from Thy sight.

5. "Our Fathers hoped in Thee." All the righteous, namely, who sought not their own praise, but Thine. "They hoped in Thee, and Thou deliveredst them" (ver. 4).

6. "They cried unto Thee, and were saved." They cried unto Thee, not in the words of sins, from which salvation is far; and therefore were they saved. "They hoped in Thee, and were not confounded" (ver. 5). "They hoped in Thee," and their hope did not deceive them. For they placed it not in themselves.

7. "But I am a worm, and no man" (ver. 6). But I, speaking now not in the person of Adam, but I in My own person, Jesus Christ, was born without human generation in the flesh, that I might be as man beyond men; that so at least human pride might deign to imitate My humility. "The scorn of men, and outcast of the people." In which humility I was made the scorn of men, so as that it should be said, as a reproachful railing, "Be thou His disciple: " and that the people despise Me.

8. "All that saw Me laughed Me to scorn" (ver. 7). All that saw Me derided Me. "And spoke with the lips, and shook the head." And they spoke, not with the heart, but with the lips.

9. For they shook their head in derision, saying, "He trusted in the Lord let Him deliver Him: " let Him save Him, since He desireth Him" (ver 8).These were their words; but they were spoken "with the lips."

10. "Since Thou art He who drew Me out of the womb" (ver. 9). Since Thou art He who drew Me, not only out of that Virgin womb (for this is the law of all men's birth, that they be drawn out of the womb), but also out of the womb of the Jewish nation; by the darkness whereof he is covered, and not yet born into the light of Christ, whosoever places his salvation in the carnal observance of the Sabbath, and of circumcision, and the like. "My hope from My mother's breasts." "My hope," O God, not from the time when I began to be fed by the milk of the Virgin's breasts; for it was even before; but from the breasts of the Synagogue, as I have said, out of the womb, Thou hast drawn Me, that I should not suck in the customs of the flesh.

11. "I have been strengthened in Thee from the womb" (ver. 10). It is the womb of the Synagogue, which did not carry Me, but threw Me out: but I fell not, for Thou heldest me. "From My mother's womb Thou art My God." "From My mother's

womb: My mother's womb did not cause that, as a babe, I should be forgetful of Thee.

12. "Thou art My God," "depart not from Me; for trouble is hard at hand" (ver. 11). Thou art, therefore, My God, depart not from Me; for trouble is nigh unto Me; for it is in My body. "For there is none to help." For who helpeth, if Thou helpest not?

13. "Many calves came about Me." The multitude of the wanton populace came about Me. "Fat bulls closed Me in" (ver. 12). And their leaders, glad at My oppression, "closed Me in."

14. "They opened their mouth upon Me" (ver. 13). They opened their mouth upon Me, not out of Thy Scripture, but of their own lusts. "As a ravening and roaring lion." As a lion, whose ravening is, that I was taken and led; and whose roaring, "Crucify, Crucify.".

15. "I was poured out like water, and all My bones were scattered" (ver. 14). "I was poured out like water," when My persecutors fell: and through fear, the stays of My body, that is, the Church, My disciples were scattered from Me. "My heart became as melting wax, in the midst of my belly." My wisdom, which was written of Me in the sacred books, was, as if hard and shut up, not understood: but after that the fire of My Passion was applied, it was, as if melted, manifested, and entertained in the memory of My Church.

16. "My strength dried up as a potsherd" (ver. 15). My strength dried up by My Passion; not as hay, but a potsherd, which is made stronger by fire. "And My tongue cleaved to My jaws." And they, through whom I was soon to speak, kept My precepts in their hearts. "And Thou broughtest Me down to the dust of death." And to the ungodly appointed to death, whom the wind casteth forth as dust from the face of the earth, Thou broughtest Me down.

17. "For many dogs came about Me" (ver. 16). For many came about Me barking, not for truth, but for custom. "The council of the malignant came about Me." The council of the malignant besieged Me. "They pierced My hands and feet." They pierced with nails My hands and feet.

18. "They numbered distinctly all My bones" (ver. 17). They numbered distinctly all My bones, while extended on the wood of the Cross. "Yea, these same regarded, and beheld Me." Yea, these same, that is, unchanged, regarded-and beheld Me.

19. "They divided My garments for themselves, and cast the lot upon My vesture" (ver. 18).

20. "But Thou, O Lord, withhold not Thy help far from Me" (ver. 19). But Thou, O Lord, raise Me up again, not as the rest of men, at the end of the world, but immediately. "Look to My defence." "Look," that they in no wise hurt Me.

21. "Deliver My soul from the sword." "Deliver My soul" from the tongue of dissension. "And My only One from the hand of the dog" (ver. 20). And from the power of the people, barking after their custom, deliver My Church.

22. "Save Me from the lion's mouth:" save Me from the mouth of the kingdom of this world: "and my humility from the horns of the unicorns " (ver. 21). And from the loftiness of the proud, exalting themselves to special pre-eminence, and enduring no partakers, save My humility.

23. "I will declare Thy name to My brethren" (ver. 22). I will declare Thy name to the humble, and to My Brethren that love one another as they have been beloved by Me. "In the midst of the Church will I sing of Thee." In the midst of the Church will I with rejoicing preach Thee.

24. "Ye that fear the Lord, praise Him." "Ye that fear the Lord," seek not your own praise, but "praise Him." "All ye seed of Jacob, magnify Him" (ver. 23). All ye seed of him whom the elder shall serve, magnify Him.

25. "Let all the seed of Israel fear Him." Let all who have been born to a new life, and restored to the vision of God "fear Him." "Since He hath not despised, nor disregarded the prayer of the poor man" (ver. 24). Since He hath not despised the prayer, not of him who, crying unto God in the words of sins was loath to overpass a vain life, but the prayer of the poor man, not swollen up with transitory pomps. "Nor hath He turned away His face from Me." As from him who said, I will cry unto Thee, but Thou wilt not hear. "And when I cried unto Him He heard Me."

26. "With Thee is My praise" (ver. 25). For I seek not Mine own praise, for Thou art My praise, who dwellest in the holy place; and, praise of Israel, Thou hearest The Holy One now beseeching Thee. "In the great Church I will confess Thee." In the Church of the whole world" I will confess Thee." "I will offer My vows in the sight of them that fear Him." I will offer the sacraments of My Body and Blood in the sight of them that fear Him.

27. "The poor shall eat, and be filled" (ver. 26). The humble and the despisers of the world shall eat, and imitate Me. For so they will neither desire this world's abundance, nor fear its want. "And they shall praise the Lord, who seek Him." For the praise of the Lord is the pouring out of that fulness. "Their hearts shall live for ever and ever." For that food is the food of the heart.

28. "All the borders of the earth shall remember themselves, and be turned to the Lord" (ver. 27). They shall remember themselves: for, by the Gentiles, born in death and bent on outward things, God had been forgotten; and then shall all the borders of the earth be turned to the Lord. "And all the kindreds of the nations shall worship in His sight." And all the kindreds of the nations shall worship in their own consciences.

29. "For the kingdom is the Lord's, and He shall rule over the nations" (ver. 28). For the kingdom is the Lord's, not proud men's: and He shall rule over the nations.

30. "All the rich of the earth have eaten, and worshipped" (ver. 29). The rich of the earth too have eaten the Body of their Lord's humiliation, and though they have not, as the poor, been filled even to imitation, yet they have worshipped. "In His sight shall fall all that descend to earth." For He alone seeth how all they fall, who abandoning a heavenly conversation, make choice, on earth, to appear happy to men, who see not their fall.

31. "And My Soul shall live to Him." And My Soul, which in the contempt of this world seems to men as it were to die, shall live, not to itself, but to Him. "And My seed shall serve Him" (ver. 30). And My deeds, or they who through Me believe on Him, shall serve Him.

32. "The generation to come shall be declared to the Lord" (ver. 31). The generation of the New Testament shall be declared to the honour of the Lord.

"And the heavens shall declare His righteousness." And the Evangelists shall declare His righteousness. "To a people that shall be born, whom the Lord hath made." To a people that shall be born to the Lord through faith.

PSALM XXIII.

A PSALM OF DAVID HIMSELF.

1. The Church speaks to Christ: "The Lord feedeth me, and I shall lack nothing" (ver. 1). The Lord Jesus Christ is my Shepherd, "and I shall lack nothing."

2. "In a place of pasture there hath He placed me" (ver. 2). In a place of fresh pasture, leading me to faith, there hath He placed me to be nourished. "By the water of refreshing hath He brought me up." By the water of baptism, whereby they are refreshed who have lost health and strength, hath He brought me up.

3. "He hath converted my soul: He hath led me forth in the paths of righteousness, for His Name's sake" (ver. 3). He hath brought me forth in the narrow ways, wherein few walk, of His righteousness; not for my merit's sake, but for His Name's sake.4. "Yea, though I walk in the midst of the shadow of death" (ver. 4). Yea, though I walk in the midst of this life, which is the shadow of death. "I will fear no evil, for Thou art with me." I will fear no evil, for Thou dwellest in my heart by faith: and Thou art now with me, that after the shadow of death I too may be with Thee. "Thy rod and Thy staff, they have comforted me." Thy discipline, like a rod for a flock of sheep, and like a staff for children of some size, and growing out of the natural into spiritual life, they have not been grievous to me; rather have they comforted me: because Thou art mindful of me.

5. "Thou hast prepared a table in my sight, against them that trouble me" (ver. 5). Now after the rod, whereby, whilst a little one, and living the natural life, I was brought up among the flock in the pastures; after that rod, I say, when I began to be under the staff, Thou hast prepared a table in my sight, that I should no more be fed as a babe with milk, but being older should take meat, strengthened against them that trouble me. "Thou hast fattened my head with oil." Thou hast gladdened my mind with spiritual joy. "And Thy inebriating cup, how excellent is it!" And Thy cup yielding forgetfulness of former vain delights, how excellent is it !

6. "And Thy mercy shall follow me all the days of my life:" that is, as long as I live in this mortal life, not Thine, but mine. "That I may dwell in the house of the Lord' for length of days" (ver. 6). Now Thy mercy shall follow me not here only, but also that I may dwell in the house of the Lord for ever.

PSALM XXIV.

A PSALM OF DAVID HIMSELF, ON THE FIRST DAY OF THE WEEK.

1. A Psalm of David himself, touching the glorifying and resurrection of the Lord, which took place catty in the morning on the first day of the week, which is now called the Lord's Day.

2. "The earth is the Lord's, and the fulness thereof, the compass of the world, and all they that dwell therein" (ver. 1); when the Lord, being glorified, is announced for the believing of all nations; and the whole compass of the world becomes His Church. "He hath founded it above the seas." He hath most firmly established it above all the waves of this world, that they should be subdued by it, and should not hurt it. "And hath prepared it above the rivers" (ver. 2). The rivers flow into the sea, and men of lust lapse into the world: these also the Church, which, when worldly lusts have been conquered by the grace of God, hath been prepared by love for the reception of immortality, subdues.

3. "Who shall ascend into the mount of the Lord?" Who shall ascend to the height of the righteousness of the Lord? "Or who shall stand in His holy place?" (ver. 3). Or who shall abide in that place, whither He shall ascend, founded above the seas, and prepared above the rivers?

4. "The innocent of hand, and the pure in heart" (ver. 4). Who then shall ascend thither, and abide there, but the guiltless in deed, and pure in thought? "Who hath not received his soul in vain." Who hath not reckoned his soul among things that pass away, but feeling it to be immortal, hath longed for an eternity stedfast and unchangeable. "And hath not sworn in deceit to his neighbour." And therefore without deceit, as things eternal are simple and undeceiving, hath so behaved himself to his neighbour.

5. "This man shall receive blessing from the Lord, and mercy from the God of his salvation" (ver. 5).

6. "This is the generation of them that seek the Lord" (ver. 6). For thus are they born that seek Him. "Of them that seek the face of the God of Jacob. Diapsalma." Now they seek the face of God, who gave the pre- eminence to the younger born.

7. "'Take away your gates, ye princes" (ver. 7). All ye, that seek rule among men, remove, that they hinder not, the entrances which ye have made, of desire and fear. "And be ye lift up, ye everlasting gates." And be ye lift up, ye entrances of eternal life, of renunciation of the world, and conversion to God. "And the King of glory shall come in." And the King, in whom we may glory without pride, shall come in: who having overcome the gates of death, and having opened for Himself the heavenly places, fulfilled that which He said, "Be of good cheer, for I have overcome the world."

8. "Who is this King of glory?" Mortal nature is awe-struck in wonder, and asks, "Who is this King of glory? " The Lord strong and mighty." He whom thou didst deem weak and overwhelmed. "The Lord mighty in battle" (ver. 8). Handle the scars, and thou wilt find them made whole, and human weakness restored to immortality. The glorifying of the Lord, which was owing to earth, where It warred with death, hath been paid.

9. "Take away your gates, ye princes." Let us go hence straightway into heaven. Again, let the Prophet's trumpet cry aloud, "Take away too, ye princes of the air, the gates, which ye have in the minds of men who 'worship the host of heaven.'" "And be ye lift up, ye everlasting gates." And be ye lift up, ye doors of everlasting righteousness, of love, and chastity, through which the soul loveth the One True God, and goeth not a-whoring with the many that are called gods. "And the King of glory shall come in" (ver. 9). "And the King of glory shall come in," that He may at the right hand of the Father intercede for us.

10. "Who is this King of glory?" What! dost thou too, prince of the power of this air, marvel and ask, "Who is this King of glory ?" "The Lord of powers, He is the King of glory" (ver. 10). Yea, His Body now quickened, He who was tempted marches above thee; He who was tempted by the angel, the deceiver, goes above all angels. Let none of you put himself before us and stop our way, that he may be worshipped as a god by us: neither principality, nor angel, nor power, separateth us from the love of Christ.' It is good to trust in the Lord, rather than to trust in a prince; that he who glorieth, should glory in the Lord. These indeed are powers in the administration of this world, but "the Lord of powers, He is the King of glory."

PSALM XXV.

TO THE END, A PSALM OF DAVID HIMSELF.

1. Christ speaks, but in the person of the Church: for what is said has reference rather to the Christian People turned unto God.

2. "Unto Thee, O Lord, have I lift up my soul" (ver. 1): with spiritual longing have I lift up the soul, that was trodden down on the earth with carnal longings. "O my God, in Thee I trust, I shall not be ashamed" (ver. 2). O my God, from trusting in myself I was brought even to this weakness of the flesh; and I who on abandoning God wished to be as God, fearing death from the smallest insect, was in derision ashamed for my pride; now, therefore, "in Thee I trust, I shall not be ashamed."

3. "And let not my enemies mock me." And let them not mock me, who by ensnaring me with serpent-like and secret suggestions, and prompting me with "Well done, well done," have brought me down to this. "For all that wait upon Thee shall not be confounded" (ver. 3).

4. "Let them be confounded who do vain things unrighteously." Let them be confounded who act unrighteously for the acquiring things that pass away. "Make Thy ways, O Lord, known to me, and teach me Thy paths" (ver. 4): not those which are broad, and lead the many to destruction; but Thy paths, narrow, and known to few, teach Thou me.

5. "In Thy truth guide me:" avoiding error. "And teach me:" for by myself I know nothing, but falsehood. "For Thou art the God of my salvation; and for Thee have I waited all the day" (ver. 5). For dismissed by Thee from Paradise, and having taken my journey into a far country? I cannot by myself return, unless Thou meetest the wanderer: for my return hath throughout the whole tract of this world's time waited for Thy mercy.

6. "Remember Thy compassions, O Lord" (ver. 6). Remember the works of Thy mercy, O Lord; for men deem of Thee as though Thou hadst forgotten. "And that Thy mercies are from eternity." And remember this, that Thy mercies are from eternity. For Thou never wast without them, who hast subjected even sinful man to

vanity indeed, but in hope; and not deprived him of so many and great consolations of Thy creation.

7. "Remember not the offences of my youth and of my ignorance" (ver. 7). The offences of my presumptuous boldness and of my ignorance reserve not for vengeance, but let them be as if forgotten by Thee. "According to Thy mercy, be mindful of me, O God." Be mindful indeed of me, not according to the anger of which I am worthy, but according to Thy mercy which is worthy of Thee. "For Thy goodness, O Lord." Not for my deservings, but for Thy goodness, O Lord.

8. "Gracious and upright is the Lord" (ver. 8). The Lord is gracious, since even sinners and the ungodly He so pitied, as to forgive all that is past; but the Lord is upright too, who after the mercy of vocation and pardon, which is of grace without merit, will require merits meet for the last judgment. "Wherefore He will establish a law for them that fail in the way." For He hath first bestowed mercy to bring them into the way.

9. "He will guide the meek in judgment." He will guide the meek, and will not confound in the judgment those that follow His will, and do not, in withstanding It, prefer their own. "The gentle He will teach His ways" (ver. 9). He will teach His ways, not to those that desire to run before, as if they were better able to rule themselves; but to those who do not exalt the neck, nor lift the heel, when the easy yoke and the light burden is laid upon them.

10. "All the ways of the Lord are mercy and truth" (ver. 10). And what ways will He teach them, but mercy wherein He is placable, and truth wherein He is incorrupt? Whereof He hath exhibited the one in forgiving sins, the other in judging deserts. And therefore "all the ways of the Lord" are the two advents of the Son of God, the one in mercy, the other in judgment. He then attaineth unto Him holding on His ways, who seeing himself freed by no deserts of his own, lays pride aside, and henceforward bewares of the severity of His trial, having experienced the clemency of His help. "To them that seek His testament and His testimonies." For they understand the Lord as merciful at His first advent, and as the Judge at His second, who in meekness and gentleness seek His testament, when with His Own Blood He redeemed us to a new life; and in the Prophets and Evangelists, His testimonies.

11. "For Thy Name's sake, O Lord, Thou wilt be favourable to my sin; for it is manifold" (ver. 11). Thou hast not only forgiven my sins, which I committed before I believed; but also to my sin, which is manifold, since even in the way there is no lack of stumbling, Thou wilt be made favourable by the sacrifice of a troubled spirit.

12. "Who is the man that feareth the Lord?" from which fear he begins to come to wisdom. "He shall establish a law for him in the way, which he hath chosen" (ver. 12). He shall establish a law for him in the way, which in his freedom he has taken, that he may not sin now with impunity.

13. "His soul shall dwell in good, and his seed shall, by inheritance, possess the earth "(ver. 13). And his work shall possess the stable inheritance of a renewed body.

14. "The Lord is the stay of them that fear Him" (ver. 14). Fear seems to belong to the weak, but the Lord is the stay of them that fear Him. And the Name of the Lord, which hath been glorified throughout the whole world, is a stay to them that fear Him. "And His testament, that it may be manifested unto them." And He maketh His testament to be manifested unto them, for the Gentiles and the bounds of the earth are Christ's inheritance.

15. "Mine eyes are ever unto the Lord; for He shall pluck my feet out of the snare" (ver. 15). Nor would I fear the dangers of earth, while I look not upon the earth: for He upon whom Look, will pluck my feet out of the snare.

16. "Look upon me, and have mercy upon me; for I am single and poor" (ver. 16). For I am a single people, keeping the lowliness of Thy single Church, which no schisms or heresies possess.

17. "The tribulations of my heart have been multiplied" (ver. 17). The tribulations of my heart have been multiplied by the abounding of iniquity and the waxing cold of love. "O bring Thou me out of my necessities." Since I must needs bear this, that by enduring unto the end I may be saved, bring Thou me out of my necessities.

18. "See my humility and my travail" (ver. 18). See my humility, whereby I never, in the boast of righteousness, break off from unity; and my travail, wherein I bear with the unruly ones that are mingled with me. "And forgive all my sins." And, propitiated by these sacrifices, forgive all my sins, not those only of youth and my ignorance before I believed, but those also which, living now by faith, I commit through infirmity, or the darkness of this life.

19. "Consider mine enemies, how they are multiplied" (ver. 19). For not only without, but even within, in the Church's very communion, they are not wanting. "And with an unrighteous hate they hate me." And they hate me who love them.

20. "Keep my soul, and deliver me." Keep my soul, that I turn not aside to imitate them; and draw me out from the confusion wherein they are mingled with me. "Let me not be confounded, for I have put my trust in Thee" (ver. 20). Let me not be confounded, if haply they rise up against me: for not in myself, but in Thee have I put my trust.

21. "The innocent and the upright have cleaved to me, for I have waited for Thee, O Lord" (ver. 21). The innocent and the upright, not in bodily presence only, as the evil, are mingled with me, but in the agreement of the heart in the same innocence and uprightness cleave to me: for I have not fallen away to imitate the evil; but I have waited for Thee, expecting the winnowing of Thy last harvest.

22. "Redeem Israel, O God, out of all his troubles" (ver. 22). "Redeem Thy people, O God," whom Thou hast prepared to see Thee, out of his troubles, not those only which he bears without, but those also which he bears within.

PSALM XXVI.

OF DAVID HIMSELF.

1. It may be attributed to David himself, not the Mediator, the Man Christ Jesus, but the whole Church now perfectly established in Christ.

2. "Judge me, O Lord, for I have walked in my innocence" (ver. 1). Judge me, O Lord, for, after the mercy which Thou first showedst me, I have some desert of my innocence, the way whereof I have kept. "And trusting in the Lord I shall not be moved." And yet not even so trusting in myself, but in the Lord, I shall abide in Him.

3. "Prove me, O Lord, and try me" (ver. 2). Lest, however, any of my secret sins should be hid from me, prove me, O Lord, and try me, making me known, not to Thee from whom nothing is hid, but to myself, and to men. "Burn my reins and my heart." Apply a remedial purgation, as it were fire, to my pleasures and thoughts. "For Thy mercy is before mine eyes" (ver. 3). For, that I be not consumed by that fire, not my merits, but Thy mercy, whereby Thou hast brought me on to such a life, is before my eyes. "And I have been pleasing in Thy truth." And since my own falsehood hath been displeasing to me, but Thy truth pleasing, I have myself been pleasing also with it and in it.

4. "I have not sat with the council of vanity" (ver. 4). I have not chosen to give my heart to them who endeavour to provide, what is impossible, how they may be blessed in the enjoyment of things transitory. "And I will not enter in with them that work wickedly." And since this is the very cause of all wickedness, therefore I will not have my conscience hid, with them that work wickedly.

5. "I have hated the congregation of evil doers." But to arrive at this council of vanity, congregations of evil doers are formed, which I have hated. "And I will not sit with the ungodly" (ver. 5). And, therefore, with such a council, with the ungodly, I will not sit, that is, I will not place my consent. "And I will not sit with the ungodly."

6. "I will wash mine hands amid the innocent" (ver. 6). I will make clean my works among the innocent: among the innocent will I wash mine hands, with which I shall embrace Thy glorious gifts. "And I will compass Thy altar, O Lord."

7. "That I may hear the voice of Thy praise." That I may learn how to praise Thee. "And that I may declare all Thy wondrous works" (ver. 7). And after I have learnt, I may set forth all Thy wondrous works.

8. "O Lord, I have loved the beauty of Thy house:" of Thy Church. "And the place of the habitation of Thy glory" (ver. 8): where Thou dwellest, and art glorified.

9. "Destroy not my soul with the ungodly" (ver. 9). Destroy not then, together with them that hate Thee, my soul, which hath loved the beauty of Thy house. "And my life with the men of blood." And with them that hate their neighbour. For Thy house is beautified with the two commandments.

10. "In whose hands is wickedness." Destroy me not then with the ungodly and the men of blood, whose works are wicked. "Their right hand is full of gifts" (ver. 10). And that which was given them to obtain eternal salvation, they have converted into the receiving this world's gifts, "supposing that godliness is a trade."

11. "But I have walked in mine innocence: deliver me, and have mercy on me" (ver. 11). Let so great a price of my Lord's Blood avail for my complete deliverance: and in the dangers of this life let not Thy mercy leave me.

12. "My foot hath stood in uprightness." My Love hath not withdrawn from Thy righteousness. "In the Churches I will bless Thee, O Lord" (ver. 12). I will not hide Thy blessing, O Lord, from those whom Thou hast called; for next to the love of Thee I join the love of my neighbour.

PSALM XXVII.

OF DAVID HIMSELF, BEFORE HE WAS ANOINTED.

1. Christ's young soldier speaketh, on his coming to the faith. "The Lord is my light, and my salvation: whom shall I fear?" (ver. 1). The Lord will give me both knowledge of Himself, and salvation: who shall take me from Him? "The Lord is the Protector of my life: of whom shall I be afraid?" The Lord will repel all the assaults and snares of mine enemy: of no man shall I be afraid.

2. "Whilst the guilty approach unto me to eat up my flesh" (ver. 2). Whilst the guilty come near to recognise and insult me, that they may exalt themselves above me in my change for the better; that with their reviling tooth they may consume not me, but rather my fleshly desires. "Mine enemies who trouble me." Not they only who trouble me, blaming me with a friendly intent, and wishing to recall me from my purpose, but mine enemies also. "They became weak, and fell." Whilst then they do this with the desire of defending their own opinion, they became weak to believe better things, and began to hate the word of salvation, whereby I do what displeases them.

3. "If camps stand together against me, my heart will not fear." But if the multitude of gainsayers conspire to stand together against me, my heart will not fear, so as to go over to their side. "If war rise up against me, in this will I trust" (ver. 3). If the persecution of this world arise against me, in this petition, which I am pondering, will I place my hope.

4. "One have I asked of the Lord, this will I require." For one petition have I asked the Lord, this will I require. "That I may dwell in the house of the Lord all the days of my life" (ver. 4). That as long as I am in this life, no adversities may exclude me from the number of them who hold the unity and the truth of the Lord's faith throughout the world. "That I may contemplate the delight of the Lord." With this end, namely, that persevering in the faith, the delightsome vision may appear to me, which I may contemplate face to face. "And I shall be protected, His temple." And death being swallowed up in victory, I shall be clothed with immortality, being made His temple.

5. "For He hath hidden me in His tabernacle in the day of my evils" (ver. 5). For He hath hidden me in the dispensation of His Incarnate Word in the time of temptations, to which my mortal life is exposed. "He hath protected me in the secret place of His tabernacle." He hath protected me, with the heart believing unto righteousness.

6. "On a rock hath He exalted me." And that what I believed might be made manifest for salvation, He hath made my confession to be conspicuous in His own strength. "And now, lo! He hath exalted mine head above mine enemies" (ver. 6). What doth He reserve for me at the last, when even now the body is dead because of sin, lo! I feel that my mind serves the law of God, and is not led captive under the rebellious law of sin? "I have gone about, and have sacrificed in His tabernacle the sacrifice of rejoicing." I have considered the circuit of the world, believing on Christ; and in that for us God was humbled in time, I have praised Him with rejoicing: for with such sacrifice He is well pleased. "I will sing and give praises to the Lord." In heart and in deed I will be glad in the Lord.

7. "Hear my voice, O Lord, wherewith I have cried unto Thee" (ver. 7). Hear, Lord, my interior voice, which with a strong intention I have addressed to Thy ears. "Have mercy upon me, and hear me." Have mercy upon me, and hear me therein.

8. "My heart hath said to Thee, I have sought Thy countenance" (ver. 8). For I have not exhibited myself to men; but in secret, where Thou alone hearest, my heart hath said to Thee; I have not sought from Thee aught without Thee as a reward, but Thy countenance. "Thy countenance, O Lord, will I seek." In thus search will I perseveringly persist: for not aught that is common, but Thy countenance, O Lord, will I seek, that I may love Thee freely, since nothing more precious do I find.

9. "Turn not away Thy face from me" (ver. 9): that I may find what I seek. "Turn not aside in anger from Thy servant:" lest, while seeking Thee, I fall in with somewhat else. For what is more grevous than this punishment to one who loveth and seeketh the truth of Thy countenance? "Be Thou my Helper." How shall I find it, if Thou help me not? "Leave me not, neither despise me, O God my Saviour." Scorn not that a mortal dares to seek the Eternal for Thou, God dost heal the wound of my sin.

10. "For my father and my mother have left me" (ver. 10). For the kingdom of this world and the city of this world, of which I was born in time and mortality, have left me seeking Thee, and despising what they promised, since they could not give what I seek. "But the Lord took me up." But the Lord, who can give me Himself, took me up.

11. "Appoint me a law, O Lord, in Thy way" (ver. 11). For me then who am setting out toward Thee, and commenting so great a profession, of arriving at wisdom, from fear, appoint, O Lord, a law in Thy way, lest in my wandering Thy rule abandon me. "And direct me in the right path because of mine enemies." And direct me in the right way of its straits. For it is not enough to begin, since enemies cease not until the end is attained.

12. "Deliver me not up unto the souls of them that trouble me" (ver. 12). Suffer not them that trouble me to be satiated with my evils. "For unrighteous witnesses have risen up against me." For there have risen up against me they that speak falsely of me, to remove and call me back from Thee, as if I seek glory of men. "And iniquity hath lied unto itself." Therefore iniquity hath been pleased with its own lie. For me it hath not moved, to whom because of this there hath been promised a greater reward in heaven.

13. "I believe to see the good things of the Lord in the land of the living" (ver. 13). And since my Lord hath first suffered these things, if I too despise the tongues of the dying ("for the mouth that lieth slayeth the soul"), I believe to see the good things of the Lord in the land of the living, where there is no place for falsity.

14. "Wait on the Lord, quit thyself like a man: and let thy heart be strong, yea wait on the Lord" (ver. 14). But when shall this be? It is arduous for a mortal, it is flow to a lover: but listen to the voice, that deceiveth not, of him that saith, "Wait on the Lord." Endure the burning of the reins manfully, and the burning of the heart stoutly. Think not that what thou dost not as yet receive is denied thee. That thou faint not in despair, see how it is said, "Wait on the Lord."

PSALM XXVIII.

OF DAVID HIMSELF.

1. It is the Voice of the Mediator Himself, strong of hand in the conflict of the Passion. Now what He seems to wish for against His enemies, is not the wish of malevolence, but the declaration of their punishment; as in the Gospel, with the dries, in which though He had performed miracles, yet they had not beloved on Him, He doth not wish in any evil will what He sixth, but predicteth what is impending over them.

2. "Unto Thee, O Lord, have I cried; My God, be not silent from me" (ver. 1). Unto Thee, O Lord, have I cried; My God, separate not the unity of Thy Word from that which as Man I am. "Lest at any time Thou be silent form me: and I shall be like them that go down into the pit." For from this, that the Eternity of Thy Word ceaseth not to unite Itself to Me, it comes that I am not such a man as the rest of men, who are born into the deep misery of this world: where, as if Thou art silent, Thy Word is not recognised. "Hear, O Lord, the voice of my supplication, whist I pray unto Thee, whilst I hold up my hands to Thy holy temple "(ver. 2). Whilst I am crucified for their salvation, who on believing become Thy holy temple.

3. "Draw not My Soul away with sinners, and destroy me not with them that work iniquity, with them that speak peace with their neighbours" (ver. 3). With them that say unto Me, "We know that Thou art a Master come from God." "But evil in their hearts." But they speak evil in their hearts.

4. "Give unto them according to their works" (ver. 4). Give unto them according to their works, for this is just. "And according to the malice of their affections." For aiming at evil, they cannot discover good. "According to the works of their hands give Thou unto them." Although what they have done may avail for salvation to others, yet give Thou unto them according to the works of their wills. "Pay them their recompense." Because, for the truth which they heard, they wished to recompense deceit; let their won deceit deceive them.

5. "For they have not had understanding in the works of the Lord" (ver. 5). And whence is it clear that this hath befallen them? From this forsooth, "for they have

not had understanding in the works of the Lord." This very thing, in truth, hath been, even now, their recompense, that in Him whom they tempted with malicious intent as a Man, they should not recognise God, with what design the Father sent Him in the Flesh. "And the works of His hands." Nor be moved by those visible works, which are laid out before their very eyes. "Thou shalt destroy them, and not build them up." Let them do Me no hurt, nay, nor again in their endeavour to raise engines against My Church, let them aught avail.

6. "Blessed be the Lord, for He hath heard the voice of My prayer" (ver. 6).

7. "The Lord My Helper and My Protector" (ver. 7). The Lord helping Me in so great sufferings, and protecting Me with immortality in My resurrection. "In Him hath My Heart trusted, and I have been helped." " And My Flesh hath flourished again:" that is, and My Flesh hath risen again. "And of my will I will confess unto Him." Wherefore, the fear of death being now destroyed, not by the necessity of fear under the Law, but with a free will with the Law, shall they who believe on Me, confess unto Him; and because I am in them, I will confess.

8. " The Lord is the strength of His people" (ver. 8). Not that people "ignorant of the righteousness of God, and willing to establish their own." For they thought not themselves strong in themselves: for the Lord is the strength of His people, struggling in this life's difficulties with the devil. "And the protector of the salvation of His Christ." That, having saved them by His Christ after the strength of war, He may protect them at the last with the immortality of peace.

9. "Save Thy people, and bless Thine inheritance (ver. 9). I intercede therefore, after My Mesh hath flourished again, because Thou hast said, "Desire of Me, and I will give Thee the heathen for Thine inheritance;" " Save Thy people, and bless Thine inheritance:" for "all Mine are Thine." "And rule them, and set them up even for even" And rule them in this temporal life, and raise them from hence into life eternal.

PSALM XXIX.

A PSALM OF DAVID HIMSELF, OF THE CONSUMMATION OF THE TABERNACLE.

1. A Psalm of the Mediator Himself, strong of hand, of the perfection of the Church in this world, where she wars in time against the devil. 5. The Prophet speaks, "Bring unto the Lord, O ye Sons of God, bring unto the Lord the young of rams" (ver. 1). Bring unto the Lord yourselves, whom the Apostles, the leaders of the flocks, have begotten by the Gospel. "Bring unto the Lord glory and honour" (ver. 2). By your works let the Lord be glorified and honoured. "Bring unto the Lord glory to His name." Let Him be made known gloriously throughout the world. "Worship the Lord in His holy court." Worship the Lord in your heart enlarged and sanctified. For ye are His regal holy habitation

3. "The Voice of the Lord is upon the waters" (ver. 3). The Voice of Christ is upon the people. "The God of majesty hath thundered. "The God of majesty, from the cloud of the flesh, hath awfully preached repentance. The Lord is upon many waters." The Lord Jesus Himself, after that He sent forth His Voice upon the people, and so.

4. "The Voice of the Lord is in power" (ver. 4). The Voice of the Lord now in them themselves, making them powerful. "The Voice of the Lord is in great might." The Voice of the Lord working great things in them.

5. "The Voice of the Lord breaking the cedars" (ver. 5). The Voice of the Lord humbling the proud in brokenness of heart. "The Lord shall break the cedars of Libanus." The Lord by repentance shall break them that are lifted on high by the splendour of earthly nobility, when to confound them He shall have "chosen the base things of this world," in the which to display His Divinity.

6. "And shall bruise them as the calf of Libanus" (ver. 6). And when their proud exaltation hath been cut off, He will lay them low after the imitation of His Own humility, who like a calf was led to slaughter by the nobility of this world. "For the kings of the earth stood up, and the rulers agreed together against the Lord, and against His Christ." "And the Beloved is as the young of the unicorns." For even He the Beloved, and the Only One of the Father, "emptied Himself" of His glory;

and was made man, like a child of the Jews, that were "ignorant of God's righteousness," and proudly boasting of their own righteousness as peculiarly theirs.

7. "The Voice of the Lord cutting short the flame of fire" (ver. 7). The Voice of the Lord, without any harm to Himself, passing through all the excited ardour of them that persecute Him, or dividing the furious rage of His persecutors, so that some should say, "Is not this haply the very Christ;" others, "Nay; but He deceiveth the people:" and so cutting short their mad tumult, as to pass some over into His love, and leave others in their malice.

8. "The Voice of the Lord moving the wilderness" (ver. 8). The Voice of the Lord moving to the faith the Gentiles once "without hope, and without God in the world;" where no prophet, no preacher of God's word, as it were, no man had dwelt. "And the Lord will move the desert of Cades." And then the Lord will cause the holy word of His Scriptures to be fully known, which was abandoned by the Jews who understood it not.

9. "The Voice of the Lord perfecting the stags" (ver. 9). For the Voice of the Lord hath first perfected them that overcame and repelled the envenomed tongues. "And will reveal the woods." And then will He reveal to them the darknesses of the Divine books, and the shadowy depths of the mysteries, where they feed with freedom. "And in His temple doth every man speak of His glory." And in His Church all born again to an eternal hope praise God, each for His own gift, which He hath received from the Holy Spirit.

10. "The Lord inhabiteth the deluge" (ver. 10). The Lord therefore first inhabiteth the deluge of this world in His Saints,, kept safely in the Church, as in the ark. "And the Lord shall sit a King for ever." And afterward He will sit reigning in them for ever.

11. "The Lord will give strength to His people" (ver. 11). For the Lord will give strength to His people fighting against the storms and whirlwinds of this world, for peace in this world He hath not promised them. "The Lord will bless His people in peace." And the same Lord will bless His people, affording them peace in Himself; for, saith He, "My peace I give unto you, My peace I leave with you."

PSALM XXX.

TO THE END, THE PSALM OF THE CANTICLE OF THE DEDICATION OF THE HOUSE, OF DAVID HIMSELF.

1. To the end, a Psalm of the joy of the Resurrection, and the change, the renewing of the body to an immortal state, and not only of the Lord, but also of the whole Church. For in the former Psalm the tabernacle was finished, wherein we dwell in the time of war: but now the house is dedicated, which will abide in peace everlasting.

2. It is then whole Christ who speaketh. "I will exalt Thee, O Lord, for Thou hast taken Me up" (ver. 1). I will praise Thy high Majesty, O Lord, for Thou hast taken Me up. "Thou hast not made Mine enemies to rejoice over Me." And those, who have so often endeavoured to oppress Me with various persecutions throughout the world, Thou hast not made to rejoice over Me.

3. "O Lord, My God, I have cried unto Thee, and Thou hast healed Me (ver. 2). O Lord, My God, I have cried unto Thee, and I no longer hear about a body enfeebled and sick by mortality.

4. "O Lord, Thou hast brought back My Soul from hell, and Thou hast saved Me from them that go down into the pit" (ver. 3). Thou hast saved Me from the condition of profound darkness, and the lowest slough of corruptible flesh.

5. "Sing to the Lord, O ye saints of His." The prophet seeing these future things, rejoiceth, and saith, "Sing to the Lord, O ye saints of His. And make confession of the remembrance of His holiness" (ver. 4). And make confession to Him, that He hath not forgotten the sanctification, wherewith He hath sanctified you, although all this intermediate period belong to your desires.

6. "For in His indignation is wrath" (ver. 5). For He hath avenged against you the first sin, for which you have paid by death. "And life in His will." And life eternal, whereunto you could not return by any strength of your own, hath He given, because He so would. "In the evening weeping will tarry." Evening began, when the light of wisdom withdrew from sinful man, when he was condemned to death: from this evening weeping will tarry, as long as God's people are, amid labours

and temptations, awaiting the day of the Lord. "And exultation in the morning." Even to the morning, when there will be the exultation of the resurrection, which hath shone forth by anticipation in the morning resurrection of the Lord.

7. "But I said in my abundance, I shall not be moved for ever" (ver. 6). But I, that people which was speaking from the first, said in mine abundance, suffering now no more any want, "I shall not be moved for ever."

8. "O Lord, in Thy will Thou hast afforded strength unto my beauty" (ver. 7). But that this my abundance, O Lord, is not of myself, but that in Thy will Thou hast afforded strength unto my beauty, I have learnt from this, "Thou turnedst away Thy Face from me, and I became troubled;" for Thou hast sometimes turned away Thy Face from the sinner, and I became troubled, when the illumination of Thy knowledge withdrew from me.

9. "Unto Thee, O Lord, will I cry, and unto my God will I pray" (ver. 8). And bringing to mind that time of my trouble and misery, and as it were established therein, I hear the voice of Thy Firs-Begotten, my Head, about to die for me, and saying "Unto Thee, O Lord, will I cry, and unto My God will I pray."

10. "What profit" is there in the shedding of My blood, whilst I go down to corruption? "Shall dust confess unto Thee?" For if I shall not rise immediately, and My body shall become corrupt, "shall dust confess unto Thee?" that is, the crowd of the ungodly, whom I shall justify by My resurrection? "Or declare Thy truth?" Or for the salvation of the rest declare Thy truth ?

11. "The Lord hath heard, and had mercy on Me, the Lord hath become My helper." Nor did "He suffer His holy One to see corruption " (ver. 10).

12. "Thou hast turned My mourning into joy to Me" (ver. 11). Whom I, the Church, having received, the First-Begotten from the dead, now in the dedication of Thine house, say, "Thou hast turned my mourning into joy to me. Thou hast put off my sackcloth, and girded me with gladness." Thou hast torn off the veil of my sins, the sadness of my mortality; and hast girded me with the first robe, with immortal gladness.

13. "That my glory should sing unto Thee, and I should not be pricked" (ver. 12). That now, not my humiliation, but my glory should not lament, but should sing unto Thee, for that now out of humiliation Thou hast exalted me; and that I should not be pricked with the consciousness of sin, with the fear of death, with the fear of judgment. "O Lord, my God, I will confess unto Thee for ever." And this is my glory, O Lord, my God, that I should confess unto Thee for ever, that I have nothing of myself, but that all my good is of Thee, who art "God, All in all."

PSALM XXXI.

TO THE END, A PSALM OF DAVID HIMSELF, AN ECSTASY.

1. To the end a Psalm of David Himself, the Mediator strong of hand in persecutions. For the word ecstasy, which is added to the title, signifies a transport of the mind, which is produced either by a panic, or by some revelation. But in this Psalm the panic of the people of God troubled by the persecution of all the heathen, and by the failing of faith throughout the world, is principally seen. But first the Mediator Himself speaks: then the People redeemed by His Blood gives thanks: at last in trouble it speaks at length, which is what belongs to the ecstasy; but the Person of the Prophet himself is twice interposed, near the end, and at the end.

2. "In Thee, O Lord, have I trusted, let Me not be put to confusion for ever" (ver. 1). In Thee, O Lord, have I trusted, let Me never be confounded, whilst they shall insult Me as one like other men. "In Thy righteousness rescue Me, and deliver Me." And in Thy righteousness rescue Me from the pit of death, and deliver Me out of their company.

3. "Bend down Thine ear unto Me" (ver. 2). Hear Me in My humiliation, nigh at hand unto Me. "Make haste to deliver Me." Defer not to the end of the world, as with all who believe on Me, My separation from sinners. "Be unto Me a God who protecteth Me." Be unto Me God, and Protector. "And a house of refuge, that Thou mayest save Me." And as a house, wherein taking refuge I may be saved.

4. "For Thou art My strength, and My refuge" (ver. 3). For Thou art unto Me My strength to bear My persecutors, and My refuge to escape them. "And for Thy Name's sake Thou shalt be My guide, and shalt nourish Me." And that by Me Thou mayest be known to all the Gentiles. I will in all things follow Thy will; and, by assembling, by degrees, Saints unto Me, Thou shall fulfil My body, and My perfect stature.

5. "Thou shalt bring Me out of this trap, which they have hidden for Me" (ver. 4). Thou shalt bring Me out of these snares, which they have hidden for Me. "For Thou art My Protector. "

6. "Into Thy hands I commend My Spirit" (ver. 5). To Thy power I commend My Spirit, soon to receive It back. "Thou hast redeemed Me, O Lord God of truth?" Let the people too, redeemed by the Passion of their Lord, and joyful in the glorifying of their Head, say, "Thou hast redeemed me, O Lord God of truth."

7. "Thou hatest them that hold to vanity uselessly" (ver. 6). Thou hatest them that hold to the false happiness of the world. "But I have trusted in the Lord."

8. "I will be glad, and rejoice in Thy mercy:" which doth not deceive me. "For Thou hast regarded My humiliation:" wherein Thou hast subjected me to vanity in hope. "Thou hast saved my soul from necessities" (ver. 7). Thou hast saved my soul from the necessities of fear, that with a free love it may serve Thee.

9. "And hast not shut me up into the hands of the enemy" (ver. 8). And hast not shut me up, that I should have no opening for recovering unto liberty, and be given over for ever into the power of the devil, ensnaring me with the desire of this life, and terrifying me with death. "Thou hast set my feet in a large room." The resurrection of my Lord being known, and mine own bring promised me, my love, having been brought out of the straits of fear, walks abroad in continuance, into the expanse of liberty.

10. "Have mercy on me, O Lord, for I am troubled" (ver. 9). But what is this unlooked-for cruelty of the persecutors, striking such dread into me? "Have mercy on me, O Lord." For I am now no more alarmed for death, but for torments and tortures. "Mine eye hath been disordered by anger." I had mine eye upon Thee, that Thou shouldest not abandon me: Thou art angry, and hast disordered it. "My soul, and my belly." By the same anger my soul hath been disturbed, and my memory, whereby I retained what my God hath suffered for me, and what He hath promised me.

11. "For my life hath failed in pain" (ver 10). For my life is to confess Thee, but it failed in pain, when the enemy had said, Let them be tortured until they deny Him. "And my years in groanings." The time that I pass in this world is not taken away from me by death, but abides, and is spent in groanings. "My strength hath been weakened by want" I want the heath of this body, and racking pains come on me: I want the dissolution of the body, and death forbears to come: and in this want my confidence hath been weakened. "And my bones have been disturbed." And my stedfastness hath been disturbed.

12. "I have been made a reproach above all mine enemies" (ver 11). All the wicked are my enemies; and nevertheless they for their wickednesses are tortured only till they confess: I then have overpassed their reproach, I, whose confession death doth not follow, but racking pains follow upon it. "And to my neighbours too much." This hath seemed too much to them, who were already drawing near to know Thee, and to hold the faith that I hold. "And a fear to mine acquaintance." And into my very acquaintance I struck fear by the example of my dreadful tribulation. "They that did see me, fled without from me." Because they did not understand my inward and invisible hope, they fled from me into things outward and visible.

13. "I have been forgotten, as one dead from the heart" (ver. 12). And they have forgotten me, as if I were dead from their hearts. "I have become as a lost vessel." I have seemed to myself to be lost to all the Lord's service, living in this world, and gaining none, when all were afraid to join themselves unto me.

14. "For I have heard the rebuking of many dwelling by in a circuit" (ver. 13). For I have heard many rebuking me, in the pilgrimage of this world near me, following the circuit of time, and refusing to return with me to the eternal country. "Whilst they were assembling themselves together against me, they conspired that they might take my soul." That my soul, which should by death easily escape from their power, might consent unto them, they imagined a device, whereby they would not suffer me even to die.

15. "But I have hoped in Thee, O Lord; I have said, Thou art my God" (ver. 14). For Thou hast not changed, that Thou shouldest not save, Who dost correct

16. "In Thy hands" are "my lots" (ver. 15). In Thy power are my lots. For I see no desert for which out of the universal ungodliness of the human race Thou hast elected me particularly to salvation. And though there be with Thee some just and secret order in my election, yet I, from whom this is hid, have attained by lot unto my Lord's vesture. "Deliver me from the hands of mine enemies, and from them that persecute me,"

17. "Make Thy Face to shine upon Thy servant" (ver. 16). Make it known to men, who do not think that I belong unto Thee, that Thy Face is bent upon me, and that I serve Thee. "Save me in Thy mercy."

18. "O Lord, let me not be confounded, for I have called upon Thee" (ver. 17). O Lord, let me not be put to shame by those who insult me, for that I have called upon Thee. "Let the ungodly be ashamed, and be brought down to hell." Let them rather who call upon stones be ashamed, and made to dwell with darkness.

19. "Let the deceitful lips be made dumb" (ver. 18). In making known to the peoples Thy mysteries wrought in me, strike with dumb amazement the lips of them that invent falsehood of me. "Which speak iniquity against the Righteous, in pride and contempt." Which speak iniquity against Christ, in their pride and contempt of Him as a crucified man.

20. "How great" is "the multitude of Thy sweetness, O Lord" (ver. 19). Here the Prophet exclaims, having sight of all this, and admiring how manifoldly plenteous is Thy sweetness, O Lord. "Which Thou hast hid for them that fear Thee." Even those, whom Thou correctest, Thou lovest much: but lest they should go on negligently from relaxed security, Thou hidest from them the sweetness of Thy love, for whom it is profitable to fear Thee. "Thou hast perfected it for them that hope in Thee." But Thou hast perfected this sweetness for them that hope in Thee. For Thou dost not withdraw from them what they look for perseveringly even unto the end. "In sight of the sons of men." For it does not escape the notice of the sons of men, who now live no more after Adam, but after the Son of Man. "Thou wilt hide them in the hidden place of Thy Countenance:" which seat Thou shalt preserve for everlasting in the hidden place of the knowledge of Thee for them that hope in Thee. "From the troubling of men." So that now they suffer no more trouble from men.

21. "Thou writ protect them in Thy tabernacle from the contradiction of tongues" (ver. 20). But here meanwhile whilst evil tongues murmur against them, saying, Who hath come thence? Thou wilt protect them in the tabernacle, that of faith in those things, which the Lord wrought and endured for us in time.

22. "Blessed be the Lord; for He hath made His mercy marvellous, in the city of compassing" (ver. 21). Blessed be the Lord, for after the correction of the sharpest persecutions He hath made His mercy marvellous to all throughout the world, in the circuit of human society.

23. "I said in my ecstasy" (ver. 22). Whence that people again speaking saith, I said in my fear, when the heathen were raging horribly against me. "I have been

cast forth from the sight of Thine eyes." For if Thou hadst regard to me, Thou wouldest not suffer me to endure these things. "Therefore Thou heardest, O Lord, the voice of my prayer, when I cried unto Thee." Therefore putting a limit to correction, and showing that I have part in Thy care, Thou heardest, O Lord, the voice of my prayer, when I raised it high out of tribulation.

24. "Love the Lord, all ye His saints" (ver. 23). The Prophet again exhorts, having sight of these things, and saith, "Love the Lord, all ye His saints; for the Lord will require truth." Since "if the righteous shall scarcely be saved, where shall the sinner and the ungodly appear?" "And He will repay them that do exceeding proudly." And He will repay them who even when conquered are not converted, because they are very proud.

25. "Quit you like men, and let your heart be strengthened" (ver. 24): working good without fainting, that ye may reap in due season. "All ye who trust in the Lord:" that is, ye who duly fear and worship Him, trust ye in the Lord.

PSALM XXXII.

TO DAVID HIMSELF; FOR UNDERSTANDING.

1. To David himself; for understanding; by which it is understood that not by the merits of works, but by the grace of God, man his delivered, confessing his sins.

2. "Blessed are they whose unrighteousness is forgiven, and whose sins are covered" (ver. 1): and whose sins are buried in oblivion. "Blessed is the man to whom the Lord hath not imputed sin, nor is there guile in his mouth" (ver. 2): nor has he in his mouth boastings of righteousness, when his conscience is full of sins.

3. "Because I kept silence, my bones waxed old:" because I made not with my mouth "confession unto salvation," all firmness in me has grown old in infirmity. "Through my roaring all the day long" (ver. 3): when I was ungodly and a blasphemer, crying against God, as though defending and excusing my sins.

4. "Because day and night Thy Hand was heavy upon me:" because, through the continual punishment of Thy scourges, "I was turned in misery, while a thorn was fixed through me" (ver. 4): I was made miserable by knowing my misery, being pricked with an evil conscience.

5. "I acknowledged my sin, and my unrighteousness have I not hid:" that is, my unrighteousuess have I not concealed. "I said, I will confess against myself my unrighteousness to the Lord :" I said, I will confess, not against God (as in my ungodly crying, when I kept silence), but against myself, my unrighteousness to the Lord. "And Thou forgavest the iniquity of my heart" (ver. 5); hearing the word of confession in the heart, before it was uttered with the voice.

6. "For this shall every one that is holy pray unto Thee in an acceptable time:" for this wickedness of heart shall every one that is righteous pray unto Thee. For not by their own merits will they be holy, but by that acceptable time, that is, at His coming, who redeemed us from sin. "Nevertheless in the flood of great waters they shall not come nigh him" (ver. 6): nevertheless, let none think, when the end has come suddenly, as in the days of Noah, that there remaineth a place of confession, whereby he may draw nigh unto God.

7. "Thou art my refuge from the pressures, which have compassed me about:" Thou art my refuge from the pressure of my sins, which hath compassed my heart. "O Thou, my Rejoicing, deliver me from them that compass me about" (ver. 7): in Thee is my joy: deliver me from the sorrow which my sins bring upon me.

8. Diapsalma. The answer of God: "I will give thee understanding, and will set thee in the way in which thou shalt go;" I will give thee understanding after confession, that thou depart not from the way in which thou shouldest go; lest thou wish to be in thine own power. "I will fix Mine Eyes upon thee" (ver. 8); so will make sure upon thee My Love.

9. "Be not ye like unto horse or mule, which have no understanding:" and therefore would govern themselves. But saith the Prophet, "Hold in their jaws with bit and bridle." Do Thou then, O God, unto them "that will not come nigh Thee" (ver. 9), what man doth to horse and mule, that by scourges Thou make them to bear Thy rule.

10. "Many are the scourges of the sinner:" much is he scourged, who, confessing not his sins to God, would be his own ruler. "But he that trusteth in the Lord, mercy compasseth him about" (ver. 10); but he that trusteth in the Lord, and submitteth himself to His rule, mercy shall compass him about.

11. "Be glad in the Lord, and rejoice, ye righteous:" be glad, and rejoice, ye righteous, not in yourselves, but in the Lord. "And glory, all ye that are right in heart" (ver. 11): and glory in Him, all ye who understand that it is right to be subject unto Him, that so ye may be placed above all things beside.

PSALM XXXIII.

1. "Rejoice in the Lord, O ye righteous:" rejoice, O ye righteous, not in yourselves, for that is not safe; but in the Lord. "For praise is comely to the upright" (ver. 1): these praise the Lord, who submit themselves unto the Lord; for else they are distorted and perverse.

2. "Praise the Lord with harp:" praise the Lord, presenting unto Him your bodies a living sacrifice. "Sing unto Him with the psaltery for ten strings" (ver. 2): let your members be servants to the love of God, and of your neighbour, in which are kept both the three and the seven commandments.

3. "Sing unto Him a new song:" sing unto Him a song of the grace of faith. "Sing skilfully unto Him with jubilation" (ver. 3): sing skillfully unto Him with rejoicing.

4. "For the Word of the Lord is right:" for the Word of the Lord is right, to make you that which of yourselves ye cannot be. "And all His works are done in faith" (ver. 4): lest any think that by the merit of works he hath arrived at faith, when in faith are done all the works which God Himself loveth.

5. "He loveth Mercy and Judgment:" for He loveth Mercy, which now He showeth first; and Judgment, wherewith He exacteth that which He hath first shown. "The earth is full is full of the Mercy of the Lord" (ver. 5): throughout the whole world are sins forgiven unto men by the Mercy of the Lord.

6. "By the Word of the Lord were the heavens made firm:" Lord were the righteous made strong. "And all the strength of them by the Breath of His Mouth" (ver. 6). And all their faith by His Holy Spirit.

7. "He gathereth the waters of the sea together as into a bottle:" He gathered the people of the world together, to confession of mortified sin, lest through pride they flow too freely. "He layeth up the up the deep in storehouses" (ver. 7): and keepeth in them His secrets for riches.

8. "Let all the earth fear the Lord:" let every sinner fear, that so he may cease to sin. "Let all the inhabitants of the world stand in awe of Him" (ver. 8): not of the terrors of men, or of any creature, but of Him let them stand in awe.

9. "For He spake, and they were made:" for no other one made those things which are to fear; but He spake, and they were made. "He commanded, and they were created" (ver. 9): He commanded by His Word, and they were created.

10. "The Lord bringeth the counsel of the heathen to nought;" of them that seek not His Kingdom, but kingdoms of their own. "He maketh the devices of the people of none effect:" of them that covet earthly happiness. "And reproveth the counsels of princes" (ver. 10): of them that seek to rule over such peoples.

11. "But the counsel of the Lord standeth for ever;" but the counsel of the Lord, whereby He maketh none blessed but him that submitteth unto Himself, standeth for ever. The thoughts of His Heart to all generations" (ver. 11): the thoughts of His Wisdom are not mutable, but endure to all generations.

12. "Blessed is the nation whose God is the Lord:" one nation is blessed, belonging to the heavenly city, which hath not chosen save the Lord for their God: "And the people whom He hath chosen for His own inheritance" (ver. 12): and which not of itself, but by the gift of God, hath been chosen, that He by possessing it may not suffer it to be uncared for and miserable.

13. "The Lord looketh from Heaven; He beholdeth all the sons of men" (ver. 13). From the souls of the righteous, the Lord looketh mercifully upon all who would rise to newness of life.

14. "From His prepared habitation:" from His habitation of assumed Humanity, which He prepared for Himself. "He looketh upon all the inhabitants of the earth" (ver. 14): He looketh mercifully upon all who live in the flesh, that He may be over them in ruling them.

15. "He fashioneth their hearts singly:" He giveth spiritually to their hearts their proper gifts, so that neither the whole body may be eye, nor the whole heating; but that one in this manner, another in that manner, may be incorporated with Christ.

"He understandeth all their works" (ver. 15). Before Him are all their works understood.

16. "A king shall not be saved by much strength:" he shall not be saved who ruleth his own flesh, if he presume much upon his own strength. "Neither shall a giant be saved by much strength" (ver. 16): nor shall he be saved whoever warreth against the habit of his own lust, or against the devil and his angels, if he trust much to his own might.

17. "A horse is a deceitful thing for safety:" he is deceived, who thinketh either that through men he gaineth salvation received among men, or that by the impetuosity of his own courage he is defended from destruction. "In the abundance of his strength shall he not be saved" (ver. 17).

18. "Behold, the Eyes of the Lord are upon them that fear Him:" because if thou seek salvation, behold, the love of the Lord is upon them that fear Him. "Upon them that hope in His mercy" (ver. 18): that hope not in their own strength, but in His mercy.

19. "To deliver their souls from death, and to keep them alive in famine" (ver. 19). To give them the nourishment of the Word, and of Everlasting Truth, which they lost while presuming on their own strength, and therefore have not even their own strength, from lack of righteousness.

20. "My soul shall be patient for the Lord:" that hereafter it may be filled with dainties incorruptible, meanwhile, whilst here it remaineth, my soul shall be patient for the Lord. "For He is our Helper and Defender" (ver. 20): our Helper He is, while we endeavour after Him; and our Defender, while we resist the adversary.

21. "For our heart shall rejoice in Him:" for not in ourselves, wherein without Him there is great need; but in Himself shall our heart rejoice. "And we have trusted in His holy Name" (ver. 21); and therefore have we trusted that we shall come to God, because unto us absent hath He sent, through faith, His own Name.

22. "Let Thy mercy, O Lord, be upon us, according as we have hoped in Thee" (ver. 22): let Thy mercy, O Lord, be upon us; for hope confoundeth not, because we have hoped in Thee.

PSALM XXXIV.

A PSALM OF DAVID, WHEN HE CHANGED HIS COUNTENANCE BEFORE ABIMELECH, AND HE SENT HIM AWAY, AND HE DEPARTED.

1. Because there was there a sacrifice after the order of Aaron, and afterwards He of His Own Body and Blood appointed a sacrifice after the order of Melchizedek; He changed then His Countenance in the Priesthood, and sent away the kingdom of the Jews, and came to the Gentiles. What then is, "He affected"? He was full of affection. For what is so full of affection as the Mercy of our Lord Jesus Christ, who, seeing our infirmity, that He might deliver us from everlasting death, underwent temporal death with such great injury and contumely? "And He drummed:" because a drum is not made, except when a skin is extended on wood; and David drummed, to signify that Christ should be crucified. But, "He drummed upon the doors of the city:" what are "the doors of the city," but our hearts which we had closed against Christ, who by the drum of His Cross hath opened the hearts of mortal men? "And was carried in His Own Hands:" how "carried in His Own Hands"? Because when He commended His Own Body and Blood, He took into His Hands that which the faithful know; and in a manner carried Himself, when He said, "This is My Body." "And He fell down at the doors of the gate;" that is, He humbled Himself. For this it is, to fall down even at the very beginning of our faith. For the door of the gate is the beginning of faith; whence beginneth the Church, and arriveth at last even unto sight: that as it believeth those things which it seeth not, it may deserve to enjoy them, when it shall have begun to see face to face. So is the title of the Psalm; briefly we have heard it; let us now hear the very words of Him that affecteth, and drummeth upon the doors of the city.

2. "I will bless the Lord at all times; His praise shall be ever in my mouth" (ver. 1). So speaketh Christ, so also let a Christian speak; for a Christian is in the Body of Christ; and therefore was Christ made Man, that that Christian might be enabled to be an Angel, who saith, "I will bless the Lord at all times." When shall I "bless the Lord"? When He blesseth thee? When the goods of this world abound? When thou hast great abundance of corn, oil, and wine, of gold and silver, of servants and cattle; when this mortal health remaineth unwounded and sound; when all that are born to thee grow up, nothing is withdrawn by immature death, happiness wholly reigneth in thy house, and all things overflow around thee; then shalt thou bless the Lord? No; but "at all times." Therefore both then, and when according to the time, or according to the scourges of our Lord God, these things are troubled, are taken away, are seldom born to thee, and born pass away. For these things come to pass, and thence followeth penury, need, labour, pain, and temptation. But thou,

156

who hast sung, "I will bless the Lord at all times: His praise shall be ever in my mouth," both when He giveth them, bless; and when He taketh them away, bless. For it is He that giveth, it is He that taketh away: but Himself from him that blesseth Him He taketh not away.

3. But who is it that blesseth the Lord at all times, except the humble in heart. For very humility taught our Lord in His Own Body and Blood: because when He commendeth His Own Body and Blood, He commendeth His Humility, in that which is written in this history, in that seeming madness of David, which we have passed by, "And his spittle ran down over his beard." When the Apostle was read, Ye heard the same spittle, but running down over the beard. One saith perhaps, What spittle have we heard? Was it not read but now, where the Apostle saith, "The Jews require a sign, and the Greeks seek after wisdom?" But now it was read, "But we preach," saith he, "Christ crucified" (for then He drummed), "unto the Jews a stumbling block, and unto the Greeks foolishness; but unto them which are called, both Jews and Greeks, Christ the Power of God, and the Wisdom of God. Because the Foolishness of God is wiser than men, and the Weakness of God is stronger than men." For spittle signifieth foolishness; spittle signifieth weakness. But if the Foolishness of God is wiser than men, and the Weakness of God is stronger than men; let not the spittle as it were offend thee, but observe that it runneth down over the beard: for as by the spittle, weakness; so by the beard, strength is signified. He covered then His Strength by the body of His Weakness, and that which without was weak, appeared as it were in spittle; but within His Divine Strength was covered as a beard. Therefore humility is commended unto us. Be humble if thou wouldest bless the Lord at all times, and that His praise should be ever in thy mouth. . .

4. But wherefore doth man bless the Lord at all times? Because he is humble. What is it to be humble? To take not praise unto himself. Who would himself be praised, is proud: who is not proud, is humble. Wouldest thou not then be proud? That thou mayest be humble, say what is here written; "In the Lord shall my soul be praised: the humble shall hear thereof and be glad" (ver. 2). Those then who will not be praised in the Lord, are not humble, but fierce, rough, lifted up, proud. Gentle cattle would the Lord have; be thou the Lord's jumentum; that is, be thou humble. He sitteth upon thee, He ruleth thee: fear not lest thou stumble, and fall headlong: that indeed is thy infirmity; but consider Who sitteth upon thee. Thou art an ass's colt, but thou carriest Christ. For even He on an ass's colt came into the city; and that beast was gentle.... "Be not ye as the horse or as the mule, which have no understanding." For horse and mule sometimes lift up their neck, and by their own fierceness throw off their rider. They are tamed with the bit, with bridle,

with stripes, until they learn to submit, and to carry their master. But thou, before thy jaws are bruised with the bridle, be humble, and carry thy Lord: wish not praise for thyself, but praised be He who sitteth upon thee, and say thou, "In the Lord shall my soul be praised; the humble shall hear thereof, and be glad."...

5. Now followeth, "O magnify the Lord with me" (ver. 3). Who is this that exhorteth us, that we should magnify the Lord with him? Whoever, Brethren, is in the body of Christ, ought for this to labour, that the Lord may be magnified with him. For he loveth the Lord, whoever he is. And how doth he love Him? So as not to envy his fellow-lover.... Let them blush who so love God as to envy others. Abandoned men love a charioteer, and whoever loveth a charioteer or hunter, wisheth the whole people to love with him, and exhorteth, saying, Love with me this pantomime, love with me this or that shame. He calleth among the people that shame may be loved with him; and doth not a Christian call in the Church, that the Truth of God may be loved with him? Stir up then love in yourselves, Brethren; and call to every one of yours, and say, "O magnify the Lord with me." Let there be in you that fervour. Wherefore are these things recited and explained? If ye love God, bring quickly to the love of God all who are joined unto you, and all who are in your house; if the Body of Christ is loved by you, that is, if the unity of the Church, bring them quickly to enjoy, and say, "O magnify the Lord with me."

6. "And let us exalt His Name together." What is, "let us exalt His Name together"? That is, in one. For many copies so have it, "O magnify the Lord with me; and let us exalt His Name in one." Whether it be said, "together," or "in one," it is the same thing. Therefore bring quickly whom ye can, by exhorting, by transporting, by beseeching, by disputing, by rendering a reason, with meekness, with gentleness. Bring them quickly unto love; that if they magnify the Lord, they may magnify Him in one....

7. "I sought the Lord, and He heard me" (ver. 4). Where heard the Lord? Within. Where giveth He? Within. There thou prayest, there thou art heard, there thou art blessed. Thou hast prayed, thou art heard, thou art blessed; and he knoweth not who standeth by thee: it is all carried on in secret, as the Lord saith in the Gospel, "Enter into thy closet, and when thou hast shut thy door, pray to thy Father which is in secret; and thy Father which seeth in secret, shall reward thee openly." When therefore thou enterest into thy chamber, thou enterest into thy heart. Blessed are they who rejoice when they enter into their heart, and find therein nought of evil....

8. "I sought the Lord, and He heard me." Who then are not heard, seek not the Lord. Attend, Holy Brethren; he said not, I sought gold from the Lord, and He heard me; I sought from the Lord long life, and He heard me; I sought from the Lord this or that, and He heard me. It is one thing to seek anything from the Lord, another to seek the Lord Himself. "I sought" (saith he) "the Lord, and He heard me." But thou, when thou prayest, saying, Kill that my enemy, seekest not the Lord, but, as it were, makest thyself a judge over thy enemy, and makest thy God an executioner. How knowest thou that he is not better than thou, whose death thou seekest? In that very thing haply he is, that he seeketh not thine. Therefore seek not from the Lord anything without, but seek the Lord Himself, and He will hear thee, and while thou yet speakest, He will say, "Lo, here I am."...

9. I have said who was the exhorter, namely, that lover who would not alone embrace what he loveth, and saith, "Approach unto Him, and be ye lightened" (ver. 5). For he saith what he himself proved. For some spiritual person in the Body of Christ, or even our Lord Jesus Christ Himself according to the flesh, the Head exhorting His Own Members, saith; what? "Approach unto Him, and be ye lightened." Or rather some spiritual Christian inviteth us to approach to our Lord Jesus Christ Himself. But let us approach to Him and be lightened; not as the Jews approached to Him, that they might be darkened; for they approached to Him that they might crucify Him: let us approach to Him that we may receive His Body and Blood. They by Him crucified were darkened; we by eating and drinking The Crucified are lightened. "Approach unto Him, and be ye lightened." Lo, this is said to the Gentiles. Christ was crucified amid the Jews raging and seeing; the Gentiles were absent; lo, they have approached who were in darkness, and they who saw not are lightened. Whereby approach the Gentiles? By following with faith, by longing with the heart, by running with charity. Thy feet are thy charity. Have two feet, be not lame. What are thy two feet? The two commandments of love, of thy God, and of thy Neighbour. With these feet run thou unto God, approach unto Him, for He hath both exhorted thee to run, and hath Himself shed His Own Light, as he hath magnificently and divinely continued. "And your faces shall not be ashamed." "Approach" (saith he) "unto Him, and be ye lightened; and your faces shall not be ashamed." No face shall be ashamed but of the proud. Wherefore? Because he would be lifted up, and when he hath suffered insult, or ignominy, or mischance in this world, or any affliction, he is ashamed. But fear not thou, approach unto Him, and thou shalt not be ashamed....

10. As the Prophet testifieth, "The poor man cried, and the Lord heard him" (ver. 6). He teacheth thee how thou mayest be heard. Therefore art thou not heard, because thou art rich. Lest haply thou say, thou criedst and wast not heard, hear

wherefore; "The poor man cried, and the Lord heard him." As poor cry thou, and the Lord heareth. And how shall I cry as poor? By not, if thou hast aught, presuming therefrom upon thy own strength: by understanding that thou art needy; by understanding that so long art thou poor, as thou hast not Him who maketh thee rich. But how did the Lord hear him? "And saved him out of all his troubles." And how saveth He men out of all their troubles? "The Angel of the Lord shall send round about them that fear Him, and shall deliver them" (ver. 7). So it is written, brethren, not as some bad copies have it, "The Lord shall send His Angel round about them that fear Him, and He shall deliver them:" but thus, "The Angel of the Lord shall send round about them that fear Him, and shall deliver them." Whom called He here the Angel of the Lord, who shall send round about them that fear Him, and shall deliver them? Our Lord Jesus Christ Himself is called in Prophecy, the Angel of the great Counsel, the Messenger of the great Counsel; so the Prophets called Him. Even He then, the Angel of the great Counsel, that is, the Messenger, shall send unto them that fear the Lord, and shall deliver them. Fear not then lest thou be hid: wheresoever thou hast feared the Lord, there doth that Angel know thee, who shall send to succour thee, and shall deliver thee.

11. Now will He speak openly of the same Sacrament, whereby He was carried in His Own Hands. "O taste and see that the Lord is good" (ver. 8). Doth not the Psalm now open itself, and show thee that seeming insanity and constant madness, the same insanity and sober inebriety of that David, who in a figure showed I know not what, when in the person of king Achis they said to him, How is it? Widen the Lord said, "Except a man eat My Flesh and drink My Blood, he shall have no life in him"? And they in whom reigned Achis, that is, error and ignorance, said; what said they? "How can this man give us his flesh to eat?" If thou art ignorant, "Taste and see that the Lord is good:" but if thou understandest not, thou art king Achis: David shall change His Countenance and shall depart from thee, and shall quit thee, and shall depart.

12. "Blessed is the man that trusteth in Him." Why needeth this to be explained at length? Whoever trusteth not in the Lord, is miserable. Who is there that trusteth not in the Lord? He that trusteth in himself. ...

13. "O fear the Lord, all ye His saints, for there is no want to them that fear Him" (ver. 9). For many therefore will not fear God the Lord, lest they suffer hunger. It is said to them, Defraud not; and they say, Whence can I feed myself? No art can be without imposture; no business can be without fraud. But fraud God punisheth: fear God. But if I should fear God, I shall not have whence to live. "O fear the Lord, all ye His saints, for there is no want to them that fear Him." He promiseth

plenty to him that trembleth, and doubteth, lest haply if he should fear God, he should lose things superfluous. The Lord fed thee despising Him, and will He desert thee fearing Him? Attend, and say not, Such an one is rich, and I am poor. I fear the Lord, he by not fearing how much has he gained, and I by fearing am bare! See what follows; "The rich do lack and suffer hunger, but they that seek the Lord shall not want any good thing" (ver. 10). If thou receive it according to the letter, He seemeth to deceive thee, for thou seest that many rich men that are wicked die in their riches, and are not made poor while they live; thou seest them grow old, and come even to the end of life amid great abundance and riches. Thou seest their funeral pomp celebrated with great profusion, the man himself brought rich even to the sepulchre, having expired in beds of ivory, his family weeping around; and thou sayest in thy mind, if haply thou knowest some both sins and crimes done by him: I know what things that man hath done; lo, he hath grown old, he hath died in his bed, his friends follow him to the grave, his funeral is celebrated with all this pomp; I know what he hath done; the Scripture has deceived me, and has spoken falsely, where I hear and sing; "The rich do lack and suffer hunger." When was this man in need? when did he suffer hunger? "But they that seek the Lord shall not want any good thing." Daily I rise up to Church, daily I bend the knee, daily I seek the Lord, and have nothing good: this man sought not the Lord, and he hath died in the midst of all these good things! Thus thinking, the snare of offence choketh him; for he seeketh mortal food on the earth, and seeketh not a true reward in heaven, and so he putteth his head into the devil's noose, his jaws are tied close, and the devil holdeth him fast unto evil doing, that so he may imitate the evil men, whom he seeth to die in such plenty.

14. Therefore understand it not so. ... When thou art filled with spiritual riches, canst thou be poor? And was he therefore rich, because he had a bed of ivory; and art thou poor who hast the chamber of thy heart filled with such jewelry of virtues, justice, truth, charity, faith, endurance? Unfold thy riches, if thou hast them, and compare them with the riches of the rich. But such an one has found in the market mules of great value, and has bought them. If thou couldest find faith to be sold, how much wouldest thou give for that, which God willeth that thou shouldest have gratis, and thou art ungrateful? Those rich then lack, they lack, and what is heavier, they lack bread. ... For He hath said, "I am the Living Bread which came down from Heaven." And again, "Blessed are they which do hunger and thirst after righteousness: for they shall be filled." "But they that seek the Lord shall not want any good thing:" but what manner of good, I have already said.

15. "Come, ye children, hearken unto me: I will teach you the fear of the Lord" (vet. 11). Ye think? brethren, that I say this: think that David saith it; think that an

Apostle saith it; nay think that our Lord Jesus Christ Himself saith it; "Come, ye children, hearken unto Me." Let us hearken unto Him together: hearken ye unto Him through us. For He would teach us; He the Humble, He that drummeth, He that affecteth, would teach us. ... 16. "What man is he that desireth life, and loveth to see good days?" (ver. 12). He asketh a question. Doth not every one among you answer, I? Is there any man among you that loveth not life, that is, that desireth not life, and loveth not to see good days? Do ye not daily thus murmur, and thus speak; How long shall we suffer these things? Daily are they worse and worse: in our fathers' time were days more joyful, were days better. O if thou couldest ask those same, thy fathers, in like manner would they murmur to thee of their own days. Our fathers were happy, miserable are we, evil days have we: such an one ruled over us, we thought that after his death might some refreshing be given to us; worse things have come: O God, show unto us good days! "What man is he that desireth life, and loveth to see good days?" Let him not seek here good days. A good thing he seeketh, but not in its right place doth he seek it. As, if thou shouldest seek some righteous man in a country, wherein he lived not, it would be said to thee, A good man thou seekest, a great man thou seekest, seek him still, but not here; in vain thou seekest him here, thou wilt never find him. Good days thou seekest, together let us seek them, seek not here. ... Read the Scriptures. ...

17. Let not a Christian then murmur, let him see whose steps he followeth: but if he loveth good days, let him hearken unto Him teaching and saying, "Come, ye children, hearken unto Me; I will teach you the fear of the Lord." What wouldest thou? Life and good days. Hear, and do. "Keep thy tongue from evil" (ver. 13). This do. I will not, saith a miserable man, I will not keep my tongue from evil, and yet I desire life and good days. If a workman of thine should say to thee, I indeed lay waste this vineyard, yet I require of thee my reward; thou broughtest me to the vineyard to lop and prune it, I cut away all the useful wood, I will cut short also the very trunks of the vines, that thou have thereon nothing to gather, and when I have done this, thou shall repay to me my labour. Wouldest thou not call him mad? Wouldest thou not drive him from thy house or ever he put his hand to the knife? Such are those men who would both do evil, and swear falsely, and speak blasphemy against God, and murmur, and defraud, and be drunken, and dispute, and commit adultery, and use charms, and consult diviners, and withal see good days. To such it is said, thou canst not doing ill seek a good reward. If thou art unjust, shall God also be unjust? What shall I do, then? What desirest thou? Life I desire, good days I desire. "Keep thy tongue from evil, and thy lips that they speak no guile," that is, defraud not any, lie not to any.

18. But what is, "Depart from evil"? (ver. 14). It is little that thou injure none, murder none, steal not, commit not adultery, do no wrong, speak no false witness; "Depart from evil." When thou hast departed, thou sayest, Now I am safe, I have done all, I shall have life, I shall see good days. Not only saith he, "Depart from evil," but also, "and do good." It is nothing that thou spoil not: clothe the naked. If thou hast not spoiled, thou hast declined from evil; but thou wilt not do good, except thou receive the stranger into thine house. So then depart from evil, as to do good. "Seek peace, and ensue it." He hath not said, Thou shalt have peace here; seek it, and ensue it. Whither shall I ensue it? Whither it hath gone before. For the Lord is our peace, hath risen again, and hath ascended into Heaven. "Seek peace, and ensue it;" because when thou also hast risen, this mortal shall be changed, and thou shall embrace peace there where no man shall trouble thee. For there is perfect peace, where thou wilt not hunger. ...

19. "The Eyes of the Lord are upon the righteous:" fear not then; labour; the eyes of the Lord are upon thee. "And His Ears are open unto their prayers" (ver. 15). What wouldest thou more? If an householder in a great house should not hearken to a servant murmuring, he would complain, and say, What hardship do we here suffer, and none heareth us. Canst thou say this of God, What hardships I suffer, and none heareth me? If He heard me, haply, sayest thou, He would take away my tribulation: I cry unto Him, and yet have tribulation. Only do thou hold fast His ways, and when thou art in tribulation, He heareth thee. But He is a Physician, and still hast thou something of putrefaction; thou criest out, but still He cutteth, and taketh not away His Hand, until He hath cut as much as pleaseth Him. For that Physician is cruel who heareth a man, and spareth his wound and putrefaction. How do mothers rub their children in the baths for their health. Do not the little ones cry out in their hands? Are they then cruel because they spare not, nor hearken unto their tears? Are they not full of affection? And yet the children cry out, and are not spared. So our God also is full of charity, but therefore seemeth He not to hear, that He may spare and heal us for everlasting.

20. Haply say the wicked, I securely do evil, because the Eyes of the Lord are not upon me: God attendeth to the righteous, me He seeth not, and whatever I do, I do securely. Immediately added the Holy Spirit, seeing the thoughts of men, and said, "But the Face of the Lord is against them that do evil; to cut off the remembrance of them from the earth" (ver. 16).

21. "The righteous cried, and the Lord heard them, and delivered them out of all their troubles" (ver. 17). Righteous were the Three Children; out of the furnace cried they unto the Lord, and in His praises their flames cooled. The flame could

not approach nor hurt the innocent and righteous Children praising God, and He delivered them out of the fire. Some one saith, Lo, truly righteous were those who were heard, as it is written, "The righteous cried, and the Lord heard them, and delivered them out of all their troubles:" but I have cried, and He delivereth me not; either I am not righteous, or I do not the things which He commandeth me, or haply He seeth me not. Fear not: only do what He commandeth; and if He deliver thee not bodily, He will deliver thee spiritually. For He who took out of the fire the Three Children, did He take out of the fire the Maccabees? Did not the first sing hymns in the flames, these last in the flames expire? The God of the Three Children, was not He the God also of the Maccabees? The one He delivered, the other He delivered not. Nay, He delivered both: but the Three Children He so delivered, that even the carnal were confounded; but the Maccabees therefore He delivered not so, that those who persecuted them should go into greater torments, while they thought that they had overcome God's Martyrs. He delivered Peter, when the Angel came unto him being in prison, and said, "Arise, and go forth," and suddenly his chains were loosed, and he followed the Angel, and He delivered him. Had Peter lost righteousness when He delivered him not from the cross? Did He not deliver him then? Even then He delivered him. Did his long life make him unrighteous? Haply He heard him more at last than at first, when truly He delivered him out of all his troubles. For when He first delivered him, how many things did he suffer afterwards! For thither He sent him at last, where he could have suffered no evil.

22. "The Lord is nigh unto them that have broken their heart; and saveth such as be lowly in spirit" (ver. 18). God is High: let a Christian be lowly. If he would that the Most High God draw nigh unto him, let him be lowly. A great mystery, Brethren. God is above all: thou raisest thyself, and touchest not Him: thou humblest thyself, and He descendeth unto thee. "Many are the troubles of the righteous" (ver. 19): doth He say, "Therefore let Christians be righteous, therefore let them hear My Word, that they may suffer no tribulation? He promiseth not this; but saith, "Many are the troubles of the righteous." Rather, if they be unrighteous they have fewer troubles, if righteous they have many. But after few tribulations, or none, these shall come to tribulation everlasting, whence they shall never be delivered: but the righteous after many tribulations shall come to peace everlasting, where they shall never suffer any evil. "Many are the tribulations of the righteous: but the Lord delivereth him out of all."

23. "The Lord keepeth all their bones: not one of them shall be broken" (ver. 20): this also, Brethren, let us not receive carnally. Bones are the firm supports of the faithful. For as in flesh our bones give firmness, so in the heart of a Christian it is

faith that gives firmness. The patience then which is in faith, is as the bones of the inner man: this is that which cannot be broken. "The Lord keepeth all their bones: not one of them shall be broken." If of our Lord God Jesus Christ he had said this, "The Lord keepeth all the bones of His Son; not one of them shall be broken;" as is prefigured of Him also in another place, when the lamb was spoken of that should be slain, and it was said of it, "Neither shall ye break a bone thereof:" then was it fulfilled in the Lord, because when He hung upon the Cross, He expired before they came to the Cross, and found His Body lifeless already, and would not break His legs, that it might be fulfilled which was written. But He gave this promise to other Christians also, "The Lord keepeth all their bones; not one of them shall be broken." Therefore, Brethren, if we see any Saint suffer tribulation, and haply either by a Physician so cut, or by some persecutor so mangled, that his bones be broken; let us not say, This man was not righteous, for this hath the Lord promised to His righteous, of whom He said, "The Lord keepeth all their bones; not one of them shall be broken." Wouldest thou see that He spoke of other bones, those which we called the firm supports of faith, that is, patience and endurance in all tribulations? For these are the bones which are not broken. Hear, and see ye in the very Passion of our Lord, what I say. The Lord was in the middle Crucified; near Him were two thieves: the one mocked, the other believed: the one was condemned, the other justified: the one had his punishment both in this world, and that which shall be, but unto the other said the Lord, "Verily I say unto thee, To-day shalt thou be with Me in Paradise;" and yet those who came brake not the bones of the Lord, but of the thieves they brake: as much were broken the bones of the thief who blasphemed, as of the thief who believed. Where then is that which is spoken, "The Lord keepeth all their bones; not one of them shall be broken"? Lo, unto whom He said, "To-day shalt thou be with Me in Paradise," could He keep all his bones? The Lord answereth thee: Yea, I kept them: for the firm support of his faith could not be broken by those blows whereby his legs were broken.

24. "The death of sinners is the worst" (ver. 21). Attend, Brethren, for the sake of those things which I said. Truly Great is the Lord, and His Mercy, truly Great is He who gave to us to eat His Body, wherein He suffered such great things, and His Blood to drink. How regardeth He them that think evil and say, "Such an one died ill, by beasts was he devoured: he was not a righteous man, therefore he perished ill; for else would he not have perished." Is he then righteous who dieth in his own house and in his own bed? This then (sayest thou) it is whereat I wonder; because I know the sins and the crimes of this same man, and yet he died well; in his own house, within his own doors, with no injury of travel, with none even in mature age. Hearken, "The death of sinners is worst." What seemeth to thee a good death, is worst if thou couldest see within. Thou seest him outwardly lying on his bed,

dost thou see him inwardly carried to hell? Hearken, Brethren, and learn from the Gospel what is the "worst death" of sinners. Were there not two in that age, a rich man who was clothed in purple and fine linen, and fared sumptuously every day; another a poor man who lay at his door full of sores, and the dogs came and licked his sores, and he desired to be fed with the crumbs which fell from the rich man's table? Now it came to pass that the poor man died (righteous was that poor man), and was carried by Angels into Abraham's bosom. He who saw his body lying at the rich man's door, and no man to bury it, what haply said he? So die he who is my enemy; and whoever persecutes me, so may I see him. His body is accursed with spitting, his wounds stink; and yet in Abraham's bosom he resteth. If we are Christians, let us believe: if we believe not, Brethren, let none feign himself a Christian. Faith bringeth us to the end. As the Lord spake these things, so are they. Doth indeed an astrologer speak unto thee, and it is true, and doth Christ speak, and it is false? But by what sort of death died the rich man? What sort of death must it not be in purple and fine linen, how sumptuous, how pompous! What funeral ceremonies were there! In what spices was that body buried! And yet when he was in hell, being in torments, from the finger of that despised poor man he desired one drop of water to be poured upon his burning tongue, and obtained it not. Learn then what meaneth, "The death of sinners is worst;" and ask not beds covered with costly garments, and to have the flesh wrapped in many rich things, friends exhibiting a show of lamentation, a household beating their breasts, a crowd of attendants going before and following when the body is carried out, marble and gilded memorials. For if ye ask those things, they answer you what is false, that of many not light sinners, but altogether wicked, the death is best, who have deserved to be so lamented, so embalmed, so covered, so carried out, so entombed. But ask the Gospel, and it will show to your faith the soul of the rich man burning in torments, which was nothing profited by all those honours and obsequies, which to his dead body the vanity of the living did afford.

25. But because there are many kinds of sinners, and not to be a sinner is difficult, or perhaps in this life impossible, he added immediately, of what kind of sinners the death is worst. "And they that hate the righteous one" (saith he) "shall perish." What righteous one, but "Him that justifieth the ungodly"? Whom, but our Lord Jesus Christ, who is also "the propitiation for our sins"? Who then hate Him, have the worst death; because they die in their sins, who are not through Him reconciled to our God. "For the Lord redeemeth the souls of His servants." But according to the soul is death to be understood either the worst or best, not according to bodily either dishonour, or honours which men see. "And none of them which trust in Him shall perish" (ver. 22); this iS the manner of human righteousness, that mortal life, however advanced, because without sin it cannot be, in this perisheth not, while it trusteth in Him, in whom is remission of sins. Amen.

PSALM XXXV.

1. ...The title of it causeth us no delay, for it is both brief, and to be understood not difficult, especially to those nursed in the Church of God. For so it is, "To David himself." The Psalm then is to David himself: now David is interpreted, Strong in hand, or Desirable. The Psalm then is to the Strong in hand, and Desirable, to Him who for us hath overcome death, who unto us hath promised life: for in this is He Strong in hand, that He hath overcome death for us; in this is He Desirable, that He hath promised unto us life eternal. For what stronger than that Hand which touched the bier, and he that was dead rose up? What stronger than that Hand which overcame the world, not armed with steel, but pierced with wood? Or what more desirable than He, whom not having seen, the Martyrs wished even to die, that they might be worthy to come unto Him? Therefore is the Psalm unto Him: to Him let our heart, to Him our tongue sing worthily: if yet Himself shall deign to give somewhat to sing. ...

2. "Judge Thou, O Lord" (saith he), "them that hurt me, and fight Thou against them that fight against me" (ver. 1). "If God be for us, who can be against us?" And whereby doth God this for us? "Take hold" (saith he) "of arms and shield, and rise up to my help" (ver. 2). A great spectacle is it, to see God armed for thee. And what is His Shield, what are His Arms? "Lord," in another place saith the man who here also speaketh, "as with the shield of Thy good-will hast Thou compassed us." But His Arms, wherewith He may not only us defend, but also strike His enemies, if we have well profited, shall we ourselves be. For as we from Him have this, that we be armed, so is He armed from us. But He is armed from those whom He hath made, we are armed with those things which we have received from Him who made us: These our arms the Apostle in a certain place calleth, "The shield of Faith, the helmet of Salvation, and the sword of the Spirit, which is the Word of God." He hath armed us with such arms as ye have heard, arms admirable, and unconquered, insuperable and shining; spiritual truly and invisible, because we have to fight also against invisible enemies. If thou seest thine enemy, let thine arms be seen. We are armed with faith in those things which we see not, and we overthrow enemies whom we see not. ...

3. "Pour forth the weapon, and stop the way against them that persecute me" (ver. 3). Who are they that persecute thee? Haply thy neighbour, or he whom thou hast offended, or to whom thou hast done wrong, or who would take away what is thine, or against whom thou preachest the truth, or whose sin thou rebukest, or whom living ill by thy well living thou offendest. There are indeed even these enemies to us, and they persecute us: but other enemies we are taught to know,

those against whom we fight invisibly, of whom the Apostle warneth us, saying, "We wrestle not against flesh and blood," that is, against men; not against those whom ye see, but against those whom ye see not; "against principalities, against powers, against the rulers of the world, of this darkness." ... "The whole world lieth in wickedness;" therefore the Apostle explained of what world they were rulers, he said, "of this darkness." The rulers of this world, I say, are the rulers of this darkness. ...

4. And what follows? "Let them be confounded and put to shame, that seek after my soul" (ver. 4): for to this end they seek after it, to destroy it. For I would that they would seek it for good! for in another Psalm he blameth this in men, that there was none who would seek after his soul: "Refuge failed me: there was none that would seek after my soul." Who is this that saith, "There was none that would seek after my soul"? Is it haply He, of whom so long before it was predicted, "They pierced My Hands and My Feet, they numbered all My Bones, they stared and looked upon Me, they have parted My Garments among them, and cast lots for My Vesture"? Now all these things were done before their eyes, and there was none who would seek after His Soul. ...

5. ...Many have been confounded to their health: many, put to shame, have passed over from the persecution of Christ to the society of His members with devoted piety; and this would not have been, had they not been confounded and put to shame. Therefore he wished well to them. ... Let them not go before, but follow; let them not give counsel, but take it. For Peter would go before the Lord, when the Lord spake of His future Passion: he would to Him as it were give counsel for His health. The sick man to the Saviour give counsel for His health! And what said he to the Lord, affirming that His future Passion? "Be it far from Thee, Lord. Be gracious to Thyself. This shall not be to Thee." He would go before that the Lord might follow; and what said He? "Get thee behind Me, Satan." By going before thou art Satan, by following thou wilt be a disciple. The same then is said to these also, "Let them be turned back and brought to confusion that think evil against me." For when they have begun to follow after, now they will not think evil against me, but desire my good.

6. What of others? For all are not so conquered as to be converted and believe: many continue in obstinacy, many preserve in heart the spirit of going before, and if they exert it not, yet they labour with it, and finding opportunity bring it forth. Of such, what followeth? "Let them be as dust before the wind" (ver. 5). "Not so are the ungodly, not so; but as the dust which the wind driveth away from the face of the earth." The wind is temptation; the dust are the ungodly. When temptation

cometh, the dust is raised, it neither standeth nor resisteth. "Let them be as dust before the wind, and let the Angel of the Lord trouble them." "Let their way be darkness and slipping "(ver. 6). A horrible way! Darkness alone who feareth not? A slippery way alone who avoids not? In a dark and slippery way how shall thou go? where set foot? These two ills are the great punishments of men: darkness, ignorance; a slippery way, luxury. "And let the Angel of the Lord persecute them;" that they be not able to stand. i For any one in a dark and slippery way, when he seeth that if he move his foot he will fall, and there is no light before his feet, haply resolveth to wait until light come; but here is the Angel of the Lord persecuting them. These things he predicted would come upon them, not as though he wished them to happen. Although the Prophet in the Spirit of God so speaketh these things, even as God doth the same, with sure judgment, with a judgment good, righteous, holy, tranquil; not moved with wrath, not with bitter jealousy, not with desire of wreaking enmities, but of punishing wickedness with righteousness; nevertheless, it is a prophecy.

7. But wherefore these so great evils? By what desert? Hear by what desert. "For without cause have they hid for me the corruption of their trap" (ver. 7). For Him that is our Head, observe, the Jews did this: they hid the corruption of their trap. For whom hid they their trap? For Him who saw the hearts of those that hid. But yet was He among them like one ignorant, as though He were deceived, whereas they were in that deceived, that they thought Him to be deceived. For therefore was He as though deceived, living among them, because we among such as they were so to live, as to be without doubt deceived. He saw His betrayer, and chose him the more to a necessary work. By his evil He wrought a great good: and yet among the twelve was he chosen, lest even the small number of twelve should be without one evil. This was an example of patience to us, because it was necessary that we should live among the evil: it was necessary that we should endure the evil, either knowing them or knowing them not: an example of patience He gave thee lest thou shouldest fail, when thou hast begun to live among the evil. And because that School of Christ in the twelve failed not, how much more ought we to be firm, when in the great Church is fulfilled what was predicted of the mixture of the evil. ...

8. But yet what is to be done? "Without a cause have they hid for me the corruption of their trap." What meaneth, "Without a cause"? I have done them no evil, I have hurt them not at all. "Vainly have they reviled my soul." What is, "Vainly"? Speaking falsely, proving nothing. "Let a trap come upon them which they know not of" (ver. 8). A magnificent retribution, nothing more just! They have hidden a trap that I might know not: let a trap come upon them which they

know not of. For I know of their trap. But what, trap is coming upon them? That which they know not of. Let us hear, lest haply he speak of that. "Let a trap come upon them, which they know not of." Perhaps that is one which they hid for him, that another which shall come upon themselves. Not so: but what? "The wicked shall be holden with the cords of his own sins." Thereby are they deceived, whereby they would deceive. Thence shall come mischief to them, whence they endeavoured mischief. For it follows, "And let the net which they have hidden catch themselves, and let them fall into their own trap." As if any one should prepare a cup of poison for another, and forgetting should drink it up himself: or as if one should dig a pit, that his enemy might fall thereinto in the darkness and himself forgetting what he had dug, should first walk that way, and fall into it. ...

9. This then for the wicked that would hurt me: what for me? "But my soul shall rejoice in the Lord" (ver. 9); as in Him from whom it hath heard, "I am thy salvation;" as not seeking other riches from without; as not seeking to abound in pleasures and good things of earth; but loving freely the true Spouse, not from Him wishing to receive aught that may delight, but Him alone proposing to itself, by whom it may be delighted. For what better than God will be given unto me? God loveth me: God loveth thee. See He hath proposed to thee, Ask what thou wilt. If the emperor should say to thee, Ask what thou wilt, what commands, what dignities, wouldest thou burst forth with! What great things wouldest thou propose to thyself, both to receive and to bestow! When God saith unto thee, Ask what thou wilt, what wilt thou ask? empty thy mind, exert thy avarice, stretch forward as far as possible, and enlarge thy desire: it is not any one, but Almighty God that said, Ask what thou wilt. If of possessions thou art a lover, thou wilt desire the whole earth, that all who are born may be thy husbandmen, or thy slaves. And what when thou hast possessed the whole earth? Thou wilt ask the sea, in which yet thou canst not live. In this greediness the fishes will have the better of thee. But perhaps thou wilt possess the islands. Pass over these also; ask the air although thou canst not fly; stretch thy desire even unto the heavens, call thine own the sun, the moon, and the stars, because He who made all said, Ask what thou wilt: yet nothing wilt thou find more precious, nothing wilt thou find better, than Himself who made all things. Him seek, who made all things, and in Him and from Him shalt thou have all things which He made. All things are precious, because all are beautiful; but what more beautiful than He? Strong are they; but what stronger than He? And nothing would He give thee rather than Himself. If aught better thou hast found, ask it. If thou ask aught else, thou wilt do wrong to Him, and harm to thyself, by preferring to Him that which He made, when He would give to thee Himself who made. ...

"But my soul shall be joyful in the Lord; it shall rejoice in His salvation." The salvation of God is Christ: "For mine eyes have seen Thy salvation."

10. "All my bones shall say, Lord, who is like unto Thee" (ver. 10). Who can speak anything worthily of these words? I think them only to be pronounced, not to be expounded. Why seekest thou this or that? What is like unto thy Lord? Him hast thou before thee. "The unrighteous have declared unto me delights, but not after Thy law, O Lord!" Persecutors have been who have said, Worship Saturn, worship Mercury. I worship not idols (saith he): "Lord, who is like unto Thee? They have eyes, and see not; ears have they, but they hear not." "Lord, who is like unto Thee," who hast made the eye to see, the ear to hear? But I (saith he) worship not idols, for them a workman made. Worship a tree or mountain; did a workman make them also? Here too, Lord, who is like unto Thee? Earthly things are shown unto me; Thou art Creator of the earth. And from these haply they turn to the higher creation, and say to me, Worship the Moon, worship this Sun, who with his light, as a great lamp in the Heavens, maketh the day. Here also I plainly say, "Lord, who is like unto Thee?" The Moon and the Stars Thou hast made, the Sun to rule the day hast Thou kindled, the Heavens hast Thou framed together. There are many invisible things better. But haply here also it is said to me, Worship Angels, adore Angels. And here also will I say, "Lord, who is like unto Thee?" Even the Angels Thou hast created. The Angels are nothing, but by seeing Thee. It is better with them to possess Thee, than by worshipping them to fall from Thee.

11. O Body of Christ, Holy Church, let all thy bones say, "Lord, who is like unto thee?" And if the flesh under persecution hath fallen away, let the bones say, "Lord, who is like unto Thee?" For of the righteous it is said, "The Lord keepeth all their bones; not one of them shall be broken." Of how many righteous have the bones under persecution been broken? Finally, "The just shall live by faith," and "Christ justifieth the ungodly." But how justifieth He any except believing and confessing? "For with the heart man believeth unto righteousness, and with the mouth confession is made unto salvation." Therefore also that thief, although from His theft led to the judge, and from the judge to the cross, yet on the very cross was justified: with his heart he believed, with his mouth he confessed. For neither to a man unrighteous and not already justified, would the Lord have said, "To-day shall thou be with Me in Paradise," and yet his bones were broken. For when they came to take down the bodies, by reason of the approaching Sabbath, the Lord was found already dead, and His Bones were not broken. But of those that yet lived, that they might be taken down, the legs were broken, that so from this pain having died, they might be buried. Were then of the one thief, who persisted in his ungodliness on the cross, the bones broken, and not also of the other who with his

heart believed, and with his mouth made confession unto salvation? Where then is that which was said, "The Lord keepeth all his bones; not one of them shall be broken;" except that in the Body of the Lord the name of bones is given to all the righteous, the firm in heart, the strong, yielding to no persecutions, no temptations, so as to consent unto evil? ...

12. "Which deliverest the poor from him that is too strong for him; yea, the poor and needy from him that spoileth him." ...Who that deliverest, but He who is Strong in hand? Even that David shall deliver the poor from him that is too strong for him. For the devil was too strong for thee, and held thee, because he conquered thee, when thou consentedst unto him. But what hath the Strong in hand done? "No man entereth into a strong man's house, to spoil his goods, except he first bind the strong man." By His own Power, most Holy, most Magnificent, hath He bound the devil by pouring forth the weapon to stop the way against him, that He may deliver the poor and needy, to whom there was no helper. For who is thy helper but the Lord to whom thou sayest, "O Lord, My Strength, and My Redeemer." If thou wilt presume of thy own strength, thereby wilt thou fall, whereof thou hast presumed: if of another's, he would lord it over thee, not succour thee. He then alone is to be sought Who hath redeemed them, and made them free, and hath given His Blood to purchase them, and of His servants hath made them His Brethren. ...

13. Let then our Head say, "False witnesses did rise up, they laid to My charge things that I knew not" (ver. 11). But let us say to our Head, Lord, what knewest Thou not? Didst Thou indeed know not anything? Didst Thou not know the hearts of them that charged Thee? Didst Thou not foresee their deceits? Didst Thou not give Thyself into their hands knowingly? Hadst Thou not come that Thou mightest suffer by them? What then knewest Thou not? He knew not sin, and thereby He knew not sin, not by not judging, but by not committing. There are phrases of this kind also in daily use, as when thou sayest of any one, He knoweth not to stand, that is, he doth not stand; and, He knoweth not to do good, because he doth not good; and, He knoweth not to do ill, because he doth not ill. ... What knew not Christ so much, as to blaspheme? Thereof was He called in question by His persecutors, and because He spake truth, He was judged to have spoken blasphemy? But by whom? By them of whom it followeth, "They rewarded Me evil for good, and barrenness to My Soul" (ver. 12). I gave unto them fruitfulness, they rewarded Me barrenness; I gave life, they death; I honour, they dishonour; I medicine, they wounds; and in all these which they rewarded Me, was truly barrenness. This barrenness in the tree He cursed, when seeking fruit He found none. Leaves there were, and fruit there was not: words there were, and deeds

there were not. See of words abundance, and of deeds barrenness. "Thou that preachest a man should not steal, stealest: thou that sayest a man should not commit adultery, committest adultery." Such were they who charged Christ with things that He knew not.

14. "But I, when they troubled me, clothed myself with sackcloth, and humbled my soul with fasting, and my prayer shall return into mine own bosom" (ver. 13). ...Brethren, if for some little space with pious curiosity we lift the veil, and search with the intent eye of the heart the inner part of this Scripture, we find that even this the Lord did. Sackcloth, haply He calleth His mortal flesh. Wherefore Sackcloth? For the likeness of sinful flesh. For the Apostle saith, "God sent His Son in the likeness of sinful flesh, that through sin He might condemn sin in the flesh:" that is, He clothed His Own Son with sackcloth, that through sackcloth" He might condemn the goats. Not that there was sin, I say not in the Word of God, but not even in that Holy Soul and Mind of a Man, which the Word and Wisdom of God had so joined to Himself as to be One Person. Nay, nor even in His very Body was any sin, but the likeness of sinful flesh there was in the Lord; because death is not but by sin, and surely that Body was mortal. For had It not been mortal, It had not died; had It not died, It had not risen again; had It not risen again, It had not showed us an example of eternal life. So then death, which is caused by sin, is called sin; as we say the Greek tongue, the Latin tongue, meaning not the very member of flesh, but that which is done by the member of flesh. For the tongue in our members is one among others, as the eyes, nose, ears, and the rest: but the Greek tongue is Greek words, not that the tongue is words, but that words are by the tongue. ... So then the sin of the Lord is that which was caused by sin; because He assumed flesh, of the same lump which had deserved death by sin. For to speak more briefly, Mary who was of Adam died for sin, Adam died for sin, and the Flesh of the Lord which was of Mary died to put away sin. With this sackcloth the Lord clothed Himself, and therefore was He not known, because He lay hid under sackcloth. "When they," saith He, "troubled Me, I clothed Myself with sackcloth:" that is, they raged, I lay hid. For had He not willed to lie hid neither could He have died, since in one moment of time one drop only of His Power, if indeed it is to be called a drop, He put forth, when they wished to seize Him, and at His one question, "Whom seek ye?" they all went back and fell to the ground. Such power could He not have humbled in passion, if He had not lain hid under sackcloth.

15. Again, if we have understood the sackcloth, how understand we the fasting? Wished Christ to eat, when He sought fruit on the tree, and if He had found, would He have eaten? Wished Christ to drink, when He said to the woman of Samaria,

"Give Me to drink"? when He said on the Cross," I thirst"? For what hungered, for what thirsted Christ, but our good works? Because in them that crucified and persecuted Him He had found no good works, He fasted; for they rewarded barrenness to His soul. For what a fast was His, who found barely one thief, whom on the Cross He might taste! For the Apostles had fled, and had hidden themselves in the multitude. And even Peter, who even to the death of his Lord had promised to persevere, had now thrice denied Him, had now wept, and still lay hid in the multitude, still feared lest He should be known. Lastly, having seen Him dead, all of them despaired of their own safety and despairing He found them, after His resurrection, and when He spake with them, found them grieving and mourning, no longer hoping anything... . In great fasting had the Lord remained, had He not refreshed them that He might feed on them. For He refreshed them, He comforted them, He confirmed them, and into His Own Body converted them. In this manner then was our Lord also in fasting.

16. "And My prayer shall return into Mine Own Bosom." In the bosom of this verse is plainly a great depth, and may the Lord grant that it be fathomable by us. For in the "bosom" a secret is understood. And we ourselves, Brethren, are here well admonished to pray within our own bosom, where God seeth, where God heareth, where no human eye penetrateth, where none seeth but He who succoureth; where Susanna prayed, and her voice, though it was not heard by men, yet by God was heard.... We read also that in the mount Jesus prayed alone, we read that He passed the night in prayer, even at the time of His Passion. What then? "And My prayer shall return into Mine Own Bosom." I know not what better to understand concerning the Lord: take meanwhile what now occurs; perhaps something better will occur hereafter, either to me or to some better: "My prayer shall return into Mine Own Bosom:" this I understand to be said, because in His Own Bosom He had the Father. "For God was in Christ reconciling the world unto Himself." In Himself He had Him to whom He prayed. He was not far from Him, for Himself had said, "I am in the Father, and the Father in Me." But because prayer rather belongeth to very Man [for according as Christ is the Word, He prayeth not, but heareth prayer; and seeketh not to be succoured for Himself, but with the Father succoureth all): what is, "My prayer shall return into Mine Own Bosom," but in Me My Manhood invoketh in Me My Godhead.

17. "As a Neighbour, as our Brother, so I pleased Him: as one mourning and sorrowful, so I humbled myself" (ver. 14). Now looketh He back to His Own Body: let us now look to this. When we rejoice m prayer, when our mind is calmed, not by the world's prosperity, but by the light of Truth: (who perceiveth this light, knoweth what I say, and he seeth and acknowledgeth what is said, "As a

Neighbour, as our Brother, so I pleased Him"): even then our soul pleaseth God, not placed afar off, for, "In Him," saith one, "we live and move and have our being," but as a Brother, as a Neighbour, as a Friend. But if it be not such that it can so rejoice, so shine, so approach, so cleave unto Him, and seeth itself far off thence, then let it do what followeth, "As one mourning and sorrowful, so I humbled Myself. As our Brother, so I pleased Him," said He, drawing near; "As one mourning and sorrowful, so I humbled Myself," said He, removed and set afar off... . Did not Peter draw near, when he said, "Thou art the Christ, the Son of the Living God"? And yet the same man became afar off by saying, "Be it far from Thee, Lord; this shall not be unto Thee." Lastly, what said He, his Neighbour, as it were, to him drawing near? "Blessed art thou, Simon, Barjona." To him afar off, as it were, and unlike, what said He? "Get thee behind Me, Satan." To him drawing near, "Flesh and blood," saith He," hath not revealed it unto thee, but My Father, which is in Heaven." His Light is shed over thee, in His Light thou shinest. But when having become afar off, he spake against the Lord's Passion, which should be for our Salvation, "Thou savourest not," said He, "the things that be of God, but those that be of men," One rightly placing together both of these saith in a certain Psalm, "I said in my ecstasy, I am cast off from before Thine Eyes." In my ecstasy, would he not have said, had he not drawn near; for ecstasy, is the transporting of the mind. He poured: over himself his own soul, and drew near unto God; and through some cloud and weight of the flesh being again cast down to earth, and recollecting where he had been, and seeing where he was, he said, "I am cast off from before Thine Eyes." This then, "As a Neighbour, as our Brother, so I pleased Him," may He grant to be done in us; but when that is not, let even this be done, "As one mourning and sorrowful, so I humbled myself."

18. And against Me they rejoiced, and gathered themselves together" (ver. 15), against Me only: they rejoicing, I sorrowful. But we heard just now in the Gospel, "Blessed are they that mourn." If they are blessed that mourn, miserable are they that laugh. "Against Me they rejoiced, and gathered themselves together: scourges were gathered together against Me, and they knew not." Because they laid to My charge things that I knew not, they also knew not Whom they charged.

19. "They tempted Me, and mocked Me with mocking" (ver. 16). That is, they derided Me, they insulted Me; this of the Head, this of the Body. Consider, Brethren, the glory of the Church which now is; remember its past dishonours, remember how once were Christians everywhere put to flight, and wherever found, mocked, beaten, slain, exposed to beasts, burned, men rejoicing against them. As it was to the Head, so it is also to the Body. For as it was to the Lord on the Cross, so has it been to His Body in all that persecution which was made but

now: nor even now cease the persecutions of the same. Wherever men find a Christian, they are wont to insult, to persecute, to deride him, to call him dull, senseless, of no spirit, of no knowledge. Do they what they will, Christ is in Heaven: do they what they will, He hath honoured His punishment, already hath He fixed His Cross in the foreheads of all; the ungodly is permitted to insult, to rage he is not permitted; but yet from that which the tongue uttereth, is understood what he beareth in his heart: "They gnashed upon Me with their teeth."

20. "Lord, when wilt Thou look on? Rescue My Soul from their deceits, My Darling from the lions" (ver. 17). For to us the time is slow; and in our person is this said, "When wilt Thou look on?" that is, when shall we see vengeance upon those who insult us? When shall the Judge, overcome by weariness, hear the widow? But our Judge, not from weariness, but from love, delayeth our salvation; from reason, not from need; not that He could not even now succour us, but that the number of us all may be filled up even to the end. And yet out of our desire, what do we say? "Lord, when wilt Thou look on? Rescue My Soul from their deceits, My Darling from the lions:" that is, My Church from raging powers.

21. Lastly, wouldest thou know what is that Darling? Read the words following: "I will confess unto Thee, O Lord, in the great Congregation; in a weighty people will I praise Thee" (ver. 18). Truly saith He," I will confess unto Thee:" for confession is made in all the multitude, but not in all is God praised: the whole multitude heareth our confession, but not in all the multitude is the praise of God. For in all the whole multitude, that is, in the Church which is spread abroad in the whole world, is chaff, and wheat: the chaff flieth, the wheat remaineth; therefore, "in a weighty people will I praise Thee." In a weighty people, which the wind of temptation carries not away, in such is God praised.For in the chaff He is ever blasphemed... .

22. "Let not them that are Mine enemies wrongfully rejoice over Me:" for they rejoice lover Me because of My chaff. "Who hate Me without a cause;" that is, whom I never hurt; "winking with their eyes" (ver. 19): that is, pretending hypocrites, "For they spake indeed peace to Me" (ver. 20). What is, "winking with their eyes"? Declaring by their looks, what they carry not in their heart. And who are these "winking with their eyes"? "For they spake indeed peace to Me; and with wrath devised craftily." "Yea they opened their mouth wide against Me" (ver. 21). First winking with their eyes, those lions sought to ravish and devour; first fawning they spake peace, and then with wrath devised craftily. What peace spake they? "Master, we know that Thou acceptest not man's person, and teachest the way of God in truth. Is it lawful to give tribute unto Caesar, or not?" They spake

indeed peace unto Me. What then? Didst not Thou know them, and deceived they Thee, winking with their eyes? Truly He knew them; therefore said He, "Why tempt ye Me, ye hypocrites?" Afterward, "they opened their mouth wide against Me," crying, "Crucify Him, Crucify Him! and said, Aha, Aha, our eyes have seen it." This, when they insulted Him, "Aha, Aha, Prophesy unto us, Thou Christ." As their peace was pretended when they tempted Him concerning the money, so now insulting was their praise. "They said, Aha, Aha, our eyes have seen it" (ver. 21): that is, Thy deeds, Thy miracles. This Man is the Christ. "If He be the Christ, let Him come down from the Cross, and we will believe Him. He saved others, Himself He cannot save." "Our eyes have seen it." This is all whereof He boasted Himself, when "He called Himself the Son of God." But the Lord was hanging patient upon the Cross: His power had He not lost, but He showed His patience. For what great thing was it for Him to come down from the Cross, who could afterward rise again from the sepulchre? But He seems to have yielded to His insulters; and this, beloved, that having risen again He should show Himself to His own, and not to them, and this is a great mystery; for His resurrection signified the New Life, but the New Life is known to His friends, not to His enemies. 23. "This Thou hast seen, O Lord; keep not silence" (ver. 22). What is, "keep not silence"? Judge Thou. For of judgment is it said in a certain place, "I have kept silence; shall I keep silence for ever?" And of the delaying of judgment it is said to the sinner, "These things hast thou done, and I kept silence;" "Thou thoughtest that I was altogether such an one as thyself." How keepeth He silence, who speaketh by the Prophets, who speaketh with His own mouth in the Gospel, who speaketh by the Evangelists, who speaketh by us, when we speak the truth? What then? He keepeth silence from judgment, not from precept, not from doctrine. But this His judgment the Prophet in a manner invoketh, and predicteth: "Thou hast seen, O Lord: keep not silence; "that is, Thou wilt not keep silence, needs must that Thou wilt judge. "O Lord, be not far from Me." Until Thy judgment come, be not far from Me, as Thou hast promised, "Lo, I am with you alway, even unto the end of the world.'"

24. "Arise, Lord, and attend to My judgment" (ver. 23). To what judgment? That Thou art in tribulation; that Thou art tormented with labours and pains? Do not even many wicked men suffer the same? To what judgment? Therefore art Thou righteous, because Thou sufferest these things? No: but what? "To My judgment." What followeth? "Attend to My judgment; even to My cause, My God, and My Lord." Not to My punishment, but to My cause: not to that which the robber hath in common with Me, but to that whereof is said, "Blessed are they which are persecuted for righteousness' sake." For this cause is distinguished. For punishment is equal to good and bad. Therefore Martyrs, not the punishment, but the cause maketh, for if punishment made Martyrs, all the mines would be full of Martyrs, every chain would drag Martyrs, all that are executed with the sword

would be crowned. Therefore let the cause be distinguished; let none say, because I suffer, I am righteous. Because He who first suffered, suffered for righteousness' sake, therefore He added a great exception, "Blessed are they which are persecuted for righteousness' sake." For many having a good cause do persecution, and many having a bad cause suffer persecution. For if persecution could not be done rightly, it had not been said in a certain Psalm, "Whoso privily slandereth his neighbour, him did I persecute." ... Let none then say, I suffer persecution: let him not sift the punishment, but prove the cause: lest if he prove not the cause, he be numbered with the ungodly. Therefore how watchfully, how excellently hath This Man recommended Himself, "O Lord, attend to My judgment," not to My punishments; "even to My cause, My God, and My Lord."

25. "Judge me, O Lord, according to My righteousness" (ver. 24); that is, attend to My cause. Not according to My punishment, but "according to My righteousness, O Lord, My God," that is, according to this judge Thou Me. "And let them not rejoice over Me;" that is, Mine enemies.

26. "Let them not say in their heart, Aha, aha, so would we have it" (ver. 25); that is, We have done what we could, we have slain him, we have taken him away. "Let them not say:" show them that they have done nothing. "Let them not say, We have swallowed him up." Whence say those Martyrs, "If the Lord had not been on our side, then they had swallowed us up quick." What is, "had swallowed us up "? Had passed into their own body. For that thou swallowest up, which thou passest into thy own body. The world would swallow thee up; swallow thou the world, pass it into thy own body: kill and eat. As it was said to Peter, "Kill and eat;" do thou kill in them what they are, make them what thou art. But if they on the other hand persuade thee to ungodliness, thou art swallowed up by them. Not when they persecute thee art thou swallowed up by them, but when they persuade thee to be what they are. "Let them not say, We have swallowed him up." Do thou swallow up the body of Pagans. Why the body of Pagans? It would swallow thee up. Do thou to it, what it would to thee. Therefore perhaps that calf, being ground to powder, was cast into the water and given to the children of Israel to drink? that so the body of ungodliness might be swallowed up by Israel. "Let them be ashamed and brought to confusion together that rejoice at mine hurt: let them be clothed with shame and dishonour" (ver. 26); so that we may swallow up them ashamed and brought to confusion. "Who speak evil against me:" let them be ashamed, let them be brought to confusion.

27. What sayest thou now, the Head with the Members? "Let them shout for joy and be glad that favour My righteous cause:" who cleave to My Body. Yea, let

them say "continually, Let the Lord be magnified, which hath pleasure in the prosperity of His servant" (ver. 27). "And my tongue shall speak of Thy righteousness, and of Thy praise all the day long" (ver. 28). And whose tongue endureth to speak the praise of God all the day long? See now I have made a discourse something longer; ye are wearied. Who endureth to praise God all the day long? I will suggest a remedy, whereby thou mayest praise God all the day long if thou wilt. Whatever thou dost, do well, and thou hast praised God. When thou singest an hymn, thou praisest God, but what doth thy tongue, unless thy heart also praise Him? Hast thou ceased from singing hymns, and departed, that thou mayest refresh thyself? Be not drunken, and thou hast praised God. Dost thou go away to sleep? Rise not to do evil, and thou hast praised God. Dost thou transact business? Do no wrong, and thou hast praised God. Dost thou till thy field? Raise not strife, and thou hast praised God. In the innocency of thy works prepare thyself to praise God all the day long.

PSALM XXXVI.

1. ... "The ungodly hath said in himself that he will sin: there is no fear of God before his eyes" (ver. 1). Not of one man, but of a race of ungodly men he speaketh, who fight against their own selves, by not understanding, that so they may live well; not because they cannot, but because they will not. For it is one thing, when one endeavours to understand some thing, and through infirmity of flesh cannot; as saith the Scripture in a certain place, "For the corruptible body presseth down the soul, and the earthly tabernacle weigheth down the mind that museth upon many things;" but another when the human heart acts mischievously against itself, so that what it could understand, if it had but good will thereto, it understandeth not, not because it is difficult, but because the will is contrary. But so it is when men love their own sins, and hate God's Commandments. For the Word of God is thy adversary, if thou be a friend to thy ungodliness; but if thou art an adversary to thy ungodliness, the Word of God is thy friend, as well as the adversary of thy ungodliness. ...

2. "For he hath wrought deceitfully in His sight" (ver. 2). In whose sight? In His, whose fear was not before the eyes of him that did work deceitfully. "To find out his iniquity, and hate it." He wrought so as not to find it. For there are men who as it were endeavour to seek out their iniquity, and fear to find it; because if they should find it, it is said to them, Depart from it: this thou didst before thou knewest; thou didst iniquity being in ignorance; God giveth pardon: now thou hast discovered it, forsake it, that to thy ignorance pardon may easily be given; and that with a clear face thou mayest say to God, "Remember not the sins of my youth, and of my ignorance." Thus he seeketh it, thus he feareth lest he find it; for he seeketh it deceitfully. When saith a man, I knew not that it was sin? When he hath seen that it is sin, and ceaseth to do the sin, which he did only because he was ignorant: such an one in truth would know his sin, to find it out, and hate it. But now many "work deceitfully to find out their iniquity:" they work not from their heart to find it out and hate it. But because in the very search after iniquity, there is deceit, in the finding it there will be defence of it. For when one hath found his iniquity, lo now it is manifest to him that it is iniquity. Do it not, thou sayest. And he who wrought deceitfully to find it out, now he hath found, hateth it not; for what saith he? How many do this! Who is there that doth it not? And will God destroy them all? Or at least he saith this: if God would not these things to be done, would men live who commit the same? Seest thou that thou didst work deceitfully to find out thy iniquity? For if not deceitfully but sincerely thou hadst wrought, thou wouldest now have found it out, and hated it; now thou hast found it

180

out, and thou defendest it; therefore thou didst work deceitfully, when thou soughtest it.

3. "The words of his mouth are iniquity and deceit: he would not understand, that he might do good" (ver. 3). Ye see that he attributeth that to the will: for there are men who would understand and cannot, and there are men who would not understand, and therefore understand not. "He would not understand, that he might do good."

4. "He hath meditated iniquity on his bed." What said He, "On his bed?" (ver. 4). "The ungodly hath said in himself, that he will sin:" what above he said, in himself, that here he said, "On his bed." Our bed is our heart: there we suffer the tossing of an evil conscience; and there we rest when our conscience is good. Whoso loveth the bed of his heart, let him do some good therein. There is our bed, where the Lord Jesus Christ commands us to pray. "Enter into thy chamber, and shut thy door." What is, "Shut thy door?" Expect not from God such things as are without, but such as are within; "and thy Father which seeth in secret, shall reward thee openly." Who is he that shutteth not the door? He who asketh much from God such things, and in such wise directeth all his prayers, that he may receive the goods that are of this world. Thy door is open, the multitude seeth when thou prayest. What is it to shut thy door? To ask that of God, which God alone knoweth how He giveth. What is that for which thou prayest, when thou hast shut the door? What "eye hath not seen, nor ear heard, or hath entered into the heart of man." And haply it hath not entered into thy very bed, that is, into thy heart. But God knoweth what He will give: but when shall it be? When the Lord shall be revealed, when the Judge shall appear... .

5. "He hath set himself in every way that is not good." What is, "he hath set himself"? He hath sinned perseveringly. Whence also of a certain pious and good man it is said, "He hath not stood in the way of sinners." As this "hath not stood," so that "hath set himself." "But wickedness hath he not hated." There is the end, there the fruit: if a man cannot but have wickedness, let him at least hate it. For when thou hatest it, it scarcely occurs to thee to do any wickedness. For sin is in our mortal body, but what saith the Apostle? "Let not sin reign in your mortal body, that ye should obey it in the lusts thereof." When beginneth it not to be therein? When that shall be fulfilled in us which he saith, "When this corruptible shall have put on incorruption, and this mortal shall have put on immortality." Before this come to pass, there is a delighting in sin in the body, but greater is the delighting and the pleasure in the Word of Wisdom, in the Commandment of God. Overcome sin and the lust thereof. Sin and iniquity do thou hate, that thou mayest

join thyself to God, who hateth it as well as thou. Now being joined in mind unto the Law of God, in mind thou servest the Law of God. And if in the flesh thou therefore servest the law of sin, because there are in thee certain carnal delightings, then will there be none when thou shalt no longer fight. It is one thing not to fight, and to be in true and lasting peace; another to fight and overcome; another to fight and to be overcome; another not to fight at all, but to be carried away. ...

6. "Thy mercy, O Lord, is in the heavens, and Thy truth reacheth even unto the clouds" (ver. 5). I know not what Mercy of Him he meaneth, which is in the heavens. For the Mercy of the Lord is also in the earth. Thou hast it written, "The earth is full of the Mercy of the Lord." Of what Mercy then speaketh He, when He saith, "Thy Mercy, O Lord, is in the heavens"? The gifts of God are partly temporal and earthly, partly eternal and heavenly. Whoso for this worshippeth God, that he may receive those temporal and earthly goods, which are open to all, is still as it were like the brutes: he enjoyeth indeed the Mercy of God, but not that which is excepted, which shall not be given, save only to the righteous, to the holy, to the good. What are the gifts which abound to all? "He maketh His sun to rise on the evil and on the good, and sendeth rain on the just and on the unjust." Who hath not this Mercy of God, first that he hath being, that he is distinguished from the brutes, that he is a rational animal, so as to understand God; secondly, that he enjoys this light, this air, rain, fruits, diversity of seasons, and all the earthly comforts, health of body, the affection of friends, the safety of his family? All these are good, and they are God's gifts... .

7. But this man rightly understood what mercy he should pray for from God. "Thy Mercy, O Lord, is in the Heavens; and Thy Truth reacheth even to the clouds." That is, the Mercy which Thou givest to Thy Saints, is Heavenly, not earthly; is Eternal, not temporal. And how couldest Thou declare it unto men? Because "Thy Truth reacheth even unto the clouds." For who could know the Heavenly Mercy of God, unless God should declare it unto men? How did He declare it? By sending His truth even unto the clouds. What are the clouds? The Preachers of the Word of God... . Truth reached even to the clouds: therefore unto us could be declared the Mercy of God, which is in Heaven and not in earth. And truly, Brethren, the clouds are the Preachers of the Word of Truth. When God threateneth through His Preachers, He thunders through the clouds. When God worketh miracles through His Preachers, He lightneth through the clouds, He terrifieth through the clouds, and watereth by the rain. Those Preachers, then, by whom is preached the Gospel of God, are the clouds of God. Let us then hope for Mercy, but for that which is in the Heavens.

8. "Thy Righteousness is like the mountains of God: Thy Judgments are a great deep" (ver. 6). Who are the mountains of God? Those who are called clouds, the same are also the mountains of God. The great Preachers are the mountains of God. And as when the sun riseth, he first clothes the mountains with light, and thence the light descends to the lowest parts of the earth: so our Lord Jesus Christ, when He came, first irradiated the height of the Apostles, first enlightened the mountains, and so His Light descended to the valley of the world. And therefore saith He in a certain Psalm, "I lifted up mine eyes unto the mountains, from whence cometh my help." But think not that the mountains themselves will give thee help: for they receive what they may give, give not of their own. And if thou remain in the mountains, thy hope will not be strong: but in Him who enlighteneth the mountains, ought to be thy hope and presumption. Thy help indeed will come to thee through the mountains, because the Scriptures are administered to thee through the mountains, through the great Preachers of the Truth: but fix not thy hope in them. Hear what He saith next following: "I lifted up mine eyes unto the mountains, from whence cometh my help." What then? Do the mountains give thee help? No; hear what follows, "My help cometh from the Lord, which made Heaven and earth." Through the mountains cometh help, but not from the mountains. From whom then? "From the Lord, which made Heaven and earth." ...

9. "Thy Judgments are like the great abyss." The abyss he calleth the depth of sin, whither every one cometh by despising God; as in a certain place it is said, "God gave them over to their own hearts' lusts, to do the things which are not convenient." ... Because then they were proud and ungrateful, they were held worthy to be delivered up to the lusts of their own hearts, and became a great abyss, so that they not only sinned, but also worked craftily, lest they should understand their iniquity, and hate it. That is the depth of wickedness, to be unwilling to find it out and to hate it. But how one cometh to that depth, see; "Thy Judgments are the great abyss." As the mountains are by the Righteousness of God, who through His Grace become great: so also through His Judgments come they unto the depth, who sink lowest. By this then let the mountains delight thee, by this turn away from the abyss, and turn thyself unto that, of which it is said, "My help cometh from the Lord." But whereby? "I have lifted up mine eyes unto the mountains." What meaneth this? I will speak plainly. In the Church of God thou findest an abyss, thou findest also mountains; thou findest there but few good, because the mountains are few, the abyss broad; that is, thou findest many living ill after the wrath of God, because they have so worked that they are delivered up to the lusts of their own heart; so now they defend their sins and confess them not; but say, Why? What have I done? Such an one did this, and such an one did that. Now will they even defend what the Divine Word reproves. This is the abyss. Therefore in a certain place saith the Scripture (hear this abyss), "The

sinner when he cometh unto the depth of sin despiseth." See, "Thy Judgments are like the great abyss." But yet not art thou a mountain; not yet art thou in the abyss; fly from the abyss, tend towards the mountains; but yet remain not on the mountains. "For thy help cometh from the Lord, which made Heaven and earth."

10. Because he said, Thy Mercy is in the Heavens, that it may be known to be also on earth, he said, "O Lord, Thou surest man and beast, as Thy Mercy is multiplied, O God" (ver. 7). Great is Thy Mercy, and manifold is Thy Mercy, O God; and that showest Thou both to man and beast. For from whom is the saving of men? From God. Is not the saving of beasts also from God? For He who made man, made also beasts; He who made both, saveth both; but the saving of beasts is temporal. But there are who as a great thing ask this of God, which He hath given to beasts. "Thy Mercy, O God, is multiplied," so that not only unto men, but unto beasts also is given the same saving which is given to men, a carnal and temporal saving.

11. Have not men then somewhat reserved with God, which beasts deserve not, and where-unto beasts arrive not? They have evidently. And where is that which they have. "The children of men put their trust under the shadow of Thy wings." Attend, my Beloved, to this most pleasant sentence; "Thou savest man and beast." First, he spake of "man and beast," then of "the children of men;" as though "men" were one, "the children of mea" other. Sometimes in Scripture children of men is said generally of all men, sometimes in some proper manner, with some proper signification, so that not all men are understood; chiefly when there is a distinction. For not without reason is it here put; "O Lord, Thou savest man and beast: but the children of men;" as though setting aside the first, he keepeth separate the children of men. Separate from whom? Not only from beasts, but also from men, who seek from God the saving of beasts, and desire this as a great thing. Who then are the children of men? Those who put their trust under the shadow of His wings. For those men together with beasts rejoice in possession, but the children of men rejoice in hope: those follow after present goods with beasts, these hope for future goods with Angels. ...

12. "They shall be satiated with the fulness of Thy House" (ver. 8). He promiseth us some great thing. He would speak it, and He speaketh it not. Can He not, or do not we receive it? I dare, my Brethren, to say, even of holy tongues and hearts, by which Truth is declared to us, that it can neither be spoken, which they declared, nor even thought of. For it is a great thing, and ineffable; and even they saw through a glass darkly, as saith the Apostle, "For now we see through a glass darkly; but then face to face." Lo, they who saw through a glass darkly, thus burst forth. What then shall we be, when we shall see face to face? That with which they

travailed in heart, and could not with their tongue bring forth, that men might receive it. For what necessity was there that he should say, "They shall be satiated with the fulness of Thy House"? He sought a word whereby to express from human things what he would say; and because he saw that men drowning themselves in drunkenness receive indeed wine without measure, but lose their senses, he saw what to say; for when shall have been received that ineffable joy, then shall be lost in a manner the human soul, it shall become Divine, and be satiated with the fulness of God's House. Wherefore also in another Psalm it is said, "Thy cup inebriating, how excellent is it!" With this cup were the Martyrs satiated when going to their passion, they knew not their own. What so inebriated as not to know a wife weeping, not children, not parents? They knew them not they thought not that they were before their eyes. Wonder not: they were inebriated Wherewith were they so? Lo, they had received a cup wherewith they were satiated Wherefore he also gives thanks to God, saying "What shall I render unto the Lord for all His benefits towards me? I will take the cup of Salvation, and call upon the Name of the Lord." Therefore, Brethren of men," let us be "children and let us trust under the shadow of His wings and be satiated with the fulness of His House As I could, I have spoken; and as far as I can I see; and how far I see, I cannot speak. "And of the torrent of Thy Pleasure shalt Thou give them to drink." A torrent we call water coming with a flood. There will be a flood of God's Mercy to overflow and inebriate those who now put their trust under the shadow of His wings. What is that Pleasure? As it were a torrent inebriating the thirsty. Let him then who thirsts now, lay up hope: whoso thirsts now, let him have hope; when inebriated, he shall have possession: before he have possession, let him thirst in hope. "Blessed are they which do hunger and thirst after righteousness, for they shall be filled."

13. With what fountain then wilt thou be overflowed, and whence runneth such a torrent of His Pleasure? "For with Thee," saith he, "is the fountain of Life." What is the fountain of Life, but Christ? He came to thee in the flesh, that He might bedew thy thirsty lips: He will satisfy thee trusting, who bedewed thee thirsting. "For with Thee is the fountain of Life; in Thy Light shall we see light" (ver. 9). Here a fountain is one thing, light another: there not so. For that which is the Fountain, the same is also Light: and whatever thou wilt thou callest It, for It is not what thou callest It: for thou canst not find a fit name: for It remaineth not in one name. If thou shouldest say, that It is Light only, it would be said to thee, Then without cause am I told to hunger and thirst, for who is there that eateth light? It is said to me plainly, directly, "Blessed are the pure in heart: for they shall see God." If It is Light, my eyes must I prepare. Prepare also lips; for That which is Light is also a Fountain: a Fountain, because It satisfieth the thirsty: Light, because It enlighteneth the blind. Here sometimes, light is in one place, a fountain in another.

For sometimes fountains run even in darkness; and sometimes in the desert thou sufferest the sun, findest no fountain: here then can these two be separated: there thou shall not be wearied, for there is a Fountain; there thou shall not be darkened, for there is Light.

14. "Show forth Thy Mercy unto them that know Thee; Thy Righteousness to them that are of a fight heart" (ver. 10). As I have said, Those are of a right heart who follow in this life the Will of God. The will of God is sometimes that thou shouldest be whole, sometimes that thou shouldest be sick. If when thou art whole God's Will be sweet, and when thou art sick God's Will be bitter; thou art not of a right heart. Wherefore? Because thou wilt not make right thy will according to God's Will, but wilt bend God's Will to thine. That is right, but thou art crooked: thy will must be made right to That, not That made crooked to thee; and thou wilt have a right heart. It is well with thee in this world; be God blessed, who comforteth thee: it goeth hardly with thee in this world; be God blessed, because He chasteneth and proveth thee; and so wilt thou be of a right heart, saying, "I will bless the Lord at all times: His Praise shall be ever in my mouth."

15. "Let not the foot of pride come against me" (ver. 11). But now he said, The children of men shall put their trust under the shadow of Thy wings: they shall be satiated with the fulness of Thy House. When one hath begun to be plentifully overflowed with that Fountain, let him take heed lest he grow proud. For the same was not wanting to Adam, the first man: but the foot of pride came against him, and the hand of the sinner removed him, that is, the proud hand of the devil. As he who seduced him, said of himself, "I will sit in the sides of the north;" so he persuaded him, by saying, "Taste, and ye shall be as gods." By pride then have we so fallen as to arrive at this mortality. And because pride had wounded us, humility maketh us whole. God came humbly, that from such great wound of pride He might heal man. He came, for "The Word was made Flesh, and dwelt among us." He was taken by the Jews; He was reviled of them. Ye heard when the Gospel was read, what they said, and to Whom they said, "Thou hast a devil:" and He said not, Ye have a devil, for ye are still in your sins, and the devil possesseth your hearts. He said not this, which if He had said, He had said truly: but it was not meet that He should say it, lest He should seem not to preach Truth, but to retort evil speaking. He let go what He heard as though He heard it not. For a Physician was He, and to cure the madman had He come. As a Physician careth not what he may hear from the madman; but how the madman may recover and become sane; nor even if he receive a blow from the madman, careth he; but while he to him giveth new wounds, he cureth his old fever: so also the Lord came to the 'sick man, to the madman came He, that whatever He might hear, whatever He might

suffer, He should despise; by this very thing teaching us humility, that being taught by humility, we might be healed from pride: from which he here prayeth to be delivered, saying, "Let not the foot of pride come against me; neither let the hand of the sinner remove me." For if the foot of pride come, the hand of the sinner removeth. What is the hand of the sinner? The working of him that adviseth ill. Hast thou become proud? Quickly he corrupteth thee who adviseth ill. Humbly fix thyself in God, and care not much what is said to thee. Hence is that which is elsewhere spoken, "From my secret sins cleanse Thou me; and from others' sins also keep Thy servant." What is, "From my secret sins"? "Let not the foot of pride come against me." What is, "From other men's sins also keep Thy servant"? "Let not the hand of the wicked remove me." Keep that which is within, and thou shall not fear from without.

16. But wherefore so greatly fearest thou this? Because it is said, "Thereby have fallen all that work iniquity" (ver. 12); so that they have come into that abyss of which it is said, "Thy judgments are like the great abyss:" so that they have come even to that deep wherein sinners who despise have fallen. "Have fallen." Whereby did they first fall? By the foot of pride. Hear the foot of pride. "When they knew God, they glorified Him not as God." Therefore came against them the foot of pride, whereby they came into the depth. "God gave them over to their own hearts' lusts, to do those things which are not convenient." The root of sin, and the head of sin feared he who said, "Let not the foot of pride come against me." Wherefore said he, "the foot"? Because by walking proudly man deserted God, and departed from Him. His foot, called he his affection. "Let not the foot of pride come against me: let not the hand of the wicked remove me:" that is, let not the works of the wicked remove me from Thee, that I should wish to imitate them. But wherefore said he this against pride, "Thereby have fallen all that work iniquity"? Because those who now are ungodly, have fallen by pride. Therefore when the Lord would caution His Church, He said, "It shall watch thy head, and thou shall watch his heel." The serpent watcheth when the foot of pride may come against thee, when thou mayest fall, that he may cast thee down. But watch thou his head: the beginning of all sin is pride. "Thereby have fallen all that work iniquity: they are driven out, and are not able to stand." He first, who in the Truth stood not, then, through him, they whom God sent out of Paradise. Whence he, the humble, who said that he was not worthy to unloose His shoe's latchet, is not driven out, but standeth and heareth Him, and rejoiceth greatly because of the Bridegroom's voice; not because of his own, lest the foot of pride come against him, and he be driven out, and be not able to stand. ...

PSALM XXXVII.

On the First Part of the Psalm.

1. With tenor do they hear of the coming of the last day, who will not be secure by living well: and who fain would live ill, long. But it was for useful purposes that God willed that day to remain unknown; that the heart may be ever ready to expect that of which it knows it is to come, but knows not when it is to come. Seeing, however, that our Lord Jesus Christ was sent to us to be our "Master," He said, that "of the day not even the Son of Man knew," because it was not part of His office as our Master that through Him it should become known to us. For indeed the Father knoweth nothing that the Son knoweth not; since that is the Very Knowledge of the Father Itself, which is His Wisdom; now His Son, His Word, is "His Wisdom." But because it was not for our good to know that, which however was known to Him who came indeed to teach us, though not to teach us that which it was not good for us to know, He not only, as a Master, taught us something, but also, as a Master, left something untaught. For, as a Master, He knew how both to teach us what was good for us, and not to teach us what was injurious. Now thus, according to a certain form of speech, the Son is said not to know what He does not teach: that is, in the same way that we are daily in the habit of speaking, He is said not to know what He causes us not to know. ...

2. This it is that disturbs you who are a Christian; that you see men of bad lives prospering, and surrounded with abundance of things like these; you see them sound in health, distinguished with proud honours; you see their family unvisited by misfortune; the happiness of their relatives, the obsequious attendance of their dependants, their most commanding influence, theirs life uninterrupted by any sad event; you see their characters most profligate, their external resources most affluent; and your heart says that there is no Divine judgment; that all things are carried to and fro by accidents, and blown about in disorderly; and irregular motions. For if God, thou sayest, regarded human affairs, would his iniquity flourish, and my innocence suffer? Every sickness of the soul hath in Scripture its proper remedy. Let him then whose sickness is of that kind that he says in his heart things like these, let him drink this Psalm by way of potion. ...

3. "Be not envious because of evil-doers, neither be envious against the workers of iniquity" (ver. 1). "For they shall soon wither like the grass, and shall fade like the herbs of the meadow" (ver. 2). That which to thee seemeth long, is "soon" in the sight of God. Conform thou thyself to God; and it will be "soon" to thee. That

which he here calls "grass," that we understand by the "herbs of the meadow." They are some worthless things, occupying the surface only of the ground, they have no depth of root. In the winter then they are green; but when the summer sun shall begin to scorch, they will wither away. For now it is the season of winter. Thy glory cloth not as yet appear. But if thy love hath but a deep root, like that of many trees during winter, the frost passes away, the summer (that is, the Day of Judgment) will come; then will the greenness of the grass wither away. Then will the glory of the trees appear. "For ye" (saith the Apostle) "are dead." even as trees seem to be in winter, as it were dead, as it were withered. What is our hope then, if we are dead? The root is within; where our root is, there is our life also, for there our love is fixed. "And your life is hid with Christ in God." When shall he wither who is thus rooted? But when will our spring be? When our summer? When will the honour of foliage clothe us around, and the fulness of fruit make us rich? When shall this come to pass? Hear what follows: "When Christ, who is our life, shall appear, then shall ye also appear with Him in glory." And what then shall we do now? "Be not envious because of the evil-doers, neither be envious against the workers of iniquity. For they shall soon wither like the grass, and fade like the herb of the meadow."

4. What shouldest thou do then? "Trust in the Lord" (ver. 3). For they too trust, but not "in the Lord." Their hope is perishable. Their hope is short-lived, frail, fleeting, transitory, baseless. "Trust thou in the Lord." "Behold," thou sayest, "I do trust; what am I to do?"

"And do good." Do not do that evil which thou beholdest in those men, who are prosperous in wickedness. "Do good, and dwell in the land." Lest haply thou shouldest be doing good without "dwelling in the land." For it is the Church that is the Lord's land. It is her whom He, the Father, the tiller of it, waters and cultivates. For there are many that, as it were, do good works, but yet, in that they do not "dwell in the land," they do not belong to the husbandman. Therefore do thou thy good, not outside of the land, but do thou "dwell in the land." And what shall I have?

"And thou shalt be fed in its riches." What are the riches of that land? Her riches are her Lord! Her riches are her God l He it is to whom it is said, "The Lord is the portion of mine inheritance, and of my cup." In a late discourse we suggested to you, dearly beloved, that God is our possession, and that we are at the same time God's possession. Hear how that He is Himself the riches of that land.

"Delight thyself in the Lord" (ver. 4). As if thou hadst put the question, and hadst said "Show me the riches of that land, in which thou biddest me dwell, he says, "Delight thyself in the Lord."

5. "And He shall give thee the desires of thine heart." Understand in their proper signification, "the desires of thine heart." Distinguish the "desires of thine heart" from the desires of thy flesh; distinguish as much as thou canst. It is not without a meaning that it is said in a certain Psalm, "God is" (the strength) "of mine heart." For there it says in what follows: "And God is my portion for ever." For instance: One labours under bodily blindness. He asks that he may receive his sight. Let him ask it; for God does that too, and gives those blessings also. But these things are asked for even by the wicked. This is a desire of the flesh. One is sick, and prays to be made sound. From the point of death he is restored to health. That too is a desire of the flesh, as are all of such a kind. What is "the desire of the heart"? As the desire of the flesh is to wish to have one's eyesight restored, to enable him, that is, to see that light, which can be seen by such eyes; so "the desire of the heart" relates to a different sort of light. For, "Blessed are the pure in heart, for they shall see God. Delight thou thyself in the Lord; and He shall give thee the desires of thine heart."

6. "Behold" (you say), "I do long after it, I do ask for it, I do desire it. Shall I then accomplish it?" No. Who shall then? "Reveal thy way unto the Lord: trust also in Him, and He shall bring it to pass" (ver. 5). Mention to Him what thou sufferest, mention to Him what thou dost desire. For what is it that thou sufferest? "The flesh lusteth against the spirit, and the spirit against the flesh." What is it then that thou dost desire? "Wretched man that I am! Who shall deliver me from the body of this death?" And because it is He "Himself" that "will bring it to pass," when thou shall have "revealed thy ways unto Him;" hear what follows: "The grace of God through Jesus Christ our Lord." What is it then that He is to bring to pass, since it is said, "Reveal thy way unto Him, and He will bring it to pass"? What will He bring to pass?

"And He shall bring forth thy righteousness as the light" (ver. 6). For now, "thy righteousness" is hid. Now it is a thing of faith; not yet of sight. You believe something that you may do it. You do not yet see that in which you believe. But when thou shall begin to see that, which thou didst believe before, "thy righteousness will be brought forth to the light," because it is thy faith that was thy righteousness. For "the just lives by faith."

7. "And He shall bring forth thy judgment as the noon-day." That is to say, "as the clear light." It was too little to say, "as the light." For we call it "light" already, even when it but dawns: we call it light even while the sun is rising. But never is the light brighter than at mid-day. Therefore He will not only "bring forth thy righteousness as the light," but "thy judgment shall be as the noon-day." For now dost thou make thy "judgment" to follow Christ. This is thy purposé: this is thy choice: this is thy "judgment."...

8. "What should I do then?" Hear what thou shouldest do. "Submit thee to the Lord, and entreat Him" (ver. 7). Be this thy life, to obey His commandments. For this is to submit thee to Him; and to entreat Him until He give thee what He hath promised. Let good works "continue;" let prayer "continue." For "men ought always to pray, and not to faint." Wherein dost thou show that thou art "submitted to Him"? In doing what He hath commanded. But haply thou dost not receive thy wages as yet, because as yet thou art not able. For He is already able to give them; but thou art not already able to receive them. Exercise thou thyself in works. Labour in the vineyard; at the close of the day crave thy wages. "Faithful is He" who brought thee into the vineyard. "Submit thee to the Lord, and entreat Him."

9. "See! I do so; I do 'submit to the Lord, and I do entreat.' But what do you think? That neighbour of mine is a wicked man, living a bad life, and prosperous! His thefts, adulteries, robberies, are known to me. Lifted up above every one, proud, and raised on high by wickedness, he deigns not to notice me. In these circumstances, how shall I hold out with patience?" This is a sickness; drink, by way of remedy. "Fret not thyself because of him who prospereth in his way." He prospereth, but it is "in his way:" thou sufferest, but it is in God's way! His portion is prosperity on his way, misery on arriving at its end: yours, toil on the road, happiness in its termination. "The Lord knoweth the way of the righteous; and the way of the ungodly shall perish." Thou walkest those ways which "the Lord knoweth," and if thou dost suffer toil in them, they do not deceive thee. The "way of the ungodly" is but a transitory happiness; at the end of the way the happiness is at an end also. Why? Because that way is "the broad road;" its termination leads to the pit of hell. Now, thy way is narrow; and "few there be" that enter in through it: but into how ample a field it comes at the last, thou oughtest to consider. "Fret not thyself at him who prospereth in his way; because of the man who bringeth wicked devices to pass."

"Cease from anger, and forsake wrath" (ver. 8). Wherefore art thou wroth? Wherefore is it that, through that passion and indignation, thou dost blaspheme, or almost blaspheme? Against "the man who bringeth wicked devices to pass, cease from anger, and forsake wrath." Knowest thou not whither that wrath tempts thee on? Thou art on the point of saying unto God, that He is unjust. It tends to that. "Look! why is that man prosperous, and this man in adversity?" Consider what thought it begets: stifle the wicked notion. "Cease from anger, and forsake wrath:" so that now returning to thy senses, thou mayest say, "Mine eye is disturbed because of wrath." What eye is that, but the eye of faith? To the eye of thy faith I appeal. Thou didst believe in Christ: why didst thou believe? What did He promise thee? If it was the happiness of this world that Christ promised thee, then murmur against Christ; yes! murmur against Him, when thou seest the wicked flourishing. What of happiness did He promise? What, save in the Resurrection of the Dead? But what in this life? That which was His portion. His portion, I say! Dost thou, servant and disciple, disdain what thy Lord, what thy Master bore? ...

"For evil-doers shall be cut off" (ver. 9). "But I see their prosperity." Believe Him who saith, "they shall be cut off;" Him who seeth better than thou, since His eye anger cannot cloud. "For evil-doers shall be cut off. But those that wait upon the Lord,"—not upon any one that can deceive them; but verily on Him who is the Truth itself,—"But those that wait upon the Lord, they shall inherit the land." What "land," but that Jerusalem, with the love of which whosoever is inflamed, shall come to peace at the last.

10. "But how long is the sinner to flourish? How long shall I have to endure?" Thou art impatient; that which seems long to thee, will soon come to pass. It is infirmity makes that seem long, which is really short, as is found in the case of the longings of sick men. Nothing seems so long as the mixing of the potion for him when athirst. For all that his attendants are making all speed, lest haply the patient be angry; "When will it be done? (he cries). When will it be drest? When will it be served?" Those who are waiting upon you are making haste, but your infirmity fancies that long which is being done with expedition. Behold ye, therefore, our Physician complying with the infirmity of the patient, saying, "How long shall I have to endure? How long will it be?"

"Yet a little while, and the sinner shall not be" (ver. 10). Is it certainly among sinners, and because of the sinner, that thou murmurest? "A little while, and he shall not be." Lest haply because I said, "They that wait upon the Lord, they shall inherit the land," thou shouldest think that waiting to be of very long duration. Wait "a little while," thou shalt receive without end what thou waitest for. A little while, a moderate space. Review the years from Adam's time up to this day; run through the Scriptures. It is almost yesterday that he fell from Paradise! So many ages have been measured out, and unrolled. Where now are the past ages? Even so, however, shall the few which remain, pass away also. Hadst thou been living throughout all that time, since Adam was banished from Paradise up to this present day, thou wouldest certainly see that the life, which had thus flown away, had not been of long duration. But how long is the duration of each individual's life? Add any number of years you please: prolong old age to its longest duration: what is it? Is it not but a morning breeze? Be it so, however, that the Day of Judgment is far off, when the reward of the righteous and of the unrighteous is to come: your last day at all events cannot be far off. Make thyself ready against this! For such as thou shall have departed from this life, shalt thou be restored to the other. At the close of that short life, you will not yet be, where the Saints shall be, to whom it shall be said, "Come, ye blessed of My Father: inherit the kingdom prepared for you from the beginning of the world." You will not yet be there? Who does not know that? But you may already be there, where that beggar, once "covered with sores," was seen at a distance, at rest, by that proud and unfruitful "rich man" in the midst of his torments. Surely hid in that rest thou waitest in security for the Day of Judgment, when thou art to receive again a body, to be changed so as to be made equal to an Angel. How long then is that for which we are impatient, and are saying, "When will it come? Will it tarry long?" This our sons will say hereafter, and our sons' sons will say too; and, though each one of these in succession will say this same thing, that "little while" that is yet to be, passes away, as all that is already past hath passed away already! O thou sick one! "Yet a little while, and the sinner shall not be. Yea, thou shalt diligently consider his place, and thou shalt not find him." ...

11. "But the meek shall inherit the land" (ver. 11). That land is the one of which we have often spoken, the holy Jerusalem, which is to be released from these her pilgrimages, and to live for ever with God, and on God. Therefore, "They shall inherit the land." What shall be their delight? "And they shall delight themselves in the abundance of peace." Let the ungodly man delight himself here in the multitude of his gold, in the multitude of his silver, in the multitude of his slaves, in the multitude, lastly, of his baths, his roses, his intoxicating wines, his most sumptuous and luxurious banquets. Is this the power thou enviest? Is this the glory- that delights thee? Would not his fate be worthy to be deplored, even if he were to be so for ever? What shall be thy delights? "And they shall delight themselves in the abundance of peace." Peace shall be thy gold. Peace shall be thy silver. Peace shall be thy lands. Peace shall be thy life, thy God Peace. Peace shall be to thee whatsoever thou dost desire. ...

On the Second Part of the Psalm.

1. Then follow these words: "The wicked plotteth against the just, and gnasheth upon him with his teeth" (ver. 12): "But the Lord shall laugh at him" (ver. 13). At whom? Surely at the sinner, "gnashing upon" the other "with his teeth." But wherefore shall the Lord" laugh at him"? "For He foreseeth that his day is coming." He seems indeed full of wrath, while, ignorant of the morrow that is in store for him, he is threatening the just. But the Lord beholds and "foresees his day." "What day?" That in which "He will render to every man according to his works." For he is "treasuring up unto himself wrath against the day of wrath, and revelation of the just judgment of God." But it is the Lord that foresees it; thou dost not foresee it. It hath been revealed to thee by Him who foresees it. Thou didst not know of the "day of the unrighteous," in which he is to suffer punishment. But He who knows it hath revealed it to thee. It is a main part of knowledge to join thyself to Him who hath knowledge. He hath the eyes of knowledge: have thou the eyes of a believing mind. That which God "sees," be thou willing to believe. For the day of the unjust, which God foresees, will come. What day is that? The day for all vengeance! For it is necessary that vengeance should be taken upon the ungodly, that vengeance be taken upon the unjust, whether he turn, or whether he turn not. For if he shall turn from his ways, that very thing, that his "injustice is come to an end," is the infliction of vengeance. ...

2. "The wicked have drawn out the sword, and have bent their bow, to cast down the poor and needy, and to slay such as be of upright heart" (ver. 14). "Their weapon shall enter into their own heart" (ver. 15). It is an easy thing for his weapon, that is, his sword, to reach thy body, even as the sword of the persecutors reached the body of the Martyrs, but when the body had been smitten, "the heart" remained unhurt; but his heart who "drew out the sword against" the body of the just did not clearly remain unhurt. This is attested by this very Psalm. It saith, Their weapon, that is, "Their sword shall," not go into their body, but, "their weapon shall go into their own heart." They would fain have slain him in the body. Let them die the death of the soul. For those whose bodies they sought to kill, the Lord hath freed from anxiety, saying, "Fear not them who kill the body, but cannot kill the soul." ...

3. "And their bows shall be broken." What is meant by, "And their bows shall be broken"? Their plots shall be frustrated. For above He haft-said, "The wicked have drawn out the sword and bent their bows." By the "drawing out of the sword" he would have understood open hostility; but by the" bending of the bow," secret conspiracies. See! His sword destroys himself, and his laying of snares is frustrated. What is meant by frustrated? That it does no mischief to the righteous. How then, for instance (you ask), did it do no mischief to the man, whom it thus

stripped of his goods, whom it reduced to straitened circumstances by taking away his possessions? He has still cause to sing, "A little that a righteous man hath, is better than great riches of the ungodly" (ver. 16).

4. ... "For the arms of the wicked shall be broken" (ver. 17). Now by "their arms" is meant their power. What will he do in hell? Will it be what the rich man had to do, he who was wont "to fare sumptuously" in the upper world, and in hell "was tormented"? Therefore their arms shall be broken; "but the Lord upholdeth the righteous." How does He "uphold" them? What saith He unto them? Even what is said in another Psalm, "Wait on the Lord, be of good courage; and let thine heart be strengthened. Wait, I say, on the Lord." What is meant by this, "Wait on the Lord"? Thou sufferest but for a time; thou shalt rest for ever: thy trouble is short; thy happiness is to be everlasting. It is but for "a little while" thou art to sorrow; thy joy shall have no end. But in the midst of trouble does thy "foot" begin to "slip"? The example even of Christ's sufferings is set before thee. Consider what He endured for thee, in whom no cause was found why He should endure it? How great soever be thy sufferings, thou wilt not come to those insults, those scourgings, to that robe of shame, to that crown of thorns, and last of all to that Cross, which He endured; because that is now removed from the number of human punishments. For though under the ancients criminals were crucified, in the present day no one is crucified. It was honoured, and it came to an end. It came to an end as a punishment; it is continued in glory. It hath removed from the place of execution to the foreheads of Emperors. He who hath invested His very sufferings with such honour, what doth He reserve for His faithful servants? ...

5. But observe whether that was fulfilled in his case which the Psalm now speaks of. "The Lord strengtheneth the righteous.—Not only so" (saith that same Paul, whilst suffering many evils), "but we glory in tribulations also: knowing that tribulation worketh patience, and patience experience; and experience hope; but hope maketh not ashamed, because the love of God is shed abroad in our hearts by the Holy Ghost, which is given unto us." Justly is it said by him, now righteous, now "strengthened." As therefore those who persecuted him did no harm to him, when now "strengthened," so neither did he himself do any harm to those whom he persecuted. "But the Lord," he saith, "strengtheneth the righteous." ...

6. Therefore "the Lord does strengthen the righteous." In what way does He strengthen them? "The Lord knoweth the ways of the spotless ones" (ver. 18). When they suffer ills, they are believed to be walking ill ways by those who are ignorant, by those who have not knowledge to discern "the ways of the spotless ones." He who "knoweth those ways," knoweth by what way to lead His own,

"them that are gentle," in the right way. Whence in another Psalm he said, "The meek shall He guide in judgment; them that are gentle will He teach His way." How, think you, was that beggar, who lay covered with sores before the rich man's door, spurned by the passers by! How did they, probably, close their nostrils and spit at him! The Lord, however, knew how to reserve Paradise for him. How did they, on the other hand, desire for themselves the life of him who was "clad in purple and fine linen, and fared sumptuously every day!" But the Lord, who foresaw that man's "day coming," knew the torments, the torments without end, that were in store for him. Therefore "The Lord knoweth the ways of the upright."

7. "And their inheritance shall be for ever" (ver. 18). This we hold by faith. Doth the Lord too know it by faith? The Lord knoweth those things with as clear a manifestation, as we cannot speak of even when we shall be made equal to the Angels. For the things that shall be manifest to us, shall not be equally manifest to us as they are now to Him, who is incapable of change. Yet even of us ourselves what is said? "Beloved, now are we the sons of God: and it doth not yet appear what we shall be: but we know that, when He shall appear, we shall be like Him, for we shall see Him as He is." There is therefore surely some blissful vision reserved for us; and if it can be now in some measure conceived, "darkly and through a glass," yet cannot we in any way express in language the ravishing beauty of that bliss, which God reserves for them that fear Him, which He consummates in those that hope in Him, It is for that destination that our hearts are being disciplined in all the troubles and trials of this life. Wonder not that it is in trouble that thou art disciplined for it. It is for something glorious that thou art being disciplined. Whence comes that speech of the now strengthened righteous man: "The sufferings of this present time are not worthy to be compared to the glory which shall be revealed in us"? What is that promised glory to be, but to be made equal to the Angels and to see God? How great a benefit doth he bestow on the blind man, who makes his eyes sound so as to be able to see the light of this life. ... What reward then shall we give unto that Physician who restores soundness to our inward eyes, to enable them to see a certain eternal Light, which is Himself? ...

8. "They shall not be ashamed in the evil time" (ver. 19). In the day of trouble, in the day of distress, they shall not be "ashamed," as he is ashamed whose hope deceives him. Who is the man that is "ashamed"? He who saith, "I have not found that which I was in hopes of." Nor undeservedly either; for thou didst hope it from thyself or from man, thy friend. But "cursed is he that putteth his trust in man." Thou art ashamed, because thy hope hath deceived thee; thy hope that was set on a lie. For "every man is a liar." But if thou dost place thy hopes on thy God, thou art

not made "ashamed." For He in whom thou hast put thy trust, cannot be deceived. Whence also the man whom we mentioned just above, the now "strengthened" righteous man, when fallen on an evil time, on the day of tribulation, what saith he to show that he was not "ashamed"? "We glory in tribulation; knowing that tribulation worketh patience, and patience experience, and experience hope; but hope maketh not ashamed." Whence is it that hope "maketh not ashamed"? Because it is placed on God. Therefore follows immediately, "Because the love of God is spread in our hearts by the Holy Spirit, which is given unto us." The Holy Spirit hath been given to us already: how should He deceive us, of whom we possess such an "earnest" already? "They shall not be ashamed in the evil time, and in the days of famine they shall be satisfied." ...

9. "For the wicked shall perish. But the enemies of the Lord, when they shall begin to glory, and to be lifted up, immediately shall consume away utterly, even as the smoke" (ver. 20). Recognise from the comparison itself the thing which he intimates. Smoke, breaking forth from the place where fire has been, rises up on high, and by the very act of rising up, it swells into a large volume: but the larger that volume is, the more unsubstantial does it become; for from that very largeness of volume, which has no foundation or consistency, but is merely loose, shifting and evanescent, it passes into air, and dissolves; so that you perceive its very largeness to have been fatal to it. For the higher it ascends, the farther it is extended, the wider the circumference which it spreads itself over, the thinner, and the more rare and wasting and evanescent does it become. "But the enemies of the Lord, when they shall begin to glory, and to be lifted up, immediately shall consume away utterly even as the smoke." Of such as these was it said, "As Jannes and Jambres withstood Moses, so do these also resist the Truth; men of corrupt minds, reprobate concerning the faith." But how is it that they resist the Truth, except by the vain inflation of their swelling pride, while they raise themselves up on high, as if great and righteous persons, though on the point of passing away into empty air? But what saith he of them? As if speaking of smoke, he says, "They shall proceed no farther, for their folly shall be manifest unto all men, even as theirs also was." ...

10. "The wicked borroweth, and payeth not again" (ver. 20). He receiveth, and will not repay. What is it he will not repay? Thanksgiving. For what is it that God would have of thee, what doth He require of thee, except that He may do thee good? And how great are the benefits which the sinner hath received, and which he will not repay! He hath received the gift of being; he hath received the gift of being a man; and of a being highly distinguished above the brutes; he hath received the form of a body, and the distinction of the senses in the body, eyes for

seeing, ears for hearing, the nostrils for smelling, the palate for tasting, the hands for touching, and the feet for walking; and even the very health and soundness of the body. But up to this point we have these things in common even with the brute; he hath received yet more than this; a mind capable of understanding, capable of Truth, capable of distinguishing right from wrong; capable of seeking after, of longing for, its Creator, of praising Him, and fixing itself upon Him. All this the wicked man hath received as well as others; but by not living well, he fails to repay that which he owes. Thus it is, "the wicked borroweth, and payeth not again:" he will not requite Him from whom he hath received; he will not return thanks; nay, he will even render evil for good, blasphemies, murmuring against God, indignation. Thus it is that he "borroweth, and payeth not again; but the righteous showeth mercy, and lendeth" (ver. 21). The one therefore hath nothing; the other hath. See, on the one side, destitution: see, on the other, wealth. The one receiveth and "payeth not again:" the "other showeth mercy, and lendeth:" and he hath more than enough. What if he is poor? Even so he is rich; do you but look at his riches with the eyes of Religion. For thou lookest at the empty chest; but dost not look at the conscience, that is full of God. ...

11. "For such as shall bless Him shall inherit the land" (ver. 23), that is, they shall possess that righteous One: the only One who both is truly righteous, and maketh righteous: who both was poor in this world, and brought great riches to it, wherewith to make those rich whom He found poor. For it is He who hath enriched the hearts of the poor with the Holy Spirit; and having emptied out their souls by confession of sins, hath filled them with the richness of righteousness: He who was able to enrich the fisherman, who, by forsaking his nets, spurned what he possessed already, but sought to draw up what he possessed not. For "God hath chosen the weak things of the world to confound the things which are mighty." And it was not by an orator that He gained to Himself the fisherman; but by the fisherman that He gained to Himself the orator; by the fisherman that He gained the Senator; by the fisherman that He gained the Emperor. For "such as shall bless Him shall inherit the land;" they shall be fellow- heirs with Him, in that "land of the living," of which it is said in another Psalm, "Thou art my hope, my portion in the land of the living." ...

12. Observe what follows: "The steps of a good man are ordered by the Lord; and he delighteth in His way" (ver. 23). That man may himself "delight in the Lord's way," his steps are ordered by the Lord Himself. For if the Lord did not order the steps of man, so crooked are they naturally, that they would always be going through crooked paths, and by pursuing crooked ways, would be unable to return again. He however came, and called us, and redeemed us, and shed His blood; He

hath given this ransom; He hath done this good, and suffered these evils. Consider Him in what He hath done, He is God! Consider Him in what He hath suffered, He is Man! Who is that God-Man? Hadst not thou, O man, forsaken God, God would not have been made Man for thee! For that was too little for thee to requite, or for Him to bestow, that He had made thee man; unless He Himself should become Man for thee also. For it is He Himself that hath "ordered our steps;" that we should "delight in His way." ...

13. Now if man were to be through the whole of his life in toil, and in sufferings, in pain, in tortures, in prison, in scourgings, in hunger, and in thirst, every day and every hour through the whole length of life, to the period of old age, yet the whole life of man is but a few days. That labour being over, there is to come the Eternal Kingdom; there is to come happiness without end; there is to come equality with the Angels; there is to come Christ's inheritance, and Christ, our "joint Heir," is to come. How great is the labour, for which thou receivest so great a recompense? The Veterans who serve in the wars, and move in the midst of wounds for so many years, enter upon the military service from their youth, and quit it in old age: and to obtain a few days of repose in their old age, when age itself begins to weigh down those whom the wars do not break down, how great hardships do they endure; what marches, what frosts, what burning suns; what privations, what wounds, and what dangers! And while suffering all these things, they fix their thoughts on nothing but those few days of repose in old age, at which they know not whether they will ever arrive. Thus it is, the "steps of a good man are ordered by the Lord, and he delighteth in His way." This is the point with which I commenced. If thou dost "delight in the way" of Christ, and art truly a Christian (for he is a Christian indeed who does not despise the way of Christ, but "delighteth in" following Christ's "way" through His sufferings), do not thou go by any other way than that by which He Himself hath also gone. It appears painful, but it is the very way of safety; another perhaps is delightful, but it is full of robbers. "And he delighteth in His way."

14. "Though he fall, he shall not be utterly cast down; for the Lord upholdeth his hand" (ver. 24). See what it is "to delight in" Christ's "way." Should it happen that he suffers some tribulation; some forfeiture of honour, some affliction, some loss, some contumely, or all those other accidents incident to mankind frequently in this life, he sets the Lord before him, what kind of trials He endured! and, "though he fall he shall not be utterly cast down, for the Lord upholdeth his hand," because He has suffered before him. For what shouldest thou fear, O man, whose steps are ordered so, that thou shouldest "delight in the way of the Lord"? What shouldest thou fear? Pain? Christ was scourged. Shouldest thou fear contumelies? He was

reproached with, "Thou hast a devil," who was Himself casting out the devils. Haply thou fearest faction, and the conspiracy of the wicked. Conspiracy was made against Him. Thou canst not make clear the purity of thy conscience in some accusation, and sufferest wrong and violence, because false witnesses are listened to against thee. False witness was borne against Him first, not only before His death, but also after His resurrection. ...

On the Third Part of the Psalm.

1. "I have been young, and now am old; yet have I not seen the righteous forsaken, nor his seed begging bread" (ver. 25).

If it is spoken but in the person of one single individual, how long is the whole life of one man? And what is there wonderful in the circumstance, that a single man, fixed in some one part of the earth, should not, throughout the whole space of his life, being so short as maws life is, have ever seen "the righteous forsaken, nor his seed begging bread," although he may have advanced from youth to age. It is not anything worthy of marvel; for it might have happened, that before his lifetime there should have been some "righteous man seeking bread;" it might have happened, that there had been some one in some other part of the earth not where he himself was. Hear too another thing, which makes an impression upon us. Any single one among you (look you) who has now grown old, may perhaps, when, looking back upon the past course of his life, he turns over in his thoughts the persons whom he has known, not find any instance of a righteous man begging bread, or of his seed begging bread, suggest itself to him; but nevertheless he turns to the inspired Scriptures, and finds that righteous Abraham was straitened, and suffered hunger in his own country, and left that land for another; he finds too that the son of the very same man, Isaac, removed to other countries in search of bread, for the same cause of hunger. And how will it be true to say, "I have never seen the righteous forsaken, nor his seed begging bread"? And if he finds this true in the duration of his own life, he finds it is otherwise in the inspired writings, which are more trustworthy than human life is.

2. What are we to do then? Let us be seconded by your pious attention, so that we may discern the purpose of God in these verses of the Psalm, what it is He would have us understand by them. For there is a fear, lest any unstable person, not capable of understanding the Scriptures spiritually, should appeal to human instances, and should observe the virtuous servants of God to be sometimes in some necessity, and in want, so as to be compelled to beg bread: should

particularly call to mind the Apostle Paul, who says, "In hunger and thirst; in cold and nakedness;" and should stumble thereat, saying to himself, "Is that certainly true which I have been singing? Is that certainly true, which I have been sounding forth in so devout a voice, standing in church? 'I have never seen the righteous forsaken, nor his seed begging bread.'" Lest he should say in his heart, "Scripture deceives us;" and all his limbs should be paralyzed to good works: and when those limbs within him, those limbs of the inner man, shall have been paralyzed (which is the more fearful paralysis), he should henceforth leave off from good works, and say to himself, "Wherefore do I do good works? Wherefore do I break my bread to the hungry, and clothe the naked, and take home to mine house him who hath no shelter, putting faith in that which is written? I have never seen the righteous forsaken, nor his seed begging bread;' whereas I see so many persons who live virtuously, yet for the most part suffering from hunger. But if perhaps I am in error in thinking the man who is living well, and the man who is living ill, to be both of them living well, and if God knows him to be otherwise; that is, knows him, whom I think just, to be unjust, what am I to make of Abraham's case, who is commended by Scripture itself as a righteous person? What am I to make of the Apostle Paul, who says, 'Be ye followers of me, even as I also am of Christ.' What? that I should myself be in evils such as he endured, 'In hunger and thirst, in cold and nakedness'?"

3. Whilst therefore he thus thinks, and whilst his limbs are paralyzed to the power of good works, can we, my brethren, as it were, lift up the sick of the palsy; and, as it were, "lay open the roof" of this Scripture, and let him down before the Lord? For you observe that it is obscure. If obscure therefore, it is covered. And I behold a certain patient paralytic in mind, and I see this roof, and am convinced that Christ is concealed beneath the roof. Let me, as far as I am able, do that which was praised in those who opened the roof, and let down the sick of the palsy before Christ; that He might say unto him, "Son, be of good cheer, thy sins be forgiven thee." For it was so that He made the inner man whole of his palsy, by loosing his sins, by binding fast his faith. ...

4. But who is "the righteous" man, who "hath never been seen forsaken, nor his seed begging bread"? If you understand what is meant by "bread," you understand who is meant by him. For the "bread" is the Word of God, which never departs from the righteous man's mouth. ... See now if "holy meditation doth 'keep thee'" in the rumination of this bread, then "hast thou never seen the righteous forsaken, nor his seed begging bread."

5. "He is always merciful, and lendeth" (ver. 26). "Foeneratur" is used in Latin indeed, both for him who lendeth, and for him who borroweth. But in this passage the meaning is more plain, if we express it by "foenerat." What matters it to us, what the grammarians please to rule? It were better for us to be guilty of a barbarism, so that ye understand, than that in our propriety of speech ye be left unprovided. Therefore, that "righteous man is all day merciful, and (foenerat) lendeth." Let not the lenders of money on usury, however, rejoice. For we find it is a particular kind of lender that is spoken of, as it was a particular kind of bread; that we may, in all passages, "remove the roof," and find our way to Christ. I would not have you be lenders of money on usury; and I would not have you be such for this reason, because God would not have you. ... Whence does it appear that God would not have it so? It is said in another place, "He that putteth not out his money to usury." And how detestable, odious, and execrable a thing it is, I believe that even usurers themselves know. Again, on the other hand, I myself, nay rather our God Himself bids thee be an usurer, and says to thee, "Lend unto God." If thou lendest to man, hast thou hope? and shalt thou not have hope, if thou lendest to God? If thou hast lent thy money on usury to man, that is, if thou hast given the loan of thy money to one, from whom thou dost expect to receive something more than thou hast given, not in money only, but anything, whether it be wheat, or wine, or oil, or whatever else you please, if you expect to receive more than you have given, you are an usurer, and in this particular are not deserving of praise, but of censure. "What then," you say, "am I to do, that I may 'lend' profitably?" Consider what the usurer does. He undoubtedly desires to give a less sum, and to receive a larger; do thou this also; give thou a little, receive much. See how thy principal grows, and increases l Give "things temporal," receive "things eternal:" give earth, receive heaven! And perhaps thou wouldest say, "To whom shall I give them?" The self-same Lord, who bade thee not lend on usury, comes forward as the Person to whom thou shouldest lend on usury! Hear from Scripture in what way thou mayest "lend unto the Lord." "He that hath pity on the poor, lendeth unto the Lord." For the Lord wanteth not aught of thee. But thou hast one who needs somewhat of thee: thou extendest it to him; he receives it. For the poor hath nothing to return to thee, and yet he would himself fain requite thee, and finds nothing wherewith to do it: all that remains in his power is the good-will that desires to pray for thee. Now when the poor man prays for thee, he, as it were, says unto God, "Lord, I have borrowed this; be Thou surety for me." Then, though you have no bond on the poor man to compel his repayment, yet you have on a sponsible security. See, God from His own Scriptures saith unto thee; "Give it, and fear not; I repay it. It is to Me thou givest it." In what way do those who make themselves sureties for others, express themselves? What is it that they say? "I repay it: I take it upon myself. It is to me you are giving it." Do we then suppose that God also says this, "I take it on Myself. It is unto me thou givest it"? Assuredly, if Christ be God, of which there is no doubt, He hath Himself said, "I

was an hungred, and ye gave Me meat." And when they said unto Him, "When saw we Thee hungry?" that He might show Himself to be the Surety for the poor, that He answers for all His members, that He is the Head, they the members, and that when the members receive, the Head receiveth also; He says, "Inasmuch as ye have done it to one of the least of these that belong to Me, ye have done it unto Me." Come, thou covetous usurer, consider what thou hast given; consider what thou art to receive. Hadst thou given a small sum of money, and he to whom thou hadst given it were to give thee for that small sum a great villa, worth incomparably more money than thou hadst given, how great thanks wouldest thou render, with how great joy wouldest thou be transported! Hear what possession He to whom thou hast been lending bestows. "Come, ye blessed of My Father, receive"—What? The same that they have given? God forbid! What you gave were earthly things, which, if you had not given them, would have; become corrupted on earth. For what could you have made of them, if you had not given them? That which on earth would have been lost, has been preserved in heaven. Therefore what we are to receive is that which hath been preserved. It is thy desert that hath been preserved, thy desert hath been made thy treasure. For consider what it is that thou art to receive. Receive—" the kingdom prepared for you from the foundation of the world." On the other hand, what shall be their sentence, who would not "lend"? "Go ye into everlasting fire, prepared for the devil and his angels." And what is the kingdom which we receive called? Consider what follows: "And these shall go into everlasting burning; but the righteous into life eternal." Make interest for this; purchase this. Give your money on usury to earn this. You have Christ throned in heaven, begging on earth. We have discovered in what way the righteous lendeth. "He is alway merciful, and lendeth."

6. "And his seed is blessed." Here too let not any carnal notion suggest itself. We see many of the sons of the righteous dying of hunger; in what sense then will his seed be blessed? His seed is that which remains of him afterwards that wherewith he soweth here, and will hereafter reap. For the Apostle says, "Let us not be weary in well-doing; for in due season we shall reap if we faint not. As we have therefore time," he says, "let us do good unto all men." This is that "seed" of thine which shall "be blessed." You commit it to the earth, and gather ever so much more; and dost thou lose it in committing it to Christ? See it expressly termed "seed" by the Apostle, when he was speaking of alms. For this he saith; "He which soweth sparingly, shall reap also sparingly and he which soweth in blessings? shall also reap in blessings." ...

7. Observe therefore what follows, and be not slothful. "Depart from evil, and do good" (ver. 27). Do not think it to be enough for thee to do, if thou dost not strip

the man who is already clothed. For in not stripping the man who is already clothed, thou hast indeed "departed from evil:" but do not be barren, and wither. So choose not to strip the man who is clothed already, as to clothe the naked. For this is to "depart from evil, and to do good." And you will say, "What advantage am I to derive from it?" He to whom thou lendest has already assured thee of what He will give thee. He will give thee everlasting life. Give to Him, and fear not! Hear too what follows: "Depart from evil, and do good, and dwell for evermore." And think not when thou givest that no one sees thee, or that God forsakes thee, when haply after thou hast given to the poor, and some loss, or some sorrow for the property thou hast lost, should follow, and thou shouldest say to thyself, "What hath it profited me to have done good works? I believe God doth not love the men who do good." Whence comes that buzz, that subdued murmur among you, except that those expressions are very common? Each one of you at this present moment recognises these expressions, either in his own lips, or on those of his friend. May God destroy them; may He root out the thorns from His field; may He plant "the good seed," and "the tree bearing fruit"! For wherefore art thou afflicted, O man, that thou hast given some things away to the poor, and hast lost certain other things? Seest thou not that it is what thou hast not given, that thou hast lost? Wherefore dost thou not attend to the voice of thy God? Where is thy faith? wherefore is it so fast asleep? Wake it up in thy heart. Consider what the Lord Himself said unto thee, while exhorting thee to good works of this kind: "Provide yourselves bags which wax not old; a treasure in the heavens that faileth not, where no thief approacheth." Call this to mind therefore when you are lamenting over a loss. Wherefore dost thou lament, thou fool of little mind, or rather of unsound mind? Wherefore didst thou lose it, except that thou didst not lend it to Me? Wherefore didst thou lose it? Who has carried it off? Thou wilt answer, "A thief." Was it not this, that I forewarned thee of? that thou shouldest not lay it up where the thief could approach? If then he who has lost anything, grieves, let him grieve for this, that he did not lay it up there, whence it could not be lost.

8. "For the Lord loveth judgment, and for-saketh not His Saints" (ver. 28). When the Saints suffer affliction, think not that God doth not judge, or doth not judge righteously. Will He, who warns thee to judge righteously, Himself judge unrighteously? He "loveth judgment, and forsaketh not His Saints." But (think) how the "life" of the Saints is "hid with Him," in such a manner, that who now suffer trouble on earth, like trees in the winter-time, having no fruit and leaves, when He, like a newly-risen sun, shall have appeared, that which before was living in their root, will show itself forth in fruits. He does then "love judgment, and doth not forsake His Saints." ...

9. "But the unrighteous shall be punished; the seed of the wicked shall be cut off." Just as the "seed of the" other "shall be blessed," so shall the "seed of the wicked be cut off." For the "seed" of the wicked is the works of the wicked. For again, on the other hand, we find the son of the wicked man flourish in the world, and sometimes become righteous, and flourish in Christ. Be careful therefore how thou takest it; that thou mayest remove the covering, and make thy way to Christ. Do not take the text in a carnal sense; for thou wilt be deceived. But "the seed of the wicked"-all the works of the wicked-" will be cut off:" they shall have no fruit. For they are effective indeed for a short time; afterwards they shall seek for them, and shall not find the reward of that which they have wrought. For it is the expression of those who lose what they have wrought, that text which says, "What hath pride profired us, or what good hath riches with our vaunting brought us? All those things are passed away like a shadow." "The seed of the wicked," then, "shall be cut off."

10. "The righteous shall inherit the land" (ver. 29). Here again let not covetousness steal on thee, nor promise thee some great estate; hope not to find there, what you are commanded to despise in this world. That "land" in the text, is a certain "land of the living," the kingdom of the Saints. Whence it is said: "Thou art my hope, my portion in the land of the living." For if thy life too is the same life as that there spoken of, think what sort of "land" thou art about to inherit. That is "the land of the living;" this the land of those who are about to die: to receive again, when dead those whom it nourished when living. Such then as is that land, such shall the life itself be also: if the life be for ever, "the land" also is to be thine "for ever." And how is "the land" to be thine "for ever"?

"And they Shall dwell therein" (it says) "for ever." It must therefore be another land, where "they are to dwell therein for ever." For of this land (of this earth) it is said, "Heaven and earth shall pass away."

11. "The mouth of the righteous speaketh wisdom" (ver. 30). See here is that "bread." Observe with what satisfaction this righteous man feedeth upon it; how he turns wisdom over and over in his mouth. "And his tongue talketh of judgment."

"The law of his God is in his heart" (ver. 31). Lest haply thou shouldest think him to have that on his lips, which he hath not in his heart, lest thou shouldest reckon him among those of whom it is said, "This people honour Me with their lips, but their heart is far from Me." And of what use is this to him?

"And none of his steps shall slide." The "word of God in the heart" frees from the snare; the "word of God in the heart" delivers from the evil way; "the word of God in the heart" delivers from "the slippery place." He is with thee, Whose word departeth not from thee. Now what evil doth he suffer, whom God keepeth? Thou settest a watchman in thy vineyard, and feelest secure from thieves; and that watchman may sleep, and may himself fall, and may admit a thief. But "He who keepeth Israel shall neither slumber nor sleep." "The law of his God is in his heart, and none of his steps shall slide." Let him therefore live free from fear; let him live free from fear even in the midst of the wicked; free from fear even in the midst of the ungodly. For what evil can the ungodly or unrighteous man do to the righteous? Lo! see what follows.

"The wicked watcheth the righteous, and seeketh to slay him" (ver. 32). For he says, what it was foretold in the book of Wisdom that he should say, "He is grievous unto us, even to behold; for his life is not like other men's." Therefore he "seeks to slay him." What? Doth the Lord, who keepeth him, who dwelleth with him, who departeth not from his lips, from his heart, doth He forsake him? What then becomes of what was said before: "And He forsaketh not His Saints"?

12. "The wicked therefore watcheth the righteous, and seeketh to slay him. But the Lord will not leave him in his hands" (ver. 33). Wherefore then did He leave the Martyrs in the hands of the ungodly? Wherefore did they do unto them "whatsoever they would "? Some they slew with the sword; some they crucified; some they delivered to the beasts; some they burnt by fire; others they led about in chains, till wasted out by a long protracted decay. Assuredly "the Lord forsaketh not His Saints." He will not "leave him in his hands." Lastly, wherefore did He leave His own Son in "the hands of the ungodly"? Here also, if thou wouldest have all the limbs of thy inner man made strong, remove the covering of the roof, and find thy way to the Lord. Hear what another Scripture, foreseeing our Lord's future suffering at the hands of the ungodly, saith. What saith it? "The earth is given into the hands of the wicked." What is meant by "earth" being "given into the hands of the ungodly"? The delivering of the flesh into the hands of the persecutors. But God did not leave "His righteous One" there: from the flesh, which was taken captive, He leads. forth the soul unconquered. ...

"The Lord will not leave him in his hand, nor condemn him when there shall be judgment for him" (ver. 33). Some copies have it, "and when He shall judge him, there shall be judgment for him." "For him," however, means when sentence is passed upon him. For we can express ourselves so as to say to a person, "Judge for me," i.e. "hear my cause." When therefore God shall begin to hear the cause of His righteous servant, since "we must all" be presented "before the tribunal of Christ," and stand before it to receive every one "the things he hath done in this body," whether good or evil, when therefore he shall have come to that Judgment, He will not condemn him; though he may seem to be condemned in this present life by man. Even though the Proconsul may have passed sentence on Cyprian, yet the earthly seat of judgment is one thing, the heavenly tribunal is another. From the inferior tribunal he receives sentence of death; from the superior one a crown, "Nor will He condemn him when there shall be judgment for him."

13. "Wait on the Lord" (ver. 34). And while I am waiting upon Him, what am I to do?—"and keep His ways." And if I keep them, what am I to receive? "And He shall exalt thee to inherit the land." "What land"? Once more let not any estate suggest itself to your mind:—the land of which it is said, "Come, ye blessed of My Father, inherit the kingdom prepared for you from the foundation of the world." What of those who have troubled us, in the midst of whom we have groaned, whose scandals we have patiently endured, for whom, while they were raging against us, we have prayed in vain? What will become of them? What follows? "When the wicked are cut off, thou shall see it." ...

"I have seen the ungodly lifted up on high, and rising above the cedars of Libanus" (ver. 35). And suppose him to be "lifted up on high;" suppose him to be towering above the "rest;" what follows?

"I passed by, and, lo, he was not! I sought him, and his place could nowhere be found!" (ver. 36). Why was he "no more, and his place nowhere to be found"? Because thou hast "passed by." But if thou art yet carnally- minded, and that earthly prosperity appears to thee to be true happiness, thou hast not yet "passed by" him; thou art either his fellow, or thou art below him; go on, and pass him; and when thou hast made progress, and hast passed by him, thou observest him by the eye of faith; thou seest his end, thou sayest to thyself, "Lo! he who so swelled before, is not!" just as if it were some smoke that thou wert passing near to. For this too was said above in this very Psalm, "They shall consume and fade away as the smoke." ...

14. "Keep innocency" (ver. 37); keep it even as thou usedst to keep thy purse, when thou wert covetous; even as thou usedst to hold fast that purse, that it might not be snatched from thy grasp by the thief, even so "keep innocency," lest that be snatched from thy grasp by the devil. Be that thy sure inheritance, of which the

rich and the poor may both be sure. "Keep innocency." What doth it profit thee to gain gold, and to lose innocence?

"Keep innocency, and take heed unto the thing which is right." Keep thou thine eyes "right," that thou mayest see "the thing which is right;" not perverted, wherewith thou lookest upon the wicked; not distorted, so that God should appear to thee distorted and wrong, in that He favours the wicked, and afflicts the faithful with persecutions. Dost thou not observe how distorted thy vision is? Set right thine eyes, and "behold the thing that is right." What "thing that is right"?. Take no heed of things present. And what wilt thou see?

"For there is a remainder for the man that maketh peace." What is meant by "there is a remainder"? When thou art dead, thou shall not be dead. This is the meaning of "there is a remainder." He will still have something remaining to him, even after this life, that is to say, that "seed," which "shall be blessed." Whence our Lord saith, "He that believeth on Me, though he die, yet shall he live;"—"seeing there is a remainder for the man that maketh peace."

15. "But the transgressors shall be destroyed in the self-same thing" (ver. 38). What is meant by, "in the self-same thing"? It means for ever: or all together in one and the same destruction.

"The remainder of the wicked shall be cut off." Now there is "(a remainder) for the man that maketh peace:" they therefore who are not peace-makers s are ungodly. For, "Blessed are the peace-makers: for they shall be called the children of God."

16. "But the salvation of the righteous is of the Lord, and He is their strength in the time of trouble" (ver. 39). "And the Lord shall help them, and deliver them; He shall deliver them from the sinners" (ver. 40). At present therefore let the righteous bear with the sinner; let the wheat bear with the tares; let the grain bear with the chaff: for the time of separation will come, and the good seed shall be set apart from that which is to be consumed with fire. The one will be consigned to the garner, the other to "everlasting burning;" for it was for this reason that the just and the unjust were at the first together; that the one should lay a stumbling-block, that the other should be proved; that afterwards the one should be condemned, the other receive a crown. ...

PSALM XXXVIII.

A PSALM TO DAVID HIMSELF, ON THE REMEMBRANCE OF THE SABBATH.

1. What doth this recollection of the Sabbath mean? What is this Sabbath? For it is with groaning that he "calls it to recollection." You have both heard already when the Psalm was read, and you will now hear it when we shall go over it, how great is his groaning, his mourning, his tears, his misery. But happy he who is wretched after this manner! Whence the Lord also in the Gospels called some who mourn blessed. "How should he be blessed if he is a mourner? How blessed, if he is miserable?" Nay rather, he would be miserable, if he were not a mourner. Such an one then let us understand here too, calling the Sabbath to remembrance (viz.), some mourner or other: and would that we were ourselves that "some one or other"! For there is here some person sorrowing, groaning, mourning, calling the Sabbath to remembrance. The Sabbath is rest. Doubtless he was in some disquietude, who with groaning was calling the Sabbath to remembrance. ...

2. "O Lord, rebuke me not in Thine indignation; neither chasten me in Thy hot displeasure" (ver. 1). For it will be that some shall be chastened in God's "hot displeasure," and rebuked in His "indignation." And haply not all who are "rebuked" will be "chastened;" yet are there some that are to be saved in the chastening. So it is to be indeed, because it is called "chastening," but yet it shall be "so as by fire." But there are to be some who will be "rebuked," and will not be "corrected." For he will at all events "rebuke" those to whom He will say, "I was an hungred, and ye gave me no meat." ... "Neither chasten me in Thy hot displeasure;" so that Thou mayest cleanse me in this life, and make me such, that I may after that stand in no need of the cleansing fire, for those "who are to be saved, yet so as by fire." Why? Why, but because they "build upon the foundation, wood, stubble, and hay." Now they should build on it, "gold, silver, and precious stones;" and should have nothing to fear from either fire: not only that which is to consume the ungodly for ever, but also that which is to purge those who are to escape through the fire. For it is said, "he himself shall be saved, yet so as by fire." And because it is said, "he shall be saved," that fire is thought lightly of. For all that, though we should be "saved by fire," yet will that fire be more grievous than anything that man can suffer in this life whatsoever. ...

3. Now on what ground does this person pray that he may not be "rebuked in indignation, nor chastened in hot displeasure"? (He speaks) as if he would say unto God, "Since the things which I already suffer are many in number, I pray Thee let

them suffice;" and he begins to enumerate them, by way of satisfying God; offering what he suffers now, that he may not have to suffer worse evils hereafter.

4. "For Thine arrows stick fast in me, and Thy hand presseth me sore" (ver. 2). "There is no soundness in my flesh, from the face of Thine anger" (ver. 3). He has now begun telling these evils, which he is suffering here: and yet even this already was from the wrath of the Lord, because it was of the vengeance of the Lord. "Of what vengeance?" That which He took upon Adam. For think not that punishment was not inflicted upon him, or that God had said to no purpose, "Thou shall surely die;" or that we suffer anything in this life, except from that death which we earned by the original sin. ... Whence then do His "arrows stick fast in" him? The very punishment, the very vengeance, and haply the pains both of mind and of body, which it is necessary for us to suffer here, these he describes by these self-same "arrows." For of these arrows holy job also made mention, and said that the arrows of the Lord stuck fast in him, whilst he was labouring under those pains. We are used, however, to call God's words also arrows; but could he grieve that he should be struck by these? The words of God are arrows, as it were, that inflame love, not pain. ... We may then understand the "arrows sticking fast," thus: Thy words are fixed fast in my heart; and by those words themselves is it come to pass, that I "called the Sabbath to remembrance:" and that very remembrance of the Sabbath, and the non-possession of it at present, prevents me from rejoicing at present; and causes me to acknowledge that there "is neither health in my very flesh," neither ought it to be so called when I compare this sort of soundness to that soundness which I am to possess in the everlasting rest; where "this corruptible shall put on incorruption, and this mortal shall put on immortality," and see that in comparison with that soundness this present kind is but sickness.

5. "Neither is there any rest in my bones, from the face of my sin." It is commonly enquired, of what person this is the speech; and some understand it to be Christ's, on account of some things which are here said of the Passion of Christ; to which we shall shortly come; and which we ourselves shall acknowledge to be spoken of His Passion. But how could He who had no sin, say, "There is no rest in my bones, from the face of my sin." ... For if we were to say that they are not the words of Christ, those words, "My God, My God, why hast Thou forsaken Me?" will also not be the words of Christ. For there too you have, "My God, My God, why hast Thou forsaken Me?" "The words of mine offences are far from my health." Just as here you have, "from the face of my sins," so there also you have, "the words of my offences." And if Christ is, for all that, without "sin," and without "offences," we begin to think those words in the Psalm also not to be His. And it is exceedingly harsh and inconsistent that that Psalm should not relate to Christ,

where we have His Passion as clearly laid open as if it were being read to us out of the Gospel. For there we have, "They parted My garments among them, and cast lots upon My vesture." Why should I mention that the first verse of that Psalm was pronounced by the Lord Himself while hanging, on the Cross, with His own mouth, saying, "My God, My God, why hast Thou forsaken Me?" What did He mean to be inferred from it, but that the whole of that Psalm relates to Him, seeing He Himself, the Head of His Body, pronounced it in His own Person? Now when it goes on to say, "the words of mine offences, it is beyond a doubt that they are the words of Christ. Whence then come "the sins," but from the Body, which is the Church? Because both the Head and the Body of Christ are speaking. Why do they speak as if one person only? Because "they twain," as He hath said, "shall be one flesh." "This" (says the Apostle) "is a great mystery; but I speak concerning Christ and the Church." ... For why should He not say, "my sins," who said, "I was an hungred, and ye gave Me no meat; I was thirsty, and ye gave Me no drink; I was a stranger, and ye took Me not in. I was sick and in prison, and ye visited Me not." Assuredly the Lord was not in prison. Why should He not say this, to whom when it was said, "When saw we Thee a hungered, and athirst, or in prison; and did not minister unto Thee?" He replied, that He spake thus in the person of His Body. "Inasmuch as ye did it not unto one of the least of Mine, ye did it not unto Me." Why should He not say, "from the face of my sins," who said to Saul, "Saul, Saul, why persecutest thou Me," who, however, being in Heaven, now suffered from no persecutors? But just as, in that passage, the Head spake for the Body, so here too the Head speaks the words of the Body; whilst you hear at the same time the accents of the Head Itself also. Yet do not either, when you hear the voice of the Body, separate the Head from it; nor the Body, when you hear the voice of the Head: because "they are no more twain, but one flesh."

6. "There is no soundness in my flesh from the face of thine anger." But perhaps God is unjustly angry with thee, O Adam; unjustly angry with thee, O son of man; because now brought to acknowledge that thy punishment, now that thou art a man that hath been placed in Christ's Body, thou hast said, "There is no soundness in my flesh from the face of Thine anger." Declare the justice of God's anger: lest thou shouldest seem to be excusing thyself, and accusing Him. Go on to tell whence the "anger" of the Lord proceeds. "There is no soundness in my flesh from the face of Thine anger; neither is there any rest in my bones." He repeats what he said before, "There is no soundness in my flesh;" for, "There is no rest in my bones," is equivalent to this. He does not however repeat "from the face of Thine anger;" but states the cause of the anger of God. "There is no rest in my bones from the face of my sins."

7. "For mine iniquities have lifted up my head; and are like a heavy burden too heavy for me to bear" (ver. 4). Here too he has placed the cause first, and the effect afterwards. What consequence followed, and from what cause, he has told us. "Mine iniquities have lift up mine head." For no one is proud but the unrighteous man, whose head is lifted up. He is "lifted up," whose "head is lifted up on high" against God. You heard when the lesson of the Book of Ecclesiasticus was read: "The beginning of pride is when a man departeth from God." He who was the first to refuse to listen to the Commandment, "his head iniquity lifted up" against God. And because his iniquities have lifted up his head, what hath God done unto him? They are "like a heavy burden, too heavy for me to bear"! It is the part of levity to lift up the head, just as if he who lifts up his head had nothing to carry. Since therefore that which admits of being lifted up is light, it receives a weight by which it may be weighed down. For "his mischief returns upon his own head, and his violent dealing comes down upon his own pate." " They are like a heavy burden, too heavy for me to bear."

8. "My wounds stink and are corrupt" (ver. 5). Now he who has wounds is not perfectly sound. Add to this, that the wounds "stink and are corrupt." Wherefore do they "stink"? Because they are "corrupt:" now in what way this is explained in reference to human life, who doth not understand? Let a man but have his soul's sense of smelling sound, he perceives how foully sins stink. The contrary to which stink of sin, is that savour of which the Apostle says, "We are the sweet savour of Christ unto God, in every place, unto them which be saved. But whence is this, except from hope? Whence is this, but from our "calling the Sabbath to remembrance"? For it is a different thing that we mourn over in this life, from that which we anticipate in the other. That which we mourn over is stench, that which we reckon upon is fragrance. Were there not therefore such a perfume as that to invite us, we should never call the Sabbath to remembrance. But since, by the Spirit, we have such a perfume, as to say to our Betrothed," Because of the savour of Thy good ointments we will run after Thee;" we turn our senses away from our own unsavourinesses, and turning ourselves to Him, we gain some little breathing-time. But indeed, unless our evil deeds also did smell rank in our nostrils, we should never confess with those groans, "My wounds stink and are corrupt." And wherefore? "from the face of my foolishness." From the same cause that he said before, "from the face of my sins;" from that same cause he now says, "from the face of my foolishness."

9. "I am troubled, I am bowed down even unto the end" (ver. 6). Wherefore was he "bowed down"? Because he had been "lifted up." If thou art "humble, thou shalt be exalted;" if thou exaltest thyself, thou shalt be "bowed down;" for God will be at

no loss to find a weight wherewith to bow thee down. ...Let him groan on these things; that he may receive the other; let him "call the Sabbath to remembrance," that he may deserve to arrive at it. For that which the Jews used to celebrate was but a sign. Of what thing was it the sign? Of that which he calls to remembrance, who saith," I am troubled, and am bowed down even unto the end." What is meant by even "unto the end"? Even to death.

"I go mourning all the day long." "All day long," that is, "without intermission." By "all the day long," he means, "all my life long." But from what time hath he known it? From the time that he began to "call the Sabbath to remembrance." For so long as he "calls to remembrance" what he no longer possesses, wouldest thou not have him "go mourning"? "All the day long have I gone mourning."

10. "For my soul is filled with illusions, and there is no soundness in my flesh" (ver. 7). Where there is the whole man, there there is soul and flesh both. The "soul is filled with illusions;" the flesh hath "no soundness." What does there remain that can give joy? Is it not meet that one should "go mourning"? "All the day long have I gone mourning." Let mourning be our portion, until our soul be divested of its illusions; and our body be clothed with soundness. For true soundness is no other than immortality. How great however are the soul's illusions, were I even to attempt to express, when would the time suffice me? For whose soul is not subject to them? There is a brief particular that I will remind yon of, to show how our soul is filled with illusions. The presence of those illusions sometimes scarcely permits us to pray. We know not how to think of material objects without images, and such as we do not wish, rush in upon the mind; and we wish to go from this one to that, and to quit that for another. And sometimes you wish to return to that which you were thinking of before, and to quit that which you are now thinking of; and a fresh one presents itself to you; you wish to call up again what you had forgotten; and it does not occur to you; and another comes instead which you would not have wished for. Where meanwhile was the one that you had forgotten? For why did it afterwards occur to you, when it had ceased to be sought after; whereas, while it was being sought for, innumerable others, which were not desired, presented themselves instead of it? I have stated a fact briefly; I have thrown out a kind of hint or suggestion to you, brethren, taking up which, you may yourselves suggest the rest to yourselves, and discover what it is to mourn over the "illusions" of our "soul." He hath received therefore the punishment of illusion; he hath forfeited Truth. For just as illusion is the soul's punishment, so is Truth its reward. But when we were set in the midst of these illusions, the Truth Itself came to us, and found us overwhelmed by illusions, took upon Itself our flesh, or rather took flesh from us; that is, from the human race. He

manifested himself to the eyes of the Flesh, that He might "by faith" heal those to whom He was going to reveal the Truth hereafter, that Truth might be manifested to the now healed eye. For He is Himself "the Truth, which He promised unto us at that time, when His Flesh was to be seen by the eye, that the foundation might be laid of that Faith, of which the Truth was to be the reward. For it was not Himself that Christ showed forth on earth; but it was His Flesh that He showed. For had He showed Himself, the Jews would have seen and known Him; but had they "known Him, they would never have crucified the Lord of Glory." But perhaps His disciples saw Him, when they said unto Him, "Show us the Father, and it sufficeth us;" and He, to show that it was not Himself that had been seen by them, added: "Have I been so long with you, and have ye not known Me, Philip? He that seeth Me, seeth the Father also." If then they saw Christ, wherefore did they yet seek for the Father? For if it were Christ whom they saw, they would have seen the Father also. They did not therefore yet see Christ, who desired that the Father should be shown unto them. To prove that they did not yet see Him, hear that, in another place, He promised it by way of reward, saying, "He who loveth Me, keepeth My commandments; and whoso loveth Me, shall be loved of My Father; and I will love Him and" (as if it were said to Him, "what wilt Thou give unto him, as Thou lovest him?" He saith), "I will manifest Myself unto him." If then He promises this by way of a reward unto them that love Him, it is manifest that the vision of the Truth, promised to us, is of such a nature, that, when we have seen it, we shall no longer say, "My soul is filled with illusions."

11. "I am become feeble, and am bowed down greatly" (ver. 8). He who calls to mind the transcendent height of the Sabbath, sees how "greatly" he is himself "bowed down." For he who cannot conceive what is that height of rest, sees not where he is at present. Therefore another Psalm hath said, "I said in my trance, I am cast out of the sight of Thine eyes." For his mind being taken up thither, he beheld something sublime; and was not yet entirely there, where what he beheld was; and a kind of flash, as it were, if one may so speak, of the Eternal Light having glanced upon him, when he perceived that he was not yet arrived at this, which he was able after a sort to understand, he saw where he himself was, and how he was cramped and "bowed down" by human infirmities. And he says, "I said in my trance, I am cast out of the sight of Thine eyes." Such is that certain something which I saw in my trance, that thence I perceive how far off I am, who am not already there. He was already there who said that he was "caught up into the third Heaven, and there heard unspeakable words, which it is not lawful for a man to utter." But he was recalled to us, in order that, as requiring to be made perfect, he might first mourn his infirmity, and afterwards be clothed with might. Yet encouraged for the ministration of his office by having seen somewhat of those things, he goes on saying, "I heard unspeakable words, which it is not lawful

for a man to utter." Now then what use is it for you to ask, either of me or of any one, the "things which it is not lawful for man to utter." If it was not lawful for him to utter them, to whom is it lawful to hear them? Let us however lament and groan in Confession; let us own where we are; let us "call the Sabbath to remembrance," and wait with patience for what He has promised, who hath, in His own Person also, showed forth an example of patience to us. "I am become feeble, and bowed down greatly."

12. "I have roared with the groaning of my heart." You observe the servants of God generally interceding with groaning; and the reason of it is asked, and there is nothing apparent, but the groaning of some servant of God, if indeed it does find its way at all to the ears of a person placed near him. For there is a secret groaning, which is not heard by man: yet if the thought of some strong desire has taken so strong hold of the heart, that the wound of the inner man finds expression in some uttered exclamation, the reason of it is asked; and a man says to himself, "Perhaps this is the cause of his groaning;" and, "Perhaps this or that hath befallen him." Who can determine, but He in whose Eyes and Ears he groaned? Therefore he says, "I roared with the groaning of mine heart;" because if men ever hear a man's groanings, they for the most part hear but the groaning of the flesh; they do not hear him who groans "with the groaning of his heart." Some one hath carried off his goods; he "roareth," but not "with the groaning of his heart:" another because he has buried his son, another his wife; another because his vineyard has been injured by a hailstorm; another because his cask has turned sour; another because some one hath stolen his beast; another because he has suffered some loss; another because he fears some man who is his enemy: all these "roar" with the "groaning of the flesh." The servant of God, however, because he "roareth" from the recollection of the Sabbath, where the Kingdom of God is, which flesh and blood shall not possess, says, "I have roared with the groaning of my heart."

13. And who observed and noticed the cause of his groaning? "All my desire is before Thee" (ver. 9). For it is not before men who cannot see the heart, but it is before Thee that all my desire is open! Let your desire be before Him; and "the Father, who seeth in secret, shall reward thee." For it is thy heart's desire that is thy prayer; and if thy desire continues uninterrupted, thy prayer continueth also. For not without a meaning did the Apostle say, "Pray without ceasing." Are we to be "without ceasing" bending the knee, prostrating the body, or lifting up our hands, that he says, "Pray without ceasing"? Or if it is in this sense that we say that we "pray," this, I believe, we cannot do "without ceasing." There is another inward kind of prayer without ceasing, which is the desire of the heart. Whatever else you are doing, if you do but long for that Sabbath, you do not cease to pray. If you

would never cease to pray, never cease to long after it. The continuance of thy longing is the continuance of thy prayer. You will be ceasing to speak, if you cease to long for it. Who are those who have ceased to speak? They of whom it is said "Because iniquity shall abound, the love of many shall wax cold." The freezing of charity is the silence of the heart; the burning of charity is the cry of the heart. If love continues still you are still lifting up your voice; if you are always lifting up your voice, you are always longing after something; if always longing for something absent, you are calling "the Sabbath rest to remembrance." And it is important you should understand too before whom the "roaring of thine heart" is open. Now then consider what sort of desires those should be, that are before the eyes of God. Should it be the desire for the death of our enemy? a thing which men flatter themselves they lawfully wish for? For sometimes we pray for what we ought not. Let us consider what they flatter themselves they pray for lawfully! For they pray that some person may die, and his inheritance come to them. But let those too, who pray for the death of their enemies, hear the Lord saying, "Pray for your enemies." Let them not pray for this, that their enemies may die; but rather pray for this, that they may be reclaimed; then will their enemies be dead; for from the time that they are reclaimed, henceforth they will be enemies no longer. "And all my desire is before Thee." What if we suppose that our desire is before Him, and that yet that very "groaning" is not before Him? How can that be, since our desire itself finds its expression in "groaning"? Therefore follows, "And my groaning is not hid from Thee."

From Thee indeed it is not hid; but from many men it is hid. The servant of God sometimes seems to be saying in humility, "And my groaning is not hid from Thee." Sometimes also he seems to smile. Is then that longing dead in his heart? If however there is the desire within, there is the "groaning" also. It does not always find its way to the ears of man; but it never ceases to sound in the ears of God.

14. "My heart is troubled" (ver. 10). Wherefore is it troubled? "And my courage hath failed me." Generally something comes upon us on a sudden; the "heart is troubled;" the earth quakes; thunder is sent from Heaven; a formidable attack is made upon us, or a horrible sound heard. Perhaps a lion is seen on the road; the "heart is troubled." Perhaps robbers lie in wait for us; the "heart is troubled:" we are filled with a panic fear; from every quarter something excites anxiety. Wherefore? Because "my courage hath failed me." For what would be feared, did that courage still remain unmoved? Whatever bad tidings were brought, whatever threatened us, whatever sound was heard, whatever were to fall, whatever appeared horrible, would inspire no terror. But whence that trouble? "My courage faileth me." Wherefore hath my courage failed me? "The light of mine eyes also is

gone from me." Thus Adam also could not see "the light of his eyes." For the "light of his eyes" was God Himself, whom when he had offended, he fled to the shade, and hid himself among the trees of Paradise. He shrunk in alarm from the face of God: and sought the shelter of the trees; thenceforth among the trees he had no more "the light of his eyes," at which he had been wont to rejoice. ...

15. "My lovers;" why should I henceforth speak of my enemies? "My lovers and my neighbours drew nigh, and stood over against me" (ver. 11). Understand this that he saith, "Stood over against me." For if they stood over against me, they fell against themselves. "My lovers and my neighbours drew nigh and stood over against me." Let us now recognise the words of the Head speaking; now let our Head in His Passion begin to dawn upon us. Yet again when the Head begins to speak, do not sever the Body from it. If the Head would not separate itself from the words of the Body, should the Body dare to separate itself from the sufferings of the Head? Do thou suffer in Christ's suffering: for Christ, as it were, sinned in thy infirmity. For just now He spoke of thy sins, as if speaking in His own Person, and called them His own. ...To those who wished to be near His exaltation, yet thought not of His humility, He answered and said to them, "Can ye drink of the cup that I shall drink of?" Those sufferings of the Lord then are our sufferings also: and were each individual to serve God well, to keep faith truly, to render to each their dues, and to conduct himself honestly among men, I should like to see if he does not suffer even that which Christ here details in the account of His Passion. "My lovers and my neighbours drew nigh, and stood over against me."

16. "And my neighbours stood afar off" Who were the "neighbours" that drew nigh, and who were those who stood afar off? The Jews were "neighbours" because "near kinsmen," they drew near even when they crucified Him: the Apostles also were His "neighbours;" and they also "stood afar off," that they might not have to suffer with Him. This may also be understood thus: "My friends," that is, those who feigned themselves" My friends:" for they feigned themselves His friends, when they said," We know that. Thou teachest the way of God in truth; " when they wished to try Him, whether tribute ought to be paid to Caesar; when He convinced them out of their own mouth, they wished to seem to be His friends. "But He needed not that any should testify of man, for He Himself knew what was in man; " so that when they spoke unto Him words of friendship, He answered them, "Why tempt ye Me, ye hypocrites?" "My friends and my neighbours" then "drew near and stood over against me, and my neighbours stood afar off." You understand what I said. I called those neighhours who "drew nigh," and at the same time "stood afar off." For they "drew nigh" in the body, but "stood afar off" in their heart. Who were in the body so near to Him as those who lifted

Him on the Cross? Who in heart so far off as those who blasphemed Him? Hear this sort of distance described by the Prophet Isaiah; observe this nearness and distance at one and the same time. "This people honours Me with their lips:" behold, with their body they draw near; "but their heart is far from Me." The same persons are at the same time "near" and "afar off" also: with their lips they are near, in heart afar off. However, because the Apostles also stood afar off, through fear, we understand it more simply and properly of them; so that we mean by it, that some drew near, and others stood afar off; since even Peter, who had followed more boldly than the rest, was still so far off, that being questioned and alarmed, he thrice denied the Lord, with whom he had promised to "be ready to die." Who afterwards that, from being afar off, he might be made to draw nigh, heard after the resurrection the question, "Lovest thou Me?" and said, "I love Thee;" and by so saying was brought "nigh," even as by denying Him, he had become "far off;" till with the threefold confession of love, he had put away from him his threefold denial. "And my neighbours stood afar off."

17. "They also that sought after my soul were preparing violence against me" (ver. 12). It is now plain who "sought after His soul;" viz. those who had not His soul, in that they were not in His Body. They who were "seeking after His soul," were far removed from His soul; but they were "seeking it" to destroy it. For His soul may be "sought after" in a right way also. For in another passage He finds fault with some persons, saying, "There is no man to care for My soul." He finds fault with some for not seeking after His soul; and again, with others for seeking after it. Who is he that seeketh after His soul in the right way? He who imitates His sufferings. Who are they that sought after His soul in the wrong way? Even those who "prepared violence against Him," and crucified Him.

18. He goes on: "Those who sought after My faults had spoken vanity." What is, "sought after My faults"? They sought after many things, and found them not. Perhaps He may have meant this: "They sought for criminal charges against me." For they sought for somewhat to say against Him, and "they found not." For they were seeking to find evil things to say of "the Good;" crimes of the Innocent; When would they find such things in Him, who had no sin? But because they had to seek for sins in Him who had no sin, it remained for them to invent that which they could not find. Therefore, "those who sought after My faults have spoken vanity," i.e., untruth, "and imagined deceit all the day long;" that is, they meditated treachery without intermission. You know how atrocious false-witness was borne against the Lord, before He suffered. You know how atrocious false-witness was borne against Him, even after His resurrection. For those soldiers who watched His sepulchre of whom Isaiah spake, "I will appoint the wicked for His burial" (for

they were wicked men, and would not speak the truth, and being bribed they disseminated a lie), consider what "vanity" they spake. They also were examined, and they said, "While we slept, His disciples came and stole Him away." This it is, "to speak vanity." For if they were sleeping, how could they know what had been done?

19. He saith then, "But I as a deaf man heard not" (ver. 13). He who replied not to what He heard, did, as it were, not hear them. "But I as a deaf man heard not. And I was as a dumb man that openeth not his mouth." And he repeats the same things again.

"And I became as a man that heareth not, and in whose mouth are no reproofs" (ver. 14). As if He had nothing to say unto them, as if He had nothing wherewith to reproach them. Had He not already reproached them for many things? Had He not said many things, and also said, "Woe unto you, Scribes and Pharisees," and many things besides? Yet when He suffered, He said none of these things; not that He had not what to say, but He waited for them to fulfil all things, and that all the prophecies might be fulfilled of Him, of whom it had been said, "And as a sheep before her shearer is dumb, so openeth He not His mouth." It behoved Him to be silent in His Passion, though not hereafter to be silent in Judgment. For He had come to be judged, then, who was hereafter coming to judge; and who was for this reason to come with great power to judge, that He had been judged in great humility.

20. "For in Thee, O Lord, do I hope; Thou wilt hear, O Lord, my God" (ver. 15). As if it were said to Him, "Wherefore openedst thou not thy mouth? Wherefore didst Thou not say, 'Refrain'? Wherefore didst Thou not rebuke the unrighteous, while hanging on the Cross?" He goes on and says," For in Thee, O Lord, do I hope; Thou, O Lord my God, wilt hear." He warns you what to do, should tribulation haply befall. For you seek to defend yourself, and perhaps your defence is not listened to by any one. Then are you confounded, as if you had lost your cause; because you have none to defend or to bear testimony in your favour. "Keep" but your "innocence" within, where no one can pervert thy cause. False-witness has prevailed against you before men. Will it then prevail before God, where your cause has to be pleaded? When God shall be Judge, there shall be no other witness than your own conscience. In the presence of a just judge, and of your own conscience, fear nothing but your own cause. If you have not a bad cause, you will have no accuser to dread; no false-witness to confute, nor witness to the truth to look for. Do but bring into court a good conscience, that you may say, "For in Thee, O Lord, do I hope; Thou, O Lord my God, wilt hear."

21. "For I said, Let not mine enemies ever rejoice over me. And when my feet slip, they magnify themselves against me" (ver. 16). Again He returns to the infirmity of His Body: and again the Head takes heed of Its "feet." The Head is not in such a manner in Heaven, as to forsake what It has on earth; He evidently sees and observes us. For sometimes, as is the way of this life, our feet are "turned aside," and they slip by falling into some sin; there the tongues of the enemy rise up with the bitterest malignity. From this then we discern what they really had in view, even while they kept silence. Then they speak with an unsparing harshness; rejoicing to have discovered what they ought to have grieved for. "And I said, Lest at any time my adversaries should rejoice over me." I said this indeed; and yet it was perhaps for my correction that Thou hast caused them to "magnify themselves against me, when my feet slipped;" that is to say, when I stumbled, they were elated, and said many things. For pity, not insult, was due from them to the weak; even as the Apostle speaks: "Brethren, if a man be overtaken in a fault, ye which are spiritual restore such an one in the spirit of meekness;" and he combines the reason why: "considering thyself also, lest thou also be tempted." Not such as these were the persons of whom He speaks: "And when my feet slipped, they rejoiced greatly against me;" but they were such as those of whom He says elsewhere: "They that hate me will rejoice if I fall?"

22. "For I am prepared for the scourges" (ver. 17). Quite a magnificent expression; as if He were saying, "It was even for this that I was born; that I might suffer." For He was not to be born, but from Adam, to whom the scourge is due. But sinners are in this life sometimes not scourged at all, or are scourged less than their deserts: because the wickedness of their heart is given over as already desperate. Those, however, for whom eternal life is prepared, must needs be scourged in this life: for that sentence is true: "My son, faint not under the chastening of the Lord, neither be weary when thou art rebuked of Him." "For whom the Lord loveth He chasteneth, and scourgeth every son whom He receiveth." Let not mine enemies therefore insult over me; let" them not magnify themselves;" and if my Father scourgeth me, "I am prepared for the scourge;" because there is an inheritance in store for me. Thou wilt not submit to the scourge: the inheritance is not bestowed upon thee. For "every son" must needs be scourged. So true it is that "every son" is scourged, that He spared not even Him who had no sin. For "I am prepared for the scourges."

23. "And my sorrow is continually before me." What "sorrow" is that? Perhaps, a sorrow for my scourge. And, in good truth, my brethren, in good truth, let me say unto you, men do mourn for their scourges, not for the causes on account of which they are scourged. Not such was the person here. Listen, my brethren: If any

person suffers any loss, he is more ready to say, "I did not deserve to suffer it," than to consider why he suffered it, mourning the loss of money, not mourning over that of righteousness. If thou hast sinned, mourn for the loss of thy inward treasure. Thou hast nothing in thy house, but perhaps thou art still more empty in heart; but if thine heart is full of its Good, even thy God, why dost thou not say, "The Lord gave, the Lord hath taken away; as it pleased the Lord was it done. Blessed be the Name of the Lord." Whence then was it that He was grieving? Was it for the "scourging" wherewith He was scourged? God forbid. "And my sorrow "(says He) "is continually before me." And as if we were to say, "What sorrow? whence comes that sorrow?" he says: "For I declare mine iniquity; and I will have a care for my sin" (ver. 18). See here the reason for the sorrow! It is not a sorrow occasioned by the scourge; not one for the remedy, not for the wound. For the scourge is a remedy against sins. Hear, brethren; We are Christians, and yet if any one's son dies, he mourns for him but does not mourn for him if he sins. It is then, when he sees him sinning, that he ought to make mourning for him, to lament over him. It is then he should restrain him, and give him a rule to live by; should impose a discipline upon him: or if he has done so, and the other has not taken heed, then was the time when he ought to have been mourned over; then he was more fatally dead whilst living in luxury, than when, by death, he brought his luxury to its close: at that time, when he was doing such things in thine house, he was not only "dead, but he stank also." These things were worthy to be lamented, the others were such as might well be endured; those, I say, were tolerable, these worthy to be mourned over. They were to be mourned over in the same way that you have heard this person mourn over them: "For I declare mine iniquity. I will have a care for my sin." Be not free from anxiety when you have confessed your sin, as if always able to confess thy sin, and to commit it again. Do thou "declare thine iniquity in such a manner, as to have a care for thy sin." What is meant by "having a care of thy sin"? To have a care of thy wound. If you were to say, "I will have a care of my wound," what would be meant by it, but I will do my endeavour to have it healed. For this is "to have a care for one's sin," to be ever struggling, ever endeavouring, ever exerting one's self, earnestly and zealously, to heal one's wound. Behold! thou art from day to day mourning over thy sins; but perhaps thy tears indeed flow, but thy hands are unemployed. Do alms, redeem thy sins, let the poor rejoice of thy bounty, that thou also mayest rejoice of the Grace of God. He is in want; so art thou in want also: he is in want at thy hands; so art thou also in want at God's hand. Dost thou despise one who needs thy aid; and shall God not despise thee when thou needest His? Do thou therefore supply the needs of him who is in want of thine aid; that God may supply thy needs within. This is the meaning of, "I will have a care for my sin." I will do all that ought to be done, to blot out and to heal my sin. "And I will have a care for my sin."

24. "But mine enemies live" (ver. 19). They are well off: they rejoice in worldly prosperity, while I am suffering, and "roaring with the groaning of my heart." In what way do His enemies "live," in that He hath said of them already, that they have "spoken vanity"? Hear in another Psalm also: "Whose sons are as young plants; firmly rooted." But above He had said, "Whose mouth speaketh vanity. Their daughters polished after the similitude of a temple: their garners full bursting forth more and more; their cattle fat, their sheep fruitful, multiplying in their streets; no hedge failing into ruin; no cry in their streets." "Mine enemies" then "live." This is their life; this life they praise; this they set their hearts upon: this they hold fast to their own ruin. For what follows? They pronounce "the people that is in such a case" blessed. But what sayest thou, who "hast a care for thy sin"? What sayest thou, who "confessest thine iniquity"? He says, "Blessed is the people whose God is the Lord."

"But mine enemies live, and are strengthened against me, and they that hate me wrongfully are multiplied." What is "hate me wrongfully"? They hate me, who wish their good, whereas were they simply requiting evil for evil, they would not be righteous; were they not to requite with good the good done to them, they would be ungrateful: they, however, who "hate wrongfully," actually return evil for good. Such were the Jews; Christ came unto them with good things; they requited Him evil for good. Beware, brethren, of this evil; it soon steals upon us. Let no one of you think himself to be far removed from the danger, because we said, "Such were the Jews." Should a brother, wishing your good, rebuke you, and you hate him, you are like them. And observe, how easily, how soon it is produced; and avoid an evil so great, a sin so easily committed.

25. "They also that render evil for good, were speaking evil of me, because I have pursued the thing that is just" (ver. 20). Therefore was it that I was requited evil for good. What is meant by "pursued after the thing that is just"? Not forsaken it. That you might not always understand persecutio in a bad sense, He means by persecutus pursued after, thoroughly followed. "Because I have followed the thing that is just." Hear also our Head crying with a lamentable voice in His Passion: "And they cast Me forth, Thy Darling, even as a dead man in abomination." Was it not enough that He was "dead"? wherefore "in abomination" also? Because He was crucified. For this death of the Cross was a great abomination in their eyes, as they did not perceive that it was spoken in prophecy, "Cursed is every one that hangeth on a tree." For He did not Himself bring death; but He found it here, propagated from the curse of the first man; and this same death of ours, which had originated in sin, He had taken upon Himself, and hung on the Tree. Lest therefore some persons should think (as some of the Heretics think), that our Lord Jesus

Christ had only a false body of flesh; and that the death by which He made satisfaction on the Cross was not a real death, the Prophet notices this, and says, "Cursed is every one that hangeth on a tree." He shows then that the Son of God died a true death, the death which was due to mortal flesh: lest if He were not "accursed," you should think that He had not truly died. But since that death was not an illusion, but had descended from that original stock, which had been derived from the curse, when He said, "Ye shall surely die:" and since a true death assuredly extended even to Him, that a true life might extend itself to us, the curse of death also did extend to Him, that the blessing of life might extend even unto us. "And they cast Me forth, Thy Darling, even as a dead man in abomination."

26. "Forsake me not, O Lord; O my God, depart not from me" (ver. 21). Let us speak in Him, let us speak through Him (for He Himself intercedeth for us), and let us say, "Forsake me not, O Lord my God." And yet He had said, "My God! My God! why hast Thou forsaken Me?" and He now says, "O My God, depart not from Me." If He does not forsake the body, did He forsake the Head? Whose words then are these but the First Man's? To show then that He carried about Him a true body of flesh derived from him, He says, "My God, My God why hast Thou forsaken Me?" God had not forsaken Him. If He does not forsake Thee, who believest in Him, could the Father, the Son, and the Holy Ghost, One God, forsake Christ? But He had transferred to Himself the person of the First Man. We know by the words of an Apostle, that "our old man is crucified with Him." We should not, however, be divested of our old nature, had He not been crucified "in weakness." For it was to this end that He came that we may be renewed in Him, because it is by aspiration after Him, and by following the example of His suffering, that we are renewed. Therefore that was the cry of infirmity; that cry, I mean, in which it was said, "Why hast Thou forsaken Me?" Thence was it said in that passage above, "the words of mine offences." As if He were saying, These words are transferred to My Person from that of the sinner.

27. "Depart not from me. Make haste to help me, Lord of my salvation" (ver. 22). This is that very "salvation," Brethren, concerning which, as the Apostle Peter saith, "Prophets have enquired diligently," and though they have enquired diligently, yet have not found it. But they searched into it, and foretold of it; while we have come and have found what they sought for. And see, we ourselves too have not as yet received it; and after us shall others also be born, and shall find, what they also shall not receive, and shall pass away, that we may, all of us together, receive the "penny of salvation in the end of the day," with the Prophets, the Patriarchs, and the Apostles. For you know that the hired servants, or labourers, were taken into the vineyard at different times; yet did they all receive

their wages on an equal footing. Apostles, then, and Prophets, and Martyrs, and ourselves also, and those who will follow us to the end of the world, it is in the End itself that we are to receive everlasting salvation; that beholding the face of God, and contemplating His Glory, we may praise Him for ever, free from imperfection, free from any punishment of iniquity, free from every perversion of sin: praising Him; and no longer longing after Him, but now clinging to Him for whom we used to long to the very end, and in whom we did rejoice, in hope. For we shall be in that City, where God is our Bliss, God is our Light, God is our Bread, God is our Life; whatever good thing of ours there is, at being absent from which we now grieve, we shall find in Him. In Him will be that "rest," which when we "call to remembrance" now, we cannot choose but grieve. For that is the "Sabbath" which we "call to remembrance;" in the recollection of which, so great things have been said already; and so great things ought to be said by us also, and ought never to cease being said by us, not with our lips indeed, but in our heart: for therefore do our lips cease to speak, that we may cry out with our hearts.

PSALM XXXIX.

1. The title of this Psalm, which we have just chanted and proposed to discuss, is, "On the end, for Idithun, a Psalm for David himself" Here then we must look for, and must attend to, the words of a certain person who is called Idithun; and if each one of ourselves may be Idithun, in that which he sings he recognises himself, and hears himself speak. For thou mayest see who was called Idithun, according to the ancient descent of man; let us, however, understand what this name is translated, and seek to comprehend the Truth in the translation of the word. According therefore to what we have been able to discover by enquiry in those names which have been translated from the Hebrew tongue into the Latin, by those who study the sacred writings, Idithun being translated is "over-leaping them." Who then is this person "over-leaping them"? or who those whom he hath "over- leaped"?... For there are some persons, yet clinging to the earth, yet bowed down to the ground, yet setting their hearts on what is below, yet placing their hopes in things that pass away, whom he who is called "over- leaping them" hath "over-leaped."

2. You know that some of the Psalms are entitled, "Songs of Degrees;" and in the Greek it is obvious enough what the word anabathmw^n means. For anabathmoi` are degrees (or steps) of them that ascend, not of them that descend. The Latin, not being able to express it strictly, expresses it by the general term; and in that it called them "steps," left it undetermined, whether they were "steps" of persons ascending or descending. But because there is no "speech or language where their voices are not heard among them," the earlier language explains the one which comes after it: and what was ambiguous in one is made certain in another. Just then as there the singer is some one who is "ascending," so here is it some one who is "over-leaping." ... Let this Idithun come still to us; let him "over-leap" those whose delight is in things below, and take delight in these things, and let him rejoice in the Word of the Lord; in the delight of the law of the Most High. ...

3. "I said, I will take heed to my ways, that I sin not with my tongue" (ver. 1). ... For it is not without reason that the tongue is set in a moist place, but because it is so prone to slip. Perceiving therefore how hard it was for a man to be under the necessity of speaking, and not to say something that he will wish unsaid, and filled with disgust at these sins, he seeks to avoid the like. To this difficulty is he exposed who is seeking to "leap beyond." ... Although I have "leaped beyond" the pleasures of earth, although the fleeting passions for things temporal ensnare me not, though now I despise these things below, and am rising up to better things than these, yet in these very better things the satisfaction of knowledge in the sight of God is enough for me. Of what use is it for me to speak what is to be laid hold

of, and to give a handle to cavillers? Therefore, "I said, I will take heed to my ways, that I sin not with my tongue. I keep my mouth with a bridle." Wherefore is this? Is it on account of the religious, the thoughtful, the faithful, the holy ones? God forbid! These persons hear in such a manner, as to praise what they approve; but as for what they disapprove, perhaps, among much that they praise they rather excuse than cavil at it; on account of what persons then dost thou "take heed to thy ways," and place a guard on thy lips "that thou mayest not sin with thy tongue"? Hear: it is, "While the wicked standeth over against me." It is not "by me" that he takes up his station, but "against me." Why? ... Even the Lord Himself says," I have yet many things to say unto you, but ye cannot bear them now." And the Apostle, "I could not speak unto you as unto spiritual, but as unto carnal." Yet not as to persons to be despaired of, but as to those who still required to be nourished. For he goes on to say, "As babes in Christ, I have fed you with milk, and not with meat; for hitherto ye were not able." Well, tell it unto us even now. "Neither yet now are ye able." Be not therefore impatient to hear that which as yet thou art not capable of; but grow that thou mayest be "able to bear it." It is thus we address the little one, who yet requires to be fed with kindly milk in the bosom of Mother Church, and to be rendered meet for the "strong meat" of the Lord's Table. But what can I say even of that kind to the sinner, who "taketh his stand against me," who either thinks or pretends himself capable of what he "cannot bear;" so that when I say anything unto him, and he has failed to comprehend it, he should not suppose that it was not he that had failed to comprehend, but I who had broken down. Therefore because of this sinner, who "taketh up his stand against me, I keep my mouth as it were with a bridle."

4. "I became deaf, and was humbled, I held my peace from good" (ver. 2). For this person, who is "leaping beyond," suffers some difficulty in a certain stage to which he hath already attained; and he desires to advance beyond, even from thence, to avoid this difficulty. I was afraid of committing a sin; so that I spoke not; that I imposed on myself the necessity of silence: for I had spoken thus, "I will take heed to my ways, that I may not sin with my tongue." Whilst I was too much afraid of saying anything wrong, I kept silence from all that is good. For whence could I say good things, except that I heard them? "It is Thou that shalt make me to hear of joy and gladness." And the "friend of the bridegroom standeth and heareth Him, and rejoiceth on account of the bridegroom's voice," not his own. That he may speak true things, he hears what he is to say. For it is he that "speaketh a lie," that "speaketh of his own." ... When therefore I had "put a bridle," as it were, "on my lips;" and constrained myself to silence, because I saw that everywhere speech was dangerous, then, says he, that came to pass upon me, which I did not wish, "I became deaf, and was humbled;" not humbled myself, but was humbled; "and I held my peace even from good." Whilst afraid of saying any

evil, I began to refrain from speaking what is good: and I condemned my determination; for "I was holding my peace even from what is good."

"And my sorrow was stirred up again" (ver. 2). Inasmuch as I had found in silence a kind of respite from a certain "sorrow," that had been inflicted upon me by those who cavilled at my words, and found fault with me: and that sorrow that was caused by the cavillers, had ceased indeed; but when "I held my peace even from good, my sorrow was stirred up again." I began to be more grieved at having refrained from saying what I ought to have said, than I had before been grieved by having said what I ought not. "And my sorrow was stirred up again.

5. "And while I was musing, the fire burned" (ver. 3). ... I reflected on the words of my Lord, "Thou wicked and slothful servant, thou oughtest to have put My money to the exchangers, and I at My coming should receive it again with usury." And that which follows may God avert from those who are His stewards! Bind him hand and foot, and let him be cast into outer darkness;" the servant, who was not a waster of his master's goods, so as to destroy them, but was slothful in laying them out to improve them. What ought they to expect, who have wasted them in luxury, if they are condemned who through slothfulness have kept them? "As I was musing, the fire burned." And as he was in this state of wavering suspense, between speaking and holding his peace, between those who are prepared to cavil and those who are anxious to be instructed, ... in this state of suspense, he prays for a better place, a place different from this his present stewardship, in which man is in such difficulty and in such danger, and sighing after a certain "end," when he was not to be subject to these things, when the Lord is to say to the faithful dispenser," Enter thou into the joy of thy Lord," he says, "Then spake I with my tongue." In this fluctuation, in the midst of these dangers and these difficulties, because, that in consequence of the abundance of offences "the love of many is waxing cold," although the law of the Lord inspires delight, in this fluctuation then, (I say), "then spake I with my tongue." To whom? not to the hearer whom I would fain instruct; but to Him who heareth and taketh heed also, by whom I would fain be instructed myself. "I spake with my tongue" to Him, from whom I inwardly hear whatever I hear that is good or true.—What saidst thou?

"Lord, make me to know mine end" (ver. 4). For some things I have passed by already; and I have arrived at a certain point, and that to which I have arrived is better than that from which I have advanced to this; but yet there remains a point, which has to be left behind. For we are not to remain here, where there are trials, offences, where we have to bear with persons who listen to us and cavil at us.

"Make me to know mine end;" the end, from which I am still removed, not the course which is already before me.

6. The "end" he speaks of, is that which the Apostle fixed his eye upon, in his course; and made confession of his own infirmity, perceiving in himself a different state of things from that which he looked for elsewhere. For he says, "Not that I have already attained, or am already perfect. Brethren, I count not myself to have apprehended." And that you might not say, "If the Apostle hath not apprehended, have I apprehended? If the Apostle is not perfect, am I perfect?" ...

7. "And the number of my days, what it is." I ask of" the number of my days, what it is." I can speak of "number" without number, and understand "number without number," in the same sense as "years without years" may be spoken of. For where there are years, there is a sort of "number" at all events, also. But yet, "Thou art the same, and Thy years shall not fail." "Make me to know the number of my days;" but "to know what it is." What then? that number in which thou art, think you that it "is" not? Assuredly, if I weigh the matter well, it has no being; if I linger behind, it has a sort of being; if I rise above it, it has none. If, shaking off the trammels of these things, I contemplate things above, if I compare things that pass away with those that endure, I see what has a true being, and what rather seems to be, than really is. Should I say that these days of mine "are;" and shall I rashly apply this word so full of meaning to this course of things passing away? To such a degree have I my own self almost ceased to "be, failing" as I am in my weakness, that He escaped from my memory, who said, "I AM HE THAT IS." Hath then any number of days any existence? In truth it hath, and it is "number without end." ... Everything is swept on by a series of moments, fleeting by, one after the other; there is a torrent of existences ever flowing on and on; a "torrent," of which He "drank in the way," who hath now "lift up His Head." These days then have no true being; they are gone almost before they arrive; and when they are come, they cannot continue; they press upon one another, they follow the one the other, and cannot check themselves in their course. Of the past nothing is called back again; what is yet to be, is expected as something to pass away again: it is not as yet possessed, whilst as yet it is not arrived; it cannot be kept when once it has arrived. He asks then concerning "the number of his days, which is;" not that which is "not:" and (which confounds me by a still greater and more perplexing difficulty) at once "is," and "is not." We can neither say that "is," which does not continue; nor that it "is not," when it has come and is passing. It is that absolute "IS," that true "IS," that "IS" in the true sense of the word, that I long for; that "IS;" which "is" in that "Jerusalem" which is "the Bride" of my Lord; where there will not be death, there will not be failing; there will be a day that passeth not away, but

continueth: which has neither a yesterday to precede it, nor a to-morrow pressing, close upon it. This "number of my days, which is," this (I say), "make Thou me to know."

8. "That I may know what is wanting to me." For while I am struggling here, "this" is wanting unto me: and so long as it is wanting unto me, I do not call myself perfect. So long as I have not received it, I say, "not that I have already attained, either am already perfect; but I am pressing towards the prize of God's high calling." This let me receive as the prize of my running the race! There will be a certain rest-ing-place, to terminate my course; and in that resting-place there will be a Country, and no pilgrimage, no dissension, no temptation. Make me then to know "this number of my days, which is, that I may know what is wanting unto me;" because I am not there yet; lest I should be made proud of what I already am, that "I may be found in Him, not having mine own righteousness." ...

9. "Behold, thou hast made my days old" (ver. 5). For these days are "waxing old." I long for new days "that never shall wax old," that I may say, "Old things have passed away; behold, things are become new." Already new in hope; then in reality. For though, in hope and in faith, made new already, how much do we even now do after our old nature! For we are not so completely "clothed upon" with Christ, as not to bear about with us anything derived from Adam. Observe that Adam is "waxing old" within us, and Christ is being "renewed" in us. "Though our outward man is perishing, yet is our inward man being renewed day by day." Therefore, while we fix our thoughts on sin, on mortality, on time, that is hastening by, on sorrow, and toil, and labour, on stages of life following each other in succession, and continuing not, passing on insensibly from infancy even to old age; whilst, I say, we fix our eyes on these things, let us see here "the old man," the "day that is waxing old;" the Song that is out of date; the Old Testament; when however we turn to the inner man, to those things that are to be renewed in place of these which are to be changed, let us find the "new man," the "new day," the "new song," the "New Testament;" and that "newness," let us so love, as to have no fears of its "waxing old." ... This man, therefore, who is hasting forward to those things which are new, and "reaching forward to those things which are before," says, "Lord, make me to know mine end, and the number of my days, which really is, that I may know what is wanting unto me." See he still drags with him Adam; and even so he is hasting unto Christ. "Behold," saith he, "thou hast made my days old." It is those days that are derived from Adam, those days, I say, that thou hast made old. They are waxing old day by day: and so waxing old, as to be at some day or other consumed also. "And my substance is as nothing before Thee." "Before Thee, O Lord, my substance is as nothing." "Before Thee;" who

seest this; and I too, when I see it, see it only when "before Thee." When "before men" I see it not. For what shall I say? What words shall I use to show, that which I now am is nothing in comparison of That which truly "IS"? But it is within that it is said; it is within that it is felt, so far as it is felt. "Before Thee, O Lord," where Thine eyes are; and not where the eyes of men are. And where Thine eyes are, what is the state of things? "That which I am is as nothing."

10. "But, verily, every man living is altogether vanity." "But, verily." For what was he saying above? Behold, I have already "leaped beyond" all mortal things, and despised things below, have trampled under foot the things of earth, have soared upwards to the delights of the law of the Lord, I have been afloat in the dispensation of the Lord, have yearned for that" End" which Itself is to know no end, have yearned for the number of my days that truly "is," because the number of days like these hath no real being. Behold, I am already such a one as this; I have already overleaped so much; I am longing for those things which abide. "But verily," in the state in which I am here, so long as I am here, so long as I am in this world, so long as I bear mortal flesh, so long as the life of man on earth is a trial, so long as I sigh among causes of offence, as long as while I "stand" I am in "fear lest I fall," as long as both my good and my ill hangs in uncertainty, "every man living is altogether vanity." ...

11. "Albeit man walketh in the Image" (ver. 6). In what "Image," save that of Him who said, "Let Us make man in Our Image, after Our Likeness." "Albeit man walks in the Image." For the reason he says "albeit," is, that this is some great thing. And this "albeit" is followed by "nevertheless," that the "albeit" which you have already heard, should relate to what is beyond the sun; but this "nevertheless," which is to follow, to what is "under the sun," and that the one should relate to the Truth, the other to "vanity." "Albeit," then, "that man walketh in the Image, nevertheless he is disquieted in vain." Hear the cause of his "disquieting," and see if it be not a vain one; that thou mayest trample it under foot, that thou mayest "leap beyond it," and mayest dwell on high, where that "vanity" is not. What "vanity" is that? "He heapeth up riches, and knoweth not for whom he may be gathering them together." O infatuated vanity! "Blessed is the man that maketh the Lord his trust, and hath not respected vanities, nor lying deceits." To you indeed, O covetous man, to you I seem to be out of my senses, these words appear to you to be "old wives' tales." For you, a man of great judgment, and of great prudence, to be sure, are daily devising methods of acquiring money, by traffic, by agriculture, by eloquence perhaps, by making yourself learned in the law, by warfare, perhaps you even add that of usury. Like a shrewd man as you are, you leave nothing untried, whereby you may pile coin on

coin; and may store it up more carefully in a place of secrecy. You plunder others; you guard against the plunderer; you are afraid lest you should yourself suffer the wrong, that you yourself do; and even what you do suffer, does not correct you. ... Examine your own heart, and that prudence of yours, which leads you to deride me, to think me out of my senses for saying these things: and tell me now, "You are heaping up treasures; for whom are you gathering them together?" I see what you would tell me; as if what you would say had not occurred to the person described here; you will say, I am keeping them for my children? This is the voice of parental affection; the excuse of injustice. "I am keeping them" (you say) "for my children." So then you are keeping them for your children, are you? Did not Idithun then know this? Assuredly he did; but he reckoned it one of the things of the "old days," that have waxed old, and therefore he despised it: because he was hastening on to the new "days." ...

12. For He, "by whom all things were made," hath built "mansions" for all of us: thither He would have that which we have go before us; that we may not lose it on earth. When, however, you have kept them on earth, tell me for whom you are to "gather them together"? You have children: add one more to their number; and give something to Christ also. "He is disquieted in vain."

13. "And now" (ver. 7). "And now," saith this Idithun,—looking back on a certain "vain" show, and looking up to a certain Truth, standing midway where he has something beyond him, and something also behind him, having below him the place from which he took his spring, having above him that toward which he has stretched forth;—"And now," when I have "over-leaped" some things, when I have trampled many things under foot, when I am no longer captivated by things temporal; even now, I am not perfect, "I have not yet apprehended." "For it is by hope that we are saved; but hope that is seen is not hope; for what a man seeth, why doth he yet hope for? But if we hope for that we see not, then do we with patience wait for it." Therefore he says: "And now what wait I for? Is it not for the Lord?" He is my expectation, who hath given me all those things, that I might despise them. He will give unto me Himself also, even He who is above all, and "by whom all things were made," and by whom I was made amongst all; even He, the Lord, is my Expectation! You see Idithun, brethren, you see in what way he waiteth for Him! Let no man therefore call himself perfect here; he deceives and imposes upon himself; he is beguiling himself, he cannot have perfection here, and what avails it that he should lose humility? ...

"And my substance is ever before Thee." Already advancing, already tending towards Him, and to some extent already beginning to "be," still (he says) "my substance is ever before Thee." Now that other substance is also before men. You have gold, silver, slaves, estates, trees, cattle, servants. These things are visible even to men. There is a certain "substance that is ever before Thee."

14. "Deliver me from all my transgressions" (ver. 8). I have "over- leaped" a great deal of ground, a very great deal of ground already; but, "If we say that we have no sin, we deceive ourselves, and the Truth is not in us." I have "over-leaped" a great deal: but still do I "beat my breast," and say, "Forgive us our debts, as we forgive our debtors." Thou therefore art "my expectation!" my "End." For "Christ is the end of the Law unto righteousness, unto every man that believeth." From all mine offences:" not only from those, that I may not relapse into those which I have already "overleaped;" but from all, without exception, of those on account of which I now beat my breast, and say, "Forgive us our debts." "Deliver me from all mine offences:" me being thus minded, and holding fast what the Apostle said, "As many of us as be perfect, let us be thus minded." For at the time that he said that he was not "already perfect," he then immediately goes on and says, "As many of us as be perfect, let us be thus minded." ... Art thou then, O Apostle, not perfect, and are we perfect? But hath it escaped you, that he did just now call himself "perfect "? For he does not say," As many of you as are perfect, be ye thus minded;" but "As many of us as be perfect, let us be thus minded;" after having said a little before, "Not that I have already attained; either am already perfect." In no other way then can you be perfect in this life, than by knowing that you cannot be perfect in this life. This then will be your perfection, so to have "over-leaped" some things, as to have still some point to which you are hastening on: so as to have something remaining, to which you will have to leap on, when everything else has been passed by. It is such faith as this that is secure; for whoever thinks that he has already attained, is "exalting himself," so as to be "abused" hereafter. ...

15. "Thou hast made me the reproach of the foolish." Thou hast so willed it, that I should live among those, and preach the Truth among those, who love vanity; and I cannot but be a laughing-stock to them. "For we have been made a spectacle unto this world, and unto angels, and unto men:" to angels who praise, to men who censure, us; or rather to angels, some of whom praise, some of whom are censuring us: and to men also, some of whom are praising, and some censuring us. ... Both the one and the other are arms to us: the one "on the right hand," the other "on the left:" arms however they are both of them; both of these kinds of arms, both those "on the right hand," and those "on the left;" both those who praise, and those who censure; both those who pay us honour, and those who heap dishonour upon us; with both these kinds I contend against the devil; with both of these I

smite him; I defeat him with prosperity, if I be not corrupted by it; by adversity, if I am not broken in spirit by it.

16. "I became dumb; and I opened not my mouth" (ver. 9). But it was to guard against "the foolish man," that "I became dumb, and opened not my mouth." For to whom should I tell what is going on within me? "For I will hear what the Lord God will speak in me; for He will speak peace unto His people." But "There is no peace," saith the Lord, "to the wicked." "I was dumb, and opened not my mouth; because it is Thou that madest me." Was this the reason that thou openedst not thy mouth, "because God made thee"? That is strange; for did not God make thy mouth, that thou shouldest speak? "He that planted the ear, doth He not hear? He that formed the eye, doth He not see?" God hath given thee a mouth to speak with; and dost thou say, "I was dumb, and opened not my mouth, because Thou madest me"? Or does the clause, "Because Thou madest me," belong to the verse that follows? "Remove Thy stroke away from me" (ver. 10). Because it is "Thou that hast made me," let it not be Thy pleasure to destroy me utterly; scourge, so that I may be made better, not so that I faint; beat me, so that I may be beaten out to a greater length and breadth, not so that I may be ground to powder. "By the heaviness of Thy hand I fainted in corrections." That is, I "fainted" while Thou wast correcting me. And what is meant by "correcting" me? except what follows.

17. "Thou with rebukes hast chastened man for iniquity; Thou hast made my life to consume away like a spider" (ver. 11). There is much that is discerned by this Idithun; by every one who discerns as he does; who overleaps as he does. For he says, that he has fainted in God's corrections; and would fain have the stroke removed away from him, "because it is He who made him." Let Him renew me, who also made me; let Him who created me, create me anew. But yet, Brethren, do we suppose that there was no cause for his fainting, so that he wishes to be "renewed," to be "created anew"? It is "for iniquity," saith he, "that Thou hast chastened man." All this, my having fainted, my being weak, my "crying out of the deep," all of this is because of "iniquity;" and in this Thou hast not condemned, but hast "chastened" me. "Thou hast chastened man for sin." Hear this more plainly from another Psalm: "It is good for me that Thou hast afflicted me, that I might learn Thy righteousness." I have been "afflicted," and at the same time "it is good for me;" it is at once a punishment, and an act of favour. What hath He in store for us after punishment is over, who inflicts punishment itself by way of favour? For He it is of whom it was said, "I was brought low, and He made me whole:" and, "It is good for me that Thou hast afflicted me, that I might learn Thy righteousness." "Thou chastenest man for iniquity." And that which is written, "Thou formest my grief in teaching me," could only be said unto God by one who

was "leaping beyond" his fellows; "Thou formest my grief in teaching me;" Thou makest, that is to say, a lesson for me out of my sorrow. It is Thou that formest that very grief itself; Thou dost not leave it unformed, but formest it; and that grief, that has been inflicted by Thee, when formed, will be a lesson unto me, that I may be set free by Thee. For the word tinges is used in the sense of "forming," as it were moulding, my grief; not in the sense of" feigning" it; in the same way that fingit is applied to the artist, in the same sense that figulus is derived from fingere. Thou therefore "hast chastened man for iniquity." I see myself in afflictions; I see myself under punishment; and I see no unrighteousness in Thee. If I therefore am under punishment, and if there is no unrighteousness with Thee, it remains that Thou must have been "chastening man for iniquity."

18. And by what means hast Thou "chastened" him? Tell us, O Idithun, the manner of thy chastening; tell us in what way thou hast been "chastened." "And Thou hast made my life consume like a spider." This is the chastening! What consumes away sooner than the spider? I speak of the creature itself; though what can be more liable to "consume away" than the spider's webs? Observe too how liable to decay is the creature itself. Do but set your finger lightly upon it, and it is a ruin: there is nothing at all more easily destroyed. To such a state hast Thou brought my life, by chastening me "because of iniquity." When chastening makes us weak, there is a kind of strength that would be a fault. ... It was by a kind of strength that man offended, so as to require to be corrected by weakness: for it was by a certain "pride" that he offended; so as to require to be chastened by humility. All proud persons call themselves strong men. Therefore have many "come from the East and the West," and have attained "to sit down with Abraham, and Isaac, and Jacob, in the kingdom of Heaven." Wherefore was it that they so attained? Because they would not be strong. What is meant by "would not be strong"? They were afraid to presume of their Own merits. They did not "go about to establish their own righteousness," that they might "submit themselves to the righteousness of God." ... Behold! you are mortal; and you bear about you a body of flesh that is corrupting away: "And ye shall fall like one of the princes. Ye shall die like men," and shall fall like the devil What good does the remedial discipline of mortality do you? The devil is proud, as not having a mortal body, as being an angel. But as for you, who have received a mortal body, and to whom even this does no good, so as to humble you by so great weakness, you shall "fall like one of the princes." This then is the first grace of God's gift, to bring us to the confession of our infirmity, that whatever good we can do, whatever ability we have, we may be that in Him; that "He that glorieth, may glory in the Lord." "When I am weak," saith he, "then am I strong."

19. "But surely every man living disquieteth himself in vain." He returns to what he mentioned a little before. Although he be improving here, yet for all that, "every man living disquieteth himself in vain;" forasmuch as he lives in a state of uncertainty. For who has any assurance even of his own goodness? "He is disquieted in vain." Let him "cast upon the Lord the burden" of his care; let him cast upon Him whatever causes him anxiety. "Let Him sustain thee;" let Him keep thee. For on this earth what is there that is certain, except death? Consider the whole sum of all the good or the ill of this life, either those belonging to righteousness, or those belonging to unrighteousness; what is there that is certain here, except death? Have you been advancing in goodness? You know what you are to-day; what you will be to-morrow, you know not! Are you a sinner? you know what you are to-day; what you will be to-morrow, you know not! You hope for wealth; it is uncertain whether it will fall to your lot. You hope to have a wife; it is uncertain whether you will obtain one, or what sort of one you will obtain. You hope for sons: it is uncertain whether they will be born to you. Are they born? it is uncertain whether they will live: if they live, it is uncertain whether they will grow up in virtue, or whether they will fall away. Whichever way you turn, all is uncertain, death alone is certain. Art thou poor? It is uncertain whether thou wilt grow rich. Art thou unlearned? It is uncertain whether thou wilt become learned. Art thou in feeble health, it is uncertain whether thou wilt regain thy strength. Art thou born? It is certain that thou wilt die: and in this certainty of death itself, the day of thy death is uncertain. Amidst these uncertainties, where death alone is certain, while even of that the hour is uncertain, and while it alone is studiously guarded against, though at the same time it is in no way to be escaped, "every man living disquieteth himself in vain." ...

20. "Hear my prayer, O Lord" (ver. 12). Whereof shall I rejoice? Whereof should I groan? I rejoice on account of what is past, I groan longing for these which are not yet come. "Hear my prayer, and give ear unto my cry. Hold not Thy peace at my tears." For do I now no longer weep, because I have already "passed by," have "left behind" so great things as these? "Do I not weep much the more?" For, "He that increaseth knowledge, increaseth sorrow." The more I long for what is not here, do I not so much the more groan for it until it comes? do I not so much the more weep until it comes? ...

21. "For I am a sojourner with Thee." But with whom am I a "sojourner"? When I was with the devil, I was a "sojourner;" but then I had a bad host and entertainer; now, however, I am with Thee; but I am a "sojourner" still. What is meant by a sojourner? I am a "sojourner" in the place from which I am to remove; not in the place where I am to dwell for ever. The place where I am to abide for ever, should

be rather called my home. In the place from which I am to remove I am a "sojourner;" but yet it is with my God that I am a sojourner, with whom I am hereafter to abide, when I have reached my home. But what home is that to which you are to remove from this estate of a sojourner? Recognise that home, of which the Apostle speaks, "We have an habitation of God, an house not made with hands, eternal in the Heavens." If this house is eternal in the Heavens, when we have come to it, we shall not be sojourners any more. For how should you be a sojourner in an eternal home? But here, where the Master of the house is some day to say to you, "Remove," while you yourself know not when He will say it, be thou in readiness. And by longing for your eternal home, you will be keeping yourself in readiness for it. And be not angry with Him, because He gives thee notice to remove, when He Himself pleases. For He made no covenant with thee, nor did He bind Himself by any engagement; nor didst thou enter upon the tenancy of this house on a certain stipulation for a definite term: thou art to quit, when it is its Master's pleasure. For therefore is it that you now dwell there free of charge. "For I am a sojourner with Thee, and a stranger." Therefore it is there is my country: it is there is my home. "I am a sojourner with Thee, and a stranger." Here too is understood "with Thee." For many are strangers with the devil: but they who have already believed and are faithful, are, it is true, "strangers" as yet, because they have not yet come to that country and to that home: but still they are strangers with God. For so long as we are in the body, we are strangers from the Lord, and we desire, whether we are strangers, or abiding here, "we may be accepted with Him." I am a "sojourner with Thee; and a stranger, as all my fathers were." If then I am as all my fathers were, shall I say that I will not remove, when they have removed? Am I to lodge here on other terms, than those on which they lodged here also? ...

22. "Grant me some remission, that I may be refreshed before I go hence" (ver. 13). Consider well, Idithun, consider what knots those are which thou wouldest have "loosed" unto thee, that thou mightest be "refreshed before thou goest hence." For thou hast certain fever-heats from which thou wouldest fain be refreshed, and thou sayest, "that I may be refreshed," and "grant me a remission." What should He remit, or loosen unto thee, save that difficulty under which, and in consequence of which, thou sayest, "Forgive us our debts. Grant me a remission before I go hence, and be no more." Set me free from my sins, "before I go hence," that I may not go hence with my sins. Remit them unto me, that I may be set at rest in my conscience, that it may be disburthened of its feverish anxiety, the anxiety with which "I am sorry for my sin. Grant me a remission, that I may be refreshed" (before everything else), "before I go hence, and be no more." For if thou grantest me not a "remission, that I may be refreshed," I shall "go and be no more." "Before I go" thither, where if I go, I shall thenceforth "be no more. Grant me a remission,

that I may be refreshed." A question has suggested itself, how he will be no more. ... What is meant then by "shall be no more," unless Idithun is alluding to what is true "being," and what is not true "being." For he was beholding with the mind, with which he could do so, with the "mind's eye," by which he was able to behold it, that end, which he had desired to have shown unto him, saying, "Lord, make me to know mine end." He was beholding "the number of his days, which truly is;" and he observed that all that is below, in comparison of that true being, has no true being. For those things are permanent; these are subject to change; mortal, and frail, and the eternal suffering, though full of corruption, is for this very reason not to be ended, that it may ever be being ended without end. He alluded therefore to that realm of bliss, to the happy country, to the happy home, where the Saints are partakers of eternal Life, and of Truth unchangeable; and he feared to "go" where that is not, where there is no true being; longing to be there, where "Being" in the highest sense is! It is on account of this contrast then, while standing midway between them, he says, "Grant me a remission, that I may be refreshed before I go hence and be no more." For if Thou "grantest me not a remission" of my sins, I shall go from Thee unto all eternity! And from whom shall I go to all eternity? From Him who said, I AM HE THAT AM: from Him who said, "Say unto the children of Israel, I Am hath sent me unto you." He then who goes from Him, in the contrary direction, goes to non- existence. ...

PSALM XL.

1. Of all those things which our Lord Jesus Christ has foretold, we know part to have been already accomplished, part we hope will be accomplished hereafter. All of them, however, will be fulfilled, because He is "the Truth" who speaks them, and requires of us to be as "faithful," as He Himself speaks them faithfully. ...

2. Let us say then what this Psalm says. "I waited patiently for the Lord" (ver. 1). I waited patiently for the promise of no mere mortal who can both deceive and be himself deceived: I waited for the consolation of no mere mortal, who may be consumed by sorrow of his own, before he gives me comfort. Should a brother mortal attempt to comfort me, when he himself is in sorrow likewise? Let us mourn in company; let us weep together, let us "wait patiently" together, let us join our prayers together also. Whom did I wait for but for the Lord? The Lord, who though He puts off the fulfilment of His promises, yet never recalls them? He will make it good; assuredly He will make it good, because He has made many of His promises good already: and of God's truth we ought to have no fears, even if as yet He had made none of them good. Lo! let us henceforth think thus, "He has promised us everything; He has not as yet given us possession of anything; He is a sponsible Promiser; a faithful Paymaster: do you but show yourself a dutiful exactor of what is promised; and if you be "weak," if you be one of the little ones, claim the promise of His mercy. Do you not see tenders lambs striking their dams' teats with their heads, in order that they may get their fill of milk? ... "And He took heed unto me, and heard my cry." He took heed to it, and He heard it. See thou hast not waited in vain. His eyes are over thee. His ears turned towards thee. For, "the eyes of the Lord are upon the righteous, and His ears are open unto their cry." What then? Did He not see thee, when thou usedst to do evil and to blaspheme Him? What then becomes of what is said in that very Psalm, "The face of the Lord is upon them that do evil"? But for what end? "that He may cut off the remembrance of them from the earth." Therefore, even when thou wert wicked, He "took heed of thee;" but He "took no heed to thee." So then to him who "waited patiently for the Lord," it was not enough to say, "He took heed of me, He says, "He took heed to me;" that is, He took heed by comforting me, that He might do me good. What was it that He took heed to? "and He heard my cry."

3. And what hath He accomplished for thee? What hath He done for thee? "He brought me up also out of a horrible pit, out of the miry clay, and set my feet upon a rock, and established my goings" (ver. 2). He hath given us great blessings already: and still He is our debtor; but let him who hath this part of the debt repaid already, believe that the rest will be also, seeing that he ought to have believed

238

even before he received anything. Our Lord has employed facts themselves to persuade us, that He is a faithful promiser, a liberal giver. What then has He already done? "He has brought me out of a horrible pit." What horrible pit is that? It is the depth of iniquity, from the lusts of the flesh, for this is meant by "the miry clay." Whence hath He brought thee out? Out of a certain deep, out of which thou criedst out in another Psalm, "Out of the deep have I called unto Thee, O Lord." And those who are already "crying out of the deep," are not absolutely in the lowest deep: the very act of crying is already lifting them up. There are some deeper in the deep, who do not even perceive themselves to be in the deep. Such are those who are proud despisers, not pious entreaters for pardon; not tearful criers for mercy: but such as Scripture thus describes. "The sinner when he comes into the depth of evil despiseth." For he is deeper in the deep, who is not satisfied with being a sinner, unless instead of confessing he even defends his sins. But he who has already "cried out of the deep," hath already lifted up his head in order that he might "cry out of the deep," has been heard already, and has been "brought out of the horrible pit, and out of the mire and clay." He already has faith, which he had not before; he has hope, which he was before without; he now walks in Christ, who before used to go astray in the devil. For on that account it is that he says, "He hath set my feet upon a rock, and established my goings." Now "that Rock was Christ." Supposing that we are "upon the rock," and that our "goings are ordered," still it is necessary that we continue to walk; that we advance to something farther. For what did the Apostle Paul say when now upon the Rock, when his "goings had now been established"? "Not as though I had already attained, either were already perfect: Brethren, I count not myself to have apprehended." What then has been done for thee, if thou hast not apprehended? On what account dost thou return thanks, saying, "But I have obtained mercy"? Because his goings are now established, because he now walks on the Rock? ... Therefore, when he was saying, "I press forward toward the prize of my high calling," because "his feet were now set on the Rock," and "his goings were ordered," because he was now walking on the right way, he had something to return thanks for; something to ask for still; returning thanks for what he had received already, while he was claiming that which still remained due. For what things already received was he giving thanks? For the remission of sins, for the illumination of faith; for the strong support of hope, for the fire of charity. But in what respects had he still a claim of debt on the Lord? "Henceforth," he says, "there is laid up for me a crown of righteousness." There is therefore something due me still. What is it that is due? "A crown of righteousness, which the Lord, the righteous Judge, shall give me at that day." He was at first a loving Father to "bring him forth from the horrible pit;" to forgive his sins, to rescue him from "the mire and clay;" hereafter he will be a "righteous Judge," requiting to him walking rightly, what He promised; to him (I say), unto whom He had at the first granted that power to walk rightly. He then as a "righteous Judge" will repay; but whom will he repay? "He that endureth unto the end, the same shall be saved."

4. "And He hath put a new song in my mouth." What new song is this? "Even a hymn unto our God" (ver. 3). Perhaps you used to sing hymns to strange gods; old hymns, because they were uttered by the "old man," not by the "new man;" let the "new man" be formed, and let him sing a "new song;" being himself made "new," let him love those "new" things by which he is himself made new. For what is more Ancient than God, who is before all things, and is without end and without beginning? He becomes "new" to thee, when thou returnest to Him; because it was by departing from Him, that thou hadst become old; and hadst said, "I have waxed old because of all mine enemies." We therefore utter "a hymn unto our God;" and the hymn itself sets us free. "For I will call upon the Lord to praise Him, and I will be safe from all mine enemies." For a hymn is a song of praise. Call on God to "praise" Him, not to find fault with Him. ...

5. If haply any one asks, what person is speaking in this Psalm? I would say briefly, "It is Christ." But as ye know, brethren, and as we must say frequently, Christ sometimes speaks in His own Person, in the Person of our Head. For He Himself is "the Saviour of the Body." He is our Head; the Son of God, who was born of the Virgin, suffered for us, "rose again for our justification," sitteth "at the right hand of God," to "make intercession for us:" who is also to recompense to the evil and to the good, in the judgment, all the evil and the good that they have done. He deigned to be come our Head; to become "the Head of the Body," by taking of us that flesh in which He should die for us; that flesh which He also raised up again for our sakes, that in that flesh He might place before us an instance of the resurrection; that we might learn to hope for that of which we heretofore despaired, and might henceforth have our feet upon the rock, and might walk in Christ. He then sometimes speaks in the name of our Head; sometimes also He speaks of us who are His members. For both when He said, "I was an hungred, and ye gave Me meat," He spoke on behalf of His members, not of Himself: and when He said, "Saul, Saul, why persecutest thou Me?" the Head was crying on behalf of its members: and yet He did not say, "Why dost thou persecute My members?" but, "Why persecutest thou Me?" If He suffers in us, then shall we also be crowned in Him. Such is the love of Christ. What is there can be compared to this? This is the thing on account of which "He hath put a hymn in our mouth," and this He speaks on behalf of His members.

6. "The just shall see, and shall fear, and shall trust in the Lord." "The just shall see." Who are the just? The faithful; because it is "by faith that the just shall live."

For there is in the Church this order, some go before, others follow; and those who go before make themselves "an example" to those who follow; and those who follow imitate those who go before. But do those then follow no one, who exhibit themselves as an ensample to them that come after? If they follow no one at all, they will fall into error. These persons then must themselves also follow some one, that is, Christ Himself. ... "The just," therefore, "shall see, and shall fear." They see a narrow way on the one hand; on the other side, "a broad road:" on this side they see few, on the other many. But thou art a just man; count them not, but weigh them; bring "a just balance," not a "deceitful" one: because thou art called just. "The just shall see, and fear," applies to thee. Count not therefore the multitudes of men that are filling the "broad ways," that are to fill the circus to-morrow; celebrating with shouts the City's Anniversary, while they defile the City itself by evil living. Look not at them; they are many in number; and who can count them? But there are a few travelling along the narrow road. Bring forth the balance, I say. Weigh them; see what a quantity of chaff you lift up on the one side, against a few grains of corn on the other. Let this be done by "the just," the "believers," who are to follow. And what shall they who precede do? Let them not be proud, let them not "exalt themselves;" let them not deceive those who follow them. How may they deceive those who follow them? By promising them salvation in themselves. What then ought those who follow to do? "The just shall see, and fear: and shall trust in the Lord;" not in those who go before them. But indeed they fix their eyes on those who go before them, and follow and imitate them; but they do so, because they consider from Whom they have received the grace to go before them; and because they trust in Him. Although therefore they make these their models, they place their trust in Him from whom the others have received the grace whereby they are such as they are. "The just shall see it, and fear, and shall trust in the Lord." Just as in another Psalm, "I lift up mine eyes unto the hills," we understand by hills, all distinguished and great spiritual persons in the Church; great in solidity, not by swollen inflation. By these it is that all Scripture hath been dispensed unto us; they are the Prophets, they are the Evangelists; they are sound Doctors: to these" I lift up mine eyes, from whence shall come my help." And lest you should think of mere human help, he goes on to say, "My help cometh from the Lord, which made heaven and earth. The just shall see it, and fear, and shall trust in the Lord." ...

7. "Blessed is that man that maketh the name of the Lord his trust, and hath not respected vanities or lying madnesses" (ver. 4). Behold the way by which thou wouldest fain have gone. Behold the "multitude that fill the Broad way." It is not without reason "that" road leads to the amphitheatre. It is not without reason it leads to Death. The "broad way" leads unto death, its breadth delights for time: its end is straitness to all eternity. Aye; but the multitudes murmur; the multitudes are

rejoicing together; the multitudes are hastening along; the multitudes are flocking together! Do not thou imitate them; do not turn aside after them: they are "vanities, and lying madnesses." Let the Lord thy God be thy hope. Hope for nothing else from the Lord thy God; but let the Lord thy God Himself be thine hope. For many persons hope to obtain from God's hands riches, and many perishable and transitory honours; and, in short, anything else they hope to obtain at God's hands, except only God Himself. But do thou seek after thy God Himself: nay, indeed, despising all things else, make thy way unto Him! Forget other things, remember Him. Leave other things behind, and "press forward" unto Him. Surely it is He Himself, who set thee right, when turned away from the right path; who, now that thou art set in the right path, guides thee aright, who guides thee to thy destination. Let Him then be thy hope, who both guides thee, and guides thee to thy destination. Whither does worldly covetousness lead thee? And to what point does it conduct thee at the last? Thou didst at first desire a farm; then thou wouldest possess an estate; thou wouldest shut out thy neighbours; having shut them out, thou didst set thy heart on the possessions of other neighbours; and didst extend thy covetous desires till thou hadst reached the shore: arriving at the shore, thou covetest the islands: having made the earth thine own, thou wouldest haply seize upon heaven. Leave thou all thy loves. He who made heaven and earth is more beautiful than all.

8. "Blessed is the man that maketh the name of the Lord his hope, and who hath not regarded vanities and lying madnesses." For whence is it that "madness" is called "lying"? Insanity is a lying thing, even as it is sanity that sees the Truth. For what thou seest as good things, thou art deceived; thou art not in thy sound senses: a violent fever has driven thee to frenzy: that which thou art in love with is not a reality. Thou applaudest the charioteer; thou cheerest the charioteer; thou art madly in love with the charioteer. It is "vanity;" it is "a lying madness." "It is 'not'" (he cries). "Nothing can be better; nothing more delightful." What can I do for one in a state of high fever? Pray ye for such persons, if you have any feelings of compassion in you. For the physician himself also in a desperate case generally turns to those in the house, who stand around weeping; who are hanging on his lips to hear his opinion of the patient who is sick and in danger. The physician stands in a state of doubt: he sees not any good to promise; he fears to pronounce evil, lest he should excite alarm. He devises a thoroughly modest sentence: "The good God can do all things. Pray ye for him." Which then of these madmen shall I check? Which of them will listen to me? Which of them would not call us miserable? Because they suppose us to have lost great and various pleasures, of which they are madly fond, in that we are not as madly in love with them as they are: and they do not see that they are "lying" pleasures. ... "And hath not respected vanities, and lying madnesses." "Such a one has won," he cries; "he harnessed

such and such a horse," he proclaims aloud. He would fain be a kind of diviner; he aspires to the honours of divination by abandoning the fountain of Divinity; and he frequently pronounces an opinion, and is frequently mistaken. Why is this? Even because they are "lying madnesses." But why is it that what they say sometimes comes true? That they may lead astray the foolish ones; that by loving the semblance of truth there, they may fall into the snare of falsehood: let them be left behind, let them be "given over," let them be "cut off." If they were members of us, they must be mortified. "Mortify," he says, "your members which are upon the earth." Let our God be our hope. He who made all things, is better than all! He who made what is beautiful, is more beautiful than all that is such. He who made whatever is mighty, is Himself mightier. He who made whatever is great, is Himself greater. He will be unto you everything that you love. Learn in the creature to love the Creator; and in the work Him who made it. Let not that which has been made by Him detain thine affections, so that thou shouldest lose Him by whom thou thyself wert made also. "Blessed," then, "is the man that maketh the Name of the Lord his trust, and hath not respected vanities and lying madnesses."...

9. We will give him other sights in exchange for such sights as these. And what sights shall we present to the Christian, whom we would fain divert from those sights? I thank the Lord our God; He in the following verse of the Psalm hath shown us what sights we ought to present and offer to spectators who would fain have sights to see? Let us now suppose him to be weaned from the circus, the theatre, the amphitheatre; let him be looking after, let him by all means be looking after, some sight to see; we do not leave him without a spectacle. What then shall we give in exchange for those? Hear what follows.

"Many, O Lord my God, are the wonderful works which Thou hast made" (ver. 5). He used to gaze at the "wonderful works" of man; let him now contemplate the wonderful works of God. "Many are the wonderful works" that God "has made." Why are they become vile in his eyes? He praises the charioteer guiding four horses; running all of them without fault and without stumbling. Perhaps the Lord has not made such "wonderful works" in things spiritual. Let him control lust, let him control cowardice, let him control injustice, let him control imprudence, I mean, the passions which falling into excess produce those vices; let him control these and bring them into subjection, and let him hold the reins, and not suffer himself to be carried away; let him guide them the way he himself would have them go; let him not be forced away whither he would not. He used to applaud the charioteer, he himself shall be applauded for his own charioteering; he used to call out that the charioteer should be invested with a dress of honour; he shall himself be clothed with immortality. These are the spectacles, these the sights that God exhibits to us. He cries out of heaven," My eyes are upon you. Strive, and 'I will' assist you; triumph, and I will crown you."

"And in Thy thought there is none that is like unto Thee." Now then look at the actor! For the man hath by dint of great pains learnt to walk upon a rope; and hanging there he holds thee hanging in suspense. Turn to Him who exhibits spectacles far more wonderful. This man hath learned to walk upon the rope; but hath he caused another to walk on the sea? Forget now thy theatre; behold our Peter; not a walker on the rope, but, so to speak, a walker on the sea. And do thou also walk on other waters (though not on those on which Peter walked, to symbolize a certain truth), for this world is a sea. It hath a deleterious bitterness; it hath the waves of tribulations, the, tempests of temptations; it hath men in it who, like fish, delight in their own ruin, and prey upon each other; walk thou here, set thou thy foot on this. Thou wouldest see sights; be thyself a "spectacle." That thy spirit may not sink, look on Him who goes before thee, and says, "We have been made a spectacle unto this world, and unto angels, and unto men." Tread thou on the waters; suffer not thyself to be drowned in the sea. Thou wilt not go there, thou wilt not "tread it under foot," unless it be His bidding, who was Himself the first to walk upon the sea. For it was thus that Peter spoke. "If Thou art, bid me come unto Thee on the waters." And because "He was," He heard him when praying; He granted his wish to him when expressing his desire; He raised him up when sinking. These are the "wonderful works" that the "Lord hath made," Look on them; let faith be the eye of him who would behold them. And do thou also likewise; for although the winds alarm thee, though the waves rage against thee, and though human frailty may have inspired thee with some doubt of thy salvation, thou hast it in thy power to "cry out," thou mayest say" Lord, I perish." He who bids thee walk there, suffers thee not to perish. For in that thou now walkest "on the Rock," thou fearest not even on the sea! If thou art without "the Rock," thou must sink in the sea; for the Rock on which thou must walk is such an one as is not sunk in the sea,

10. Observe then the "wonderful works" of God. "I have declared, and have spoken; they are multiplied beyond number." There is "a number," there are some over and above the number. There is a fixed number that belongs to that heavenly Jerusalem. For "'the Lord knoweth them that are His;" the Christians that fear Him, the Christians that believe, the Christians that keep the commandments, that walk in God's ways, that keep themselves from sins; that if they fall confess: they belong to "the number." But are they the only ones? There are also some "beyond the number." For even if they be but a few (a few in comparison of the numbers of

the larger majority), with how great numbers are our Churches filled, crowded up to the very walls; to what a degree do they annoy each other by the pressure, and almost choke each other by their overflowing numbers. Again, out of these very same persons, when there is a public spectacle, there are numbers flocking to the amphitheatre; these are over and above "the number." But it is for this reason that we say this, that they may be in "the number." Not being present, they do not hear this from us; but when ye have gone from hence, let them hear it from you. "I have declared," he says, "and have spoken." It is Christ who speaks. "He hath declared it," in His own Person, as our Head. He hath Himself declared it by His members. He Himself hath sent those who should "declare" it; He Himself hath sent the Apostles. "Their sound is gone out into all lands, and their words unto the ends of the world." How great the number of believers that are gathered together; how great the multitudes that flock together; many of them truly converted, many but in appearance: and those who are truly converted are the minority; those who are so but in appearance are the majority: because "they are multiplied beyond the number."

11. ... These are the "wonderful works" of God; these are the "thoughts" of God, to which "no man's thoughts are like;" that the lover of sight-seeing may be weaned from curiosity: and with us may seek after those more excellent, those more profitable things, in which, when he shall have attained unto them, he will rejoice. ...

12. "Sacrifice and offering Thou didst not desire" (ver, 6), saith the Psalm to God. For the men of old time, when as yet the true Sacrifice, which is known to the faithful, was foreshown in figures, used to celebrate rites that were figures of the reality that was to be hereafter; many of them understanding their meaning; but more of them in ignorance of it. For the Prophets and the holy Patriarchs understood what they were celebrating; but the rest of the "stiff-necked people" were so carnal, that what was done by them was but to symbolize the things that were to come afterwards; and it came to pass, when that first sacrifice was abolished; when the burnt-offerings of "rams, of goats, and of calves," and of other victims, had been abolished, "God did not desire them." Why did God not desire them? And why did He at the first desire them? Because all those things were, as it were, the words of a person making a promise; and the expressions conveying a promise, when the thing that they promise is come, are no longer uttered. ... Those sacrifices then, as being but expressions of a promise, have been abrogated. What is that which has been given as its fulfilment? That "Body;" which ye know; which ye do not all of you know; which, of you who do know it, I pray God all may not know it unto condemnation. Observe the time when it was said; for the person is

Christ our Lord, speaking at one time for His members, at another in His own person. "Sacrifice and offering," said He, "Thou didst not desire." What then? Are we left at this present time without a sacrifice? God forbid!

"But a Body hast Thou perfected for me." It was for this reason that Thou didst not desire the others; that Thou mightest "perfect" this; before Thou "perfectedst" this, Thou didst desire the others. The fulfilment of the promise has done away with the words that express the promise. For if they still hold out a promise, that which was promised is not yet fulfilled. This was promised by certain signs; the signs that convey the promise are done away; because the Substance that was promised is come. We are in this "Body." We are partakers of this "Body." We know that which we ourselves receive; and ye who know it not yet, will know it bye and bye; and when ye come to know it, I pray ye may not receive it unto condemnation. "For he that eateth and drinketh unworthily, eateth and drinketh damnation unto himself." "A Body" hath been "perfected" for us; let us be made perfect in the Body.

13. "Burnt-offerings also for sin hast Thou not required." "Then said I, Lo, I come!" (ver. 7). It is time that what "was promised should come;" because the signs, by means of which they were promised, have been put away. And indeed, Brethren, observe these put away; those fulfilled. Let the Jewish nation at this time show me their priest, if they can! Where are their sacrifices? They are brought to an end; they are put away now. Should we at that time have rejected them? We do reject them now; because, if you chose to celebrate them now, it were unseasonable; unfitting at the time; incongruous. You are still making promises; I have already received! There has remained to them a certain thing for them to celebrate; that they might not remain altogether without a sign. ... In such a case then are they; like Cain with his mark. The sacrifices, however, which used to be performed there, have been put away; and that which remained unto them for a sign like that of Cain, hath by this time been fulfilled; and they know it not. They slay the Lamb; they eat the unleavened bread. "Christ has been sacrificed for us, as our Passover." Lo, in the sacrifice of Christ, I recognise the Lamb that was slain! What of the unleavened bread? "Therefore," says he, "let us keep the feast; not with old leaven, neither with the leaven of wickedness" (he shows what is meant by "old;" it is "stale" flour; it is sour), "but in the unleavened bread of sincerity and truth." They have continued in the shade; they cannot abide the Sun of Glory. We are already in the light of day. We have "the Body" of Christ, we have the Blood of Christ. If we have a new life, let us "sing a new song, even a hymn unto our God." "Burnt offerings for sin Thou didst not desire. Then said I, Lo, I come!"

14. "In the head of the Book it is written of me, that I should fulfil Thy will: O my God, I am willing, and Thy Law is within my heart" (ver. 8). Behold! He turns His regards to His members. Behold! He hath Himself" fulfilled the will" of the Father. But in what "beginning of a Book" is it written of Him? Perhaps in the beginning of this Book of Psalms. For why should we seek far for it, or examine into other books for it? Behold! It is written in the beginning of this Book of Psalms! "His will is in the Law of the Lord;" that is," ' O my God, I am willing,' and 'Thy Law is within my heart ;'" that is the" same as, "And in His Law doth he meditate day and night."

15. "I have well declared Thy righteousness in the great congregation" (ver. 9). He now addresses His members. He is exhorting them to do what He has already done. He has "declared;" let us declare also. He has suffered; let us "suffer with Him." He has been glorified; we shall be "glorified with Him." "I have declared Thy righteousness in the great congregation." How great an one is that? In all the world. How great is it? Even among all nations. Why among all nations? Because He is "the Seed of Abraham, in whom all nations shall be blessed." Why among all nations? "Because their sound hath gone forth into all lands." "Lo! I will not refrain my lips, O Lord, and that Thou knowest." My lips speak; I will not "refrain" them from speaking. My lips indeed sound audibly in the ears of men; but "Thou knowest" mine heart. "I will not refrain my lips, O Lord; that Thou knowest." It is one thing that man heareth; another that God "knoweth." That the "declaring" of it should not be confined to the lips alone, and that it might not be said of us," Whatsoever things they say unto you, do; but do not after their works;" or lest it should be said to the people, "praising God with their lips, but not with their heart," "This people honoureth Me with their lips, but their heart is far from Me;" do thou make audible confession with thy lips; draw nigh with thine heart also. "For with the heart man believeth unto righteousness; but with the mouth confession is made unto salvation." In case like unto which that thief was found, who, hanging on the Cross with the Lord, did on the Cross acknowledge the Lord. Others had refused to acknowledge Him while working miracles; this man acknowledged Him when hanging on the Cross. That thief had every other member pierced through; his hands were fastened by the nails; his feet were pierced also; his whole body was fastened to the tree; the body was not disengaged in its other members; the heart and the tongue were disengaged; "with the heart" he "believed; with the tongue" he made "confession." "Remember me, O Lord," he said, "when Thou comest into Thy kingdom." He hoped for the coming of his salvation at a time far remote; he was content to receive it after a long delay; his hope rested on an object far remote. The day, however, was not postponed! The answer was, "This day shalt thou be with Me in Paradise." Paradise hath happy

trees! This day hast thou been with Me on "the Tree" of the Cross. This day shalt thou be with Me on "the Tree" of Salvation. ...

16. "I have not hid my righteousness within my heart" (ver. 10). What is meant by "my righteousness"? My faith. For," the just shall live by faith." As suppose the persecutor under threat of punishment, as they were once allowed to do, puts you to the question, "What art thou? Pagan or Christian?" "A Christian." That is his "righteousness." He believeth; he "lives by faith." He doth not "hide his righteousness within his heart." He has not said in his heart, "I do indeed believe in Christ; but I will not tell what I believe to this persecutor, who is raging against me, and threatening me. My God knoweth that inwardly, within my heart, I do believe. He knoweth that I renounce Him not." Lo! you say that you have this inwardly within your heart! What have you upon your lips? "I am not a Christian." Your lips bear witness against your heart. "I have not hid my righteousness within my heart." ...

17. "I have declared Thy Truth and. Thy Salvation." I have declared Thy Christ. This is the meaning of, "I have declared Thy Truth and Thy Salvation." How is "Thy Truth" Christ? "I am the Truth." How is Christ "His Salvation"? Simeon recognised the infant in His Mother's hands in the Temple, and said, "For mine eyes have seen Thy Salvation." The old man recognised the little child; the old man having himself "become a little child" in that infant, having been renewed by faith. For he had received an oracle from God; and it said this, "The Lord had said unto him, that he was not to depart out of this life, until he had seen the "Salvation of God." This "Salvation of God" it is a good thing to have shown unto men; but let them cry, "Show us Thy mercy, O Lord, and grant us Thy Salvation." ...

18. "I have not concealed Thy mercy and Thy Truth from the great congregation." Let us be there; let us also be numbered among the members of this Body: let us not keep back "the mercy" of the Lord, and "the Truth" of the Lord. Wouldest thou hear what "the mercy of the Lord" is? Depart from thy sins; He will forgive thy sins. Wouldest thou hear what "the truth" of the Lord is? Hold fast righteousness. Thy righteousness shall receive a crown. For mercy is announced to you now; "Truth" is to be shown unto thee hereafter. For God is not merciful in such a way as not to be just, nor just in such a way as not to be merciful. Does that mercy seem to thee an inconsiderable one? He will not impute unto thee all thy former sins: thou hast lived ill up to this present clay; thou art still living; this day live well; then thou wilt not "conceal" this" mercy." If this is meant by "mercy," what is meant by "truth"? ...

19. "Remove not Thou Thy mercies far from me, O Lord" (ver. 11). He is turning his attention to the wounded members. Because I have not "concealed Thy mercy and Thy Truth from the great congregation," from the Unity of the Universal Church, look Thou on Thy afflicted members, look on those who are guilty of sins of omission, and on those who are guilty of sins of commission: and withhold not Thou Thy mercies. "Thy mercy and Thy Truth have continually preserved me." I should not dare to turn from my evil way, were I not assured of remission; I could not endure so as to persevere, if I were not assured of the fulfilment of Thy promise. ...

"Innumerable evils have compassed me about" (ver. 12). Who can number sins? Who can count his own sins, and those of others? A burden under which he was groaning, who said, "Cleanse Thou me from my secret faults; and from the faults of others, spare Thou Thy servant, O Lord." Our own are too little; those "of others" are added to the burden. I fear for myself; I fear for a virtuous brother, I have to bear with a wicked brother; and under such burthen what shall we be, if God's mercy were to fail? "But Thou, Lord, remove not afar off." Be Thou near unto us! To whom is the Lord near? "Even" unto them that" are of a broken heart." He is far from the proud: He is near to the humble. "For though the Lord is high, yet hath He respect unto the lowly." But let not those that are proud think themselves to be unobserved: for the things that are high, He "beholdeth afar off." He "beheld afar off" the Pharisee, who boasted himself; He was near at hand to succour the Publican, who made confession The one extolled his own merits, and concealed his wounds; the other boasted not of his merits, but laid bare his wounds. He came to the Physician; he knew that he was sick, and that he required to be made whole; he" dared not lift up his eyes to Heaven: he smote upon his breast." He spared not himself, that God might spare him; he acknowledged himself guilty, that God might "ignore" the charge against him. He punished himself, that God might free him from punishment. ...

20. "Mine iniquities have taken hold upon me, so that I could not see." There is a something for us "to see;" what prevents us so that we see it not? Is it not iniquity? From beholding this light your eye is prevented perhaps by some humour penetrating into it; perhaps by smoke, or dust, or by something else that has been thrown into it: and you have not been able to raise your wounded eye to contemplate this light of day. What then? Will you be able to lift up your wounded heart unto God? Must it not be first healed, in order that thou mayest see? Do you not show your pride, when you say, "First let me see, and then I will believe"? Who is there who says this? For who that would fain see, says, "Let me see, and then I will believe"? I am about to manifest the Light unto thee; or rather the Light

Itself would fain manifest Itself to thee! To whom? It cannot manifest Itself to the blind. He does not see. Whence is it that he seeth not? It is that the eye is clogged by the multitude of sins. ...

21. "They are more than the hairs of my head." He subjects the number of the "hairs of his head" to calculation. Who is there can calculate the number of the hairs of his head? Much less can he tell the number of his sins, which exceed the number of the hairs of his head. They seem to be minute; but they are many in number. You have guarded against great ones; you do not now commit adultery, or murder; you do not plunder the property of others; you do not blaspheme; and do not bear false witness; those are the weightier kind of sins. You have guarded against great sins, what are you doing about your smaller ones? You have cast off the weight; beware lest the sand overwhelm you. "And my heart hath forsaken me." What wonder if thine heart is forsaken by thy God, when it is even "forsaken" by itself? What is meant by "faileth me," "forsaketh me"? Is not capable of knowing itself. He means this: "My heart hath forsaken me." I would fain see God with mine heart, and cannot from the multitude of my sins: that is not enough; mine heart does not even know itself. For no one thoroughly knows himself: let no one presume upon his own state. Was Peter able to comprehend with his own heart the state of his own heart, who said, "I will be with Thee even unto death"? There was a false presumption in the heart; there was lurking in that heart at the same time a real fear: and the heart was not able to comprehend the state of the heart. Its state was unknown to the sick heart itself: it was manifest to the physician. That which was foretold of him was fulfilled. God knew that in him which he knew not in himself: because his heart had forsaken him, his heart was unknown to his heart.

22. "Be pleased, O Lord, to deliver me" (ver. 13). As if he were saying, "' If Thou wilt, Thou canst make me clean.' Be pleased to deliver me. O Lord, look upon me to help me." Look, that is, on the penitent members, members that lie in pain, members that are writhing under the instruments of the surgeon; but still in hope.

23. "Let them be ashamed and confounded together that seek after my soul to destroy it" (ver. 14). For in a certain passage he makes an accusation, and says, "I looked upon my right hand, and beheld; and there was no man who sought after my soul;" that is, there was no man to imitate Mine example. Christ in His Passion is the Speaker. "I looked on my right hand," that is, not on the ungodly Jews, but on Mine own right hand, the Apostles,—"and there was no man who sought after My soul." So thoroughly was there no man to "seek after My soul," that he who had presumed on his own strength, "denied My soul." But because a man's soul is

sought after in two ways, either in order that you may enjoy his society; or that you may persecute him; therefore he here speaks of others, whom he would have "confounded and ashamed," who are "seeking after his soul." But lest you should understand it in the same way as when he complains of some who did not "seek after his soul," He adds, "to destroy it;" that is, they seek after my soul in order to my death. ...

24. "Let them be turned backward and put to shame that wish me evil." "Turned backwards." Let us not take this in a bad sense. He wishes them well; and it is His voice, who said from the Cross, "Father, forgive them; for they know not what they do." Wherefore then cloth he, say to them, that they should return "backwards"? Because they who before were proud, so that they fell, are now become humble, so that they may rise again. For when they are before, they are wishing to take precedence of their Lord; to be better than He; but if they go behind Him, they acknowledge Him to be better than they; they acknowledge that He ought to go before; that He should precede? they follow. Thence He thus rebukes Peter giving Him evil counsel. For the Lord, when about to suffer for our salvation, also foretold what was to happen concerning that Passion itself; and Peter says, "Be it far from Thee," "God forbid it!" "This shall not be!" He would fain have gone before his Lord; would have given counsel to his Master! But the Lord, that He might make him not go before Him, but follow after Him, says, "Get thee behind, Satan !" It is for this reason He said "Satan," because thou art seeking to go before Him, whom thou oughest to follow; but if thou art behind, if thou follow Him, thou wilt henceforth not be "Satan." What then? "Upon this Rock I will build My Church." ...

25. "Let them speedily bear away their own confusion, that say unto me, Well done! Well done!" (ver. 15). They praise you without reason. "A great man! A good man! A man of education and of learning; but why a Christian?" They praise those things in you which you should wish not to be praised; they find fault with that at which you rejoice. But if perhaps you say, "What is it you praise in me, O man? That I am a virtuous man? A just man? If you think this, Christ made me this; praise Him." But the other says, "Be it far from you. Do yourself no wrong! You yourself made yourself such." "Let them be confounded who say unto me, Well done! Well done!" And what follows?

"Let all those that seek Thee, O Lord, rejoice and be glad" (ver. 16). Those who "seek" not me, but "Thee;" who say not to me, "Well done! Well done!" but see me "glory in Thee," if I have anything whereof to glory; for "he who glories, let him glory in the Lord." "Let all those who seek Thee, Lord, rejoice and be glad."

"And say continually, the Lord be magnified." For even if the sinner becometh righteous, thou shouldest give the glory to "Him who justifieth the ungodly." Whether therefore it be a sinner, let Him be praised who calls him to forgiveness; or one already walking in the way of righteousness, let Him be praised who callus him to receive the crown! Let the Name of the Lord be magnified continually by "such as love Thy salvation."

"But I" (ver. 17). I for whom they were seeking evil, I whose "life they were seeking, that they might take it away." But turn thee to another description of persons. But I to whom they said, "Well done! Well done!" "I am poor and needy." There is nothing in me that may be praised as mine own. Let Him rend my sackcloth in sunder, and cover me with His robe, For, "Now I live, not I myself; but Christ liveth in me." If it is Christ that "liveth in thee," and all that thou hast is Christ's, and all that thou art to have hereafter is Christ's also; what art thou in thyself? "I am poor and needy." Now I am not rich, because I am not proud. He was rich who said, "Lord, I thank Thee that I am not as other men are;" but the publican was poor, who said, "Lord, be merciful to me a sinner!" The one was belching from his fulness; the other from want was crying piteously, "I am poor and needy!" And what wouldest thou do, O poor and needy man? Beg at God's door; "Knock, and it shall be opened unto thee."—"As for me, I am poor and needy. Yet the Lord careth for me."—"Cast thy care upon the Lord, and He shall bring it to pass." What canst thou effect for thyself by taking care? what canst thou provide for thyself? Let Him who made thee "care for thee." He who cared for thee before thou wert, how shall He fail to have a care of thee, now that thou art what He would have thee be? For now thou art a believer, now thou art walking in the "way of righteousness." Shall not He have a care for thee, who "maketh His sun rise on the good and on the evil, and sendeth rain on the just and on the unjust"? ...

"Thou art my Help, and my Deliverer; make no tarrying, O my God" (ver. 17). He is calling upon God, imploring Him, fearing lest he should fall away: "Make no tarrying." What is meant by "make no tarrying"? We lately read concerning the days of tribulation: "Unless those days should be shortened, there should no flesh be saved." The members of Christ—the Body of Christ extended everywhere—are asking of God, as one single person, one single poor man, and beggar! For He too was poor, who "though He was rich, yet became poor, that ye through His poverty might be made rich." It is He that maketh rich those who are the true poor; and maketh poor those who are falsely rich. He crieth unto Him; "From the end of the earth I cried unto Thee, when my heart was in heaviness." There will come days of tribulations, and of greater tribulations; they will come even as the Scripture speaks: and as days advance, so are tribulations increased also. Let no one promise himself what the Gospel doth not promise. ...

PSALM XLI.

TO THE PEOPLE, ON THE FEAST OF THE MARTYRS.

1. The solemn day of the Martyrs hath dawned; therefore to the glory of the Passion of Christ, the Captain of Martyrs, who spared not Himself, ordering His soldiers to the fight; but first fought, first conquered, that their fighting He might encourage by His example, and aid with His majesty, and crown with His promise: let us hear somewhat from this Psalm pertaining to His Passion. I commend unto you oftentimes, nor grieve I to repeat, what for you is useful to retain, that our Lord Jesus Christ speaketh often Of Himself, that is, in His own Person, which is our Head; often in the person of His Body, which are we and His Church; but so that the words sound as from the mouth of one, that we may understand the Head and the Body to consist together in the unity of integrity, and not be separated the one from the other; as in that marriage whereof it is said, "They two shall be one flesh." If then we acknowledge two in one flesh, let us acknowledge two in one voice. First, that which responding to the reader we have sung, though it be from the middle of the Psalm, from that I will take the beginning of this Sermon.

"Mine enemies speak evil of Me, When He shall die, then shall His Name perish" (ver. 5). This is the Person of our Lord Jesus Christ: but see if herein are not understood the members also. This was spoken also when our Lord Himself walked in the flesh here on earth. ... When they saw the people go after Him, they said, "When He shall die, then shall His Name perish;" that is, when we have slain Him, then shall His Name be no more in the earth, nor shall He seduce any, being dead; but by that very slaying of Him shall men understand, that He was but a man whom they followed, that there was in Him no hope of salvation, and shall desert His Name, and it shall no more be. He died, and His Name perished not, but His Name was sown as seed: He died, but He was a grain, which dying, the corn immediately sprang up. When glorified then was our Lord Jesus Christ, began they much more, and much more numerously to trust in Him; then began His members to hear what the Head had heard. Now then our Lord Jesus Christ being in heaven set down, and Himself in us labouring on earth, still spake His enemies, "When He shall die, then shall His Name perish." For hence stirred up the devil persecutions in the Church to destroy the Name of Christ. Unless haply ye think, brethren, that those Pagans, when they raged against Christians, said not this among themselves, "to blot out the Name of Christ from the earth." That Christ might die again, not in the Head, but in His Body, were slain also the Martyrs. To the multiplying of the Church availed the Holy Blood poured forth, to help Its seminating came also the death of the Martyrs. "Precious in the sight of the Lord is the death of His Saints."

More and more were the Christians multiplied, nor was it fulfilled which spake the enemies, "When He shall die, then shall His Name perish." Even now also is it spoken. Down sit the Pagans, and compute them the years, they hear their fanatics saying, A time shall come when Christians shall be none, and those idols must be worshipped as before they were worshipped: still say they, "When He shall die, then shall His Name perish." Twice conquered, now the third time be wise! Christ died, His Name has not perished: the Martyrs died, multiplied more is the Church, groweth through all nations the Name of Christ. He who foretold of His own Death, and of His Resurrection, He who foretold of His Martyrs' death, and of their crown, He Himself foretold of His Church things yet to come, if truth He spake twice, has He the third time lied? Vain then is what ye believe against Him; better is it that ye believe in Him, that ye may "understand upon the needy and poor One;" that "though He was rich, yet for your sakes He became poor, that ye through His poverty might be rich." ...

2. "Blessed is he that understandeth upon the needy and poor One: in the evil day shall the Lord deliver him" (ver. 1). For the evil day will come: will thou, hill thou, come it will: the Day of Judgment will come upon thee, an evil day if thou "understand not the needy and poor." For what now thou wilt not believe, shall be made manifest in the end. But neither shalt thou escape, when it shall be made manifest, because thou believest not, when it is kept secret. Invited art thou, what thou seest not to believe, lest when thou see, thou be put to the blush. "Understand then upon the needy and poor One," that is, Christ: understand in Him the hidden riches, whom poor thou seest. "In Him are hid all the treasures of wisdom and knowledge." For thereby in the evil day shall He deliver thee, in that He is God: but in that He is man, and that which in Him is human hath raised to life, and changed for the better, He hath lifted (thee) to heaven. But He who is God, who would have one person in man and with man, could neither decrease nor increase, neither die nor rise again. He died out of man's infirmity, but God dieth not. ... But as we rightly say, Such a man died, though his soul dieth not; so we rightly say, Christ died, though His Divinity dieth not. Wherefore died? Because needy and poor. Let not His death offend thee, and avert thee from beholding His Divinity. "Blessed is he that understandeth upon the needy and poor One." Consider also the poor, the needy, the hungry and thirsty, the naked, the sick, the prisoners; understand also upon such poor, for if upon such thou understand, thou understandest upon Him who said, "I was an hungred, I was thirsty, I was a stranger, naked, sick, in prison;" so in the evil day shall the Lord deliver thee. ...

3. "And deliver him not into the hand of his enemy" (ver. 2). The enemy is the devil. Let none think of a man his enemy, when he hears these words. Haply one

thought of his neighbour, of him who had a suit with him in court, of him who would take from him his own possession, of him who would force him to sell to him his house. Think not this; but that enemy think of, of whom said the Lord, "an enemy hath done this." For He it is who suggests that for things earthly he be worshipped, for overthrow the Christian Name this enemy cannot. For he hath seen himself conquered by the fame and praises of Christ, he hath seen, whereas he slew Christ's Martyrs, that they are crowned, he triumphed over. He hath begun to be unable to persuade men that Christ is nought; and because by reviling Christ, he now with difficulty deceives, by lauding Christ, he endeavours to deceive. Before this what said he? Whom worship ye? A Jew, dead, crucified, a man of no moment, who could not even from himself drive away death. When after His Name he saw running the whole human race, saw that in the Name of the Crucified temples are thrown down, idols are broken, sacrifices abolished; and that all these things predicted in the Prophets are considered by men, by men with wonder astonished, and closing now their hearts against the reviling of Christ; he clothes himself with praise of Christ, and begins to deter from the faith in another manner. Great is the law of Christ, powerful is that law, divine, ineffable! but who fulfilleth it? In the name of our Saviour, "tread upon the lion and the dragon." By reviling openly roared the lion; by lauding craftily lurks the dragon. Let them come to the faith, who doubted; and not say, Who fulfilleth it? If on their own strength they presume, they will not fulfil it. Presuming on the grace of God let them believe, presuming (on it) let them come; to be aided come, not to be judged. So live all the faithful in the Name of Christ, each one in his degree fulfilling the commands of Christ, whether married, or celibates and virgins, they live as much as God granteth them to live; neither presume they in their own strength, but know that in Him they ought to glory. ...

4. "The Lord help him" (ver. 3). But when? Haply in heaven, haply in the life eternal, that so it remain to worship the devil for earthly needs, for the necessities of this life. Far be it! Thou hast "promise of the life that now is, and of that which is to come." He came unto thee on earth, by Whom were made heaven and earth. Consider then what He saith, "The Lord help him, on his bed of pain." The bed of pain is the infirmity of the flesh; lest thou shouldest say, I cannot hold, and carry, and tie up my flesh; thou art aided that thou mayest. The Lord help thee on thy bed of pain. Thy bed did carry thee, thou carriedst not thy bed, but wast a paralytic inwardly; He cometh who saith to thee, "Take up thy bed, and go thy way into thy house." "The Lord help him on his bed of pain." Then to the Lord Himself He turneth, as though it were asked, Why then, since the Lord helpeth us, suffer we such great ills in this life, such great scandals, such great labours, such disquiet from the flesh and the world? He turneth to God, and as though explaining to us the counsel of His healing, He saith, "Thou hast turned all his bed in his infirmity."

By the bed is understood anything earthly. Every soul that is infirm in this life seeketh for itself somewhat whereon to rest, because intensity of labour, and of the soul extended toward God, it can hardly endure perpetually, somewhat it seeketh on earth whereon to rest, and in a manner with a kind of pausing to recline, as are those things which innocent ones love. ... The innocent man resteth in his house, his family, his wife, his children; in his poverty, his little farm, his orchard planted with his own hand, in some building fabricated with his own study; in these rest the innocent. But yet God willing us not to have love but of life eternal, even with these, though innocent delights, mixeth bitterness, that even in these we may suffer tribulation, and so He turneth all our bed in our infirmity. "Thou hast turned all his bed in his infirmity." Let him not then complain, when in these things which he hath innocently, he suffereth some tribulations. He is taught to love the better, by the bitterness of the worse; lest going a traveller to his country, he choose the inn instead of his own home.

5. But why this? Because He "scourgeth every son whom He receiveth." Why this? Because to men sinning was it said, "In the sweat of thy face shall thou eat bread." Therefore because all these chastisements, in which all our bed is turned in our infirmity, man ought to acknowledge that he suffers for sin; let him turn himself, and say what follows: "I said, Lord, be merciful unto me; heal my soul, for I have sinned against Thee" (ver. 4). O Lord, by tribulations do Thou exercise me; to be scourged Thou judgest every son whom Thou wilt receive, who sparedst not even the Only- Begotten. He indeed without sin was scourged; but I say, "I have sinned against Thee." ...

6. "Mine enemies speak evil of Me, When He shall die, then shall His Name perish" (ver. 5). Of this we have already spoken, and from this began.

7. "And entered in to see" (ver. 6). What Christ suffered, that suffereth also the Church; what the Head suffered, that suffer also the Members. "For the disciple is not above his Master, nor the servant above his Lord." ...

If to Christ's Members thou belongest, come within, cling to the Head. Endure the tares if thou art wheat, endure the chaff if thou art grain. Endure the bad fish within the net if thou art a good fish. Wherefore before the time of winnowing dost thou fly away? Wherefore before the time of harvest, dost thou root up the corn also with thyself? Wherefore before thou art come to the shore, hast thou broken the nets? "They go abroad, and tell it."

8. "All mine enemies whisper against Me unto the same thing" (ver. 7). Against Me all unto the same thing. How much better with me unto the same thing, than against me "unto the same thing." What is, "Against me unto the same thing"? With one counsel, with one conspiring. Christ then speaketh unto thee, Ye consent against Me, consent ye to Me: why against Me? wherefore not with Me? That same thing if ye had always had, ye had not divided you into schisms. For, saith the Apostle, "I beseech you, brethren, that ye all speak the same thing, and that there be no division among you." "All mine enemies whisper against Me unto the same thing:" against Me do they "devise evil to Me." To themselves rather, for "they have gathered iniquity to themselves;" but therefore to Me, because by their intention they are to be weighed: for not because to do nothing was in their power, to do nothing was in their will. For the devil lusted to extinguish Christ, and Judas would slay Christ; yet Christ slain and rising again, we are made alive, but to the devil and to Judas is rendered the reward of their evil will, not of our salvation. ... The intention wherewith they spake, not what they spake, did He consider, who related that they spake evil of Him, "Against Me they devised evil to Me." And what evil to Christ, to the Martyrs what evil? All hath God turned to good.

9. "An ungodly word do they set forth against Me" (ver. 8). What sort of ungodly word? Listen to the Head Itself. "Come, let us kill Him, and the inheritance shall be ours." Fools! How shall the inheritance be yours? Because ye killed Him? Lo! ye even killed Him; yet shall not the inheritance be yours. "Shall not He that sleepeth add this also, that He rise again"? When ye exulted that ye had slain Him, He slept; for He saith in another Psalm, "I slept." They raged and would slay Me; "I slept." If I had not willed, I had not even slept. "I slept," because "I have power to lay down My life, and I have power to take it again." "I laid Me down and slept, and rose up again." Rage then the Jews; be "the earth given into the hands of the wicked," be the flesh left to the hands of persecutors, let them on wood suspend it, with nails transfix it, with a spear pierce it. "Shall He that sleepeth, not add this, that He rise up again?" Wherefore slept He? Because "Adam is the figure of Him that was to come." And Adam slept, when out of his side was made Eve. Adam in the figure of Christ, Eve in the figure of the Church; whence she was called "the mother of all living." When was Eve created? While Adam slept. When out of Christ's side flowed the Sacraments of the Church? While He slept upon the Cross. ...

10. "The man of My peace, in whom I: trusted, which did eat of My bread, hath enlarged his heel against Me" (ver. 9): hath raised up his foot against Me: would trample upon Me. Who is this man of His peace? Judas. And in him did Christ trust, that He said, "in whom I trusted"? Did He not know: him from the

beginning? Did He not before he was born know that he would be? Had He not said to all His disciples," I have chosen you twelve, and one of you is a devil"? How then trusted He in him, but that He is in His Members, and that because many faithful trusted in Judas, the Lord transferred this to Himself? ... "The man of My peace, in whom I trusted, which did eat of My bread." How showed He him in His Passion? By the words of His prophecy: by the sop He marked Him out, that it might appear said of him, "Which did eat of My bread." Again, when he came to betray Him, He granted him a kiss, that it might appear said of him, "The man of My peace."

11. "But Thou, O Lord, be merciful unto Me" (ver. 10). This is the person of a servant, this is the person of the needy and poor for, "Blessed is he that understandeth upon the needy and poor One." See, as it was spoken, "Be merciful unto Me, and raise Me up, and I will requite them," so is it done. For the Jews slew Christ, lest they should lose their place. Christ slain, they lost their place. Rooted out of the kingdom were they, dispersed were they. He, raised up, requited them tribulation, He requited them unto admonition, not yet unto condemnation. For the city wherein the people raged, as a ramping and a roaring lion, crying out, "Crucify Him, Crucify Him," the Jews rooted out therefrom, hath now Christians, by not one Jew is inhabited. There is planted the Church of Christ, whence were rooted out the thorns of the synagogue. For truly this fire blazed "as the fire of thorns." But the Lord was as a green tree. This said Himself, when certain women mourned Christ as dying. ... "For if they do these things in a green tree, what shall be done in a dry?" When can a green tree be consumed by the fire of thorns? For they blazed as fire among thorns. Fire consumeth thorns, but whatsoever green tree it is applied to, is not easily kindled. ... Yet lest ye think that God the Father of Christ could raise up Christ, that is, the Flesh of His Son, and that Christ Himself, though He be the Word equal with the Father, could not raise up His own Flesh; hear out of the Gospel, "Destroy this temple, and in three days I will raise it up." "But," said the Evangelist (lest even after this we should doubt), "He spake of the temple of His Body. Raise Me up, and I will requite them."

12. "By this I know that Thou favourest Me, that Mine enemies shall not triumph over Me" (ver. 11.) Because the Jews did triumph, when they saw Christ crucified; they thought that they had fulfilled their will to do Him hurt: the fruits of their cruelty they saw in effect, Christ hanging on the Cross: they shook their heads, saying, "If Thou be the Son of God, come down from the Cross." He came not down, who could; His Potency He showed not, but patience taught. For if, on their saying these things, He had come down from the Cross, He would have seemed as it were to yield to them insulting, and not being able to endure reproach, would

have been believed conquered: more firm remained He upon the Cross, than they insulting; fixed was He, they wavering. For therefore shook they their heads, because to the true Head they adhered not. He taught us plainly patience. For mightier is that which He did, who would not do what the Jews challenged. For much mightier is it to rise from the sepulchre, than to come down from the Cross. "That Mine enemies shall not triumph over Me." They triumphed then at that time. Christ rose again, Christ was glorified. Now see they in His Name the human race converted: now let them insult, now shake the head: rather now let them fix the head, or if they shake the head, in wonder and admiration let them shake. ...

13. "But as for Me, Thou upholdest Me, because of Mine innocence" (ver. 12). Truly innocence; integrity without sin, requiting without debt, scourging without desert. "Thou upholdest Me because of Mine innocence, and hast made Me strong in Thy sight for ever." Thou hast made Me strong for ever, Thou madest Me weak for a time: Thou hast made Me strong in Thy sight, Thou madest Me weak in sight of men. What then? Praise to Him, glory to Him. "Blessed be the Lord God of Israel." For He is the God of Israel, our God, the God of Jacob, the God of the younger son, the God of the younger people. Let none say, Of the Jews said He this, I am not Israel; rather the Jews are not Israel. For the elder son, he is the elder people reprobated; the younger, the people beloved. "The elder shall serve the younger:" now is it fulfilled: now, brethren, the Jews serve us, they are as our satchellers, we studying, they carry our books. Hear wherein the Jews serve us, and not without reason. ... With them are the Law and the Prophets, in which. Law, and in which Prophets, Christ is preached. When we have to do with Pagans, and show this coming to pass in the Church of Christ, which before was predicted of the Name of Christ, of the Head and Body of Christ, lest they think that we have forged these predictions, and from things which have happened, as though they were future, had made them up, we bring forth the books of the Jews. The Jews forsooth are our enemies, from an enemy's books convince we the adversary. ... If any enemy clamour and say," Ye for yourselves have forged prophecies;" be the books of the Jews brought forth, because the elder shall serve the younger. Therein let them read those predictions, which now we see fulfilled; and let us all say, "Blessed be the Lord God of Israel, from everlasting to everlasting, and all the people shall say, So be it, So be it."

PSALMS 42-72: THE 2ND BOOK OF THE PSALMS

PSALM XLII.

1. We have undertaken the exposition of a Psalm corresponding to your own "longings," on which we propose to speak to you. For the Psalm itself begins with a certain pious "longing;" and he who sings so, says, "Like as the hart desireth the water-brooks, so longeth my soul after Thee, O God" (ver. 1). Who is it then that saith this? It is ourselves, if we be but willing! And why ask, who it is other than thyself, when it is in thy power to be the thing which thou art asking about? It is not however one individual, but it is "One Body;" but "Christ's Body is the Church." Such "longing" indeed is not found in all who enter the Church: let all however who have "tasted" the sweetness "of the Lord," and who own in Christ that for which they have a relish, think that they are not the only ones; but that there are such seeds scattered throughout "the field" of the Lord, this whole earth: and that there is a certain Christian unity, whose voice thus speaks, "Like as the hart desireth the water-brooks, so longeth my soul after Thee, O God." And indeed it is not ill understood as the cry of those, who being as yet Catechumens, are hastening to the grace of the holy Font. On which account too this Psalm is ordinarily chanted on those occasions, that they may long for the Fountain of remission of sins, even "as the hart for the water-brooks." Let this be allowed; and this meaning retain its place in the Church; a place both truthful and sanctioned by usage. Nevertheless, it appears to me, my brethren, that such "a longing" is not fully satisfied even in the faithful in Baptism: but that haply, if they know where they are sojourning, and whither they have to remove from hence, their "longing" is kindled in even greater intensity.

2. The title then of it is, "On the end: a Psalm for understanding for the sons of Korah." We have met with the sons of Korah in other titles of Psalms: and remember to have discussed and stated already the meaning of this name. Yet we must even now take notice of this title in such a way, that what we have said already should be no prejudice against our saying it again: for all were not present in every place where we said it. Now Korah may have been, as indeed he was, a certain definite person; and have had sons, who might be called "the sons of Korah;" let us however search for the secret of which this is the sacrament, that this name may bring to light the mystery with which it is pregnant. For there is some great mystery in the matter that the name "sons of Korah" is given to Christians. Why "sons of Korah"? They are "sons of the bridegroom, sons of Christ," Why then does "Korah" stand for Christ? Because "Korah" is equivalent

to" Calvaria." ... Therefore, the "sons of the bridegroom," the sons of His Passion, the sons redeemed by His Blood, the sons of His Cross, who bear on their forehead that which His enemies erected on Calvary, are called "the sons of Korah; to them is this Psalm sung as a Psalm for "understanding." Let then our understanding be roused: and if the Psalm be sung to us, let us follow it with our "understanding." ... Run to the brooks; long after the water-brooks. "With God is the fountain of Life;" a "fountain" that shall never be dried up: in His "Light" is a Light that shall never be darkened. Long thou for this light: for a certain fountain, a certain light, such as thy bodily eyes know not; a light to see which the inward eye must be prepared; a fountain, to drink of which the inward thirst is to be kindled. Run to the fountain; long for the fountain; but do it not anyhow, be not satisfied with running like any ordinary animal; run thou "like the hart." What is meant by "like the hart"? Let there be no sloth in thy running; run with all thy might: long for the fountain with all thy might. For we find in "the hart" an emblem of swiftness.

3. But perhaps Scripture meant us to consider in the stag not this point only, but another also. Hear what else there is in the hart. It destroys serpents, and after the killing of serpents, it is inflamed with thirst yet more violent; having destroyed serpents, it runs to "the water-brooks," with thirst more keen than before. The serpents are thy vices, destroy the serpents of iniquity; then wilt thou long yet more for "the Fountain of Truth." Perhaps avarice whispers in thine ear some dark counsel, hisses against the word of God, hisses against the commandment of God. And since it is said to thee, "Disregard this or that thing," if thou prefer working iniquity to despising some temporal good, thou choosest to be bitten by a serpent, rather than destroy it. Whilst, therefore, thou art yet indulgent to thy vice, thy covetousness or thy appetite, when am I to find in thee "a longing" such as this, that might make thee run to the water-brooks? ...

4. There is another point to be observed in the hart. It is reported of stags ... that when they either wander in the herds, or when they are swimming to reach some other parts of the earth, that they support the burdens of their heads on each other, in such a manner as that one takes the lead, and others follow, resting their heads upon him, as again others who follow do upon them, and others in succession to the very end of the herd; but the one who took the lead in bearing the burden of their heads, when tired, returns to the rear, and rests himself after his fatigue by supporting his head just as did the others; by thus supporting what is burdensome, each in turn, they both accomplish their journey, and do not abandon each other. Are they not a kind of "harts" that the Apostle addresses, saying, "Bear ye one another's burdens, and so fulfil the Law of Christ"? ...

5. "My soul is athirst for the living God" (ver. 2). What I am saying, that "as the hart panteth after the water-brooks, so longs my soul after Thee, O God," means this, "My soul is athirst for the living God." For what is it athirst? "When shall I come and appear before God?" This it is for which I am athirst, to "come and to appear before Him." I am athirst in my pilgrimage, in my running; I shall be filled on my arrival. But "When shall I come?" And this, which is soon in the sight of God, is late to our "longing." "When shall I come and appear before God?" This too proceeds from that "longing," of which in another place comes that cry, "One thing have I desired of the Lord; that will I seek after; that I may dwell in the house of the Lord all the days of my life." Wherefore so? "That I may behold" (he saith) "the beauty of the Lord." "When shall I come and appear before the Lord?"

6. "My tears have been my meat day and night, while they daily say unto me, Where is thy God?" (ver. 3). My tears (he saith) have been not bitterness, but "my bread." Those very tears were sweet unto me: being athirst for that fountain, inasmuch as I was not as yet able to drink of it, I have eagerly made my tears my meat. For he said not, "My tears became my drink," lest he should seem to have longed for them, as for "the water- brooks:" but, still retaining that thirst wherewith I burn, and by which I am hurried away towards the water-brooks, "My tears became my meat," whilst I am not yet there. And assuredly he does but the more thirst for the water-brooks from making his tears his meat. ... "And they daily say unto me, Where is thy God?" For if a Pagan should say this to me, I cannot retort it upon him, saying, "Where is thine?" inasmuch as he points with his finger to some stone, and says, "Lo, there is my God!" When I have laughed at the stone, and he who pointed to it has been put to the blush, he raises his eyes from the stone, looks up to heaven, and perhaps says, pointing his finger to the Sun, "Behold there my God! Where, I pray, is your God?" He has found something to point out to the eyes of the flesh; whereas I, on my part, not that I have not a God to show to him, cannot show him what he has no eyes to see. For he indeed could point out to my bodily eyes his God, the Sun; but what eyes hath he to which I might point out the Creator of the Sun? ...

7. "I thought on these things, and poured out my soul above myself" (ver. 4). When would my soul attain to that object of its search, which is "above my soul," if my soul were not to "pour itself out above itself"? For were it to rest in itself, it would not see anything else beyond itself; and in seeing itself, would not, for all that, see God. Let then my insulting enemies now say, "Where is thy God?" aye, let them say it! I, so long as I do not "see," so long as my happiness is postponed, make my tears my "bread day and night." Let them still say, "Where is thy God?" I seek my God in every corporeal nature, terrestrial or celestial, and find Him not: I

seek His Substance in my own soul, and I find it not, yet still I have thought on these things, and wishing to "see the invisible things of my God, being understood by the things made," I have poured forth my soul above myself, and there remains no longer any being for me to attain to, save my God. For it is "there" is the "house of my God." His dwelling-place is above my soul; from thence He beholds me; from thence He created me; from thence He directs me and provides for me; from thence he appeals to me, and calls me, and directs me; leads me in the way, and to the end of my way. ...

8. For when I was "pouring out my soul above myself," in order to reach my God, why did I do so? "For I will go into the place of Thy Tabernacle." For I should be in error were I to seek for my God without" the place of His tabernacle." "For I will go into the place of Thy wonderful tabernacle, even unto the house of God."

"I will go," he says, "into the place of the wonderful tabernacle, even unto the house of God!" For there are already many things that I admire in "the tabernacle." See how great wonders I admire in the tabernacle! For God's tabernacle on earth is the faithful; I admire in them the obedience of even their bodily members: that in them "Sin does not reign so that they should obey its lusts; neither do they yield their members instruments of unrighteousness unto sin; but unto the living God in good works." I admire the sight of the bodily members warring in the service of the soul that serves God. ... And wonderful though the tabernacle be, yet when I come to "the house of God," I am even struck dumb with astonishment. Of that "house" he speaks in another Psalm, after he had put a certain abstruse and difficult question to himself (viz., why is it that it generally goes well with the wicked on earth, and ill with the good?), saying, "I thought to know this; it is too painful for me, until I go into the sanctuary of God, and understand of the last things." For it is there, in the sanctuary of God, in the house of God, is the fountain of "understanding." There he "understood of the last things;" and solved the question concerning the prosperity of the unrighteous, and the sufferings of the righteous. How does he solve it? Why, that the wicked, when reprieved here, are reserved for punishments without end; and the good when they suffer here, are being tried in order that they may in the end obtain the inheritance. And it was in the sanctuary of God that he understood this, and "understood of the last things." ... For he tells us of his progress, and of his guidance thither; as if we had been saying, "You are admiring the tabernacle here on earth; how came you to the sanctuary of the house of God?" he says, "In the voice of joy and praise; the sound of keeping holiday." Here, when men keep festival simply for their own indulgence, it is their custom to place musical instruments, or to station a chorus of singers, before their houses, or any kind of music that serves and allures to wantonness. And when these are heard, what do we passers by say? "What is going on here?" And we are told in answer, that it is some festival. "It is a birthday that is being celebrated" (say they)," there is a marriage here;" that those songs may not appear out of place, but the luxurious indulgence may be excused by the festive occasion. In the "house of God" there is a never-ending festival: for there it is not an occasion celebrated once, and then to pass away. The angelic choir makes an eternal "holiday:" the presence of God's face, joy that never fails. This is a "holiday" of such a kind, as neither to be opened by any dawn, nor terminated by any evening. From that everlasting perpetual festivity, a certain sweet and melodious strain strikes on the ears of the heart, provided only the world do not drown the sounds. As he walks in this tabernacle, and contemplates God's wonderful works for the redemption of the faithful, the sound of that festivity charms his ears, and bears the "hart" away to "the water-brooks."

9. But seeing, brethren, so long as "we are at home in this body, we are absent from the Lord;" and "the corruptible body presseth down the soul, and the earthly tabernacle weigheth down the mind that museth on many things;" even though we have some way or other dispersed the clouds, by walking as "longing" leads us on, and for a brief while have come within reach of that sound, so that by an effort we may catch something from that "house of God," yet through the burden, so to speak, of our infirmity, we sink back to our usual level, and relapse to our ordinary state. And just as there we found cause for rejoicing, so here there will not be wanting an occasion for sorrow. For that hart that made "tears" its "bread day and night," borne along by "longing to the water-brooks" (that is, to the spiritual delights of God), "pouring forth his soul above himself," that he may attain to what is "above" his own soul, walking towards "the place of the wonderful tabernacle, even unto the house of God," and led on by the sweetness of that inward spiritual sound to feel contempt for all outward things, and be borne on to things spiritual, is but a mortal man still; is still groaning here, still bearing about the frailty of flesh, still in peril in the midst of the "offences" of this world. He therefore glances back to himself? as if he were coming from that world; and says to himself, now placed in the midst of these sorrows, comparing these with the things, to see which he had entered in there, and after seeing which he had come forth from thence;

"Why art thou cast down, O my soul, and why dost thou disquiet me?" (ver. 5). Lo, we have just now been gladdened by certain inward delights: with the mind's eye we have been able to behold, though but with a momentary glance, something not susceptible of change: why dost thou still "disquiet me, why art thou" still "cast down"? For thou dost not doubt of thy God. For now thou art not without somewhat to say to thyself, in answer to those who say, "Where is thy God?" I have now had the perception of something that is unchangeable; why dost thou disquiet me still?

"Hope in God." Just as if his soul was silently replying to him, "Why do I disquiet thee, but because I am not yet there, where that delight is, to which I was, as it were, rapt for a moment? Am I already 'drinking' from this 'fountain' with nothing to fear?" ... Still "Hope in God," is his answer to the soul that disquiets him, and would fain account for her disquiet from the evils with which this world abounds. In the mean while dwell in hope: for "hope that is seen is not hope; but if we hope for that we see not, then do we with patience wait for it."

10. "Hope in God." Why "hope"? "For I will confess unto Him." What wilt thou "confess"? "My God is the saving health of my countenance." My "health" (my salvation) cannot be from myself; this it is that I will say, that I will "confess." It is my God that is "the saving health of my countenance." For to account for his fears, in the midst of those things, which he now knows, having come after a sort to the "understanding" of them, he has been looking behind him again in anxiety, lest the enemy be stealing upon him: he cannot yet say, "I am made whole every whit." For having but "the first-fruits of the Spirit, we groan within ourselves; waiting for the adoption, to wit, the redemption of the body." When that "health" (that salvation) is perfected in us, then shall we be living in the house of God for ever, and praising for ever Him to whom it was said, "Blessed are they that dwell in Thy house, they will be praising Thee world without end." This is not so yet, because the salvation which is promised, is not as yet in being; but it is "in hope" that I confess unto God, and say, "My God is the saving health of my countenance." For it is "in hope" that "we are saved; but hope that is seen, is not hope." ...

11. "My soul is disquieted on account of myself" (ver. 6). Is it disquieted on account of God? It is on my own account it is disquieted. By the Unchangeable it was revived; it is by the changeable it is disquieted. I know that the righteousness of God remaineth; whether my own will remain stedfast, I know not. For I am alarmed by the Apostle's saying, "Let him that thinketh he standeth, take heed lest he fall." Therefore since "there is no soundness in me for myself," there is no hope either for me of myself. "My soul is disquieted on account of myself." ... "Therefore I remember Thee, O Lord, from the land of Jordan, and from the little hill of Hermon." From whence did I remember thee? From the "little hill," and from the "land of Jordan." Perhaps from Baptism, where the remission of sins is given. For no one runs to the remission of sins, except he who is dissatisfied with himself; no one runs to the remission of sins, but he who confesses himself a

sinner; no one confesses himself a sinner, except by humbling himself before God. Therefore it is from "the land of Jordan I have remembered thee, and from the hill;" observe, not "of the great hill," that thou mayest make of the "little hill" a great one: for "whoso exalteth himself shall be abased, and whoso humbleth himself shall be exalted." If you would also ask the meanings of the names, Jordan means "their descent." Descend then, that thou mayest be "lifted up:" be not lifted up, lest thou be cast down. "And the little hill of Hermon." Hermon means "anathematizing." Anathematize thyself, by being displeased with thyself; for if thou art pleased with thyself, God will be displeased with thee. Because then God gives us all good things, because He Himself is good, not because we are worthy of it; because He is merciful, not because we have in anything deserved it; it is from "the land of Jordan, and from Hermon," that I remember thee. And because he so remembers with humility, he shall earn his exaltation to fruition, for he is not "exalted" in himself, who "glories in the Lord."

12. "Deep calleth unto deep with the voice of thy water-spouts" (ver. 7). I may perhaps finish the Psalm, aided as I am by your attention, whose fervour I perceive. As for your fatigue in hearing, I am not greatly solicitous, since you see me also, who speak, toiling in the heat of these exertions. Assuredly it is from your seeing me labouring, that you labour with me: for I am labouring not for myself, but for you. "Deep calleth unto deep with the voice of thy water-spouts." It was God whom he addressed, who "remembered him from the land of Jordan and Hermon." It was in wonder and admiration he spake this: "Abyss calleth unto abyss with the voice of Thy water-spouts." What abyss is this that calls, and to what other abyss? Justly, because the "understanding" spoken of is an "abyss." For an "abyss" is a depth that cannot be reached or comprehended; and it is principally applied to a great body of water. For there is a "depth," a "profound," the bottom of which cannot be reached by sounding. Furthermore, it is said in a certain passage. "Thy judgments are a mighty abyss," Scripture meaning to suggest that the judgments of God are incomprehensible. What then is the "abyss" that calls, and to what other "abyss" does it call? If by "abyss" we understand a great depth, is not man's heart, do you not suppose, "an abyss"? For what is there more profound than that "abyss"? Men may speak, may be seen by the operations of their members, may be heard speaking in conversation: but whose thought is penetrated, whose heart seen into? What he is inwardly engaged on, what he is inwardly capable of, what he is inwardly doing or what purposing, what he is inwardly wishing to happen, or not to happen, who shall comprehend? I think an "abyss" may not unreasonably be understood of man, of whom it is said elsewhere, "Man shall come to a deep heart, and God shall be exalted." If man then is an "abyss," in what way doth "abyss" call on "abyss"? Does man "call on" man as God is called upon? No, but "calls on" is equivalent to "calls to him." For it was

said of a certain person, he calls on death; that is, lives in such a way as to be inviting death; for there is no man at all who puts up a prayer, and calls expressly on death: but men by evil-living invite death. "Deep calls on deep," then, is, "man calls to man." Thus is it wisdom is learnt, and thus faith, when "man calls to man." The holy preachers of God's word call on the "deep:" are they not themselves "a deep" also? ...

13. "Deep calleth to deep with the voice of Thy water-spouts" I, who tremble all over, when my soul was disquieted on account of myself, feared greatly on account of Thy "judgments." ... Are those judgments slight ones? They are great ones, severe, hard to bear; but would they were all. "Deep calls to deep with the voice of Thy water-spouts," in that Thou threatenest, Thou sayest, that there is another condemnation in store even after those sufferings. "Deep calls on deep with the voice of Thy water- spouts." "Whither then shall I go from Thy presence? And whither shall I flee from Thy Spirit?" seeing that deep calls to deep, and after those sufferings severer ones are to be dreaded.

14. "All Thy overhangings and Thy waves are come upon me." The "waves" in what I already feel, the "overhangings" in that Thou denouncest. All my sufferings are Thy waves; all Thy denouncements of judgments are Thy "overhangings." In the "waves" that deep "calleth;" in the "overhangings" is the other "deep" which it "calls to." In this that I suffer are all Thy waves; in the severer punishment that Thou threatenest, all Thy "overhangings" are come unto me. For He who threatens does not let His judgments fall upon us, but keeps them suspended over us." But inasmuch as Thou sittest at liberty, I have thus spoken unto my soul. "Hope in God: for I will confess unto Him. My God is the saving health of my countenance." The more numerous my sufferings, the sweeter will be Thy mercy.

15. Therefore follows: "The Lord will commend His loving-kindness in the day-time; and in the night-time will He declare it"(ver. 8). In tribulation no man has leisure to hear: attend, when it is well with you; hear, when it is well with you; learn, when you are in tranquillity, the discipline of wisdom, and store up the word of God as you do food. For in tribulation every one must be profiled by what he heard in the time of security. For in prosperity God "commends to thee His mercy," in case thou serve Him faithfully, for He frees thee from tribulation; but it is "in the night" only that He "declares" His mercy to thee, which He "commended" to thee by day. When tribulation shall actually come, He will not leave thee destitute of His help; He will show thee that which He commended to thee in the daytime is true. For it is written in a certain passage, "The mercy of the Lord is seasonable in the time of affliction, as clouds of rain in the time of

drought." "The Lord hath commended His loving-kindness in the day-time, and in the night will He declare it." He does not showy that He is thine Helper, unless tribulation come, from whence thou must be rescued by Him who promised it to thee "in the day-time." Therefore we are warned to be like "the ant." For just as worldly prosperity is signified by "the day," adversity by the night, so again in another way worldly prosperity is expressed by "the summer," adversity by the winter. And what is it that the ant does? She lays up in summer what will be useful to her in winter. Whilst therefore it is summer, whilst it is well with you, whilst you are in tranquillity, hear the word of the Lord. For how can it be that in the midst of these tempests of the world, you should pass through the whole of that sea, without suffering? How could it happen? To what mortal's lot has it fallen? If even it has been the lot of any, that very calm is more to be dreaded. "The Lord hath commended His loving-kindness in the day-time, and in the night-time will He declare it." ... "There is with me prayer unto the God of my life." This I make my business here; I who am the "hart thirsting and longing for the water-brooks," calling to mind the sweetness of that strain, by which I was led on through the tabernacle even to the house of God; whilst this "corruptible body presseth down the soul," there is yet with me "prayer unto the God of my life." For in order to making supplication unto God, I have not to buy aught from places beyond the sea; or in order that He may hear me, have I to sail to bring from a distance frankincense and perfumes, or have I to bring "calf or ram from the flock." There is "with me prayer to the God of my life." I have within a victim to sacrifice; I have within an incense to place on the altar; I have within a sacrifice wherewith to propitiate my God. "The sacrifice of God is a troubled spirit." What sacrifice of a "troubled spirit" I have within, hear.

16. "I will say unto God, Thou art my lifter up. Why hast Thou forgotten me?" (ver. 9). For I am suffering here, even as if Thou hadst forgotten me. But Thou art trying me, and I know that Thou dost but put off, not take utterly from me, what Thou hast promised me. But yet, "Why hast Thou forgotten me?" So cried our Head also, as if speaking in our name. "My God, my God, why hast Thou forsaken me?" I will say unto God, "Thou art my lifter up; why hast Thou forgotten me?"

17. "Why hast Thou rejected me?" "Rejected" me, that is to say, from that height of the apprehension of the unchangeable Truth. "Why hast Thou rejected me?" Why, when already longing for those things, have I been cast down to these, by the weight and burden of my iniquity? This same voice in another passage said, "I said in my trance" (i.e., in my rapture, when he had seen some great thing or other), "I said in my trance, I am cast out of the sight of Thine eyes." For he compared these things in which he found himself, to those toward which he had

been raised; and saw himself cast out far "from the sight of God's eyes," as he speaks even here, "Why hast Thou rejected me? Why go I mourning, while mine enemy troubleth me, while he breaketh my bones?" Even he, my tempter, the devil; while offences are everywhere on the increase, because of the abundance of which "the love of many is waxing cold." When we see the strong members of the Church generally giving way to the causes of offence, does not Christ's body say, "The enemy breaketh my bones"? For it is the strong members that are "the bones;" and sometimes even those that are strong sink under their temptations. For whosoever of the body of Christ considers this, does he not exclaim, with the voice of Christ's Body, "Why hast Thou rejected me? Why go I mourning, while mine enemy troubleth me, while he breaketh my bones?"

You may see not my flesh merely, but even my "bones." To see those who were thought to have some stability, giving way under temptations, so that the rest of the weak brethren despair when they see those who are strong succumbing; how great, my brethren, are the dangers:

18. "They who trouble me cast me in the teeth." Again that voice! "While they say daily unto me, Where is thy God?" (ver. 10). And it is principally in the temptations of the Church they say this," Where is thy God?" How much was this cast in the teeth of the Martyrs! Those men so patient and courageous for the name of Christ, how often was it said to them, "Where is your God?" "Let Him deliver you, if He can." For men saw their torments outwardly; they did not inwardly behold their crowns! "They who trouble me cast me in the teeth, while they say daily unto me, Where is thy God?" And on this account, seeing "my soul is disquieted on account of myself," what else should I say unto it than those words:

"Why art thou cast down, O my soul; and why dost thou disquiet me?" (ver. 11). And, as it seems to answer, "Wouldest thou not have me disquiet thee, placed as I am here in so great evils? Wouldest thou have me not disquiet thee, panting as I am after what is good, thirsting and labouring as I am for it?" What should I say, but,

"Hope thou in God; for I will yet confess unto Him" (ver. 11). He states the very words of that confession; he repeats the grounds on which he fortifies his hope. "He is the health of my countenance, and my God."

PSALM XLIII.

1. This Psalm is a short one; it satisfies the mental cravings of the hearers, without imposing too severe a trial on the hunger of those fasting. Let our soul feed upon it; our soul, which he who sings in this Psalm, speaks of as "cast down;" cast down, I suppose, either in consequence of some fist, or rather in consequence of some hunger he was in. For fasting is a voluntary act; being an-hungered is an involuntary thing. That which is an-hungered, is the Church, is the Body of Christ: and that "Man" who is extended throughout the whole world, of which the Head is above, the limbs below: it is His voice which ought by this time to be perfectly known, and perfectly familiar, to us, in all the Psalms; now chanting joyously, now sorrowing; now rejoicing in hope, now sighing at its actual state, even as if it were our own. We need not then dwell long on pointing out to you, who is the speaker here: let each one of us be a member of Christ's Body; and he will be speaker here. ...

2. "Judge me, O Lord, and separate my cause from the ungodly nation" (ver. 1). I do not dread Thy judgment, because I know Thy mercy. "Judge me, O God," he cries. Now, meanwhile, in this state of pilgrimage, Thou dost not yet separate my place, because I am to live together with the "tares" even to the time of the "harvest:" Thou dost not as yet separate my rain from theirs; my light from theirs: "separate my cause." Let a difference be made between him who believes in Thee, and him who believes not in Thee. Our infirmity is the same; but our consciences not the same:our sufferings the same; but our longings not the same. "The desire of the ungodly shall perish," but as to the desire of the righteous, we might well doubt, if He were not "sure" who promised. The object of our desires is He Himself, who prom-iseth: He will give us Himself, because He has already given Himself to us; He will give Himself in His immortality to us then immortal, even because He gave Himself in His mortality to us when mortal. ...

3. And since patience is needful in order to endure, until the harvest, a certain distinction without separation, if we may so speak (for they are together with us, and therefore not yet separated; the tares however being still tares, and the corn still corn, and therefore they are already distinct); since then a kind of strength is needful, which must be implored of Him who bids us to be strong, and without whose making us strong, we should not be what He bids us to be; of Him who said, "He that endures unto the end shall be saved," lest the soul's powers should be impaired in consequence of her ascribing any strength to herself, he subjoins immediately,

"For Thou, O God, art my strength: why hast Thou cast me off, and why go I mourning, while the enemy harasseth me?" (ver. 2). I go mourning: the enemy is harassing me with daily temptations: inspiring either some unlawful love, or some ungrounded cause of fear; and the soul that fights against both of them, though not taken prisoner by them, yet being in danger from them, is contracted with sorrow, and says unto God, "Why?"

Let her then ask of Him, and hear "Why?" For she is in the Psalm enquiring the cause of her dejection; saying, "Why hast Thou cast me off? and why go I mourning?" Let her hear from Isaiah; let the lesson which has just been read, suggest itself to her. "The spirit shall go forth from me, and every breath have I made. For iniquity have I a little afflicted him; I hid my face from him, and he departed from me sorrowful in the ways of his heart." Why then didst thou ask, "Why hast Thou cast me off, and why go I mourning?" Thou hast heard, it was "for iniquity." "Iniquity" is the cause of thy mourning; let "Righteousness" be the cause of thy rejoicing! Thou wouldest sin; and yet thou wouldest fain not suffer; so that it was too little for thee to be thyself unrighteous, without also wishing Him to be unrighteous, in that thou wouldest fain not be punished by Him. Consider a speech of a better kind in another Psalm. "It is good for me that Thou hast humbled me, that I might learn Thy righteousnesses." By being lifted up, I had learned my own iniquities; let me by being "humbled," learn "Thy righteousnesses." "Why go I mourning, while the enemy harasses me?" Thou complainest of the enemy. It is true he does harass thee; but it was thou didst "give place" to him. And even now there is a course open to thee; choose the course of prudence; admit thy King, shut the tyrant out.

4. But in order that she may do this, hear what she says, what she supplicates, what she prays for. Pray thou for what thou hearest; pray for it when thou hearest it; let these words be the voice of us all: "O send out Thy Light and Thy Truth. They have led me, and brought me on unto Thy holy hill, and into Thy Tabernacles" (ver. 3). For that very "Light" and "Truth" are indeed two in name; the reality expressed is but One. For what else is the "Light" of God, except the "Truth" of God? Or what else is the "Truth" of God, except the "Light" of God? And the one Person of Christ is both of these. "I am the Light of the world: he that believeth on Me, shall not walk in darkness." "I am the Way, the Truth, and the Life." He is Himself "the Light:" He is Himself "the Truth." Let Him come then and rescue us, and "separate at once our cause from the ungodly nation; let Him deliver us from the deceitful and unjust man," let him separate the wheat from the tares, for at the time of harvest He will Himself send His Angels, that they may "gather out of His kingdom all things that offend," and cast them into flaming fire, while they gather

together the corn into the garner. He will send out His" Light," and His "Truth;" for that they have already "brought us and led us to His holy hill, and into His Tabernacles." We possess the "earnest;" we hope for the prize. "His holy Hill" is His holy Church. It is that mountain which, according to Daniel's vision, grew from a very small "stone," till it crushed the kingdoms of the earth; and grew to such a size, that it "filled the face of the earth." This is the "hill," from which he tells us that his prayer was heard, who says, "I cried unto the Lord with my voice, and He heard me out of His holy hill." s Let no one of those that are without that mountain, hope to be heard unto eternal life. For many are heard in their prayers for many things. Let them not congratulate themselves on being heard; the devils were heard in their prayer, that they might be sent into the swine. Let us desire to be heard unto eternal life, by reason of our longing, through which we say, "Send out Thy Light and Thy Truth." That is a "Light" which requires the eye of the heart. For "Blessed" (He saith) "are the pure in heart, for they shall see God." We are now on His Hill, that is, in His Church, and in His Tabernacle. The "tabernacle" is for persons sojourning; the house, for those dwelling in one community. The tabernacle is also for those who are both from home, and also in a state of warfare. When thou hearest of a tabernacle, form a notion of a war; guard against an enemy. But what shall the house be? "Blessed are they that dwell in Thine house: they will be alway praising Thee."

5. Now then that we have been led on even to "the Tabernacle," and are placed on "His holy Hill," what hope do we carry with us?

"Then will I go in unto the Altar of God" (ver. 4). For there is a certain invisible Altar on high, which the unrighteous man approaches not. To that Altar he alone draws nigh, who draws nigh to this one without cause to fear. There he shall find his Life, who in this one "separates his cause." "And I will go in unto the Altar of God." From His holy Hill, and from His Tabernacle, from His Holy Church, I will go in unto the Altar of God on High. What manner of Sacrifice is there? He himself who goeth in is taken for a burnt-offering. "I will go in unto the Altar of God." What is the meaning of what he says, "The Altar of my God"?

"Unto God, who makes glad my youth." Youth signifies newness: just as if he said, "Unto God, who makes glad my newness." It is He who makes glad my newness, who hath filled my old estate" with mourning. For now "I go mourning" in oldness, then shall "I stand," exulting in newness!

"Yea, upon the harp will I praise Thee, O God my God." What is the meaning of "praising on the harp," and praising on the psaltery? For he does not always do so with the harp, nor always with the psaltery. These two instruments of the musicians have each a distinct meaning of their own, worthy of our consideration and notice. They are both borne in the hands, and played by the touch; and they stand for certain bodily works of ours. Both are good, if one knows how to play the psaltery, or to play the harp. But since the psaltery is that instrument which has the shell (i.e. that drum, that hollow piece of wood, by straining on which the chords resound) on the upper part of it, whereas the harp has that same concave sounding-board on the lower part, there is to be a distinction made between our works, when they are" upon the harp," when "on the psaltery:" both however are acceptable to God, and grateful to His ear. When we do anything according to God's Commandments, obeying His commands and hearkening to Him, that we may fulfil His injunctions, when we are active and not passive, it is the psaltery that is playing. For so also do the Angels: for they have nothing to suffer. But when we suffer anything of tribulation, of trials, of offences on this earth (as we suffer only from the inferior part of ourselves; i.e. from the fact that we are mortal, that we owe somewhat of tribulation to our original cause, and also from the fact of our suffering much from those who are not "above"); this is "the harp." For there rises a sweet strain from that part of us which is "below:" we "suffer," and we strike the psaltery, or shall I rather say we sing and we strike the harp. ...

6. And again, in order that he may draw the sound from that sounding- board below, he addresses his soul: he says, "Why art thou sorrowful, O my soul, and why dost thou disquiet me?" (ver. 5). I am in tribulations, in weariness, in mourning, "Why dost thou disquiet me, O my soul?" Who is the speaker, to whom is he speaking? That it is the soul to which he is speaking, everybody knows: for it is obvious: the appeal is addressed to it directly: "Why art thou sorrowful, O my soul, and why dost thou disquiet me?" The question is as to the speaker. It is not the flesh addressing the soul, surely, since the flesh cannot speak without the soul. For it is more appropriate for the soul to address the flesh, than for the flesh to address the soul. ... We perceive then that we have a certain part, in which is "the image of God;" viz. the mind and reason. It was that same mind that prayed for "God's Light" and "God's Truth." It is the same mind by which we apprehend right and wrong: it is by the same that we discern truth from falsehood. It is this same that we call "understanding;" which "understanding," indeed, is wanting to the brutes. And this "understanding" whoever neglects in himself, and holds it in less account than the other parts of his nature, and casts it off, just as if he had it not, is addressed in the Psalm, "Be ye not as the horse and the mule, which have no understanding." It is our "understanding" then that is addressing our soul. The latter is withered away from tribulations, worn out in anguish, made "sorrowful" in

temptations, fainting in toils. The mind, catching a glimpse of Truth above, would fain rouse her spirits, and she says, "Why art thou sorrowful, O my soul?" ...

7. These expressions, brethren, are safe ones: but yet be watchful in good works. Touch "the psaltery," by obeying the Commandments; touch the harp, by patiently enduring your sufferings. You have heard from Isaiah, "Break thy bread to the hungry;" think not that fasting by itself is sufficient. Fasting chasteneth thine own self: it does not refresh others. Thy distress will profit thee, if thou affordest comfort to others. See, thou hast denied thyself; to whom wilt thou give that of which thou hast deprived thyself? Where wilt thou bestow what thou hast denied thyself? How many poor may be filled by the breakfast we have this day given up? Fast in such a way that thou mayest rejoice, that thou hast breakfasted, while another has been eating; fast on account of thy prayers, that thou mayest be heard in them. For He says in that passage, "Whilst thou art yet speaking I will say, Here I am," provided thou wilt with cheerful mind "break thy bread to the hungry." For generally this is done by men reluctantly and with murmurs, to rid themselves of the wearisome importunity of the beggar, not to refresh the bowels of him that is needy. But it is "a cheerful giver" that "God loves." If thou givest thy bread reluctantly, thou hast lost both the bread, and the merit of the action. Do it then from the heart: that He "who seeth in secret," may say, "whilst thou art yet speaking, Here I am." How speedily are the prayers of those received, who work righteousness! And this is man's righteousness in this life, fasting, alms, and prayer. Wouldest thou have thy prayer fly upward to God? Make for it those two wings of alms and fasting. Such may God's "Light" and God's "Truth" find us, that He may find us without cause for fear, when He comes to free us from death, who has already come to undergo death for us. Amen.

PSALM XLIV.

1. This Psalm is addressed "to the sons of Korah," as its title shows. Now Korah is equivalent to the word baldness; and we find in the Gospel that our Lord Jesus Christ was crucified in "the place of a skull." It is clear then that this Psalm is sung to the "sons of His 'Passion.'" Now we have on this point a most certain and most evident testimony from the Apostle Paul; because that at the time when the Church was suffering under the persecutions of the Gentiles, he quoted from hence a verse, to insert by way of consolation, and encouragement to patience. For that which he inserted in his Epistle, is said here: "For Thy sake are we killed all the day long; we are counted as sheep for the slaughter." Let us then hear in this Psalm the voice of the Martyrs; and see how good is the cause which the voice of the Martyrs pleads, saying, For Thy sake, etc. ...

2. The title then is not simply "To the sons of Korah," but, "For understanding, to the sons of Korah." This is the case also with that Psalm, the first verse of which the Lord Himself uttered on the Cross: "My God, My God, look upon Me; why hast Thou forsaken Me?" For "transferring us in a figure" to what He was saying, and to His own Body (for we are also "His Body," and He is our "Head"), He uttered from the Cross not His own cry, but ours. For God never "forsook" Him: nor did He Himself ever depart from the Father; but it was in behalf of us that He spake this: "My God, My God, why hast thou forsaken Me?" For there follows, "Far from My health are the words of My offences:" and it shows in whose person He said this; for sin could not be found in Him. ...

3. "O God, we have heard with our ears; our fathers have told us the work that Thou didst in their days, and in the days of old" (ver. 1). Wondering wherefore, in these days, He has seemingly forsaken those whom it was His will to exercise in sufferings, they recall the past events which they have heard of from their fathers; as if they said, It is not of these things that we suffer, that our fathers told us! For in that other Psalm also, He said this, "Our fathers trusted in Thee; they trusted, and Thou didst deliver them. But I am a worm and no man; a reproach of men, and the outcast of the people." They trusted, and Thou didst deliver them; have I then hoped, and hast Thou forsaken me? And have I believed upon Thee in vain? And is it in vain that my name has been written in Thy Book, and Thy name has been inscribed on me? What our fathers told us was this:

"Thy hand destroyed the nations; and Thou plantedst them: Thou didst weaken the peoples, and cast them out" (ver. 2). That is to say: "Thou didst drive out 'the peoples' from their own land, that Thou mightest bring 'them' in, and plant them; and mightest by Thy mercy stablish their kingdom." These are the things that we heard from our fathers. But perhaps it was because they were brave, were men of battle, were invincible, were well-disciplined, and warlike, that they could do these things. Far from it. This is not what our fathers told us; this is not what is contained in Scripture. But what does it say, but what follows?

"For they gat not the land in possession by their own sword, neither did their own arm save them; but Thy right hand, and Thine arm, and the light of Thy countenance" (ver. 3). Thy "right hand" is Thy Power: Thine "arm" is Thy Son Himself. And "the light of Thy countenance." What means this, but that Thou wert present with them, in miracles of such a sort that Thy presence was perceived. For when God's presence with us appears by any miracle, do we see His face with our own eyes? No. It is by the effect of the miracle He intimates to man His presence. In fact, what do all persons say, who express wonder at facts of this description? "I saw God present." "But Thy right hand, and Thine arm, and the light of Thy countenance; because Thou pleasedst in them:" i.e. didst so deal with them, that Thou wert well-pleasing in them: that whoso considered how they were being dealt with, might say, that "God is with them of a truth;" and it is God that moves them.

4. "What? Was He then other than now He is?" Away with the supposition. For what follows?

"Thou art Thyself my King and my God." (ver. 4). "Thou art Thyself;" for Thou art not changed. I see that the times are changed; but the Creator of times is unchanged. "Thou art Thyself my King and my God." Thou art wont to guide me: to govern me, to save me. "Thou who commandest salvation unto Jacob." What is, "Thou who commandest"? Even though in Thine own proper Substance and Nature, in which Thou art whatsoever Thou art, Thou wast hid from them; and though Thou didst not converse with the fathers in that which Thou art in Thyself, so that they could see Thee "face to face," yet by any created being whatsoever "Thou commandest salvation unto Israel." For that sight of Thee "face to face" is reserved for those set free in the Resurrection. And the very "fathers" of the New Testament too, although they saw Thy mysteries revealed, although they preached the secret things so revealed to them, nevertheless said that they themselves saw but "in a glass, darkly," but that "seeing face to face" is reserved to a future time, when what the Apostle himself speaks of shall have come. "When Christ our life shall appear, then shall ye also appear with Him in glory." It is against that time then that vision "face to face" is reserved for you, of which John also speaks:

277

"Beloved, we are now the sons of God: and it doth not yet appear what we shall be. We know that, when He shall appear, we shall be like Him; for we shall see Him as He is." Although then at that time our fathers saw Thee not as Thou art, "face to face," although that vision is reserved against the resurrection, yet, even though they were Angels who presented themselves, it is Thou, "Who commandest salvation unto Jacob." Thou art not only present by Thine own Self; but by whatsoever created being Thou didst appear, it is Thou that dost "command" by them, that which Thou doest by Thine own Self in order to the salvation of Thy servants: but that which they do whom Thou "commandest" it, is done to procure the salvation of Thy servants. Since then Thou art Thyself" my King and my God, and Thou commandest salvation unto Jacob," wherefore are we suffering these things?

5. But perhaps it is only what is past that has been described to us: but nothing of the kind is to be hoped for by us for the future. Nay indeed, it is still to be hoped for. "Through Thee will we winnow away our enemies" (ver. 5). Our fathers then have declared to us a work that Thou didst "in their days, and in the days of old," that Thy hand destroyed the Gentiles: that Thou "didst cast out the peoples; and didst plant them." Such was the past; but what is to be hereafter? "Through Thee we shall winnow away our enemies." A time will come, when all the enemies of Christians will be winnowed away like chaff, be blown like dust, and be cast off from the earth. ... Thus much of the future. "I will not trust in my bow," even as our fathers did not in "their sword. Neither shall my sword help me" (ver. 6).

6. "For Thou hast saved us from our enemies" (ver. 7). This too is spoken of the future under the figure of the past. But this is the reason that it is spoken of as if it were past, that it is as certain as if it were past. Give heed, wherefore many things are expressed by the Prophets as if they were past; whereas it is things future, not past facts that are the subject of prophecy. For the future Passion of our Lord Himself was foretold: and yet it says, "They pierced My hands and My feet. They told all My bones;" not, "They shall pierce," and "shall tell." "They looked and stared upon Me;" not "They shall look and stare upon Me." "They parted My garments among them." It does not say, "They shall part" them. All these things are expressed as if they were past, although they were yet to come: because to God things to come also are as certain as if they were past. ... It is for this reason, in consequence of their certainty, that those things which are yet future, are spoken of as if past. This it is then that we hope. For it is, "Thou hast saved us from our enemies, and hast put them to shame that hated us."

7. "In God will we boast all the day long" (ver. 8). Observe how he intermingles words expressive of a future time, that you may perceive that what was spoken of before as in past time was foretold of future times. "In God will we boast all day long; and in Thy name will we confess for ever." What is, "We shall boast"? What, "We shall confess"? That Thou hast "saved us from our enemies;" that Thou art to give us an everlasting kingdom: that in us are to be fulfilled the words," Blessed are they that dwell in Thine house: they will be always praising Thee."

8. Since then we have the certainty that these things are to be hereafter, and since we have heard from our fathers that those we spoke of were in time past, what is our state at present? "But now Thou hast cast us off, and put us to shame" (ver. 9). Thou hast "put us to shame" not before our own consciences, but in the sight of men. For there was a time when Christians were persecuted; when in every place they were outcasts, when in every place it used to be said, "He is a Christian!" as if it conveyed an insult and reproach. Where then is He, "our God, our King," who "commands salvation unto Jacob"? Where is He who did all those works, which "our fathers have told us"? Where is He who is hereafter to do all those things which He revealed unto us by His Spirit? Is He changed? No. These things are done in order to "understanding, for the sons of Korah." For we ought to "understand" something of the reason, why He has willed we should suffer all these things in the mean time. What "all things"? "But now Thou hast cast us off and put us to shame: and goest not forth, O God, in our powers." We go forth to meet our enemies, and Thou goest not forth with us. We see them: they are very strong, and we are without strength. Where is that might of Thine? Where Thy "right hand," and Thy power? Where the sea dried up, and the Egyptian pursuers overwhelmed with the waves? Where Amalek's resistance subdued by the sign of the Cross? "And Thou, O God, goest not forth in our powers."

9. "Thou hast turned us away backward in presence of our enemies" (ver. 10), so that they are, as it were, before; we, behind; they are counted as conquerors, we as conquered. "And they which hate us spoiled for themselves." What did they "spoil" but ourselves?

10. "Thou has given us like sheep appointed for meat, and hast scattered us among the nations" (ver. 11). We have been "devoured" by "the nations." Those persons are meant, who, through their sufferings, have by process of assimilation, becomes part of the "body" of the Gentile world. For the Church mourns over them, as over members of her body, that have been devoured.

11. "Thou hast sold Thy people for no price" (ver. 12). For we see whom Thou hast made over; what Thou hast received, we have not seen. "And there was no multitude in their jubilees." For when the Christians were flying before the pursuit of enemies, who were idolaters, were there then held any congregations and "jubilees" to the honour of God? Were those Hymns chanted in concert from the Churches of God, that are wont to be sung in concert in time of peace, and to be sounded in a sweet accord of the brotherhood in the ears of God?

12. "Thou madest us a reproach to our neighbours; a scorn and a derision to them that are round about us" (ver. 13). "Thou madest us a similitude among the heathen" (ver. 14). What is meant by a "similitude"? It is when men in imprecating a curse make a "similitude" of his name whom they detest. "So mayest thou die;" "So mayest thou be punished!" What a number of such reproaches were then uttered! "So mayest thou be crucified!" Even in the present day there are not wanting enemies of Christ (those very Jews themselves), against whom whensoever we defend Christ, they say unto us, "So mayest thou die as He did." For they would not have inflicted that kind of death had they not an intense horror of dying by such a death: or had they been able to comprehend what mystery was contained in it. When the ointment is applied to the eyes of the blind man, he does not see the eye-salve in the physician's hand. For the very Cross was made for the benefit even of the persecutors themselves. Hereby they were healed afterwards; and they believed in Him whom they themselves had slain. "Thou madest us a similitude among the heathen; a shaking of the head among the peoples," a "shaking of the head" by way of insult. "They spake with their lips, they shook the head." This they did to the Lord: this to all His Saints also, whom they were able to pursue, to lay hold of, to mock, to betray, to afflict, and to slay.

13. "My shame is continually before me; and the confusion of my face has covered me" (ver. 15). "For the voice of him that reproacheth and blasphemeth" (ver. 16): that is to say, from the voice of them that insult over me, and who make it a charge against me that I worship Thee, that I confess Thee! and who make it a charge against me that I bear that name by which all charges against me shall be blotted out. "For the voice of him that reproacheth and blasphemeth," that is, of him that speaketh against me. "By reason of the enemy and the persecutor." And what is the "understanding" conveyed here? Those things which are told us of the time past, will not be done in our case: those which are hoped for, as to be hereafter, are not as yet manifest. Those which are past, as the leading out of Thy people with great glory from Egypt; its deliverance from its persecutors; the guiding of it through the nations, the placing of it in the kingdom, whence the nations had been expelled. What are those to be hereafter? The leading of the people out of this

Egypt of the world, when Christ, our "leader" shall appear in His glory: the placing of the Saints at His right hand; of the wicked at His left; the condemnation of the wicked with the devil to eternal punishment; the receiving of a kingdom from Christ with the Saints to last for ever. These are the things that are yet to be: the former are what are past. In the interval, what is to be our lot? Tribulations! "Why so?" That it may be seen with respect to the soul that worships God, to what extent it worships God; that it may be seen whether it worships Him "freely" from whom it received salvation "freely." ... What hast thou given unto God? Thou wert wicked, and thou wert redeemed! What hast thou given unto God? What is there that thou hast not "received" from Him "freely"? With reason is it named "grace," because it is bestowed (gratis, i.e.) freely. What is required of thee then is this, "that thou too shouldest worship "Him freely;" not because He gives thee things temporal, but because He holds out to thee things eternal. ...

14. "All this is come upon us; yet have we not forgotten Thee" (ver. 17). What is meant by, "have not forgotten Thee"? "Neither have we behaved ourselves frowardly in Thy covenant."

"Our heart has not turned back; and Thou hast turned aside our goings out of Thy way" (ver. 18). See here is "understanding," in that "our heart has not gone back;" that we have not" forgotten Thee, have not behaved frowardly in Thy covenant;" placed as we are in great tribulations, and persecutions of the Gentiles. "Thou hast turned aside our goings out of Thy way." Our "goings" were in the pleasures of the world; our "goings" were in the midst of temporal prosperities. Thou hast taken "our goings out of Thy way;" and hast shown us how "strait and narrow is the way that leadeth unto life." What is meant by, "hast turned aside our goings out of Thy way"? It is as if He said, "Ye are placed in the midst of tribulation; ye are suffering many things; ye have already lost many things that ye loved in this life: but I have not abandoned you on the way, the narrow way that I am teaching you. Ye were seeking "broad ways." What do I tell you? This is the way we go to everlasting life; by the way ye wish to walk, ye are going to death. How "broad and wide is the road that leads to destruction: and" how "many there be that find it! How strait and narrow the way that leadeth unto life, and" how "few there be" that walk therein! Who are the few? They who patiently endure tribulations, patiently endure temptations; who in all these troubles do not "fall away:" who do not rejoice in the word "for a season" only; and in the time of tribulation fade away, as on the sun's arising; but who have the "root" of "love," according to what we have lately heard read in the Gospel. ...

15. "For Thou hast brought us low in the place of infirmity" (ver. 18): therefore Thou wilt exalt us in the place of strength. "And the shadow of death has covered us" (ver. 19). For this mortality of ours is but the "shadow" of death. The true death is condemnation with the devil.

16. "If we have forgotten the Name of our God." Here is the "understanding" of the "sons of Korah." "And stretched out our hands to a strange God" (ver. 20). "Shall not God search this out? For He knoweth the secrets of the heart" (ver. 21). He "knows," and yet He "searches them out"? If He knows the secrets of the heart, what do the words, "Shall not God search it out," do there? He "knows" it in Himself; He "searches it out" for our sakes. For it is for this reason God sometimes "searches a thing out;" and speaks of that becoming known to Himself, which He is Himself making known to thee. He is speaking of His own work, not of His knowledge. We commonly say, "A gladsome day," when it is fine. Yet is it the day itself that experiences delight? No: we speak of the day as gladsome, because it fills us with delight. And we speak of a "sullen sky." Not that there is any such feeling in the clouds, but because men are affected with sullenness at the sight of such an appearance of the skies, it is called sullen for this reason, that it makes us sullen. So also God is said to "know" when He causes us to know. God says to Abraham, "Now I know that thou fearest God." Did He then not know it before then? But Abraham did not know himself till then: for it was in that very trial he came to know himself. ... And God is said to "know" that which He had caused him to know. Did Peter know himself, when he said to the Physician, "I will be with Thee even unto death?" The Physician had felt his pulse, and knew what was going on within His patient's soul: the patient knew it not. The crisis of trial came; and the Physician approved the correctness of His opinion: the sick man gave up his presumption. Thus God at once "knows" it and "searches it out." "He knows it already. Why does He 'search it out'?" For thy sake: that thou mayest come to know thine own self, and mayest return thanks to Him that made thee. "Shall not God search it out?"

17. "For, for Thy sake we are killed all the day long: we are counted as sheep for the slaughter" (ver. 22). For you may see a man being put to death; you do not know why he is being put to death. God knoweth this. The thing in itself is hid. But some one will say to me, "See, he is detained in prison for the name of Christ, he is a confessor for the name of Christ." Why do not heretics also confess the name of Christ, and yet they do not die for His sake? Nay more; let me say it, in the Catholic Church itself, do you think there either are, or have been wanting persons such as would suffer for the sake of glory among men? Were there no such persons, the Apostle would not say, "Though I give my body to be burned,

and have not charity, it profiteth me nothing." He knew therefore that there might be some persons, who did this not from "charity," but out of vainglory. It is therefore hid from us; God alone sees this; we cannot see it. He alone can judge of this, who "knoweth the secrets of the heart." "For," for Thy sake "are we killed all the day long; we are counted as sheep for the slaughter." I have already mentioned that from hence the Apostle Paul had borrowed a text for the encouragement of the Martyrs: that they might not "faint in the tribulations" undergone by them for the name of Christ.

18. "Awake; why sleepest Thou, O Lord?" (ver. 23). Who is addressed, and who is the speaker? Would not he be more correctly said to sleep and slumber, who speaks such words as these? He replies to you, I know what I am saying: I know that "He that keepeth Israel doth not sleep:" but yet the Martyrs cry, "Awake; why sleepest Thou, O Lord?" O Lord Jesus, Thou wast slain; Thou didst "sleep" in Thy Passion; to us Thou hast now "awaked" from sleep. For "we" know that Thou hast now "awaked" again. To what purpose hast Thou awaked and risen again? The Gentiles that persecute us, think Thee to be dead; do not believe Thee to have risen again. "Arise Thou" then to them also! "Why sleepest Thou," though not to us, yet to them? For if they already believed Thee to have risen again, could they persecute us who believe in Thee? But why do they persecute? "Destroy, slay so and so, whoever have believed in Thee, such an one, who died an ill death!" As yet to them "Thou sleepest;" arise to them, that they may perceive that Thou hast "awaked" again; and may be at rest. Lastly, it has come to pass, while the Martyrs die, and say these things; while they sleep, and "awaken" Christ, truly dead in their sleepings, Christ has, in a certain sense, risen again in the Gentiles; i.e. it becomes believed, that He has risen again; so by degrees they themselves, becoming converted to Christ by believing, collected a numerous body: such as the persecutors dreaded; and the persecutions have come to an end. Why? Because Christ, who before was asleep to them, as not believing, bath risen in the Gentiles. "Arise, and cast us not off for ever!"

19. "Wherefore hidest Thou Thy face:" as if Thou wert not present; as if thou hadst forgotten us? "And forgettest our misery and trouble?" (ver. 24).

20. "For our soul is bowed down to the dust" (ver. 25). Where is it bowed down? "To the dust:" i.e. dust persecutes us. They persecute us, of whom Thou hast said, "The ungodly are not so; but are like the dust, which the wind driveth away from the face of the earth." "Our belly hath cleaved to the earth." He seems to me to have expressed the punishment of the extreme of humiliation, in which, when any one prostrates himself, "his belly cleaveth to the earth." For whosoever is humbled

so as to be on his knees, has yet a lower degree of humiliation to which he can come: but he who is so humbled, that his "belly cleaveth to the ground," there is no farther humiliation for him. Should one wish to do still farther, it will, after that point, be not bowing him down, but crushing him. Perhaps then he may have meant this We are "bowed down very low" in this dust; there is no farther point to which humiliation can go. Humiliation has now reached its highest point: let mercy then come also. ...

21. "Arise, O Lord, help us" (ver. 26). And indeed, dearly beloved, He has arisen and helped us. For when he awaked (i.e. when He arose again, and became known to the Gentiles) on the cessation of persecutions, even those who had cleaved to the earth were raised up from the earth, and on performing penance, have been restored to Christ's body, feeble and imperfect though they were: so that in them was fulfilled the text, "Thine eyes did see my substance yet being imperfect; and in Thy book shall they all be written."

"Arise, O Lord, help us, and redeem us for Thy Name's sake ;" that is to say, freely; for Thy Name's sake, not for the sake of my merits: because Thou hast vouchsafed to do it, not because I am worthy that Thou shouldest do it unto me. For this very thing, that "we have not forgotten Thee;" that "our heart hath not gone back;" that we "have not stretched out our hands to any strange god;" how should we have been able to achieve, except with Thy help? How should we have strength for it, except through Thy appealing to us within, exhorting us, and not forsaking us? Whether then we suffer in tribulations, or rejoice in prosperities, redeem Thou us, not for our merits, but for Thy Name's sake.

PSALM XLV.

1. This Psalm, even as we ourselves have been singing with gladness together with you, we would beg you in like manner to consider with attention together with us. For it is sung of the sacred Marriage-feast; of the Bridegroom and the Bride; of the King and His people; of the Saviour and those who are to be saved. ... His sons are we, in that we are the "children of the Bridegroom;" and it is to us that this Psalm is addressed, whose title has the words, "For the sons of Korah, for the things that shall be changed."

2. Why need I explain what is meant by, "for the things that shall be changed "? Every one who is himself "changed," recognises the meaning of this. Let him who hears this, "for the things that shall be changed," consider what was before, and what is now. And first let him see the world itself to be changed, lately worshipping idols, now worshipping God; lately serving things that they themselves made, now serving Him by whom they themselves were made. Observe at what time the words, "for the things that shall be changed," were said. Already by this time the Pagans that are left are in dread of the "changed" state of things: and those who will not suffer themselves to be "changed" see the churches full; the temples deserted; see crowds here, and there solitude They marvel at the things so changed; let them read that they were foretold; let them lend their ears to Him who promised it; let them believe Him who fulfils that promise. But each one of us, brethren, also undergoes a change from "the old" to "the new man:" from an infidel to a believer: from a thief to a giver of alms: from an adulterer to a man of chastity; from an evildoer to a doer of good. To us then be sung the words, "for the things that shall be changed;" and so let the description of Him by whom they were changed, begin.

3. For it goes on, "For the things that shall be changed, to the sons of Korah for understanding; a song for the beloved." For that "beloved" One was seen by His persecutors, but yet not for "understanding." For "had they known Him, they would never have crucified the Lord of Glory." In order to this "understanding," other eyes were required by Him when He said, "He that seeth Me, seeth My Father also." Let the Psalm then now sound of Him, let us rejoice in the marriage-feast, and we shall be with those of whom the marriage is made, who are invited to the marriage; and the very persons invited are the Bride herself. For the Church is "the Bride," Christ the Bridegroom. There are commonly spoken by balladists certain verses to Bridegrooms and Brides, called Epithalamia. Whatever is sung there, is sung in honour of the Bride and Bridegroom. Is there then no Bridechamber in that marriage-feast to which we are invited? Whence then does

another Psalm say, "He hath set up His tabernacle in the Sun; and He is even as a bridegroom coming out of his chamber." The nuptial union is that of "the Word," and the flesh. The Bridechamber of this union, the Virgin's womb. For the flesh itself was united to the Word: whence also it is said, "Henceforth they are not twain, but one flesh." The Church was assumed unto Him out of the human race: so that the Flesh itself, being united to the Word, might be the Head of the Church: and the rest who believe, members of that Head. ...

4. "Mine heart hath uttered a good word" (ver. 1). Who is the speaker? The Father, or the Prophet? For some understand it to be the Person of the Father, which says, "Mine heart hath uttered a good word," intimating to us a certain unspeakable generation. Lest you should haply think something to have been taken unto Him, out of which God should beget the Son (just as man takes something to himself out of which he begets children, that is to say, an union of marriage, without which man cannot beget offspring), lest then you should think that God stood in need of any nuptial union, to beget "the Son," be says, "Mine heart hath uttered a good word." This very day thine heart, O man, begets a counsel, and requires no wife: by the counsel, so born of thine heart, thou buildest something or other, and before that building subsists, the design subsists; and that which thou art about to produce, exists already in that by which thou art going to produce it; and thou praisest the fabric that as yet is not existing, not yet in the visible form of a building, but on the projecting of a design: nor does any one else praise thy design, unless either thou showest it to him, or he sees what thou hast done. If then by the Word "all things were made," and the Word is of God, consider the fabric reared by the Word, and learn from that building to admire His counsels! What manner of Word is that by which heaven and earth were made; and all the splendour of the heavens; all the fertility of the earth; the expanse of the sea; the wide diffusion of air; the brightness of the constellations; the light of sun and moon? These are visible things: rise above these also; think of the Angels," Principalities, Thrones, Dominions, and Powers." All were made by Him. How then were these good things made? Because there was "uttered forth 'a good Word,' " by which they were to be made. ...

5. It proceeds: "I speak of the things which I have made unto the King." Is the Father still speaking? If the Father is still speaking, let us enquire how this also can be understood by us, consistently with the true Catholic Faith, "I speak of the things that I have made unto the King." For if it is the Father speaking of His own works to His Son, our "King," what works is the Father to speak of to the Son, seeing that all the Father's works were made by the Son's agency? Or, in the words, "I speak of My works unto the King," does the word, "I speak," itself

signify the generation of the Son? I fear whether this can ever be made intelligible to those slow of comprehension: I will nevertheless say it. Let those who can follow me, do so: lest if it were left unsaid, even those who can follow should not be able. We have read where it is said in another Psalm, "God hath spoken once." So often has He spoken by the Prophets, so often by the Apostles, and in these days by His Saints, and does He say, "God has spoken once "? How can He have spoken but "once," except with reference to His" Word "? But as the "Mine heart hath uttered a good Word," was understood by us in the other clause of the generation of the Son, it seems that a kind of repetition is made in the following sentence, so that the "Mine heart hath uttered a good Word," which had been already said, is repeated in what He is now saying, "I speak." For what does "I speak" mean? "I utter a Word." And whence but from His heart, from His very inmost, does God utter the Word? You yourself do not speak anything but what you bring forth from your "heart," this word of yours which sounds once and passes away, is brought forth from no other place: and do you wonder that God "speaks" in this manner? But God's "speaking" is eternal. You are speaking something at the present moment, because you were silent before: or, look you, you have not yet brought forth your word; but when you have begun to bring it forth, you as it were "break silence;" and bring into being a word, that did not exist before. It was not so God begat the "Word." God's "speaking" is without beginning, and without end: and yet the "Word" He utters is but "One." Let Him utter another, if what He has spoken shall have passed away. But since He by whom it is uttered abideth, and That which is uttered abideth; and is uttered but once, and has no end, that very "once" too is said without beginning, and there is no second speaking, because that which is said once, does not pass away. The words "Mine heart hath uttered a good Word," then, are the same thing with, "I speak of the things which I have made unto the King." Why then, "I speak of the things which I have made"? Because in the Word Itself are all the works of God. For whatever God designed to make in the creation already existed in "the Word;" and would not exist in the reality, had it not existed in the Word, just as with you the thing would not exist in the building, had it not existed in your design: even as it is said in the Gospel: "That which was made in Him was life." That which was made then was m existence; but it had its existence in the Word: and all the works of God existed there, and yet were not as yet "works." "The Word" however already was, as this "Word was God, and was with God:" and was the Son of God, and One God with the Father. "I speak of the things I have made unto the King." Let him hear Him "speaking," who apprehends "the Word:" and let him see together with the Father the Everlasting Word; in whom exist even those things that are yet to come: in whom even those things that are past have not passed away. These "works" of God are in "the Word," as in the Word, as in the Only-Begotten, as in the "Word of God."

6. What follows then? "My tongue is the pen of a writer writing rapidly." What likeness, my brethren, what likeness, I ask, has the "tongue" of God with a transcriber's pen? What resemblance has "the rock" to Christ? What likeness does the "lamb" bear to our Saviour, or what "the lion" to the strength of the Only-Begotten? Yet such comparisons have been made; and were they not made, we should not be formed to a certain extent by these visible things to the knowledge of the "Invisible One:" So then with this mean simile of the pen; let us not compare it to His excellent greatness, so let us not reject it with contempt. For I ask, why He compares His "tongue" to "the pen of a writer writing rapidly "? But how swiftly soever the transcriber writes, still it is not comparable to that swiftness of which another Psalm says, "His word runneth very swiftly." But it appears to me (if human understanding may presume so far) that this too may be understood as spoken in the Person of the Father: "My tongue is the pen of a writer." Inasmuch as what is spoken by the "tongue," sounds once and passes away, what is written, remains; seeing then that God uttereth "a Word," and the Word which is uttered does not sound once and pass away, but is uttered and yet continues, God chose rather to compare this to words written than to sounds. But what He added, saying, "of one writing swiftly," stimulates the mind unto "understanding." Let it however not slothfully rest here, thinking of transcribers, or thinking of some kind of quick shorthand writers: if it be this it sees in the passage, it will be resting there. Let it think swiftly what is the meaning of that word "swiftly." The "swiftly" of God is such that nothing exceeds in swiftness. For in writings letter is written after letter; syllable after syllable; word after word: nor do we pass to the second except when the first is written out. But there nothing can exceed the swiftness, where there are not several words; and yet there is not anything omitted: since in the One are contained all things.

7. Lo! now then that Word, so uttered, Eternal, the Co-eternal Offspring of the Eternal, will come as "the Bridegroom;" "Fairer than the children of men" (ver. 2). "Than the children of men." I ask, why not than the Angels also? Why did he say, "than the children of men," except because He was Man? Lest you should think "the Man Christ" to be any ordinary man, he says, "Fairer than the children of men." Even though Himself" Man," He is "fairer than the children of men;" though among the children of men, "fairer than the children of men:" though of the children of men, "fairer than the children of men." "Grace is shed abroad on Thy lips." "The Law was given by Moses. Grace and Truth came by Jesus Christ." ...

8. There have not been wanting those who preferred understanding all the preceding passage also of the Prophet's own person; and would have even this verse, "Mine heart hath uttered forth a good word," understood as spoken by the

Prophet, supposed to be uttering a hymn. For whoever utters a hymn to God, his heart is, as it were, "uttering forth a good word," just as his heart who blasphemes God, is uttering forth an evil word. So that even by what follows, "I speak of the things which I have made unto the King," he meant to express that man's chief work was but to praise God. To Him it belongs to satisfy thee, by His beauty; to thee to praise Him with thanksgiving. ...

9. "My tongue is the pen of a writer writing quickly." There have been persons who have understood the Prophet to have been describing in this manner what he was writing; and therefore to have compared his tongue to "the pen of a writer writing quickly:" but that he chose to express himself in the words "writing quickly," to signify, that he was writing of things which were to come" quickly;" that "writing quickly" should be understood to be equivalent to "writing things that are quick;" i.e. writing things that would not long tarry. For God did not tarry long to manifest Christ. How quickly is that perceived to have rolled by, which is acknowledged to be already past! Call to mind the generations before thee; thou wilt find that the making of Adam is but a thing of yesterday. So do we read that all things have gone on from the very beginning: they were therefore done "quickly." The day of Judgment also will be here "quickly." Do thou anticipate its "quick" coming. It is to come "quickly;" do thou become converted yet more "quickly." The Judge's face will appear: but observe thou what the Prophet says, "Let us come before" (let us "prevent ") "His face with confession."

10. "Gird Thy sword upon Thy thigh, O most Mighty" (ver. 3). What is meant by "Thy sword, but "Thy word"? It was by that sword He scattered His enemies; by that sword he divided the son from the father, "the daughter from the mother, the daughter-in-law from the mother-in-law." We read these words in the Gospel, "I came not to send peace, but a sword." And, "In one house shall five be divided against each other; three against two, and two against three;" i.e. "the father against the son, the daughter against the mother, the daughter-in-law against the mother-in-law." By what "sword," but that which Christ brought, was this division wrought? And indeed, my brethren, we see this exemplified daily. Some young man is minded to give himself up to God's service; his father is opposed to it; they are "divided against each other:" the one promises an earthly inheritance, the other loves an heavenly; the one promises one thing, the other prefers another. The father should not think himself wronged: God alone is preferred to him. And yet he is at strife with the son, who would fain give himself to God's service. But the spiritual sword is mightier to separate them, than the ties of carnal nature to bind them together. This happens also in the case of a mother against her daughter; still more also in that of a daughter-in-law against a mother-in-law. For sometimes in

one house mother-in-law and daughter-in law are found orthodox and heretical respectively. And where that sword is forcibly felt, we do not dread the repetition of Baptism. Could daughter be divided against mother; and could not daughter-in-law be divided against mother-in law? ...

11. What does he mean to express by the "thigh"? The flesh. Whence those words, " A prince shall not depart from Judah; and a lawgiver from his thighs"? Did not Abraham himself (to whom was promised the seed in which "all the nations of the earth were to be blessed"), when he sent his servant to seek and to bring home a wife for his son, being by faith fully persuaded, that in that, so to speak, contemptible seed was contained the great Name; that is, that the Son of God was to come of the seed of Abraham, out of all the children of men; did not he, I say, cause his servant to swear unto him in this manner, saying, "Put thy hand under my thigh," and so swear; as if he had said, "Put thy hand on the altar, or on the Gospel, or on the Prophet, or on any holy thing." "Put" (he says) "thy hand under my thigh;" having full confidence, not ashamed of it as unseemly, but understanding therein a truth. "With Thy beauty and Thy glory." Take to Thee that righteousness, in which Thou art at all times beautiful and glorious. "And speed on, and proceed prosperously, and reign" (ver. 4). Do we not see it so? Is it not already come to pass? He has "sped on; has proceeded prosperously, and He reigns ;" all nations are subdued unto Him. What a thing was it to see that "in the Spirit," of which same thing it is now in our power to experience in the reality! At the time when these words were said, Christ did not yet "reign" thus; had not yet sped on, nor "proceeded prosperously." They were then being preached, they have now been fulfilled: in many things we have God's promise fulfilled already; in some few we have to claim its fulfilment yet.

12. "Because of truth, meekness, and righteousness." Truth was restored unto us, when "the Truth sprung out of the earth: and Righteousness looked out from heaven." Christ was presented to the expectation of mankind, that in Abraham's Seed "all nations should be blessed." The Gospel has been preached. It is "the Truth." What is meant by" meekness"? The Martyrs have suffered; and the kingdom of God has made much progress from thence, and advanced throughout all nations; because the Martyrs suffered, and neither "fell away," nor yet offered resistance; confessing everything, concealing nothing; prepared for everything, shrinking from nothing. Marvellous "meekness"! This did the body of Christ, by its Head it learned. He was first "led as a sheep to the slaughter, and as a lamb before his shearer is dumb, even so opened not His mouth;" meek to that degree, that while hanging on the Cross, He said, "Father, forgive them, for they know not what they do." Why because of "righteousness"? He will come also to judge, and

to "render to every man according to his works." He spake "the truth;" He patiently endured unrighteousness: He is to bring "righteousness" hereafter.

13. "And Thy right hand shall lead Thee on marvellously." We shall be guided on by His right hand: He by His own. For He is God, we mortal men. He was led on by His own right hand; i.e. by His own power. For the power which the Father hath, He hath also; the Father's immortality He hath also; He hath the Father's Divinity, the Fathers Eternity, the Father's Power. Marvellously will His right hand lead Him on, performing the works of God; undergoing human sufferings, overthrowing the evil wills of men by His own goodness. Even now, He is being led on even to places where as yet He is not; and it is His own right hand that is leading Him on. For that is leading Him thither which He has Himself bestowed upon His Saints. "Thy right hand shall lead Thee on marvellously."

14. "Thine arrows are sharp, are most powerful" (ver. 5); words that pierce the heart, that kindle love. Whence in the Song of Songs it is said, "I am wounded with love." For she speaks of being "wounded with love;" that is, of being in love, of being inflamed with passion, of sighing for the Bridegroom, from whom she received the arrow of the Word. "Thine arrows are sharp, are most powerful;" both piercing, and effective; "sharp, most powerful." "The peoples shall fall under Thee." Who have "fallen"? They who were "wounded" have also "fallen." We see the nations subdued unto Christ; we do not see them "fall." He explains where they "fall," viz. "in the heart." It was there they lifted themselves up against Christ, there they "fall" down before Christ. Saul was a blasphemer of Christ: he was then lifted up, he prays to Christ, "he is fallen," he is prostrate before Him: the enemy of Christ is slain, that the disciple of Christ may live! By an arrow launched from heaven, Saul (not as yet Paul, but still Saul), still lifted up, still not yet prostrate, is wounded in "the heart:" he received the arrow, he fell "in heart." For though he fell prostrate on his face, it was not there that he fell down in heart: but it was there where he said aloud, "Lord, what dost Thou bid me do?" But just now thou weft going to bind the Christians, and to bring them to punishment: and now thou sayest unto Christ, "What dost Thou bid me do?" O arrow sharp and most mighty, by whose stroke "Saul" fell, so as to become "Paul." As it was with him, so was it also with "the peoples;" consider the nations, observe their subjection unto Christ. "The peoples" (then) "shall fall under Thee in the heart of the King's enemies;" that is, in the heart of Thine enemies. For it is Him that he calls King, Him that he recognises as King. "The peoples shall fall under Thee in the heart of the King's enemies." They were "enemies" before; they have been stricken by thine arrows: they have fallen before Thee. Out of enemies they have been made friends: the enemies are dead, the friends survive. This is the meaning of, "for those which

shall be changed." We are seeking to "understand" each single word, and each separate verse; yet so far only are we to seek for their "understanding," as to leave no one to doubt that they are spoken of Christ.

15. "Thy throne, O God, is for ever and ever" (ver. 6). Because God has "'blessed Thee' for ever," on account of the" grace poured over Thy lips." Now the throne of the Jewish Kingdom was a temporal one; belonging to those who were under the Law, not to those who were under "grace:" He came to "redeem those who were under the Law," and to place them under "Grace." His "Throne is for ever and ever." Why? for that first throne of the Kingdom was but a temporal one: whence then have we a "throne for ever and ever"? Because it is God's throne. O divine Attribute of Eternity! for God could not have a temporal throne. "Thy throne, O God, is for ever and ever- -a sceptre of direction is the sceptre of Thy Kingdom." "The sceptre of direction" is that which directs mankind: they were before crooked, distorted; they sought to reign for themselves: they loved themselves, loved their own evil deeds: they submitted not their own will to God; but would fain have bent God's will to conformity with their own lusts. For the sinner and the unrighteous man is generally angry with God, because it rains not! and yet would have God not be angry with himself, because he is profligate. And it is pretty much for this very reason that men daily sit, to dispute against God: "This is what He ought to have done: this He has not well done." Thou forsooth seest what thou doest; He knows not what He does! It is thou that art crooked! His ways are right. When wilt thou make the crooked coincide with the straight? It cannot be made to coincide with it. Just as if you were to place a crooked stick on a level pavement; it does not join on to it; it does not cohere; it does not fit into the pavement. The pavement is even in every part: but that is crooked; it does not fit into that which is level. The will of God then is "equal," thine own is "crooked:" it is because thou canst not be conformed unto it, that it seems "crooked" unto thee: rule thou thyself by it; seek not to bend it to thine own will: for thou canst not accomplish it; that is at all times "straight"! Wouldest thou abide in Him? "Correct thou thyself;" so will the sceptre of Him who rules thee, be unto thee "a rule of direction." Thence is He also called King, from "ruling." For that is no "ruler" that does not correct. Hereunto is our King a King of "right ones." Just as He is a Priest (Sacerdos) by sanctifying us, so is He our King, our Ruler, by "ruling" us. ...

16. Thou hast loved righteousness, and hated iniquity" (ver. 7). See there "the rod of direction" described. "Thou hast loved righteousness, and hated iniquity." Draw near to that "rod;" let Christ be thy King: let Him "rule" thee with that rod, not crush thee with it. For that rod is "a rod of iron;" an inflexible rod. "Thou shalt rule them with a rod of iron: and break them in pieces like a potter's vessel." Some He

rules; others He "breaks in pieces:" He "rules" them that are spiritual: He "breaks in pieces" them that are carnal. ... Would He so loudly declare that He was about to smite thee, if He wished to smite thee? He is then holding back His hand from the punishment of thine offences; but do not thou hold back. Turn thou thyself to the punishment of thine offences: for unpunished offences cannot be: punishment therefore must be executed either by thyself, or by Him: do thou then plead guilty, that He may reprieve thee. Consider an instance in that penitential Psalm: "Hide Thy face from my sins." Did he mean "from me"? No: for in another passage he says plainly, "Hide not Thy face from me." "Turn" then "Thy face from my sins." I would have Thee not see my sins. For God's "seeing" is animadverting upon. Hence too a Judge is said to "animadvert" on that which he punishes; i.e. to turn his mind on it, to bend it thereon, even to the punishment of it, inasmuch as he is the Judge. So too is God a Judge. "Turn Thou Thy face from my sins." But thou thyself, if thou wouldest have God turn "His face" from them, turn not thine own face from them. Observe how he proposes this to God in that very Psalm: "I acknowledge," he says, "my transgression, and my sin is ever before me." He would fain have that which he wishes to be ever before his own eyes, not be before God's eyes. Let no one flatter himself with fond hopes of God's mercy. His sceptre is "a sceptre of righteousness." Do we say that God is not merciful? What can exceed His mercy, who shows such forbearance to sinners; who takes no account of the past in all that turn unto Him? So love thou Him for His mercy, as still to wish that He should be truthful. For mercy cannot strip Him of His attribute of justice: nor justice of that of mercy. Meanwhile during the time that He postpones thy punishment, do not thou postpone it.

17. "Therefore, God, Thy God, hath anointed Thee." It was for this reason that He anointed thee, that thou mightest love righteousness, and hate iniquity. And observe in what way he expresses himself. "Therefore, God, Thy God, hath anointed Thee:" i.e. "God hath anointed Thee, O God." "God" is "anointed" by God. For in the Latin it is thought to be the same case of the noun repeated: in the Greek however there is a most evident distinction; one being the name of the Person addressed; and one His who makes the address, saying, "God hath anointed Thee." "O God, Thy God hath anointed Thee," just as if He were saying, "Therefore hath Thy God, O God, anointed Thee." Take it in that sense, understand it in that sense; that such is the sense is most evident in the Greek. Who then is the God that is "anointed" by God? Let the Jews tell us; these Scriptures are common to us and them. It was God, who was anointed by God: you hear of an "Anointed" one; understand it to mean "Christ." For the name of "Christ" comes from "chrism;" this name by which He is called "Christ" expresses "unction:" nor were kings and prophets anointed in any kingdom, in any other place, save in that kingdom where Christ was prophesied of, where He was

anointed, and from whence the Name of Christ was to come. It is found nowhere else at all: in no one nation or kingdom. God, then, was anointed by God; with what oil was He anointed, but a spiritual one? For the visible oil is in the sign, the invisible oil is in the mystery; the spiritual oil is within. "God" then was "anointed" for us, and sent unto us; and God Himself was man, in order that He might be "anointed:" but He was man in such a way as to be God still. He was God in such a way as not to disdain to be man. "Very man and very God;" in nothing deceitful, in nothing false, as being everywhere true, everywhere "the Truth" itself. God then is man; and it was for this cause that "God" was "anointed," because God was Man, and became "Christ."

18. This was figured in Jacob's placing a stone at his head, and so sleeping. The patriarch Jacob had placed a stone at his head: sleeping with that stone at his head, he saw heaven opened, and a ladder from heaven to earth, and Angels ascending and descending; after this vision he awaked, anointed the stone, and departed. In that "stone" he understood Christ; for that reason he anointed it. Take notice what it is whereby Christ is preached. What is the meaning of that anointing of a stone, especially in the case of the Patriarchs who worshipped but One God? It was however done as a figurative act: and he departed. For he did not anoint the stone, and come to worship there constantly, and to perform sacrifice there. It was the expression of a mystery; not the commencement of sacrilege. And notice the meaning of "the stone." "The Stone which the builders refused, this is become the head of the corner." Notice here a great mystery. The "Stone" is Christ. Peter calls Him "a living Stone, disallowed indeed of men, but chosen of God." And the stone is set at "the head," because "Christ is the Head of the man." And "the stone" was anointed, because "Christ" was so called from His being anointed. And in the revelation of Christ, the ladder from earth to heaven is seen, or from heaven to earth, and the Angels ascending and descending. What this means, we shall see more clearly, when we have quoted the testimony from the Lord Himself in the Gospel. You know that Jacob is the same as Israel. For when he wrestled with the Angel, and "prevailed," and had been blest by Him over whom he prevailed, his named was changed, so that he was called "Israel;" just as the people of Israel "prevailed" against Christ, so as to crucify Him, and nevertheless was (in those who believed in Christ) blest by Him over whom it prevailed. But many believed not; hence the halting of Jacob. Here we have at once, blessing and halting. Blessing on those who became believers; for we know that afterward many of that people did believe: Halting on the other hand in those who believed not. And because the greater part believed not, and but few believed, therefore that a halting might be produced, He touched "the breadth of his thigh." What is meant by the breadth of the thigh? The great multitude of his descendants. ...

19. "God, Thy God, hath anointed Thee." We have been speaking of God, who was "anointed;" i.e. of Christ. The name of Christ could not be more clearly expressed than by His being called "God the Anointed." In the same way in which He was" beautiful before the children of men," so is He here "anointed with the oil of gladness above His fellows." Who then are His "fellows"? The children of men; for that He Himself (as the Son of Man) became partaker of their mortality in order to make them partakers of His Immortality.

20. "Out of Thy garments is the smell of myrrh, amber, and cassia" (ver. 8). Out of Thy garments is perceived the smell of fragrant odours. By His garments are meant His Saints, His elect, His whole Church, which he shows forth, as His garment, so to speak; His robe "without spot and wrinkle," which on account of its spots He has "washed" in His blood; on account of its "wrinkles" extended on His Cross. Hence the sweet savour which is signified by certain perfumes there mentioned. Hear Paul, that "least of the Apostles" (that "hem of that garment," which the woman with the issue of blood touched, and was healed), hear him saying: "We are a sweet savour of Christ, in every place, both in them that are saved, and in them that perish." He did not say, "We are a sweet savour in them that are saved, and a foul savour in them that are lost:" but, as far as relates to ourselves, "we are a sweet savour both in them that are saved, and in them that perish." ... They who loved him were saved by the odour of "sweet savour;" they who envied him, perished by means of that "sweet savour." To them that perished then he was not a foul "savour," but a "sweet savour." For it was for this very reason they the more envied him, the more excellent that grace was which reigned in him: for no man envies him who is unhappy. He then was glorious in the preaching of God's Word, and in regulating his life according to the rule of that "rod of direction;" and he was loved by those who loved Christ in him, who followed after and pursued the odour of sweet savour; who loved the friend of the bridegroom: that is to say, by the Bride Herself, who says in the Song of Songs, "We will run after the sweet savour of thy perfumes." But the others, the more they beheld him invested with the glory of the preaching of the Gospel, and of an irreproachable life, were so much the more tortured with envy, and found that sweet savour prove death to them.

21. "Out of thy ivory palaces, whereby kings' daughters have made Thee glad." Choose whichever you please, "ivory" palaces, or "magnificent," or "royal" palaces, it is out of these that the kings' daughters have made Christ glad. Would you understand the spiritual sense of "ivory palaces"? Understand by them the magnificent houses, and tabernacles of God, the hearts of the Saints; and by these self-same "kings" those who rule their flesh; who bring into subjection to

themselves the rebellious commonalty of human affections, who chastise the body, and reduce it to bondage: for it is from these that the daughters of kings have made Him glad. For all the souls that have been born through their preaching and evangelizing are "daughters of kings:" and the Churches, as the daughters of Apostles, are daughters of kings. For He is "King of kings;" they themselves kings, of whom it was said, "Ye shall sit upon twelve thrones, judging the twelve tribes of Israel." They preached the "Word of Truth;" and begat Churches not for themselves, but for Him. ... Therefore as "raising up seeds to their brother," to as many as they begat, they gave the name not of "Paulians" or "Petrians," but of "Christians." Observe whether that sense is not wakefully kept in these verses. For when he said, "out of the ivory palaces, he spake of mansions royal, ample, honourable, peaceful, like the heart of the Saints; he added, "Whereby the kings' daughters have made Thee glad in Thine honour." They are indeed daughters of kings. daughters of thine Apostles, but still "in Thine honour:" for they raised up seed to their brother. Hence Paul, when he saw those whom he had raised up unto his Brother, running after his own name, exclaimed, "Was Paul crucified for you? " ... No; for he says, "Or were ye baptized in the name of Paul?"

"The daughters of kings have made Thee glad in Thine honour." Keep, hold fast this "in Thine honour." This is meant by having "a wedding garment;" seeking His honour, His glory. Understand moreover by "kings' daughters" the cities, which were founded by kings, and have received the faith: and out of the ivory palaces (palaces rich, the proud, the lifted up). "Kings' daughters have made Thee glad in Thine honour;" in that they sought not the honour of their founders, but have sought Thine honour. Show me at Rome a temple of Romulus held in so great honour as I can show you the Monument of Peter. In Peter, who is honoured but He who died for us? For we are followers of Christ, not followers of Peter. And even if we were born from the brother of Him that is dead, yet are we named after the name of Him who is dead. We were begotten by the one, but begotten to the other. Behold, Rome, Carthage, and several other cities are the daughters of kings, and yet have they "made glad the King in His honour:" and all these make up one single Queen.

22. What a nuptial song! Behold in the midst of songs full of rejoicing, comes forth the Bride herself. For the Bridegroom was coming. It was He who was being described: it was on Him all our attention was fixed.

"Upon Thy right hand did stand the Queen" (ver. 9). She which stands on the left is no Queen. For there will be one standing on "the left" also, to whom it will be said, "Go into everlasting fire." But she shall stand on the right hand, to whom it will be said, "Come, ye blessed of My Father, inherit the kingdom prepared for you from the foundation of the world." On Thy right hand did stand the Queen, "in a vesture of gold, clothed about with divers colours." What is the vesture of this Queen? It is one both precious, and also of divers colours: it is the mysteries of doctrine in all the various tongues: one African, one Syrian, one Greek, one Hebrew, one this, and one that; it is these languages that produce the divers colours of this vesture. But just as all the divers colours of the vesture blend together in the one vesture, so do all the languages in one and the same faith. In that vesture, let there be diversity, let there be no rent. See we have "understood" the divers colours of the diversity of tongues; and the vesture to refer to unity: but in that diversity itself, what is meant by the "gold "? Wisdom itself. Let there be any diversity of tongues you please, but there is but one "gold" that is preached of: not a different gold, but a different form of that gold. For it is the same Wisdom, the same doctrine and discipline that every language preaches. In the languages there is diversity; gold in the thoughts.

23. The Prophet addresses this Queen (for he delights in singing to her), and moreover each one of us, provided, however, we know where we are, and endeavour to belong to that body, and do belong to it in faith and hope, being united in the membership of Christ. For it is us whom he addresses, saying, "Hearken, O daughter, and behold" (ver. 10), as being one of the "Fathers" (for they are "daughters of kings"), although it be a Prophet, or although it be an Apostle that is addressing her; addressing her, as a daughter, for we are accustomed to speak in this way, "Our fathers the Prophets, our fathers the Apostles;" if we address them as "fathers," they may address us as children: and it is one father's voice addressing one daughter. "Hearken, O daughter, and see." "Hear" first; afterward "see." For they came to us with the Gospel; and that has been preached to us, which as yet we do not see, and which on hearing of it we believed, which by believing it, we shall come to see: even as the Bridegroom Himself speaks in the Prophet, "A people whom I have not known served me. In the hearing of me with the ear it obeyed me." What is meant by on "hearing of me with the ear"? That they did not "see." The Jews saw Him, and crucified Him; the Gentiles saw Him not, and believed. Let the Queen who comes from the Gentiles come in "the vesture of gold, clothed with divers colours;" let her come from among the Gentiles clad in all languages, in the unity of Wisdom: let it be said unto her, "Hearken, O daughter, and see." If thou wilt not hear, thou shalt not "see." ...

"And incline thine ear." It is not enough to "hearken;" hearken with humility: bow down thine ear. "Forget also thine own people, and thy father's house." There was a certain "people," and a certain house of thy father, in which thou wast born, the people of Babylon, having the devil for thy king. Whencesoever the Gentiles came, they came from their father the devil; but they have renounced their sonship to the devil. "Forget also thine own people, and thy father's house." He, in making thee a sinner, begat thee loathsome: the Other, in that "He justifies the ungodly," begetteth thee again in beauty.

24. "For the King hath greatly desired thy beauty" (ver. 11). What "beauty" is that, save that which is His own work? "Greatly desired the beauty"—Of whom? Of her the sinner, the unrighteous, the ungodly, such as she was with her "father," the devil, and among her own "people"? No, but hers of whom it is said, "Who is this that cometh up made white?" She was not white then at the first, but was "made" white afterwards. For "though your sins shall be as scarlet, I will make them white as snow." "The king has greatly desired thy beauty." What King is this? "For He is the Lord thy God." Now consider whether thou oughtest not to forego that thy father, and thy own people, and to come to this King, who is thy God? Thy God is "thy King," thy" King" is also thy Bridegroom. Thou weddest to thy King, who is thy God: being endowed by Him, being adorned by Him; redeemed by Him, and healed by Him. Whatever thou hast, wherewith to be pleasing to Him, thou hast from Him.

25. "And the daughters of Tyre shall worship Him with gifts" (ver. 12). It is that selfsame "King, who is thy God," that the daughters of Tyre shall worship with gifts. The daughters of Tyre are the daughters of the Gentiles; the part standing for the whole. Tyre, a city bordering on this country, where the prophecy was delivered, typified the nations that were to believe in Christ. Thence came that Canaanitish woman, who was at first called "a dog;" for that ye may know that she was from thence, the Gospel speaks thus. "He departed into the parts of Tyre and Sidon, and behold a woman of Canaan came out of the same coasts," with all the rest that is related there. She who at first, at the house of her "father," and among her "own people," was but "a dog," who by coming to, and crying after that "King," was made beautiful by believing in Him, what did she obtain to hear? "O woman, great is thy faith.'" "The King has greatly desired thy beauty. And the daughters of Tyre shall worship with gifts." With what gifts? Even so would this King be approached, and would have His treasuries filled: and it is He Himself who has given us that wherewith they may be filled, and may be filled by you. Let them come (He says) and "worship Him with gifts." What is meant by "with gifts"? ... "Give alms, and all things are clean unto you." Come with gifts to Him that saith, "I will have mercy rather than sacrifice." To that Temple that existed aforetime as a shadow of that which was to come, they used to come with bulls,

and rams, and goats, with every different kind of animal for sacrifice: that with that blood one thing should be done, and another be typified by it. Now that very blood, which all these things used to figure, hath come: the King Himself hath come, and He Himself would have your "gifts." What gifts? Alms. For He Himself will judge hereafter, and will Himself hereafter account "gifts" to certain persons "Come" (He says), "ye blessed of My Father." Why? "I was an hungred, and ye gave Me meat," etc. These are the gifts with which the daughters of Tyre worship the King; for when they said, "When saw we Thee?" He who is at once above and below (whence those "ascending" and "descending" are spoken of), said, "Inasmuch as ye have done it unto one of the least of Mine, ye have done it unto Me."

26. ... "The rich among the people shall entreat Thy face." Both they who shall entreat that face, and He whose face they will entreat, are all collectively but one Bride, but one Queen, mother and children belonging all together unto Christ, belonging unto their Head. ...

27. "All the glory of her, the King's daughter, is from within" (ver. 13). Not only is her robe, outwardly, "of gold, and of divers colours;" but He who loved her beauty, knew her to be also beautiful within. What are those inward charms? Those of conscience. It is there Christ sees; it is there Christ loves her: it is there He addresses her, there punishes, there crowns. Let then thine alms be done in secret; for "all the glory of her, the King's daughter, is from within." "With fringes of gold, clothed with divers colours" (ver. 14). Her beauty is from within; yet in the" fringes of gold" is the' diversity of languages: the beauty of doctrine. What do these avail, if them be not that beauty "from within"? "The virgins shall be brought unto the King after her." It has been fulfilled indeed. The Church has believed; the Church has been formed throughout all nations. And to what a degree do virgins now seek to find favour in the eyes of that King! Whence are they moved to do so? Even because the Church preceded them. "The virgins shall be brought unto the King after her. Her near kinswomen shall be brought unto Thee." For they that are brought unto Him are not strangers, but her "near kinswomen," that belong to her. And because he had said, "unto the King," he says, turning the discourse to Him, "her near kinswomen shall be brought unto Thee."

28. "With gladness and rejoicing shall they be brought and shall be led into the Temple of the King" (ver. 15). The "Temple of the King" is the Church itself: it is the Church itself that enters into "the Temple of the King." Whereof is that Temple constructed? Of the men who enter the Temple? Who but God's "faithful" ones are its "living stones"? "They shall be led into the Temple of the King. For there are

virgins without the Temple of the King, the nuns among the heretics: they are virgins, it is true; but what will that profit them, unless they be led into the "Temple of the King"? The "Temple of the King" is in unity: the "Temple of the King" is not ruinous, is not rent asunder, is not divided. The cement of those living stones is "charity."

29. "Instead of thy fathers, children are born to thee" (ver. 16). Nothing can be more manifest. Now consider the "Temple of the King" itself, for it is on its behalf he speaks, on account of the unity of the body that is spread throughout all the world: for those very persons who have chosen to be virgins, cannot find favour with the King unless they be led into the Temple of the King. "Instead of thy fathers, are thy children born to thee." It was the Apostles begat thee: they were "sent:" they were the preachers: they are "the fathers." But was it possible for them to be with us in the body for ever? Although one of them said, "I desire to depart, and to be with Christ, which is far better: to abide in the flesh is necessary for your sakes." It is true he said this, but how long was it possible for him to remain here? Could it be till this present time, could it be to all futurity? Is the Church then left desolate by their departure? God forbid. "Instead of thy fathers, children have been born to thee." What is that? The Apostles were sent to thee as "fathers," instead of the Apostles sons have been born to thee: there have been appointed Bishops. For in the present day, whence do the Bishops, throughout all the world, derive their origin? The Church itself calls them fathers; the Church itself brought them forth, and placed them on the thrones of "the fathers." Think not thyself abandoned then, because thou seest not Peter, nor seest Paul: seest not those through whom thou wert born. Out of thine own offspring has a body of "fathers" been raised up to thee. "Instead of thy fathers, have children been born to thee." Observe how widely diffused is the "Temple of the King," that "the virgins that are not led to the Temple of the King," may know that they have nothing to do with that marriage. "Thou shall make them princes over all the earth." This is the Universal Church: her children have been made "princes over all the earth:" her children have been appointed instead of the "fathers." Let those who are cut off own the truth of this, let them come to the One Body: let them be led into the Temple of the King. God hath established His Temple everywhere: hath laid everywhere "the foundations of the Prophets and Apostles." The Church has brought "forth sons;" has made them "instead of her fathers" to be "princes over all the earth."

30. "They shall be mindful of thy name in every generation and generation; therefore shall the peoples confess unto Thee" (ver. 17). What does it profit then to "confess" indeed and yet to confess out of "the Temple"? What does it profit to pray, and yet not to pray on the Mount? "I cried," says he, "unto the Lord with my

voice: and He heard me out of His holy hill." Out of what "hill"? Out of that of which it is said, "A city set upon a hill cannot be hid." Of what" hill"? Out of that hill which Daniel saw "grow out of a small stone, and break all the kingdoms of the earth; and cover all the face of the earth." There let him pray, who hopes to receive: there let him ask, who would have his prayer heard: there let him confess, who wishes to be pardoned. "Therefore shall the peoples confess unto thee for ever, world without end." For in that eternal life it is true indeed there will no longer be the mourning over sins: but yet in the praises of God by that everlasting City which is above, there will not be wanting a perpetual confession of the greatness of that happiness. For to that City itself, to which another Psalm sings, "Glorious things are spoken of thee, O City of God," to her who is the very Bride of Christ, the very Queen, a "King's daughter, and a King's consort;" ... the peoples shall for this very cause confess even to herself; the hearts of all, now enlightened by perfect charity, being laid bare, and made manifest, that she may know the whole of herself most completely, who here is, in many parts of her, unknown to herself. ...

PSALM XLVI.

1. It is called, "A Psalm, to the end, for the sons of Korah, for things secret." Secret is it then; but He Himself, who in the place of Calvary was crucified, ye know, hath rent the veil, that the secrets of the temple might he discovered. Furthermore since the Cross of our Lord was a key, whereby things closed might be opened; let us trust that He will be with us, that these secrets may be revealed. What is said, "To the end," always ought to be understood of Christ. For "Christ is the end of the law for righteousness to every one that believeth." But The End He is called, not because He consumeth, but because He perfecteth. For ended call we the food which is eaten, and ended the coat which is woven, the former to consumption, the latter to perfection. Because then we have not where to go farther when we have come to Christ, Himself is called the end of our course. Nor ought we to think, that when we have come to Him, we ought to strive any further to come also to the Father. For this thought Philip also, when he said to Him, "Lord, show us the Father, and it sufficeth us." When he said, "It sufficeth us," he sought the end of satisfaction and perfection. Then said He, "Have I been so long time with you, and hast thou not known Me, Philip: be that hath seen Me, hath seen the Father." In Him then have we the Father, because He is in the Father, and the Father in Him, and He and His Father are One.

2. "Our God is a refuge and strength" (ver. 1). There are some refuges wherein is no strength, whereto when any fleeth, he is more weakened than strengthened. Thou fleest, for example, to some one greater in the world, that thou mayest make' thyself a powerful friend; this seemeth to thee a refuge. Yet so great are this world's uncertainties, and so frequent grow the ruins of the powerful day by day, that when to such refuge thou art come, thou beginnest to fear more than ever therein. ... Our refuge is not such, but our refuge is strength. When thither we have fled, we shall be firm.

3. "A helper in tribulations, which find us out too much." Tribulations are many, and in every tribulation unto God must we flee; whether it be a tribulation in our estate, or in our body's health, or about the peril of those dearest to us, or any other thing necessary to the sustaining of this life, refuge ought there to be none at all to a Christian man, other than his Saviour, other than his God, to whom when he has fled, he is strong. For he will not in himself be strong, nor will he to himself be strength, but He will be his strength, who has become his refuge. But, dearly beloved, among all tribulations of the human soul is no greater tribulation than the consciousness of sin. For if there be no wound herein, and that be sound within man which is called conscience, wherever else he may suffer tribulation, thither

302

will he flee, and there find God. ... Ye see, dearly beloved, when trees are cut down and proved by the carpenters, sometimes in the surface they seem as though injured and rotten; but the carpenter looks into the inner marrow as it were of the tree, and if within he find the wood sound, he promises that it will last in a building; nor will he be very anxious about the injured surface, when that which is within he declares sound. Furthermore, to man anything more inward than conscience is not found; what then profits it, if what is without is sound, and the marrow of conscience has become rotton? These are close and vehement overmuch, and as this Psalm saith, too great tribulations; yet even in these the Lord hath become a helper by forgiving sin. For the consciences of the ungodly hateth nothing save indulgence; for if one saith he hath great tribulations, being a confessed debtor to the treasury, when he beholdeth the narrowness of his estate, and seeth that he cannot be solvent; if on account of the distrainers every year hanging over him, he saith that he suffereth great tribulations, and doth not breathe freely except in hope of indulgence, and that in things earthly; how much more the debtor of penalties out of the abundance of sins: when shall he pay what he owes out of his evil conscience, when if he pay, he perisheth? For to pay this debt, is to undergo the penalties. Remaineth then that of His indulgence, we may be secure, get so that, indulgence received, we return not again to contract debts. ...

4. Now then, such security received, what say they? "Therefore will not we fear, when the earth shall be confounded" (ver. 2). Just before anxious, suddenly secure; out of too great tribulations set in great tranquillity. For in them Christ was sleeping, therefore were they tossed: Christ awoke (as but now we heard out of the Gospel), He commanded the winds, and they were still. Since Christ is in each man's heart by faith, it is signified to us, that his heart as a ship in this world's tempest is tossed, who forgetteth his faith: as though Christ sleeping it is tossed, but Christ awaking cometh tranquillity. Nay, the Lord Himself, what said He? "Where is your faith?" Christ aroused, aroused up faith, that what had been done in the ship, might be done in their hearts. "A helper in tribulations, which found us s out too much." He caused that therein should be great tranquillity.

5. See what tranquillity: "Therefore will not we fear when the earth shall be confounded, and the mountains shall be carried into the heart of the sea." Then we shall find not fear. Let us seek mountains carried, and if we can find, it is manifest that this is our security. The Lord truly said to His disciples, "If ye have faith as a grain of mustard seed, ye shall say to this mountain, Be Thou removed, and be Thou cast into the sea, and it shall be done." Haply "to this mountain," He said of Himself; for He is called a Mountain: "It shall come to pass in the last days, that the mountain of the Lord shall be manifest." But this Mountain is placed above

other mountains; because the Apostles also are mountains, supporting this Mountain. Therefore followeth, "In the last days the Mountain of the Lord shall be manifest, established in the top of the mountains." Therefore passeth It the tops of all mountains, and on the top of all mountains is It placed; because the mountains are preaching The Mountain. But the sea signifieth this world, in comparison of which sea, like earth seemed the nation of the Jews. For it was not covered over with the bitterness of idolatry, but, like dry land, was surrounded with the bitterness of the Gentiles as with sea. It was to be, that the earth be confounded, that is, that nation of the Jews; and that the mountains be carried into the heart of the sea, that is, first that great Mountain established in the top of the mountains. For He deserted the nation of the Jews, and came among the Gentiles. He was carried from the earth into the sea. Who carrying Him? The Apostles, to whom He had said, "If ye have faith as a grain of mustard seed, ye shall say to this mountain, Be thou removed, and be thou cast into the sea, and it shall be done:" that is, through your most faithful preaching it shall come to pass, that this mountain, that is, I Myself, be preached among the Gentiles, be glorified among the Gentiles, be acknowledged among the Gentiles, and that be fulfilled which was predicted of Me, "A people whom I have not known shall serve Me." ...

6. "The waters thereof roared, and were troubled" (ver. 3): when the Gospel was preached, "What is this? He seemeth to be a setter forth of strange gods:" this the Athenians; but the Ephesians, with what tumult would they have slain the Apostles, when in the theatre, for their goddess Diana, they made such an uproar, as to be shouting, "Great is Diana of the Ephesians! " Amidst which waves and roaring of the sea, feared not they who to that refuge had fled. Nay, the Apostle Paul would enter in to the theatre, and was kept back by the disciples, because it was necessary that he should still abide in the flesh for their sakes. But yet, "the waters thereof roared, and were troubled: the mountains shook at the mightiness thereof." Whose might? The sea's? or rather God's, of whom was said, "refuge and strength, a helper in tribulations, which have found us out too much?" For shaken were the mountains, that is, the powers of this world. For one thing are the mountains of God, another the mountains of the world: the mountains of the world, they whose head is the devil, the mountains of God, they whose Head is Christ. But by these mountains were shaken those mountains. Then gave they their voices against Christians, when the mountains were shaken, the waters roaring; for the mountains were shaken, and there was made a great earthquake, with quaking of the sea. But against whom this? Against the City founded upon a rock. The waters roar, the mountains shake, the Gospel being preached. What then, the City of God? Hear what followeth.

7. "The streams of the river make glad the City of God" (ver. 4). When the mountains shake, when the sea rages, God deserteth not His City, by the streams of the river. What are these streams of the river? That overflowing of the Holy Spirit, of which the Lord said, "If any man thirst, let him come unto Me, and drink. He that believeth on Me, out of his bosom shall flow rivers of living water." These rivers then flowed out of the bosom of Paul, Peter, John, the other Apostles, the other faithful Evangelists. Since these rivers flowed from one river, many "streams of the river make glad the City of God." For that ye might know this to be said of the Holy Spirit, in the same Gospel next said the Evangelist, "But this spake He of the Spirit, which they that were to believe on Him should receive. For the Holy Ghost was not yet given, because that Jesus was not yet glorified." Jesus being glorified after His Resurrection, glorified after His Ascension, on the day of Pentecost came the Holy Spirit, and filled the believers, who spake with tongues, and began to preach the Gospel to the Gentiles. Hence was the City of God made glad, while the sea was troubled by the roaring of its waters, while the mountains were confounded, asking what they should do, how drive out the new doctrine, how root out the race of Christians from the earth. Against whom? Against the streams of the river making glad the City of God. For thereby showed He of what river He spake; that He signified the Holy Spirit, by "the streams of the river make glad the City of God." And what follows? "The Most High hath sanctified His tabernacle:" since then there followeth the mention of Sanctification, it is manifest that these streams of the river are to be understood of the Holy Spirit, by whom is sanctified every godly soul believing in Christ, that it may be made a citizen of the City of God.

8. "God is in the midst of her: she shall not be moved "(ver. 5). Let the sea rage, the mountains shake; "God is in the midst of her: she shall not be moved." What is, "in the midst of her"? That God stands in any one place, and they surround Him who believe in Him? Then is God circumscribed by place; and broad that which surroundeth, narrow that which is surrounded? God forbid. No such thing imagine of God, who is contained in no place, whose seat is the conscience of the godly: and so is God's seat in the hearts of men, that if man fall from God, God in Himself abideth, not falleth like one not finding where to be. For rather doth He lift up thee, that thou mayest be in Him, than so lean upon thee, as if thou withdraw thyself, to fall. Himself if He withdraw, fall wilt thou: thyself if thou withdraw, fall will not He. What then is, "God is in the midst of her"? It signifieth that God is equal to all, and accepteth not persons. For as that which is in the middle has equal distances to all the boundaries, so God is said to be in the middle, because He consulteth equally for all. "God is in the midst of her: she shall not be moved." Wherefore shall she not be moved? Because God is in the midst of her. He is "the Helper in tribulations that have found us out too much. God shall help

her with His Countenance." What is, "with His Countenance"? With manifestation of Himself. How manifests God Himself, so as that we see His Countenance? I have already told you; ye have learned God's Presence; we have learned it through His works. When from Him we receive any help so that we cannot at all doubt that it was granted to us by the Lord, then God's Countenance is with us.

9. "The heathen are troubled" (ver. 6). And how troubled? why troubled? To cast down the City of God, in the midst whereof is God? To overthrow the tabernacle sanctified, which God helpeth with His Countenance? No: with a wholesome trouble are the heathen now troubled. For what followeth? "And the kingdoms are bowed." Bowed, saith He, are the kingdoms; not now erected that they may rage, but bowed that they may adore. When were the kingdoms bowed? When that came to pass which was predicted in another Psalm, "All kings shall fall down before Him, all nations shall serve Him." What cause made the kingdoms to bow? Hear the cause. "The Most High gave His Voice, and the earth was moved." The fanatics of idolatry, like frogs in the marshes, clamoured, the more tumultuously, the more sordidly, in filth and mire. And what is the brawling of frogs to the thunder of the clouds? For out of them "the Most High gave His Voice, and the earth was moved:" He thundered out of His clouds. And what are His clouds? His Apostles, His preachers, by whom He thundered in precepts, lightened in miracles. The same are clouds who are also mountains: mountains for their height and firmness, clouds for their rain and fruitfulness. For these clouds watered the earth, of which it was said, "The Most High gave His Voice, and the earth was moved." For it is of those clouds that He threateneth a certain barren vineyard, whence the mountains were carried into the heart of the sea; "I will command," saith He, "the clouds that they rain no rain upon it." This was fulfilled in that which I have mentioned, when the mountains were carried into the heart of the sea; when it was said, "It was necessary that the word of God should have been spoken first to you; but seeing ye put it from you, we turn to the Gentiles;" then was fulfilled, "I will command the clouds that they rain no rain upon it." The nation of the Jews hath just so remained as a fleece dry upon the ground. For this, ye know, happened in a certain miracle, the ground was dry, the fleece only was wet, yet rain in the fleece appeared not. So also the mystery of the New Testament appeared not in the nation of the Jews. What there was the fleece, is here the veil. For in the fleece was veiled the mystery. But on the ground, in all the nations open lieth Christ's Gospel; the rain is manifest, the Grace of Christ is bare, for it is not covered with a veil. But that the rain might come out of it, the fleece was pressed. For by pressure they from themselves excluded Christ, and the Lord now from His clouds raineth on the ground, the fleece hath remained dry. But of them then "the Most High gave His Voice," out of those clouds; by which Voice the kingdoms were bowed and worshipped.

10. "The Lord of Hosts is with us; the God of Jacob is our taker up" (ver. 7). Not any man, not any power, not, in short, Angel, or any creature either earthly or heavenly, but "the Lord of Hosts is with us; the God of Jacob is our taker up." He who sent Angels, came after Angels, came that Angels might serve Him, came that men He might make equal to Angels. Mighty Grace! If God be for us, who can be against us? "The Lord of Hosts is with us." What Lord of Hosts is with us? "If" (I say) "God be for us, who can be against us? He that spared not His own Son, but delivered Him up for us all; how hath He not with Him also freely given us all things." Therefore be we secure, in tranquillity of heart nourish we a good conscience with the Bread of the Lord. "The Lord of Hosts is with us; the God of Jacob is our taker up." However great be thy infirmity, see who taketh thee up. One is sick, a physician is called to him. His own taken- up, the Physician calleth the sick man. Who hath taken him up? Even He. A great hope of salvation; a great Physician hath taken him up. What Physician? Every Physician save He is man: every Physician who cometh to a sick man, another day can be made sick, beside Him. "The God of Jacob is our taker up." Make thyself altogether as a little child, such as are taken up by their parents. For those not taken up, are exposed; those taken up are nursed. Thinkest thou God hath so taken thee up, as when an infant thy mother took thee up? Not so, but to eternity. For thy voice is in that Psalm, "My father and my mother forsake me, but the Lord hath taken me up."

11. "Come and see the works of the Lord" (ver. 8). Now of this taking up, what hath the Lord done? Consider the whole world, come and see. For if thou comest not, thou seest not; if thou seest not, thou believest not; if thou believest not, thou standest afar off: if thou believest thou comest, if thou believest thou seest. For how came we to that mountain? Not on foot? Is it by ship? Is it on the wing? Is it on horses? For all that pertain to space and place, be not concerned, trouble not thyself, He cometh to thee. For out of a small stone He hath grown, and become a great mountain, so that He hath filled all the face of the earth. Why then wouldest thou by land come to Him, who filleth all lands? Lo, He hath already come: watch thou. By growing He waketh even sleepers; if yet there is not in them so deep sleep, as that they be hardened even against the mountain coming; but they hear, "Awake, thou that sleepest, and arise from the dead, and Christ shall give thee light." For it was a great thing for the Jews to see the stone. For the stone was yet small: and small they deservedly despised it, and despising they stumbled, and stumbling they were broken; remains that they be ground to powder. For so was it said of the stone, "Whosoever shall fall upon that stone shall be broken; but on whomsoever it shall fall, it will grind him to powder." It is one thing to be broken, another to be ground to powder. To be broken is less than to be ground to powder: but none grindeth He coming exalted, save whom He brake lying low. For now before His coming He lay low before the Jews, and they stumbled at Him, and

were broken; hereafter shall He come in His Judgment, glorious and exalted, great and powerful, not weak to be judged, but strong to judge, and grind to powder those who were broken stumbling at Him. For" A stone of stumbling and a rock of offence," is He to them that believe not. Therefore, brethren, no wonder if the Jews acknowledged not Him, whom as a small stone lying before their feet they despised. They are to be wondered at, who even now so great a mountain will not acknowledge. The Jews at a small stone by not seeing stumbled; the heretics stumble at a mountain. For now that stone hath grown, now say we unto them, Lo, now is fulfilled the prophecy of Daniel, "The stone that was small became a great mountain, and filled the whole earth." Wherefore stumble ye at Him, and go not rather up to Him? Who is so blind as to stumble at a mountain? Came He to thee that thou shouldest have whereat to stumble, and not have whereto to go up? "Come ye, and let us go up to the mountain of the Lord." Isaiah saith this: "Come ye, and let us go up." What is, "Come ye, and let us go up"? "Come ye," is, Believe ye. "Let us go up," is, Let us profit. But they will neither come, nor go up, nor believe, nor profit. They bark against the mountain. Even now by so often stumbling on Him they are broken, and will not go up, choosing always to stumble. Say we to them, "Come ye, and see the works of the Lord:" what "prodigies He hath set forth through the earth." Prodigies are called, because they portend something, those signs of miracles which were done when the world believed. And what thereafter came to pass, and what did they portend?

12. "He maketh wars to cease unto the end of the earth" (ver. 9). This not yet see we fulfilled: yet are there wars, wars among nations for sovereignty; among sects, among Jews, Pagans, Christians, heretics, are wars, frequent wars, some for the truth, some for falsehood contending. Not yet then is this fulfilled, "He maketh wars to cease unto the end of the earth;" but haply it shall be fulfilled. Or is it now also fulfilled? In some it is fulfilled; in the wheat it is fulfilled, in the tares it is not yet fulfilled. What is this then, "He maketh wars to cease unto the end of the earth"? Wars He calleth whereby it is warred against God. But who warreth against God? Ungodliness. And what to God can ungodliness do? Nothing. What doth an earthen vessel dashed against the rock, however vehemently dashed? With so much greater harm to itself it cometh, with how much the greater force it cometh. These wars were great, frequent were they. Against God fought ungodliness, and earthen vessels were dashed in pieces, even men by presuming on themselves, by too much prevailing by their own strength. This is that, the shield whereof Job also named concerning one ungodly. "He runneth against God, upon the stiff neck of his shield." What is, "upon the stiff neck of his shield"? Presuming too much upon his own protection. Were they such who said, "God is our refuge and strength, a Helper in tribulations which have found us out too much"? or in another Psalm, "For I will not trust in my bow, neither shall my

sword save me." When one learneth that in himself he is nothing, and help in himself has none, arms in him are broken in pieces, wars are made to cease. Such wars then destroyed that Voice of the Most High out of His holy clouds, whereby the earth was moved, and the kingdoms were bowed. These wars hath He made to cease unto the end of the earth. "He shall break the bow, and dash in pieces the arms, and burn the shield with fire." Bow, arms, shield, fire. The bow is plots; arms, public warfare; shields, vain presuming of self-protection: the fire wherewith they are burned, is that whereof the Lord said, "I am come to send fire on the earth; " of which fire saith the Psalm, "There is nothing hid from the heat thereof." This fire burning, no arms of ungodliness shall remain in us, needs must all be broken, dashed in pieces, burned. Remain thou unharmed, not having any help of thine own; and the more weak thou art, having no arms thine own, the more He taketh thee up, of whom it is said, "The God of Jacob is our taker up." ... But when God taketh us up, doth He send us away unarmed? He armeth us, but with other arms, arms Evangelical, arms of truth, continence, salvation, faith, hope, charity. These arms shall we have, but not of ourselves: but the arms which of ourselves we had, are burnt up: yet if by that fire of the Holy Spirit we are kindled, whereof it is said, "He shall burn the shields with fire;" thee, who didst wish to be powerful in thyself, hath God made weak, that He may make thee strong in Him, because in thyself thou wast made weak.

13. What then followeth? "Be still." To what purpose? "And see that I am God" (ver. 10). That is, Not ye, but I am God. I created, I create anew; I formed, I form anew; I made, I make anew. If thou couldest not make thyself, how canst thou make thyself anew? This seeth not the contentious tumult of man's soul; to which contentious tumult is it said, "Be still." That is, restrain your souls from contradiction. Do not argue, and, as it were, arm against God. Else yet live thy arms, not yet burned up with fire. But if they are burned, "Be still;" because ye have not wherewith to fight. But if ye be still in yourselves, and from Me seek all, who before presumed on yourselves, then shall ye "see that I am God." "I will be exalted among the heathen, I will be exalted in the earth." Just before I said, by the name of earth is signified the nation of the Jews, by the name of sea the other nations. The mountains were carried into the heart of the sea; the nations are troubled, the kingdoms are bowed; the Most High gave His Voice, and the earth was moved. "The Lord of Hosts is with us, the God of Jacob is our taker up" (ver. 11). Miracles are done among the heathen, full filled is the faith of the heathen; burned are the arms of human presumption. Still are they, in tranquillity of heart, to acknowledge God the Author of all their gifts. And after this glorifying, doth He yet desert the people of the Jews? of which saith the Apostle, "I say unto you, lest ye should be wise in your own conceits; that blindness in part is happened unto Israel, until the fulness of the Gentiles be come in." That is, until the mountains be

carried hither, the clouds rain here, the Lord here bows the kingdoms with His thunder, "until the fulness of the Gentiles be come in." And what thereafter? "And so all Israel shall be saved." Therefore, here too observing the same order, "I will be exalted" (saith He) "among the heathen, I will be exalted in the earth;" that is, both in the sea, and in the earth, that now might all say what followeth: "the God of Jacob is our taker up."

PSALM XLVII.

1. The title of the Psalm goeth thus. "To the end: for the sons of Korah: a Psalm of David himself." These sons of Korah have the title also of some other Psalms, and indicate a sweet mystery, insinuate a great Sacrament: wherein let us willingly understand ourselves, and let us acknowledge in the title us who hear, and read, and as in a glass set before us behold who we are. The sons of Korah, who are they? ... Haply the sons of the Bridegroom. For the Bridegroom was crucified in the place of Calvary. Recollect the Gospel, where they crucified the Lord, and ye will find Him crucified in the place of Calvary. Furthermore, they who deride His Cross, by devils, as by beasts, are devoured. For this also a certain Scripture signified. When God's Prophet Elisha was going up, children called after him mocking, "Go up thou bald head, Go up thou bald head:" but he, not so much in cruelty as in mystery, made those children to be devoured by bears out of the wood. If those children had not been devoured, would they have lived even till now? Or could they not, being born mortal, have been taken off by a fever? But so in them had no mystery been shown, whereby posterity might be put in fear. Let none then mock the Cross of Christ. The Jews were possessed by devils, and devoured; for in the place of Calvary, crucifying Christ, and lifting on the Cross, they said as it were with childish sense, not understanding what they said, "Go up, thou bald head." For what is, "Go up"? "Crucify Him, Crucify Him." For childhood is set before us to imitate humility, and childhood is set before us to beware of foolishness. To imitate humility, childhood was set before us by the Lord, when He called children to Him, and because they were kept from Him, He said, "Suffer them to come unto Me, for of such is the Kingdom of Heaven." The example of childhood is set before us to beware of foolishness by the Apostle, "Brethren, be not children in understanding:" and again he proposeth it to imitate, "Howbeit in malice be ye children, that in understanding ye may be men." "For the sons of Korah" the Psalm is sung; for Christians then is it sung. Let us hear it as sons of the Bridegroom, whom senseless children crucified in the place of Calvary. For they earned to be devoured by beasts; we to be crowned by Angels. For we acknowledge the humility of our Lord, and of it are not ashamed. We are not ashamed of Him called in mystery "the bald" (Calvus), from the place of Calvary. For on the very Cross whereon He was insulted, He permitted not our forehead to be bald; for with His own Cross He marked it. Finally, that ye may know that these things are said to us, see what is said.

2. "O clap your hands, all ye nations" (ver. 1). Were the people of the Jews all the nations? No, but blindness in part is happened to Israel, that senseless children might cry, "Calve," "Calve;" and so the Lord might be crucified in the place of

Calvary, that by His Blood shed He might redeem the Gentiles, and that might be fulfilled which saith the Apostle, "Blindness in part is happened unto Israel, until the fulness of the Gentiles be come in." Let them insult, then, the vain, and foolish, and senseless, and say, "Calve," "Calve;" but ye redeemed by His Blood which was shed in the place of Calvary, say, "O clap your hands, all ye nations;" because to you hath come down the Grace of God. "O clap your hands." What is "O clap"? Rejoice. But wherefore with the hands? Because with good works. Do not rejoice with the mouth while idle with the hands. If ye rejoice, "clap your hands." The hands of the nations let Him see, who joys hath deigned to give them. What is, the hands of the nations? The acts of them doing good works. "O clap your hands, all ye nations shout unto God with the voice of triumph." Both with voice and with hands. If with the voice only it is not well, because the hands are slow; if only with the hands it is not well, because the tongue is mute. Agree together must the hands and tongue. Let this confess, these work. "Shout unto God with the voice of triumph."

3. "For the Lord Most High is terrible" (ver. 2). The Most High in descending made like one ludicrous, by ascending into Heaven is made terrible. "A great King over all the earth." Not only over the Jews; for over them also He is King. For of them also the Apostles believed and of them many thousands of men sold their goods, and laid the price at the Apostles' feet, and in them was fulfilled what in the title of the Cross was written, "The King of the Jews." For He is King also of the Jews. But "of the Jews" is little. "O clap your hands, all ye nations: for God is the King of all the earth." For it sufficeth not Him to have under Him one nation: therefore such great price gave He out of His side, as to buy the whole world.

4. "He hath subdued the people under us, and the nations under our feet" (ver. 3). Which subdued, and to whom? Who are they that speak? Haply Jews? Surely, if Apostles; surely, if Saints. For under these God hath subdued the people and the nations, that to-day are they honoured among the nations, who by their own citizens earned to be slain: as their Lord was slain by His citizens, arid is honoured among the nations; was crucified by His own, is adored by aliens, but those by a price made His own. For therefore bought He us, that aliens from Him we might not be. Thinkest thou then these are the words of Apostles, "He hath subdued the people under us, and the nations under our feet"? I know not. Strange that Apostles should speak so proudly, as to rejoice that the nations were put under their feet, that is, Christians under the feet of Apostles. For they rejoice that we are with them under the feet of Him who died for us. For under Paul's feet ran they, who would be of Paul, to whom He said, "Was Paul crucified for you?" What then here, what are we to understand? "He hath subdued the people under us, and the

nations under our feet." All pertaining to Christ's inheritance are among "all the nations," and all not pertaining to Christ's inheritance are among "all the nations:" and ye see so exalted in Christ's Name is Christ's Church, that all not yet believing in Christ lie under the feet of Christians. For what numbers now run to the Church; not yet being Christians, they ask aid of the Church; to be succoured by us temporally they are willing, though eternally to reign with us as yet they are unwilling. When all seek aid of the Church, even they who are not yet in the Church, hath He not "subdued the people under us, and the nations under our feet"?

5. "He hath chosen an inheritance for us, the excellency of Jacob, whom He loved" (ver. 4). A certain beauty of Jacob He hath chosen for our inheritance. Esau and Jacob were two brothers; in their mother's womb both struggled, and by this struggle their mother's bowels were shaken; and while they two were yet therein, the younger was elected and preferred to the elder, and it was said, "Two peoples are in thy womb, and the eider shall serve the younger." Among all nations is the elder, among all nations the younger; but the younger is in good Christians, elect, godly, faithful; the elder in the proud, unworthy, sinful, stubborn, defending rather than confessing their sins: as was also the very people of the Jews, "being ignorant of God's righteousness, and going about to establish their own righteousness." But for that it is said, "The elder shall serve the younger;" it is manifest that under the godly are subdued the ungodly, under the humble are subdued the proud. Esau was born first, and Jacob was born last; but he who was last born, was preferred to the first-born, who through gluttony lost his birthright. So thou hast it written, He longed for the pottage, and his brother said to him, If thou wilt that I give it thee, give me thy birthright. He loved more that which carnally he desired, than that which spiritually by being born first he had earned: and he laid aside his birthright, that he might eat lentils. But lentils we find to be the food of the Egyptians, for there it abounds in Egypt. Whence is so magnified the lentil of Alexandria, that it comes even to our country, as if here grew no lentil. Therefore by desiring Egyptian food he lost his birthright. So also the people of the Jews, of whom it is said, "in their hearts they turned back again into Egypt." They desired in a manner the lentil, and lost their birthright.

6. "God is gone up with jubilation" (ver. 5). Even He our God, the Lord Christ, is gone up with jubilation; "the Lord with the sound of a trumpet." "Is gone up:" whither, save where we know? Whither the Jews followed Him not, even with their eyes. For exalted on the Cross they mocked Him, ascending into Heaven they did not ,see Him. "God hath gone up with jubilation. What is jubilation, but admiration of joy which cannot be expressed in words? As the disciples in joy

admired, seeing Him go into Heaven, whom they had mourned dead; truly for the joy, words sufficed not: remained to jubilate what none could express. There was also the voice of the trumpet, the voice of Angels. For it is said, "Lift up thy voice like a trumpet." Angels preached the ascension of the Lord: they saw the Disciples, their Lord ascending, tarrying admiring, confounded, nothing speaking, but in heart jubilant: and now was the sound of the trumpet in the clear voice of the Angels, "Ye men of Galilee, why stand ye gazing up into Heaven? this is Jesus." As if they knew not that it was the same Jesus. Had they not just before seen Him before them? Had they not heard Him speaking with them? Nay, they not only saw the figure of Him present, but handled also His limbs. Of themselves then knew they not, that it was the same Jesus? But they being by very admiration, from joy of jubilation, as it were transported in mind, the Angels said, "that same is Jesus." As though they said, If ye believe Him, this is that same Jesus, whom crucified, your feet stumbled, whom dead and buried, ye thought your hope lost. Lo, this is the same Jesus. He hath gone up before you, "He shall so come in like manner as ye have seen Him go into Heaven." His Body is removed indeed from your eyes, but God is not separated from your hearts: see Him going up, believe on Him absent, hope for Him coming; but yet through His secret Mercy, feel Him present. For He who ascended into Heaven that He might be removed from your eyes, promised unto you, saying, "Lo, I am with you always, even unto the end of the world." Justly then the Apostle so addressed us, "The Lord is at hand; be careful for nothing." Christ sitteth above the Heavens; the Heavens are far off, He who there sitteth is near. ...

7. "Sing praises to our God, sing praises" (ver. 6). Whom as Man mocked they, who from God were alienated. "Sing praises to our God." For He is not Man only, but God. Man of the seed of David, God the Lord of David, of the Jews having flesh. "Whose" (saith the Apostle) "are the fathers, of whom as concerning the flesh Christ came." Of the Jews then is Christ, but according to the flesh. But who is this Christ who is of the Jews according to the flesh? "Who is over all, God blessed for ever." God before the flesh, God in the flesh, God with the flesh. Nor only God before the flesh, but God before the earth whence flesh was made; nor only God before the earth whereof flesh was made, but even God before the Heaven which was first made; God before the day which was first made; God before Angels; the same Christ is God: for "In the beginning was the Word, and the Word was with God, and the Word was God."

8. "For God is the King of all the earth" (ver. 7). What? And before was He not God of all the earth? Is He not God of both heaven and earth, since by Him surely were all things made? Who can say that He is not his God? But not all men

acknowledged Him their God; and where He was acknowledged, there only, so to say, He was God. "In Judah is God known." Not yet was it said to the sons of Korah, "O clap your hands, all ye nations." For that God known in Judah, is King of all the earth: now by all He is acknowledged, for that is fulfilled which Isaiah saith, "He is thy God who hath delivered thee, the God of the whole earth shall He be called." "Sing ye praises with understanding." He teacheth us and warneth us to sing praises with understanding, not to seek the sound of the ear, but the light of the heart. The Gentiles, whence ye were called that ye might be Christians, adored gods made with hands, and sang praises to them, but not with understanding. If they had sung with understanding, they had not adored stones. When a man sensible sang to a stone insensible, did he sing with understanding? But now, brethren, we see not with our eyes Whom we adore, and yet correctly we adore. Much more is God commended to us, that with our eyes we see Him not. If with our eyes we saw Him, haply we might despise. For even Christ seen, the Jews despised; unseen, the Gentiles adored.

9. "God shall reign over all nations" (ver. 8). Who reigned over one nation, "shall reign" (saith He) "over all nations." When this was said, God reigned over one nation. It was a prophecy, the thing was not yet shown. Thanks be to God, we now see fulfilled what before was prophesied. A written promise God sent unto us before the time, the time fulfilled He hath repaid us. "God shall reign over all nations," is a promise. "God sitteth upon His Holy Seat." What then was promised to come, now being fulfilled, is acknowledged and held. "God sitteth upon His Holy Seat." What is His Holy Seat? Haply saith one, The Heavens, and he understandeth well. For Christ hath gone up, as we know, with the Body, wherein He was crucified, and sitteth at the right hand of the Father; thence we expect Him to come to judge the quick and the dead. "God sitteth upon His Holy Seat." The Heavens are His Holy Seat. Wilt thou also be His Seat? think not that thou canst not be; prepare for Him a place in thy heart. He cometh, and willingly sitteth. The same Christ is surely "the Power of God, and the Wisdom of God:" and what saith the Scripture of Wisdom Herself? The soul of the righteous is the seat of Wisdom. If then the soul of the righteous is the seat of Wisdom, be thy soul righteous, and thou shalt be a royal seat of Wisdom. And truly, brethren, all men who live well, who act well, converse in godly charity, doth not God sit in them, and Himself command? Thy soul obeyeth God sitting in it, and itself commandeth the members. For thy soul commandeth thy members, that so may move the foot, the hand, the eye, the ear, and itself commandeth the members as its servants, but yet itself serveth its Lord sitting within. It cannot well rule its inferior, unless its superior it have not disdained to serve.

10. "The princes of the peoples are gathered together unto the God of Abraham" (ver. 9). The God of Abraham, and the God of Isaac, and the God of Jacob. True it is, God said this, and thereupon the Jews prided themselves, and said, "We are Abraham's children; " priding themselves in their father's name, carrying his flesh, not holding his faith; by seed cleaving to Him, in manners degenerating. But the Lord, what said He to them so priding themselves? "If ye are Abraham's children, do the works of Abraham." Again ... "The princes of the peoples:" the princes of the nations: not the princes of one people, but the princes of all people have "gathered together unto the God of Abraham." Of these princes was that Centurion too, of whom but now when the Gospel was read ye heard. For he was a Centurion having honour and power among men, he was a prince among the princes of the peoples. Christ coming to him, he sent his friends to meet Him, nay unto Christ truly passing over to him he sent his friends, and asked that He would heal his servant who was dangerously sick. And when the Lord would come, he sent to Him this message: "I am not worthy that Thou shouldest enter under my roof, but say in a word only, and my servant shall be healed." "For I also am a man set under authority, having under me soldiers." See how he kept his rank! first he mentioned that he was under another, and afterwards that another was under him. I am under authority, and I am in authority; both under some I am, and over some I am. ... As though he said, If I being set under authority command those who are under me, Thou who art set under no man's authority, canst not Thou command Thy creature, since all things were made by Thee, and without Thee was nothing made. "Say," then, said he, "in a word, and my servant shall be healed. For I am not worthy that Thou shouldest enter under my roof." ... Admiring at his faith, Jesus reprobates the Jews' misbelief. For sound to themselves they seemed, whereas they were dangerously sick, when their Physician not knowing they slew. Therefore when He reprobated, and repudiated their pride what said he? "I say unto you, that many shall come from the east and west," not belonging to the kindred of Israel: many shall come to whom He said, "O clap your hands, all ye nations;" "and shall sit down with Abraham, and Isaac, and Jacob, in the kingdom of heaven." Abraham begat them not of his own flesh; yet shall they come and sit down with him in the kingdom of heaven, and be his sons. Whereby his sons? Not as born of his flesh, but by following his faith. "But the children of the kingdom," that is, the Jews, "shall be cast into outer darkness, there shall be weeping and gnashing of teeth." They shall be condemned to outer darkness who are born of the flesh of Abraham, and they shall sit down with him in the kingdom of heaven, who have imitated Abraham's faith.

11. And what they who belonged to the God of Abraham? "For the mighty gods of the earth are greatly lifted up." They who were gods, the people of God, the vineyard of God, whereof it is said, "Judge betwixt Me and My vineyard," shall go

into outer darkness, shall not sit down with Abraham, and Isaac, and Jacob, are not gathered unto the God of Abraham. Wherefore? "For the mighty gods of the earth;" they who were mighty gods of the earth, presuming upon earth. What earth? Themselves; for every man is earth. For to man was it said, "Dust thou art, and unto dust shalt thou return." But man ought to presume upon God, and thence to hope for help, not from himself. For the earth raineth not upon itself, nor shineth for itself; but as the earth from heaven expecteth rain and light, so man from God ought to expect mercy and truth. They then, "the mighty gods of the earth, were greatly lifted up," that is, greatly prided themselves: they thought no physician necessary for themselves, and therefore remained in their sickness, and by their sickness were brought down even to death. The natural branches were broken off that the humble wild olive tree might be grafted in. Hold we fast then, brethren, humility, charity, godliness: since we are called, on their proving reprobate, even by their example let us fear to pride ourselves.

PSALM XLVIII.

1. The title of this Psalm is, "A song of praise, to the sons of Korah, on the second day of the week." Concerning this what the Lord deigneth to grant receive ye like sons of the firmament. For on the second day of the week, that is, the day after the first which we call the Lord's day, which also is called the second week-day, was made the firmament of Heaven. ... The second day of the week then we ought not to understand but of the Church of Christ: but the Church of Christ in the Saints, the Church of Christ in those who are written in Heaven, the Church of Christ in those who to this world's temptations yield not. For they are worthy of the name of "firmament." The Church of Christ, then, in those who are strong, of whom saith the Apostle, "We that are strong ought to bear the infirmities of the weak," is called the firmament. Of this it is sung in this Psalm. Let us hear, acknowledge, associate, glory, reign. For Her called firmament, hear also in the Apostolic Epistles, "the pillar and firmament of the truth." ...

2. "Great is the Lord, and greatly to be praised" (ver. 1). ... That is, "in the city of our God, in His holy mountain." This is the city set upon an hill, which cannot be hid: this is the candle which is not hidden under a bushel, to all known, to all proclaimed. Yet are not all men citizens thereof, but they in whom "great is the Lord, and greatly to be praised." What then is that city: let us see whether perhaps, since it is said, "In the city of our God, in His holy mountain," we ought not to enquire for this mountain where also we may be heard. ... What then is that mountain, brethren? One is it with great care to be enquired for, with great solicitude investigated, with labour also to be occupied and ascended. But if in any part of the earth it is, what shall we do? Shall we go abroad out of our own country, that to that mountain we may arrive? Nay, then we are abroad, when in it we are not. For that is our city, if we are members of the King, who is the head of the same city. ... For there was a certain corner-stone contemptible, whereat the Jews stumbled,' cut out of a certain mountain without hands, that is, coming of the kingdom of the Jews without hands, because human operation went not with Mary of whom was born Christ. But if that stone, when the Jews stumbled thereat, had remained there, thou hadst not had whither to ascend. But what was done? What saith the prophecy of Daniel? What but that the stone grew, and became a great mountain? How great? So that it filled the whole face of the earth. By growing, then, and by filling the whole face of the earth, that mountain came to us. Why then seek we the mountain as though absent, and not as being present ascend to it; that in us the Lord may be "great, and greatly to be praised"?

3. Further, ... when he had said, "in the city of our God, in His holy mountain," what added he? "Spreading abroad the joys of the whole earth, the mountains of Sion" (ver. 2). Sion is one mountain, why then "mountains"? Is it that to Sion belonged also those which came from the other side, so as to meet together on the Corner Stone, and become two walls, as it were two mountains, one of the circumcision, the other of the uncircumcision; one of the Jews, the other of the Gentiles: no longer adverse, although diverse, because from different sides, now in the corner not even diverse. "For He is our peace, who hath made both one." The same Corner Stone "which the builders rejected, is become the Head Stone of the corner." The mountain hath joined in itself two mountains; one house there is, and two houses; two, because coming from different sides; one, because of the Corner Stone, wherein both are joined together. Hear also this, "the mountains of Sion: the sides of the North are the city of the great King." ... See the Gentiles; "the sides of the North:" the sides of the North are joined to the city of the great King. The North is wont to be contrary to Sion: Sion forsooth is in the South, the North over against the South. Who is the North, but He who said, "I will sit in the sides of the North, I will be like the Most High"? The devil had held dominion over the ungodly, and possessed the nations serving images, adoring demons; and all whatsoever them was of human kind anywhere throughout the world, by cleaving to Him, had become North. But since He who binds the strong man, taketh away his goods? and maketh them His own goods; men delivered from infidelity and superstition of devils, believing in Christ, are fitted on to that city, have met in the corner that wall that cometh from the circumcision, and that was made the city of the great King, which had been the sides of the North. Therefore also in another Scripture is it said, "Out of the North come clouds of golden colour: great is the glory and honour of the Almighty." For great is the glory of the physician, when from being despaired of the sick recovers. "Out of the North come clouds," and not black clouds, not dark clouds, not lowering, but "of golden colour." Whence but by grace illumined through Christ? See, "the sides of the North are the city of the great King." ...

4. Let the Psalm then follow, and say, "God shall be known in her houses." Now in her "houses," because of the mountains, because of the two walls, because of the two sons. "God shall be known in her houses," but he commendeth grace, therefore he added, "when He shall take her up." For what would that city have been, unless He had taken her up? Would it not immediately have fallen, unless it had such foundation? For "other foundation can no man lay than that is laid, which is Jesus Christ." Let none then glory in his own merits; but "he that glorieth, let him glory in the Lord." ... The Lord then hath taken up this city, and is known therein, that is, His grace is known in that city: for whatever that city hath, which

glorieth in the Lord, it hath not of itself. For because of this it is said, "What hast thou that thou didst not receive?"

5. "For, lo, the kings of the earth are gathered together" (ver. 3). Behold now those sides of the North, see how they come, see how they say, "Come ye, and let us go up to the mountain of the Lord: and He will teach us His way, and we will walk in it." "And have come together in one." In what one, but :hat "corner-stone"? "They saw it, and so they marvelled" (ver. 4). After their marvelling at the miracles and glory of Christ, what followed? "They were troubled, they were moved" (ver. 5), "trembling took hold upon them." Whence took trembling hold upon them, but from the consciousness of sins? Let them run then, king after a king; kings, let them acknowledge the King. Therefore saith He elsewhere, "Yet have I been set by Him a King upon His holy hill of Sion." ... A King then was heard of, set up in Sion, to Him were delivered possessions even to the uttermost parts of the earth. Kings behoved to fear lest they should lose the kingdom, lest the kingdom be taken from them. As wretched Herod feared, and for the Child slew the children. But fearing to lose his kingdom, he deserved not to know the King. Would that he too had adored the King with the Magi: not by ill-seeking the kingdom, slain the Innocents, and perished guilty. For as concerning him, he destroyed the Innocents: but as for Christ, even a Child, the children dying for Him did He crown. Therefore behoved kings to fear when it was said, "Yet have I been set a King by Him upon His holy sill of Sion," and inheritance. to the uttermost parts of the earth shall He give Him, who set Him up King. ... Thence also this is said to them, "Understand now therefore, O ye kings; be instructed, ye judges of the earth. Serve the Lord with fear, and rejoice unto Him with trembling." And what did they? "There pains as of a woman in travail." What are the pains "as of a woman in travail," but the pangs of a penitent? See the same conception of pain and travail: "Of Thy fear" (saith Isaiah) "we have conceived, we have travailed of the Spirit of salvation." So then the kings conceived from the fear of Christ, that by travailing they brought forth salvation by believing on Him whom they had feared. "There pains as of a woman in travail:" when of travail thou hearest, expect a birth. The old man travaileth, but the new man is born.

6. "With a strong wind Thou shalt break the ships of Tarshish" (ver. 6). Briefly understood, this is, Thou shalt overthrow the pride of the nations. But where in this history is mentioned the overthrowing of the pride of the nations? Because of "the ships of Tarshish." Learned men have enquired for Tarshish a city, that is, what city was signified by this name: and to some it has seemed that Cilicia is called Tarshish, because its metropolis is called Tarsus. Of which city was the Apostle Paul, being born in Tarsus of Cilicia. But some have understood by it

Carthage, being haply sometimes so named, or in some language so signified. For in the Prophet Isaiah it is thus found: "Howl, ye ships of Carthage." But in Ezekiel by some interpreters the word is translated Carthage, by some Tarshish: and from this diversity it can be understood that the same which was called Carthage, is called Tharsus. But it is manifest, that in the beginning of its reign Carthage flourished with ships, and so flourished, that among other nations they excelled in trafficking and navigation. For when Dido, flying from her brother, escaped to the parts of Africa, where she built Carthage, the ships which had been prepared for commerce in his country she had taken with her for her flight, the princes of the country consenting to it; and the same ships also when Carthage was built failed not in traffic. And hence that city became too proud, so that justly by its ships may be understood the pride of the nations, presuming on things uncertain, as on the breath of the winds. Now let none presume on full sails, and on the seeming fair state of this life, as of the sea. Be our foundation in Sion: there ought we to be stablished, not to be "carried about with every wind of doctrine." Whoso then by the uncertain things of this life had been puffed up, let them be overthrown, and be all the pride of the nations subjected to Christ. who shall "with a strong wind break all the ships of Tarshish:" not of any city, but of "Tarshish." How "with a strong wind"? With very strong fear. For so all pride feared Him that shall judge, as on Him humble to believe, lest Him exalted it should fear.

7. "As we have heard, so have we seen" (ver. 7). Blessed Church! at one time thou hast heard, at another time thou hast seen. She heard in promises, seeth in performance: heard in Prophecy, seeth in the Gospel. For all things which are now fulfilled were before prophesied. Lift up thine eyes then, and stretch them over the world; see now His "inheritance even to the uttermost parts of the earth: " see now is fulfilled what was said, "All kings shall fall down before Him: all nations shall serve Him :" see fulfilled what was said, "Be Thou exalted, O God, above the heavens, and Thy glory above all the earth." See Him whose feet and hands were pierced with nails, whose bones hanging on the tree were counted, upon whose vesture lots were cast: see reigning whom they saw hanging; see sitting in Heaven whom they despised walking on earth: see thus fulfilled, "All the ends of the earth shall remember, and turn to the Lord, and all the kindreds of the nations shall worship before Him." Seeing all this, exclaim with joy, "As we have heard, so have we seen." Justly the Church herself is so called out of the Gentiles. ... They to whom the Prophets were not sent, first heard and understood the Prophets: they who first heard not, afterwards hearing marvelled. They remained behind to whom they were sent, carrying the books, understanding not the truth: having the tables of the Testament, and not holding the inheritance. But we, ... "As we have heard, so have we seen." And where hearest thou? where seest thou? "In the city of the Lord of Hosts, in the city of our God. God hath founded it for ever." Let not

heretics insult, divided into parties, let them not exalt themselves who say, "Lo, here is Christ, or lo, there." Whoso saith, "Lo, here is Christ, or lo, there," inviteth to parties. Unity God promised. The kings are gathered together in one, not dissipated through schisms. But haply that city which hath held the world, shall sometime be overthrown? Far be the thought! "God hath founded it for ever." If then God hath founded it for ever, why fearest thou lest the firmament should fall?

8. "We have received Thy mercy, O God, in the midst of Thy people" (ver. 8). Who have received, and where received? Hath not the same Thy people received Thy mercy. If Thy people hath received Thy mercy, how then, "in the midst of Thy people"? As if they who received were one party, they in the midst of whom they received another. A great mystery, but yet welt known. When hence also, that is, out of these verses, hath been extracted and brought forth what ye know; it will be not ruder, but sweeter. Now forsooth all are reckoned the people of God, who carry His Sacraments, but not all belong to His Mercy. All forsooth receiving the Sacrament of the Baptism of Christ, are called Christians, but not all live worthily of that Sacrament. There are some of whom saith the Apostle, "Having a form of godliness, but denying the power thereof." Yet on account of this form of godliness they are named among God's people. As to the floor, until the corn is threshed, belongs not the wheat only, but the chaff. But will it also belong to the garner? In the midst then of an evil people is a good people, which hath received the Mercy of God. He liveth worthily of the Mercy of God who heareth, and holdeth, and doeth what the Apostle saith, "We beseech you that ye receive not the Grace of God in vain." Whoso then receiveth not the Grace of God in vain, the same receiveth not only the Sacrament, but also the Mercy of God as well. ... So those who have the Sacraments, and have not good manners, are both said to be of God, and not of God; are both said to be His, and to be strangers: His because of His own Sacraments, strangers because of their own vice. So also strange daughters: daughters, because of the form of godliness; strange, because of their loss of virtue. Be the lily there; let it receive the Mercy of God: hold fast the root of a good flower, be not ungrateful for soft rain coming from heaven. Be thorns ungrateful, let them grow by the showers: for the fire they grow, not for the garner. In the midst of Thy people not receiving Thy mercy, we have received Thy mercy. For" He came unto His own, and His own received Him not," yet, in the midst of them, "as many as received Him, to them gave He power to become the sons of God." ....

9. For when he had said, "We have received Thy mercy in the midst of Thy people," he signified that there is a people not receiving the mercy of God, in the midst of whom some do receive the mercy of God: and then lest it should occur to

men that there are so few, as to be nearly none, how did He console them in the words following? "According to Thy Name, O God, so is Thy praise unto the ends of the earth" (ver. 9). What is this? ... That is, as Thou art known through all the earth, so Thou art also praised through all the earth, nor are there wanting who now praise Thee through all the earth. But they praise Thee who live well. For, "According to Thy Name, O God, so is Thy praise," not in a part, but "unto the ends of the earth." "Thy right hand is full of righteousness." That is, many are they also who shall stand at Thy right hand. Not only shall they be many who shall stand at Thy left hand, but there also shall be a full heap set at Thy right hand.

10. "Let mount Zion rejoice, and the daughters of Judah be glad, because of Thy judgments, O Lord" (ver. 10). O mount Zion, O daughters of Judah, ye labour now among tares, among chaff, among thorns ye labour: yet be glad because of God's judgments. God erreth not in judgment. Live ye separate, though separate ye were not born; not vainly hath a voice gone forth from your mouth and heart, "Destroy not my soul with sinners, nor my life with bloody men." He shall winnow with such art, carrying in His hand a fan, that not one grain of wheat shall fall into the heap of chaff prepared to be burned, nor one beard of chaff pass to the heap to be laid up in the garner. Be glad, O ye daughters of Judaea, because of the judgments of God that erreth not, and do not yet judge rashly. To you let it belong to collect, to Him let it belong to separate. But think not that the "daughters of Judah" are Jews. Judah is confession; all the sons of confession are all the sons of Judah. For "salvation is of the Jews," is nothing else than that Christ is of the Jews. This saith also the Apostle, "He is not a Jew which is one outwardly; neither is that circumcision which is outward in the flesh: but he is a Jew which is one inwardly, and circumcision is that of the heart, in the spirit, and not in the letter, whose praise is not of men, but of God." Be such a Jew; glory in the circumcision of the heart, though thou hast not the circumcision of the flesh. Let the daughters of Judah be glad, because of Thy judgments, O Lord.

11. "Walk about Zion, and embrace her" (ver. 11). Be it said to them who live ill, in the midst of whom is the people, which hath received the mercy of God. In the midst of you is a people living well, "Walk about Zion." But how? "embrace her." Not with scandals, but with love go round about her: that so those who live well in the midst of you ye may imitate, and by imitation of them, be incorporate with Christ, whose members they are. "Walk about Zion, go round about her: speak in the towers thereof." In the height of her bulwarks, set forth the praises thereof.

12. "Set your hearts upon her might" (ver. 12). Not that ye may have the form of godliness. deny the power thereof, but, "upon her might set your hearts. Speak ye

in her towers." What is the might of this city? Whoso would understand the might of this city, let him understand the force of love. That is a virtue which none conquereth. Love's flame no waves of the world, no streams of temptation, extinguish. Of this it is said, "Love is strong as death." For as when death cometh, it cannot be resisted; by whatever arts, whatever medicines, you meet it; the violence of death can none avoid who is born mortal; so against the violence of love can the world do nothing. For from the contrary the similitude is made of death; for as death is most violent to take away, so love is most violent to save. Through love many have died to the world, to live to God; by this love inflamed, the martyrs, not pretenders, not puffed up by vain-glory, not such as they of whom it is written, "Though I give. my body to be burned, and have not charity, it profiteth me nothing," but men whom truly a love of Christ and of the truth led on to this passion; what to them were the temptations of the tormentors? Greater violence had the eyes of their weeping friends, than the persecutions of enemies. For how many were held by their children, that they might not suffer? to how many did their wives fall upon their knees, that they might not be left widows? How many have their parents forbidden to die; as we know and read in the Passion of the Blessed Perpetua! All this was done; but tears, however great, and with whatever force flowing, when did they extinguish the ardour of love? This is the might of Sion, to whom elsewhere it is said, "Peace. be within thy walls, and prosperity within thy palaces."

13. What here understand we, "Set your hearts upon her might, and distribute her houses"? That is, distinguish house from house. Do not confound. For there is a house having the form of godliness, and not having godliness; but there is a house having both form and godliness. Distribute, confound not. But then ye distribute and confound not, when ye "set your hearts upon her might;" that is, when through love ye are made spiritual. Then ye will not judge rashly, then ye will see that the evil harms not the good as long as we are in this floor. "Distribute her houses." There can be also another understanding. The two houses, one coming of the circumcision, one of the uncircumcision, it is commanded the Apostles to distribute. For when Saul was called, and made the Apostle Paul, agreeing in unity with his fellow Apostles, he so with thorn determined, that they should go to the circumcision, he to the uncircumcision. By that dispensation of their Apostleship, they distributed the houses of the city of the great King; and meeting in the corner, divided the Gospel in dispensation, in love united it. And truly this is rather to be understood; for it followeth and showeth that it is here said to the preachers, "distribute her houses: that ye may tell it to the generation following:" that is, that even to us, who were to come after them, their dispensation of the Gospel should reach: For not for those only they laboured, with whom they lived in the earth; nor the Lord for those Apostles only to whom He deigned to show Himself alive after

His Resurrection, but for us also. For to them He spake, and signified us when He spake, "Lo, I am with you alway, even to the end of the world." Were they then to be here alway, even to the end of the world? Also He said, "Neither pray I for these alone, but for them also which shall believe on Me through their word." Therefore He considereth us, because He suffered on account of us. Justly then it is said, "That ye may tell it to the generation following."

14. Tell what? "For this is God, even our God" (ver. 13). The earth was seen, the earth's Creator was not seen; the flesh was held, God in the flesh was not acknowledged. For the flesh was held by those from whom had been taken the same flesh, for of the seed of Abraham was the Virgin Mary. At the flesh they stayed, the Divinity they did not understand. O Apostles, O mighty city, preach thou on the towers, and say, "This is God, even our God." So, even so as He was despised, as He lay a stone before the feet of the stumbling, that He might humble the hearts of the confessing; even so, "This is God, even our God." Certainly He was seen, as was said, "Afterward did He show Himself upon earth, and conversed with men." "This is God, even our God." He is also Man, and who is there will know Him? "This is God, even our God." But haply for a time as the false gods. For because they can be called gods, but cannot be so, for a time they are even called so. For what saith the Prophet, or what warneth He to be said to them? This shall ye say to them, "The gods that have not made the heavens and the earth, even they shall perish from the earth, and from those that are under the heavens." He is not such a god: for our God is above all gods. Above all what gods? "For all the gods of the nations are idols, but the Lord made the heavens." The same then is our God. "This is God, even our God." For how long? "For ever and ever: He shall role us for ever." If He is our God, He is also our King. He protecteth us, being our God, lest we die; He ruleth us, being our King, lest we fall. But by ruling us He doth not break us; for whom He ruleth not, He breaketh. "Thou shalt rule them," saith He, "with a rod of iron, and dash them in pieces like a potter's vessel." But there are whom He ruleth not; these He spareth not, as a potter's vessel dashing them in pieces. By Him then let us wish to be ruled and delivered, "for He is our God for ever and ever, and He shall rule us for ever."

PSALM XLIX.

The First Part.

1. ..."Hear ye these things, all ye nations" (ver. 1). Not then you only who are here. For of what power is our voice so to cry out, as that all nations may hear? For Our Lord Jesus Christ hath proclaimed it through the Apostles, hath proclaimed it in so many tongues that He. sent; and we see this Psalm, which before was only repeated in one nation, in the Synagogue of the Jews, now repeated throughout the whole world, throughout all Churches; and that fulfilled which is here spoken of, "Hear ye these words, all ye nations." ... Of whom ye are: "With ears ponder, all ye that dwell in the world." This He seemeth to have repeated a second time, lest to have said "hear," before, were too little. What I say, he saith, "hear, with ears ponder," that is, hear not cursorily. What is, "with ears ponder"? It is what the Lord said, "he that hath ears to hear, let him hear:" for as all who were in His presence must have had ears, what ears did He require save those of the heart, when He said, "he that hath ears to hear, let him hear"? The same ears also this Psalm doth smite. "With ears ponder, all ye that dwell in the world." Perhaps there is here some distinction. We ought not indeed to narrow our view, but there is no harm in explaining even this view of the sense. Perhaps there is some difference between the saying, "all nations," and the saying, "all ye that dwell in the world." For perchance he would have us understand the expression, "dwell in," with a further meaning, so as to take all nations for all the wicked, but the dwellers of the world all the just. For he doth inhabit who is not held fast: but he that is occupied is inhabited, and doth not inhabit. Just as he doth possess whatever he hath, who is master of his property: but a master is one who is not held in the meshes of covetousness: while he that is held fast by covetousness is the possessed, and not the possessor. ...

2. Therefore let even the ungodly hear: "Hear ye this, all ye nations." Let the just also hear, who have not heard to no purpose, and who rather rule the world than are ruled by the world: "with ears ponder, all ye that dwell in the world."

3. And again he saith, "both all ye earthborn, and sons of men" (ver. 2). The expression "earthborn" he cloth refer to sinners; the expression "sons of men" to the faithful and righteous. Ye see then that this distinction is observed. Who are the "earthborn"? The children of the earth. Who are the children of the earth? They who desire earthly inheritances. Who are the "sons of men"? They who appertain to the Son of Man. We have already before explained this distinction to your

326

Sanctity, and have concluded that Adam was a man, but not the son of man; that Christ was the Son of Man, but was God also. For whosoever pertain to Adam, are "earthborn:" whosoever pertain to Christ, are "sons of men." Nevertheless, let all hear, I withhold my discourse from no one. If one is "earthborn," let him hear, because of the judgment: another is a "son of man," let him hear for the kingdom's sake. "The rich and poor together." Again, the same words are repeated. The expression "rich" refers to the "earthborn;" but the word "poor" to the "sons of men." By the "rich" understand the proud, by the "poor" the humble. ... He saith in another Psalm, "The poor shall eat and be satisfied." How hath he commended the poor? "The poor shall eat and be satisfied." What eat they? That Food which the faithful know. How shall they be satisfied? By imitating the Passion of their Lord, and not without cause receiving their recompense. "The poor shall eat and be satisfied, and they shall praise the Lord who seek Him." What of the rich? Even they eat. But how eat they? "All the rich upon the earth have eaten and worshipped." He said not, "Have eaten and are satisfied;" but, "have eaten and worshipped." They worship God indeed, but they will not display brotherly humaneness. These eat and worship; those eat and are filled: yet both eat. Of the eater what he eateth is required: let him not be forbidden by the distributor to eat, but let him be admonished to fear him who doth require his account. Let these words then be heard by sinners and righteous, nations, and those who inhabit the world, "earthborn and sons of men, the rich and the poor together:" not divided, not separated. That is for the time of the harvest to do, the hand of the winnower will effect that Now together let rich and poor hear, let goats and sheep feed in the same pasture, until He come who shah separate the one on His right hand, the other on His left. Let them all hear together the teacher, lest separated from one another they hear the voice of the Judge.

4. And what is it they are now to hear? "My mouth shall speak of wisdom, and the meditation of my hear understanding" (ver. 3). And this repetition is perhaps made, lest perchance if he had said only "my mouth," thou shouldest suppose that one spake to thee who had understanding but in his lips. For many have understanding in their lips, but have not in their heart, of whom the Scripture saith, "This people honoureth me with their lips, but their heart is far from me." What saith he then who speaketh to thee? when he hath said, "My mouth shall speak of wisdom," in order that thou mayest know that what is poured forth from the mouth floweth from the bottom of the heart, he hath added, "And the meditation of my heart of understanding."

5. "I will incline mine ear to the parable, I will show my proposition upon the harp" (ver. 4). ... And why "to a parable"? Because "now we see through a glass

darkly," as saith the Apostle; "whilst we are at home in the body, we are absent from the Lord." For our vision is not yet that face to face, where there are no longer parables, where there no longer are riddles and comparisons. Whatever now we understand we behold through riddles. A riddle is a dark parable which it is hard to understand. Howsoever a man may cultivate his heart and apply himself to apprehend mysteries, so long as we see through the corruption of this flesh, we see but in part. ... But as He was seen by those who believed, and by those who crucified Him, when He was judged; so will He be seen, when He shall have begun to be judge, both by those whom He shall condemn, and by those whom He shall crown. But that vision of divinity, which He hath promised to them that love Him, when He saith, "He that loveth Me shall be loved of My Father, and he that loveth Me keepeth My commandments, and I will love him, and will manifest Myself to him:" this the ungodly shall not see. This manifestation is in a certain way familiar: He keepeth it for His own, He will not show it to the ungodly. Of what sort is the vision itself? Of what sort is Christ? Equal to the Father. Of what sort is Christ? "In the beginning was the Word, and the Word was with God, and the Word was God." For this vision we sigh now, and groan so long as we sojourn here; to this vision we shall be brought home at the last, this vision now we see but darkly. If then we see now darkly, let us "incline our ear to the parable," and then let us "show our proposition upon the harp:" let us hear what we say, do what we enjoin.

6. And what hath he said? "And wherefore shall I fear in the evil day? The iniquity of my heel shall compass me" (ver. 5). He beginneth something obscurely. Therefore he ought the rather to fear if the iniquity of his heel shall compass him. Nay, for let not man fear, he saith, who hath not power to escape. For example, he who feareth death, what shall he do to escape death? Let him tell me how he is to escape what Adam oweth, he who is born of Adam. But let him consider that he is born of Adam, and hath followed Christ, and ought to pay what Adam oweth, and obtain what Christ hath promised. Therefore, he who feareth death can no wise escape: but he who feareth the damnation which the ungodly shall hear, "Go ye into everlasting fire," hath an escape. Let him not fear then. For why should he fear? Will the iniquity of his heel compass him? If then he avoid "the iniquity of his heel," and walk in the ways of God, he shall not come to the evil day: the evil day, the last day, shall not be evil to him. ... Now while they live, let them take heed to themselves, let them put away iniquity from their heel: let them walk in that way, let them walk in the way of which He saith Himself, "I am the way, the truth, and the life: " and let them not fear in the evil day, for He giveth them safety who became "The Way." Therefore let them avoid the iniquity of their heel. With the heel a man slippeth. Let your Love observe. What was said by God to the Serpent? "She shall mark thy head, and thou shalt mark her heel." The devil

marketh thy heel, in order that when thou slippest he may overthrow thee. He marketh thy heel, do thou mark his head. What is his head? The beginning of an evil suggestion. When he beginneth to suggest evil thoughts, then do thou thrust him away before pleasure ariseth, and consent followeth; and so shalt thou avoid his head, and he shall not grasp thy heel. But wherefore said He this to Eve? Because through the flesh man doth slip. Our flesh is an Eve within us. "He that loveth his wife," he saith, "loveth himself." What meaneth "himself"? He continueth, and saith, "For no man ever yet hath hated his own flesh." Because then the devil would make us slip through the flesh, just as he made that man Adam to slip, through Eve; Eve is bidden to mark the head of the devil, because the devil marketh her heel. "If then the iniquity of our heel shall compass us, why fear we in the evil day," since being converted to Christ we are able not to do iniquity; and there will be nothing to compass us, and we shall joy and not sorrow in the last day?

7. But who are they whom the "iniquity of their heel shall compass"? "They who trust in their virtue, and in the abundance of their riches do glory" (ver. 6). Therefore such sins will I avoid, and the "iniquity of my heel" shall never compass me. What is avoiding such sins? Let us not trust in our own virtue, let us not glory in the abundance of our own riches, but let us glory in Him who hath promised to us, being humble, exaltation, and hath threatened condemnation to men exalted; and then iniquity of our heel shall never compass us.

8. There are some who rely on their friends, others rely on their virtue, others on their riches. This is the presumption of mankind which relieth not on God. He hath spoken of virtue, he hath spoken of riches, he speaketh of friends. "Brother redeemeth not, shall man redeem?" (ver. 7). Dost thou expect that man shall redeem thee from the wrath to come? If brother redeem thee not, shall man redeem thee? Who is the brother, who if He hath not redeemed thee, no man will redeem? It is He who said after His resurrection, "Go, tell My brethren." Our Brother He hath willed to be: and when we say to God, "Our Father," this is manifested in us. For he that saith to God, "Our Father;" saith to Christ, "Brother." Therefore let him that hath God for his Father and Christ for his Brother, not fear in the evil day. "For the iniquity of his heel shall not compass him;" for he relieth not on his virtue, nor glorieth in the abundance of his riches, nor vaunteth himself of his powerful friends. Let him rely on Him who died for him, that he might not die eternally: who for his sake was humbled, in order that he might be exalted; who sought him ungodly, in order that He might be sought by him faithful. Therefore if He redeem not, shall man redeem? Shall any man redeem, if the Son of man

redeem not? If Christ redeem not, shall Adam redeem? "Brother redeemeth not, shall man redeem?"

9. "He shall not give to God his propitiation, and the price of the redemption of his soul" (ver. 8). He trusteth in his virtue, and in the abundance of his riches doth glory, who "shall not give to God his propitiation :" that is, satisfaction whereby he may prevail with God for his sins: "nor the price of the redemption of his soul," who relieth on his virtue, and on his friends, and on his riches. But who are they that give the price of the redemption of their souls? They to whom the Lord saith, "Make to yourselves friends of the Mammon of unrighteousness, that they may receive you into everlasting habitations." They give the price of the redemption of their soul who cease not to do almsdeeds. So those whom the Apostle chargeth by Timothy he would not have to be proud, lest they should glory in the abundance of their riches. Lastly, what they possessed he would not have to grow old in their hands: but that something should be made of it to be for the price of the redemption of their souls. For he saith, "Charge them that are rich in this world, that they be not high- minded: nor trust in uncertain riches, but in the living God, who giveth us richly all things to enjoy." And as if they had said, "What shall we then make of our riches?" he continueth, "Let them be rich in good works, ready to distribute, willing to communicate," and they will not lose that. How know we? Hear what followeth. "Let them lay up for themselves a good foundation against the time to come, that they may lay hold on the true life." So shall they give the price of the redemption of their soul. And our Lord counselleth this: "Make for yourselves bags which wax not old, a treasure in the heavens that faileth not. where thief approacheth not, neither moth corrupteth." God would not have thee lose thy wealth, but He hath given thee counsel to change the place thereof. Let your love understand. Suppose thy friend were just now to enter thy house, and find thou hadst placed thy store of grain in a damp place, and he knew the natural proneness of grain to decay, which thou perchance knewest not, he would give thee counsel of this sort, saying, "Brother, thou art losing what with great toil thou hast gathered, thou hast placed it in a damp place, in a few days this grain will decay." "And what am I to do, brother? "Raise it into a higher place." Thou wouldest hearken to thy friend suggesting that thou shouldest raise grain from a lower to a higher chamber, and dost thou not hearken to Christ charging thee to lift thy treasure from earth to heaven, where not what thou keepest in store may be paid to thee, but that thou mayest keep in store earth, mayest receive heaven, mayest keep in store things mortal, mayest receive things everlasting, that while thou lendest Christ to receive at thy hands but a small loan upon earth, He may repay thee a great recompense in Heaven? Nevertheless, they whom "the iniquity of their heel shall compass," because they trust in their virtue, and in the abundance of their riches do glory, and rely on human friends who are able to help

them in nothing, "shall not give to God their propitiation, and the price of the redemption of their souls."

10. And what hath he said of such a man? "Yea, he hath laboured for ever, and shall live till the end" (ver. 9). His labour shall be without end, his life shall have an end. Wherefore saith he, "He shall live till the end"? Because such men think life to be nought but daily enjoyments. So when many poor and needy men of our times, unstable, and not looking to what God doth promise them for their labours, see rich men in daily feastings, in the splendour and glitter of gold and of silver, they say what? "These are the only people; they really live!" This is a saying, be it said no longer: we both warn you, and it remains to warn you, that it be said by fewer persons than it would be said, if we had not warned you. For we do not presume to say that we so say these words, as that it be not said, but that it be said by fewer persons: for it will be said even unto the end of the world. It is too little that he saith, "he liveth;" he addeth and saith, he thundereth thinkest thou that he alone liveth? Let him live! his life will be ended: because he giveth not the price of the redemption of his soul, his life will end, his labour will not end. "He laboured for ever, and shall live till the end." How shall he live till the end? As he lived that was "clothed with purple and fine linen, and fared sumptuously every day," who, being proud and puffed up, spurned the man full of sores lying before his gate, whose sores the dogs licked, and who longed for the crumbs which fell from his table. What did those riches profit him? Both changed places: the one was borne from the rich man's gate into Abraham's bosom, the other from his rich feasts was cast into the fire; the one was in peace, the other burned; the one was sated, the other thirsted; the one had laboured till the end, but he lived for ever; the other had lived till the end, but he laboured for ever. And what did it profit the rich man, who asked, while lying in torments in hell, that a drop of water should be poured upon his tongue from the finger of Lazarus, saying, "For I am burning here in this flame," and it was not granted to him? One longed for the drop from the finger, as the other had for the crumbs from the rich man's table; but the labour of the one is ended, and the life of the other is ended: the labour of this is for ever, the life of that is for ever. We who labour perchance here on the earth, have not our life here: and shall not be so placed hereafter, for our life shall be Christ for ever: while they who "will" have their life here, shall labour for ever and live till the end.

11. "For he shall not see death, though he shall have seen wise men dying" (ver. 10). The man who laboured for ever and shall live till the end, "shall not see death, though he shall have seen wise men dying." What is this? He shall not comprehend what death is, whenever he shall have seen wise men dying. For he saith to himself, "this fellow, for all he was wise and dwelled with wisdom and

worshipped God with piety, is he not dead? Therefore I will enjoy myself while I live; for if they that are wise in other respects, could do anything, they would not have died." Just as the Jews saw Christ hanging on the Cross and despised Him, saying, "If this Man were the Son of God, He would come down from the Cross:" not seeing what death is. If they had seen what death is; if they had seen, I say, He died for a time, that He might live again for ever: they lived for a time, that they might die for ever. But because they saw Him dying, they saw not death, that is to say, they understood not what was very death. What say they even in Wisdom? "Let us condemn Him with a most shameful death, for by His own sayings He shall be respected;" for if he is indeed the Son of God, He will deliver Him from the hands of His adversaries: He will not suffer His Son to die, if He is truly His Son. But when they saw themselves insulting Him upon the Cross, and Him not descending from the Cross, they said, He was indeed but a Man. Thus was it spoken: and surely He could have come down froth the Cross, He that could rise again from the tomb: but He taught us to bear with those who insult us; He taught us to be patient of the tongues of men, to drink now the cup of bitterness, and afterwards to receive everlasting salvation. ...

12. "The imprudent and unwise shall perish together." Who is "the imprudent"? He that looketh not out for himself for the future. Who is "the unwise"? He that perceiveth not in what evil case he is. But do thou perceive in what evil case thou art now, and look out that thou be in a good case for the future. By perceiving in what evil case thou art, thou wilt not be unwise: by looking out for thyself for the future, thou wilt not be imprudent. Who is he that looketh out for himself? That servant to whom his master gave what he should expend, and afterwards said to him, "Thou canst not be my steward, give an account of thy stewardship;" and who answered, "What shall I do? I cannot dig, to beg I am ashamed;" had, nevertheless, by even his master's goods made to himself friends, who might receive him when he was put out of his stewardship. Now he cheated his master in order that he might get to himself friends to receive him: fear not thou lest thou be cheating, the Lord Himself exhorteth thee to do so: He saith Himself to thee, "Make to thyself friends of the mammon of unrighteousness." Perhaps what thou hast got, thou hast gotten of unrighteousness: or perhaps this very thing is unrighteousness, that thou hast and another hath not, thou aboundest and another needeth. Of this mammon of unrighteousness, of these riches which the unrighteous call riches, make to thyself friends, and thou shalt be prudent: thou art gaining for thyself, and art not cheating. For now thou seemest to lose it. Wilt thou lose it if thou place it in a treasury? For boys, my brethren, no sooner find some money, wherewith to buy something, than they put it in a money-box, which they open not until afterwards: do they, because they see not what they have got, on that account lose it? Fear not: boys put in a money-box, and are secure: dost thou

place it in the hand of Christ, and fear? Be prudent, and provide for thyself against the future in Heaven. Be therefore prudent, copy the ant, as saith the Scripture: "Store in summer, lest thou hunger in winter;" the winter is the last day, the day of tribulation; the winter is the day of offences and of bitterness: gather what may be there for thee for the future: but if thou doest not so, thou wilt perish both imprudent and unwise.

13. But that rich man too died, and a like funeral was made for him. See to what men have brought themselves: they regard not what a wicked life he led while he lived, but what pomp followed him when he died! O happy he, whom so many lament! But the other lived in such sort, that few lament. For all ought to lament a man living so sadly. But there is the funeral train; he is received in a costly tomb, he is wound in costly robes, he is buried in perfumes and spices. Secondly, what a monument he hath! How marbled! Doth he live in that same monument? He is therein dead. Men deeming these to be good things, have strayed from God, and have not sought the true good things, and have been deceived with the false. To this end see what followeth. He who gave not the price of the redemption of his soul, who understood not death, because he saw wise men dying, he became imprudent and unwise, in order that he might die with them. And how shall they perish, who "shall leave their riches to aliens"? ...

14. But do those same aliens indeed serve them who are called their own? Hear in what they serve them, observe how they are ridiculed why hath he said, "to strangers"? Because they can do them no good. Nevertheless, wherein do they seem to themselves to do good? "And their tombs shall be their house for ever" (ver. 11). Now because these tombs are erected the tombs are a house. For often thou hearest a rich man saying, I have a house of marble which I must quit, and I think not for myself of an eternal house, where I shall alway be. When he thinketh to make for himself a monument of marble or of sculpture, he is deeming as it were of an eternal house: as if therein this rich man would abide! If he would abide there, he would not burn in hell. We must consider that the place where the spirit of an evil doer abideth, is not where the mortal body is laid: but "their tombs shall be their house for ever. Their dwelling places are from generation to generation." "Dwelling places" are wherein they abode for a season: "house" is wherein they will abide as it were for ever, that is to say, their tombs. Thus they leave their dwelling places, where they abode while they lived, to their families, and they pass as it were to everlasting houses, to their tombs. What profit to them are "their dwelling places, from generation to generation"? Now suppose a generation and generation are sons, grandsons there will be, and great grandsons; what do their dwelling places, what do they profit them? What? Hear: "they shall

invoke their names in their lands." What is this? They shall take bread and wine to their tombs, and there they shall invoke the names of the dead. Dost thou consider how loudly was invoked the name of the rich man after his death, when men drank them drunk at his monument, and there came down not one drop upon his own burning tongue? Men minister to their own belly, not to the ghosts of their friends. The souls of the dead nothing doth reach, but what they have done of themselves while alive: but if they have done nought of themselves while alive, nothing doth reach them dead. But what do the survivors? They will but "invoke their names in their lands."

15. "And man though he was in honour perceived not, he was compared to the beasts without sense, and was made like to them" (ver. 12). ... They ought, on the contrary, to have made ready for themselves an eternal house in good works, to have made ready for themselves everlasting life, to have sent before them expenditure, to have followed their works, to have ministered to a needy companion, to have given to him with whom they were walking, not to have despised Christ covered with sores before their gate, who hath said, "Inasmuch as ye have done it unto one of the least of these My brethren, ye have done it unto Me." However, "man being in honour hath not understood." What is, "being in honour"? Being made after the image and likeness of God, man is preferred to beasts. For God hath not so made man as He made a beast: but God hath made man for beasts to minister to: is it to his strength then, and not to his understanding? Nay. But he "understood not;" and he who was made after the image of God, "is compared to the beasts without sense, and is made like unto them." Whence it is said elsewhere, "Be ye not like to horse and mule, in which there is no understanding."

16. "This their own way is an offence to them" (ver. 13). Be it an offence to them, not to thee. But when will it be so to thee too? If thou thinkest such men to be blessed. If thou perceivest that they be not blessed, their own way will be an offence to themselves; not to Christ, not to His Body, not to His members. "And afterwards they shall bless with their mouth." What meaneth, "Afterwards they shall bless with their mouth"? Though they have become such, that they seek nothing but temporal goods, yet they become hypocrites: and when they bless God, with lips they bless, and not with heart. Christians like these, when to them eternal life is commended, and they are told, that in the name of Christ they ought to be despisers of riches, do make grimaces in their hearts: and if they dare not do it with open face, lest they blush, or lest they should be rebuked by men, yet they do it in heart, and scorn; and there remaineth in their mouth blessing, and in their heart cursing.

The Second Part.

1. "Like sheep laid in hell, death is their shepherd" (ver. 14). Whose? Of those whose way is a stumbling-block to themselves. Whose? Of those who mind only things present, while they think not of things future: of those who think not of any life, but of that which must be called death. Not without cause, then, like sheep in hell, have they death to their shepherd. What meaneth, "they have death to their shepherd"? For is death either some thing or some power? Yea, death is either the separation of the soul from the body, or a separation of the soul from God, and that indeed which men fear is the separation of the soul from the body: but the real death, which men do not fear, is the separation of the soul from God. And ofttimes when men fear that which doth separate the soul from the body, they fall into that wherein the soul is separated from God. This then is death. But how is "death their shepherd"? If Christ is life, the devil is death. But we read in many places in Scripture, how that Christ is life. But the devil is death, not because he is himself death, but because through him is death. For whether that (death) wherein Adam fell was given man to drink by the persuasion of him: or whether that wherein the soul is separated from the body, still they have him for the author thereof, who first falling through pride envied him who stood, and overthrew him who stood with an invisible death, in order that he might have to pay the visible death. They who belong to him have death to their shepherd: but we who think of future immortality, and not without reason do wear the sign of the Cross of Christ on the forehead, have no shepherd but life. Of unbelievers death is the shepherd, of believers life is the shepherd. If then in hell are the sheep, whose shepherd is death, in heaven are the sheep, whose shepherd is life. What then? Are we now in heaven? In heaven we are by faith. For if not in heaven, where is the "Lift up your heart"? If not in heaven, whence with the Apostle Paul, "For our conversation is in heaven"? In body we walk on earth, in heart we dwell in heaven. We dwell there, if thither we send anything which holdeth us there. For no one dwelleth in heart, save where thought is: but there his thought is, where his treasure is. He hath treasured on earth, his heart doth not withdraw from earth: he hath treasured in heaven, his heart from heaven doth not come down: for the Lord saith plainly, "Where thy treasure is, there will thy heart be also."

2. They, then, whose shepherd is death, seem to flourish for a time, and the righteous to labour: but why? Because it is yet night. What meaneth, it is night? The merits of the righteous appear not, and the felicity of the unrighteous hath, as it were, a name. So long as it is winter, grass appeareth more verdant than a tree. For grass flourisheth through the winter, a tree is as it were dry through the winter: when in summer time the sun hath come forth with greater heat, the tree, which

seemed dry through the winter, is bursting with leaves, and putteth forth fruits, but the grass withereth: thou wilt see the honour of the tree, the grass is dried. So also now the righteous labour, before that summer cometh. There is life in the root, it doth not yet appear in the branches. But our root is love. And what saith the Apostle? That we ought to have our root above, in order that life may be our shepherd, because our dwelling ought not to quit heaven, because in this earth we ought to walk as if dead; so that living above, below we may be dead; not so as that being dead above, we may live below. ... Our labour shall appear in the morning, and there shall be fruit in the morning: so that they that now labour shall hereafter reign, and they that now boast them and are proud, shall hereafter be brought under. For what followeth? "Like sheep laid in hell, death is their shepherd; and the righteous shall reign over them in the morning."

3. Endure thou the night, yearn for the morning. Think not because the night hath life, the morning too hath not life. Doth then he that sleepeth live, and he that riseth live not? Is not he that sleepeth more like death? And who are they that sleep? They whom the Apostle Paul rouseth, if they choose but to awake. For to certain he saith, "Awake, thou that sleepest, and arise from the dead, and Christ shall give thee light." They then that are lightened by Christ watch now, but the fruit of their watchings appeareth not yet: in the morning it shall appear, that is, when doubtful things of this world shall have passed away. For these are very night: for do they not appear to thee like darkness? ... But they on whom men have trampled, and who were ridiculed for believing, shall hear from Life Itself, whom they have for shepherd, "Come, ye blessed of My Father, receive the kingdom which was prepared for you from the foundation of the world." Therefore the righteous" shall reign over them," not now, but "in the morning." Let no one say, Wherefore am I a Christian? I rule no one, I would rule the wicked. Be not in haste, thou shalt reign, but "in the morning." "And the help of them shall grow old in hell from their glory." Now they have glory, in hell they shall grow old. What is "the help of them"? Help from money, help from friends, help from their own might. But when a man shall be dead, "in that day shall perish all his thoughts." How great glory he seemed to have among men, while he lived, so great oldness and decay of punishments shall he have, when he shall be dead in hell.

4. "Nevertheless, God shall redeem my soul" (ver. 15). Behold the voice of one hoping in the future: "Nevertheless, God shall redeem my soul." Perhaps it is the voice of one still wishing to be relieved from oppression. Some one is in prison, he saith, "God shall redeem my soul:" some one is in bond, "God shall redeem my soul:" some one is suffering peril by sea, is being tossed by waves and raging tempests, what saith he? "God shall redeem my soul." They would be delivered for

the sake of this life. Not such is the voice of this man. Hear what followeth: "God shall redeem my soul from the hand of hell, when He shall have received me." He is speaking of this redemption, which Christ now showeth in Himself. For He hath descended into hell, and hath ascended into heaven. What we have seen in the Head we have found in the Body. For what we have believed in the Head, they that have seen, have themselves told us, and by themselves we have seen: "For we are" all "one body." But are they better that hear, we worse to whom it hath been told? Not so saith The Life Itself, Our Shepherd Himself. For He rebuketh a certain disciple of His, doubting and desiring to handle His scars, and when he had handled the scars and had cried out, saying, "My Lord and my God," seeing His disciple doubting, and looking to the whole world about to believe, "Because thou hast seen Me," He saith, "thou hast believed: blessed are they that see not, and believe." "But God shall redeem my soul from the land of hell, when He hath received me." Here then what? Labour, oppression, tribulation, temptation: expect nothing else. Where joy? In future hope. ...

5. ... Perchance thy heart saith, Wretch that I am, I suppose to no purpose I have believed, God doth not regard things human. God therefore doth awaken us: and He saith what? "Fear not, though a man have become rich" (ver. 16). For why didst thou fear, because a man hath become rich? Thou didst fear that thou hadst believed to no purpose, that perchance thou shouldest have lost the labour for thy faith, and the hope of thy conversion: because perchance there hath come in thy way gain with guilt, and thou couldest have been rich, if thou hadst seized upon that same gain with the guilt, and neededst not have laboured; and thou, remembering what God hath threatened, hast refrained from guilt, and hast contemned the gain: thou seest another man that hath made gain by guilt, and hath suffered no harm; and thou fearest to be good. "Fear not," saith the Spirit of God to thee, "though a man shall have become rich." Wouldest thou not have eyes but for things present? Things future He hath promised, who hath risen again; peace in this world, and repose in this life, He hath not promised. Every man doth seek repose; a good thing he is seeking, but not in the proper region thereof he is seeking it. There is no peace in this life; in Heaven hath been promised that which on earth we are seeking: in the world to come hath been promised that which in this world we are seeking.

6. "Fear not, though a man be made rich, and though the glory of his house be multiplied." Wherefore "fear not"? "For when he shall die, he shall not receive anything" (ver. 17). Thou seest him living, consider him dying. Thou markest what he hath here, mark what he taketh with him. What cloth he take with him? He hath store of gold, he hath store of silver, numerous estates, slaves: he dieth, these

remain, he knoweth not for whom. For though he leaveth them for whom he will, he keepeth them not for whom he will. For many have gained even what was not left them, and many have lost what was left them. All these things then remain, and he taketh with him what? Perhaps some one saith, He taketh that with him in which he is wound, and that which is expended upon him for a costly and marble tomb. to erect a monument, this he taketh with him. I say, not even this. For these things are presented to him without his feeling them. If thou deckest a man sleeping and not awake, he hath the decorations with him on the couch perhaps the decorations are resting upon the body of him as he lieth, and perhaps he seeth himself in tatters during sleep. What he feeleth is more to him than what he feeleth not Though even this when he shall have awaked will not be: yet to him sleeping, that which he saw in sleep was more than that which he felt not. Why then, brethren, should men say to themselves, Let money be spent at my death: why do I leave my heirs rich? Many things will they have of mine, let me too have something of my own for my body. What shall a dead body have? what shall rotting flesh have? what shall flesh not feeling have? If that rich man had anything, whose tongue was dry, then man hath something of his own. My brethren, do we read in the Gospel, that this rich man appeared in the fire with all-silken and fine-linen coverings? Was he of such sort in hell as he was in feastings at table? When he thirsted and desired a drop, all those things were not there. Therefore man carrieth not with him anything, nor doth the dead take with him that which the burial taketh. For where feeling is, there is the man; where is no feeling, the man is not. There lieth fallen the vessel which contained the man, the house which held the man. The body let us call the house, the spirit let us call the inhabitant of the house. The spirit is tormented in hell: what doth it profit him, that the body lieth in spices and perfumes, wound in costly linens? just as if the master of the house should be sent into banishment, and thou shouldest garnish the walls of his house. He in banishment is in need, and doth faint with hunger, he scarce findeth to himself one hovel where he may snatch a sleep, and thou sayest, "Happy is he, for his house hath been garnished." Who would not judge that thou wast either jesting or wast mad? Thou dost garnish the body, the spirit is tormented. Give something to the spirit, and ye have given something to the dead man. But what wilt thou give him, when he desired one drop, and received not? For the man scorned to send before him anything. Wherefore scorned? "because this their way is a stumbling-block to them." He minded not any but the present life, he thought not but how he might be buried, wound in costly vestments. His soul was taken from him, as the Lord saith: "Thou fool, this night thy soul shall be taken from thee, and whose shall those things be which thou hast provided?" And that is fulfilled which this Psalm saith: "Fear not, though a man be made rich, and though the glory of his house be multiplied: for when he shall die he shall not receive anything, nor shall his glory descend together with him."

7. Let your love observe: "For his soul shall be blessed in his life" (ver. 18). As long as he lived he did well for himself. This all men say, but say falsely. It is a blessing from the mind of the blesser, not from the truth itself. For what sayest thou? Because he ate and drank, because he did what he chose, because he feasted sumptuously, therefore he did well with himself. I say, he did ill for himself. Not I say, but Christ. He did ill for himself. For that rich man, when he feasted sumptuously every day, was supposed to do well with himself: but when he began to burn in hell, then that which was supposed to be well was found to be ill. For what he had eaten with men above, he digested in hell beneath. Unrighteousness I mean, brethren, on which he used to feast. He used to eat costly banquets with the mouth of flesh, with his heart's mouth he used to eat unrighteousness. What he ate with his heart's mouth with men above, this he digested amid those punishments in the places beneath. And verily he had eaten for a time, he digested ill for everlasting. Is then unrighteousness eaten? perhaps some one saith: what is it that he saith? Unrighteousness eaten? It is not I that say: hear the Scripture: "As a sour grape is vexation to the teeth, and smoke to the eyes, so is unrighteousness to them that use it." For he that shall have eaten unrighteousness, that is, he that shall have had unrighteousness wilfully, shall not be able to eat righteousness. For righteousness is bread. Who is bread? "I am the living bread which came down from heaven." Himself is the bread of our heart. ... Is then even righteousness eaten? If it were not eaten, the Lord would not have said, "Blessed are they which do hunger and thirst after righteousness." Therefore "since his soul shall be blessed in life," in life it "shall" be blessed, in death it shall be tormented. ...

8. "He shall confess to Thee, when Thou shalt have done him good." Be not of such sort, brethren: see ye how that to this end we say these words, to this end we sing, to this end we treat, to this end toil—do not these things. Your business doth prove you: sometimes in your business ye hear the truth, and ye blaspheme. The Church ye blaspheme. Wherefore? Because ye are Christians. "If so it be, I betake myself to Donatus's party: I will be a heathen." Wherefore? Because thou hast eaten bread, and the teeth are in pain. When thou sawest the bread itself, thou didst praise; thou beginnest to eat, and the teeth are in pain; that is, when thou wast hearing the Word of God thou didst praise: when it is said to thee, "Do this," thou blasphemest: do not so ill: say this, "The bread is good, but I cannot eat it." But now if thou seest with the eyes, thou praisest: when thou beginnest to close the teeth thou sayest, "Bad is this bread, and like him that made it." So it cometh to pass that thou confessest to God, when God doeth thee good and thou liest when thou singest, "I will alway bless God, His praise is ever in my mouth." How alway? If alway gain, alway He is blessed if sometime there is loss, He is not blessed, but blasphemed. Forsooth thou blessest alway, forsooth His praise is ever

in thy mouth! Thou wilt be such as just now he describeth: "He will confess to Thee, when Thou shalt have done him good."

9. "He shall enter even unto the generations of his fathers" (ver. 19): that is, he shall imitate his fathers. For the unrighteous, that now are, have brothers, have fathers. Unrighteous men of old, are the fathers of the present; and they that are now unrighteous, are the fathers of unrighteous posterity: just as the fathers of the righteous, the righteous of old, are the fathers of the righteous that now are; and they that now are, are the fathers of them that are to be. The Holy Spirit hath willed to show that righteousness is not evil when men murmur against her: but these men have their father from the beginning, even to the generation of their fathers. Two men Adam begat, and in one was unrighteousness, in one was righteousness: unrighteousness in Cain, righteousness in Abel Unrighteousness seemed to prevail over righteousness, because Cain unrighteous slew Abel righteous in the night. Is it so in the morning? Nay, "but the righteous shall reign over them in the morning." The morning shall come, and it shall be seen where Abel is, and where Cain. So all men who are after Cain, and so all who are after Abel, even unto the end of the world. "He shall enter even unto the generations of his fathers: even to eternity he shall not see light." Because even when he was here, he was in darkness, taking pleasure in false goods, and not loving real goods: even so he shall go hence into hell: from the darkness of his dreams the darkness of torments shall receive him. Therefore, "even to eternity he shall not see light."

But wherefore this? What he hath written in the middle of the Psalm, the same also he hath writ at the end: "Man, though he was in honour, understood not, was compared to the beasts without sense, and was made like to them" (ver. 20). But ye, brethren, consider that ye be men made after the image and likeness of God. The image of God is within, is not in the body; is not in these ears which ye see, and eyes, and nostrils, and palate, and hands, and feet; but is made nevertheless: wherein is the intellect, wherein is the mind, wherein the power of discovering truth, wherein is faith, wherein is your hope, wherein your charity, there God hath His Image: there at least ye perceive and see that these things pass away; for so he hath said in another Psalm, "Though man walketh in an image, yet he is disquieted in vain: he heapeth up treasures, and knoweth not for whom he shall gather them." Be not disquieted, for of whatsoever kind these things be, they are transitory, if ye are men who being in honour understand. For if being men in honour ye understand not, ye are compared to the beasts without sense, and are made like to them.

PSALM L.

1. How much availeth the Word of God to us for the correction of our life, both regarding His rewards to be expected, and His punishments to be feared, let each one measure in himself; and let him put his conscience without deceit before His eyes, and not flatter himself in a danger so great: for ye see that even our Lord God Himself doth flatter no one: though He comforteth us by promising His blessings, and by strengthening our hope; yet them that live ill and despise His word He assuredly spareth not. Let each one examine himself, while it is time, and let him see where he is, and either persevere in good, or be changed from evil. For as he saith in this Psalm, not any man whatever nor any angel whatever, but, "The Lord, the God of gods, hath spoken" (ver. 1). But in speaking, He hath done what? "He hath called the earth from the rising of the sun unto the going down." He that "hath called the world from the rising of the sun unto the going down," is Our Lord and Saviour Jesus Christ, "the Word made Flesh," in order that He might dwell in us. Our Lord Jesus Christ then is the "God of gods;" because by Himself were all things made, and without Himself was nothing made. The Word of God, if He is God, is truly the God of gods; but whether He be God the Gospel answereth, "In the beginning was the Word, and the Word was with God, and the Word was God." And if all things were made by Himself, as He saith in the sequel, then if any were made gods, by Himself were they made. For the one God was not made, and He is Himself alone truly God. But Himself the only God, Father and Son and Holy Ghost, is one God.

2. But then who are those gods, or where are they, of whom God is the true God? Another Psalm saith, "God hath stood in the synagogue of gods, but in the midst He judgeth gods." As yet we know not whether perchance any gods be congregated in heaven, and in their congregation, for this is "in the synagogue," God hath stood to judge. See in the same Psalm those to whom he saith, "I have said, Ye are gods, and children of the Highest all; but ye shall die like men, and fall like one of the princes." It is evident then, that He hath called men gods, that are deified of His Grace, not born of His Substance. For He doth justify, who is just through His own self, and not of another; and He doth deify who is God through Himself, not by the partaking of another. But He that justifieth doth Himself deify, in that by justifying He doth make sons of God. "For He hath given them power to become the sons of God." If we have been made sons of God, we have also been made gods: but this is the effect of Grace adopting, not of nature generating. For the only Son of God, God, and one God with the Father, Our Lord and Saviour Jesus Christ, was in the beginning the Word, and the Word with God, the Word God. The rest that are made gods, are made by His own Grace, are not

born of His Substance, that they should be the same as He, but that by favour they should come to Him, and be fellow-heirs with Christ. For so great is the love in Him the Heir, that He hath willed to have fellow-heirs. What covetous man would will this, to have fellow- heirs? But even one that is found so to will, will share with them the inheritance, the sharer having less himself, than if he had possessed alone: but the inheritance wherein we are fellow-heirs of Christ, is not lessened by multitude of possessors, nor is it made narrower by the number of fellow-heirs: but is as great for many as it is for few, as great for individuals as for all. "See," saith the Apostle, "what love God hath bestowed upon us, that we should be called, and be, the sons of God." And in another place, "Dearly beloved, we are the sons of God, and it doth not yet appear what we shall be." We are therefore in hope, not yet in substance. "But we know," he saith, "that when He shall have appeared, we shall be like Him, for we shall see Him as He is." The Only Son is like Him by birth, we like by seeing. For we are not like in such sort as He, who is the same as He is by whom He was begotten: for we are like, not equal: He, because equal, is therefore like. We have heard who are the gods that being made are justified, because they are called the sons of God: and who are the gods that are not Gods, to whom the God of gods is terrible? For another Psalm saith, "He is terrible over all gods." And as if thou shouldest enquire, what gods? He saith, "For all the gods of the nations are devils." To the gods of the nations, to the devils, terrible: to the gods made by Himself, to sons, lovely. Furthermore, I find both of them confessing the Majesty of God, both the devils confessed Christ, and the faithful confessed Christ. "Thou art Christ, the Son of the living God," said Peter. "We know who Thou art, Thou art the Son of God," said the devils. A like confession I hear, but like love I find not; nay even here love, there fear. To whom therefore He is lovely, the same are sons; to whom He is terrible, are not sons; to whom He is lovely, the same He hath made gods; those to whom He is terrible He doth prove not to be gods. For these are made gods, those are reputed gods; these Truth maketh gods, those error doth so account.

3. "The God," therefore, "of gods, the Lord hath spoken" (ver. 1). Hath spoken many ways. By Angels He hath Himself spoken, by Prophets He hath Himself spoken, by His own mouth He hath Himself spoken, by His faithful He doth Himself speak, by our lowliness, when we say anything true, He doth Himself speak. See then, by speaking diversely, many ways, by many vessels, by many instruments, yet He doth Himself sound everywhere, by touching, moulding, inspiring: see what He hath done. For "He hath spoken, and hath called the world." What world? Africa, perhaps! for the sake of those that say, the Church of Christ is the portion of Donatus. Africa indeed alone He hath not called, but even Africa He hath not severed. For He that "hath called the world from the rising of the sun unto the going down," leaving out no parts that He hath not called, in His calling hath

found Africa. Let it rejoice therefore in unity, not pride itself in division. We say well, that the voice of the God of gods hath come even into Africa, hath not stayed in Africa. For "He hath called the world from the rising of the sun unto the going down." There is no place where may lurk the conspiracies of heretics, they have no place wherein they may hide themselves under the shadow of falsehood; for "there is none that can hide himself from the heat thereof." He that hath called the world, hath called even the whole world: He that hath called the world, hath called as much as He hath formed. Why do false christs and false prophets rise up against me? why is it that they strive to ensnare me with captious words, saying, "Lo! here is Christ, Lo! He is there! " I hear not them that point out portions: the God of gods hath pointed out the whole: "He" that "hath called the world from the rising of the sun unto the going down," hath redeemed the whole; but hath condemned them that lay false claim to portions.

4. But we have heard the world called from the rising of the sun unto the going down: whence doth He begin to call, who hath called? This thing also hear ye: "Out of Sion is the semblance of His beauty" (ver. 2). Evidently the Psalm doth agree with the Gospel, which saith, "Throughout all nations, beginning at Jerusalem." Hear, "Throughout all nations:" He hath called the world from the rising of the sun unto the going down." Hear, "Beginning at Jerusalem:" "Out of Sion is the semblance of His beauty." Therefore, "He hath called the world from the rising of the sun unto the going down," agreeth with the words of the Lord, who saith," It behoved Christ to suffer, and to rise from the dead the third day; and that repentance and remission of sins should be preached in His Name throughout all nations." For all nations are from the rising of the sun unto the going down. But that, "Out of Sion is the semblance of His beauty," that thence beginneth the beauty of His Gospel, that thence He began to be preached, being "beautiful in form beyond the sons of men," agreeth with the words of the Lord, who saith, "Beginning at Jerusalem." New things are in tune with old, old things with new: the two Seraphim say to one another," Holy, holy, holy, Lord God of Sabaoth." The two Testaments are both in tune, and the two Testaments have one voice: let the voice of the Testaments in tune be heard, not that of pretenders disinherited. This thing then hath the God of gods done, "He hath called the world from the rising of the sun unto the going down, His semblance going before out of Sion." For in that place were His disciples, who received the Holy Ghost sent from heaven on the fiftieth day after His resurrection. Thence the Gospel, thence the preaching, thence the whole world filled, and that in the Grace of Faith.

5. For when the Lord Himself had come, because He came to suffer, He came hidden: and though He was strong in Himself, He appeared in the flesh weak. For

He must needs appear in order that He might not be perceived; be despised, in order that He might be slain. There was semblance of glory in divinity, but it lay concealed in flesh. "For if they had known, they would never have crucified the Lord of glory." So then He walked hidden among the Jews, among His enemies, doing marvels, suffering ills, until He was hanged on the tree, and the Jews seeing Him hanging both despised Him the more, and before the Cross wagging their heads they said, "If He be the Son of God, let Him come down from the Cross." Hidden then was the God of gods, and He gave forth words more out of compassion for us than out of His own majesty. For whence, unless assumed from us, were those words, "My God, My God, why hast Thou forsaken me? But when hath the Father forsaken the Son, or the Son the Father? Are not Father and Son one God? Whence then, "My God, My God, why hast Thou forsaken Me," save that in the Flesh of infirmity there was acknowledged the voice of a sinner? For as He took upon Him the likeness of the flesh of sin," why should He not take upon Him the voice of sin? Hidden then was the God of gods, both when He walked among men, and when He hungered, and when He thirsted, and when fatigued He sat, and when with wearied body He slept, and when taken, and when scourged, and when standing before the judge, and when He made answer to him in his pride, "Thou couldest have no power against Me, except it had been given thee from above;" and while led as a victim "before His shearer He opened not His mouth," and while crucified, and while buried, He was always hidden God of gods. What took place after He rose again? The disciples marvelled, and at first believed not, until they touched and handled. But flesh had risen, because flesh had been dead: Divinity which could not die, even still lay hid in the flesh of Him rising. Form could be seen, limbs held, scars handled: the Word by whom all things were made, who doth see? who doth hold? who doth handle? And yet "the Word was made flesh, and dwelled among us." And Thomas, that was holding Man, understood God as he was able. For when he had handled the scars, he cried out, "My Lord, and my God." Yet the Lord was showing that form, and that flesh, which they had seen upon the Cross, which had been laid in the sepulchre. He stayed with them forty days. ... But what was said to Thomas handling? "Because thou hast seen, thou hast believed; blessed are they that see not, and believe." We are foretold. That world called from the rising of the sun unto the going down seeth not, and believeth. Hidden then is the God of gods, both to those among whom He walked, and to those by whom He was crucified, and to those before whose eyes He rose, and to us who believe on Him in heaven sitting, whom we have not seen on earth walking. But even if we were to see, should we not see that which the Jews saw and crucified? It is more, that not seeing we believe Christ to be God, than that they seeing deemed Him only to be man. They in a word by thinking evil slew, we by believing well are made alive.

6. What then, brethren? This God of gods, both then hidden, and now hidden, shall He ever be hidden? Evidently not: hear what followeth: "God shall come manifest" (ver. 3). He that came hidden, shall come manifest. Hidden He came to be judged, manifest He shall come to judge: hidden He came that He might stand before a judge, manifest He shall come that He may be judge even of judges: "He shall come manifest, and shall not be silent." But why? Is He now silent? And whence are all the words that we say? whence those precepts? whence those warnings? whence that trumpet of terror? He is not silent, and is silent: is not silent from warning, is silent from avenging: is not silent from precept, is silent from judgment. For He suffereth sinners daily doing evil things, not caring for God, not in their conscience, not in heaven, not in earth: all these things escape Him not, and universally He doth admonish all; and whenever He chastiseth any on earth, it is admonition, not yet condemnation. He is silent then from judgment, He is hidden in heaven, as yet He intercedeth for us: He is long- suffering to sinners, not putting forth His wrath, but awaiting penitence. He saith in another place: "I have held my peace, shall I always hold my peace?" When then He shall not hold His peace, "God shall come manifest." What God? "Our God." And the God Himself, who is our God: for he is not God, who is not our God. For the gods of the nations are devils: the God of Christians is very God. Himself shall come, but "manifest," not still to be mocked, not still to be buffeted and scourged: He shall come, but "manifest," not still to be smitten with a reed upon the head, not still to be crucified, slain, buried: for all these things God being hidden hath willed to suffer. "He shall come manifest, and shall not be silent."

7. But that He shall come to judgment, the following words teach. "Fire shall go before Him." Do we fear? Be we changed, and we shall not fear. Let chaff fear the fire: what doth it to gold? What thou mayest do is now in thy power, so thou mayest not experience, for want of being corrected, that which is to come even against thy will. For if we might so bring it about, brethren, that the day of judgment should not come; I think that even then it were not for us to live ill. If the fire of the day of judgment were not to come, and over sinners there impended only separation from the face of God, in whatever affluence of delights they might be, not seeing Him by whom they were created, and separated from that sweetness of His ineffable countenance, in whatever eternity and impunity of sin, they ought to bemoan themselves. But what shall I say, or to whom shall I say? This is a punishment to lovers, not to despisers. They that have begun to feel in any degree the sweetness of wisdom and truth, know what I say, how great a punishment it is to be only separated from the face of God: but they that have not tasted that sweetness, if not yet they yearn for the face of God, let them fear even fire; let punishments terrify those, whom rewards win not. Of no value to thee is what God promiseth, tremble at what He threateneth. The sweetness of His presence shall

come; thou art not changed, thou art not awakened, thou sighest not, thou longest not: thou embracest thy sins and the delights of thy flesh, thou art heaping stubble to thyself, the fire will come. "Fire shall burn in His presence." This fire will not be like thy hearth-fire, into which nevertheless, if thou art compelled to thrust thy hand, thou wilt do whatsoever he would have thee who doth threaten this alternative. If he say to thee, "write against the life of thy father, write against the lives of thy children, for if thou do not, I thrust thy hand into thy fire:" thou wilt do it in order that thy hand be not burned, in order that thy member be not burned for a time, though it is not to be ever in pain. Thine enemy threateneth then but so light an evil, and thou doest evil; God threateneth eternal evil, and doest thou not good? To do evil not even menaces should compel thee: from doing good not even menaces should deter thee. But by the menaces of God, by menaces of everlasting fire, thou art dissuaded from evil, invited to good. Wherefore doth it grieve thee, except because thou believest not? Let each one then examine his heart, and see what faith doth hold there. If we believe a judgment to come, brethren, let us live well. Now is time of mercy, then will be time of judgment. No one will say, "Call me back to my former years." Even then men will repent, but will repent in vain: now let there be repentance, while there is fruit of repentance; now let there be applied to the roots of the tree a basket of dung, sorrow of heart and tears; lest He come and pluck up by the roots. For when He shall have plucked up, then the fire is to be looked for. Now, even if the branches have been broken, they can again be grafted in; then, "every tree which bringeth not forth good fruit, shall be cut down, and shall be cast into the fire." "Fire shall burn in His presence."

8. "And a mighty tempest round about Him" (ver. 3). "A mighty tempest," in order to winnow so great a floor. In this tempest shall be that winnowing whereby from the saints shall be put away everything impure, from the faithful every unreality; from godly men and them that fear the Word of God, every scorner and every proud man. For now a sort of mixture doth lie there, from the rising of the sun unto the going down. Let us see then how He will do that is to come, what He will do with that tempest which "shall be a mighty tempest round about Him." Doubtless this tempest is to make a sort of separation. It is that separation which they waited not for, who brake the nets, before they came to land. But in this separation there is made a sort of distinction between good men and bad men. There be some that now follow Christ with lightened shoulders without the load of the world's cares, who have not heard in vain, "If thou wilt be perfect, go and sell all that thou hast, and give to the poor, and thou shall have treasure in heaven: and come, follow Me;" to which sort is said, "Ye shall sit upon twelve thrones, judging the twelve tribes of Israel." Some then shall be judging with the Lord: but others to be judged, but to be placed on the right hand. For that there will be certain judging

with the Lord, we have most evident testimony, which I have but now quoted: "Ye shall sit upon twelve thrones, judging the twelve tribes of Israel." ...

9. But what the Lord did after His resurrection, signified what is to be to us after our resurrection, in that number of the kingdom of heaven, where shall be no bad man. ... Lastly, those seven thousand of whom reply was made to Elias, "I have left me seven thousand men that have not bowed knees before Baal," far exceed that number of fishes. Therefore the hundred and fifty-three fishes doth not alone express just such a number of saints, but Scripture doth express the whole number of saints and righteous men by so great a number for a particular reason; to wit, in order that in those hundred and fifty-three all may be understood that pertain to the resurrection to eternal life. For the Law hath ten commandments: but the Spirit of Grace, through which alone the Law is fulfilled," is called sevenfold. The number then must be examined, what mean ten and seven: ten in commandments, seven in the grace of the Holy Spirit: by which grace the commandments are fulfilled. Ten then and seven contain all that pertain to the resurrection, to the right hand, to the kingdom of heaven, to life eternal, that is, they that fulfil the Law by the Grace of the Spirit, not as it were by their own work or their own merit. But ten and seven, if thou countest from one unto seventeen, by adding all the numbers by steps, so that to one thou mayest add two, add three, add four, that they may become ten, by adding five that they may become fifteen, by adding six that they may become twenty-one, by adding seven that they may become twenty-eight, by adding eight that they may become thirty-six, by adding nine that they may become forty-five, by adding ten that they may become fifty-five, by adding eleven that they may become sixty-six, by adding twelve that they may become seventy-eight, by adding thirteen that they may become ninety-one, by adding fourteen that they may become one hundred and five, by adding fifteen that they may become one hundred and twenty, by adding sixteen that they may become one hundred and thirty-six, by adding seventeen, make up one hundred and fifty- three, thou wilt find a vast number of all saints to belong to this number of a few fishes. In like manner then as in five virgins, countless virgins; as in five brethren of him that was tormented in hell, thousands of the people of the Jews; as in the number of one hundred and fifty-three fishes, thousands of thousands of saints: so in twelve thrones, not twelve men, but great is the number of the perfect.

10. But I see what is next required of us; in like manner as in the case of the five virgins, a reason was given why many should belong to five, and why to those five many Jews, and why to a hundred and fifty-three many perfect—to show why and how to the twelve thrones not twelve men, but many belong. What mean the twelve thrones, which signify all men everywhere that have been enabled to be so

perfect as they must be perfect, to whom it is said, "Ye shall sit over the twelve tribes of Israel"? And why do all men everywhere belong to the number twelve? Because the very "everywhere" which we say, we say of the whole world: but the compass of lands is contained in four particular quarters, East, West, South, and North: from all these quarters they being called in the Trinity and made perfect in the faith and precept of the Trinity,—seeing that three times four are twelve, ye perceive wherefore the saints belong to the whole world; they that shall sit upon twelve thrones to judge the twelve tribes of Israel, since the twelve tribes of Israel, also, are the twelve tribes of the whole of Israel. For like as they that are to judge are from the whole world, so also they that are to be judged are from the whole world. The Apostle Paul of himself, when he was reproving believing laymen, because they referred not their causes to the Church, but dragged them with whom they had matters before the public, said, "Know ye not that we shall judge Angels?" See after what sort He hath made Himself judge: not only himself, but also all that judge aright in the Church.

11. Since then it is evident, that many are to judge with the Lord, but that others are to be judged, not however on equality, but according to their deserts; He will come with all His Angels, when before Him shall be gathered all nations, and among all the Angels are to be reckoned those that have been made so perfect, that sitting upon twelve thrones they judge the twelve tribes of Israel. For men are called Angels: the Apostle saith of himself, "As an angel of God ye received me." Of John Baptist it is said, "Behold, I send My Angel before Thy face, that shall prepare Thy way before Thee." Therefore, coming with all Angels, together with Him He shall have the Saints also. For plainly saith Isaias also, "He shall come to judgment with the elders of the people." Those "elders of the people," then, those but now named Angels, those thousands of many men made perfect coming from the whole world, are called Heaven. But the others are called earth, yet fruitful. Which is the earth that is fruitful? That which is to be set on the fight hand, unto which it shall be said, "I was an hungred, and ye gave Me to eat:" truly fruitful earth in which the Apostle doth joy, when they sent to him to supply his necessities: "Not because I ask a gift," he saith, "but I require fruit." And he giveth thanks, saying, "Because at length ye have budded forth again to be thoughtful for me." He saith, "Ye have budded forth again," as to trees which had withered away with a kind of barrenness. Therefore the Lord coming to judgment (that we may now hear the Psalm, brethren), He will do what? "He will call the heaven from above" (ver. 4). The heaven, all the Saints, those made perfect that shall judge, them He shall call from above, to be sitters with Him to judge the twelve tribes of Israel. For how shall "He call the heaven from above," when the heaven is always above? But those that He here calleth heaven, the same elsewhere He calleth heavens. What heavens? That tell out the glory of God: for, "The heavens tell out

the glory of God:" whereof is said, "Into all the earth their sound hath gone forth, and into the ends of the world their words." For see the Lord severing in judgment: "He shall call the heaven from above and the earth, to sever His people." From whom but from evil men? Of whom here afterwards no mention is made, now as it were condemned to punishment. See these good men, and distinguish. "He shall call the heaven from above, and the earth, to sever His people." He calleth the earth also, not however to be associated, but to be dissociated. For at first He called them together, "when the God of gods spake and called the world from the rising of the sun unto the going down," He had not yet severed: those servants had been sent to bid to the marriage, who had gathered good and bad. But when the God of gods shall come manifest and shall not keep silence, He shall so call the "heaven from above" that it may judge with Him. For what the heaven is, the heavens themselves are; just as what the earth is, the lands themselves, just as what the Church is, the Churches themselves: "He shall call the heaven from above, and the earth, to sever His people." Now with the heaven He severeth the earth, that is, the heaven with Him doth sever the earth. How doth He sever the earth? In such sort that He setteth on the right hand some, others on the left. But to the earth severed, He saith what? "Come, ye blessed of My Father, receive the kingdom which was prepared for you from the beginning of the world. For I was an hungred, and ye gave me to eat," and so forth. But they say, "When saw we Thee an hungred?" And He, "Inasmuch as ye have done it unto one of the least of Mine, ye have done it unto Me." "He shall call therefore the heaven from above, and the earth, to sever His people."

12. "Gather to Him His righteous" (ver. 5). The voice divine and prophetic, seeing future things as if present doth exhort the Angels gathering. For He shall send His Angels, and before Him shall be gathered all nations. Gather to Him His righteous. What righteous men save those that live of faith and do works of mercy? For those works are works of righteousness. Thou hast the Gospel: "Beware of doing your righteousness before men to be seen of them." And as if it were inquired, What righteousness? "When therefore thou doest alms," He saith. Therefore alms He hath signified to be works of righteousness. Those very persons gather for His righteous: gather those that have had compassion on the "needy," that have considered the needy and poor: gather them, "The Lord preserve them, and make them to live;" "Gather to Him His righteous: who order His covenant above sacrifices:" that is, who think of His promises above those things which they work. For those things are sacrifices, God saying, "I will have mercy more than sacrifice." "Who keep His covenant more than sacrifice."

13. "And the Heaven shall declare His righteousness" (ver. 6). Truly this righteousness of God to us the "heavens have declared," the Evangelists have foretold. Through them we have heard that some will be on the right hand, to whom the Householder saith, "Come, ye blessed of My Father, receive. Receive what? "A kingdom." In return for what thing? "I was an hungred, and ye gave Me to eat." What so valueless, what so earthly, as to break bread to the hungry? At so much is valued the kingdom of heaven. "Break thy bread to the hungry, and the needy without covering bring into thy house; if thou seest one naked, clothe him." If thou hast not the means of breaking bread, hast not house into which thou mayest bring, hast not garment wherewith thou mayest cover: give a cup of cold water? cast two mites into the treasury. As much the widow doth buy with two mites, as Peter buyeth, by leaving the nets, as Zacchaeus buyeth by giving half his goods. Of so much worth is all that thou hast. "The heavens shall declare His righteousness, for God is Judge." Truly judge not confounding but severing. For "the Lord knoweth them that are His." Even if grains lie hid in the chaff, they are known to the husbandman. Let no one fear that he is a grain even among the chaff; the eyes of our winnower are not deceived. Fear not lest that tempest, which shall be round about Him, should confound thee with chaff. Certainly mighty will be the tempest; yet not one grain will it sweep from the side of the corn to the chaff: because not any rustic with three-pronged fork, but God, Three in One, is Judge. And the heavens shall declare His righteousness: for God is Judge. Let heavens go, let the heavens tell, into every land let their sound go out, and unto the ends of the world their words: and let that body say, "From the ends of the world unto Thee have I cried, when my heart was in heaviness." For now mingled it groaneth, divided it shall rejoice. Let it cry then and say, "Destroy not my soul with ungodly men, and with men of blood my life." He destroyeth not together, because God is Judge. Let it cry to Him and say, "Judge me, O Lord, and sever my cause from the nation unholy: " let it say, He shall do it: there shall be gathered to Him His righteous ones. He hath called the earth that He may sever His people.

14. "Hear, my people, and I will speak to thee" (ver. 7). He shall come and shall not keep silence; see how that even now, if ye hear, He is not silent. Hear, my people, and I will speak to thee. For if thou hearest not, I will not speak to thee. "Hear, and I will speak to thee." For if thou hearest not, even though I shall speak, it will not be to thee. When then shall I speak to thee? If thou hearest. When hearest thou? If thou art my people. For, "Hear, my people:" thou hearest not if thou art an alien people. "Hear, my people, and I will speak to thee: Israel, and I will testify to thee." ... For "Thy God," is properly said to that man whom God doth keep more as one of His family, as though in His household, as though in His peculiar: "Thy God am I." What wilt thou more? Requirest thou a reward from God, so that God may give thee something; so that what He hath given thee may

be thine own? Behold God Himself, who shall give, is thine own. What richer than He? Gifts thou wast desiring, thou hast the Giver Himself. "God, thy God, I am."

15. What He requireth of man, let us see; what tribute our God, our Emperor and our King doth enjoin us; since He hath willed to be our King, and hath willed us to be His province? Let us hear His injunctions. Let not a poor man tremble beneath the injunction of God: what God enjoineth to be given to Himself, He doth Himself first give that enjoineth: be ye only devoted. God doth not exact what He hath not given, and to all men hath given what He doth exact. For what doth He exact? Let us hear now: "I will not reprove thee because of thy sacrifices" (ver. 8). I will not say to thee, Wherefore hast thou not slain for me a fat bull? why hast thou not selected the best he-goat from thy flock? Wherefore doth that ram amble among thy sheep, and is not laid upon mine altar? I will not say, Examine thy fields and thy pen and thy walls, seeking what thou mayest give Me. "I will not reprove thee because of thy sacrifices." What then: Dost Thou not accept my sacrifices? "But thy holocausts are always in My sight" (ver. 9). Certain holocausts concerning which it is said in another Psalm, "If Thou hadst desired sacrifice, I would surely have given, with holocausts Thou wilt not be delighted:" and again he turneth himself," Sacrifice to God is a troubled spirit, a heart broken and humbled God doth not despise." Which be then holocausts that He despiseth not? Which holocausts that are always in His sight? "Kindly, O Lord," he saith, "deal in Thy good will with Sion, and be the walls of Jerusalem builded, then shall Thou accept the sacrifice of righteousness, oblations, and holocausts." He saith that certain holocausts God will accept. But what is a holocaust? A whole consumed with fire: causis is burning, holon is whole: but a "holocaust" is a whole consumed with fire. There is a certain fire of most burning love: be the mind inflamed with love, let the same love hurry off the limbs to its use, let it not allow them to serve cupidity, in order that we may wholly glow with fire of divine love that will offer to God a holocaust. Such "holocausts of thine are in My sight always."

16. As yet that Israel perchance doth not understand what are the holocausts thereof which He hath in His sight always, and is still thinking of oxen, of sheep, of he-goats: let it not so think: "I will not accept calves of thy house." Holocausts I named; at once in mind and thought to earthly flocks thou wast running, therefrom thou wast selecting for Me some fat thing: "I will not accept calves of thy house." He is foretelling the New Testament, wherein all those sacrifices have ceased. For they were then foretelling a certain Sacrifice which was to be, with the Blood whereof we should be cleansed. "I will not accept calves of thy house, nor he-goats of thy flocks."

17. "For mine are all the beasts of the wood" (ver. 10). Why should I ask of thee what I have made? Is it more thine, to whom I have given it to possess, than Mine, who have made it? "For mine are all the beasts of the wood." But perchance that Israel saith, The beasts are God's, those wild beasts which I enclose not in my pen, which I bind not to my stall; but this ox and sheep and he-goat—these are mine own. "Cattle on the mountain, and oxen." Mine are those which thou possessest not, Mine are these which thou possessest. For if thou art My servant, the whole of thy property is Mine. For it cannot be, that is the property of the master which the servant hath gotten to himself, and yet that not be the property of the Master which the Master Himself hath created for the servant. Therefore Mine are the beasts of the wood which thou hast not taken; Mine are also the cattle on the mountains which are thine, and the oxen which are at thy stall: all are Mine own, for I have created them.

18. "I know all the winged creatures of heaven" (ver. 11). How doth He know? He hath weighed them, hath counted. Which of us knoweth all the winged creatures of heaven? But even though to some man God give knowledge of all the winged creatures of heaven, He doth not Himself know in the same manner as He giveth man to know. One thing is God's knowledge, another man's: in like manner as there is one possession of God's, another of man's: that is, God's possessing is one thing, man's another. For what thou possessest thou hast not wholly in thy power, or else thy ox, so long as it liveth, is in thy power; so as that it either die not, or be not to be fed. With whom there is the highest power, there is highest and most secret cognition. Let us ascribe tiffs to God, while praising God. Let us not dare to say, How knoweth God? Do not, I pray you, brethren, of me expect this, that I should unfold to you, how God doth know: this only I say, He doth not so know as a man, He doth not so know as an Angel: and how He knoweth I dare not say, because also I cannot ken. One thing, nevertheless, I ken, that even before all the winged creatures of heaven were, God knew that which He was to create. What is that knowledge? O man, thou beginnest to see, after that thou hadst been formed, after that thou hadst received sense of seeing. These fowls sprung of the water at the word of God, saying, "Let the waters bring forth fowls." Whereby did God know the things which He commanded the water to bear forth? Now surely He knew what He had created, and before He created He knew. So great then is the knowledge of God, so that with Himself they were in a certain ineffable manner before they were created: and of thee doth He expect to receive what He had, before He created? "I know all the winged creatures of heaven," which thou to Me canst not give. The things which thou wast about to slay for Me, I know all: not because I made I know, but in order that I might make. "And the beauty of the field is with Me." The fairness of the field, the abundance of all things engendering upon earth, "is with Me," He saith. How with Him? Were they so,

even before they were made? Yea, for with Him were all things to come, and with Him are all things by-gone: things to come in such sort, that there be not withdrawn from Him all things by-gone. With Him are all things by a certain cognition of the ineffable wisdom of God residing in the Word, and the Word Himself is all things. Is not the beauty of the field in a manner with Him, inasmuch as He is everywhere, and Himself hath said, "Heaven and earth I fill "? What with Him is not, of whom it is said, "If I shall have ascended into heaven, Thou art there; and if I shall have descended into hell, Thou art present"? With Him is the whole: but it is not so with Him as that He doth suffer any contamination from those things which He hath created, or any want of them. For with thee, perchance, is a pillar near which thou art standing, and when thou art weary, thou leanest against it. Thou needest that which is with thee, God needeth not the field which is which Him. With Him is field, with Him beauty of earth, with Him beauty of heaven, with Him all winged creatures, because He is Himself everywhere. And wherefore are all things near Him? Because even before that all things were, or were created, to Him were known all things.

19. Who can explain, who expound that which is said to Him in another Psalm, "For my goods Thou needest not"? He hath said that He needeth not from us any necessary thing. "If I shall be hungry, I will not tell thee" (ver. 12). He that keepeth Israel shall neither hunger nor thirst, nor be weary, nor fall asleep. But, lo! according to thy carnality I speak: because thou wilt suffer hunger when thou hast not eaten, perhaps thou thinkest even God doth hunger that He may eat. Even though He shall be hungry, He telleth not thee: all things are before Him, whence He will He taketh what is needful for Him. These words are said to convince little understanding; not that God hath declared His hunger. Though for our sake this God of gods deigned even to hunger. He came to hunger, and to fill; He came to thirst, and give drink; He came to be clothed with mortality, and to clothe with immortality; He came poor, to make rich. For He lost not His riches by taking to Him our poverty, for, "In him are all the treasures of wisdom and knowledge hidden." "If I shall be hungry, I will not tell thee. For Mine is the whole world, and the fulness thereof." Do not then labour to find what to give Me, without whom I have what I will.

20. Why then dost still think of thy flocks? "Shall I eat the flesh of bulls, or shall I drink the blood of he-goats?" (ver. 13). Ye have heard what of us He requireth not, who willeth to enjoin us somewhat. If of such things ye were thinking, now withdraw your thoughts from such things: think not to offer God any such thing. If thou hast a fat bull, kill for the poor: let them eat the flesh of bulls, though they shall not drink the blood of he-goats. Which, when thou shalt have done, He will

account it to thee, that hath said," If I shall be hungry, I will not tell thee:" and He shall say to thee, "I was hungry, and thou gavest Me to eat." "Shall I eat the flesh of bulls, or shall I drink the blood of he-goats ?"

21. Say then, Lord our God, what dost Thou enjoin thy people, Thy Israel? "Immolate to God the sacrifice of praise" (ver. 14). Let us also say to Him, "In me, O God, are thy vows, which I will render of prose to Thee." I had feared lest Thou mightest enjoin something which would be out of my power, which I was counting to be in my pen, and but now perchance it had been taken away by a thief. What dost Thou enjoin me? "Immolate to God the sacrifice of praise" Let me revert to myself, wherein I may find what I may immolate: let me revert to myself; in myself may I find immolation of praise: be Thy altar my conscience. We are without anxiety, we go not into Arabia in quest of frankincense: not any bags of covetous dealer do we sift: God requireth of us the sacrifice of praise. Zacchaeus had the sacrifice of praise in his patrimony; the widow had it in her bag; some poor host or other hath had it in his jar: another neither in patrimony, nor in bag, nor in jar, hath had anything, had it wholly in his heart: salvation was to the house of Zacchaeus; and more this poor widow cast in than those rich men: this man, that doth offer a cup of cold water, shall not lose his reward: but there is even "peace on earth to men of good will." "Immolate to God the sacrifice of praise. O sacrifice gratuitous, by grace given! I have not indeed bought this to offer, but Thou hast given: for not even this should I have had. And this is the immolation of the sacrifice of praise, to render thanks to Him from whom thou hast whatever of good thou hast, and by whose mercy is forgiven thee whatsoever of evil of thine thou hast. "Immolate to God the sacrifice of praise: and render to the Highest thy prayers." With this odour the Lord is well pleased.

22. "And call thou upon Me in the day of thy tribulation: and I will draw thee forth, and thou shall glorify Me" (ver. 15). For thou oughtest not to rely on thy powers, all thy aids are deceitful. "Upon Me call thou in the day of tribulation: I will draw thee forth, and thou shalt glorify Me." For to this end I have allowed the day of tribulation to come to thee: because perchance if thou wast not troubled, thou wouldest not call on Me: but when thou art troubled, thou callest on Me; when thou callest upon Me, I will draw thee forth; when I shah draw thee forth, thou shalt glorify Me, that thou mayest no more depart from Me. A certain man had grown dull and cold in fervour of prayer, and said, "Tribulation and grief I found, and on the Name of the Lord I called." He found tribulation as it were some profitable thing; he had rotted in the slough of his sins; now he had continued without feeling, he found tribulation to be a sort of caustic and cutting. "I found," he saith, "tribulation and grief, and on the Name of the Lord I called." And truly,

brethren, tribulations are known to all men. Behold those afflictions that abound in mankind; one afflicted with loss bewaileth; another smitten with bereavement mourneth; another exiled from country grieveth and desireth to return, deeming sojourning intolerable; another's vineyard is hailed upon, he observeth his labours and all his toil spent in vain. When can a human being not be made sad? An enemy he findeth in a friend. What greater misery in mankind? These things all men do deplore and grieve at, and these are tribulations: in all these they call upon the Lord, and they do rightly. Let them call upon God, He is able either to teach how it must be borne, or to heal it when borne. He knoweth how not to suffer us to be tried above that we are able to bear. Let us call upon God even in those tribulations: but these tribulations do find us; as in another Psalm is written, "Helper in tribulations which have found us too much: " there is a certain tribulation which we ought to find. Let such tribulations find us: there is a certain tribulation which we ought to seek and to find. What is that? The above-named felicity in this world, abundance of temporal things: that is not indeed tribulation, these are the solaces of our tribulation. Of what tribulation? Of our sojourning. For the very fact that we are not yet with God, the very fact that we are living amid trials and difficulties, that we cannot be without fear, is tribulation: for there is not that peace which is promised us. He that shall not have found this tribulation in his sojourning, doth not think of going home to his father-land. This is tribulation, brethren. Surely now we do good works, when we deal bread to the hungry, home to the stranger, and the like: tribulation even this is. For we find pitiful objects upon whom we show pity; and the pitiful case of pitiful objects maketh us compassionate. How much better now would it be with thee in that place, where thou findest no hungry man whom thou mayest feed, where thou findest no stranger whom thou mayest take in, no naked man whom thou mayest cover, no sick man whom thou mayest visit, no litigant whom thou mayest set at one! For all things in that place are most high, are true, are holy, are everlasting. Our bread in that place is righteousness, our drink there is wisdom, our garment there is immortality, our house is everlasting in the heavens, our stedfastness is immortality: doth sickness come over? Doth weariness weigh down to sleep? No death, no litigation: there peace, quiet, joy, righteousness. No enemy hath entrance, no friend falleth away. What is the quiet there? If we think and observe where we are, and where He that cannot He hath promised that we are to be, from His very promise we find in what tribulation we are. This tribulation none findeth, but he that shall have sought it. Thou art whole, see if thou art miserable; for it is easy for him that is sick to find himself miserable: when thou art whole, see if thou art miserable; that thou art not yet with God. "Tribulation and grief I found, and on the Name of the Lord I called." "Immolate," therefore, "to God the sacrifice of praise." Praise Him promising, praise Him calling, praise Him exhorting, praise Him helping: and understand in what tribulation thou art placed. Call upon (Him), thou shalt be drawn forth, thou shalt glorify, shalt abide.

23. But see what followeth, my brethren. For now some one or other, because God had said to him, "Immolate to God the sacrifice of praise," and had enjoined in a manner this tribute, did meditate to himself and said, I will rise daily, I will proceed to Church, I will say one hymn at matins, another at vespers, a third or fourth in my house, daily I do sacrifice the sacrifice of praise, and immolate to my God. Well thou doest indeed, if thou doest this: but take heed, lest now thou be careless, because now thou doest this: and perchance thy tongue bless God, and thy life curse God. O my people, saith to thee the God of gods, the Lord that spake, "calling the earth from the rising of the sun unto the setting," though yet thou art placed amid the tares, "Immolate the sacrifice of praise to thy God, and render to Him thy prayers:" but take heed lest thou live ill, and chant well. Wherefore this? For, "Unto the sinner, saith God, why dost thou tell out My judgments, and takest My Covenant in thy mouth?" (ver. 16). Ye see, brethren, with what trembling we say these words. We take the Covenant of God in our mouth, and we say these words. We take the Covenant of God in our mouth, and we preach to you the instruction and judgment of God. And what saith God to the sinner? "Why dost thou?" Doth He then forbid preachers that be sinners? And where is that, "What they say do, but what they do, do not "? Where is that, "Whether in truth or on occasion Christ be preached "? But these words were said, lest they should fear that hear, from whomsoever it be that they hear: not that they should be without care that speak good words, and do evil deeds. Now therefore, brethren, ye are without care: if ye hear good words ye hear God, through whomsoever it be that ye may hear. But God would not dismiss without reproof them that speak: lest with their speaking alone, without care for themselves they should slumber in evil life, and say to themselves, "For God will not consign us to perdition, through whose mouth He has willed that so many good words should be spoken to His people." Nay, but hear what thou speakest, whoever thou art that speakest: and thou that writ be heard thyself, first hear thyself; and speak what a certain man doth speak in another Psalm, "I will hear what in me speaketh the Lord God, for He shall speak peace to His people." What am I then, that hear not what in me He speaketh, and will that other hear what through me He speaketh? I will hear first, will hear, and chiefly I will hear what speaketh in me the Lord God, for He shall speak peace to His people. Let me hear, and "chasten my body, and to servitude subject it, lest perchance to others preaching, myself be found a cast-away." "Why dost thou tell out my judgments?" Wherefore to thee what profiteth not thee? He admonisheth him to hear: not to lay down preaching, but to take up obedience. "But thou, why dost thou take My Covenant in they mouth?"

24. "But thou hatest instruction" (ver. 17). Thou hatest discipline. When I spare, thou singest and praisest: when I chasten, thou murmurest: as though, when I spare, I am thy God: and, when I chasten, I am not thy God. "I rebuke and chasten

those whom I love." "But thou hatest instruction: and hast thrown My sayings behind thee." The words that are said through thee, thou throwest behind thee. "And thou hast thrown My sayings behind thee:" to a place where they may not be seen by thee, but may load thee. "And thou hast thrown My sayings behind thee."

25. "If thou sawest a thief, thou didst consent unto him, and with adulterers thou didst make thy portion" (ver. 18). Lest perchance thou shouldest say, I have not committed theft, I have not committed adultery. What if he pleased thee that hath committed? Hast thou not with the very pleasing consented? Hast thou not by approval made thy portion with him that hath committed? For this is , brethren, to consent with a thief, and to make with an adulterer thy portion: for even if thou committest not, and approvest what is committed, thou art an accessory in the deed: for "the sinner is praised in the longings of his soul, and he that doeth iniquity shall be blessed." Thou doest not evil things, thou praisest evil-doers. For is this a small evil? "Thou didst make thy portion with adulterers."

26. "Thy mouth hath abounded in malice, and thy tongue hath embraced deceit" (ver. 19). Of the malevolence and deceit, brethren, of certain men he speaketh, who by adulation, though they know what they hear to be evil, yet lest they offend those from whom they hear, not only by not reproving but by holding their peace do consent. Too little is it, that they do not say, Thou hast done evil: but they even say, Thou hast done even well: and they know it to be evil: but their mouth aboundeth in malice, and their tongue embraceth deceit. Deceit is a sort of guile in words, of uttering one thing, thinking another. He saith not, thy tongue hath committed deceit or perpetrated deceit, but is order to point out to thee a kind of pleasure taken in the very evil doing, He hath said, "Hath embraced." It is too little that thou doest it, thou art delighted too; thou praisest openly, thou laughest to thyself. Thou dost push to destruction a man heedlessly putting forth his faults, and knowing not whether they be faults: thou that knowest it to be a fault, sayest not, "Whither art thou rushing?" If thou wert to see him heedlessly walk in the dark, where thou knewest a well to be, and wert to hold thy peace, of what sort wouldest thou be? wouldest thou not be set down for an enemy of his life ? And yet if he were to fall into a well, not in soul but in body he would die. He doth fall headlong into his vices, he doth expose before thee his evil doings: thou knowest them to be evil, and praisest and laughest to thyself. Oh that at length he were to be turned to God at whom thou hughest, and whom thou wouldest not reprove, and that he were to say, "Let them be confounded that say to me, Well, well."

27. "Sitting against thy brother thou didst detract" (ver. 20). And this "sitting" doth belong to that whereof he hath spoken above in, "hath embraced." For he that

doeth anything while standing or passing along, doth it not with pleasure: but if he for this purpose sitteth, how much leisure cloth he seek out to do it! That very evil detraction thou wast making with diligence, thou wast making sitting; thou wouldest thereon be wholly engaged; thou wast embracing thy evil, thou wast kissing thy craftiness. "And against thy mother's son thou didst lay a stumbling-block." Who is "mother's son "? Is it not brother? He would repeat then the same that he had said above, "thy brother." Hath he intimated that any distinction must be perceived by us? Evidently, brethren, I think a distinction must be made. Brother against brother doth detract, for example's sake, as though for instance one strong, and now a doctor and scholar of some weight, doth detract from his brother, one perchance that is teaching well and walking well: but another is weak, against him he layeth a stumbling-block by detracting from the former. For when the good are detracted from by those that seem to be of some weight and to be learned, the weak fall upon the stumbling-block, who as yet know not how to judge. Therefore this weak one is called "mother's son," not yet father's, still needing milk, and hanging on the breast. He is borne as yet in the bosom of his mother the Church, he is not strong enough to draw near to the solid food of his Fathers table, but from the mother's breast he draweth sustenance, unskilled in judging, inasmuch as yet he is animal and carnal. "For the spiritual man judgeth all things," but "the animal man perceiveth not those things which are of the Spirit of God; for they are foolishness to him." To such men saith the Apostle, "I could not speak unto you as unto spiritual, but as unto carnal, as to babes in Christ I gave you milk to drink, not meat; for ye were not able, but not even now are ye able." A mother I have been to you: as is said in another place, "I became a babe among you, even as a nurse cherishing her own children." Not a nurse nursing children of others, but a nurse cherishing her own children. For there are mothers who when they have borne give to nurses: they that have borne cherish not their children, because they have given them to be nursed; but those that cherish, cherish not their own, but those of others: but he himself had borne, he was himself cherishing, to no nurse did commit what he had borne; for he had said, "Of whom I travel again until Christ be formed in you." He did cherish them, and gave milk. But there were some as it were learned and spiritual men who detracted from Paul. "His letters indeed, say they, are weighty and powerful; but the presence of his body weak, and speech contemptible: " he saith himself in his Epistle, that certain his detractors had said these words. They were sitting, and were detracting against their brother, and against that their mother's son, to be fed with milk, they were laying a stumbling-block. "And against thy mothers son thou didst lay a stumbling-block."

28. "These things hast thou done, and I held my tongue" (ver. 21). Therefore the Lord our God shall come, and shall not keep silence. Now, "These things hast thou

done, and I held my tongue" What is , "I held my tongue "? From vengeance I have desisted, my severity I have deferred, patience to thee I have prolonged, thy repentance I have long looked for ... "Thou hast imagined iniquity, that I shall be like unto thee;" Thou hast s imagined that I shall be like unto thee, while thou wilt not be like unto Me. For, "Be ye," he saith, "perfect, even as your Father, which is in the heavens, who maketh His sun to rise on the good and evil." Him thou wouldest not copy, who giveth good things even to evil men, insomuch that sitting thou dost detract even from good men. "I will reprove thee," when "God manifest shall come, our God, and shall not keep silence," "I will reprove thee." And what to thee shall I do in reproving thee? what to thee shall I do? Now thyself thou seest not, I will make thee see thyself. Because if thou shouldest see thyself, and shouldest displease thyself, thou wouldest please Me: but because not seeing thyself thou hast pleased thyself, thou wilt displease both Me and thyself; Me when thou shalt be judged; thyself when thou shalt burn. But what to thee shall I do? He saith. "I will set thee before thy face." For why wouldest thou escape thyself? At thy back thou art to thyself, thou seest not thyself: I make thee see thyself: what behind thy back thou hast put, before thy face will I put; thou shalt see thy uncleanness, not that thou mayest amend, but that thou mayest blush . ...

29. But, "understand these things, ye that forget God" (ver. 22). See how He crieth, and keepeth not silence, spareth not. Thou hadst forgotten the Lord," didst not think of thy evil life. Perceive how thou hast forgotten the Lord. "Lest at length He seize like a lion, and there be none to driven" What is "like a lion"? Like a brave one, like a mighty one, like him whom none can withstand. To this he made reference when he said, "Lion." For it is used for praise, it is used also for showing evil. The devil hath been called lion: "Your adversary," He saith, "like a roaring lion, goeth about seeking whom He may devour?" May it not be that whereas he hath been called lion because of savage fierceness, Christ hath been called Lion for wondrous mightiness? And where is that, "The Lion hath prevailed of the tribe of

30. "Sacrifice of praise shall glorify Me" (ver. 23). How shall "sacrifice of praise glorify Me"? Assuredly sacrifice of praise doth no wise profit evil men, because they take Thy Covenant in their mouth, and do damnable things that displease Thine eyes. Straightway, he saith, even to them this I say, "Sacrifice of praise shall glorify Me." For if thou livest ill and speakest good words, not yet dost thou praise: but again, if, when thou beginnest to live well, to thy merits thou dost ascribe thy living well, not yet dost thou praise. ... Therefore the Publican went down justified, rather than that Pharisee. Therefore hear ye that live well, hear ye that live ill: "Sacrifice of praise shall glorify Me." No one offereth Me this

sacrifice, and is evil. I say not, Let there not offer Me this any one that is evil; but no one doth offer Me this, that is evil. For he that praiseth, is good: because if he praiseth, he doth also live well, because if he praiseth, not only with tongue he praiseth, but life also with tongue doth agree.

31. "And there is the way whereby I will show him the salvation of God." In sacrifice of praise" is the way." What is "the salvation of God "? Christ Jesus. And how in sacrifice of praise to us is shown Christ? Because Christ with grace came to us. These words saith the Apostle: "But I live, now not I, but Christ liveth in me: but that in flesh I live, in faith I live of the Son of God, who loved me, and gave Himself for me." Acknowledge then sinners, that there would not need physician, if they were whole. For Christ died for the ungodly. When then they acknowledge their ungodlinesses, and first copy that Publican, saying, "Lord, be merciful to me a sinner: " show wounds, beseech Physician: and because they praise not themselves, but blame themselves,—"So that he that glorieth, not in himself but in the Lord may glory,"—they acknowledge the cause of the coming of Christ, because for this end He came, that He might save sinners: for "Jesus Christ came," he saith, "into this world to save sinners; of whom I am chief." Further, those Jews, boasting of their work, thus the same Apostle doth rebuke, in saying, that they to grace belonged not, who to their merits and their works thought that reward was owing. He therefore that knoweth himself to belong to grace, doth know what is Christ and what is Christ's because he needeth grace. If grace it is called, gratis it is given; if gratis it is given, not any merits of time have preceded that it should be given. ...

PSALM LI.

1. Neither must this multitude's throng be defrauded, nor their infirmity burthened. Silence we ask, and quiet, in order that our voice, after yesterday's labour, be able with some little vigour to last out. It must be believed, that your love hath met together in greater numbers to- day for nothing else, but that ye may pray for those whom an allen and perverse inclination doth keep away. For we are speaking neither of heathens nor of Jews, but of Christians: nor of those that are yet Catechumens, but of many that are even baptized, from the Layer of whom ye do no wise differ, and yet to their heart ye are unlike. For to-day how many brethren of ours we think of, and deplore their going unto vanities and lying insanities, to the neglect of that to which they have been called. Who, if in the very circus from any cause they chance to be startled, do immediately cross themselves, and stand bearing It on the forehead, in the very place, from whence they had withdrawn, if they had borne It in heart. God's mercy must be implored, that He may give understanding for condemning these things, inclination to flee them, and mercy to forgive. Opportunately, then, of Penitence a Psalm to-day has been chanted. Speak we even with the absent: there will be to them for our voice your memory. Neglect not the wounded and feeble, but that ye may more easily make whole, whole ye ought to abide. Correct by reproving, comfort by addressing, set an example by living well, He will be with them that hath been with you. For now that ye have overpassed these dangers, the fountain of God's mercy is not closed Where ye have come they will come; where ye have passed they will pass. A grievous thing it is indeed, and exceeding perilous, nay ruinous, and for certain a deadly thing, that witting they sin. For in one way to these vanities doth he run that despiseth the voice of Christ; in another way, he that knoweth from what he is fleeing. But that not even of such men we ought to despair, this Psalm doth show.

2. For there is written over it the title thereof, "A Psalm of David himself, when there came to him Nathan the prophet, when he went in unto Bersabee." Bersabee was a woman, wife of another. With grief indeed we speak, and with trembling; but yet God would not have to be hushed what He hath willed to be written. I will say then not what I will, but what I am obliged; I will say not as one exhorting to imitation, but as one instructing you to real Captivated with this woman's beauty, the wife of another, the king and prophet David, from whose seed according to the flesh the Lord was to come, committed adultery with her. This thing in this Psalm is not read, but in the title thereof it appeareth; but in the book of Kings it is more fully read. Both Scriptures are canonical, to both without any doubt by Christians credit must be given. The sin was committed, and was written down. Moreover her

husband in war he caused to be killed: and after this deed there was sent to him Nathan the prophet; sent by the Lord, to reprove him for so great an outrage.

3. What men should beware of, we have said; but what if they shall have fallen they should imitate, let us hear. For many men will to fall with David, and will not to rise with David. Not then for falling is the example set forth, but if thou shalt have fallen for rising again. Take heed lest thou fall. Not the delight of the younger be the lapse of the elder, but be the fall of the elder the dread of the younger. For this it was set forth, for this was written, for this in the Church often read and chanted: let them hear that have not fallen, lest they fall; let them hear that have fallen, that they may rise. So great a man's sin is not hushed, is proclaimed in the Church. There men hear that are ill hearers, and seek for themselves countenance for sinning: they look out for means whereby they may defend what they have made ready to commit, not how they may beware of what they have not committed, and they say to themselves, If David, why not I too? Thence that soul is more unrighteous, which, forasmuch as it hath done it because David did, therefore hath done worse than David. I will say this very thing, if I shall be able, more plainly. David had set forth to himself none for a precedent as thou hast: he had fallen by lapse of concupiscence, not by the countenance of holiness: thou dost set before thine eyes as it were a holy man, in order that thou mayest sin: thou dost not copy his holiness, but dost copy his fall Thou dost love that in David, which in himself David hated: thou makest thee ready to sin, thou inclinest to sin: in order that thou mayest sin thou consultest the book of God: the Scriptures of God for this thou hearest, that thou mayest do what displeaseth God. This did not David; he was reproved by a Prophet, he stumbled not over a Prophet. But others hearing to their health, by the fall of a strong man measure their weakness: and desiring to avoid what God condemneth, from careless looking do restrain their eyes. Them they fix not upon the beauty of another's flesh, nor make themselves carries with perverse simpleness; they say not, "With good intent I have observed, of kindness I have observed, of charity I have long looked." For they set before themselves the fall of David, and they see that this great man for this purpose hath fallen, in order that little men may not be willing to look on that whereby they may fall. For they restrain their eyes from wantonness, not readily do they join themselves in company, they do not mingle with strange women, they raise not complying eyes to strange balconies, to strange terraces. For from afar David saw her with whom he was captivated. Woman afar, lust near. What he saw was elsewhere, in himself that whereby he fell. This weakness of the flesh must be therefore minded, the words of the Apostle recollected, "Let not sin therefore reign in your mortal body." He hath not said, let there not be; but, "let there not reign." There is sin in thee, when thou takest pleasure; there reigneth, if thou shalt have consented. Carnal pleasure, especially if proceeding unto unlawful and strange

objects, is to be bridled, not let loose: by government to be tamed, not to be set up for government. Look and be without care, if thou hast nothing whereby thou mayest be moved. But thou makest answer, "I contain with strong resolution." Art thou any wise stronger than David ?

4. He admonisheth, moreover, by such an example, that no one ought to lift himself up in prosperous circumstances. For many fear adverse circumstances, fear not prosperous circumstances. Prosperity is more perilous to soul than adversity to body. First, prosperity doth corrupt, in order that adversity may find something to break. My brethren, stricter watch must be kept against felicity. Wherefore, see ye after what manner the saying of God amid our own felicity doth take from us security: "Serve ye," He saith, "the Lord in fear, and exult unto Him with trembling." In exultation, in order that we may render thanks; in trembling, lest we fall This sin did not David, when he was suffering Saul for persecutor. When holy David was suffering Saul his enemy, when he was being vexed by his persecutions, when he was fleeing through divers places, in order that he might not fall into his hands, he lusted not for her that was another's, he slew not husband after committing adultery with wife. He was in the infirmity of his tribulation so much the more intimate with God as he seemed more miserable. Something useful is tribulation; useful the surgeon's lancet rather than the devil's temptation. He became secure when his enemies were overthrown, pressure was removed, swelling grew out. This example therefore doth avail to this end, that we should fear felicity. "Tribulation," he sixth, "and grief I found, and on the name of the Lord I called. "

5. But it was done; I would say these words to those that have not done the like, in order that they should watch to keep their uncorruptness, and that while they take heed how a great one has fallen, they that be small should fear. But if any that hath already fallen heareth these words, and that hath in his conscience any evil thing; to the words of this Psalm let him advert; let him heed the greatness of the wound, but not despair of the majesty of the Physician. Sin with despair is certain death. Let no one therefore say, If already any evil thing I have done, already I am to be condemned: God pardoneth not such evil things, why add I not sins to sins? I will enjoy this word in pleasure, in wantonness, in wicked cupidity: now hope of amendment having been lost, let me have even what I see, if I cannot have what I believe. This Psalm then, while it maketh heedful those that have not believed, so doth not will them that have fallen to be despaired of. Whoever thou art that hast sinned, and hesitatest to exercise penitence for thy sin, despairing of thy salvation, hear David groaning. To thee Nathan the prophet hath not been sent, David himself hath been sent to thee Hear him crying, and with him cry: hear him

groaning, and with him groan; hear him weeping, and mingle tears; hear him amended, and with him rejoice. If from thee sin could not be excluded, be not hope of pardon excluded. There was sent to that man Nathan the prophet, observe the king's humility. He rejected not the words of him giving admonition, he said not, Darest thou speak to me, a king? An exited king heard a prophet, let His humble people hear Christ.

6. Hear therefore these words, and say thou with him: "Have pity upon me, O God, after Thy great mercy" (ver. 1). He that imploreth great mercy, confesseth great misery. Let them seek a little mercy of Thee, that have sinned in ignorance: "Have pity," he sixth, "upon me, after Thy great mercy." Relieve a deep wound after Thy great healing. Deep is what I have, but in the Almighty I take refuge. Of my own so deadly wound I should despair, unless I could find so great a Physician. "Have pity upon me, O God, after Thy great mercy: and after the multitude of Thy pities, blot out my iniquity." What he saith, "Blot out my iniquity," is this, "Have pity upon me, O God." And what he saith, "After the multitude of Thy pities," is this, "After Thy great mercy." Because great is the mercy, many are the mercies; and of Thy great mercy, many are Thy pitying. Thou dost regard mockers to amend them, dost regard ignorant men to teach them, dost regard men confessing to pardon. Did he this in ignorance? A certain man had done some, aye many evil things he had done; "Mercy," he saith, "I obtained, because ignorant I did it in unbelief." This David could not say, "Ignorant I did it." For he was not ignorant how very evil a thing was the touching of another's wife, and how very evil a thing was the killing of the husband, who knew not of it, and was not even angered. They obtain therefore the mercy of the Lord that have in ignorance done it; and they that have knowing done it, obtain not any mercy it may chance, but "great mercy."

7. "More and more wash me from mine unrighteousness" (ver. 2). What is , "More and more wash "? One much stained. More and more wash the sins of one knowing. Thou that hast washed off the sins of one ignorant. Not even thus is it to be despaired of Thy mercy. "And from my delinquency purge Thou me." According to the manner in which He is physician, offer a recompense. He is God, offer sacrifice. What wilt thou give that thou mayest be purged? For see upon whom thou callest; upon a Just One thou callest. He hateth sins, if He is just; He taketh vengeance upon sins, if He is just; thou wilt not be able to take away from the Lord God His justice: entreat mercy, but observe the justice: there is mercy to pardon the sinner, there is justice to punish the sin. What then? Thou askest mercy; shall sin unpunished abide? Let David answer, let those that have fallen answer, answer with David, and say, No, Lord, no sin of mine shall be unpunished; I know the justice of Him whose mercy I ask: it shall not be unpunished, but for this

reason I will not that Thou punish me, because I punish my sin: for this reason I beg that Thou pardon, because I acknowledge.

8. "For mine iniquity I acknowledge, and my delinquency is before me ever" (ver. 3). I have not put behind my back what I have done, I look not at others, forgetful of myself, I pretend not to pull out a straw from my brother's eye, when there is a beam in my eye; my sin is before me, not behind me. For it was behind me when to me was sent the Prophet, and set before me the parable of the poor man's sheep. For saith Nathan the Prophet to David, "There was a certain rich man having very many sheep; but a poor man his neighbour had one little ewe sheep, which in his bosom and of his own food he was feeding: there came a stranger to the rich man, nothing from his flock he took, for the lithe ewe sheep of the poor man his neighbour he lusted; her he slew for the stranger: what doth he deserve?" But the other being angry doth pronounce sentence: then the king, evidently knowing not wherein he had been taken, declared the rich man deserving of death, and that the sheep be restored fourfold. Most sternly and most justly. But his sin was not yet before him, behind his back was what he had done: his own iniquity he did not yet acknowledge, and therefore another's he did not pardon. But the Prophet, being for this purpose sent, took from his back the sin, and before his eyes placed it, so that he might see that sentence so stern to have been pronounced against himself. For cutting and healing his heart's wound, he made a lancet of his tongue. ...

9. "Against Thee alone have I sinned, and before Thee an evil thing have I done" (ver. 4). What is this? For before men was not another's wife debauched and husband slain? Did not all men know what David had done? What is, "Against Thee alone have I sinned, and before Thee an evil thing have I done." Because Thou alone art without sin. He is a just punisher that hath nothing in Him to be punished; He is a just reprover that hath nothing in Him to be reproved. "That thou mayest be justified in Thy sayings, and conquer when Thou art judged." To whom he speaketh, brethren, to whom he speaketh, is difficult to understand. To God surely he speaketh, and it is evident that God the Father is not judged. What is, "And conquer when Thou art judged"? He seeth the future Judge to be judged, one just by sinners to be judged, and therein conquering, because in Him was nothing to be judged. For alone among men could truly say the God-Man, "If ye have found in Me sin, say." But perchance there was what escaped men, and they found not what was really there, but was not manifest. In another place He saith, "Behold there cometh the Prince of the world," being an acute observer of all sins; "Behold," He saith, "there cometh the Prince of this world," with death afflicting sinners, presiding over death: for, "By the malice of the devil death came into the world." "Behold," He saith, "there cometh the Prince of the world:"—He said

these words dose upon His Passion:—" and in Me he shall find nothing," nothing of sin, nothing worthy of death, nothing worthy of condemnation. And as if it were said to Him, Why then dost Thou die? He continueth and saith, "But that all men may know that I do the will of My Father; arise, let us go hence." I suffer, He saith, undeserving, for men deserving, in order that them I may make deserving of My Life, for whom I undeservedly suffer their death. To Him then, having no sin, saith on the present occasion the Prophet David, "Against Thee only have I sinned, and before Thee an evil thing have I done, that Thou mayest be justified in Thy sayings, and conquer when Thou art judged." For Thou overcomest all men, all judges; and he that deemeth himself just, before Thee is unjust: Thou alone justly judgest, having been unjustly judged, That hast power to lay down Thy life, and hast power again to take it. Thou conquerest, then, when Thou art judged. All men Thou overcomest, because Thou art more than men, and by Thee were men made.

10. "For, behold, in iniquities I was conceived" (ver. 6). As though he were saying, They are conquered that have done what thou, David, hast done: for this is not a little evil and little sin, to wit, adultery and man- slaying. What of them that from the day that they were born of their mother's womb, have done no such thing? even to them dost thou ascribe some sins, in order that He may conquer all men when He beginneth to be judged. David hath taken upon him the person of mankind, and hath heeded the bonds of all men, hath considered the offspring of death, hath adverted to the origin of iniquity, and he saith, "For, behold, in iniquities I was conceived." Was David born of adultery; being born of Jesse, a righteous man, and his own wife? What is it that he saith himself to have been in iniquity conceived, except that iniquity is drawn from Adam? Even the very bond of death, with iniquity itself is engrained? No man is born without bringing punishment, bringing desert of punishment. A Prophet saith also in another placer "No one is clean in Thy sight, not even an infant, whose life is of one day upon earth." For we know both by the Baptism of Christ that sins are loosed, and that the Baptism of Christ availeth the remission of sins. If infants are every way innocent, why do mothers run with them when sick to the Church? What by that Baptism, what by that remission is put away? An innocent one I see that rather weeps than is angry. What doth Baptism wash off? what doth that Grace loose? There is loosed the offspring of sin. For if that infant could speak to thee, it would say, and if it had the understanding which David had, it would answer thee, Why heedest thou me, an infant? Thou dost not indeed see my actions: but I in iniquity have been conceived, "And in sins hath my mother nourished me in the womb."

Apart from this bond of mortal concupiscence was Christ horn without a male, of a virgin conceiving by the Holy Ghost. He cannot be said to have been conceived in iniquity, it cannot be said, In sins His mother nourished Him in the womb, to whom was said," The Holy Ghost shall come upon thee, and the Virtue of the Highest shall overshadow thee." It is not therefore because it is sin to have to do with wives that men are conceived in iniquity, and in sins nourished in the womb by their mother; but because that which is made is surely made of flesh deserving punishment. For the punishment of the flesh is death, and surely there is in it liability to death itself. Whence the Apostle spoke not of the body as if to die, but as if dead: "The body indeed is dead," he saith, "because of sin, but the Spirit is life because of righteousness." How then without bond of sin is born that which is conceived and sown of a body dead because of sin? This chaste operation in a married person hath not sin, but the origin of sin draweth with it condign punishment. For there is no husband that, because he is an husband, is not subject to death, or that is subject to death for any other reason but because of sin. For even the Lord was subject to death, but not on account of sin: He took upon Him our punishment, and so looseth our guilt. With reason then, "In Adam all die, but in Christ shall all be made alive." For, "Through one man," saith the Apostle, "sin hath entered into this world, and through sin death, and so hath passed unto all men, in that all have sinned." Definite is the sentence: "In Adam," he saith, "all have sinned." Alone then could such an infant be innocent, as hath not been born of the work of Adam.

11. "For, behold, truth Thou hast loved uncertain and hidden things of Thy wisdom, Thou hast manifested to me" (ver. 6). That is, Thou hast not left unpunished even the sins of those whom Thou dost pardon. "Truth Thou hast loved:" so mercy Thou hast granted first, as that Thou shouldest also preserve truth. Thou pardonest one confessing, pardonest, but only if he punisheth himself: so there are preserved mercy and truth: mercy because man is set free; truth, because sin is punished. "Uncertain and hidden things of Thy wisdom Thou hast manifested to me." What "hidden things"? What "uncertain things"? Because God pardoneth even such. Nothing is so hidden, nothing so uncertain. For this uncertainty the Ninevites repented, for they said, though after the threatenings of the Prophet, though after that cry, "Three clays and Nineve shall be overthrown:" they said to themselves, Mercy must be implored; they said in this sort reasoning among themselves, "Who knoweth whether God may turn for the better His sentence, and have pity?" It was "uncertain," when it is said, "Who knoweth?" on an uncertainty they did repent, certain mercy they earned: they prostrated them in tears, in fastings, in sackcloth and ashes they prostrated them, groaned, wept, God spared. Nineve stood: was Nineve overthrown? One way indeed it seemeth to men, and another way it seemed to God. But I think that it was fulfilled that the Prophet had foretold. Regard what Nineve was, and see how it was overthrown; overthrown in evil, builded in good; just as Saul the persecutor was overthrown,

Paul the preacher builded. Who would not say that this city, in which we now are, was happily overthrown, if all those madmen, leaving their triflings, were to run together to the Church with contrite heart, and were to call upon God's mercy for their past doings? Should we not say, Where is that Carthage? Because there is not what there was, it is overthrown: but if there is what there was not, it is builded. So is said to Jeremiah, "Behold, I will give to thee to root up, to dig under, to overthrow, to destroy," and again, "to build, and to plant." Thence is that voice of the Lord, "I will smite and I will heal." He smiteth the rottenness of the deed, He healeth the pain of the wound. Physicians do thus when they cut; they smite and heal; they arm themselves in order to strike, they carry steel, and come to cure. But because great were the sins of the Ninevites, they said, "Who knoweth?" This uncertainty had God disclosed to His servant David. For when he had said, before the Prophet standing and convicting him, "I have sinned:" straightway he heard from the Prophet, that is, from the Spirit of God which was in the Prophet, "Thy sin is put away from thee." "Uncertain and hidden things" of His wisdom He manifested to him.

12. "Thou shall sprinkle me," he saith, "with hyssop, and I shall be cleansed" (ver. 7). Hyssop we know to be a herb humble but healing: to the rock it is said to adhere with roots. Thence in a mystery the similitude of cleansing the heart has been taken. Do thou also take hold, with the root of thy love, on thy Rock: be humble in thy humble God, in order that thou mayest be exalted in thy glorified God. Thou shalt be sprinkled with hyssop, the humility of Christ shall cleanse thee. Despise not the herb, attend to the efficacy of the medicine. Something further I will say, which we are wont to hear from physicians, or to experience in sick persons. Hyssop, they say, is proper for purging the lungs. In the lung is wont to be noted pride: for there is inflation, there breathing. It was said of Saul the persecutor as of Saul the proud, that he was going to bind Christians, breathing slaughter: he was breathing out slaughter, breathing out blood, his lung not yet cleansed. Hear also in this place one humbled, because with hyssop purged: "Thou shalt wash me," that is, shalt cleanse the: "and above snow I shall be whitened." "Although," he saith, "your sins shall have been like scarlet, like snow I will whiten." Out of such men Christ doth present to Himself a vesture without spot and wrinkle. Further, His vesture on the mount, which shone forth like whitened snow, signified the Church cleansed from every spot of sin.

13. But where is humility from hyssop? Hear what followeth: "To my hearing Thou shall give exultation and gladness, and bones humbled shall exult" (ver. 8). I will rejoice in hearing Thee, not in speaking against Thee. Thou hast sinned, why defendest thou thyself? Thou wilt speak: suffer thou; hear, yield to divine words,

lest thou be put to confusion, and be still more wounded: sin hath been committed, be it not defended: to confession let it come, not to defence. Thou engagest thyself as defender of thy sin, thou art conquered: no innocent patron hast thou engaged, thy defence is not profitable to thee. For who art thou that defendest thyself? Thou art meet to accuse thyself. Say not, either, "I have done nothing;" or, "What great thing have I done?" or, "Other men as well have done." If in doing sin thou sayest thou hast done nothing, thou wilt be nothing, thou wilt receive nothing: God is ready to give indulgence, thou closest the door against thyself: He is ready to give, do not oppose the bar of defence, but open the bosom of confession. "To my hearing Thou shall give exultation and gladness." ...

14. "Turn Thou away Thy face from my sins, and all mine iniquities blot out" (ver. 9). For now bones humbled exult, now with hyssop cleansed, humble I have become. "Turn Thou away Thy face," not from me, but "from my sins." For in another place praying he saith, "Turn not away Thy face from me." He that would not that God's face be turned away from himself, would that God's face be turned away from his sins. For to sin, when God turneth not Himself away, he adverteth: if he adverteth, he animadverteth. "And all mine iniquities blot out." He is busied with that capital sin: he reckoneth on more, he would have all his iniquities to be blotted out: he relieth on the Physician's hand, on that "great mercy," upon which he hath called in the beginning of the Psalm: "All mine iniquities blot out." God turneth away His face, and so blotteth out; by "turning away" His face, sins He blotteth out. By "turning towards," He writeth them. Thou hast heard of Him blotting out by turning away, hear of Him by turning towards, doing what? "But the countenance of the Lord is upon men doing evil things, that He may destroy from the earth the remembrance of them: " He shall destroy the remembrance of them, not by "blotting out their sins." But here he doth ask what? "Turn away Thy face from my sins." Well he asketh. For he himself doth not turn away his face from his own sins, saying, "For my sin I acknowledge." With reason thou askest and well askest, that God turn away from thy sin, if thou from thence dost not turn away thy face: but if thou settest thy sin at thy back, God doth there set His face. Do thou turn sin before thy face, if thou wilt that God thence turn away His face; and then safely thou askest, and He heareth.

15. "A clean heart create in me, O God" (ver. 10). "Create"—he meant to say, "as it were begin something new." But, because repentant he was praying (that had committed some sin, which before he had committed, he was more innocent), after what manner he hath said "create" he showeth. "And a right spirit renew in my inner parts." By my doing, he saith, the uprightness of my spirit hath been made old and bowed. For he saith in another Psalm, "They have bowed my soul." And

when a man cloth make himself stoop unto earthly lusts, he is "bowed" in a manner, but when he is made erect for things above, upright is his heart made, in order that God may be good to him. For, "How good is the God of Israel to the upright of heart! "Moreover, brethren, listen. Sometimes God in this world chastiseth for his sin him that He pardoneth in the world to come. For even to David himself, to whom it had been already said by the Prophet, "Thy sin is put away," there happened certain things which God had threatened for that very sin. For his son Abessalom against him waged bloody war, and many ways humbled his father. He was walking in grief, in the tribulation of his humiliation, so resigned to God, that, ascribing to Him all that was just, he confessed that he was suffering nothing underservedly, having now an heart upright, to which God was not displeasing. A slanderous person and one throwing in his teeth harsh curses he patiently heard, one of the soldiers on the opposite side, that were with his unnatural son. And when he was heaping curses upon the king, one of the companions of David, enraged, would have gone and smitten him; but he is kept back by David. And he is kept back how? For that he said, God sent him to curse me. Acknowledging his guilt he embraced his penance, seeking glory not his own, praising the Lord in that good which he had, praising the Lord in that which he was suffering, "blessing the Lord alway, ever His praise was in his mouth." Such are all the upright in heart: not those crooked persons who think themselves upright and God crooked: who when they do any evil thing, rejoice; when they suffer any evil thing, blaspheme; nay, if set in tribulation and scourging, they say from their distorted heart, "O God, what have I done to Thee?" Truly it is because they have done nothing. to God, for they have done all to themselves. "And an upright spirit, renew in my inner parts."

16. "Cast me not forth from Thy face" (ver. 11). Turn away Thy face from my sins: and "cast me not forth from Thy face." Whose face he feareth, upon the face of the Same he calleth. "And Thy Holy Spirit take not away from me." For in one confessing there is the Holy Spirit. Even now, to the gift of the Holy Spirit it belongeth, that what thou hast done displeaseth thee. The unclean spirit sins do please; the Holy One they displease. Though then thou still implore pardon, yet thou art joined to God on the other part, because the evil thing that thou hast committed displeaseth thee: for the same thing displeaseth both thee and Him. Now, to assail thy fever, ye are two, thou and the Physician. For the reason that there cannot be confession of sin and punishment of sin in a man of himself: when one is angry with himself, and is displeasing to himself, then it is not without the gift of the Holy Spirit, nor doth he say, Thy Holy Spirit give to me, but, "Take not away from me."

17. "Give back to me the exultation of Thy salvation'" (ver. 12). "Give back" what I had; what by sinning I had lost: to wit, of Thy Christ. For who without Him can be made whole? Because even before that He was Son of Mary, "In the beginning He was the Word, and the Word was with God, and the Word was God;" and so, by the holy fathers a future dispensation of flesh taken upon Him, was looked for; as is believed by us to have been done. Times are changed, not faith. "And with Principal Spirit confirm me." Some have here understood the Trinity in God, Itself God; the dispensation of Flesh being excepted therefrom: since it is written, "God is a Spirit." For that which is not body, and yet is, seemeth to exist in such sort as that it is spirit. Therefore some understand here the Trinity spoken of: "In upright Spirit," the Son; in "Holy Spirit," Holy Ghost; in "Principal Spirit," Father. It is not any heretical opinion, therefore, whether this be so, or whether "upright Spirit" He would have to be taken of man himself (when He saith, "An upright spirit renew in my inner parts"), which I have bowed and distorted by sinning, so that in that case the Holy Spirit be Himself the Principal Spirit: which also he would not have to be taken away from him, and thereby would have himself to be confirmed therein.

18. But see what he annexeth: "With Principal Spirit," he saith, "confirm Thou me." Wherein "confirm"? Because Thou hast pardoned me, because I am secure, that what Thou hast forgiven is not to be ascribed, on this being made secure and with this grace confirmed, therefore I am not ungrateful. But I shall do what? "I would teach unrighteous men Thy ways" (ver. 13). Being myself of the unrighteous" (that is, one that was myself an unrighteous man, now no longer unrighteous; the Holy Spirit not having been taken away from me, and I being confirmed with Principal Spirit). "I would teach unrighteous men Thy ways." What ways wilt thou teach unrighteous men? "And ungodly men to Thee shall be converted." If David's sin is counted for ungodliness, let not ungodly men despair of themselves, forasmuch as God hath spared an ungodly man; but let them take heed that to Him they be converted, that His ways they learn. But if David's deed is not counted for ungodliness, but this is properly call ungodliness, namely, to apostatize from God, not to worship one God, or never to have worshipped, or to have forsaken, Him whom one did worship, then what he saith hath the force of superabundance, "And ungodly men shall to Thee be converted." So full art thou of the fatness of mercy, that for those converted to Thee, not only sinners of any sort, but even ungodly, there is no cause for despair. Wherefore? That believing on Him that justifieth an ungodly man, their faith may be counted for righteousness.

19. "Deliver me from bloods, O God, God of my health" (ver. 14). The Latin translator hath expressed, though by a word not Latin, yet an accuracy from the Greek. For we all know that in Latin, sanguines (bloods) are not spoken of, nor yet

sanguina (bloods in the neuter), nevertheless because the Greek translator hath thus used the plural number, not without reason, but because he found this in the original language the Hebrew, a godly translator hath preferred to use a word not Latin, rather than one not exact. Wherefore then hath he said in the plural number, "From bloods"? In many bloods, as in the origin of the sinful flesh, many sins he would have to be understood. The Apostle having regard to the very sins which come of the corruption of flesh and blood, saith, "Flesh and blood shall not possess the kingdom of God." For doubtless, after the true faith of the same Apostle, that flesh shall rise again and shall itself gain incorruption, as He saith Himself, "This corruptible must put on incorruption, and this mortal put on immortality." Because then this corruption is of sin, by the name thereof sins are called. In like manner as both that morsel of flesh and member which playeth in the mouth when we articulate words is called a tongue, and that is called a tongue which by the tongue is made, so we call one tongue the Greek, another the Latin; for the flesh is not diverse, but the sound. In the same manner, then, as the speech which is made by the tongue is called a tongue; so also the iniquity which is made by blood is called blood. Heeding, then, his many iniquities, as in the expression above, "And all my iniquities blot out," and ascribing them to the corruption of flesh and blood, "Free me," he saith, "from bloods: "that is, free me from iniquities, cleanse me from all corruption. ... Not yet is the substance, but certain hope. "And my tongue shall exult of Thy righteousness."

20. "O Lord, my lips Thou shall open, and my mouth shall tell of Thy praise" (ver. 15). "Thy praise," because I have been created: "Thy praise," because sinning I have not been forsaken: "Thy praise," because I have been admonished to confess: "Thy praise," because in order that I might be secured I have been cleansed.

21. "Because if Thou hadst willed sacrifice, I would have given it surely" (ver. 16). David was living at that time when sacrifices of victim animals were offered to God, and he saw these times that were to be. Do we not perceive ourselves in these words? Those sacrifices were figurative, foretelling the One Saving Sacrifice. Not even we have been left without a Sacrifice to offer to God. For hear what he saith, having a concern for his sin, and wishing the evil thing which he hath done to be forgiven him: "If Thou hadst willed;" he saith, "sacrifice, I would have given it surely. With holocausts Thou wilt not be delighted." Nothing shall we therefore offer? So shall we come to God? And whence shall we propitiate Him? Offer; certainly in thyself thou hast what thou mayest offer. Do not from without fetch frankincense, but say, "In me are, O God, Thy vows, which I will render of praise to Thee." Do not from without seek cattle to slay, thou hast in thyself what thou mayest kill. "Sacrifice to God is a spirit troubled, a heart contrite

and humbled God despiseth not" (ver. 17). Utterly he despiseth bull, he-goat, ram: now is not the time that these should be offered. They were offered when they indicated something, when they promised something; when the things promised come, the promises are taken away. "A heart contrite and humbled God despiseth not." Ye know that God is high: if thou shalt have made thyself high, He will be from thee; if thou shall have humbled thyself, He will draw near to thee.

22. See who this is: David as one man was seeming to implore; see ye here our image and the type of the Church.

"Deal kindly, O Lord, in Thy good will with Sion" (ver. 18). With this Sion deal kindly. What is Sion? A city holy. What is a city holy? That which cannot be hidden, being upon a mountain established. Sion in prospect, because it hath prospect of something which it hopeth for. For Sion is interpreted" prospect," and Jerusalem, "vision of peace." Ye perceive then yourselves to be in Sion and in Jerusalem, if being sure ye look for hope that is to be, and if ye have peace with God. "And be the walls of Jerusalem builded." "Deal kindly, O Lord, in Thy good will with Sion, and be the walls of Jerusalem builded." For not to herself let Sion ascribe her merits: do Thou with her deal kindly, "Be the walls of Jerusalem builded:" be the battlements of our immortality laid, in faith and hope and charity.

23. "Then Thou shalt accept the sacrifice of righteousness" (ver. 19). But now sacrifice for iniquity, to wit, a spirit troubled, and a heart humbled; then the sacrifice of righteousness, praises alone. For, "Blessed they that dwell in Thy house, for ever and ever they shall praise Thee:" for this is the sacrifice of righteousness. "Oblations and holocausts." What are "holocausts"? A whole victim by fire consumed. When a whole beast was laid upon the altar with fire to be consumed, it was called a holocaust. May divine fire take us up whole, and that fervour catch us whole. What fervour? "Neither is there that hideth himself from the heat thereof." What fervour? That whereof speaketh the Apostle:" In spirit fervent." Be not merely our soul taken up by that divine fire of wisdom, but also our body; that it may earn their immortality; so be it lifted up for a holocaust, that death be swallowed into victory. "Oblations and holocausts." "Then shall they lay upon thine altar calves." Whence "calves"? What shall He therein choose? Will it be the innocence of the new age, or necks freed from the yoke of the law? ...

PSALM LII.

1. The title of the Psalm hath: "At the end, understanding of David, when there came Doeg the Edomite arid told Saul, David hath come into the house of Abimelech:" whereas we read that he had come into the house of Achimelech. And it may chance that we do not unreasonably suppose, that because of the similarity of a name and the difference of one syllable, or rather of one letter, the titles have been varied. In the manuscripts, however, of the Psalms, when we looked into them, rather Abimelech we have found than Achimelech. And since in another place thou hast a most evident Psalm, intimating not a dissimilarity of name, but an utterly different name; when, for instance, David changed his face before King Achish, not before king Abimelech, and he sent him away, and he departed: and yet the title of the Psalm is thus written, "When he changed his countenance in the presence of Abimelech"—the very change of name maketh us the rather intent upon a mystery, lest thou shouldest pursue the quasi-facts of history, and despise the sacred veilings. ...

2. Observe ye two kinds of men; the one of men labouring, the other of those among whom they labour: the one of men thinking of earth, the other of heaven: the one of men weighing down their heart unto the deep, the other of men with Angels their heart conjoining: the one trusting in earthly things, wherein this world aboundeth, the other confiding in heavenly things, which God, who lieth not, hath promised. But mingled are these kinds of men. We see now the citizen of Jerusalem, citizen of the kingdom of heaven, have some office upon earth: to wit, one weareth purple, is a Magistrate, is Aedile, is Proconsul, is Emperor, doth direct the earthly republic: but he hath his heart above, if he is a Christian, if he is a believer, if he is godly, if he is despising those things wherein he is, and trusteth in that wherein he is not yet. Of which kind was that holy woman Esther, who, though she was wife of a king, incurred the danger of interceding for her countrymen: and when she was praying before God, where she could not lie, in her prayer said, that her royal ornaments were to her but as the cloth of a menstruous woman. Despair we not then of the citizens of the kingdom of heaven, when we see them engaged in any of Babylon's matters, doing something earthly in republic earthly: nor again let us forthwith congratulate all men that we see doing matters heavenly; because even the sons of pestilence sit sometimes in the seat of Moses, of whom is said, "What things they say, do ye: but what things they do, do not: for they say, and do not." Those, amid earthly things, lift up heart unto heaven, these, amid heavenly words, trail heart upon earth. But there will come time of winnowing, when both are to be severed with greatest diligence, in order that no grain may pass over unto the heap of chaff that is to be burned, that not one single

straw may pass over to the mass that is to be stored in the barn. So long as then now it is mingled, hear we thence our voice, that is, voice of the citizens of the kingdom of heaven (for to this we ought to aspire, to bear with evil men here, rather than be borne with by good men): and let us conjoin ourselves to this voice, both with ear and with tongue, and with heart and work. Which if we shall have done, we are here speaking in those things which we hear. Let us therefore speak first of the evil body of kingdom earthly.

3. "Why doth he glory in malice that is mighty?" (ver. 1). Observe, my brethren, the glorying of malignity, the glorying of evil men. Where is glorying? "Why doth he glory in malice that is mighty?" That is, he that in malice is mighty, why doth he glory? There is need that a man be mighty, but in goodness, not in malice. Is it any great thing to glory in malice? To build a house doth belong to few men, any ignorant man you please can pull down. To sow wheat, to dress the crop, to wait until it ripen, and in that fruit on which one has laboured to rejoice, doth belong to few men: with one spark any man you please can burn all the crop. To breed an infant, when born to feed him, to educate, to bring him on to youth's estate, is a great task: to kill him in one moment of time any one you please is able. Therefore those things which are done for destruction, are most easily done. "He that glorieth, let him glory in the Lord: " he that glorieth, let him glory in goodness. Thou gloriest, because thou art mighty in evil. What art thou about to do, O mighty man, what art thou about to do, boasting thyself much? Thou art about to kill a man: this thing also a scorpion, this also one fever, this also a poisonous fungus can do. To this is thy mightiness reduced, that it be made equal to a poisonous fungus? This therefore do the good citizens of Jerusalem, who not in malice but in goodness glory: firstly, that not in themselves, but in the Lord they glory. Secondly, that those things which make for edification they earnestly do, and do such things as are strong to abide: but things which make for destruction they may do, for the discipline of men advancing, not for the oppression of the innocent. To this mightiness then that earthly body being compared, why may it not hear out of these words, "Why doth he glory in malice that is mighty?"

4. "In iniquity the whole day upon injustice hath thy tongue thought" (ver. 2): that is, in the whole of time, without weariness, without intermission, without cessation. And when thou doest not, thou thinkest; so that when anything of evil is away from thy hands, from thy heart it is not away; either thou doest an evil thing, or while thou canst not do, thou sayest an evil thing, that is, thou evil-speakest: or when not even this thou canst do, thou wiliest and thinkest an evil thing. "The whole day," then, that is, without intermission. We expect punishment to this man. Is he to himself a small punishment? Thou threatenest him: thou, when thou

threatenest him, wilt send him whither? Unto evil? Send him away unto himself. In order that thou mayest vent much rage, thou art going to give him into the power of beasts: unto himself he is worse than beasts. For a beast can mangle his body: of himself he cannot leave his heart whole. Within, against himself he doth rage of himself, and dost thou from without seek for stripes? Nay, pray God for him, that he may be set free from himself. Nevertheless in this Psalm, my brethren, there is not a prayer for evil men, or against evil men, but a prophecy of what is to result to evil men. Think not therefore that the Psalm of ill-will saith anything: for it is said in the spirit of prophecy.

5. There followeth then what? All thy might and all thy thought of iniquity all the day, and meditation of malignity in thy tongue without intermission, hath performed what, done what? "As with a sharp razor thou hast done deceit" (ver. 3). See what do evil men to Saints, they scrape their hair. What is it that I have said? If there be such citizens of Jerusalem, that hear the voice of their Lord, of their King, saying, "Fear not them which kill the body, but are not able to kill the soul:" that hear the voice which but now from the Gospel hath been read, " What doth it profit a man, if he shall gain the whole world, and of himself make wreck:" they despise all present good things, and above all life itself. And what is Doeg's razor to do to a man on this earth meditating on the kingdom of heaven, and about to be in the kingdom of heaven, having with him God, and about to abide with God? What is that razor to do? Hair it is to scrape, it is to make a man bald. And this belongeth to Christ, who in the Place of a Skull was crucified. It maketh also the son of Core, which is interpreted baldness. For this hair signifieth a superfluity of things temporal. Which hairs indeed are not made by God superfluously on the body of men, but for a sort of ornament: yet because without feeling they are cut off, they that cleave to the Lord with their heart, so have these earthly things as they have hair. But sometimes even something of good with "hair" is wrought, when thou breakest bread to the hungry, the poor without roof thou bringest into thy house; if thou shalt have seen one naked, thou coverest him: lastly, the Martyrs themselves also imitating the Lord, blood for the Church shedding, hearing that voice, "As Christ laid down His life for us, so also ought we also to lay down for the brethren," in a certain way with their hair did good to us, that is, with those things which that razor can lop off or scrape. But that therefore even with the very hair some good can be done, even that woman a sinner intimated, who, when she had wept over the feet of the Lord, with her hair wiped what with tears she wetted? Signifying what? That when thou shalt have pitied any one, thou oughtest to relieve him also if thou canst. For when thou hast pity, thou sheddest as it were tears: when thou relievest, thou wipest with hair. And if this to any one, how much more to the feet of the Lord. The feet of the Lord are what? The holy Evangelists, whereof is said, "How beautiful are the feet of them that tell of peace, that tell of

good things!" Therefore like a razor let Doeg whet his tongue, let him whet deceit as much as he may: he will take away superfluous temporal things; will he necessary things everlasting?

6. "Thou hast loved malice above benignity" (ver. 4). Before thee was benignity; herself thou shouldest have loved. For thou wast not going to expend anything, nor wast thou going to fetch something to love by a distant voyage. Benignity is before thee, iniquity before thee: compare and choose. But perchance thou hast an eye wherewith thou seest malignity, and hast no eye wherewith thou seest benignity. Woe to the iniquitous heart. What is worse, it doth turn away itself, that it may not see what it is able to see. For what of such hath been said in another place? "He would not understand that he might do good." For it is not said, he could not: but "he would not," he saith, "understand that he might do good," he closed his eyes from present light. And what followeth? "Of iniquity he hath meditated in his bed;" that is, in the inner secrecy of his heart. Some reproach of this kind is heaped upon this Doeg the Edomite, a malignant body, a motion of earth, not abiding, not heavenly. "Thou hast loved malignity above benignity." For wilt thou know how an evil man doth see both, and the former he doth rather choose, from the other doth turn himself away? Wherefore doth he cry out when he suffereth anything unjustly? Wherefore doth he then exaggerate as much as he can the iniquity, and praise benignity, censuring him that hath wrought in him malignity above benignity? Be he then a rule to himself for seeing: out of himself he shall be judged. Moreover, if he do what is written, "Thou shalt love thy neighbour as thyself;" and, "Whatsoever good things ye will that men should do unto you, these also do ye do unto them:" at home he hath means of knowing, because what on himself he will not have to be done, he ought not to do to another. "Thou hast loved malice above benignity." Iniquitously, inordinately, perversely thou wouldest raise water above oil: the water will be sunk, the oil will remain above. Thou wouldest under darkness place a light: the darkness will be put to flight, the light will remain. Above heaven thou wouldest place earth, by its weight the earth will fall into its place. Thou therefore wilt be sunk by loving malice above benignity. For never will malice overcome benignity. "Thou hast loved malice above benignity: iniquity more than to speak of equity." Before thee is equity, before thee is iniquity: one tongue thou hast, whither thou wilt thou turnest it: wherefore then rather to iniquity and not to equity? Food of bitterness dost thou not give to thy belly, and food of iniquity dost thou give to thy malignant tongue? As thou choosest whereon to live, so choose what thou mayest speak. Thou preferrest iniquity to equity, and preferrest malice to benignity; thou indeed preferrest, but above what can ever He but benignity and equity? But thou, by placing thyself in a manner upon those things which it is necessary should go

beneath, wilt not make them to be above good things, but thou with them wilt be sunk unto evil things.

7. Because of this there followeth in the Psalm, "Thou hast loved all words of sinking under" (ver. 5). Rescue therefore thyself, if thou canst, from sinking-under. From shipwreck thou art fleeing, and dost embrace lead! If thou wilt not sink, catch at a plank, be borne on wood, let the Cross carry thee through. But now because thou art a Doeg the Edomite, a "motion," and "of earth," thou doest what? "Thou hast loved all words of sinking-under, a tongue deceitful." This hath preceded, words of sinking- under have followed a tongue deceitful. What is a tongue deceitful? A minister of guile is a tongue deceitful, of men bearing one thing in heart, another thing from mouth bringing forth. But in these is overthrowing, in these sinking under.

8. "Wherefore God shall destroy thee at the end" (ver. 6): though now thou seemest to flourish like grass in the field before the heat of the sun. For, "All flesh is grass, and the brightness of man as the bloom of grass: the grass hath withered, and the bloom hath fallen down: but the word of the Lord abideth for everlasting." Behold that to which thou mayest bind thyself, to what "abideth for everlasting." For if to grass, and to the bloom of grass, thou shalt have bound thyself, since the grass shall wither, and the bloom shall fall down, "God shall destroy thee at the end: "and if not now, certainly at the end He shall destroy, when that winnowing shall have come, and the heap of chaff from the solid grain shall have been separated. Is not the solid grain for the barns, and the chaff for the fire? Shall not the whole of that Doeg stand at the left hand, when the Lord is to say, "Go ye into fire everlasting, which hath been prepared for the devil and his angels"? Therefore "God shall destroy at the end: shall pluck thee out, and shall remove thee from thy dwelling." Now then this Doeg the Edomite is in a dwelling: "But a servant abideth not in the house for ever." Even he worketh something of good, even if not with his doings, at least with the words of God, so that in the Church, when he "seeketh his own," he would say, at least, those things which are of Christ.

"But He shall remove thee from thy dwelling." "Verily, verily, I say unto you, they have received their reward." "And thy root from the land of the living." Therefore in the land of the living we ought to have root. Be our root there. Out of sight is the root: fruits may be seen, root cannot be seen. Our root is our love, our fruits are our works: it is needful that thy works proceed from love, then is thy root in the land of the living. Then shall be rooted up that Doeg, nor any wise shall he be able there to abide, because neither more deeply there hath he fixed a root: but it shall be with him in like manner as it is with those seeds on the rock, which even if a root they throw out, yet, because moisture they have not, with the risen sun forthwith do wither. But, on the other hand, they that fix a root more deeply, hear from the Apostle what? "I bow my knees for you to the Father of our Lord Jesus Christ, that ye may be in love rooted and grounded." And because there now is root, "That ye may be able," he saith, "to comprehend what is the height, and breadth, and length, and depth: to know also the super-eminent knowledge of the love of Christ, that ye may be filled unto all the fulness of God." Of such fruits so great a root is worthy, being so single, so budding, for buddings so deeply grounded. But truly this man's root shall be rooted up from the land of the living.

9. "And the just shall see, and shall fear; and over him they shall laugh" (ver. 7). Shall fear when? Shall laugh when? Let us therefore understand, and make a distinction between those two times of fearing and laughing, which have their several uses. For so long as we are in this world, not yet must we laugh, lest hereafter we mourn. We have read what is reserved at the end for this Doeg, we have read and because we understand and believe, we see but fear. This, therefore, hath been said, "The just shall see, and shall fear." So long as we see what will result at the end to evil men, wherefore do we fear? Because the Apostle hath said, "In fear and trembling work out your own salvation:" because it hath been said in a Psalm, "Serve the Lord in fear, and exult unto Him with trembling." Wherefore "with fear"? "Wherefore let him that thinketh himself to stand, see that he fall not." Wherefore "with trembling"? Because he saith in another place: "Brethren, if a man shall have been overtaken in any delinquency, ye that are spiritual instruct such sort in the spirit of gentleness; heeding thyself, lest thou also be tempted." Therefore, the just that are now, that live of faith, so see this Doeg, what to him is to result, that nevertheless they fear also for themselves: for what they are to-day, they know; what to-morrow they are to be, they know not. Now, therefore, "The just shall see, and they shall fear." But when shall they laugh? When iniquity shall have passed over; when it shall have flown over; as now to a great degree hath flown over the time uncertain; when shall have been put to flight the darkness of this world, wherein now we walk not but by the lamp of the Scriptures, and therefore fear as though in night. For we walk by prophecy; whereof saith the Apostle Peter, "We have a more sure prophetic word, to which giving heed ye do well, as to a lamp shining in a dark place, until the day shine, and the day-star arise in your hearts." So long then as by a lamp we walk, it is needful that with fear we should live. But when shall have come our day, that is, the manifestation of Christ, whereof the same Apostle saith, "When Christ shall have appeared, your life, then ye also shall appear with Himself in glory," then the just shall laugh at that Doeg. ...

10. But what shall they then say that shall laugh? "And over him they shall laugh; and shall say, Behold a man that hath not set God for his helper" (ver. 8). See ye the body earthly! "As much as thou shalt have, so great shalt thou be," is a proverb of covetous men, of grasping men, of men oppressing the innocent, of men seizing upon other men's goods, of men denying things entrusted to their care. Of what sort is this proverb? "As much as thou shalt have, so great shalt thou be;" that is, as much as thou shall have had of money, as much as thou shalt have gotten, by so much the more mighty shall thou be. "Behold a man that hath not set God for his helper, but hath trusted in the multitude of his riches." Let not a poor man, one perchance that is evil, say, I am not of this body. For he hath heard the Prophet saying, "He hath trusted in the multitude of his riches:" forthwith if he is poor, he heedeth his rags, he hath observed near him perchance a rich man among the people of God more richly apparelled, and he saith in his heart, Of this man he speaketh; doth he speak of me? Do not thence except thyself, do not separate thyself, unless thou shalt have seen and feared, in order that thou mayest hereafter laugh. For what doth it profit thee, if thou dost want means, and thou burnest with cupidity? When our Lord Jesus Christ to that rich man that was grieved, and that was departing from Him, had said, "Go, sell all that thou hast, and give to the poor, and thou shall have treasure in heaven, and come follow Me:" and great hopelessness for rich men foretold, so that He said, more easily could a camel pass through the eye of a needle, than a rich man enter into the kingdom of Heaven, were not forthwith the disciples grieved, saying with themselves, "Who shall be able to be saved?" Therefore when they were saying, "Who shall be able to be saved?" did they think of the few rich men, did there escape them so great a multitude of poor men? Could they not say to themselves, If it is hard, aye an impossible thing, that rich men should enter into the kingdom of heaven, as it is impossible that a camel should enter through the eye of a needle, let all poor men enter into the kingdom of heaven, be the rich alone shut out? For how few are the rich men? But of poor men are thousands innumerable. For not the coats are we to look upon in the kingdom of heaven; but for every one's garment shall be reckoned the effulgence of righteousness: there shall be therefore poor men equal to Angels of God, clothed with the stoles of immortality, they shall shine as the sun in the kingdom of their Father: what reason is there for us about a few rich men to be concerned, or distressed? This thought not the Apostles; but when the Lord had spoken this, "It is easier for a camel to go through the eye of a needle, than for a rich man to enter into the kingdom of heaven:" they saying to themselves, "Who shall be able to be saved," meant what? Not means, but desires; for they saw even poor men themselves, even if not having money, yet to have covetousness. And that ye may know, that not money in a rich man, but covetousness is condemned, attend to what I say; Thou observest that rich man standing near thee, and perchance in him is money, and is not covetousness; in thee is not money, and is covetousness. A poor man full of sores, full of woe, licked by dogs, having no

help, having no morsel, not having perchance a mere garment, was borne by the Angels unto Abraham's bosom. Ho! being a poor man, art thou glad now; for are even sores by thee to be desired? Is not thy patrimony soundness? There is not in this Lazarus the merit of poverty, but that of godliness. For thou seest who was borne up, thou seest not whither he was borne up. Who was borne up by Angels? A poor man, full of woe, full of sores. Whither was he borne up? Unto Abraham's bosom. Read the Scriptures, and thou shall find Abraham to have been a rich man. In order that thou mayest know, that not riches are blamed; Abraham had much gold, silver, cattle, household, was a rich man, and unto his bosom Lazarus, a poor man, was borne up. Unto bosom of rich man, poor man: are not rather both unto God rich men, both in cupidity poor men? ...

11. Therefore that man having been condemned that "hath trusted in the multitude of his riches, and hath prevailed in his vanity:" for what more vain, than he that thinketh coin more to avail than God? Therefore that man having been condemned that said, blessed of the people to whom these things are: thou that sayest, "Blessed the people of whom is the Lord their own God," dost think of thyself what? dost hope for thyself what? "But I;" now at length hear that body: "But I am like an olive, fruit-bearing in the house of God" (ver. 9). Not one man speaketh, but that olive fruit-bearing, whence have been pruned the proud branches, and the humble wild olive grafted in. "Like an olive, fruit-bearing in the house of God, I have trusted in the mercy of God." He did what? "In the multitude of his riches:" therefore his root shall be plucked out from the land of the living. "But I," because "like an olive, fruit-bearing in the house of God," the root whereof is nourished, is not rooted out, "have trusted in the mercy of God." But perchance now? For even herein men err sometimes. God indeed they worship, and are not now like to that Doeg: but though on God they rely, it is for temporal things nevertheless; so that they say to themselves, I Worship my God, who will make me rich upon earth, who to me will give sons, who to me will give a wife. Such things indeed giveth none but God, but God would not have Himself for the sake of such things to be loved. For to this end oftentimes those things He giveth even to evil men, in order that some other thing good men of Him may learn to seek. In what manner then sayest thou, "I have trusted in the mercy of God "? Perchance for obtaining temporal things? Nay but, "For everlasting and world without end." The expression, "For everlasting," he willed to repeat by adding, "world without end," in order that by there repeating he might affirm how rooted he was in the love of the kingdom of heaven, and in the hope of everlasting felicity.

12. "I will confess to Thee for ever, because Thou hast done" (ver. 10). "Hast done what?" Doeg Thou hast condemned, David Thou hast crowned. "I will confess to

Thee for ever, because Thou hast done." Great confession, "Because thou hast done"! "Hast done" what? except these very things which above have been spoken of, that like an olive fruit-bearing in the house of God, I should trust in the mercy of God for everlasting and world without end? Thou hast done: an ungodly man cannot justify himself. But who is He that justifieth? "Believing," he saith, "on Him" that justifieth "the ungodly." " For what hast thou which thou hast not received? But if thou hast received, why dost thou glory as if thou hast not received, as if of thyself thou hast?" Be it far from me that I should so glory, saith he, that is opposed against Doeg, that beareth with Doeg upon earth, until he remove from his dwelling, and be rooted up from the land of the living. I glory not as if I have not received, but in God I glory. "And I will confess to Thee because Thou hast done," that is, because Thou hast done not according to my merits, but according to Thy mercy. But I have done what? If thou recollectest, "Before, I was a blasphemer, and a persecutor, and injurious." But thou, what hast thou done? "But mercy I have obtained, because ignorant I did it." " I will confess to Thee for ever, because Thou hast done."

13. "And I will look for Thy name, for it is pleasant." Bitter is the world, but Thy name is pleasant. Even if certain sweet things are in the world, yet with bitterness they are digested. Thy name is preferred, not only for greatness but also for pleasantness. "For unjust men have told to me their delights, but it is not as Thy law, O Lord." For if there were nothing sweet to the Martyrs, they would not have suffered with equanimity so great bitterness of tribulations. Their bitterness by any one was experienced, their sweetness easily could no one taste. The name of God therefore is pleasant to men loving God above all pleasantnesses. "I will look for Thy name, for it is pleasant." And to what dost Thou prove that it is pleasant? Give me a palate to which it is pleasant. Praise honey as much as thou art able, exaggerate the sweetness thereof with what words thou shalt have the power: a man knowing not what honey is, unless he shall have tasted, what thou sayest knoweth not. Therefore the rather to the proof the Psalm inviting thee saith what? "Taste and see that sweet is the Lord." Taste thou wilt not, and thou sayest, Is it pleasant? What is pleasant? If thou hast tasted, in thy fruit be it found, not in words alone, as it were only in leaves, lest by the curse of the Lord, to wither like that fig- tree thou shouldest deserve. "Taste," he saith," and see, that sweet is the Lord." Taste and see: then ye shall see, if ye shall have tasted. But to a man not tasting, how provest thou? By praising the pleasantness of the name of God, whatsoever things thou shall have said are words: something else is taste. The words of His praise there hear even the ungodly, but none taste how sweet it is, but the Saints. Further, a man discerning the sweetness of the name of God, and wishing to unfold and wishing to show the same, and not finding persons to whom he may unfold it; for to the Saints there is no need that he show it, because they

even of themselves taste and know, but the ungodly cannot discern what they will not taste: doth, I say, what, because of the sweetness of the name of God? He hath borne him forthwith away from the crowds of the ungodly. "And I will look," he saith, "for Thy name, for it is pleasant, in the sight of Thy Saints." Pleasant is Thy name, but not in the sight of the ungodly. I know how sweet a thing it is, but it is to them that have tasted.

PSALM LIII.

1. Of this Psalm we undertake to treat with you, as far as the Lord supplieth us. A brother biddeth us that we may have the will, and prayeth that we may have the power. If anything in haste perchance I shall have passed over, He that even to us deigneth to give what we shall be enabled to say, will supply it in you. The title of it is: "At the end, for Maeleth, understanding to David himself." "For Maeleth," as we find in interpretations of Hebrew names, seemeth to say, For one travailing, or in pain. But who there is in this world that travaileth and is in pain, the faithful acknowledge, because thereof they are. Christ here travaileth, Christ here is in pain: the Head is above, the members below. For one not travailing nor in pain would not say, "Saul, Saul, why persecutest thou me?" Him, with whom when persecuting He was travailing, being converted, He made to travail. For he also was himself afterwards enlightened, and grafted on those members which he used to persecute; being pregnant with the same love, he said, "My little children, of whom again I travail, until Christ be formed in you." For the members therefore of Christ, for His Body which is the Church, for that same One Man, that is, for that very unity, whereof the Head is above, this Psalm is sung. ... Who are they, then, amid whom we travail and groan, if in the Body of Christ we are, if under Him, the Head, we live, if amongst His members we are counted? Who they are, hear ye.

2. "The unwise man hath said in his heart, There is no God" (ver. 1). Such sort is it of men amid whom is pained and groaneth the Body of Christ. If such is this sort of men, of not many do we travail; as far as seemeth to occur to our thoughts, very few there are; and a difficult thing it is to meet with a man that saith in his heart, "There is no God;" nevertheless, so few there are, that, fearing amid the many to say this, in their heart they say it, for that with mouth to say it they dare not. Not much then is that which we are bid to endure, hardly is it found: uncommon is that sort of men that say in their heart, "There is no God." But, if it he examined in another sense, is not that found to be in more men, which we supposed to be in men few and uncommon, and almost in none? Let them come forth into the midst that live evil lives, let us look into the doings of profligate, daring, and wicked men, of whom there is a great multitude; who foster day by day their sins, who, their acts having been changed into habit, have even lost sense of shame: this is so great a multitude of men, that the Body of Christ, set amid them, scarce dareth to censure that which it is not constrained to commit, and deemeth it a great matter for itself that the integrity of innocence be preserved in not doing that which now, by habit, either it doth not dare to blame, or if it shall have dared, there breaketh out the censure and recrimination of them that live evil lives, more readily than the

free voice of them that live good lives. And those men are such as say in their heart, "There is no God." Such men I am confuting. Whence confuting? That their doings please God, they judge. He doth not therefore affirm, "some say," but "The unwise man hath said in his heart, There is no God." Which men do so far believe there is a God, that the same God they judge with what they do to be pleased. But if thou being wise dost perceive, how "the unwise man hath said in his heart, There is no God," if thou give heed, if thou understand, if thou examine; he that thinketh that evil doings please God, Him he doth not think to be God. For if God is, He is just; if He is just, injustice displeaseth Him, iniquity displeaseth. But thou, when thou thinkest that iniquity pleaseth Him, dost deny God. For if God is one Whom iniquity displeaseth, but God seemeth not to thee to be one whom iniquity displeaseth, and there is no God but one whom iniquity displeaseth, then when thou sayest in thy heart, God doth countenance my iniquities, thou sayest nothing else than, "There is no God."

3. Let us advert also to that sense, which concerning Christ our Lord Himself, our Head Himself, doth present itself. For when Himself in form of a servant appeared on earth, they that crucified Him said," He is not God." Because Son of God He was, truly God He was. But they that are corrupted and have become abominable said what? "He is not God:" let us slay Him, "He is not God." Thou hast the voice of these very men in the book of Wisdom. For after there had gone before the verse, "The unwise man hath said in his heart, There is no God ;" as if reasons were required why the unwise man could say this, he hath subjoined, "Corrupted they are, and abominable have become in their iniquities" (ver. 2). Hear ye those corrupted men. "For they have said with themselves, not rightly thinking:" corruption beginneth with evil belief, thence it proceedeth to depraved morals, thence to the most flagrant iniquities, these are the grades. But what with themselves said they, thinking not rightly? "A small thing and with tediousness is our life." From this evil belief followeth that which also the Apostle hath spoken of, "Let us eat and drink, for to- morrow we shall die." But in the former passage more diffusely luxury itself is described: "Let us crown us with roses, before they be withered; in every place let us leave the tokens of our gladness." After the more diffuse description of that luxury, what followeth? "Let us slay the poor just man:" this is therefore saying, "He is not God." Soft words they seemed but now to say:" Let us crown us with roses, before they be withered." What more delicate, what more soft? Wouldest thou expect, out of this softness, Crosses, swords? Wonder not, soft are even the roots of brambles; if any one handle them, he is not pricked: but that wherewith thou shall be pricked from thence hath birth. "Corrupted," therefore, are those men, "and abominable have become in their iniquities." They say, "If Son of God He is, let Him come down from the Cross." Behold them openly saying, "He is not God." ...

4. "The Lord from Heaven hath looked forth upon the sons of men, that He might see if there is one understanding and seeking after God" (ver. 3). What is this? "Corrupted they are," all these that say, "There is no God"? And what? Did it escape God, that they were become such? Or indeed to us would their inward thought be opened, except by Him it were told? If then He understood, if then He knew, what is this which hath been said, "that He might see "? For the words are of one inquiring, of one not knowing. "God from Heaven hath looked forth," etc. And as though He had found what He sought by looking upon, and by looking down from Heaven, He giveth sentence: "All men have gone aside, together useless they have become: there is not one that doeth good, not so much as one" (ver. 4). Two questions arise somewhat difficult: for if God looketh out from Heaven, in order that He may see if there is one understanding or seeking after God; there stealeth upon an unwise man the thought, that God knoweth not all things. This is one question: what is the other? If there is not one that doeth good, is not so much as one; who is he that travaileth amid bad men? The former question then is solved as followeth: ofttimes the Scripture speaketh in such manner, that what by the gift of God a creature doth, God is said to do. ... For hence has been said the following also, "For the Spirit searcheth all things, even the depth of God; " not because He that knoweth all things searcheth, but because to thee hath been given the Spirit, which maketh thee also to search: and that which by His own gift thou doest, He is said to do; because without Him thou wouldest not do it: therefore God is said to do, when thou doest. ... And because this by the gift of God thou doest, God from heaven is "looking forth upon the sons of men." The former question then, according to our measure, thus hath been solved.

5. What is that which looking forth we acknowledge? What is that which looking forth God acknowledgeth? What (because here He giveth it) doth He acknowledge? Hear what it is; that "All have gone aside, together useless they have become: there is not one that doeth good, there is not so much as one." What then is that other question, but the same whereof a little before I have made mention? If, "There is not one that doeth good, is not so much as one," no one remaineth to groan amid evil men. Stay, saith the Lord, do not hastily give judgment. I have given to men to do well; but of Me, He saith, not of themselves: for of themselves evil they are: sons of men they are, when they do evil; when well, My sons. For this thing God doth, out of sons of men He maketh sons of God: because out of Son of God He hath made Son of Man. See what this participation is: there hath been promised to us a participation of Divinity: He lieth that hath promised, if He is not first made partaker of mortality. For the Son of God hath been made partaker of mortality, in order that mortal man may be made partaker of divinity. He that hath promised that His good is to be shared with thee,

first with thee hath shared thy evil: He that to thee hath promised divinity, showeth in thee love. Therefore take away that men are sons of God, there remaineth that they are sons of men: "There is none that doeth good, is not so much as one."

6. "Shall not all know that work iniquity, that devour My people for the food of bread "? (ver. 5). ...There is therefore here a people of God that is being devoured. Nay, "There is not one that doeth good, there is not so much as one." We reply by the rule above. But this people that is devoured, this people that suffereth evil men, this that groaneth and travaileth amid evil men, now out of sons of men have been made sons of God: therefore are they devoured. For, "The counsel of the needy man thou hast confounded, because the Lord is his hope." For ofttimes, in order that the people of God may be devoured, this very thing in it is despised, that it is the people of God. I will pillage, he saith, and despoil; if he is a Christian, what will he do to me? ... But what followeth? "I will convince thee, and will set thee before thy face." Thou wilt not now know so as thou shouldest be displeasing to thyself, thou shall know so as thou mayest mourn. For God cannot but show to the unrighteous their iniquity. If He is not to show, who will they be that are to say, "What hath profiled us pride, and what hath boasting of riches bestowed upon us?" For then shall they know, that now will not know. "Shall not all know?" etc. Why hath He added, "for the food of bread "? As it were as bread, they eat My people. For all other things which we eat, we can eat now these, now those; not always this vegetable, not always this flesh, not always these apples: but always bread. What is then, "Devour My people for the food of bread "? Without intermission, without cessation they devour.

7. "On God they have not called." He is comforting the man that groaneth, and chiefly by an admonition, lest by imitating evil men, who ofttimes prosper, they delight in evil doing. There is kept for thee that which to thee hath been promised: their hope is present, thine is future, but theirs is transient, thine sure; theirs false, thine true. For they "upon God have not called." Do not daily such men ask of God? They do "not" ask of God. Give heed, if I am able to say this by the aid of God Himself. God gratuitously will have Himself to be worshipped, gratuitously will have Himself to be loved, that is chastely to be loved; not Himself to be loved for the reason that He giveth anything besides Himself, but because He giveth Himself. He then that calleth upon God in order that He may be made rich, On God doth not call: for upon that He calleth which to himself he willeth to come. ... But now thou wouldest have coffer full, and conscience void: God filleth not coffer, but breast. What do outward riches profit thee, if inward need presseth thee? Therefore those men that for the sake of worldly comforts, that for the sake

of earthly good things, that for the sake of present life and earthly felicity, call upon God, do not call upon God.

8. For this reason what followeth concerning them? "There have they feared with fear, where there was no fear" (ver. 6). For is there fear, if a man lose riches? There is no fear there, and yet in that case men are afraid. But if a man lose wisdom, truly there is fear, and in that case he is not afraid. ... Thou hast feared to give back money, and hast willed to lose fidelity. The Martyrs took not away property of other persons, but even their own they despised that they might not lose fidelity: and it was too little to lose money, when they were proscribed; they took also their life when they suffered: they lost life, in order that unto everlasting life they might find it. Therefore there they feared, where they ought to have been afraid. But they that of Christ have said, "He is not God," have there feared where was no fear. For they said, "If we shall have let Him go, there will come the Romans, and will take away from us both place and kingdom." O folly and imprudence saying in its heart, "He is not God"! Thou hast feared to lose earth, thou hast lost Heaven: thou hast feared lest there should come the Romans, and take away from thee place and kingdom! Could they take away from thee God? What then remaineth? what but that thou confess, that thou hast willed to keep, and by keeping ill hast lost? For thou hast lost both place and nation by slaying Christ. For ye did will rather to slay Christ, than to lose place; and ye have lost place, and nation, and Christ. In fearing, they have slain Christ: but wherefore this? "For God hath scattered the bones of them that please men." Willing to please men, they feared to lose their place. But Christ Himself, of whom they said, "He is not God," willed rather to displease such men, as they were: sons of men, not sons of God, He willed rather to displease. Thence were scattered their bones, His bones no one hath broken. "They were confounded, for God hath despised them." In very deed, brethren, as far as regardeth them, great confusion hath come to them. In the place where they crucified the Lord, whom for this cause they crucified, that they might not lose both place and nation, the Jews are not. "God," therefore," hath despised them:" and yet in despising He warned them to be converted. Let them now confess Christ, and say, He is God, of whom they said, "He is not God." Let them return to the inheritance of their fathers, to the inheritance of Abraham, of Isaac, and of Jacob, let them possess with these very persons life eternal: though they have lost life temporal. Wherefore this? Because out of sons of men have been made sons of God. For so long as they remain, and will not, there is not one that doeth good, there is not so much as one. "They were confounded, for God hath despised them." And as though to these very persons He were turned, He saith, "Who shall give out of Sion salvation to Israel?" (ver. 7). O ye fools, ye revile, insult, buffet, besmear with spittings, with thorns ye crown, upon the Cross ye lift up; whom? "Who shall give out of Sion salvation to Israel?"

Shall not That Same of whom ye have said, "He is not God "? "In God's turning away the captivity of His people." For there turneth away the captivity of His people, no one but He that hath willed to be a captive in your own hands. But what men shall understand this thing? "Jacob shall exult, and Israel shall rejoice." "Israel;" the true Jacob, and the true Israel, that younger, to whom the eider was servant shall himself exult, for he shall himself understand.

PSALM LIV.

1. The title of this Psalm hath fruit in the prolixity thereof, if it be understood: and because the Psalm is short, let us make up our not having to tarry over the Psalm by tarrying over the title. For upon this dependeth every verse which is sung. If any one, therefore, observe that which on the front of the house is fixed, secure he will enter; and, when he shall have entered, he will not err. For this on the post itself is prominently marked, namely, in what manner within he may not be in error. The title thereof standeth thus: "At the end, in hymns, understanding to David himself, when there came the Ziphites, and said to Saul, Behold, is not David hidden with us?" That Saul was persecutor of the holy man David, very well we know: that Saul was bearing the figure of a temporal kingdom, not to life but to death belonging, this also to your Love we remember to have imparted. And also that David himself was bearing the figure of Christ, or of the Body of Christ, ye ought both to know and to call to mind, ye that have already learned. What then of the Ziphites? There was a certain village, Ziph, whereof the inhabitants were Ziphites, in whose country David had hidden himself, when Saul would find and slay him. These Ziphites then, when they had learned this, betrayed him to the king his persecutor, saying, "Behold, is not David hidden with us?" Of no good to them indeed was their betrayal, and to David himself of no harm. For their evil disposition was shown: but Saul not even after their betrayal could seize David; but rather in a certain cave in that very country, when into his hands Saul had been given to slay, David spared him, and that which he had in his power he did not But the other was seeking to do that which he had not in his power. Let them that have been Ziphites take heed: let us see those whom to us the Psalm presenteth to be understood by the occasion of those same men.

2. If we inquire then by what word is translated Ziphites, we find, "Men flourishing." Flourishing then were certain enemies to holy David, flourishing before him hiding. We may find them in mankind, if we are willing to understand the Psalm. Let us find here at first David hiding, and we shall find his adversaries flourishing. Observe David hiding: "For ye are dead," saith the Apostle to the members of Christ," and your life is hid with Christ in God." These men, therefore, that are hiding, when shall they be flourishing? "When Christ," he saith, "your life, shall have appeared, then ye also with Him shall appear in glory." When these men shall be flourishing, then shall be those Ziphites withering. For observe to what flower their glory is compared: "All flesh is grass, and the honour of flesh as the flower of grass." What is the end? "The grass hath withered, and the flower hath fallen off." Where then shall be David? See what followeth: "But the Word of the Lord abideth for ever." ...

3. These men sometimes are observed of the weak sons of light, and their feet totter, when they have seen evil men in felicity to flourish, and they say to themselves, "Of what profit to me is innocence? What doth it advantage me that I serve God, that I keep His commandments, that I oppress no one, from no one plunder anything, hurt no one, that what I can I bestow? behold, all these things I do, and they flourish, I toil." But why? Wouldest thou also wish to be a Ziphite? They flourish in the world, wither in judgment, and after withering, into fire everlasting shall be cast: wouldest thou also choose this? Art thou ignorant of what He hath promised thee, who to thee hath come, what in Himself here He displayed? If the flower of the Ziphites were to be desired, would not Himself thy Lord also in this world have flourished? Or indeed was there wanting to Him the power to flourish? Nay but here He chose rather amid the Ziphites to hide, and to say to Pontius Pilate, as if to one being himself also a flower of the Ziphites, and in suspicion about His kingdom, "My kingdom is not of this world." Therefore here He was hidden: and all good men are hidden here, because their good is within, it is concealed, in the heart it is, where is faith, where charity, where hope, where their treasure is. Do these good things appear in the world? Both these good things are hidden, and the reward of these good things is hidden. ...

4. "O God, in Thy name make me safe, and in Thy virtue judge me" (ver. 1). Let the Church say this, hiding amid the Ziphites. Let the Christian body say this, keeping secret the good of its morals, expecting in secret the reward of its merits, let it say this: "In Thy virtues judge me." Thou hast come, O Christ, humble Thou hast appeared, despised Thou hast been, scourged hast been, crucified hast been slain hast been; but, on the third day hast risen, on the fortieth day into Heaven hast ascended: Thou sittest at the right hand of the Father, and no one seeth: Thy Spirit thence Thou hast sent, which men that were worthy have received; fulfilled with Thy love, the praise of that very humility of Thine throughout the world and nations they have preached: Thy name I see to excel among mankind, but nevertheless as weak to us hast Thou been preached. For not even did that Teacher of the Gentiles say, that among us he knew anything, "Save Christ Jesus, and Him crucified;" in order that of Him we might choose the reproach, rather than the glory of the flourishing Ziphites. Nevertheless, of Him he saith what? "Although He died of weakness, yet He liveth of the power of God." He came then that He might die of weakness, He is to come that He may judge in the power of God: but through the weakness of the Cross His name hath been illustrious. Whosoever shall not have believed upon the name made illustrious through weakness, shall stand in awe at the Judge, when He shall have come in power. But, lest He that once was weak, when He shall have come strong, with that fan send us to the left hand; may He "save us in His name, and judge us in His virtue." For who so rash as to have desired this, as to say to God, for instance "Judge me"? Is it not wont to

be said to men for a curse, "God judge thee"? So evidently it is a curse, if He judge thee in His virtue; and shall not have saved thee in His name: but when in name precedent He shall have saved thee, to thy health in virtue consequent He shall judge. Be thou without care: that judgment shall not to thee be punishment, but dividing. For in a certain Psalm s thus is said: "Judge me, O God, and divide my cause from the nation unholy." ...

5. "O God, hearken to my prayer, in Thy ears receive the words of my mouth" (ver. 2). ... To Thee may my prayer attain, driven forth and darted out from the desire of Thy eternal blessings: to Thy ears I send it forth, aid it that it may reach, lest it fall short in the middle of the way, and fainting as it were it fall down. But even if there result not to me now the good things which I ask, I am secured nevertheless that hereafter they will come. For even in the case of transgressions a certain man is said to have asked of God, and not to have been hearkened to for his good. For privations of this world had inspired him to prayer, and being set in temporal tribulations he had wished that temporal tribulations should pass away, and there should return the flower of grass; and he saith, "My God, my God, why hast Thou forsaken me?" The very voice of Christ it is, but for His members' sake. "The words," he saith, "of my transgressions I have cried to Thee throughout the day, and Thou hast not hearkened: and by night, and not for the sake of folly to me:" that is, "and by night I have cried, and Thou hast not hearkened; and nevertheless in this very thing that Thou hast not hearkened, it is not for the sake of folly to me that Thou hast not hearkened, but rather for the sake of wisdom that Thou hast not hearkened, that I might perceive what of Thee I ought to ask. For those things I was asking which to my cost perchance I should have received." Thou askest riches, O man; how many have been overset through their riches? Whence knowest thou whether to thee riches may profit? Have not many poor men more safely been in obscurity; having become rich men, so soon as they have begun to blaze forth, they have been a prey to the stronger? How much better they would have lain concealed, how much better they would have been unknown, that have begun to be inquired after not for the sake of what they were, but for the sake of what they had! In these temporal things therefore, brethren, we admonish and exhort you in the Lord, that ye ask not anything as if it were a thing settled, but that which God knoweth to be expedient for you. For what is expedient for you, ye know not at all. Sometimes that which ye think to be for you is against you, and that which ye think to be against you is for you. For sick ye are; do not dictate to the physician the medicines he may choose to set beside you. If the teacher of the Gentiles, Paul the Apostle, saith, "For what we should pray for as we ought, we know not," how much more we? Who nevertheless, when he seemed to himself to pray wisely, namely, that from him should be taken away the thorn of the flesh, the angel of Satan, that did buffet him, in order that he might not in the greatness

of the revelations be lifted up, heard from the Lord what? Was that done which he wished? Nay, in order to that being done which was expedient, he heard from the Lord, I say, what? "Thrice," he saith, "I besought the Lord that He would take it from me; and He said to me, My Grace sufficeth for thee: for virtue in weakness is made perfect." Salve to the wound I have applied; when I applied it I know, when it should be taken away I know. Let not a sick man draw back from the hands of the physician, let him not give advice to the physician. So it is with all these things temporal. There are tribulations; if well thou worshippest God, thou wilt know that He knoweth what is expedient for each man: there are prosperities; take the more heed, lest these same corrupt thy soul, so that it withdraw from Him that hath given these things. ...

6. "For aliens have risen up against me" (ver. 3). What "aliens"? Was not David himself a Jew of the tribe of Judah? But the very place Ziph belonged to the tribe of Judah; it was of the Jews. How then "aliens "? Not in city, not in tribe, not in kindred, but in flower. ... But see the Ziphites, see them for a time flourishing. With reason "alien" sons. Thou amid the Ziphites hiding saidst what? "Blessed the people whereof the Lord is its God." Out of this affection this prayer is being sent forth into the ears of the Lord, when it is said, "for aliens have risen up against me."

7. "And mighty men have sought after my soul." For in a new manner, my brethren, they would destroy the race of holy men, and the race of them that abstain from hoping in this world, all they that have hope in this world. Certainly commingled they are, certainly together they live. Very much to one another are opposed these two sorts: the one of those that place no hope but in things secular, and in temporal felicity, and the other of those that do firmly place their trope in the Lord God. And though concordant are these Ziphites, do not much trust to their concord: temptations are wanting; when there shall have come any temptation, so as that a person may be reproved for the flower of the world, I say not to thee he will quarrel with the Bishop, but not even to the Church Herself will he draw near, lest there fall any part of the grass. Wherefore have I said these words, brethren? Because now gladly ye all hear in the name of Christ, and according as ye understand, so ye shout out at the word; ye would not indeed shout at it unless ye understood. This your understanding ought to be fruitful. But whether it is fruitful, temptation doth try; lest suddenly when ye are said to be ours, through temptation ye be found aliens, and it be said, "Aliens have risen up against me, and mighty men have sought my soul." Be not that said which followeth, "They have not set forth God before their face." For when will he set God before his face, before whose eyes there is nought but the world? namely,

how he may have coin upon coin, how flocks may be increased, how barns may be filled, how it may be said to his soul, "Thou hast many good things, be merry, feast, take thy fill." Doth he set before his face Him, that unto one so boasting and so blooming with the flower of the Ziphites saith, "Fool" (that is, "man not understanding," "man unwise"), "this night shall be taken from thee thy soul; all these things which thou hast prepared, whose shall they be?"

8. "For behold, God helpeth me" (ver. 4). Even themselves know not themselves, amid whom I am hiding. But if they too were to set God before their face, they would find in what manner God helpeth me. For all holy men are helped by God, but within, where no one seeth For in like manner as the conscience of ungodly men is a great punishment, so a great joy is the very conscience of godly men. "For our glory this is," saith the Apostle, "the testimony of our conscience." In this within, not in the flower of the Ziphites without, doth glory that man that now saith, "For behold God helpeth me." Surely though afar off are to be those things which He promiseth, this day have I a sweet and present help; to-day in my heart's joy I find that without cause certain say, "Who doth show to us good things? For there is signed upon us the light of Thy countenance, O Lord, Thou hast put pleasantness into my heart." Not into my vineyard, not into my flock, not into my cask, not into my table, but" into my heart." "For behold God helpeth me." How doth He help thee? "And the Lord is the lifter up of my soul."

9. "Turn away evil things unto mine enemies" (ver. 5). So however green they are, so however they flourish, for the fire they are being reserved. "In Thy virtue destroy Thou them." Because to wit they flourish now, because to wit they spring up like grass: do not thou be a man unwise and foolish, so that by giving thought to these things thou perish for ever and ever. For, "Turn Thou away evil things unto mine enemies." For if thou shalt have place in the body of David Himself, in His virtue He will destroy them. These men flourish in the felicity of the world, perish in the virtue of God. Not in the same manner as they flourish, do they also perish: for they flourish for a time, perish for everlasting: flourish in unreal good things, perish in real torments. "In Thy strength destroy," whom in Thy weakness Thou hast endured.

10. "Voluntarily I will sacrifice to Thee" (ver. 6). Who can even understand this good thing of the heart, at another's speaking thereof, unless in himself he hath tasted it? What is, "Voluntarily I will sacrifice to Thee"?... For what sacrifice here shall I take, brethren? or what worthily shall I offer to the Lord for His mercy? Victims shall. I seek from flock of sheep, ram shall I select, for any bull in the herds shall I look out, frankincense indeed from the land of the Sabaeans shall I

bring? What shall I do? What offer; except that whereof He speaketh, "Sacrifice of praise shall honour Me"? Wherefore then "voluntarily"? Because truly I love that which I praise. I praise God, and in the self-same praise I rejoice: in the praise of Himself I rejoice, at whom being praised, I blush not. For He is not praised in the same manner as by those who love the theatrical follies is praised either by a charioteer, or a hunter, or actor of any kind, and by their praisers, other praisers are invited, are exhorted, to shout together: and when all have shouted, ofttimes, if their favourite is overcome, they are all put to the blush. Not so is our God: be He praised with the will, loved with charity: let it be gratuitous (or voluntary) that He is loved and that He is praised. What is "gratuitous "? Himself for the sake of Himself, not for the sake of something else. For if thou praisest God in order that He may give thee something else, no longer freely dost thou love God. Thou wouldest blush, if thy wife for the sake of riches were to love thee, and perchance if poverty should befall thee, should begin to think of adultery. Seeing that therefore thou wouldest be loved by thy partner freely, wilt thou for anything else love God? What reward art thou to receive of God, O covetous man? Not earth for thee, but Himself He keepeth, who made heaven and earth. "Voluntarily I will sacrifice to Thee:" do it not of necessity. For if for the sake of anything else thou praisest God, out of necessity thou praisest. ... These things also which He hath given, because of the Giver are good things. For He giveth entirely, He giveth these temporal things: and to certain men to their good, to certain men to their harm, after the height and depth of His judgments. ... "Voluntarily I will sacrifice to Thee." Wherefore "voluntarily"? Because gratis. What is gratis? "And I will confess to Thy name, O Lord, for it is a good thing:" for nothing else, but because a "good thing" it is. Doth he say, "I will confess to Thy name, O Lord," because Thou givest me fruitful manors, because Thou givest me gold and silver, because Thou givest me extended riches, abundant money, most exalted dignity? Nay. But what? "For it is a good thing." Nothing I find better than Thy name.

11. "For out of all tribulation Thou hast delivered me" (ver. 7). For this cause I have perceived how good a thing is Thy name: for if this I were able before tribulations to acknowledge, perchance for me there had been no need of them. But tribulation hath been applied for admonition, admonition hath redounded to Thy praise. For I should not have understood where I was, except of my weakness I had been admonished. "Out of all tribulations," therefore, "Thou hast delivered me. And upon mine enemies mine eye hath looked back:" upon those Ziphites "mine eye hath looked back." Yea, their flower I have passed over in loftiness of heart, unto Thee I have come, and thence I have looked back upon them, and have seen that "All flesh is grass, and all the glory of man as the flower of grass:" as in a certain place is also said, "I have seen the ungodly man to be exalted and raised up like the cedars of Lebanon: I passed by, and, lo! he was not." Wherefore "he

was not"? Because thou hast passed by. What is," because thou hast passed by"? Because not to no purpose hast thou heard "Lift up thy heart;" because not on earth, where thou wouldest have rotted, thou hast remained; because thou hast lifted thy soul to God, and thou hast mounted beyond the cedars of Lebanon, and from that elevation hast observed: and "Lo! he was not;" and thou hast sought him, and there hath not been found place for him. No longer is labour before thee; because thou hast entered into the sanctuary of God, and hast understood for the last things. So also here thus he concludeth. "And upon mine enemies mine eye hath looked back." This do ye therefore, brethren, with your souls; lift up your hearts, sharpen the edge of your mind, learn truly to love God, learn to despise the present world, learn voluntarily to sacrifice the offerings of praise; to the end that, mounting beyond the flower of the grass, ye may look back upon your enemies.

PSALM LV.

1. Of this Psalm the title is: "At the end, in hymns, understanding to David himself." What the "end" is, we will briefly call to your recollection, because ye have known it. "For the end of the Law is Christ, for righteousness unto every man believing." Be the attention therefore directed unto the End, directed unto Christ. Wherefore is He called the end? Because whatever we do, to Him we refer it, and when to Him we shall have come home, more to ask we shall not have. For there is an end spoken of which doth consume, there is an end spoken of which doth make perfect. In one sense, for instance, we understand it, when we hear, there is ended the food which was in eating; and in another sense we understand it when we hear, there is ended the vesture which was in weaving: in each case we hear, there is ended; but the food so that it no longer is, the vesture so that it is perfected. Our end therefore ought to be our perfection, our perfection Christ. For in Him we are made perfect, because of Himself the Head, the Members are we. And he hath been spoken of as "the End of the Law," because without Him no one doth make perfect the Law. When therefore ye hear in the Psalms, "At the end,"—for many Psalms are thus superscribed,—be not your thought upon consuming, but upon consummation.

2. "In hymens:" in praises. For whether we are troubled and are straitened, or whether we rejoice and exult, He is to be praised, who both in tribulations doth instruct, and in gladness doth comfort. For the praise of God from the heart and mouth of a Christian man ought not to depart; not that he may be praising in prosperity, and speaking evil in adversity; but after the manner that this Psalm doth prescribe, "I will speak good of the Lord in every time, alway the praise of Him is in my mouth." Thou dost rejoice; acknowledge a Father indulging: thou art troubled; acknowledge a Father chastening. Whether He indulge, or whether He chasten, He is instructing one for whom He is preparing an inheritance.

3. What then is, "Understanding to David himself"? David indeed was, as we know, a holy prophet, king of Israel, son of Jesse: but because out of his seed there came for our salvation after the flesh the Lord Jesus Christ, often under that name He is figured, and David instead of Christ is in a figure set down, because of the origin of the Flesh of the Same. For after some sort He is Son of David, after some sort He is the Lord of David; Son of David after the flesh, Lord of David after the divinity. For if by Him have been made all-things, by Him also David himself hath been made, out of whose seed He came to men. Moreover, when the Lord had questioned the Jews, whose Son they affirmed Christ to be, they made answer, "David's:" where the Lord chides the Jews, when they said that He was the Son of

David. He saw that they had stayed at the flesh, and had lost sight of the divinity; and He reproveth them by propounding a question: "How then doth David himself in spirit call Him Lord, 'The Lord hath said unto my Lord.' ... If then He in spirit calleth Him Lord, how is He is Son?" A question He propounded; His being Son He denied not. Ye have heard "Lord;" say ye how He is his "Son:" ye have heard "Son; say how He is "Lord." This question the Catholic Faith solveth. How "Lord"? Because "In the beginning was the Word, and the Word was with God, and the Word was God." How "Son"? Because "The Word was made flesh, and dwelt among us. Because then David in a figure is Christ, but Christ, as we have often reminded your Love, is both Head and Body; neither ought we to speak of ourselves as alien from Christ, of whom we are members, nor to count ourselves as if we were any other thing: because "The two shall be in one flesh." "This is a great Sacrament," saith the Apostle, "but I speak in regard of Christ and the Church." Because then whole Christ is" Head and Body;" when we hear, "Understanding to David himself," understand we ourselves also in David. Let the members of Christ understand, and Christ in His members understand, and the members of Christ in Christ understand: because Head and Members are one Christ. The Head was in heaven, and was saying, "Why dost thou persecute Me?" We with Him are in heaven through hope, Himself is with us on earth through love. Therefore "understanding to David himself." Be we admonished when we hear, and let the Church understand: for there belongeth to us great diligence to understand in what evil we now are, and from what evil we desire to be delivered, remembering the Prayer of the Lord, where at the end we say," Deliver us from evil." Therefore amid many tribulations of this world, this Psalm complaineth somewhat of understanding. He lamenteth not with it, who hath not understanding. But furthermore, dearly beloved, we ought to remember, that after the image of God we have been made, and that not in any other part than in the understanding itself. For in many things by beasts we are surpassed: but when a man knoweth himself to have been made after the image of God, therein something in himself he acknowledgeth to be more than hath been given to dumb animals. But on consideration of all those things which a man hath, he findeth himself in this thing peculiarly distinguished from a dumb animal, in that he hath himself an understanding. Whence certain men despising in themselves that peculiar and especial thing which from their Maker they had received, the Maker Himself reproveth, saying, "Do not become like horse and mule, in which there is no understanding." ...

4. "Hear Thou, O God, my entreaty, and despise not my prayer: give heed unto me, and hearken unto me" (ver. 1). Of one earnest, anxious, of one set in tribulation, are these words. He is praying, suffering many things, from evil yearning to be delivered: it remaineth that we hear in what evil he is, and when he

beginneth to speak, let us acknowledge there ourselves to be; in order that the tribulation being shared, we may conjoin prayer. "I have been made sad in my exercise, and have been troubled" (ver. 2). Where made sad, where troubled? "'In my exercise," he saith. Of evil men, whom he suffereth, he hath made mention, and the same suffering of evil men he hath called his "exercise." Think ye not that without profit there are evil men in this world, and that no good God maketh of them. Every evil man either on this account liveth that he may be corrected, or on this account liveth that through him a good man may be exercised. O that therefore they that do now exercise us would be converted, and together with us be exercised! Nevertheless, so long as they are such as to exercise, let us not hate them: because in that wherein any one of them is evil, whether unto the end he is to persevere, we know not; and ofttimes when to thyself thou seemest to have been hating an enemy, thou hast been hating a brother, and knowest not. The devil and his angels in the holy Scriptures have been manifested to us, that for fire everlasting they have been destined. Of them only must amendment be despaired of. ... Therefore since this rule of Love for thee is fixed, that imitating the Father thou shouldest love an enemy: for, He saith, "love your enemies:" in this precept how wouldest thou be exercised, if thou hadst no enemy to suffer? Thou seest then that he profiteth thee somewhat: and let God sparing evil men profit thee, so that thou show mercy: because perchance thou too, if thou art a good man, out of an evil man hast been made a good man: and if God spared not evil men, not even thou wouldest be found to return thanks. May He therefore spare others, that hath spared thee also. For it were not right, when thou hadst passed through, to close up the way of godliness.

5. Whence then doth this man pray, set among evil men, with whose enmities he was being exercised? Why saith he, "I have been made sad in my exercise, and have been troubled"? While he is extending his love so as to love enemies, he hath been affected with disgust, being bayed at all around by the enmities of many men, by the frenzy of many and under a sort of human infirmity he hath sunk. He hath seen himself now begin to be pierced through with an evil suggestion of the devil, to bring on hatred against his enemies: wrestling against hatred in order to perfect love herself, in the very fight, and in the wrestling, he hath been troubled. For there is his voice in another Psalm, "Mine eye hath been troubled, because of anger." And what followeth there? "I have waxen old among all mine enemies." As if in storm and waves he were beginning to sink, like Peter. For he doth trample the waves of this world, that loveth enemies. Christ on the sea was walking fearless, from whose heart there could not by any means be taken away the love of an enemy, who hanging on the Cross did say, "Father, forgive them, for they know not what they do." Peter too would walk. He as Head, Peter as Body: because, "Upon this rock," He saith, "I will build My Church." He was bidden to

walk, and he was walking by the Grace of Him bidding, not by his own strength. But when he saw the wind mighty, he feared; and then he began to sink, being troubled in his exercise. By what mighty wind? "By the voice of the enemy, and by the tribulation of the sinner" (ver. 3). Therefore, in the same manner as he cried out on the waves, "Lord, I perish, save me," a similar voice from this man hath preceded, "Hearken unto me." Wherefore? For what sufferest thou? Of what dost thou groan? "I have been made sad in my exercise." To be exercised indeed among evil men Thou hast set me, but too much they have risen up, beyond my powers: calm Thou one troubled, stretch forth a hand to one sinking. "For they have brought down upon me iniquity, and in anger they were shadowing me." Ye have heard of waves and winds: one as it were humbled they were insulting, and he was praying: on every side against him with the roar of insult they were raging, but he within was calling upon Him whom they did not see. ...

6. But this man being troubled and made sad was praying, his eye being disturbed as it were on account of anger. But the anger of a brother if it shall have been inveterate is then hatred. Anger doth trouble the eye, hatred doth quench it: anger is a straw, hatred is a beam. Sometimes thou hatest and chidest an angry man: in thee is hatred, in him whom thou chidest anger: with reason to thee is said, "Cast out first the beam from thine own eye, and so thou shall see to cast out the straw from thy brother's eye." For that ye may know how much difference there is between anger and hatred: day by day men are angry with their sons, show me them that hate their sons! This man being troubled was praying even when made sad, wrestling against all revilings of all revilers; not in order that he might conquer any one of them by giving back reviling, but that he might not hate any one of them. Hence he prayeth, hence asketh: "From the voice of the enemy and from the tribulation of the sinner." "My heart hath been troubled in me" (ver. 4). This is the same as elsewhere hath been said," Mine eye because of anger hath been troubled." And if eye hath been troubled, what followeth? "And fear of death hath fallen upon me." Our life is love: if life is love, death is hatred. When a man hath begun to fear lest he should hate him that he was loving, it is death he is fearing; and a sharper death, and a more inward death, whereby soul is killed, not body. Thou didst mind a man raging against thee; what was he to do, against whom thine own Lord had given thee security, saying, "Fear not them that kill the body"? He by raging killeth body, thou by keeping hatred hast killed soul; and he the body of another, thou thine own soul. "Fear," therefore, "of death hath fallen upon me."

7. "Fearfulness and trembling have come upon me, and darkness hath covered me" (ver. 5). "And I have said," "He that hateth his brother, is in darkness until now."

400

If love is light, hatred is darkness. And what saith to himself one set in that weakness and troubled in that exercise? "Who shall give me wings as to a dove, and I shall fly and shall rest?" (ver. 6). Either for death he was wishing, or for solitude he was longing. So long, he saith, as this is the work with me, as this command is given me, that I should love enemies, the revilings of these men, increasing and shadowing me, do derange mine eye, perturb my sight, penetrate my heart, slay my soul. I could wish to depart, but weak I am, lest by abiding I should add sins to sins: or at least may I be separated for a little space from mankind, lest my wound suffer from frequent blows, in order that when it hath been made whole it may be brought back to the exercise. This is what takes place, brethren, and there ariseth ofttimes in the mind of the servant of God a longing for solitude, for no other reason than because of the multitude of tribulations and scandals, and he saith, "Who shall give me wings?" Doth he find himself without wings, or rather with bound wings? If they are wanting, be they given; if bound, be they loosed; because even he that looseth a bird's wings, either giveth, or giveth back to it its wings. For it had not as though its own them, wherewith it could not fly. Bound wings make a burden. "Who," he saith, "shall give me wings as to a dove, and I shall fly and shall rest?" Shall rest, where? I have said there are two senses here: either, as saith the Apostle, "To be dissolved and to be with Christ, for it is by far the best thing." ... Even he that amended cannot be, is thine, either by the fellowship of the human race, or ofttimes by Church Communion; he is within, what wilt thou do? whither wilt go? whither separate thyself, in order that these things thou mayest not suffer? But go to him, speak, exhort, coax, threaten, reprove. I have done all things, whatever powers I had I have expended and have drained, nothing I see have I prevailed; all my labour hath been spent out, sorrow hath remained. How then shall my heart rest from such men, except I say, "Who shall give me wings?" "As to a dove," however, not as to a raven. A dove seeketh a flying away from troubles, but she loseth not love. For a dove as a type of love is set forth, and in her the plaint is loved. Nothing is so fond of plaints as a dove: day and night she complaineth, as though she were set here where she ought to complain. What then saith this lover? Revilings of men to bear I am unable, they roar, with frenzy are carried away, are inflamed with indignation, in anger they shadow me; to do good to them I am unable; O that I might rest somewhere, being separated from them in body, not in love; lest in me there should be troubled love itself: with my words and my speech no good can I do them, by praying for them perchance I shall do good. These words men say, but ofttimes they are so bound, that to fly they are not able. For perchance they are not bound with any birdlime, but are bound by duty. But if they are bound with care and duty, and to leave it are unable, let them say," I was wishing to be dissolved and to be with Christ, for it is by far the best thing: to abide in the flesh is necessary because of you." A dove bound back by affection, not by cupidity, was not able to fly away because of duty to be fulfilled, not because of little merit. Nevertheless a longing in heart must needs be; nor doth any man suffer this longing, but he that hath begun to walk in that narrow way: in order that he may know that there are not wanting to the Church persecutions, even in this time, when a calm is seen in the Church, at least with respect to those persecutions which our Martyrs have suffered. But there are not wanting persecutions, because a true saying is this, "All that will godly to live in Christ, shall suffer persecution." ...

8. "Behold I have gone afar fleeing, and have abode in the desert" (ver. 7). In what desert? Wherever thou shalt be, there will gather them together other men, the desert with thee they will seek, will attach themselves to thy life, thou canst not thrust back the society of brethren: there are mingled with thee also evil men; still exercise is thy due portion," Behold I have gone afar, and have abode in the desert." In what desert? It is perchance in the conscience, whither no man entereth, where no one is with thee, where thou art and God. For if in the desert, in any place, what wilt thou do with men gathering themselves together? For thou wilt not be able to be separated from mankind, so long as among men thou livest. ...

9. "I was looking for him that should save me from weakness of mind and tempest (ver. 8). Sea there is, tempest there is: nothing for thee remaineth but to cry out, "Lord, I perish." Let Him stretch forth hand, who doth the waves tread fearlessly, let Him relieve thy dread, let Him confirm in Himself thy security, let Him speak to thee within, and say to thee, "Give heed to Me, what I have borne:" an evil brother perchance thou art suffering, or an enemy without art suffering; which of these have I not suffered? There roared without Jews, within a disciple was betraying. There rageth therefore tempest, but He doth save men from weakness of mind, and tempest. Perchance thy ship is being troubled, because He in thee is sleeping. The sea was raging, the bark wherein the disciples were sailing was being tossed; but Christ was sleeping: at length it was seen by them that among them was sleeping the Ruler and Creator of winds; they drew near and awoke Christ; He commanded the winds, and there was a great calm. With reason then perchance thy heart is troubled, because thou hast forgotten Him on whom thou hast believed: beyond endurance thou art suffering, because it hath not come into thy mind what for thee Christ hath borne. If unto thy mind cometh not Christ, He sleepeth: awake Christ, recall faith. For then in thee Christ is sleeping, if thou hast forgotten the sufferings of Christ: then in thee Christ is watching, if thou hast remembered the sufferings of Christ. But when with full heart thou shalt have considered what He hath suffered, wilt not thou too with equanimity endure? and perchance rejoicing, because thou hast been found in some likeness of the sufferings of thy King. When therefore on these things thinking thou hast begun to be comforted and to rejoice, He hath arisen, He hath commanded the winds;

therefore there is a great calm. "I was looking for Him that should save me from weakness of mind and tempest."

10. "Sink, O Lord, and divide the tongues of them" (ver. 9). He is referring to men troubling him and shadowing him, and he hath wished this thing not of anger, brethren. They that have wickedly lifted up themselves, for them it is expedient that they be sunk. They that have wickedly conspired, it is expedient for them that their tongues should be divided: to good let them consent, and let their tongues agree together. But if to one purpose there were a whispering against me, he saith, all mine enemies, let them lose their "one purpose" in evil, divided be the tongues of them, let them not with themselves agree together. "Sink, O Lord, and divide the tongues of them." Wherefore "sink"? Because themselves they have lifted up. Wherefore "divide"? Because for an evil thing they have united. Recollect that tower of proud men made after the deluge: what said the proud men? Lest we perish in a deluge, let us make a lofty tower. In pride they were thinking themselves to be fortified, they builded up a lofty tower, and the Lord divided the tongues of them. Then they began not to understand one another; hence arose the beginning of many tongues. For before, one tongue there was: but one tongue for men agreeing was good, one tongue for humble men was good: but when that gathering together did into a union of pride fall headlong, God spared them; even though He divided the tongues, lest by understanding one another they should make a destructive unity. Through proud men, divided were the tongues; through humble Apostles, united were the tongues. Spirit of pride dispersed tongues, Spirit Holy united tongues. For when the Holy Spirit came upon the disciples, with the tongues of all men they spake, by all men they were understood: tongues dispersed, into one were united. Therefore if still they rage and are Gentiles, it is expedient for them divided to have their tongues. They would have one tongue; let them come to the Church; because even among the diversity of tongues of flesh, one is the tongue in faith of heart.

11. "For I have seen iniquity and contradiction in the city." With reason this man was seeking the desert, for he saw iniquity and contradiction in the city. There is a certain city turbulent: the same it was that was building a tower, the same was confounded and called Babylon, the same through innumerable nations dispersed: thence is gathered the Church into the desert of a good conscience. For he saw contradiction in the city. "Christ cometh."—"What Christ?" thou contradictest.—"Son of God."—" And hath God a Son?" thou contradictest.—"He was born of a virgin, suffered, rose again."—"And whence is it possible for this to be done?" thou contradictest.—Give heed at least to the glory of the Cross itself. Now on the brow of kings that Cross hath been fixed, over which enemies insulted. The effect

hath proved the virtue. It hath subdued the world, not with steel, but with wood. The wood of the Cross deserving of insults hath seemed to enemies, and before the wood itself standing they were wagging the head, and saying, "If Son of God He is, let Him come down from the Cross." He was stretching forth His hands to a people unbelieving and contradicting. For if just he is that of faith liveth, unjust he is that hath not faith. By that which here he saith "iniquity," I understand unbelief. The Lord therefore was seeing in the city iniquity and contradiction, and was stretching forth His hands to a people unbelieving and contradicting: and nevertheless waiting for these same, He was saying, "Father, forgive them, for they know not what they do." Even now indeed there rage the remnant of that city, even now they contradict. From the brows of all men now He is stretching forth hands to the remnant unbelieving and contradicting.

12. "Day and night there will compass it upon the walls thereof iniquity, and labour." "Upon the walls thereof;" upon the fortifications thereof, holding as it were the heads thereof, the noble men thereof. If that noble man were a Christian, not one would remain a pagan! Oft-times men say, "no one would remain a pagan, if he were a Christian." Ofttimes men say, "If he too were made a Christian, who would remain a pagan?" Because therefore not yet they are made Christians, as if walls they are of that city unbelieving and contradicting. How long shall these walls stand? Not always shall they stand. The Ark is going around the walls of Jericho: there shall come a time at the seventh going round of the Ark, when all the walls of the city unbelieving and contradicting shall fall. Until it come to pass, this man is being troubled in his exercise; and enduring the remains of men contradicting, he would choose wings for flying away, would choose the rest of the desert. Yea let him continue amid men contradicting, let him endure menaces, drink revilings, and look for Him that will save him from weakness of mind and tempest: let him look upon the Head, the pattern for his life, let him be made calm in hope, even if he is troubled in fact. "Day and night there will compass it upon the walls thereof iniquity; and labour in the midst thereof and injustice." And for this reason labour is there, because iniquity is there: because injustice is there, therefore also labour is there. But let them hear him stretching forth hands. "Come unto Me, all ye that labour." Ye cry, ye contradict, ye revile: He on the contrary, "Come unto Me, all ye that labour," in your pride, and ye shall rest in My humility. "Learn of Me," He saith, "for meek I am and humble in heart, and ye shall find rest unto your souls." For whence do they labour, but because they are not meek and humble in heart? God humble was made, let man blush to be proud.

13. "There hath not failed from the streets thereof usury and deceit" (ver. 11). Usury and deceit are not hidden at least, because they are evil things, but in public

they rage. For he that in his house doth any evil thing, however for his evil thing doth blush: "In the streets thereof usury and deceit." Money-lending even hath a profession, Money-lending also is called a science; a corporation is spoken of, a corporation as if necessary to the state, and of its profession it payeth revenue; so entirely indeed in the streets is that which should have been hidden. There is also another usury worse, when thou forgivest not that which to thee is owed; and the eye is disturbed in that verse of the prayer, "Forgive us our debts—as we too forgive our debtors." For what there wilt thou do, when thou art going to pray, and coming to that same verse? An insulting word thou hast heard: thou wouldest exact the punishment of condemnation. Do but consent to exact just so much as thou hast given, thou usurer of injuries! With the fist thou hast been smitten, slaying thou seekest. Evil usury! How wilt thou go to prayer? If thou shall have left praying, which way wilt thou come round unto the Lord? Behold thou wilt say: "Our Father which art in heaven, hallowed be Thy Name, Thy kingdom come, Thy will be done, as in heaven so on earth." Thou wilt say, "Our daily bread give us to-day." Thou wilt come to, "Forgive us our debts, as we also forgive our debtors." Even in that evil city let there abound these usuries; let them not enter the walls where the breast is smitten! What wilt thou do? because there thou and that verse are in the midst? Petitions for thee hath a heavenly Lawyer composed. He that knew what used there to be done, said to thee, "Otherwise thou shall not obtain." "Verily, verily, I say unto you, that if ye shall have forgiven men sins, they shall be forgiven you; but if ye shall not have forgiven sins unto men, neither will your Father forgive you." Who saith this? He that knoweth what there is being done, in the place whereat thou art standing to make request. See how Himself hath willed to be thy Advocate; Himself thy Counsellor? Himself the Assessor of the Father Himself thy Judge hath said, "Otherwise thou shalt not receive." What wilt thou do? Thou wilt not receive, unless thou shall speak; wilt not receive if falsely thou shall speak. Therefore either thou must do and speak, or else what thou askest thou wilt not earn; because they that this do not do, are in the midst of those evil usuries. Be they engaged therein, that yet do idols either adore or desire: do not thou, O people of God, do not thou, O people of Christ, do not thou the Body of Him the Head! Give heed to the bond s of thy peace, give heed to the promise of thy life. For what doth it profit thee, that thou exactest for injuries which thou hast endured? doth vengeance refresh thee? Therefore, over the evil of another shalt thou rejoice? Thou hast suffered evil; pardon thou; be not ye two. ...

14. "For if an enemy had upbraided me" (ver. 12). And indeed above he was "troubled in his exercise" by the voice of the enemy and by the tribulation of the sinner, perhaps being placed in that city, that proud city that was building a tower, which was "sunk," that divided might be the tongues: give heed to his inward groaning because of perils from false brethren. "For if an enemy had upbraided

me, I would have undergone it assuredly, and if he that did hate me had over me spoken great words," that is, through pride had on me trampled, did magnify himself above me, did threaten me all in his power: "I would hide myself assuredly from him." From him that is abroad, thou wouldest hide thyself where? Amid those that are within. But now see whether anything else remaineth, but that thou seek solitude. "But thou," he saith, "man of one mind, my guide and my friend" (ver. 13). Perchance sometimes good counsel thou hast given, perchance sometimes thou hast gone before me, and some wholesome advice thou hast given me: in the Church of God together we have been. "But thou, ... that together with me didst take sweet morsels" (ver. 14). What are the sweet morsels? Not all they that are present know: but let them not be soured that do know, in order that they may be able to say to them that as yet know not: "Taste ye and see, how sweet is the Lord." "In the House of God we have walked with consent." Whence then dissension? Thou that wast within, hast become one without. He hath walked with me in the House of God with consent: another house hath he set up against the House of God. Wherefore hath that been forsaken, wherein we have walked with consent? wherefore hath that been deserted, wherein together we did take sweet morsels?

15. "Let there come death upon them, and let them go down unto Hell living" (ver. 15). How hath he cited and hath made us call to mind that first beginning of schism, when in that first people of the Jews certain proud men separated themselves, and would without have sacrificed? A new death upon them came: the earth opened herself, and swallowed them up alive. "Let there come," he saith, "death upon them, and let them go down into Hell living." What is "living"? knowing that they are perishing, and yet perishing. Hear of living men perishing and being swallowed up in a gulf of the earth, that is, being swallowed up in the voraciousness of earthly desires. Thou sayest to a man, What aileth thee, brother? Brethren we are, one God we invoke, in one Christ we believe, one Gospel we hear, one Psalm we sing, one Amen we respond, one Hallelujah we sound, one Easter we celebrate: why art thou without and I am within? Ofttimes one straitened, and perceiving how true are the charges which are made, saith, May God requite our ancestors! Therefore alive he perisheth. In the next place thou continuest and thus givest warning. At least let the evil of separation stand alone, why dost thou adjoin thereto that of rebaptism? Acknowledge in me what thou hast; and if thou hatest me, spare thou Christ in me. And this evil thing doth frequently and very greatly displease them. ... Because they themselves have the Scriptures in their hands, and know well by daily reading how the Church Catholic through the whole world is so spread, that in a word all contradiction is void; and that there cannot be found any support for their schism they know well: therefore unto the lower places living they go down, because the evil which they do, they

know evil to be. But the former a fire of divine indignation consumed. For being inflamed with desire of strife, from their evil leaders they would not depart. There came upon fire a fire, upon the heat of dissension the heat of consuming. "For naughtiness is in their lodgings, in the midst of them." "In their lodgings," wherein they tarry and pass away. For here they are not alway to be: and nevertheless in defence of a temporal animosity they are fighting so fiercely. "In their lodgings is iniquity; in the midst of them is iniquity:" no part of them is so near the middle of them as their heart.

16. "Therefore to the Lord I have cried out" (ver. 16). The Body of Christ and the oneness of Christ in anguish, in weariness, in uneasiness, in the tribulation of its exercise, that One Man, Oneness in One Body set, when He was wearying His soul in crying out from the ends of the earth; saith, "From the ends of the earth to Thee I have cried out, when My heart was being vexed." Himself one, but a oneness s that One! and Himself one, not in one place one, but from the ends of the earth is crying as one. How from the ends of the earth should there cry one, except in many there were one? "I to the Lord have cried out." Rightly do thou cry out to the Lord, cry not to Donatus: lest for thee he be instead of the Lord a lord, that under the Lord would not be a fellow-servant.

17. "In evening, in morning, at noon-day I will recount and will tell forth, and He shall hearken to my voice" 6 (ver. 18). Do thou proclaim glad tidings, keep not secret that which thou hast received, "in evening" of things gone by, "in morning" of things to be, at "noonday" of things ever to be. Therefore, to that which he saith "in evening" belongeth that which he recounteth: to that which he saith, "in morning," belongeth that which he telleth forth: to that which he saith "at noon-day," belongeth that wherein his voice is hearkened to. For the end is at noon-day; that is to say, whence there is no going down unto setting. For at noon-day there is light full high, the splendour of wisdom, the fervour of love. "In evening and in morning and at noon-day." "In evening," the Lord on the Cross; "in morning," in Resurrection; "at noon-day," in Ascension. I will recount in evening the patience of Him dying, I will tell forth in morning the life of Him rising, I will pray that He hearken at noon-day sitting at the right hand of the Father. He shall hearken to my voice, That intercedeth for us. How great is the security of this man. How great the consolation, how great the refuge "from weakness of mind and tempest," against evil men, against ungodly men both without and within, and in the case of those that are without though they had been within.

18. Therefore, my Brethren, those that in the very congregation of these walls ye see to be rebellious men, proud, seeking their own, lifted up; not having a zeal for

God that is chaste, sound, quiet, but ascribing to themselves much; ready for dissension, but not finding opportunity; are the very chaff of the Lord's floor. From hence these few men the wind of pride hath dislodged: the whole floor will not fly, save when He at the last shall winnow. But what shall we do, save with this man sing, with this man pray, with this man mourn and say securely, "He shall redeem in peace my soul" (ver. 18). Against them that love not peace: "in peace He shall redeem my soul." "Because with those that hated peace I was peace-making." "He shall redeem in peace my soul, from those that draw near to me." For from those that are afar from me, it is an easy case: not so soon doth he deceive me that saith, Come, pray to an idol: he is very far from me. Art thou a Christian? A Christian, he saith. Out of a neighbouring place he is my adversary, he is at hand. "He shall redeem in peace my soul, from those that draw near to me: for in many things they were with me." Wherefore have I said, "draw near to me"? Because "in many things they were with me." In this verse two propositions occur. "In many things they were with me." Baptism we had both of us, in that they were with me: the Gospel we both read, they were in that with me: the festivals of martyrs we celebrated, they were there with me: Easter's solemnity we attended, they were there with me. But not entirely with me: in schism not with me, in heresy not with me. In many things with me, in few things not with me. But in these few things wherein not with me, there is no profit to them of the many things wherein they were with me. For see, brethren, how many things hath recounted the Apostle Paul: one thing, he hath said, if it shall have been wanting, in vain are those things. "If with the tongues of men and of angels I shall speak," he saith, "if I have all prophecy, and all faith, and all knowledge; if mountains I shall remove, if I shall bestow all my goods upon the poor, if I shall deliver my body even so that it be burned. How many things he hath enumerated! To all these many things let there be wanting one thing, charity; the former in number are more, the latter in weight is greater. Therefore in all Sacraments they are with me, in one charity not with me: "In many things they were with me." Again, by a different expression: "For in many things they were with me." They that themselves have separated from me, with me they were, not in few things, but in many things. For throughout the whole world few are the grains, many are the chaffs. Therefore he saith what? In chaff with me they were, in wheat with me they were not. And the chaff is nearly related to the wheat, from one seed it goeth forth, in one field is rooted, with one rain is nourished, the same reaper it suffereth, the same threshing sustaineth, the same winnowing awaiteth, but not into one barn entereth.

19. "God will hear me, and He shall humble them That is before ages" (ver. 19). For they rely on some leader or other of theirs that hath begun but yesterday. "He shall humble them That is before ages." For even if with reference to time Christ is of Mary the Virgin, nevertheless before ages: "In the beginning He is the Word

and the Word with God, and the Word God." "He shall humble them That is before ages. For to them is no changing:" of them I "speak to whom is no changing." He knew of some to persevere, and in the perseverance of their own wickedness to die. For we see them, and to them is no changing: they that die in that same perverseness, in that same schism, to them is no changing. God shall humble them, shall humble them in damnation, because they are exalted in dissension. To them is no changing, because they are not changed for the better, but for the worse: neither while they are here, nor in the resurrection. For all we shall rise again, but not all shall be changed. Wherefore? Because "'To them is no changing: and they have not feared God." ...

20. "He stretcheth forth His hand in requiting" (ver. 20). "They have polluted His Testament." Read the testament which they have polluted: "In thy seed shall be blessed all nations." Thou against these words of the Testator sayest what? The Africa of holy Donatus hath alone deserved this grace, in him hath remained the Church of Christ. Say at least the Church of Donatus. Wherefore addest thou, of Christ? Of whom it is said, "In thy seed shall be blessed all nations." After Donatus wilt thou go? Set aside Christ, and then secede. See therefore what followeth: "They have polluted His Testament." What Testament? To Abraham have been spoken the promises, and to his seed. The Apostle saith, "Nevertheless, a man's testament confirmed no one maketh void, or super-addeth to: to Abraham have been spoken the promises, and to his seed. He saith not, And to seeds, as if in many; but as if in one, And to thy Seed, which is Christ." In this Christ, therefore, what Testament hath been promised? "In thy seed shall be blessed all nations." Thou that hast given up the unity of all nations, and in a part hast remained, hast polluted His Testament. ...

21. "And His heart hath drawn near" (ver. 22). Of whom do we understand it, except of Him, by the anger of whom they have been divided? How "hath his heart drawn near"? In such sort, that we may understand His will. For by Keretics hath been vindicated the Catholic Church, and by those that think evil have been proved those that think well. For many things lay hid in the Scriptures: and when heretics had been cut off, with questions they troubled the Church of God: then those things were opened which lay hid, and the will of God was understood. Thence is said in another Psalm, "In order that they might be excluded that have been proved with silver." For let them be excluded, He hath said, let them come forth, let them appear. Whence even in silver-working men are called "excluders," that is, pressers out of form from the sort of confusion of the lump. Therefore many men that could understand and expound the Scriptures very excellently, were hidden among the people of God: but they did not declare the solution of

difficult questions, when no reviler again urged them. For was the Trinity perfectly treated of before the Arians snarled thereat? Was repentance perfectly treated of before the Novatians opposed? So not perfectly of Baptism was it treated, before rebaptizers removed outside contradicted; nor of the very oneness of Christ were the doctrines clearly stated which have been stated, save after that this separation began to press upon the weak: in order that they that knew how to treat of and solve these questions (lest the weak should perish vexed with the questions of the ungodly), by their discourses and disputations should bring out unto open day the dark things of the Law. ... This obscure sense see in what manner the Apostle bringeth out into light; "It is needful," he saith, "that also heresies there be, in order that men proved may be made manifest among you." What is "men proved"? Proved with silver, proved with the word. What is "may be made manifest"? May be brought out. Wherefore this? Because of heretics. So therefore these also "have been divided because of the anger of His countenance, and His heart hath drawn near."

22. "His discourses have been softened above oil, and themselves are darts" (ver. 21). For certain things in the Scriptures were seeming hard, while they were obscure; when explained, they have been softened. For even the first heresy in the disciples of Christ, as it were from the hardness of His discourse arose. For when He said, "Except a man shall have eaten My flesh and shall have drunk My blood, he shall not have life in himself:" they, not understanding, said to one another, "Hard is this discourse, who can hear it?" Saying that, "Hard is this discourse," they separated from Him: He remained with the others, the twelve. When they had intimated to Him, that by His discourse they had been scandalized, "Will ye also," He saith, "choose to go?" Then Peter: "Thou hast the Word of life eternal: to whom shall we go?" Attend, we beseech you, and ye little ones learn godliness. Did Peter by any means at that time understand the secret of that discourse of the Lord? Not yet he understood: but that good were the words which he understood not, godly he believed. Therefore if hard is a discourse, and not yet is understood, be it hard to an ungodly man, but to thee be it by godliness softened: for whenever it is solved, it both will become for thee oil, and even unto the bones it will penetrate.

23. Furthermore, just as Peter, after their having been scandalized by the hardness, as they thought, of the discourse of the Lord, even then said, "to whom shall we go?" so he hath added, "Cast upon the Lord thy care, and He shall Himself nourish thee up" (ver. 22). A little one thou art, not yet thou understandest the secret things of words: perchance from thee the bread is hidden, and as yet with milk thou must be fed: be not angry with the breasts: they will make thee fit for the table, for

which now little fitted thou art. Behold by the division of heretics many hard things have been softened: His discourses that were hard have been softened above oil, and they are themselves darts. They have armed men preaching the Gospel: and the very discourses are aimed at the breast of every one that heareth, by men instant in season and out of season: by those discourses, by those words, as though by arrows, hearts of men unto the love of peace are smitten. Hard they were, and soft they have been made. Being softened they have not lost their virtue, but into darts have been converted. ... Upon the Lord cast thyself. Behold thou wilt cast thyself upon the Lord, let no one put himself in the place of the Lord. "Cast upon the Lord thy care." ...

24. But to the others what? "But Thou, O God, shall bring them down unto the pit of corruption" (ver. 23). The pit of corruption is the darkness of sinking under. When blind leadeth blind, they both fall into a ditch. God bringeth them down into the pit of corruption, not because He is the author of their own guilt, but because He is Himself the judge of their iniquities. "For God hath delivered them unto the desires of their heart." For they have loved darkness, and not light; they have loved blindness, and not seeing. For behold the Lord Jesus hath shone out to the whole world, let them sing in unity with the whole world: "For there is not one that can hide himself from the heat of Him." But they passing over from the whole to a part, from the body to a wound, from life to a limb cut off, shall meet with what, but going into the pit of corruption?

25. "Men of bloods and of deceitfulness." Men of bloods, because of slayings he calleth them: and O that they were corporal and not spiritual slayings. For blood from the flesh going forth, is seen and shuddered at: who seeth the blood of the heart in a man rebaptized? Those deaths require other eyes. Although even about these visible deaths Circumcelliones armed everywhere remain not quiet. And if we think of these visible deaths, there are men of bloods. Give heed to the armed man, whether he is a man of peace and not of blood. If at least a club only he were to carry, well; but he carrieth a sling, carrieth an axe, carrieth stones, carrieth lances; and carrying these weapons, wherever they may they scour, for the blood of innocent men they thirst. Therefore even with regard to these visible deaths there are men of bloods. But even of them let us say, O that such deaths alone they perpetrated, and souls they slew not. These that are men of bloods and of deceit, let them not suppose that we thus wrongly understand men of bloods, of them that kill souls: they themselves of their Maximianists have so understood it. For when they condemned them, in the very sentence of their Council they have set down these words: "Swift are the feet of them to shed the blood" (of the proclaimers), "tribulation and calamity are in the ways of them, and the way of peace they have

not known." This of the Maximianists they have said. But I ask of them, when have the Maximianists shed the body's blood; not because they too would not shed, if there were so great a multitude as could shed, but because of the fear in their minority rather they have suffered somewhat from others, than have themselves at any time done any such thing. Therefore I question the Donatist and say: In thy Council thou hast set down of the Maximianists, "Swift are the feet of them to shed blood." Show me one of whom the Maximianists have hurt so much as a finger! What other thing to me is he to answer, than that which I say? They that have separated themselves from unity, and who slay souls by leading astray, spiritually, not carnally, do shed blood. Very well thou hast expounded, but in thy exposition acknowledge their own deeds. "Men of bloods and of deceitfulness." In guile is deceitfulness, in dissimulation, in seduction. What therefore of those very men that have been divided because of the anger of His countenance? They are themselves men of bloods and of deceit.

26. But of them he saith what? "They shall not halve their days." What is, "They shall not halve their days"? They shall not make progress as much as they think: within the time which they expect, they shall perish. For he is that partridge, whereof hath been said, "In the half of his days they shall leave him, and in his last days he shall be an unwise one." They make progress, but for a time. For what saith the Apostle? "But evil men and seducers shall make progress for the worse, themselves erring, and other men into error driving." But "a blind man leading a blind man, together into a ditch they fall." Deservedly they fall "into the pit of corruption." What therefore saith he? They shall make progress for the worse: not however for long. For a little before he hath said, "But further they shall not make progress:" that is, "shall not halve their days." Let the Apostle proceed and tell wherefore: "For the madness of them shall be manifest to all men, as also was that of the others." "But I in Thee will hope, O Lord." But deservedly they shall not halve their days, because in man they have hoped. But I from days temporal have reached unto day eternal. Wherefore? Because in Thee I have hoped, O Lord.

PSALM LVI.

1. Just as when we are going to enter into any house, we look on the title to see whose it is and to whom it belongeth, lest perchance inopportunely we burst into a place whereunto we ought not; and again, in order that we may not through timidity withdraw from that which we ought to enter: as if in a word we were to read, These estates belong to such an one or to such an one: so on the lintel of this Psalm we have inscribed, "At the end, for the people that from holy men were put afar off, to David himself, at the inscription of the Title, when the Allophyli held him in Gath." Let us therefore take knowledge of the people that from holy men were put afar off at the inscription of the Title. For this doth belong to that David whom now ye know how to understand spiritually. For there is here commended to our notice no other than He of whom hath been said, "The end of the Law is Christ for righteousness to every man believing." Therefore when thou hearest "at the end," unto Christ give heed, lest tarrying in the way thou arrive not at the end.
...

2. Who are then the people that from holy men were put afar off at the inscription of the Title? Let the Title itself declare to us that people. For there was written a certain title at the Passion of the Lord, when the Lord was crucified: there was in that place a Title inscribed in Hebrew, in Greek, and in Latin, "The King of the Jews;" in three tongues as though by three witnesses the Title was confirmed: because "in the mouth of two or three witnesses shall stand every word."...

3. What therefore meaneth that which to the title itself still belongeth, namely, that "the Allophyli held him in Geth"? Geth was a certain city of the Allophyli, that is, of strangers, to wit, of people afar from holy men. All they that refuse Christ for King become strangers. Wherefore strangers are they made? Because even that vine, though by Him planted, when it had become sour what heard it? "Wherefore hast thou been turned into sourness, O alien vine?" It hath not been said, My vine: because if Mine, sweet; if sour, not Mine; if not Mine, surely alien. "There held him," then, "Allophyli in Geth." We find indeed, brethren, David himself, son of Jesse, king of Israel, to have been in a strange land among the Allophyli, when he was sought by Saul, and was in that city and with the king of that city, but that there he was detained we read not. Therefore our David, the Lord Jesus Christ out of the seed of that David, not alone they held, but there hold Him still Allophyli in Geth. Of Geth we have said that it is a city. But the interpretation of this name, if asked for, signifieth "press." ... How therefore here is He held in Geth? Held in a winepress is His Body, that is, His Church. What is, in a winepress? In pressings. But in a winepress fruitful is the pressing. A grape on the vine sustaineth no

pressing, whole it seemeth, but nothing thence floweth: it is thrown into a winepress, is trodden, is pressed; harm seemeth to be done to the grape, but this harm is not barren; nay, if no harm had been applied, barren it would have remained.

4. Let whatsoever holy men therefore that are suffering pressing from those that have been put afar off from the saints, give heed to this Psalm, let them perceive here themselves, let them speak what here is spoken, that suffer what here is spoken of. ... Private enmities therefore let no one think of, when about to hear the words of this Psalm: "Know ye that for us the wrestling is not against flesh and blood, but against princes and powers, and spiritual things of wickedness," that is, against the devil and his angels; because even when we suffer men that annoy us, he is instigating, he is inflaming, as it were his vessels he is moving. Let us give heed therefore to two enemies, him whom we see, and him whom we see not; man we see, the devil we see not; man let us love, of the devil beware; for man pray, against the devil pray, and let us say to God, "Have pity on me, O Lord, for man hath trodden me down" (ver. 1). Fear not because man hath trodden thee clown: have thou wine, a grape thou hast become in order that thou shouldest be trodden. "All day long warring he hath troubled me," every one that hath been put afar off from the saints. But why should not here be understood even the devil himself? Is it because mention is made of "man"? doth therefore the Gospel err, because it hath said, "A man that is an enemy hath done this"? But by a kind of figure may he also be called a man, and yet not be a man. Whether therefore it was him whom he that said these words was beholding, or whether it was the people and each one that was put afar off from holy men, through which kind the devil troubleth the people of God, who cleave to holy men, who cleave to the Holy One, who cleave to the King, at the title of which King being indignant they were as though beaten back, and put afar off: let him say, "Have pity on me, O Lord, for man hath trodden me down:" and let him faint not in this treading down, knowing Him on whom he is calling, and by whose example he hath been made strong. The first cluster in the winefat pressed is Christ. When that cluster by passion was pressed Out, there flowed that whence "the cup inebriating is how passing beautiful!" Let His Body likewise say, looking upon its Head, "Have pity on me, O Lord, for man hath trodden me down: all day long warring he hath troubled me." "All day long," at all times. Let no one say to himself, There have been troubles in our fathers' time, in our time there are not. If thou supposest thyself not to have troubles, not yet hast thou begun to be a Christian. And where is the voice of the Apostle, "But even all that will live godly in Christ, persecutions shall suffer." If therefore thou sufferest not any persecution for Christ, take heed lest not yet thou hast begun godly to live in Christ. But when thou hast begun godly to live in Christ, thou hast

entered into the winepress; make ready thyself for pressings: but be not thou dry, lest from the pressing nothing go forth.

5. "Mine enemies have trodden me down all day long" (ver. 2). They that have been put afar off from holy men, these are mine enemies. All day long: already it hath been said, "From the height of the day." What meaneth, "from the height of the day"? Perchance it is a high thing to understand. And no wonder, because the height of the day it is. For perchance they for this reason have been put afar off from holy men, because they were not able to penetrate the height of the day, whereof the Apostles are twelve shining hours. Therefore they that crucified Him, as if man, in the day have erred. But why have they suffered darkness, so that they should be put afar off from holy men? Because on high the day was shining, Him in the height hidden they knew not. "For if they had known, never the Lord of Glory would they have crucified." ...

6. "For many men that war against me, shall fear" (ver. 3). Shall fear when? When the day shall have passed away, wherein they are high. For for a time high they are, when the time of their height is finished they will fear. "But I in Thee will hope, O Lord." He saith not, "But I will not fear:" but, "Many men, that war against me, shall fear." When there shall have come that day of Judgment, then "shall mourn for themselves all the tribes of the earth." When there shall have appeared the sign of the Son of Man in heaven, then secure shall be all holy men. For that thing shall come which they hoped for, which they longed for, the coming whereof they prayed for: but to those men no place for repentance shall remain, because in that time wherein fruitful might have been repentance, their heart they hardened against a warning Lord. Shall they too raise up a wall against a judging God? The godliness of this man do thou indeed acknowledge, and if in that Body thou art, imitate him. When he had said, "Many men, that war against me, shall fear:" he did not continue, "But I will not fear;" lest to his own powers ascribing his not fearing, he too should be amid high temporal things, and through pride temporal he should not deserve to come to rest everlasting: rather he hath made thee to perceive whence he shall not fear. "But I," he saith, "in thee will hope, O Lord:" he hath not spoken of his confidence: but of the cause of his confidence. For if I shall not fear, I may also by hardness of heart not fear, for many men by too much pride fear nothing. ...

7. "In God I will praise my discourses, in God I have hoped: I will not fear what flesh doeth to me" (ver. 4). Wherefore? Because in God I will praise my discourses. If in thyself thou praisest thy discourses: I say not that thou art not to fear; it is impossible that thou have not to fear. For thy discourses either false thou

wilt have, and therefore thine own, because false: or if thy discourses shall be true, and thou shalt deem thyself not to have them from God but of thyself to speak; true they will be, but thou wilt be false: but if thou shalt have known that thou canst say nothing true in the wisdom of God, in the faith of the Truth, save that which From Him thou hast received, of whom is said, "For what hast thou which thou hast not received?" Then in God thou art praising thy discourses, in order that in God thou mayest be praised by the discourses of God. ... "In God I have hoped, I will not fear what flesh doeth to me." Wast thou not the same that a little before wast saying, "Have pity on me, O Lord, for man hath trodden me down; all day long warring he hath troubled me"? How therefore here, "I will not fear what flesh doeth to me"? What shall he do to thee? Thou thyself a little before hast said, "Hath trodden me down, hath troubled me." Nothing shall he do, when these things he shall do? He hath had regard to the wine which floweth from treading, and hath made answer, Evidently he hath trodden down, evidently hath troubled; but what to me shall he do? A grape I was, wine I shall be: "In God I have hoped, I will not fear what flesh doeth to me."

8. "All day long my words they abhorred" (ver. 5). Thus they are, ye know. Speak truth, preach truth, proclaim Christ to the heathen, proclaim the Church to heretics, proclaim to all men salvation: they contradict, they abhor my words. But when my words they abhor, whom think ye they abhor, save Him in whom I shall praise my discourses? "All day long my words they abhorred." Let this at least suffice, let them abhor words, no farther let them proceed, censure, reject! Be it far from them! Why should I say this? When words they reject, when words they hate, those words which from the fount of truth flow forth, what would they do to him through whom the very words are spoken? what but that which followeth, "Against me all the counsels of them are for evil?" If the bread itself they hate, how spare they the basket wherein it is ministered? "Against me all the counsels of them are for evil." If so even against the Lord Himself, let not the Body disdain that which hath gone before in the Head, to the end that the Body may cleave to the Head. Despised hath been thy Lord, and wilt thou have thyself be honoured by those men that have been put afar off from holy men? Do not for thyself wish to claim that which in Him hath not gone before. "The disciple is not greater than his Master; the servant is not greater than his Lord. If the Master of the family they have called Beelzebub, how much more them of His household?" Against me all the counsels of them are for evil."

9. "They shall sojourn, and shall hide" (ver. 6). To sojourn is to be in a strange land. Sojourners is a term used of those then that live in a country not their own. Every man in this life is a foreigner: in which life ye see that with flesh we are

covered round, through which flesh the heart cannot be seen. Therefore the Apostle saith, "Do not before the time judge anything, until the Lord come, and He shall enlighten the hidden things of darkness, and shall manifest the thoughts of the heart; and then praise shall be to each one from God." Before that this be done, in this sojourning of fleshly life every one carrieth his own heart, and every heart to every other heart is shut. Furthermore, those men of whom the counsels are against this man for evil, "shall sojourn, and shall hide:" because in this foreign abode they are, and carry flesh, they hide guile in heart; whatsoever of evil they think, they hide. Wherefore? Because as yet this life is a foreign one. Let them hide; that shall appear which they hide, and they too will not be hidden. There is also in this hidden thing another interpretation, which perchance will be more approved of. For out of those men that have been put afar off from holy men, there creep in certain false brethren, and they cause worse tribulations to the Body of Christ; because they are not altogether avoided as if entirely aliens. ... Not even those men nevertheless let us fear, brethren: "I will not fear what flesh doeth to me." Even if they sojourn, even if they go in, even if they feign, even if they hide, flesh they are: do thou in the Lord hope, nothing to thee shall flesh do. But he bringeth in tribulation, bringeth in treading down. There is added wine, because the grape is pressed: thy tribulation will not be unfruitful: another seeth thee, imitateth thee: because thou also in order that thou mightest learn to bear such a man, to thy Head hast looked up, that first cluster, unto whom there hath come in a man that he might see, hath sojourned, and hath hidden, to wit, the traitor Judas. All men, therefore, that with false heart go in, sojourning and hiding, do not thou fear: the father of these same men, Judas, with thy Lord hath been: and He indeed knew him; although Judas the traitor was sojourning and hiding, nevertheless, the heart of him was open to the Lord of all: knowingly He chose one man, whereby He might give comfort to thee that wouldest not know whom thou shouldest avoid. For He might have not chosen Judas, because He knew Judas: for He saith to His disciples, "Have not I chosen you twelve, and one out of you is a devil?" Therefore even a devil was chosen. Or if chosen he was not, how is it that He hath chosen twelve, and not rather eleven? Chosen even he is, but for another purpose. Chosen were eleven for the work of probation, chosen one for the work of temptation. Whence could He give an example to thee, that wouldest not know what men thou shouldest avoid as evil, of what men thou shouldest beware as false and artificial, sojourning and hiding, except He say to thee, Behold, with Myself I have had one of those very men! There hath gone before an example, I have borne, to suffer I have willed that which I knew, in order that to thee knowing not I might give consolation. That which to Me he hath done, the same he will do to thee also: in order that he may be able to do much, in order that he may make much havoc, he will accuse, false charges he will allege. ...

10. "These same men shall mark my heel." For they shall sojourn and hide in such sort, that they may mark where a man slippeth. Intent they are upon the heel, to see when a slip may chance to be made; in order that they may detain the foot for a fall, or trip up the foot for a stumble; certes that they may find that which they may accuse. And what man so walketh, that nowhere he slippeth? For example, how speedily is a slip made even in tongue? For it is written, "Whosoever in tongue stumbleth not, the same is a perfect man." What man I pray would dare himself to call or deem perfect? Therefore it must needs be that every one slip in tongue. But let them that shall sojourn and shall hide, carp at all words, seeking somewhere to make snares and knotty false accusations, wherein they are themselves entangled before those whom they strive to entangle: in order that they may themselves be taken and perish before that they catch other men in order to destroy them. ... Whatever good thing I have said, whatever true thing I have said, of God I have said it, and from God have said it: whatever other thing perchance I have said, which to have said I ought not, as a man I have said, but under God I have said. He that strengtheneth one walking, doth menace one straying, forgive one acknowledging, recalleth the tongue, recalleth him that slipped. ... Attend thou unto the discourses of him whom thou blamest, whether perchance he may teach thee something to thy health. And what, he saith, shall he be able to teach to my health, that hath so slipped in word? This very thing perchance he is teaching thee to thy health, that thou be not a carper at words, but a gatherer of precepts. "As my soul hath undergone." I speak of that which I have undergone. He was speaking as one experienced: "As my soul hath undergone. They shall sojourn and hide." Let my soul undergo all men, men without barking, men within hiding, let it undergo. From without coming, like a river cometh temptation: on the Rock let it find thee, let it strike against, not throw thee down; the house hath been founded upon a Rock. Within he is, he shall sojourn and hide: suppose chaff is near thee, let there come in the treading of oxen, let there come in the roller of temptations; thou art cleansed, the other is crushed.

11. "For nothing Thou shalt save them" (ver. 7). He hath taught us even for these very men to pray. However "they shall sojourn and hide," however deceitful they be, however dissemblers and liers in wait they be; do thou pray for them, and do not say, Shall God amend even such a man, so evil, so perverse? Do not despair: give heed to Him whom thou askest, not him for whom thou askest. The greatness of the disease seest thou, the might of the Physician seest thou not? "They shall sojourn and hide: as my soul hath undergone." Undergo, pray: and there is done what? "For nothing Thou shalt save them." Thou shalt make them safe so as that nothing to Thee it may be, that is, so that no labour to Thee it may be. With men they are despaired of, but Thou with a word dost heal; Thou wilt not toil in healing, though we are astounded in looking on. There is another sense in this

verse, "For nothing Thou shalt save them:" with not any merits of their going before Thou shall save them. ... They shall not bring to Thee he-goats, rams, bulls, not gifts and spices shall they bring Thee in Thy temple, not anything of the drink-offering of a good conscience do they pour thereon; all in them is rough, all foul, all to be detested: and though they to Thee bring nothing whereby they may be saved; "For nothing Thou shall save them," that is, with the free gift of Thy Grace. ...

12. "In anger the peoples Thou shall bring down." Thou art angry and dost bring down, dost rage and save, dost terrify and call. Thou fillest with tribulations all things, in order that being set in tribulations men may fly to Thee, lest by pleasures and a wrong security they be seduced. From Thee anger is seen, but that of a father. A father is angry with a son, the despiser of his injunctions: being angry with him he boxeth him, striketh, pulleth the ear, draggeth with hand, leadeth to school. How many men have entered, how many men have filled the House of the Lord, in the anger of Him brought down, that is, by tribulations terrified and with faith filled? For to this end tribulation stirreth up; in order to empty the vessel which is full of wickedness, so as that it may be filled with grace.

13. "O God, my life I have told out to Thee" (ver. 8). For that I live hath been Thy doing, and for this reason I tell out my life to Thee. But did not God know that which He had given? What is that which thou tellest out to Him? Wilt thou teach God? Far be it. Therefore why saith he, "I have told out to Thee"? Is it perchance because it profiteth Thee that I have told out my life? And what doth it profit God? To the advantage of God it doth profit. I have told out to God my life, because that life hath been God's doing. In like manner as his life Paul the Apostle did tell out, saying, "I that before was a blasphemer and a persecutor and injurious," he shall tell out his life. "But mercy I have obtained." He hath told out his life, not for himself, but for Him: because he hath told it out in such sort, that in Him men believe, not for his own advantages, but for the advantages of Him. ... "O God, my life I have told out to Thee. Thou hast put my tears in Thy sight." Thou hast hearkened to me imploring Thee. "As also in Thy promise." Because as Thou hadst promised this thing, so Thou hast done. Thou hast said Thou wouldest hearken to one weeping. I have believed, I have wept, I have been hearkened unto; I have found Thee merciful in prommising, true in repaying.

14. "Turned be mine enemies backward" (ver. 9). This thing to these very men is profitable, no ill to these men he is wishing. For to go before they are willing, therefore to be amended they are not willing. Thou warnest thine enemy to live well, that he amend himself: he scorneth, he rejecteth thy word: "Behold him that

adviseth me; behold him from whom I am to hear the commandments whereby I shall live!" To go before thee he willeth, and in going before is not amended. He mindeth not that thy words are not thine, he mindeth not that thy life to God thou tellest out, not to thyself. In going before therefore he is not amended: it is a good thing for him that he be turned backward, and follow him whom to go before he willed. The Lord to His disciples was speaking of His Passion that was to be. Peter shuddered, and saith," Far be it, O Lord;" he that a little before had said, "Thou art the Christ, Son of the living God," having confessed God, feared for Him to die, as if but a man. But the Lord who so came that He might suffer (for we could not otherwise be saved unless with His blood we were redeemed), a little before had praised the confession of Peter. ... But immediately when the Lord beginneth to speak of His Passion, he feared lest He should perish by death, whereas we ourselves should perish unless He died; and he saith, "Far be it, O Lord, this thing shall not be done." And the Lord, to him to whom a little before He had said, "Blessed thou art, and upon this Rock I will build my Church," saith, "Go back behind, Satan, an offence thou art to Me." Why therefore "Satan" is he, that a little before was "blessed," and a "Rock"? "For thou savourest not the things which are of God," He saith, "but those things which are of man. A little before he savoured the things which are of God: because "not flesh and blood hath revealed to thee, but My Father which is in the Heavens." When in God he was praising his discourse, not Satan but Peter, from petra: but when of himself and out of human infirmity, carnal love of man, which would be for an impediment to his own salvation, and that of the rest, Satan he is called. Why? Because to go before the Lord he willed, and earthly counsel to give to the heavenly Leader. "Far be it, O Lord, this thing shall not be done." Thou sayest, "Far be it," and thou sayest, "O Lord:" surely if Lord He is, in power He doeth: if Master He is, He knoweth what He doeth, He knoweth what He teacheth. But thou wiliest to lead thy Leader, teach thy Master, command thy Lord, choose for God: much thou goest before, go back behind. Did not this too profit these enemies? "Turned be Mine enemies backward;" but let them not remain backward. For this reason let them be turned backward, lest they go before; but so that they follow, not so that they remain.

15. "In whatsoever day I shall have called upon Thee, behold I have known that my God art Thou" (ver. 9). A great knowledge. He saith not, "I have known that God Thou art:" but, "that my God art Thou." For thine He is, when thee He succoureth: thine He is, when thou to Him art not an alien. Whence is said, "Blessed the people of whom is the Lord the God of the same." Wherefore "of whom is"? For of whom is He not? Of all things indeed God He is: but of those men the God peculiarly He is said to be, that love Him, that hold Him, that possess Him, that worship Him, as though belonging to His own House: the great family of Him are they, redeemed by the great blood of the Only Son. How great a thing

hath God given to us, that His own we should be, and He should be ours! But in truth foreigners afar have been put from holy men, sons alien they are. See what of them is said in another Psalm: "0 Lord, deliver me," he saith, "from the hand of alien sons, of whom the mouth hath spoken vanity, and the right hand of them is a right hand of iniquity." ...

16. Let us therefore love God, brethren, purely and chastely. There is not a chaste heart, if God for reward it worshippeth. How so? Reward of the worship of God shall not we have? We shall have evidently, but it is God Himself whom we worship. Himself for us a reward shall be, because "we shall see Him as He is." Observe that a reward thou shalt obtain. ... I will tell you, brethren: in these human alliances consider a chaste heart, of what sort it is towards God: certainly human alliances are of such sort, that a man doth not love his wife, that loveth her because of her portion: a woman her husband doth not chastely love, that for these reasons loveth him, because something he hath given, or because much he hath given. Both a rich man is a husband, and one that hath become a poor man is a husband. How many men proscribed, by chaste wives have been the more beloved! Proved have been many chaste marriages by the misfortunes of husbands: that the wives might not be supposed to love any other object more than their husband, not only have they not forsaken, but the more have they obeyed. If therefore a husband of flesh freely is loved, if chastely he is loved; and a wife of flesh freely is loved, if chastely she is loved; in what manner must God be loved, the true and truth-speaking Husband of the soul, making fruitful unto the offspring of everlasting life, and not suffering us to be barren? Him, therefore, so let us love, as that any other thing besides Himself be not loved: and there takes place in us that which we have spoken of, that which we have sung, because even here the voice is ours: "In whatsoever day I shall have called upon Thee, behold, I have known that my God art Thou." This is to call upon God, freely to call upon Him. Furthermore, of certain men hath been said what? "Upon the Lord they have not called." The Lord they seemed as it were to call unto themselves and they besought Him about inheritances, about increasing money, about lengthening this life, about the rest of temporal things: and concerning them the Scripture saith what? "Upon the Lord they have not called." Therefore there followeth what? "There they have feared with fear, where there was no fear." What is, "where there was no fear"? Lest money should be stolen from them, lest anything in their house should be made less; lastly, lest they should have less of years in this life, than they hoped for themselves: but there have they trembled with fear, where there was no fear. ... "In God I will praise the word, in the Lord I will praise the discourse" (ver. 10): "in God I have hoped, I will not fear what man doeth unto me" (ver. 11). Now this is the very sense which above hath been repeated.

17. "In me, O God, are Thy vows, which I will render of praise to Thee" (ver. 12). "Vow ye, and render to the Lord your God." What vow, what render? Perchance those animals which were offered at the altars aforetime? No such thing offer thou: in thyself is what thou mayest vow and render. From the heart's coffer bring forth the incense of praise; from the store of a good conscience bring forth the sacrifice of faith. Whatsoever thing thou bringest forth, kindle with love. In thyself be the vows, which thou mayest render of praise to God. Of what praise? For what hath He granted thee? "For Thou hast rescued my soul from death" (ver. 13). This is that very life which he telleth out to Him: "O God, my life I have told out to Thee." For I was what? Dead. Through myself I was dead: through Thee I am what? Alive. Therefore "in me, O God, are Thy vows, which I will render of praise to Thee." Behold I love my God: no one doth tear Him from me: that which to Him I may give, no one doth tear front me, because in the heart it is shut up. With reason is said with that former confidence, "What should man do unto me?" Let man rage, let him be permitted to rage, be permitted to accomplish that which he attempteth: what is he to take away? Gold, silver, cattle, men servants, maid servants, estates, houses, let him take away all things: doth he by any means take away the vows, which are in me, which I may render of praise to God? The tempter was permitted to tempt a holy man, Job; in one moment he took away all things: whatever of possessions he had had, he carried off: took away inheritance, slew heirs; and this not little by little, but in a crowd, at one blow, at one swoop, so that all things were on a sudden announced: when all was taken away, alone there remained Job, but in him were vows of praise, which he might render to God, in him evidently there were: the coffer of his holy breast the thieving devil had not rifled, full he was of that wherefrom he might sacrifice. Hear what he had, hear what he brought forth: "The Lord hath given, the Lord hath taken away; as hath pleased the Lord, so hath been done: be the name of the Lord blessed." O riches interior, whither thief doth not draw near! God Himself had given that whereof He was receiving; He had Himself enriched him with that whereof to Him he was offering that which He loved. Praise from thee God requireth, thy confession God requireth. But from thy field wilt thou give anything? He hath Himself rained in order that thou mayest have. From thy coffer wilt thou give anything? He hath Himself put in that which thou art to give. What wilt thou give, which from Him thou hast not received? "For what hast thou which thou hast not received?" From the heart wilt thou give? He too hath given faith, hope, and charity: this thou must bring forth: this thou must sacrifice. But evidently all the other things the enemy is able to take away against thy will; this to take away he is not able, unless thou be willing. These things a man will lose even against his will: and wishing to have gold, will lose gold; and wishing to have house, will lose house: faith no one will lose, except him that shall have despised her.

18. "Because Thou hast rescued my soul from death, mine eyes from tears, and my feet from slipping: that I may be pleasing before God in the light of the living" (ver. 13). With reason he is not pleasing to alien sons, that are put afar off from holy men, because they have not the light of the living, whence they may see that which to God is pleasing. "Light of the living," is light of the immortal, light of holy men. He that is not in darkness, is pleasing in the light of the living. A man is observed, and the things which belong to him; no one knoweth of what sort he is: God seeth of what sort he is. Sometimes even the devil himself he escapeth; except he tempt, he findeth not: just as concerning that man of whom just now I have made mention: ... "Doth Job by any means worship God for nought?" For this was true light, this the light of the living, that gratis he should worship God. God saw in the heart of His servant His gratuitous worship. For that heart was pleasing in the sight of the Lord in the light of the living: the devil's sight he escaped, because in darkness he was. God admitted the tempter, not in order that He might Himself know that which He did know, but in order that to us to be known and imitated He might set it forth. Admitted was the tempter; he took away everything, there remained the man bereft of possessions, bereft of family, bereft of children, full of God. A wife certainly was left. Merciful do ye deem the devil, that he left him a wife? He knew through whom he had deceived Adam. ... With wound smitten from head even unto feet, whole nevertheless within, he made answer to the woman tempting, out of the light of the living, out of the light of his heart: "thou hast spoken as though one of the unwise women," that is, as though one that hath not the light of the living. For the light of the living is wisdom, and the darkness of unwise men is folly. Thou hast spoken as though one of the unwise women: my flesh thou seest, the light of my heart thou seest not. For she then might more have loved her husband, if the interior beauty she had known, and had beheld the place where he was beautiful before the eyes of God: because in Him were vows which he might render of praise to God. How entirely the enemy had forborne to invade that patrimony! How whole was that which he was possessing, and that because of which yet more to be possessed he hoped for, being to go on" from virtues unto virtue." Therefore, brethren, to this end let all these things serve us, that God grates we love, in Him hope always, neither man nor devil fear. Neither the one nor the other doeth anything, except when it is permitted: permitted for no other reason can it be, except because it doth profit us. Let us endure evil men, let us be good men: because even we have been evil. Even as nothing God shall save men, of whom we dare to despair. Therefore of no one let us despair, for all men whom we suffer let us pray, from God let us never depart. Our patrimony let Him be, our hope let Him be, our safety let Him be. He is Himself here a comforter, there a remunerator, everywhere Maker-alive, and of life the Giver, not of another life, but of that whereof hath been said, "I am the Way, and the Truth, and the Life:" in order that both here in the light of faith, and there in the light of sight, as it were in the light of the living, in the sight of the Lord we may be pleasing.

PSALM LVII.

1. We have heard in the Gospel just now, brethren, how loveth us our Lord and Saviour Jesus Christ, God with the Father, Man with us, out of our own selves, now at s the right hand of the Father; ye have heard how much He loveth us. ...

2. Because then this Psalm is singing of the Passion of the Lord, see what is the title that it hath: "at the end." The end is Christ? Why hath He been called end? Not as one that consumeth, but one that consummateth. ...

3. "At the end, corrupt not, for David himself, for the inscription of the title; when he fled from the face of Saul into a cavern." We referring to holy Scripture, do find indeed how holy David, that king of Israel, from whom too the Psalter of David hath received the name thereof, had suffered for persecutor Saul the king of his own people, as many of you know that have either read or have heard the Scriptures. King David had then for persecutor Saul: and whereas the one was most gentle, the other most ferocious: the one mild, the other envious; the one patient, the other cruel; the one beneficent, the other ungrateful: he endured him with so much mildness, that when he had gotten him into his hands him he touched not hurt not. ... What reference hath this to Christ? If all things which then were being done, were figures of things future, we find there Christ, and by far in the greatest degree. For this, "corrupt not for the inscription of the title," I see not how it belongeth to that David. For not any "title" was inscribed over David himself which Saul would "corrupt." But we see in the Passion of the Lord that there had been written a title, "King of the Jews:" in order that this title might put to the blush these very men, seeing that from their King they withheld not their hands. For in them Saul was, in Christ David was. For Christ, as saith the Apostolic Gospel, is, as we know, as we confess, of the seed of David after the flesh; for after the Godhead He is above David, above all men, above heaven and earth, above angels, above all things visible and invisible. ... And because already it had been sung through the Holy Spirit, "Unto the end, corrupt not, for the inscription of the title:" Pilate answered them, "What I have written, I have written:" why do ye suggest to me falsehood? I corrupt not truth.

4. What therefore is, "When he fled from the face of Saul into a cavern"? Which thing indeed the former David also did: but because in him we find not the inscription of the title, in the latter let us find the flight into the cavern. For that cavern wherein David hid himself did figure somewhat. But wherefore hid he himself? It was in order that he might be concealed and not be found. What is to

be hidden in a cavern? To be hidden in earth. For he that fleeth into a cavern, with earth is covered so that he may not be seen. But Jesus did carry earth, flesh which He had received from earth: and in it He concealed Himself, in order that by Jews He might not be discovered as God. "For if they had known, never the Lord of glory would they have crucified." Why therefore the Lord of glory found they not? Because in a cavern He had hidden Himself, that is, the flesh's weakness to their eyes He presented, but the Majesty of the Godhead in the body's clothing, as though in a hiding-place of the earth, He hid. ... But wherefore even unto death willed He to be patient? It was in order that He might flee from the face of Saul into a cavern. For a cavern may be understood as a lower part of the earth. And certainly, as is manifest and certain to all, His Body in a Tomb was laid, which was cut in a Rock. This Tomb therefore was the Cavern; thither He fled from the face of Saul. For so long the Jews did persecute Him, even until He was laid in a cavern. Whence prove we that so long they persecuted Him, until therein He was laid? Even when dead, and, on the Cross hanging, with lance they wounded Him. But when shrouded, the funeral celebrated, He was laid in a cavern, no longer had they anything which to the Flesh they might do. Rose therefore the Lord again out of that cavern unhurt, uncorrupt, from that place whither He had fled from the face of Saul: concealing Himself from ungodly men, whom Saul prefigured, but showing Himself to His members. For the members of Him rising again by His members were handled: for the members of Him, the Apostles, touched Him rising again and believed; and behold nothing profited the persecution of Saul. Hear we therefore now the Psalm; because concerning the title thereof enough we have spoken, as far as the Lord hath deigned to give.

5. "Have pity on me, O God, have pity on me, for in Thee hath trusted my Soul" (ver. 1). Christ in the Passion saith, "Have pity on Me, O God." To God, God saith, "Have pity on Me!" He that with the Father hath pity on thee, in thee crieth, "Have pity on Me." For that part of Him which is crying, "Have pity on Me," is thine: from thee this He received, for the sake of thee, that thou shouldest be delivered, with Flesh He was clothed. The flesh itself crieth: "Have pity on Me, O God, have pity on me:" Man himself, soul and flesh. For whole Man did the Word take upon Him, and whole Man the Word became. Let it not therefore be thought that there Soul was not, because the Evangelist thus saith: "The Word was made flesh, and dwelled in us." For man is called flesh, as in another place saith the Scripture, "And all flesh shall see the salvation of God." Shall anywise flesh alone see, and shall Soul not be there? ... Thou hearest the Master praying, learn thou to pray. For to this end He prayed, in order that He might teach how to pray: because to this end He suffered, in order that He might teach how to suffer; to this end He rose again, in order that He might teach how to hope for rising again. "And in the shadow of Thy wings I will hope, until iniquity pass over." This now evidently

whole Christ doth say: here is also our voice. For not yet hath passed over, still rife is iniquity. And in the end our Lord Himself said there should be an abounding of iniquity: "And since iniquity shall abound, the love of many shall wax cold; but he that shall have persevered unto the end, the same shall be saved." But who shall persevere even unto the end, even until iniquity pass over? He that shall have been in the Body of Christ, he that shall have been in the members of Christ, and from the Head shall have learned the patience of persevering. Thou passest away, and behold passed are thy temptations; and thou goest into another life whither have gone holy men, if holy thou hast been. Into another life have gone Martyrs; if Martyr thou shalt have been, thou also goest into another life. Because "thou" hast passed away hence, hath by any means iniquity therefore passed away? There are born other unrighteous men, as there die some unrighteous men. In like manner therefore as some unrighteous men die and others are born: so some just men go, and others are born. Even unto the end of the world neither iniquity will be wanting to oppress, nor righteousness to suffer. ...

6. "I will cry to God most high" (ver. 2). If most high He is, how heareth He thee crying? Confidence hath been engendered by experience: "to God," he saith, "who had done good to me." If before that I was seeking Him, He did good to me, when I cry shall He not hearken to me? For good to us the Lord God hath done in sending to us our Saviour Jesus Christ, that He might die for our offences, and rise again for our justification. For what sort of men hath He willed His Son to die? For ungodly men. But ungodly men were not seeking God, and have been sought of God. For He is Most High in such sort, as that not far from Him is our misery and our groaning: because "near is the Lord to them that have bruised the heart." "God that hath done good to me."

7. "He hath sent from heaven and hath saved me" (ver. 3). Now the Man Himself, now the Flesh Itself, now the Son of God after His partaking of ourselves, of Him it is manifest, how He was saved, and hath sent from heaven the Father and hath saved Him, hath sent from heaven, and hath raised Him again: but in order that ye may know, that also the Lord Himself hath raised again Himself both truths are written in Scripture, both that the Father hath raised Him again, and that Himself Himself hath raised again. Hear ye how the Father hath raised Him again: the Apostle saith, "He hath been made," he saith, "obedient unto death, even the death of the Cross: wherefore God also hath exalted Him, and hath given Him a name which is above every name." Ye have heard of the Father raising again and exalting the Son; hear ye how that He too Himself His flesh hath raised again. Under the figure of a temple He saith to the Jews, "Destroy this Temple, and in three days I will raise it up." But the Evangelist hath explained to us what it was

that He said: "But this," he saith, "He spake of the Temple of His Body." Now therefore out of the person of one praying, out of the person of a man, out of the person of the flesh, He saith, "He hath saved me. He hath given unto reproach those that trampled on me." Them that have trampled on Him, that over Him dead have insulted, that Him as though man have crucified, because God they perceived not, them He hath given unto reproach. See ye whether it has not been so done. The thing we do not believe as yet to come, but fulfilled we acknowledge it. The Jews raged against Christ, they were overbearing against Christ. Where? In the city of Jerusalem. For where they reigned, there they were puffed up, there their necks they lifted up. After the Passion of the Lord thence they were rooted out; and they lost the kingdom, wherein Christ for King they would not acknowledge. In what manner they have been given unto reproach, see ye: dispersed they have been throughout all nations, nowhere having a settlement, nowhere a sure abode. But for this reason still Jews they are, in order that our books they may carry to their confusion. For whenever we wish to show Christ prophesied of, we produce to the heathen these writings. And lest perchance men hard of belief should say that we Christians have composed these books, so that together with the Gospel which we have preached we have forged the Prophet, through whom there might seem to be foretold that which we preach: by this we convince them; namely, that all the very writings wherein Christ hath been prophesied are with the Jews, all these very writings the Jews have. We produce documents from enemies, to confound other enemies. In what sort of reproach therefore are the Jews? A document the Jew carrieth, wherefrom a Christian may believe. Our librarians they have become, just as slaves are wont behind their masters to carry documents, in such sort that these faint in carrying, those profit by reading. Unto such a reproach have been given the Jews: and there hath been fulfilled that which so long before hath been foretold, "He hath given unto reproach those that trampled on me." But how great a reproach it is, brethren, that this verse they should read, and themselves being blind should look upon their mirror! For in the same manner the Jews appear in the holy Scripture which they carry, as appeareth the face of a blind man in a mirror: by other men it is seen, by himself not seen.

8. Thou wast inquiring perhaps when he said, "He hath sent from heaven and hath saved me." What hath He sent from heaven? Whom hath He sent from heaven? An Angel hath He sent, to save Christ, and through a servant is the Lord saved? For all Angels are creatures serving Christ. For obedience there might have been sent Angels, for service they might have been sent, not for succour: as is written, "Angels ministered unto Him," not like men merciful to one indigent, but like subjects to One Omnipotent. What therefore "hath He sent from heaven, and hath saved me"? Now we hear in another verse what from heaven He hath sent. "He hath sent from heaven His mercy and His truth." For what purpose? "And hath

drawn out my soul from the midst of the lions' whelps." "Hath sent," he saith, "from heaven His mercy and His truth:" and Christ Himself saith, "I am Truth." There was sent therefore Truth, that it should draw out my soul hence from the midst of the lions' whelps: there was sent mercy. Christ Himself we find to be both mercy and truth; mercy in suffering with us, and truth in requiting us. ... Who are the lions' whelps? That lesser people, unto evil deceived, unto evil led away by the chiefs of the Jews: so that these are lions, those lions' whelps. All roared, all slew. For we are to hear even here the slaying of these very men, presently in the following verses of this Psalm.

9. "And hath drawn out," he saith, "my soul from the midst of the lions' whelps" (ver. 4). Why sayest thou, "And hath drawn out my soul"? For what hadst thou suffered, that thy soul should be drawn out? "I have slept troubled." Christ hath intimated His death. ...

10. Whence "troubled"? Who troubling? Let us see in what manner he brandeth an evil conscience upon the Jews, wishing to excuse themselves of the slaying of the Lord. For to this end, as the Gospel speaketh, to the judge they delivered Him, that they might not themselves seem to have killed Him. ... Let us question Him, and say, since Thou hast slept troubled, who have persecuted Thee? who have slain Thee? was it perchance Pilate, who to soldiers gave Thee, on the Tree to be hanged, with nails to be pierced? Hear who they were, "Sons of men" (ver. 5). Of them He speaketh, whom for persecutors He suffered. But how did they slay, that steel bare not? They that sword drew not, that made no assault upon Him to slay; whence slew they? "Their teeth are arms and arrows, and their tongue a sharp sword." Do not consider the unarmed hands, but the mouth armed: from thence the sword proceeded, wherewith Christ was to be slain: in like manner also as from the mouth of Christ, that wherewith the Jews were to be slain. For He hath a sword twice whetted: and rising again He hath smitten them, and hath severed from them those whom He would make His faithful people. They an evil sword, He a good sword: they evil arrows, He good arrows. For He hath Himself also arrows good, words good, whence He pierceth the faithful heart, in order that He may be loved. Therefore of one kind are their arrows, and of another kind their sword. "Sons of men, their teeth are arms and arrows, and their tongue a sharp sabre." Tongue of sons of men is a sharp sabre, and their teeth arms and arrows. When therefore did they smite, save when they clamoured, "Crucify, crucify"?

11. And what have they done to Thee, O Lord? Let the Prophet here exult! For above, all those verses the Lord was speaking: a Prophet indeed, but in the person of the Lord, because in the Prophet is the Lord. ... "Be exalted," he saith, "above

the Heavens, O God" Man on the Cross, and above the Heavens, God. Let them continue on the earth raging, Thou in Heaven be judging. Where are they that were raging? where are their teeth, the arms and arrows? Have not "the stripes of them been made the arrows of infants"? For in another place a Psalm this saith, desiring to prove them vainly to have raged, and vainly unto frenzies to have been driven headlong: for nothing they were able to do to Christ when for the time crucified, and afterwards when He was rising again, and in Heaven was sitting. How do infants make to themselves arrows? Of reeds? But what arrows? or what powers? or what bows? or what wound? "Be Thou exalted above the Heavens, O God, and above all the earth Thy glory" (ver. 6). Wherefore exalted above the Heavens, O God? Brethren, God exalted above the Heavens we see not, but we believe: but above all the earth His glory to be not only we believe, but also see. But what kind of madness heretics are afflicted with, I pray you observe. They being cut off from the bond of the Church of Christ, and to a part holding, the whole losing, will not communicate with the whole earth, where is spread abroad the glory of Christ. But we Catholics are in all the earth, because with all the world we communicate, wherever the Glory of Christ is spread abroad. For we see that which then was sung, now fulfilled. There hath been exalted above the Heavens our God, and above all the earth the Glory of the Same. O heretical insanity! That which thou seest not thou believest with me, that which thou seest thou deniest: thou believest with me in Christ exalted above the Heavens, a thing which we see not; and deniest His Glory over all the earth, a thing which we see.

12. ... Let your Love see the Lord speaking to us, and exhorting us by His example: "A trap they have prepared for My feet, and have bowed down My Soul" (ver. 7). They wished to bring It down as if from Heaven, and to the lower places to weigh It down: "They have bowed My Soul: they have digged before My face a pit and themselves have fallen into it." Me have they hurt, or themselves? Behold He hath been exalted above the Heavens, God, and behold above all the earth the Glory of the Same: the kingdom of Christ we see, where is the kingdom of the Jews? Since therefore they did that which to have done they ought not, there hath been done in their case that which to have suffered they ought: themselves have dug a ditch, and themselves have fallen into it. For their persecuting Christ, to Christ did no hurt, but to themselves did hurt. And do not suppose, brethren, that themselves alone hath this befallen. Every one that prepareth a pit for his brother, it must needs be that himself fall into it. ...

13. But the patience of good men with preparation of heart accepteth the will of God: and glorieth in tribulations, saying that which followeth: "Prepared is my heart, O God, I will sing and play" (ver. 8). What hath he done to me? He hath

prepared a pit, my heart is prepared. He hath prepared pit to deceive, shall I not prepare heart to suffer? He hath prepared pit to oppress, shall I not prepare heart to endure? Therefore he shall fall into it, but I will sing and play. Hear the heart prepared in an Apostle, because he hath imitated his Lord: "We glory," he saith, "in tribulations: because tribulation worketh patience: patience probation, probation hope, but hope maketh not ashamed: because the love of God is shed abroad in our hearts through the Holy Spirit, which hath been given to us." He was in oppressions, in chains, in prisons, in stripes, in hunger and thirst, in cold and nakedness, in every wasting of toils and pains, and he was saying, "We glory in tribulations." Whence, but that prepared was his heart? Therefore he was singing and playing.

14. "Rise up, my glory" (ver. 9). He that had fled from the face of Saul into a cavern, saith, "Rise up, my glory:" glorified be Jesus after His Passion. "Rise up, psaltery and harp." He calleth upon what to rise? Two organs I see: but Body of Christ one I see, one flesh hath risen again, and two organs have risen. The one organ then is the psaltery, the other the harp. Organs is the word used for all instruments of musicians. Not only is that called an organ, which is great, and blown into with bellows; but whatsoever is adapted to playing and is corporeal, whereof for an instrument the player maketh use, is said to be an organ. But distinguished froth one another are these organs. ... What therefore do these two organs figure to us? For Christ the Lord our God is waking up His psaltery and His harp; and He saith, "I will rise up at the dawn." I suppose that here ye now perceive the Lord rising. We have read thereof in the Gospel: see the hour of the Resurrection. How long through shadows was Christ being sought? He hath shone, be He acknowledged; "at the dawn" He rose again. But what is psaltery? what is harp? Through His flesh two kinds of deeds the Lord hath wrought, miracles and sufferings: miracles from above have been, sufferings from below have been. But those miracles which He did were divine; but through Body He did them, through flesh He did them. The flesh therefore working things divine, is the psaltery: the flesh suffering things human is the harp. Let the psaltery sound, let the blind be enlightened, let the deaf hear, let the paralytics be braced to strength, the lame walk, the sick rise up, the dead rise again; this is the sound of the Psaltery. Let there sound also the harp, let Him hunger, thirst, sleep, be held, scourged, derided, crucified, buried. When therefore thou seest in that Flesh certain things to have sounded from above, certain things from the lower part, one flesh hath risen again, and in one flesh we acknowledge both psaltery and harp. And these two kinds of things done have fulfilled the Gospel, and it is preached in the nations: for both the miracles and the sufferings of the Lord are preached.

15. Therefore there hath risen psaltery and harp in the dawn, and he confesseth to the Lord; and saith what? "I will confess to Thee among the peoples, O Lord, and will play to Thee among the nations: for magnified even unto the Heavens hath been Thy mercy, and even unto the clouds Thy truth" (ver. 10). Heavens above clouds, and clouds below heavens: and nevertheless to this nearest heaven belong clouds. But sometimes clouds rest upon the mountains, even so far in the nearest air are they rolled. But a Heaven above there is, the habitations of Angels, Thrones, Dominions, Principalities, Powers. This therefore may perchance seem to be what should have been said: "Unto the Heavens Thy truth, and even unto the clouds Thy mercy." For in Heaven Angels praise God, seeing the very form of truth, without any darkness of vision, without any admixture of unreality: they see, love, praise, are not wearied. There is truth: but here in our own misery surely there is mercy. For to a miserable one must be rendered mercy. For there is no need of mercy above, where is no miserable one. I have said this because that it seemeth as though it might have been more fittingly said, "Magnified even unto the Heavens hath been Thy truth, and even unto the clouds Thy mercy." For" clouds" we understand to be preachers of truth, men bearing that flesh in a manner dark, whence God both gleameth in miracles, and thundereth in precepts. ... Glory to our Lord, and to the Mercy of the Same, and to the Truth of the Same, because neither hath He forsaken by mercy to make us blessed through His Grace, nor defrauded us of truth: because first Truth veiled in flesh came to us and healed through His flesh the interior eye of our heart, in order that hereafter face to face we may be able to see It. Giving therefore to Him thanks, let us say with the same Psalm the last verses, which sometime since too I have said, "Be Thou exalted above the Heavens, O God, and above all the earth Thy glory" (ver. 11). For this to Him the Prophet said so many years before; this now we see; this therefore let us also say.

PSALM LVIII.

1. The words which we have sung must be rather hearkened to by us, than proclaimed. For to all men as it were in an assemblage of mankind, the Truth crieth, "If truly indeed justice ye speak, judge right things, ye sons of men" (ver. 1). For to what unjust man is it not an easy thing to speak justice? or what man if questioned about justice, when he hath not a cause, would not easily answer what is just? Inasmuch as the hand of our Maker in our very hearts hath written this truth, "That which to thyself thou wouldest not have done, do not thou to another." Of this truth, even before that the Law was given, no one was suffered to be ignorant, in order that there might be some rule whereby might be judged even those to whom Law had not been given. But lest men should complain that something had been wanting for them, there hath been written also in tables that which in their hearts they read not. For it was not that they had it not written, but read it they would not. There hath been set before their eyes that which in their conscience to see they would be compelled; and as if from without the voice of God were brought to them, to his own inward parts hath man been thus driven, the Scripture saying," For in the thoughts of the ungodly man there will be questioning." Where questioning is, there is law. But because men, desiring those things which are without, even from themselves have become exiles, there hath been given also a written law: not because in hearts it had not been written, but because thou wast a deserter from thy heart, thou art seized by Him that is everywhere, and to thyself within art called back. Therefore the written law, what crieth it, to those that have deserted the law written in their hearts? "Return ye transgressors to the heart." For who hath taught thee, that thou wouldest have no other man draw near thy wife? Who hath taught thee, that thou wouldest not have a theft committed upon thee? Who hath taught thee, that thou wouldest not suffer wrong, and whatever other thing either universally or particularly might be spoken of? For many things there are, of which severally if questioned men with loud voice would answer, that they would not suffer. Come, if thou art not willing to suffer these things, art thou by any means the only man? dost thou not live in the fellowship of mankind? He that together with thee hath been made, is thy fellow; and all men have been made after the image of God, unless with earthly coverings they efface that which He hath formed. That which therefore to thyself thou wilt not have to be done, do not thou to another. For thou judgest that there is evil in that, which to suffer thou art not willing: and this thing thou art constrained to know by an inward law; that in thy very heart is written. Thou wast doing somewhat, and there was a cry raised in thy hands: how art thou constrained to return to thy heart when this thing thou sufferest in the hands of others? Is theft a good thing? No! I ask, is adultery a good thing? All cry, No! Is man-slaying a good thing? All cry, that they abhor it. Is coveting the property of a neighbour a

good thing? No! is the voice of all men. Or if yet thou confessest not, there draweth near one that coveteth thy property: be pleased to answer what thou wilt have. All men therefore, when of these things questioned, cry that these things are not good. Again, of doing kindnesses, not only of not hurting, but also of conferring and distributing, any hungry soul is questioned thus: "thou sufferest hunger, another man hath bread, and there is abundance with him beyond sufficiency, he knoweth thee to want, he giveth not: it displeaseth thee when hungering, let it displease thee when full also, when of another's hungering thou shalt have known. A stranger wanting shelter cometh into thy country, he is not taken in: he then crieth that inhuman is that city, at once among barbarians he might have found a home. He feeleth the injustice because he suffereth; thou perchance feelest not, but it is meet that thou imagine thyself also a stranger; and that thou see in what manner he will have displeased thee, who shall not have given that, which thou in thy country wilt not give to a stranger." I ask all men. True are these things? True. Just are these things? Just. But hear ye the Psalm. "If truly therefore justice ye speak, judge right things, ye sons of men." Be it not a justice of lips, but also of deeds. For if thou actest otherwise than thou speakest, good things thou speakest, and ill thou judgest. ...

2. But now to the present case let us come, if ye please. For the voice is that sweet voice, so well known to the ears of the Church, the voice of our Lord Jesus Christ, and the voice of His Body, the voice of the Church toiling, sojourning upon earth, living amid the perils of men speaking evil and of men flattering. Thou wilt not fear a threatener, if thou lovest not a flatterer. He therefore, of whom this is the voice, hath observed and hath seen, that all men speak justice. For what man doth dare not to speak it, lest he be called unjust? When, therefore, as though he were hearing the voices of all men, and were observing the lips of all men, he cried out to them, "If truly indeed justice ye speak,"—if not falsely justice ye Speak, if not one thing on lips doth sound, whilst another thing is concealed in hearts,—"judge right things, ye sons of men," Hear out of the Gospel His own voice, the very same as is in this Psalm: "Hypocrites," saith the Lord to the Pharisees, "how are ye able good things to speak, when ye are evil men?. ... Either make the tree good, and the fruit thereof good: or make the tree evil, and the fruit thereof evil." Why wilt thou whiten thee, wall of mud? I know thy inward parts, I am not deceived by thy covering: I know what thou holdest forth, I know what thou coverest. "For there was no need for Him, that any one to Him should bear testimony of man: for He knew Himself what was in man." For He knew what was in man, who had made man, and who had been made Man, in order that He might seek man. ...

3. But now ye do what? Why these things to you do I speak? "Because in heart iniquities ye work on earth" (ver. 2). Iniquities perchance in heart alone? Hear what followeth: both their heart hands do follow, and their heart hands do serve, the thing is thought of, and it is done; or else it is not done, not because we would not, but because we could not, WHATEVER THOU WILLEST AND CANST NOT, FOR DONE GOD DOTH COUNT IT. "For in heart Iniquities ye work on earth." What next? "Iniquities your hands knit together." What is, "knit together"? From sin, sin, and to sin, sin, because of sin. What is this? A theft a man hath committed, a sin it is: he hath been seen, he seeketh to slay him by whom he hath been seen: there hath been knit together sin with sin: God hath permitted him in His hidden judgment to slay that man whom he hath willed to slay: he perceiveth that the thing is known, he seeketh to slay a second also; he hath knit together a third sin: while these things he is planning, perchance that he may not be found out, or that he may not be convicted of having done it, he consulteth an astrologer; there is added a fourth sin: the astrologer answereth perchance with some hard and evil responses, he runneth to a soothsayer, that expiation may be made; the soothsayer maketh answer that he is not able to expiate: a magician is sought. And who could enumerate those sins which are knit together with sins? "Iniquities your hands do knit together." So long as thou knittest together, thou bindest sin upon sin. Loose thyself from sins. But I am not able, thou sayest. Cry to Him. "Unhappy man I, who shall deliver me from the body of this death?" For there shall come the Grace of God, so that righteousness shall be thy delight, as much as thou didst delight in iniquity; and thou, a man that out of bonds hast been loosed, shall cry out to God, "Thou hast broken asunder my bonds." "Thou hast broken asunder my bonds," is what else but, "Thou hast remitted my sins"? Hear why chains they are: the Scripture maketh answer, "with the chains of his sins each one is bound fast." Not only bonds, but chains also they are. Chains are those which are made by twisting in: that is, because with sins sins thou wast knitting together. ...

4. "Alienated are sinners from the womb, they have gone astray from the belly, they have spoken false things" (ver. 3). And when iniquity they speak, false things they speak; because deceitful is iniquity: and when justice they speak, false things they speak; because one thing with mouth they profess, another thing in heart they conceal. "Alienated are sinners from the womb." What is this? Let us search more diligently: for perhaps he is saying this, because God hath foreknown men that are to be sinners even in the wombs of their mothers. For whence when Rebecca was yet pregnant, and in womb was bearing twins, was it said, "Jacob I have loved, but Esau I have hated"? For it was said, "The elder shall serve the younger." Hidden at that time was the judgment of God: but yet from the womb, that is, from the very origin, alienated are sinners. Whence alienated? From truth. Whence alienated? From the blessed country, from the blessed life. Perchance alienated they are from

the very womb. And what sinners have been alienated from the womb? For what men would have been born, if therein they had not been held? Or what men to-day would be alive to hear these words to no purpose, unless they were born? Perchance therefore sinners have been alienated from a certain womb, wherein that charity was suffering pains, which speaketh through the Apostle, "Of whom again I am in labour, until Christ be formed in you." Expect thou therefore; be formed: do not to thyself ascribe a judgment which perchance thou knowest not. Carnal thou art as yet, conceived thou hast been: from that very time when thou hast received the name of Christ, by a sort of sacrament thou hast been born in the bowels of a mother. For not only out of bowels a man is born, but also in bowels. First he is born in bowels, in order that he may be able to be born of bowels. Wherefore it hath been said even to Mary, "For that which is born in thee, is of the Holy Spirit." Not yet of Her It had been born, but already in Her It had been born. Therefore there are born within the bowels of the Church certain little ones, and a good thing it is that being formed they should go forth, so that they drop not by miscarriage. Let the mother bear thee, not miscarry. If patient thou shall have been, even until thou be formed, even until in thee there be the sure doctrine of truth, the maternal bowels ought to keep thee. But if by thy impatience thou shall have shaken the sides of thy mother, with pain indeed she expelleth thee out, but more to thy loss than to hers.

5. For this reason therefore have they gone astray from the belly, because "they have spoken false things"? Or rather have they not for this reason spoken false things, because they have gone astray from the belly? For in the belly of the Church truth abideth. Whosoever from this belly of the Church separated shall have been, must needs speak false things: must needs, I say, speak false things; whoso either conceived would not be, or whom when conceived the mother hath expelled. Thence heretics exclaim against the Gospel (to speak in preference of those whom expelled we lament). We repeat to them: behold Christ hath said, "It behoved Christ to suffer, and from the dead to rise again the third day." I acknowledge there our Head, I acknowledge there our bridegroom: acknowledge thou also with me the Bride. ...

6. "Indignation to them after the similitude of a serpent" (ver. 4). A great thing ye are to hear. "Indignation to them after the similitude of a serpent." As if we had said, What is that which thou hast said? there followeth, "As if of a deaf asp." Whence deaf? "And closing its ears." Therefore deaf, because it closeth its ears. "And closing its ears." "Which will not hearken to the voice of men charming, and of the medicine medicated by the wise man" (ver. 5). As we have heard, because even men speak who have learned it with such research as they were able, but

nevertheless it is a thing which the Spirit of God knoweth much better than any men. For it is not to no purpose that of this he hath spoken, but because it may chance that true is even that which we have heard of the asp. When the asp beginneth to be affected by the Marsian charmer, who calleth it forth with certain peculiar incantations, hear what it doeth. ... Give heed what is spoken to thee for a simile's sake, what is noted thee for avoidance. So therefore here also there hath been given a certain simile derived from the Marsian, who maketh incantation to bring forth the asp from the dark cavern; surely into light he would bring it: but it loving its darkness, wherein coiled up it hideth itself, when it will not choose to come forth, nevertheless refusing to hear those words whereby it feeleth itself to be constrained, is said to press one ear against the ground, and with its tail to stop up the other, and therefore as much as possible escaping those words, it cometh not forth to the charmer. To this as being like, the Spirit of God hath spoken of certain persons hearing not the Word of God, and not only not doing, but altogether, that they may not do it, refusing to hear.

7. This thing hath been done even in the first times of the faith. Stephen the Martyr was preaching the Truth, and to minds as though dark, in order to bring them forth into light, was making incantation: when he came to make mention of Christ, whom they would not hear at all, of them the Scripture saith what? of them relateth what? "They shut," he saith, "their ears." But what they did afterwards, the narrative of the passion of Stephen doth publish. They were not deaf, but they made themselves deaf. ... For this thing they did at the point where Christ was named. The indignation of these men was as the indignation of a serpent. Why your ears do ye shut? Wait, hear, and if ye shall be able, rage. Because they chose not to do aught but rage, they would not hear. But if they had heard, perchance they would have ceased to rage. The indignation of them was as the indignation of a serpent. ...

8. "God hath broken utterly the teeth of them in their own mouth" (ver. 6). Of whom? Of them to whom indignation is as the similitude of a serpent, and of an asp closing up its ears, so that it heareth not the voice of men charming, and of medicine medicated by the wise man. The Lord hath done to them what? "Hath broken utterly the teeth of them in their own mouth." It hath been done, this at first hath been done, and now is being done. But it would have sufficed, my brethren, that it should have been said, "God hath broken utterly the teeth of them." The Pharisees would not hear the Law, would not hear the precepts of truth from Christ, being like to that serpent and asp. For in their past sins they took delight, and present life they would not lose, that is, joys earthly for joys heavenly. ... What is, "in their own mouth"? In such sort, that with their own mouth against

themselves they should make declaration: He hath compelled them with their mouth against themselves to give sentence. They would have slandered Him, because of the tribute: He said not," It is lawful to pay tribute," or, "It is not lawful to pay tribute." And He willed to break utterly their teeth, wherewith they were gaping in order to bite; but in their own mouth He would do it. If He said, Let there be paid to Caesar tribute, they would have slandered Him, because He had spoken evil to the nation of the Jews, by making it a tributary. For because of sin they were paying tribute, having been humbled, as to them in the Law had been foretold. We have Him, say they, a maligner of our nation, if He shall have bidden us to pay tribute: but if He say, Do not pay, we have Him for saying that we should not be under allegiance to Caesar. Such a double noose as it were to catch the Lord they laid. But to whom had they come? To Him that knew how to break utterly the teeth of them in their own mouth. "Show to Me the coin," He saith. Why tempt ye Me, ye hypocrites?" Of paying tribute do ye think? To do justice are ye willing? the counsel of justice do ye seek? "If truly justice ye speak, judge right things, ye sons of men." But now because in one way ye speak, in another way judge, hypocrites ye are: "Why tempt ye Me, ye hypocrites?" Now I will break utterly your teeth in your mouth: "show to Me the coin." And they showed it to Him. And He saith not, it is Caesar's: but asketh Whose it is? in order that their teeth in their own mouth might be utterly broken. For on His inquiring, of whom it had the image and inscription, they said, of Caesar. Even now the Lord shall break utterly the teeth of them in their own mouth. Now ye have made answer, now have been broken utterly your teeth in your mouth. "Render unto Caesar the things which are of Caesar, and unto God the things which are of God." Caesar seeketh his image; render it: God seeketh His image; render it. Let not Caesar lose from you his coin: let not God lose in you His coin. And they found not what they might answer. For they had been sent to slander Him: and they went back, saying, that no one to Him could make answer. Wherefore? Because broken utterly had been the teeth of them in their own mouth. Of that sort is also the following: "In what power doest Thou these things? I also will ask of you one question, answer me." And He asked them of John, whence was the Baptism of John, from heaven, or of men? so that whatever they might answer might tell against themselves. ...

9. The Lord displeased that Pharisee, who to dinner had bidden Him, because a woman that was a sinner drew near to His feet, and he murmured against Him, saying, "If this man were a prophet, He would know what woman drew near to His feet." O thou that art no prophet, whence knowest thou that He knew not what woman drew near to His feet? Because indeed He kept not the purifying of the Jews, which outwardly was as it were kept in the flesh, and was afar from the heart, this thing he suspected of the Lord. And in order that I may not speak at length on this point, even in his mouth He willed to break utterly the teeth of him.

For He set forth to him: "A certain usurer had two debtors, one was owing five hundred pence, the other fifty: both had not wherewithal to pay, he forgave both. Which loved him the more?" To this end the one asketh, that the other may answer: to this end he answereth that the teeth of him in his mouth may be broken utterly. ...

10. "The jaw-bones of lions the Lord hath broken utterly." Not only of asps. What of asps? Asps treacherously desire to throw in their venom, and scatter it, and hiss. Most openly raged the nations, and roared like lions. "Wherefore have raged the nations, and the peoples meditated empty things?" When they were lying in wait for the Lord. Is it lawful to give tribute to Caesar, or is it not lawful? Asps they were, serpents they were, broken utterly were the teeth of them in their own mouth. Afterwards they cried out, "Crucify, Crucify." Now is there no tongue of asp, but roar of lion. But also "the jaw-bones of lions the Lord hath broken utterly." Perchance here there is no need of that which he hath not added, namely, "in the mouth of them." For men lying in wait with captious questions, were forced to be conquered with their own answer: but those men that openly were raging, were they by any means to be confuted with questions? Nevertheless, even their jaw-bones were broken utterly: having been crucified, He rose again, ascended into heaven, was glorified as the Christ, is adored by all nations, adored by all kings. Let the Jews now rage, if they are able. We have also in the case of heretics this as a warning and precedent, because themselves also we find to be serpents with indignation made deaf, not choosing to hear the "medicine medicated by the wise man:" and in their own mouth the Lord hath broken utterly the teeth of them. ...

11. "They shall be despised like water running down" (ver. 7). Be not terrified, brethren, by certain streams, which are called torrents: with winter waters they are filled up; do not fear: after a little it passeth by, that water runneth down; for a time it roareth, soon it will subside: they cannot hold long. Many heresies now are utterly dead: they have run in their channels as much as they were able, have run down, dried are the channels, scarce of them the memory is found, or that they have been. "They shall be despised like water running down." But not they alone; the whole of this age for a time is roaring, and is seeking whom it may drag along. Let all ungodly men, all proud men resounding against the rocks of their pride as it were with waters rushing along and flowing together, not terrify you, winter waters they are, they cannot alway flow: it must needs be that they run down unto their place, unto their end. And nevertheless of this torrent of the world the Lord hath drunk. For He hath suffered here, the very torrent He hath drunk, but in the way He hath drunk, but in the passage over: because in way of sinners He hath not

stood. But of Him saith the Scripture what? "Of the torrent in the way He shall drink, therefore He shall lift up His Head;" that is, for this reason glorified He hath been, because He hath died; for this reason hath risen again, because He hath suffered. ...

12. "Like wax melted they shall be taken away" (ver. 8). For thou wast about to say, all men are not so made weak, like myself, in order that they may believe: many men do persevere in their evil, and in their malice. And of the same fear thou nothing: "Like wax melted they shall be taken away." Against thee they shall not stand, they shall not continue: with a sort of fire of their own lusts they shall perish. For there is here a kind of hidden punishment, of it the Psalm is about to speak now, to the end of it. There are but a few verses; be attentive. There is a certain punishment future, fire of hell, fire everlasting. For future punishment hath two kinds: either of the lower places it is, where was burning that rich man, who was wishing for himself a drop of water to be dropped on his tongue off the finger of the poor man, whom before his gate he had spurned, when he saith, "For I am tormented in this flame." And the second is that at the end, whereof they are to hear, that on the left hand are to be set: "Go ye into fire everlasting, that hath been prepared for the devil and his angels." Those punishments shall be manifest at that time, when we shall have departed out of this life, or when at the end of the world men shall have come to the resurrection of the dead. Now therefore is there no punishment, and doth God suffer sins utterly unpunished even unto that day? There is even here a sort of hidden punishment, of the same he is treating no. ... We see nevertheless sometimes with these punishments just men to be afflicted, and to these punishments unjust men to be strangers: for which reason did totter the feet of him that afterwards rejoicing saith, "How good is the God of Israel to men right in heart! But my own feet have been almost shaken, because I have been jealous in the case of sinners, beholding the peace of sinners." For he had seen the felicity of evil men, and well-pleased he had been to be an evil man, seeing evil men to reign, seeing that it was well with them, that they abounded in plenty of all things temporal, such as he too, being as yet but a babe, was desiring from the Lord: and his feet did totter, even until he saw what at the end is either to be hoped for or to be feared. For he saith in the same Psalm, "This thing is a labour before me, until I enter into the sanctuary of God, and understand unto the last things." It is not therefore the punishments of the lower places, not the punishments of that fire everlasting after the resurrection, not those punishments which as yet in this world are common to just men and unjust men, and ofttimes more heavy are those of just men than those of unjust men; but some punishment or other of the present life the Spirit of God would recommend to our notice. Give heed, hear ye me about to speak of that which ye know: but a more sweet thing it is when it is declared in a Psalm, which, before it was declared, was deemed obscure. For

behold I bring forth that which already ye knew: but because these things are brought forth from a place where ye have never yet seen them, it cometh to pass that even known things, as if they were new things, do delight you. Hear ye the punishment of ungodly men: "Like wax," he saith, "melted they shall be taken away." I have said that through their lusts this thing to them is done. Evil lust is like a burning and a fire. Doth fire consume a garment, and doth not the lust of adultery consume the soul? Of meditated adultery when the Scripture was speaking it saith, "Shall one bind fire in his bosom, and his garments shall he not burn up?" Thou bearest in thy bosom live coals; burned through is thy vest; thou bearest in thought adultery, and whole then is thy soul? But these punishments few men do see: therefore them the Spirit of God doth exceedingly recommend to our notice. Hear the Apostle saying, "God hath given them up unto the lusts of their heart." Behold, the fire from the face of which like wax they are melting. For they loose themselves from a certain continence of chastity; therefore even these same men, going unto their lusts, as loose and melting are spoken of. Whence melting? whence loose? From the fire of lusts. "God hath given them up unto the lusts of their heart, so that they do those things which beseem not, being filled full of all iniquity." ...

13. "There hath fallen upon them fire, and they have not seen the sun." Ye see in what manner he speaketh of a certain punishment of darkening. "Fire hath fallen upon them," fire of pride, a smoky fire, fire of lust, fire of wrath. How great a fire is it? He upon whom it shall have fallen, shall not see the sun. Therefore hath it been said, "Let not the sun go down upon your wrath." Therefore, brethren, fire of evil lust fear ye, if ye will not melt like wax, and to perish from the face of God. For there falleth upon you that fire, and the sun ye shall not see. What sun? Not that which together with thee see both beasts and insects, and good men and evil men: because "He maketh His sun to rise upon good men and evil men." But there is another sun, whereof those men are to speak, "And the sun hath not risen to us, passed away are all those things as it were a shadow. Therefore we have strayed from the way of truth, and the light of righteousness hath not shone to us, and the sun hath not risen to us."

14. "Before that the bramble bringeth forth your thorns: as though living, as though in anger, it shall drink them up" (ver. 9). What is the bramble? Of prickly plants it is a kind, upon which there are said to be certain of the closest thorns. At first it is a herb; and while it is a herb, soft and fair it is: but thereon there are nevertheless thorns to come forth. Now therefore sins are pleasant, and as it were they do not prick. A herb is the bramble; even now nevertheless there is a thorn. "Before that the bramble bringeth forth thorns:" is before that of miserable delights

and pleasures the evident tortures come forth. Let them question themselves that love any object, and to it cannot attain; let them see if they are not racked with longing: and when they have attained to that which unlawfully they long for, let them mark if they are not racked with fear. Let them see therefore here their punishments; before that there cometh that resurrection, when in flesh rising again they shall not be changed. "For all we shall rise again, but not all we shall be changed." For they shall have the corruption of the flesh wherein to be pained, not that wherein to die: otherwise even those pains would be ended. Then the thorns of that bramble, that is, all pains and piercings of tortures shall be brought forth. Such thorns as they shall suffer that are to say, "These are they whom sometimes we had in derision:" thorns of the piercing of repentance, but of one too late and without fruit like the barrenness of thorns. The repentance of this time is pain healing: repentance of that time is pain penal. Wouldest thou not suffer those thorns? here be thou pierced with the thorns of repentance; in such sort that thou do that which hath been spoken of, "Turned I have been in sorrow, when the thorn was piercing: my sin I have known, and mine iniquity I have not covered: I have said, I will declare against me my shortcoming to the Lord, and Thou hast remitted the ungodliness of my heart." Now do so, now be pierced through, be there not in thee done that which hath been said of certain execrable men, "They have been cloven asunder, and have not been pierced through." Observe them that have been cloven asunder and have not been pierced through. Ye see men cloven asunder, and ye see them not pierced through. Behold beside the Church they are, and it doth not repent them, so as they should return whence they have been cloven asunder. The bramble hereafter shall bring forth their thorns. They will not now have a healing piercing through, they shall have hereafter one penal. But even now before that the bramble produceth thorns, there hath fallen upon them fire, that suffereth them not to see the sun, that is, the wrath of God is drinking up them while still living: fire of evil lusts, of empty honours, of pride, of their covetousness: and whatsoever is weighing them down, that they should not know the truth, so that they seem not to be conquered, so that they be not brought into subjection even by truth herself. For what is a more glorious thing, brethren, than to be brought in subjection and to be overcome by truth? Let truth overcome thee willing: for even unwilling she shall of herself overcome thee. ...

15. As yet the punishments of the lower places have not come, as yet fire everlasting hath not come: let him that is growing in God compare himself now with an ungodly man, a blind heart with an enlightened heart: compare ye two men, one seeing and one not seeing in the flesh. And what so great thing is vision of the flesh? Did Tobias by any means have fleshly eyes? His own son had, and he had not; and the way of life a blind man to one seeing did show. Therefore when ye see that punishment, rejoice, because in it ye are not.

Therefore saith the Scripture, "The just man shall rejoice when he shall have seen vengeance" (ver. 10). Not that future punishment; for see what followeth: "his hands he shall wash in the blood of the sinner." What is this? Let your love attend. When man-slayers are smitten, ought anywise innocent men to go thither and wash their hands? But what is, "in the blood of the sinner he shall wash his hands"? When a just man seeth the punishment of a sinner, he groweth himself; and the death of one is the life of another. For if spiritually blood runneth from those that within are dead, do thou, seeing such vengeance, wash therein thy hands; for the future more cleanly live. And how shall he wash his hands, if a just man he is? For what hath he on his hands to be washed, if just he is? "But the just man of faith shall live." Just men therefore he hath called believers: and from the time that thou hast believed, at once thou beginnest to be called just. For there hath been made a remission of sins. Even if out of that remaining part of thy life some sins are thine, which cannot but flow in, like water from the sea into the hold; nevertheless, because thou hast believed, when thou shalt have seen him that altogether is turned away from God to be slain in that blindness, there falling upon him that fire so that he see not the sun—then do thou that now through faith seest Christ, in order that thou mayest see in substance (because the just man liveth of faith), observe the ungodly man dying, and purge thyself from sins. So thou shalt wash in a manner thy hands in the blood of the sinner.

16. "And a man shall say, If therefore there is fruit to a just man" (ver. 10). Behold, before that there cometh that which is promised, before that there is given life everlasting, before that ungodly men are cast forth into fire everlasting, here in this life there is fruit to the just man. What fruit? "In hope rejoicing, in tribulation enduring." What fruit to the just man? "We glory in tribulations, knowing that tribulation worketh patience, but patience probation, but probation hope: but hope confoundeth not: because the love of God is shed abroad in our hearts through the Holy Spirit, that hath been given to us." Doth he rejoice that is a drunkard; and doth he not rejoice that is just? In love there is fruit to a just man. Miserable the one, even when he maketh himself drunken: blessed the other, even when he hungereth and thirsteth. The one wine-bibbing doth gorge, the other hope doth feed. Let him see therefore the punishment of the other, his own rejoicing, and let him think of God. He that hath given even now such joy of faith, of hope, of charity, of the truth of His Scriptures, what manner of joy is He making ready against the end? In the way thus He feedeth, in his home how shall He fill him? "And a man shall say, If therefore there is fruit to the just man." Let them that see believe, and see, and perceive. Rejoice shall the just man when he shall have seen vengeance. But if he hath not eyes whence he may see vengeance, he will be made sad, and will not be amended by it. But if he seeth it, he seeth what difference there is between the darkened eye of the heart, and the eye enlightened of the

heart: between the coolness of chastity and the flame of lust, between the security of hope and the fear there is in crime. When he shall have seen this, let him separate himself, and wash his hands in the blood of the same. Let him profit by the comparison, and say, "Therefore there is fruit to the just man: therefore there is a God judging them in the earth." Not yet in that life, not yet in fire eternal, not yet in the lower places, but here in earth. ...

17. If somewhat too prolix we have been, pardon us. We exhort you in the name of Christ, to meditate profitably on those things which ye have heard. Because even to preach the truth is nought, if heart from tongue dissenteth; and to hear the truth nothing profiteth, if a man upon the rock build not. He that buildeth upon a Rock, is the same that heareth and doeth: but he that heareth and doeth not, buildeth upon sand: he that neither heareth nor doeth, buildeth nothing. ...

PSALM LIX.

The First Part.

1. As the Scripture is wont to set mysteries of the Psalms on the titles, and to deck the brow of a Psalm with the high announcement of a Mystery, in order that we that are about to go in may know (when as it were upon the door-post we have read what within is doing) either of whom the house is, or who is the owner of that estate: so also in this Psalm there hath been written a title, of a title. For it hath, "At the end, corrupt not for David himself unto the inscription of the title." This is that which I have spoken of, title of Title. For what the inscription of this title is, which to be corrupted he forbiddeth, the Gospel to us doth indicate. For when the Lord was being crucified, a title by Pilate was inscribed and set, "King of the Jews," in three tongues, Hebrew, Greek, and Latin: which tongues in the whole world mostly do prevail. ... Therefore "corrupt not" is most proper and prophetic; since indeed even those Jews made suggestion at that time to Pilate, and said, "Do not write King of the Jews, but write, that Himself said that He was King of the Jews:" for this title, say they, hath established Him King over us. And Pilate, "What I have written, I have written." And there was fulfilled, "corrupt not."

2. Nor is this the only Psalm which hath an inscription of such sort, that the Title be not corrupted. Several Psalms thus are marked on the face, but however in all the Passion of the Lord is foretold. Therefore here also let us perceive the Lord's Passion, and let there speak to us Christ, Head and Body. So always, or nearly always, let us hear the words of Christ from the Psalm, as that we look not only upon that Head, the one mediator between God and man, the Man Christ Jesus. ... But let us think of Christ, Head and whole Body, a sort of entire Man. For to us is said, "But ye are the Body of Christ and members," by the Apostle Paul. If therefore He is Head, we Body; whole Christ is Head and Body. For sometimes thou findest words which do not suit the Head, and unless thou shalt have attached them to the Body, thy understanding will waver: again thou findest words which are proper for the Body, and Christ nevertheless is speaking. In that place we must have no fear lest a man be mistaken for quickly he proceedeth to adapt to the Head, that which he seeth is not proper for the Body. ...

3. Let us hear, therefore, what followeth: "When Saul sent and guarded his house in order that he might kill him." This though not to the Cross of the Lord, yet to the Passion of the Lord doth belong. For Crucified was Christ, and dead, and buried. That sepulchre was therefore as it were the house: to guard which the

government of the Jews sent, when guards were set to the sepulchre of Christ. There is indeed a story in the Scripture of the Reigns, of the occasion when Saul sent to guard the house in order that he might kill David. ... But in like manner as Saul effected not his purpose of slaying David: so this could not the government of the Jews effect, that the testimony of guards sleeping should avail more than that of Apostles watching. For what were the guards instructed to say? We give to you, they say, as much money as ye please; and say ye, that while ye were sleeping there came His disciples, and took Him away. Behold what sort of witnesses of falsehood against truth and the Resurrection of Christ, His enemies, through Saul figured, did produce. Enquire, O unbelief, of sleeping witnesses, let them reply to thee of what was done in the tomb. Who, if they were sleeping, whence knew it? If watching, wherefore detained they not the thieves? Let him say therefore what followeth.

4. "Deliver me from mine enemies, my God, and from men rising up upon me, redeem Thou me" (ver. 1). There hath been done this thing in the flesh of Christ, it is being done in us also. For our enemies, to wit the devil and his angels, cease not to rise up upon us every day, and to wish to make sport of our weakness and our frailness, by deceptions, by suggestions, by temptations, and by snares of whatsoever sort to entangle us, while on earth we are still living. But let our voice watch unto God, and cry out in the members of Christ, under the Head that is in heaven, "Deliver me from mine enemies, my God, and from men rising up upon me, redeem Thou me."

5. "Deliver me from men working iniquity, and from men of bloods, save Thou me" (ver. 2). They indeed were men of bloods, who slew the Just One, in whom no guilt they found: they were men of bloods, because when the foreigner washed his hands, and would have let go Christ, they cried, "Crucify, Crucify:" they were men of bloods, on whom when there was being charged the crime of the blood of Christ, they made answer, giving it to their posterity to drink, "His blood be upon us and upon our sons." But neither against His Body did men of bloods cease to rise up; for even after the Resurrection and Ascension of Christ, the Church suffered persecutions, and she indeed first that grew out of the Jewish people, of which also our Apostles were. There at first Stephen was stoned, and received that of which he had his name. For Stephanus doth signify a crown. Lowly stoned but highly crowned. Secondly, among the Gentiles rose up kingdoms of Gentiles, before that in them was fulfilled that which had been foretold, "There shall adore Him all the kings of the earth, all nations shall serve Him:" and there roared the fierceness of that kingdom against the witnesses of Christ: there was shed largely and frequently the blood of Martyrs: wherewith when it had been shed, being as it

were sown, the field of the Church more productively put forth, and filled the whole world as we now behold. From these therefore, men of bloods, is delivered Christ, not only Head, but also Body. From men of bloods is delivered Christ, both from them that have been, and from them that are, and from them that are to be; there is delivered Christ, both He that hath gone before, and He that is, and He that is to come. For Christ is the whole Body of Christ; and whatsoever good Christians that now are, and that have been before us, and that after us are to be, are an whole Christ, who is delivered from men of bloods; nor is this voice void, "And from men of bloods save Thou me."

6. "For behold they have hunted my soul. ... There have rushed upon me strong men" (ver. 3). We must not however pass on from these strong men: diligently we must trace who are the strong men rising up. Strong men, upon whom but upon weak men, upon powerless men, upon men not strong? And praised nevertheless are the weak men, and condemned are the strong men. If it would be perceived who are strong men, at first the devil himself the Lord hath called a strong man: "No one," He saith, "is able to go into the house of a strong man, and to carry off his vessels, unless first he shall have bound the strong man." He hath bound therefore the strong man with the chains of His dominion: and his vessels He hath carried off, and His own vessels hath made them. For all unrighteous men were vessels of the devil. ... But there are among mankind certain strong men of a blameable and damnable strength, that are confident indeed, but on temporal felicity. That man doth not seem to you to have been strong, of whom now from the Gospels hath been read: how his estate brought forth abundance of fruits, and he being troubled, hit upon the design of rebuilding, so that, having pulled down his old barns, he should construct new ones more capacious, and, these having been finished, should say to his soul, "Thou hast many good things, soul, feast, be merry, be filled." ...There are also other men strong, not because of riches, not because of the powers of the body, not because of any temporally pre-eminent power of station, but relying on their righteousness. This sort of strong men must be guarded against, feared, repulsed, not imitated: of men relying, I say, not on body, not on means, not on descent, not on honour; for all such things who would not see to be temporal, fleeting, falling, flying? but relying on their own righteousness. ... "Wherefore," say they, doth your Master eat with publicans and sinners? O ye strong men, to whom a Physician is not needful! This strength to soundness belongeth not, but to insanity. For even than men frenzied nothing can be stronger, more mighty they are than whole men: but by how much greater their powers are, by so much nearer is their death. May God therefore turn away from our imitation these strong men. ... The same are therefore the strong men, that assailed Christ, commending their own justice. Hear ye these strong men: when certain men of Jerusalem were speaking, having been sent by them to take Christ,

446

and not daring to take Him (because when he would, then was He taken, that truly was strong): Why therefore, say they, "could ye not take Him?" And they made answer, "No one of men did ever so speak as He." And these strong men, "Hath by any means any one of the Pharisees believed on Him, or any one of the Scribes, but this people knowing not the Law?" They preferred themselves to the sick multitude, that was running to the Physician: whence but because they were themselves strong? and what is worse, by their strength, all the multitude also they brought over unto themselves, and slew the Physician of all. ...

7. What next? "Neither iniquity is mine, nor sin mine, O Lord" (ver. 4). There have rushed on indeed strong men on their own righteousness relying, they have rushed on, but sin in me they have not found. For truly those strong men, that is, as it were righteous men, on what account would they be able to persecute Christ, unless it were as if a sinner? But, however, let them look to it how strong they be, in the raging of fever not in the vigour of soundness: let them look to it how strong they be, and how as though just against an unrighteous man they have raged. But, however, "neither iniquity is mine, nor sin mine, O Lord. Without iniquity I did run, and I was guided." Those strong men therefore could not follow me running: therefore a sinner they have deemed me, because my steps they have not seen.

8. "Without iniquity I did run, and was guided; rise up to meet me, and see." To God is said this. But why? If He meet not, is He unable to see? It is just as if thou wast walking in a road, and from afar by some one thou couldest not be recognised, thou wouldest call to him and wouldest say, Meet me, and see how I am walking; for when from afar thou espiest me, my steps thou art not able to see. So also unless God were to meet, would He not see how without iniquity he was guided, and how without sin he was running? This interpretation indeed we can also accept, namely, "Rise up to meet me," as if "help me." But that which he hath added, "and see," must be understood as, make it to be seen that I run, make it to be seen that I am guided: according to that figure wherein this also hath been said to Abraham, "Now I know that thou fearest God." God saith, "Now I know:" whence, but because I have made thee to know? For unknown to himself every one is before the questioning of temptation: just as of himself Peter s in his confidence was ignorant, and by denying learned what kind of powers he had, in his very stumbling he perceived that it was falsely he had been confident: he wept, and in weeping he earned profitably to know what he was, and to be what he was not. Therefore Abraham when tried, became known to himself: and it was said by God, "Now I know," that is, now I have made thee to know. In like manner as glad is the day because it maketh men glad; and sad is bitterness because it maketh sad one tasting thereof: so God's seeing is making to see. "Rise up, therefore," he saith,

"to meet me, and see" (ver. 5). What is, "and see"? And help me, that is, in those men, in order that they may see my course, may follow me; let not that seem to them to be crooked which is straight, let not that seem to them to be curved which keepeth the rule of truth.

9. Something else I am admonished to say in this place of the loftiness of our Head Himself: for He was made weak even unto death, and He took on Him the weakness of flesh, in order that the chickens of Jerusalem He might gather under His wings, like a hen showing herself weak with her little ones. For have we not observed this thing in some bird at some time or other, even in those which build nests before our eyes, as the house- sparrows, as swallows, so to speak, our annual guests, as storks, as various sorts of birds, which before our eyes build nests, and hatch eggs, feed chickens, as the very doves which daily we see; and some bird to become weak with her chickens, have we not known, have we not looked upon, have we not seen? In what way doth a hen experience this weakness? Surely a known fact I am speaking of, which in our sight is daily taking place. How her voice groweth hoarse, how her whole body is made languid? The wings droop, the feathers are loosened, and thou seest around the chickens some sick thing, and this is maternal love which is found as weakness. Why was it therefore, but for this reason, that the Lord willed to be as a Hen, saying in the Holy Scripture, "Jerusalem, Jerusalem, how often have I willed to gather thy sons, even as a hen her chickens under her wings, and thou hast not been willing." But He hath gathered all nations, like as a hen her chickens. ...

10. "And Thou, Lord God of virtues, God of Israel." Thou God of Israel, that art thought to be but God of one nation, which worshippeth Thee, when all nations worship idols, Thou God of Israel, "Give heed unto the visiting all nations." Fulfilled be that prophecy wherein Isaiah in Thy person speaketh to Thy Church, Thy holy City, that barren one of whom many more are the sons of Her forsaken than of her that hath a husband. To Her indeed hath been said, "Rejoice, thou barren, that bearest not," etc., more than of the Jewish nation which hath a Husband, which hath received the Law, more than of that nation which had a visible king. For thy king is hidden, and more sons to thee there are by a hidden Bridegroom. ... The Prophet addeth, "Enlarge the place of Thy tabernacle, and Thy courts fix thou: there is no cause for thee to spare, extend further thy cords, and strong stakes set thou again and again on the right and on the left." Upon the right keep good men, on the left keep evil men, until there come the fan: occupy nevertheless all nations; bidden to the marriage be good men and evil men, filled be the marriage with guests; it is the office of servants to bid, of the Lord to sever. "Cities which had been forsaken Thou shall inhabit:" forsaken of God, forsaken of

Prophets, forsaken of Apostles, forsaken of the Gospel, full of demons. For Thou shalt prevail; and blush not because abominable Thou hast been. Therefore though there have risen up upon thee strong men, blush not: when against the name of Christ laws were enacted, when ignominy and infamy it was to be a Christian. "Blush not because abominable Thou hast been: for confusion for everlasting Thou shalt forget, of the ignominy of Thy widowhood Thou shall not be mindful." ...

11. "Have not pity upon all men that work iniquity." Here evidently He is terrifying. Whom would He not terrify? What man falling back upon his own conscience would not tremble? Which even if to itself it is conscious of godliness, strange if it be not in some sort conscious of iniquity. For whosoever doeth sin, also doeth iniquity. "For if Thou shalt have marked iniquities, O Lord, what man shall abide it?" And nevertheless a true saying it is, and not said to no purpose, and neither is nor will it be possible to be void, "Have not pity upon all men that work iniquity." But He had pity even upon Paul, who at first as Saul wrought iniquity. For what good thing did he, whence he might deserve of God? Did he not hate His Saints unto death? did he not bear letters from the chief of the priests, to the end that wheresoever he might find Christians, to punishment he should hurry them? When bent upon this, when thither proceeding, breathing and panting slaughter, as the Scripture testified of him, was he not from Heaven with a mighty voice summoned, thrown down, raised up; blinded, lightened; slain, made alive; destroyed, restored? In return for what merit? Let us say nothing; himself rather let us hear: "I that before have been," he saith, "a blasphemer, and persecutor; and injurious, but mercy I have obtained." Surely "Thou wouldest not have pity upon all men that work iniquity:" this in two ways may be understood: either that in fact not any sins doth God leave unpunished; or that there is a sort of iniquity, on the workers whereof God hath indeed no pity.

12. All iniquity, be it little or great, punished must needs be, either by man himself repenting, or by God avenging. For even he that repenteth punisheth himself. Therefore, brethren, let us punish our own sins, if we seek the mercy of God. God cannot have mercy on all men working iniquity as if pandering to sins, or not rooting out sins. In a word, either thou punishest, or He punisheth. ...

13. But let us see now another way in which this sentence may be understood. There is a certain iniquity, on the worker whereof it cannot be that God have mercy. Ye enquire, perchance, what that is? It is the defending of sins. When a man defendeth his sins, great iniquity he worketh: that thing he is defending which God hateth. And see how perversely, how iniquitously. Whatever of good he hath

done, to himself he would have it to be ascribed; whatever of evil, to God. For in this manner men defend sins in the person of God, which is a worse sin. ...Therefore thou defendest thy sin in such sort, that thou layest blame on God. So the guilty is excused, so that the Judge may be charged. However on men working iniquity God hath no pity at all.

14. "Let them be converted at the evening" (ver. 6). Of certain men he is speaking that were once workers of iniquity, and once darkness, being converted in the evening. What is, "in the evening"? Afterward. What is "at the evening"? Later. For before, before that they crucified Christ, they ought to have acknowledged their Physician. Wherefore, when He had been crucified—rising again, into Heaven ascending—after that He sent His Holy Spirit, wherewith were fulfilled they that were in one house, and they began to speak with the tongues of all nations, there feared the crucifiers of Christ; they were pricked through with their consciences, they besought counsel of safety from the Apostles, they heard, "Repent, and be baptized each one of you in the name of our Lord Jesus Christ, and your sins shall be remitted unto you." After the slaying of Christ, after the shedding of the blood of Christ, remitted are your sins. ... "Let these be converted," therefore, they also "at evening." Let them yearn for the grace of God, perceive themselves to be sinners; let those strong men be made weak, those rich men be made poor, those just men acknowledge themselves sinners, those lions be made dogs. "Let them be converted at evening, and suffer hunger as dogs. And they shall go around the city." What city? That world, which in certain places the Scripture calleth "the city of standing round:" that is, because in all nations everywhere the world had encompassed the one nation of Jews, where such words were being spoken, and it was called "the city of standing round." Around this city shall go those men, now having become hungry dogs. In what manner shall they go around? By preaching. Saul out of a wolf was made a dog at evening, that is, being late converted by the crumbs of his Lord, in His grace he ran, and went around the city.

15. "Behold, themselves shall speak in their mouth, and a sword is on the lips of them" (ver. 7). Here is that sword twice whetted, whereof the Apostle saith, "And the sword of the Spirit, which is the Word of God." Wherefore twice whetted? Wherefore, but because smiting out of both Testaments? With this sword were slain those whereof it was said to Peter, "Slay, and eat." "And a sword is on the lips of them. For who hath heard?" They all speak in their mouth, "Who hath heard?" That is, they shall be wroth with men that are slow to believe. They that a little before were even themselves unwilling to believe, do feel disgust from men not believing. And truly, brethren, so it is. Thou seest a man slow before he is

made a Christian; thou criest to him daily, hardly he is converted: suppose him to be converted, and then he would have all men to be Christians, and wondereth that not yet they are. It hath chanced out to him at evening to have been converted: but because he hath been made hungering like a dog, he hath also on his lips a sword; he saith, "Who hath heard?" What is, "Who hath heard?" "Who hath believed our hearing, and to whom hath the arm of the Lord been revealed?" "For who hath heard?" The Jews believe not: they have turned them to the nations, and have preached. The Jews did not believe; and nevertheless through believing Jews the Gospel went around the city, and they said, "For who hath heard?" "And Thou, Lord, shall deride them" (ver. 8). All nations are to be Christian, and ye say, "Who hath heard?" What is, "shall deride them"? "As nothing Thou shall esteem all nations." Nothing for Thee it shall be; because a most easy thing it will be for all nations to believe in Thee.

16. "My strength to Thee I will keep" (ver. 9). For those strong men have fallen for this reason; because their strength to Thee they have not kept: that is, they that upon me have risen up and rushed, on themselves have relied. But I "my strength to Thee will keep:" because if I withdraw, I fall; if I draw near, stronger I am made. For see, brethren, what there is in a human soul. It hath not of itself light, hath not of itself powers: but all that is fair in a soul, is virtue and wisdom: but it neither is wise for itself, nor strong for itself, nor itself is light to itself, nor itself is virtue to itself. There is a certain origin and fountain of virtue, there is a certain root of wisdom, there is a certain, so to speak, if this also must be said, region of unchangeable truth: from this the soul withdrawing is made dark, drawing near is made light. "Draw near to Him, and be made light:" because by withdrawing ye are made dark. Therefore, "my strength, I will keep to, Thee:" not from Thee will I withdraw, not on myself will I rely. "My strength, to Thee I will keep: because, O God, my lifter up Thou art." For where was I, and where am I? Whence hast Thou taken me up? What iniquities of mine hast Thou remitted? Where was I lying? To what have I been raised up? I ought to have remembered these things: because in another Psalm is said, "For my father and my mother have forsaken me, but the Lord hath taken me unto Him."

17. "My God, the mercy of Him shall come before me" (ver. 10). Behold what is, "My strength, to Thee I will keep:" on myself I will in no ways at all rely. For what good thing have I brought, that thou shouldest have mercy on me, and shouldest justify me? What in me hast Thou found, save sins alone? Of Thine there is nothing else but the nature which Thou hast created: the other things are mine own evil things which Thou hast blotted out. I have not first risen up to Thee, but to awake me Thou hast come: for "His mercy shall come before me." Before

that anything of good I shall do, "His mercy shall come before me." What answer here shall the unhappy Pelagius make? "My God hath shown to me among mine enemies" (ver. 11). How great mercy He hath put forth concerning me, among mine enemies He hath showed. Let one gathered compare himself with men forsaken, and one elect with men rejected: let the vessel of mercy compare itself with the vessels of wrath; and let it see how out of one lump God hath made one vessel unto honour, another unto dishonour. "For so God, willing to show wrath, and to manifest His power, hath brought in, in much patience, the vessels of wrath, which have been perfected unto perdition." And wherefore this? "In order that He might make known His riches upon the vessels of mercy." If therefore vessels of wrath He hath brought in, wherein He might make known His riches upon the vessels of mercy, most rightly hath been said, "His mercy shall come before me: My God hath showed to me among mine enemies:" that is however great mercy He hath had concerning me, to me He hath showed it among these men concerning whom He hath not had mercy. For unless the debtor be in suspense, he is less grateful to him by whom the debt hath been forgiven."My God hath showed to me among mine enemies."

18. But of the enemies themselves what? "Slay them not, lest sometime they forget Thy law." He is making request for his enemies, he is fulfilling the commandment. ... Slay not them of whom the sins Thou slayest. But what is it to be slain? To forget the law of the Lord. It is real death, to go into the pit of sin; this indeed may be also understood of the Jews. Why of the Jews, "Slay not them, lest sometime they forget Thy law"? Those very enemies of mine, that have slain me, do not Thou slay. Let the nation of the Jews remain: certes conquered it hath been by the Romans certes effaced is the city of them, Jews are not admitted into their city, and yet Jews there are. For all those provinces by the Romans have been subjugated. Who now can distinguish the nations in the Roman empire the one from the other, inasmuch as all have become Romans and all are called Romans? The Jews nevertheless remain with a mark; nor in such sort conquered have they been, as that by the conquerors they have been swallowed up. Not without reason is there that Cain, on whom, when he had slain his brother, God set a mark in order that no one should slay him. This is the mark which the Jews have: they hold fast by the remnant of their law, they are circumcised, they keep Sabbaths, they sacrifice the Passover; they eat unleavened bread. These are therefore Jews, they have not been slain, they are necessary to believing nations. Why so? In order that He may show to us among our enemies His mercy. "My God hath shown to me in mine enemies." He showeth His mercy to the wild-olive grafted on branches that have been cut off because of pride. Behold where they lie, that were proud, behold where thou hast been grafted, that didst lie: and be not thou proud, lest thou shouldest deserve to be cut off.

19. "Scatter them abroad in Thy virtue" (ver. 11). Now this thing hath been done: throughout all nations there have been scattered abroad the Jews, witnesses of their own iniquity and our truth. They have themselves writings, out of which hath been prophesied Christ, and we hold Christ. And if sometime perchance any heathen man shall have doubted, when we have told him the prophecies of Christ, at the clearness whereof he is amazed, and wondering hath supposed that they were written by ourselves, then out of the copies of the Jews we prove, how this thing so long time before had been foretold. See after what sort by means of our enemies we confound other enemies. "Scatter them abroad in Thy virtue:" take away from them "virtue," take away from them their strength. "And bring them down, my protector, O Lord." "The transgressions of their mouth, the discourse of their lips: and let them be taken in their pride: and out of cursing and lying shall be declared consummations, in the anger of consummation, and they shall not be" (ver. 12). Obscure words these are, and I fear lest they be not well instilled. ...

The Second Part.

1. For, behold, the Jews are enemies, whom this Psalm seemeth to imply; the law of God they hold, and therefore of them hath been said, "Slay not them, lest sometime they forget Thy law:" in order that the nation of Jews might remain, and by it remaining the number of Christians might increase. Throughout all nations they remain certainly, and Jews they are, nor have they ceased to be what they were: that is, this nation hath not so yielded to Roman institutions, as to have lost the form of Jews; but hath been subjected to the Romans so as that it still retaineth its own laws; which are the laws of God. But what in their case hath been done? "Ye tithe mint and cummin, and have forsaken the weightier matters of the law, mercy, and judgment, straining a gnat, but swallowing a camel." This to them the Lord saith. And in truth so they are; they hold the law, hold the Prophets; read all things, sing all things: the light of the Prophets therein they see not, which is Christ Jesus. Not only Him now they see not, when he is sitting in Heaven: but not even at that tithe saw they Him, when among them humble He was walking, and they were made guilty by shedding the blood of the Same; but not all. This even to-day we commend to the notice of your Love. Not all: because many of them were turned to Him whom they slew, and by believing on Him, they obtained pardon even for the shedding of His blood: and they have given an example for men; how they ought not to despair that sin of whatsoever kind would be remitted to them, since even the killing of Christ was remitted to them confessing. ...

2. What in them wilt Thou slay? The Crucify, Crucify, which they cried out, not them that cried out. For they willed to blot out, cut off, destroy Christ: but Thou,

by raising to life Christ, whom they willed to destroy, dost slay the "transgressions of their mouth, the discourse of their lips." For in that He whom they cried out should be destroyed, liveth, they are taken with dread: and that He whom on earth they despised, in heaven is adored by all nations, they wonder: thus are there slain the transgressions of them, and the discourse of their lips. What is, "let them be taken in their pride"? Because to no purpose have strong men rushed on, and it hath fallen out to them as it were to think themselves to have done somewhat, and they have prevailed against the Lord. They were able to crucify a man, weakness might prevail and virtue be slain; and they thought themselves somewhat, as it were strong men, as it were mighty men, as it were prevailing, as it were a lion prepared for prey, as it were fat bulls, as of them in another place he maketh mention: "Fat bulls have beset me." But what have they done in the case of Christ? Not life, but death they have slain. ... And what now hath come to pass in those men that have been converted? For it was told to them that He whom they slew rose again. They believed Him to have risen again, because they saw that He, being in Heaven, thence sent the Holy Spirit, and filled those that on Him believed; and they found themselves to have condemned nought, and to have done nought. Their doing issued in emptiness, the sin remained. Because therefore the doing was made void, but the sin remained upon the doers; they were taken in their pride, they saw themselves under their iniquity. It remained therefore for them to confess the sin, and for Him to pardon, that had given Himself up to sinners, and to forgive His death, having been slain by men dead, and making alive men dead. They were taken therefore in their pride.

3. "And out of cursing and lying shall be declared consummations, in anger of consummation, and they shall not be." This too with difficulty is understood, to what is joined the "and they shall not be." What shall they not be? Let us therefore examine the context above: when they shall have been taken in their pride, "there shall be declared out of cursing and lying consummations." What are consummations? Perfections: for to be consummated, is to be perfected. One thing it is to be consummated, another thing to be consumed. For a thing is consummated which is so finished as that it is perfected: a thing is consumed which is so finished that it is not. Pride would not suffer a man to be perfected, nothing so much hindereth perfection. For let your Love attend a little to what I am saying; and see an evil very pernicious, very much to be guarded against. What sort of evil do ye think it is? How long could I enlarge upon how much evil there is in pride? The devil on that account alone is to be punished. Certes he is the chief of all sinners: certes he is the tempter to sin: to him is not ascribed adultery, not wine-bibbing, not fornication, not the robbing of others' goods: by pride alone he fell. And since pride's companion is envy, it must needs be that a proud man should envy. ... In a word, all vices in evil-doings are to be feared, pride in well-

doings is more to be feared. It is no wonder, then, that so humble is the Apostle, as to say, "When I am made weak, then I am strong." For lest he should himself be tempted by this sin, what sort of medicine doth he say was applied to him against swelling by the Physician, who knew what He was healing? "Lest by the greatness," he saith, "of the revelations I should be exalted, there was given to me a thorn of my flesh, the angel of Satan, to buffet me: wherefore thrice the Lord I besought, that it should depart from me: and He said to me, My grace is sufficient for thee, for virtue in weakness is made perfect." See what the consummations are. An Apostle, the teacher of Gentiles, father of the faithful through the Gospel, received a thorn of the flesh whereby he might be buffeted. Which of us would dare to say this, unless he had not been ashamed to confess this? For if we shall have said that Paul had not suffered this; while to him as it were honour we give, a liar we make him. But because truthful he is, and truth he hath spoken; it behoveth us to believe that there was given to him an angel of Satan, lest by the greatness of the revelations he should be exalted. Behold how much to be feared is the serpent of pride. ...

4. What is, "in the anger of consummation shall be declared consummations"? There is an anger of consummation, and there is an anger of consuming. For every vengeance of God is called anger: sometimes God avengeth, to the end that He may make perfect; sometimes He avengeth, to the end that He may condemn. How doth He avenge, to the end that He may make perfect? "He scourgeth every son whom He receiveth." How doth He avenge, to the end that He may condemn? When He shall have set ungodly men on the left hand, and shall have said to them, "Go ye into fire everlasting, that hath been prepared for the devil and his angels." This is the anger of consuming, not that of consummation. But "there shall be declared consummations in the anger of consummation;" it shall be preached by the Apostles, that "where sin hath abounded, grace shall much more abound," and the weakness of man hath belonged to the healing of humility. Those men thinking of this, and finding out and confessing their iniquities, "shall not be." "Shall not be" what? In their pride.

5. "And they shall know how God shall have dominion of Jacob, and of the ends of the earth" (ver. 13). For before they thought themselves just men, because the Jewish nation had received the Law, because it had kept the commandments of God: it is proved to them that it hath not kept them, since in the very commandments of God Christ it perceived not, because "blindness in part has happened to Israel." Even the Jews themselves see that they ought not to despise the Gentiles, of whom they deemed as of dogs and sinners. For just as alike they have been found in iniquity, so alike they will attain unto salvation. "Not only to

Jews," saith the Apostle, "but also even to Gentiles." For to this end the Stone which the builders set at nought, hath even been made for the Head of the corner, in order that two in itself It might join: for a corner doth unite two walls. The Jews thought themselves exalted and great: of the Gentiles they thought as weak, as sinners, as the servants of demons, as the worshippers of idols, and yet in both was there iniquity. Even the Jews have been proved sinners; because "there is none that doeth good, there is not even so much as one:" they have laid down their pride, and have not envied the salvation of the Gentiles, because they have known their own and their weakness to be alike: and in the Corner Stone being united, they have together worshipped the Lord. ...

6. "They shall be converted at evening" (ver. 14): that is, even if late, that is, after the slaying of our Lord Jesus Christ: "They shall be converted at evening: and hereafter they shall suffer hunger as dogs." But "as dogs," not as sheep or calves: "as dogs," as Gentiles, as sinners; because they too have known their sin that thought themselves righteous. ... It is a good thing therefore for a sinner to be humbled; and no one is more incurable than he that thinketh himself whole. "And they shall go around the city." Already we have explained "city;" it is the "city of standing round;" all nations.

7. "They shall be scattered abroad in order that they may eat" (ver. 15); that is, in order that they may gain others, in order that into their Body they may change believers. "But if they shall not be filled, they shall murmur." Because above also he had spoken of the murmur of them, saying, "For who hath heard?" "And Thou, O Lord," he saith, "shall deride them, saying, Who hath heard?" Wherefore? Because, as nothing Thou shall count all nations. Let the Psalm be concluded. See ye the Corner exulting, now with both walls rejoicing. The Jews were proud, humbled they have been; Gentiles were despairing, raised up they have been: let them come to the Corner, there let them meet, there run together, there find the kiss of peace; from different parts let them come, but with differing not come, those of Circumcision, these of uncircumcision. Far apart were the walls, but before that to the Corner they came: but in the Corner let them hold themselves, and now let the whole Church from both walls, say what? "But I will sing of Thy power, and I will exult in the morning of Thy mercy" (ver. 16). In the morning when temptations have been overcome, in the morning when the night of this world shall have passed away; in the morning when no longer the lyings in wait of robbers and of the devil and of his angels we dread, in the morning when no longer by the lamp of prophecy we walk, but Himself the Word of God as it were a Sun we contemplate. "And I will exult in the morning of Thy mercy." With reason in another Psalm is said, "In the morning I will stand by Thee, and I will meditate."

With reason also of the Lord Himself the Resurrection was at dawn, that there should be fulfilled that which hath been said in another Psalm, "In the evening shall tarry weeping and in the morning exultation." For at even the disciples mourned our Lord Jesus Christ as dead, at dawn at Him rising again they exulted. "For Thou hast become my taker up, and my refuge in the day of my tribulation."

8. "My Helper, to Thee I will play, because Thou, O God, art my taker up" (ver. 17). What was I, unless Thou didst succour? How much despaired of was I, unless Thou didst heal? Where was I lying, unless Thou didst come to me? Certes with a huge wound I was endangered, but that wound of mine did call for an Almighty Physician. To an Almighty Physician nothing is incurable. ... Lastly, thinking of all good things whatsoever we may have, either in nature or in purpose, or in conversion itself, in faith, in hope, in charity, in good morals, in justice, in fear of God; all these to be only by His gifts, he hath thus concluded: "My God is my mercy:" He being filled with the good things of God hath not found what he might call his God, save "his mercy." O name, under which no one must despair! If thou say, my salvation, I perceive that He giveth salvation; if thou say, my refuge, I perceive that thou takest refuge in Him; if thou say, my strength, I perceive that He giveth to thee strength: "my mercy," is what? All that I am is of Thy mercy. ...

PSALM LX.

1. David the king was one man, but not one man he figured; sometimes to wit he figured the Church of many men consisting, extended even unto the ends of the earth: but sometimes One Man he figured, Him he figured that is Mediator of God and men, the Man Christ Jesus. In this Psalm therefore, or rather in this Psalm's title, certain victorious actions of David are spoken of: ... "To the end, in behalf of those men that shall be changed unto the title's inscription, unto teaching for David himself, when he burned up Mesopotamia in Syria, and Syria Sobal, and turned Joab, and smote Edom, in the valley of salt-pits twelve thousand." We read of these things in the books of the Reigns, that all those persons whom he hath named, were defeated by David, that is, Mesopotamia in Syria, and Syria Sobal, Joab, Edom. These things were done, and just as they were done, so there they have been written, so they are read: let him read that will. Nevertheless, as the Prophetic Spirit in the Psalms' titles is wont to depart somewhat from the expression of things done, and to say something which in history is not found, and hence rather to admonish us that titles of this kind have been written not that we may know things done, but that things future may be prefigured. ... But here this thing is inserted for this especial reason, that there it is not written s that he burned up Mesopotamia in Syria, and Syria Sobal. But now let us begin to examine these things after the significations of things future, and to bring out the dimness of shadows into the light of the word.

2. What is "to the end" ye know. For "the end of the law is Christ." Those that are changed ye know. For who but they that do pass from old life into new? ... "For ye were sometime darkness, but now light in the Lord." But they are changed "into the title's inscription," ... who into the kingdom of Christ do pass over from the kingdom of the devil. It is well that they are changed unto this title's inscription. But they are changed, as followeth, "unto teaching." He added, "for David himself unto teaching:" that is, are changed not for themselves, but for David himself, and are changed unto teaching. ... When therefore would Christ have changed us, unless He had done that which He spake of, "Fire I have come to send into the world"? If therefore Christ came to send into the world fire, to wit to its health and profit, we must inquire not how He is to send the world into fire, but how into the world fire. Inasmuch as therefore He came to send fire into the world, let us inquire what is Mesopotamia which was burned up, what is Syria Sobal? The interpretations therefore of the names let us examine according to the Hebrew language, wherein first this Scripture was written. Mesopotamia they say is interpreted, "exalted calling." Now the whole world by calling hath been exalted, Syria is interpreted "lofty." But she which was lofty, burned up hath been and

humbled. Sobal is interpreted "empty antiquity." Thanks to Christ that hath burned her. Whenever old bushes are burned up, green places succeed; and more speedily and more plentifully, and more fully green, fresh ones spring out, when fire hath gone before them to the burning up of the old. Let not therefore the fire of Christ be feared, hay it consumeth. "For all flesh is hay, and all the glory of man as flower of hay." He burneth up therefore those things with that fire. "And turned Joab." Joab is interpreted enemy. There was turned an enemy, as thou wilt understand it. If turned unto flight, the devil it is: if converted to the faith, a Christian it is. How unto flight? From the heart of a Christian: "The Prince of this world," He saith, "now hath been cast out." But how can a Christian turned to the Lord be an enemy turned? Because he hath become a believer that had been an enemy. "Smote Edom." Edom is interpreted "earthly." That earthly one ought to be smitten. For why should one live earthly, that ought to live heavenly? There hath been slain therefore life earthly, let there live life heavenly. "For as we have borne the image of the earthly, let us bear also the image of Him that is from Heaven." See it slain: "Mortify your members which are upon earth." But when he had smitten Edom, he smote "twelve thousand in the valley of salt-pits." Twelve thousand is a perfect number, to which perfect number also the number of the twelve Apostles is ascribed: for not to no purpose is it, but because through the whole world was to be sent the Word. But the Word of God, which is Christ, is in clouds, that is, in the preachers of truth. But the world of four parts doth consist. The four parts thereof are exceeding well known to all, and often in the Scriptures they are mentioned: they are the same as the name of the four winds, East, West, North, and South. To all these four parts was sent the Word, so that in the Trinity all might be called. The number twelve four times three do make. With reason therefore twelve thousand earthly things were smitten, the whole world was smitten: for from the whole world was chosen out the Church, mortified from earthly life. Why "in the valley of salt-pits"? A valley is humility: salt- pits signify savour. For many men are humbled, but emptily and foolishly, in empty oldness they are humbled. One suffereth tribulation for money, suffereth tribulation for temporal honour, suffereth tribulation for the comforts of this life; he is to suffer tribulation and to be humbled: why not for the sake of God? why not for the sake of Christ? why not for the savour of salt? Knowest thou not that to thee hath been said, "Ye are the salt of earth," and, "If the salt shall have been spoiled, for no other thing will it be of use, but to be cast out"? A good thing it is therefore wisely to be humbled. Behold now are not heretics being humbled? Have not laws been made even by men to condemn them, against whom divine laws do reign, which even before had condemned them? Behold they are humbled, behold they are put to flight, behold persecution they suffer, but without savour; for folly, for emptiness. For now the salt hath been spoiled: therefore it hath been cast out, to be trodden down of men. We have heard the title of the Psalm, let us hear also the words of the Psalm.

3. "God, Thou hast driven us back, and hast destroyed us" (ver. 1). Is that David speaking that smote, that burned up, that defeated, and not they to whom He did these things, that is to say, their being smitten and driven back, that were evil men, and again their being made alive and returning in order that they might be good men? That destruction indeed that David made, strong of hand, our Christ, whose figure that man was bearing; He did those things, He made this destruction with His sword and with His fire: for both He brought into this world. Both "Fire I am come to send into the world," thou hast in the Gospel: and "A sword I have come to send into the earth," thou hast in the Gospel. He brought in fire, whereby might be burned up Mesopotamia in Syria, and Syria Sobal: He brought in a sword whereby might be smitten Edom. Now again this destruction was made for the sake of "those that are changed unto the title's inscription." Hear we therefore the voice of them: to their health smitten they were, being raised up let them speak. Let them say, therefore, that are changed into something better, changed unto the title's inscription, changed unto teaching for David himself; let them say, "Thou hast had mercy upon us." Thou hast destroyed us, in order that Thou mightest build us; Thou hast destroyed us that were ill builded, hast destroyed empty oldness; in order that there may be a building unto a new man, building to abide for everlasting. ...

4. "Thou hast moved the earth, and hast troubled it" (ver. 2). How hath the earth been troubled? In the conscience of sinners. Whither go we? Whither flee we, when this sword hath been brandished, "Repent, for near hath drawn the kingdom of Heaven"? "Heal the crushings thereof, for moved it hath been." Unworthy it is to be healed, if moved it hath not been: but thou speakest, preachest, threatenest us with God, of coming judgment holdest not thy peace, of the commandment of God thou warnest, from these things thou abstainest not; and he that heareth, if he feareth not, if he is not moved, is not worthy to be healed. Another heareth, is moved, is stung, smiteth the breast, sheddeth tears. ...

5. The first labour is, that thou shouldest be displeasing to thyself, that sins thou shouldest battle out, that thou shouldest be changed into something better: the second labour, in return for thy having been changed, is to bear the tribulations and temptations of this world, and amid them to hold on even unto the end. Of these things therefore when he was speaking, while pointing out such things, he addeth what? "Thou hast shown to Thy people hard things" (ver. 3): to Thy people now, made tributary after the victory of David. "Thou hast shown to Thy people hard things." Wherein? In persecutions which the Church of Christ hath endured, when so much blood of martyrs was spilled. "Thou hast given us to drink of the wine of goading." "Of goading" is what? Not of killing. For it was not a killing

that destroyeth, but a medicine that smarteth. "Thou hast given us to drink of the wine of goading."

6. Wherefore this? "Thou hast given to men fearing Thee, a sign that they should flee from the face of the bow" (ver. 4). Through tribulations temporal, he saith, Thou hast signified to Thine own to flee from the wrath of fire everlasting. For, saith the Apostle Peter, "Time it is that Judgment begin with the House of God." And exhorting the Martyrs to endurance, when the world should rage, when slaughters should be made at the hands of persecutors, when far and wide blood of believers should be spilled, when in chains, in prisons, in tortures, many hard things Christians should suffer, in these hard things, I say, lest they should faint, Peter saith to them, "Time it is that Judgment begin with the House of God," etc. What therefore is to be in the Judgment? The bow is bended, still in menacing posture it is, not yet in aiming. And see what there is in the bow: is there not an arrow to be shot forward? The string however is stretched back in a contrary direction to that in which it is going to be shot; and the more the stretching thereof hath gone backward, with the greater swiftness it starteth forward. What is it that I have said? The more the Judgment is deferred, with so much the greater swiftness it is to come. Therefore even for temporal tribulations to God let us render thanks, because He hath given to His people a sign, "that they should flee from the face of the bow:" in order that His faithful ones having been exercised in tribulations temporal, may be worthy to avoid the condemnation of fire everlasting, which is to find out all them that do not believe these things.

7. "That Thy beloved may be delivered: save me with Thy right hand, and hearken unto me" (ver. 5). With Thy right hand save me, Lord: so save me as that at the right hand I may stand. Not any safety temporal I require, in this matter Thy Will be done. For a time what is good for us we are utterly ignorant: for "what we should pray for as we ought we know not:" but "save me with Thy right hand," so that even if in this time I suffer sundry tribulations, when the night of all tribulations hath been spent, on the right hand I may be found among the sheep, not on the left hand among the goats. "And hearken, unto me." Because now I am deserving that which Thou art willing to give; not "with the words of my transgressions" I am crying through the day, so that Thou hearken not, and "in the night so that Thou hearken not," and that not for folly to me," but truly for my warning, by adding savour from the valley of salt-pits, so that in tribulation I may know what to ask: but I ask life everlasting; therefore hearken unto me, because Thy right hand I ask. ...

8. "God hath spoken in His Holy One" (ver. 6). ... In what Holy One of His? "God was in Christ reconciling the world to Himself." In that Holy One, of whom elsewhere ye have heard, "O God, in the Holy One is Thy way." "I will rejoice and will divide Sichima. ... and the valley of tabernacles I will measure out." Sichima is interpreted shoulders. But according to history, Jacob returning from Laban his father-in-law with all his kindred, hid the idols in Sichima which he had from Syria, where for a long time he had dwelled, and at length was coming from thence. But tabernacles he made there because of his sheep and herds, and called the place Tabernacles. And these I will divide, saith the Church. What is this, "I will divide Sichima"? If to the story where the idols were hidden is the reference, the Gentiles it signifieth; I divide the Gentiles. I divide, is what? "For not in all men is there faith." I divide, is what? Some will believe, others will not believe. ... The shoulders are divided, in order that their sins may burthen some men, while others may take up the burden of Christ. For godly shoulders He was requiring when He said," For My yoke is gentle, and My burden is light." Another burden oppresseth and loadeth thee, but Christ's burden relieveth thee: another burden hath weight, Christ's burden hath wings. For even if thou pull off the wings from a bird, thou dost remove a kind of weight; and the more weight thou hast taken away, the more on earth it will abide. She that thou hast chosen to disburden lieth there: she flieth not, because thou hast taken off a weight: let there be given back the weight, and she flieth. Such is Christ's burden; let men carry it, and not be idle: let them not be heeded that will not bear it; let them bear it that will, and they shall find how light it is, how sweet, how pleasant, how ravishing unto Heaven, and from earth how transporting. ... Perchance because of the sheep of Jacob, "the valley of Tabernacles" is to be understood of the nation of the Jews, and the same is divided: for they have passed from thence that have believed, the rest have remained without.

9. "Mine is Galaad" (ver. 7). These names are read in the Scriptures of God. Galaad hath the voice of an interpretation of its own and of a great Mystery: for it is interpreted "the heap of testimony." How great a heap of testimony in the Martyrs? "Mine is Galaad," mine is a heap of testimony, mine are the true Martyrs. ... Then meanly esteemed was the Church among men, then reproach on Her a Widow was being thrown, because Christ's She was, because the sign of the Cross on her brow She was wearing: not yet was there honour, censure there was then: when therefore not honour, but censure there was, then was made a heap of witness; and through the heap of witness was the Love of Christ enlarged; and through the enlargement of the Love of Christ, were the Gentiles possessed. There followeth, "And mine is Manasses;" which is interpreted forgotten. For to Her had been said, "Confusion for everlasting Thou shall forget, and of the reproach of Thy widowhood Thou shall not be mindful." There was therefore a confusion of the

Church once, which now hath been forgotten: for of Her confusion and of the "reproach" of Her widow-hood now She is not mindful. For when there was a sort of confusion among men, a heap of witness was made. Now no longer doth any even remember that confusion, when it was a reproach to be a Christian, now no one remembereth, now all have forgotten, now "Mine is Manasses, and Ephraim the strength of My head." Ephraim is interpreted fruitfulness. Mine, he saith, is fruitfulness, and this fruitfulness is the strength of My Head. For My Head is Christ. And whence is fruitfulness the strength of Him? Because unless a grain were to fall into the earth, it would not be multiplied, alone it would remain. Fall then to earth did Christ in His Passion, and there followed fruit-bearing in the Resurrection. He was hanging and was being despised: the grain was within, it had powers to draw after it all things. How in a grain do numbers of seeds lie hid, something abject it appeareth to the eyes, but a power turning into itself matter and bringing forth fruit is hidden; so in Christ's Cross virtue was hidden, there appeared weakness. O mighty grain! Doubtless weak is He that hangeth, Doubtless before Him that people did wag the head, Doubtless they said, "If Son of God He is, let Him come down from the Cross." Hear the strength of Him: that which is a weak thing of God, is stronger than men. With reason so great fruitfulness hath followed: it is mine, saith the Church.

10. "Juda is my king: Moab the pot of my hope" (ver. 7). What Juda? He that is of the tribe of Juda. What Juda, but He to whom Jacob himself said, "Juda, thy brethren shall praise thee"? What therefore should I fear, when Juda my king saith, "Fear not them that kill the body"? Moab the pot of my hope" Wherefore "pot"? Because tribulation. Wherefore "of my hope"? Because there hath gone before Juda my king. ... Moab is perceived in the Gentiles. For that nation was born of sin, that nation was born of the daughters of Lot, who lay with their father drunken, abusing a father. Better were it to have remained barren, than thus to have become mothers. But this was a kind of figure of them that abuse the law. For do not heed that law in the Latin language is of the feminine gender: in Greek of the masculine gender it is: but whether it be of the feminine gender in speaking, or of the masculine, the expression maketh no difference to the truth. For law hath rather a masculine force, because it ruleth, is not ruled. But moreover, the Apostle Paul saith what? "Good is the law, if any one use it lawfully." But those daughters of Lot unlawfully used their father. But in the same manner as good works begin to grow when a man useth well the law: so arise evil works, when a man ill useth the law. Furthermore, they ill using their father, that is, ill using the law, engendered the Moabites, by whom are signified evil works. Thence the tribulation of the Church, thence the pot boiling up. Of this pot in a certain place of prophecy is said, "A pot heated by the North wind." Whence but by the quarters of the devil, who hath said, "I will set my seat at the North"? The chiefest

tribulations therefore arise against the Church from none except from those that ill use the law. ...

11. "Into Idumaea I will stretch out my shoe" (ver. 8). The Church speaketh, "I will come through even unto Idumaea." Let tribulations rage, let the world boil with offences, even unto those very persons that lead an earthly life (for Idumaea is interpreted earthly), even unto those same," even unto Idumaea, I will stretch out my shoe." Of what thing the shoe except of the Gospel? "How beautiful the feet of them that tell of peace, that tell of good things," and "the feet shod unto the preparation of the Gospel of peace."... In these times we see, brethren, how many earthly men do perpetrate frauds for the sake of gain, for frauds perjuries; on account of their fears they consult fortune-tellers, astrologers: all these men are Edomites, earthly; and nevertheless all these men adore Christ, under His own shoe they are; now even unto Idumaea is stretched out His shoe. "To Me Allophyli have been made subject." Who are "Allophyli"? Men of other race, not belonging to My race. They "have been made subject," because many men adore Christ, and are not to reign with Christ.

12. "Who will lead Me down into the city of standing round?" (ver. 9). What is the city of standing round? If ye remember already, I have made mention thereof in another Psalm, wherein hath been said, "And they shall go around the city." For the city of standing round is the compassing around of the Gentiles, which compassing around of the Gentiles in the middle thereof had the one nation of the Jews, worshipping one God: the rest of the compassing around of the Gentiles to idols made supplication, demons they did serve. And mystically it was called the city of standing round; because on all sides the Gentiles had poured themselves around, and had stood around that nation which did worship one God. ... "Who will lead me down even unto Idumaea?"

13. "Wilt not Thou, O God, that hast driven us back? And wilt not Thou, O God, march forth in our powers?" (ver. 10). Wilt not Thou lead us down, that hast driven us back? But wherefore "hast driven us back"? Because Thou hast destroyed us. Wherefore hast destroyed us? Because angry Thou hast been, and hast had pity on us. Thou therefore wilt lead down, that hast driven back; Thou, O God, that wilt not march forth in our powers, wilt lead down. What is, "wilt not march forth in our powers"? The world is to rage, the world is to tread us down, there is to be a heap of witnesses, builded of the spilled blood of martyrs, and the raging heathen are to say, "Where is the God of them?" Then "Thou wilt not march forth in our powers:" against them Thou wilt not show Thyself, Thou wilt not show Thy power, such as Thou hast shown in David, in Moses, in Joshua the

son of Nun, when to their might the Gentiles yielded, and when the slaughter had been ended, and the great laying waste repaired, into the land which Thou promisedst Thou leddest in Thy people. This thing then Thou wilt not do, "Thou wilt not march forth in our powers," but within Thou wilt work. What is, "wilt not march forth"? Wilt not show Thyself. For indeed when in chains the Martyrs were being led along, when they were being shut up in prison, when they were being led forth to be mocked, when to the beasts they were exposed, when they were being smitten with the sword, when with fire they were being burned, were they not despised as though forsaken, as though without helper? In what manner was God working within? in what manner within was He comforting? in what manner to these men was He making sweet the hope of life everlasting? in what manner was He not forsaking the hearts of them, where the man was dwelling in silence, well if good, ill if evil? Was He then by any means forsaking, because He was not marching forth in the powers of them? By not marching forth in the powers of them, did He not the more lead down the Church even unto Idumaea, lead down the Church even unto the city of standing around? For if the Church chose to war and to use the sword, She would seem to be fighting for life present: but because she was despising life present, therefore there was made a heap of witness for the life that shall be.

14. Thou therefore, O God, that wilt not march forth in our powers, "Give to us aid from tribulation, and vain is the safety of man" (ver. 11). Go now they that salt have not, and desire safety temporal for their friends, which is empty oldness. "Give to us aid:" from thence whence Thou wast supposed to forsake, thence succour. "In God we will do valour, and Himself to nothing shall bring down our enemies" (ver. 12). We will not do valour with the sword, not with horses, not with breastplates, not with shields, not in the mightiness of an army, not abroad. But where? Within, where we are not seen. Where within? "In God we will do virtue:" and as if abjects, and as if trodden down, men as if of no consideration we shall be, but "Himself to nothing shall bring down our enemies." In a word, this thing hath been done to our enemies. Trodden down have been the Martyrs: by suffering, by enduring, by persevering even unto the end, in God they have done valour. Himself also hath done that which followeth: to nothing He hath brought down the enemies of them. Where are now the enemies of the Martyrs, except perchance that now drunken men with their cups do persecute those whom at that time frenzied men did use with stones to persecute?

PSALM LXI.

1. The title of it doth not detain us. For it is "Unto the end, in hymns, to David himself. "In hymns," to wit in praises. "Unto the end," to wit unto Christ. ... But the voice in this Psalm (if we are among the members of Him, and in the Body, even as upon His exhortation we have the boldness to trust) we ought to acknowledge to be our own, not that of any foreigner. But I have not so called it our own, as if it were of those only that are now in presence; but our own, as being of us that are throughout the whole world, that are from the East even unto the West. And in order that ye may know it thus to be our voice, He speaketh here as if one Man: but He is not One Man; but even as One, the Unity is speaking. But in Christ we all are one man: because of this One Man the Head is in Heaven, and the members are yet toiling on earth: and because they are toiling see what He saith.

2. "Hearken, O God, to my supplication, give heed to my prayer" (ver. 1). Who saith? He, as if One. See whether one: "From the ends of the earth to Thee I have cried, while my heart was being vexed" (ver. 2). Now therefore not one: but for this reason one, because Christ is One, of whom all we are the members. For what one man crieth from the ends of the earth? There crieth not from the ends of the earth any but that inheritance, of which hath been said to the Son Himself, "Demand of Me, and I will give to Thee the nations for Thine inheritance, and for Thy possession the boundaries of the earth." This therefore Christ's possession, this Christ's inheritance, this Christ's Body, this Christ's one Church, this the Unity which we are, is crying from the ends of the earth. ... But wherefore have I cried this thing? "While my heart was being vexed." He showeth himself to be throughout all nations in the whole round world, in great glory, but in great tribulation. For our life in this sojourning cannot be without temptation: because our advance is made through our temptation, nor does a man become known to himself unless tempted, nor can he be crowned except he shall have conquered, nor can he conquer except he shall have striven, nor can he strive except he shall have experienced an enemy, and temptations. This Man therefore is being vexed, that from the ends of the earth is crying, but nevertheless He is not forsaken. For ourselves who are His Body He hath willed to prefigure also in that His Body wherein already He hath both died and hath risen again, and into Heaven hath ascended, in order that whither the Head hath gone before, thither the members may be assured that they shall follow. Therefore us He did transfer by a figure into Himself, when He willed to be tempted of Satan.

3. But now there was read in the Gospel, how the Lord Jesus Christ in the wilderness was being tempted of the devil. Christ entirely was tempted of the

devil. For in Christ thou wast being tempted, because Christ of thee had for Himself flesh, of Himself for thee salvation; of thee for Himself death, of Himself for thee life; of thee for Himself revilings, of Himself for thee honours; therefore of thee for Himself temptation, of Himself for thee victory. If in Him tempted we have been, in Him we overcome the devil. ... "On the Rock Thou hast exalted me." Now therefore here we perceive who is crying from the ends of the earth. Let us call to mind the Gospel: "Upon this Rock I will build My Church." Therefore She crieth from the ends of the earth, whom He hath willed to be builded upon a Rock. But in order that the Church might be builded upon the Rock, who was made the Rock? Hear Paul saying: "But the Rock was Christ." On Him therefore builded we have been. For this reason that Rock whereon we have been builded, first hath been smitten with winds, flood, rain, when Christ of the devil was being tempted. Behold on what firmness He hath willed to stablish thee. With reason our voice is not in vain, but is hearkened unto: for on great hope we have been set: "On the Rock Thou hast exalted me." ...

4. "Thou hast led me down, because Thou hast been made my hope: a tower of strength from the face of the enemy" (ver. 3). My heart is vexed, saith that Unity from the ends of the earth, and I toil amid temptations and offences: the heathen envy, because they have been conquered; the heretics lie in wait, hidden in the cloak of the Christian name: within in the Church itself the wheat suffereth violence from the chaff: amid all these things when my heart is vexed, I will cry from the ends of the earth. But there forsaketh me not the Same that hath exalted me upon the Rock, in order to lead me down even unto Himself, because even if I labour, while the devil through so many places and times and occasions lieth in wait against me, He is to me a tower of strength, to whom when I shall have fled for refuge, not only I shall escape the weapons of the enemy, but even against him securely I shall myself hurl whatever darts I shall please. For Christ Himself is the tower, Himself for us hath been made a tower from the face of the enemy, who is also the Rock whereon hath been builded the Church. Art thou taking heed that thou be not smitten of the devil? Flee to the Tower; never to that tower will the devil's darts follow thee: there thou wilt stand protected and fixed. But in what manner shalt thou flee to the Tower? Let not a man, set perchance in temptation, in body seek that Tower, and when he shall not have found it, be wearied, or faint in temptation. Before thee is the Tower: call to mind Christ, and go into the Tower. ...

5. "A sojourner I will be in Thy tabernacle even unto ages" (ver. 4). Ye see how he, of whom we have spoken, is he that crieth. Which of us is a sojourner even unto ages? For a few days here we live, and we pass away: for sojourners here we

are, inhabitants in Heaven we shall be. Thou art a sojourner in that place where thou art to hear the voice of the Lord thy God, "Remove." For from that Home everlasting in the Heavens no one will bid thee to remove. Here therefore a sojourner thou art. Whence also is said in another Psalm, "A sojourner I am with Thee and a stranger, as all my fathers were." Here therefore sojourners we are; there the Lord shall give to us mansions everlasting: "Many are," He saith, "the mansions in My Father's house." Those mansions not as though to sojourners He will give, but as though to citizens to abide for everlasting. Here however, brethren, because for no small time the Church was to be on this earth, but because here shall be the Church even unto the end of the world: therefore here He hath said, "A dweller I will be in Thy tabernacle even unto ages." ... Well, of a few days thou wouldest choose that the temptations should be: but how would She gather together all Her sons, unless for a long time She were to be here, unless even unto the end She were to be prolonged? Do not envy the rest of mankind that hereafter shall be: do not, because thou hast already passed over, wish to cut down the bridge of mercy: be it here even for ever. And what of temptations, which needs must abound, by how much the more offences come? For Himself saith "Because iniquity hath abounded, the love of many shall wax cold." But that Church, which crieth from the ends of the earth, is in these circumstances whereof he speaketh in continuation. "But he that shall have persevered even unto the end, the same shall be saved." But whence shalt thou persevere? ... "I shall be covered up in the veiling of Thy wings." Behold the reason why we are in safety amid so great temptations, until there come the end of the world, and ages everlasting receive us; namely, because we are covered up in the veiling of His Wings. There is heat in the world, but there is a great shade under the wings of God.

6. "For Thou, O God, hast hearkened to my prayer" (ver. 5). What prayer? That wherewith he beginneth: "Hearken, O God, to my supplication." ... "Thou hast given inheritance to men fearing Thy name." Let us continue therefore in the fear of God's name: the eternal Father deceiveth us not. Sons labour, that they may receive the inheritance of their parents, to whom when dead they are to succeed: are we not labouring to receive an inheritance from that Father, to whom not dying we succeed; but together with Him in the very inheritance for everlasting are to live?

7. "Days upon days of the King Thou shall add to the years of Him" (ver. 6). This is therefore the King of whom we are the members. A King Christ is, our Head, our King. Thou hast given to Him days upon days; not only those days in that time that hath end, but days upon those days without end. "I will dwell," he saith, "in the house of the Lord, for length of days," Wherefore for length of days, but

because now is the shortness of days? For everything which hath an end, is short: but of this King are days upon days, so that not only while these days pass away, Christ reigneth in His Church, but the Saints shall reign together with Him in those days which have no end. ... For years of God have been also spoken of: "But Thou art the very Same, and Thy years shall not fail." In the same manner as years, so days, so one day. Whatsoever thou wilt thou sayest of eternity. Whatever thou wilt thou sayest for this reason, because whatever thou shalt have said, it is too little that thou hast said. For thou must needs say somewhat, to the end that there may be something whereby thou mayest meditate on that which cannot be told. "Even unto the day of generation and of generation." Of this generation and of the generation that shall be: of this generation which is compared to the moon, because as the moon is new, waxeth, is full, waneth, and vanisheth, so are these mortal generations; and of the generation wherein we are born anew by rising again, and shall abide for everlasting with God, when now no longer we are like the moon, but like that of which saith the Lord, "Then the righteous shall shine like the sun in the kingdom of their Father." For the moon by a figure in the Scriptures is put for the mutability of this mortal state. ...

8. "He shall abide for everlasting in the sight of God" (ver. 7); according to what, or because of what? "His mercy and truth who shall seek for Him?" He saith also in another place, "All the ways of the Lord are mercy and truth, to men seeking His testament and His testimonies." Large is the discourse of truth and mercy, but shortness we have promised. Briefly hear ye what is truth and mercy: because no small thing is that which hath been said, "All the ways of the Lord are mercy and truth." Mercy is spoken of, because our merits God regarded not, but His own goodness, in order that He might forgive us all our sins, and might promise life everlasting: but truth is spoken of, because He faileth not to render those things which He hath promised. Let us acknowledge it here, and let us do it; so that, just as to us God hath shown forth His mercy and His truth, mercy in forgiving our sins, truth in showing forth His promises; so also, I say, let us execute mercy and truth, mercy concerning the weak, concerning the needy, concerning even our enemies; truth in not sinning, and in not adding sin upon sin. ...Who is therefore he that doeth this, save one out of those few, of whom is said, "He that shall have continued unto the end, the same shall be saved"? With reason here also "His mercy and truth who shall seek for Him?" Why is there" for Him"? "Who shall seek," would be sufficient. Why hath he added, "for Him," but because many men seek to learn His mercy and truth in His books? And when they have learned, for themselves they live, not for Him; their own things they seek, not the things which are of Jesus Christ: they preach mercy and truth, and do not mercy and truth. But by preaching it, they know it: for they would not preach it, unless they knew it. But he that loveth God and Christ, in preaching the mercy and truth of the Same,

doth himself seek her for Him, not for himself: that is, not in order that himself may have by this preaching temporal advantages, but in order that he may do good to His members, that is, His faithful ones, by ministering with truth of that which he knoweth: in order that he that liveth, no longer for himself may live, but for Him that for all men hath died.

9. "So I will play music to Thy name, that I may render my vows from day unto day" (ver. 8). If thou playest music to the name of God, play not for a time. Wilt thou for ever play? wilt thou for everlasting play? Render to Him thy vows from day unto day. What is, render to Him thy vows from day unto day? From this day unto that day. Continue to render vows in this day, until thou come to that day: that is," He that shall have continued even unto the end, the same shall be saved."

PSALM LXII.

1. The title of it is, "Unto the end, in behalf of Idithun, a Psalm to David himself." I recollect that already s to you hath been explained what Idithun is. ... Let us see how far he hath leaped over, and whom he hath "leaped over," and in what place, though he hath leaped over certain men, he is situate, whence as from a kind of spiritual and secure position he may behold what is below. ... He being set, I say, in a certain fortified place, doth say, "Shall not my soul be subject to God?" (ver. 1). For he had heard, "He that doth exalt himself shall be humbled; and he that humbleth himself shall be exalted:" and fearful lest by leaping over he should be proud, not elated by those things which were below, but humble because of Him that was above; to envious men, as it were threatening to him a fall, who were grieved that he had leaped over, he hath made answer, "Shall not my soul be subject to God?" ... "For from Himself is my salvation." "For Himself is my God and thy salvation, my taker up, I shall not be moved more" (ver. 2). I know who is above me, I know who stretcheth forth His mercy to men that know Him, I know under the coverings of whose wings I should hope: "I shall not be moved more." ...

2. Therefore, down from the higher place fortified and protected, he, to whom the Lord hath been made a refuge, he, to whom is God Himself for a fortified place, hath regard to those whom he hath leaped over, and looking down upon them speaketh as though from a lofty tower: for this also hath been said of Him, "A Tower of strength from the face of the enemy:" he giveth heed therefore to them, and saith," How long do ye lay upon a man?" (ver. 3). By insulting, by hurling reproaches, by laying wait, by persecuting, ye lay upon a man burthens, ye lay upon a man as much as a man can bear: but in order that a man may bear, under him is He that hath made man. If to a man ye look, "slay ye, all of you." Behold, lay upon, rage, "slay ye, all of you." "As though a wall bowed down, and as a fence smitten against;" lean against, smite against, as if going to throw down. And where is, "I shall not be moved more"? But wherefore? "I shall not be moved more." Because Himself is God my Saving One, my taker up, therefore ye men are able to lay burdens upon a man; can ye anywise lay upon God, who protecteth man? "Slay ye, all of you." What is that size of body in one man so great as that he may be slain by all? But we ought to perceive our person, the person of the Church, the person of the Body of Christ. For one Man with His Head and Body is Jesus Christ, the Saviour of the Body and the Members of the Body: two in one Flesh, and in one voice, and in one passion, and, when iniquity shall have passed over, in one rest. The sufferings therefore of Christ are not in Christ alone; nay, there are not any save in Christ. For if Christ thou understandest to be Head and Body, the sufferings of Christ are not, save in Christ: but if Christ thou understand

of Head alone, the sufferings of Christ are not in Christ alone. For if the sufferings of Christ are in Christ alone, to wit in the Head alone; whence saith a certain member of Him, Paul the Apostle, "In order that I may supply what are wanting of the oppressions of Christ in my flesh"? If therefore in the members of Christ thou art, whatsoever man thou art that art hearing these words, whosoever thou art that dost hear these words (but however, thou dost hear, if in the members of Christ thou art): whatsoever thing thou sufferest from those that are not in the members of Christ, was wanting to the sufferings of Christ. Therefore it is added because it was wanting; thou fillest up the measure, thou causest it not to run over: thou sufferest so much as was to be contributed out of thy sufferings to the whole suffering of Christ, that hath suffered in our Head, and doth suffer in His members, that is, in our own selves. Unto this our common republic, as it were each of us according to our measure payeth that which we owe, and according to the powers which we have, as it were a quota of sufferings we contribute. The storehouse of all men's sufferings will not be completely made up, save when the world shall have been ended. ... That whole City therefore is speaking, from the blood of righteous Abel even to the blood of Zacharias. Thence also hereafter from the blood of John, through the blood of the Apostles, through the blood of Martyrs, through the blood of the faithful ones of Christ, one City speaketh, one man saith, "How long do ye lay upon a man? Slay ye, all of you." Let us see if ye efface, let us see if ye extinguish, let us see if ye remove from the earth the name thereof, let us see if ye peoples do not meditate of empty things, saying, "When shall She die, and when shall perish the name of Her?" "As though She were a wall bowed down, and a fence smitten against," lean ye against Her, smite against Her. Hear from above: "My taker up, I shall not be moved more:" for as though a heap of sand I have been smitten against that I might fall, and the Lord hath taken me up.

3. "Nevertheless, mine honour they have thought to drive back" (ver. 4). Conquered while they slay men yielding, by the blood of the slain multiplying the faithful, yielding to these and no longer being able to kill; "Nevertheless, mine honour they have thought to drive back." Now because a Christian cannot be killed, pains are taken that a Christian should be dishonoured. For now by the honour of Christians the hearts of ungodly men are tortured: now that spiritual Joseph, after his selling by his brethren, after his removal from his home into Egypt as though into the Gentiles, after the humiliation of a prison, after the made-up tale of a false witness, after that there had come to pass that which of him was said, "Iron passed through the soul of him:" now he is honoured, now he is not made subject to brethren selling him, but corn he supplieth to them hungering. Conquered by his humility and chastity, uncorruptness, temptations, sufferings, now honoured they see him, and his honour they think to check. ... Is it all against

one man, or one man against all; or all against all, or one against one? Meanwhile, when he saith, "ye lay upon a man," it is as it were upon one man: and when he saith, "Slay all ye," it is as if all men were against one man: but nevertheless it is also all against all, because also all are Christians, but in One. But why must those divers errors hostile to Christ be spoken of as all together? Are they also one? Truly them also as one I dare to speak of: because there is one City and one city, one People and one people, King and king. One City and one city is what? Babylon one, Jerusalem one. By whatsoever other mystical names besides She is called, yet One City there is and one city; over this the devil is king, over that Christ is King. ...

4. Give heed, brethren, give heed, I entreat you. For it delighteth me yet to speak a few words to you of this beloved City. For "most glorious things of Thee have been spoken, City of God." And, "if I forget Thee, O Jerusalem, let mine own right hand forget me." For dear is the one Country, and truly but one Country, the only Country: besides Her whatsoever we have, is a sojourning in a strange land. I will say therefore that which ye may acknowledge, that of which ye may approve: I will call to your minds that which ye know, I will not teach that which ye know not. "Not first," saith the Apostle, "that which is spiritual, but that which is natural, afterwards that which is spiritual." Therefore the former city is greater by age, because first was born Cain, and afterwards Abel: but in these the elder shall serve the younger. The former greater by age, the latter greater in dignity. Wherefore is the former greater by age? Because "not first that which is spiritual, but that which is natural." Wherefore is the latter greater in dignity? Because "the eider shall serve the younger." ... Cain first builded a city, and in that place he builded where no city was. But when Jerusalem was being builded, it was not builded in a place where there was not a city, but there was a city at first which was called Jebus, whence the Jebusites. This having been captured, overcome, made subject, there was builded a new city, as though the old were thrown down; and it was called Jerusalem, vision of peace, City of God. Each one therefore that is born of Adam, not yet doth belong to Jerusalem: for he beareth with him the offshoot of iniquity, and the punishment of sin, having been consigned to death, and he belongeth in a manner to a sort of old city. But if he is to be in the people of God; his old self will be thrown down, and he will be builded up new. For this reason therefore Cain builded a city where there was not a city. For from mortality and from naughtiness every one setteth out, in order that he may be made good hereafter. "For as by the disobedience of one man many were made sinners, so by the obedience of One Man many shall be made just." And all we in Adam do die: and each one of us of Adam was born. Let him pass over to Jerusalem, he shall be thrown down old, and shall be builded new. As though to conquered Jebusites, in order that there may be builded up Jerusalem, is said, "Put ye off the old man, and put on the new." And

now to them builded in Jerusalem, and shining by the light of Grace, is said, "Ye have been sometime darkness, but now light in the Lord." The evil city therefore from the beginning even unto the end doth run on, and the good City by the changing of evil men is builded up. And these two cities are meanwhile mingled, at the end to be severed; against each other mutually in conflict, the one for iniquity, the other for the truth. And sometimes this very temporal mingling bringeth it to pass that certain men belonging to the city Babylon, do order matters belonging to Jerusalem, and again certain men belonging to Jerusalem, do order matters belonging to Babylon. Something difficult I seem to have propounded. Be ye patient, until it be proved by examples. "For all things" in the old people, as writeth the Apostle, "in a figure used to befall them: but they have been written for our amendment, upon whom the end of the world hath come." Regard therefore that people as also set to intimate an after people; and see then what I say. There were great kings in Jerusalem: it is a known fact, they are enumerated, are named. They all were, I say, wicked citizens of Babylon, and they were ordering matters of Jerusalem: all men from thence to be dissevered at the end, to no one but to the devil do belong. Again we find citizens of Jerusalem to have ordered certain matters belonging to Babylon. For those three children, Nabuchodonosor, overcome by a miracle, made the ministers of his kingdom, and set them over his Satraps; and so there were ordering the matters of Babylon citizens of Jerusalem. Observe now how this is being fulfilled and done in the Church, and in these times. ... Every earthly commonwealth, sometime assuredly to perish, whereof the kingdom is to pass away, when there shall come that kingdom, whereof we pray, "Thy kingdom come;" and whereof hath been foretold, "And of His kingdom shall be no end:" an earthly commonwealth, I say, hath our citizens conducting the affairs of it. For how many faithful, how many good men, are both magistrates in their cities, and are judges, and are generals, and are counts, and are kings? All that are just and good men, having not anything in heart but the most glorious things, which of Thee have been said, City of God. And as if they were doing bond-service in the city which is to pass away, even there by the doctors of the Holy City they are bidden to keep faith with those set over them, "whether with the king as supreme, or with governors as though sent by God for the punishment of evil men, but for the praise of good men:" or as servants, that to their masters they should be subject, even Christians to Heathens, and the better should keep faith with the worse, for a time to serve, for everlasting to have dominion. For these things do happen until iniquity do pass away. Servants are commanded to bear with masters unjust and capricious: the citizens of Babylon are commanded to be endured by the citizens of Jerusalem, showing even more attentions, than if they were citizens of the same Babylon, as though fulfilling the precept, "He that shall have exacted of thee a mile, go with him other twain."...

5. "I have run in thirst." For they were rendering evil things for good things: for them was I thirsting: mine honour they thought to drive back: I was thirsting to bring them over into my body. For in drinking what do we, but send into our members liquor that is without, and suck it into our body? Thus did Moses in that head of the calf. The head of the calf is a great sacrament. For the head of the calf was the body of ungodly men, in the similitude of a calf eating hay, seeking earthly things: because all flesh is hay. ... And what now is more evident, than that into that City Jerusalem, of which the people Israel was a type, by Baptism men were to be made to pass over? Therefore in water it was scattered, in order that for drink it might be given. For this even unto the end this man thirsteth; he runneth and thirsteth. For many men He drinketh, but never will He be without thirst. For thence is, "I thirst, woman, give Me to drink." That Samaritan woman at the well found the Lord thirsting, and by Him thirsting she was filled: she first found Him thirsting, in order that He might drink her believing. And when He was on the Cross, "I thirst," He said, although they gave not to Him that for which He was thirsting. For for themselves He was thirsting: but they gave vinegar, not new wine, wherewith are filled up the new bottles, but old wine, but old to its loss. For old vinegar also is said of the old men, of whom hath been said, "For to them is no changing;" namely, that the Jebusites should be overthrown, and Jerusalem be builded.

6. So also the Head of this body even unto the end from the beginning runneth in thirst. And as if to Him were being said, Why in thirst? what is wanting to Thee, O Body of Christ, O Church of Christ? in so great honour, in so great exaltation, in so great height also even in this world established, what is wanting to Thee? There is fulfilled that which hath been foretold of thee, "There shall adore Him all kings of the earth, all nations shall serve Him." ... They that at Jerusalem's festivals fill up the Churches, at Babylon's festivals fill up the theatres: and for all they serve, honour, obey Her—not only those very persons that bear the Sacraments of Christ, and hate the commandments of Christ, but also they, that bear not even the mere Sacraments, Heathen though they be, Jews though they be,—they honour, praise, proclaim, "but with their mouths they were blessing." I heed not the mouth, He knoweth that hath instructed me, "with their heart they were cursing." In that place they were cursing, where "mine honour they thought to drive back."

7. What dost Thou, O Idithun, Body of Christ, leaping over them? What dost Thou amid all these things? What wilt Thou? wilt faint? wilt Thou not persevere even unto the end? wilt Thou not hearken, "He that shall have persevered even unto the end, the same shall be saved," though for that iniquity aboundeth, the love of many shall wax cold? And where is it that Thou hast leaped over them? where is it that

Thy conversation is in Heaven? But they cleave unto earthly things, as though earthborn they mind the earth, and are earth, the serpent's food. What dost thou amid these things? ... "Nevertheless, to God my soul shall be made subject" (ver. 5). And who would endure so great things, either open wars, or secret lyings-in-wait? Who would endure so great things amid open enemies, amid false brethren? Who would endure so great things? Would a man? and if a man would, would a man of himself? I have not so leaped over that I should be lifted up, and fall: "To God my soul shall be made subject: for from Himself is my patience." What patience is there amid so great scandals, except that "if for that which we do not see we hope, through patience we look for it"? There cometh my pain, there will come my rest also; there cometh my tribulation, there will come my cleansing also. For doth gold glitter in the furnace of the refiner? In a necklace it will glitter, in an ornament it will glitter: let it suffer however the furnace, in order that being cleansed from dross it may come into light. This is the furnace, there is there chaff, there gold, there fire, into this bloweth the refiner: in the furnace burneth the chaff, and the gold is cleansed; the one into ashes is turned, of dross the other is cleansed. The furnace is the world, the chaff unrighteous men, the gold just men; the fire tribulation, the refiner God: that which therefore the refiner willeth I do; wherever the Maker setteth me I endure it. I am commanded to endure, He knoweth how to cleanse. Though there burn the chaff to set me on fire, and as if to consume me; that into ashes is burned, I of dross am cleansed. Wherefore? Because "to God my soul shall be made subject: for from Himself is my patience."

8. "For Himself is my God and My Saving One, my Taker up, I will not remove hence" (ver. 6). Because "Himself is my God," therefore He calleth me: "and my Saving One," therefore He justifieth me: "and my Taker up," therefore He glorifieth me. For here I am called and am justified, but there I am glorified; and from thence where I am glorified, "I will not remove." For a sojourner I am with Thee on earth as all my fathers were. Therefore from my lodging I shall remove, from my Heavenly home I shall not remove. "In God is my salvation and my glory" (ver. 7). Saved I shall be in God, glorious I shall be in God: for not only saved, but also glorious, saved, because a just man I have been made out of an ungodly man, by Him justified; but glorious, because not only justified, but also honoured. For "those whom He hath predestined, those also He hath called." Calling them, what hath He done here? "Whom He hath called, the same also He hath justified; but whom He hath justified, the same also He hath glorified." Justification therefore to salvation belongeth, glorifying to honour. How glorifying to honour belongeth, it is not needful to discuss. How justification belongeth to salvation, let us seek some proof. Behold there cometh to mind out of the Gospel: there were some who to themselves were seeming to be just men, and they were finding fault: with the Lord because He admitted to the feast sinners, and with

publicans and sinners was eating; to such men therefore priding themselves, strong men of earth very much lifted up, much glorying of their own soundness, such as they counted it, not such as they had, the Lord answered what? "They that are whole need not a Physician, but they that are sick." Whom calleth He whole, whom calleth He sick? He continueth and saith, "I have not come to call just men, but sinners unto repentance." He hath called therefore "the whole" just men, not because the Pharisees were so, but because themselves they thought so to be; and for this reason were proud, and grudged sick men a physician, and being more sick than those, they slew the Physician. He hath called whole, however, righteous men, sick, the sinners. My being justified therefore, saith that man that leapeth over, from Himself I have: my being glorified, from Himself I have: "For God is my salvation and my glory." "My salvation," so that saved I am: "my glory," so that honoured I am. This thing hereafter: now what? "God of my help, and my hope is in God;" until I attain unto perfect justification and salvation. "For by hope we are saved: but hope which is seen, is not hope." ...

9. "Hope ye in Him all the council of the people" (ver. 8). Imitate ye Idithun, leap over your enemies; men fighting against you, stopping up your way, men hating you, leap ye over: "Hope in Him all the council of the people: pour out before Him your hearts:" ... By imploring, by confessing, by hoping. Do not keep back your hearts within your hearts: "Pour out before Him your hearts." That perisheth not which ye pour out. For He is my Taker up. If He taketh up, why fearest thou to pour out? "Cast upon the Lord thy care, and hope in Him." What fear ye amid whisperers, slanderers hateful to God, where they are able openly assailing, where they are unable secretly lying in wait, falsely praising, truly at enmity, amid them what fear ye? "God is our Helper." Do they anywise equal God? Are they anywise stronger than He? "God is our Helper," be ye without care. "If God is for us, who is against us?" "Pour out before Him your hearts," by leaping over unto Him, by lifting up your souls: "God is our helper." ... "Nevertheless, vain are the sons of men, and liars are the sons of men in the balances, in order that they may deceive, being at one because of vanity" (ver. 9). Certainly many men there are: behold there is that one man, that one man that was cast forth from the multitude of guests. They conspire, they all seek things temporal, and they that are carnal things carnal, and for the future they hope them, whosoever do hope: even if because of variety of opinions they are in division, nevertheless because of vanity they are at one. Divers indeed are errors and of many forms, and the kingdom against itself divided shall not stand: but alike in all is the will vain and lying, belonging to one king, with whom into fire everlasting it is to be thrown headlong—"these men because of vanity are at one." And for them see how the thirsteth, see how He runneth in thirst.

10. He turneth therefore Himself to them, thirsting for them: "Do not hope in iniquity" (vet. 10). For my hope is in God. Ye that will not draw near and pass over, "do not hope in iniquity." For I that have leapt over, my hope is in God; and is there anywise iniquity with God? This thing let us do, that thing let us do, of that thing let us think, thus let us adjust our lyings in wait; "Because of vanity being at one." Thou thirstest: they that think of those things against thee are given up by those whom thou drinkest, "Do not hope in vanity." Vain is iniquity, nought is iniquity, mighty is nothing save righteousness. Truth may be hidden for a time, conquered it cannot be. Iniquity may flourish for a time, abide it cannot. "Do not hope upon iniquity: and for robbery be not covetous." Thou art not rich, and wilt thou rob? What findest thou? What losest thou? O losing gains! Thou findest money, thou losest righteousness. "For robbery be not covetous." ... Therefore, vain sons of men, lying sons of men, neither rob, nor, if there flow riches, set heart upon them: no longer love vanity, and seek lying. For "blessed is the man who hath the Lord God for his hope, and who hath not had regard unto vanities, and lying follies." Ye would deceive, ye would commit a fraud, what bring ye in order that ye may cheat. Deceitful balances. For "lying," he saith, "are the sons of men in the balances," in order that they may cheat by bringing forth deceitful balances. By a false balance ye beguile men looking on: know ye not that one is he that weigheth, Another He that judgeth of the weight? He seeth not, for whom thou weighest, but He seeth that weigheth thee and him. Therefore neither fraud nor robbery covet ye any longer, nor on those things which ye have set your hope: I have admonished, have foretold, saith this Idithun.

11. What followeth? "Once hath God spoken, these two things I have heard, that power is of God (ver. 11), and to Thee, O Lord, is mercy, for Thou shall render to each one after his works" (ver. 12). ..."Once hath God spoken." What sayest thou, Idithun? If thou that hadst leapt over them art saying, "Once He hath spoken;" I turn to another Scripture and it saith to me, "In many quarters and in many ways formerly God hath spoken to the fathers in the prophets." What is, "Once hath God spoken"? Is He not the God that in the beginning of mankind spake to Adam? Did not the Selfsame speak to Cain, to Noe, to Abraham, to Isaac, to Jacob, to all the Prophets, and to Moses? One man Moses was, and how often to him spake God? Behold even to one man, not once but ofttimes God hath spoken. Secondly, He hath spoken to the Son when standing here, "Thou art My beloved Son." God hath spoken to the Apostles, He hath spoken to all the Saints, even though not with voice sounding through the cloud, nevertheless in the heart where He is Himself Teacher. What is therefore, "Once hath God spoken"? Much hath that man leapt over in order to arrive at that place, where once God hath spoken. Behold briefly I have spoken to your Love. Here among men, to men ofttimes, in many ways, in many quarters, through creatures of many forms God hath spoken: by Himself

once God hath spoken, because One Word God hath begotten. ... For it could not be but that God did Himself know that which by the Word He made: but if that which He made He knew, in Him there was that which was made before it was made For if in Him was not that which was made before it was made, how knew He that which He made? For thou canst not say that God made things He knew not. God therefore hath known that which He hath made. And how knew He before He made, if there cannot be known any but things made? But by things made there cannot be known any but things previously made, by thee, to wit, who art a man made in a lower place, and set in a lower place: but before that all these things were made, they were known by Him by whom they were made, and that which He knew He made. Therefore in that Word by which He made all things, before that they were made, were all things; and after they have been made there are all things; but in one way here, in another there, in one way in their own nature wherein they have been made, in another in the art by which they have been made. Who could explain this? We may endeavour: go ye with Idithun, and see.

12. ... For even the Lord saith, "Many things I have to say to you, but ye cannot bear them now." What is therefore, "These two things I, have heard"? These two things which to you I am about to say not of myself to you I say, but what things I have heard I say. "Once hath God spoken:" One Word hath He, the Only-begotten God. Ill that Word are all things, because by the Word were made all things. One Word hath He, "in whom all the treasures of wisdom and knowledge are hidden." One Word He hath, "once hath God spoken." "These two things," which to you I am about to say, these I have heard: not of myself I speak, not of myself I say: to this belongeth the "I have heard." But the friend of the Bridegroom standeth and heareth Him, that he may speak the truth. For he heareth Him, lest by speaking a lie, of his own he should speak: lest thou shouldest say, Who art thou that sayest this thing to me? whence dost thou say this to me? I have heard these two things, and I that speak to thee that I have heard these two things, am one who also doth know that once God hath spoken. Do not despise a hearer saying to thee certain two things for thee so necessary; him, I say, that by leaping over the whole creation hath attained unto the Only-begotten Word of God, where he hath learned that "once God hath spoken."

13. Let him therefore now say certain two things. For greatly to us belong these two things. "For power is of God, and to Thee, O Lord, is mercy." Are these the two things, power and mercy? These two evidently: perceive ye the power of God, perceive ye the mercy of God. In these two things are contained nearly all the Scriptures. Because of these two things are the Prophets, because of these two, the Patriarchs, because of these the Law, because of these Himself our Lord Jesus

Christ, because of these the Apostles, because of these all the preaching and spreading of the word of God in the Church, because of these two, because of the power of God, and His mercy. His power fear ye, His mercy love ye. Neither so on His mercy rely, as that His power ye despise: nor so the power fear ye, as that of mercy ye despair. With Him is power, with Him mercy. This man He humbleth, and that man He exalteth:" this man He humbleth with power, that man He exalteth in mercy. "For if God, willing to show wrath and to prove His power, hath in much patience borne with the vessels of wrath, which have been perfected unto perdition"—thou hast heard of power: inquire for mercy—"and that He might make known," He saith, "His riches unto the vessels of mercy." It belongeth therefore to His power to condemn unjust men. And to Him who would say, What hast thou done? "For thou, O man, who art thou that should make answer to God?" Fear therefore and tremble at His power: but hope for His mercy. The devil is a sort of power; ofttimes however he wisheth to hurt, and is not able, because that power is under power. For if the devil could hurt as much as he would; no one of just men would remain, nor could any one of the faithful be on earth. The same through his vessels smiteth against, as it were, a wall bowed down: but he only smiteth against, so far as he receiveth power. But in order that the wall may not fall, the Lord will support: for He that giveth power to the tempter, doth Himself to the tempted extend mercy. For according to measure the devil is permitted to tempt. And, "Thou wilt give us to drink in tears in a measure." Do not therefore fear the tempter permitted to do somewhat: for thou hast a most merciful Saviour. So much he is permitted to tempt as is profitable for thee, that thou mayest be exercised, mayest be proved; in order that by thyself thou mayest be found out, that knowest not thyself. For where, or from whence, ought we to be secure, except by this power and mercy of God? After that Apostolic saying, "Faithful is God, that doth not suffer you to be tempted above that which ye are able." ... Fear not the enemy: so much he doeth as he hath received power to do, Him fear thou that hath the chief power: Him fear, that doeth as much as He willeth, and that doeth nothing unjustly, and whatever He shall have done, is just. We might suppose something or other to be unjust: inasmuch as God hath done it, believe it to be just.

14. Therefore, thou sayest, if any one slay an innocent man, doeth he justly or unjustly? Unjustly certainly. Wherefore doth God permit this? ... The counsel of God to tell to thee, O man, I am not able: this thing however I say, both that the man hath done unjustly that hath slain an innocent person, and that it would not have been done unless God permitted it: and though the man hath done unjustly, yet God hath not unjustly permitted this. Let the reason lie concealed in that person whoever it be, for whose sake thou art moved, whose innocence doth much move thee. For to thee speedily I might make answer. He would not have been

slain unless he were guilty: but thou thinkest him innocent. I might speedily say this to thee. For thou couldest not examine his heart, sift his deeds, weigh his thoughts, so that thou couldest say to me, unjustly he was slain. I might easily therefore make answer: but there is forced upon my view a certain Just One, without dispute just, without doubt just, who had no sin, slain by sinners, betrayed by a sinner; Himself Christ the Lord, of whom we cannot say that He hath any iniquity, for "those things which He robbed not He paid," is made an objection to my answer. And why should I speak of Christ? "With thee I am dealing," thou sayest. And I with thee. About Him thou proposest a question, about Him I am solving the question. For therein the counsel of God we know, which except by His own revealing we should not know: so that when thou shall have found out that counsel of God, whereby He hath permitted His innocent Son to be slain by unjust men, and such a counsel as pleaseth thee, and such a counsel as cannot displease thee, if thou art just, thou mayest believe that in other things also by His counsel God doeth the same, but it escaped thee. Ah! brethren, need there was of the blood of a just one to blot out the handwriting of sins; need there was of an example of patience, of an example of humility; need there was of the Sign of the Cross to beat down the devil and his angels; need for us there was of the Passion of our Lord; for by the Passion of the Lord redeemed hath been the world. How many good things hath the Passion of the Lord done! And yet the Passion of this Just One would not have been, unless unrighteous men had slain the Lord. What then? is this good thing which to us hath been granted by the Lord's Passion to be ascribed to the unjust slayers of Christ? Far be it. They willed, God permitted. They guilty would have been, even if only they had willed it: but God would not have permitted it, unless just it had been. ... Accordingly, my brethren, both Judas the foul traitor to Christ, and the persecutors of Christ, malignant all, ungodly all, unjust all, are to be condemned all: and nevertheless the Father His own proper Son hath not spared, but for the sake of us all He hath delivered Him up. Order if thou art able; distinguish if thou art able (these things): render to God thy vows, which thy lips have uttered: see what the unjust hath here done, what the Just One. The one hath willed, the Other hath permitted: the one unjustly hath willed, the Other justly hath permitted. Let unjust will be condemned, just permission be glorified. For what evil thing hath befallen Christ, in that Christ hath died? Both evil were they that evil willed to do, and yet nothing of evil did He suffer on whom they did it. Slain was mortal flesh, slaying death by death, giving a lesson of patience, sending before an example of Resurrection. How great good things of the Just One were wrought by the evil things of the unjust! This is the great mystery s of God: that even a good thing which thou doest He hath Himself given it to thee, and by thy evil He doeth good Himself. Do not therefore wonder, God permitteth, and in judgment permitteth: He permitteth, and in measure, number, weight, He permitteth. With Him is not iniquity: do thou only belong to Him; on Himself thy hope set thou, let Himself be thy Helper, thy Salvation: in Him be there the fortified place, the tower of strength, thy refuge let Himself be, and He will not suffer thee to be tempted above that which thou art able to bear, but will make with the temptation also an escape, that thou mayest be able to support it: so that His suffering thee to bear temptation, be His power; His suffering not any more on thee to be done than thou art able to bear, be His mercy: "for power is of God, and to Thee, O Lord, is mercy, because Thou wilt render to each one after his works."

15. That thirst of the Church, would fain drink up that man also whom ye see. At the same time also, in order that ye may know how many in the mixed multitude of Christians with their mouth do bless, and in their heart curse, this man having been a Christian and a believer returneth as a penitent, and being terrified by the power of the Lord, turneth him to the mercy of the Lord. For having been led astray by the enemy when he was a believer, long time he hath been an astrologer, led astray, leading astray, deceived, deceiving, he hath allured, hath beguiled, many lies he hath spoken against God, That hath given to men power of doing that which is good, and of not doing that which is evil. He used to say, that one's own will did not adultery, but Venus; one's own will did not manslaying, but Mars; and God did not what is just, but Jupiter; and many other blasphemous things, and not light ones. From how many Christians do ye think he hath pocketed money? How many from him have bought a lie, to whom we used to say, "Sons of men, how long are ye dull of heart, wherefore love ye vanity, and seek a lie" ? Now, as of him must be believed, he hath shuddered at his lie, and being the allurer of many men, he hath perceived at length that by the devil he hath himself been allured, and he turneth to God a penitent. We think, brethren, that because of great fear of heart it hath come to pass. For what must we say? If out of a heathen an astrologer were converted, great indeed would be the joy: but nevertheless it might appear, that, if he had been converted, he was desiring the clerical office in the Church. A penitent he is, he seeketh not anything save mercy alone. He must be recommended therefore both to your eyes and hearts. Him whom ye see in hearts love ye, with eyes guard ye. See ye him, mark ye him, and whithersoever he shall have gone his way, to the rest of the brethren that now are not here, point him out: and such diligence is mercy; lest that leader astray drag back his heart and take it by storm. Guard ye him, let there not escape you his conversation, his way: in order that by your testimony it may be proved to us that truly to the Lord he hath been turned. For report will not be silent about his life, when to you he is thus presented both to be seen and to be pitied. Ye know in the Acts of the Apostles how it is written, that many lost men, that is, men of such arts, and followers of naughty doctrines, brought unto the Apostles all their books; and there were burned so many volumes, that it was the writer's task to make a valuation of them, and write down the sum of the price. This truly was for the glory of God, in order

that even such lost men might not be despaired of by Him that knew how to seek that which had been lost. Therefore this man had been lost, is now sought, found, led hither, he bringeth with him books to be burned, by which he had been to be burned, so that when these have been thrown into the fire, he may himself pass over into a place of refreshment. Know ye that he, brethren, once knocked at the Church door before Easter: for before Easter he began to ask of the Church Christ's medicine. But because the art wherein he had been practised is of such sort as that it was suspected of lying and deceit, he was put off that he might not tempt; at length however he was admitted, that he might not more dangerously be tempted. Pray for him through Christ. Straightway to-day's prayer pour out for him to the Lord our God. For we know and are sure, that your prayer effaceth all his impieties. The Lord be with you.

PSALM LXIII.

1. This psalm hath the title, "For David himself, when he was in the desert of Idumaea." By the name of Idumaea is understood this world. For Idumaea was a certain nation of men going astray, where idols were worshipped. In no good sense is put this Idumaea. If not in a good sense it is put, it must be understood that this life, wherein we suffer so great toils, and wherein to so great necessities we are made subject, by the name of Idumaea is signified. Even here is a desert where there is much thirst, and ye are to hear the voice of One now thirsting in the desert. But if we acknowledge ourselves as thirsting, we shall acknowledge ourselves as drinking also. For he that thirsteth in this world, in the world to come shall be satisfied, according to the Lord's saying, "Blessed are they that hunger and thirst after righteousness, for the same shall be satisfied." Therefore in this world we ought not to love fulness. Here we must thirst, in another place we shall be filled. But now in order that we may not faint in this desert, He sprinkleth upon us the dew of His word, and leaveth us not utterly to dry up, so that there should not be in our case any seeking of us again, but that we may so thirst as that we may drink. But in order that we may drink, with somewhat of His Grace we are sprinkled: nevertheless we thirst. And what saith our soul to God?

2. "God, my God, unto Thee from the light I watch" (ver. 1). What is to watch? It is, not to sleep. What is to sleep? There is a sleep of the soul; there is a sleep of the body. Sleep of body we all ought to have: because if sleep of body is not taken, a man fainteth, the body itself fainteth. For our frail body cannot long sustain a soul watching and on the stretch on active works; if for a long time the soul shall have been intent on active pursuits, the body being frail and earthly holdeth her not, sustaineth her not for ever in activity, and fainteth and falleth. Therefore God hath granted sleep to the body, whereby are recruited the members of the body, in order that they may be able to sustain the soul watching. But of this let us take heed, namely, that our soul herself sleep not: for evil is the sleep of the soul. Good is the sleep of the body, whereby is recruited the health of the body. But the sleep of the soul is to forget her God. Whatsoever soul shall have forgotten her God, sleepeth. Therefore the Apostle saith to certain persons that forgot their God, and being as it were in sleep, did act the follies of the worship of idols—the Apostle, I say, saith to certain persons, "Rise, thou that sleepest, and rise up from the dead, and Christ shall enlighten thee." Was the Apostle waking up one sleeping in body? Nay, but he was waking a soul sleeping, inasmuch as he was waking her, in order that she might be lightened by Christ. Therefore as to these same watchings saith this man, "God, my God, unto Thee from the light I watch." For thou wouldest not watch of thyself, unless there should arise thy Light, to wake thee from sleep. For Christ

lighteneth souls, and maketh them to watch: but if His light He taketh away, they slumber. For for this cause to Him there is said in another psalm, "Lighten mine eyes, that I may never slumber in death." ...

3. "My soul hath thirsted for Thee" (ver. 2). Behold that desert of Idumaea. See how here he thirsteth: but see what good thing is here, "Hath thirsted for Thee." For there are they that thirst, but not for God. For every one that willeth anything to be granted to him, is in the heat of longing; the longing itself is the thirst of the soul. And see ye what longings there are in the hearts of men: one longeth for gold, another longeth for silver, another longeth for possessions, another inheritance, another abundance of money, another many herds, another a wife, another honours, another sons. Ye see those longings, how they are in the hearts of men. All men are inflamed with longing, and scarce is found one to say, "My soul hath thirsted for Thee." For men thirst for the world: and perceive not themselves to be in the desert of Idumaea, where their souls ought to thirst for God. ...

4. Wisdom therefore must be thirsted after, righteousness must be thirsted after. With it we shall not be satisfied, with it we shall not be filled, save when this life shall have been ended, and we shall have come to that which God hath promised. For God hath promised equality with Angels: and now the Angels thirst not as we do, they hunger not as we do; but they have the fulness of truth, of light, of immortal wisdom. Therefore blessed they are, and out of so great blessedness, because they are in that City, the Heavenly Jerusalem, afar from whence we now are sojourning in a strange land, they observe us sojourners, and they pity us, and by the command of the Lord they help us, in order that to this common country sometime we may return, and there with them sometime with the Lord's fountain of truth and eternity we may be filled. Now therefore let our soul thirst: whence doth our flesh also thirst, and this in many ways? "In many ways for Thee," he saith, "my flesh also." Because to our flesh also is promised Resurrection. As to our soul is promised blessedness, so also to our flesh is promised resurrection. ... For if God hath made us that were not, is it a great thing for Him to make again us that were? Therefore let not this seem to you to be incredible, because ye see dead men as it were decaying, and passing into ashes and into dust. Or if any dead man be burned, or if dogs tear him in pieces, do ye think that from this he will not rise again? All things which are dismembered, and into a sort of dust do decay, are entire with God. For into those elements of the world they pass, whence at first they have come, when we were made: we do not see them; but yet God will bring them forth, He knoweth whence, because even before we were, He created us from whence He knew. Such a resurrection of the flesh therefore to us is promised, as that, although it be the same flesh that now we carry which is to rise again, yet it

hath not the corruption which now it hath. For now because of the corruption of frailty, if we eat not, we faint and are hungry; if we drink not, we faint and are thirsty; if long time we watch we faint and sleep; if long time we sleep, we faint, therefore we watch. ... Secondly, see how without any standing is our flesh: for infancy passeth away into boyhood, and thou seekest infancy, and infancy is not, for now instead of infancy is boyhood: again this same also passeth into youth, thou seekest boyhood and findest not: the young man becometh a middle-aged man, thou seekest the young man and he is not: the middle-aged man becometh an old man, thou seekest a middle-aged man and findest not: and an old man dieth, thou seekest an old man and findest not: our age therefore standeth not still: everywhere is weariness, everywhere faintness, everywhere corruption. Observing what a hope of resurrection God promiseth to us, in all those our manifold faintings we thirst for that incorruption: and so our flesh manifoldly doth thirst for God.

5. Nevertheless, my brethren, the flesh of a good Christian and a believer even in this world for God doth thirst: for if the flesh hath need of bread, if it hath need of water, if it hath need of wine, if it hath need of money, if this flesh hath need of a beast, from God it ought to seek it, not from demons and idols and I know not what powers of this world. For there are certain who when they suffer hunger in this world, leave God and ask Mercury or ask Jove to give unto them, or her whom they call "Heavenly," or any the like demons: not for God their flesh thirsteth. But they that thirst for God, everywhere ought to thirst for Him, both soul and flesh: for to the soul also God giveth His bread, that is the Word of Truth: and to the flesh God giveth the things which are necessary, for God hath made both soul and flesh. For the sake of thy flesh thou askest of demons: hath God made the soul, and the demons made the flesh? He that hath made the soul, the Same hath made the flesh also: He that hath made both of them, the Same feedeth both of them. Let either part of us thirst for God, and after labour manifold let either simply be filled.

6. But where thirsteth our soul, and our flesh manifoldly, not for any one but for Thee, O Lord, that is our God? it thirsteth where? "In a land desert, and without way, and without water." Of this world we have spoken, the same is Idumaea, this is the desert of Idumaea, whence the Psalm hath received its title. "In a land desert." Too little it is to say "desert," where no man dwelleth; it is besides, both "without way, and without water." O that the same desert had even a way: O that into this a man running, even knew where he might thence get forth! ... Evil is the desert, horrible, and to be feared: and nevertheless God hath pitied us, and hath made for us a way in the desert, Himself our Lord Jesus Christ: and hath made for us a consolation in the desert, in sending to us preachers of His Word: and hath

given to us water in the desert, by fulfilling with the Holy Spirit His preachers, in order that there might be created in them a well of water springing up unto life everlasting. And, lo! we have here all things, but they are not of the desert. ...

7. "Thus in a holy thing I have appeared to Thee, that I might see Thy power and Thy glory" (ver. 3). ...Unless a man first thirst in that desert, that is in the evil wherein he is, he never arriveth at the good, which is God. But "I have appeared to Thee," he saith, "in a holy thing." Now in a holy thing is there great consolation. "I have appeared to Thee," is what? In order that Thou mightest see me: and for this reason Thou hast seen me, in order that I might see Thee. "I have appeared to Thee, that I might see." He hath not said, "I have appeared to Thee, that Thou mightest see:" but, "I have appeared to Thee, that I might see Thy power and Thy glory." Whence also the Apostle, "But now," he saith, "knowing God, nay, having been known of God." For first ye have appeared to God, in order that to you God might be able to appear. "That I might see Thy power and Thy glory." In truth in that forsaken place, that is, in that desert, if as though from the desert a man striveth to obtain enough for his sustenance, he will never see the power of the Lord, and the glory of the Lord, but he will remain to die of thirst, and will find neither way, nor consolation, nor water, whereby he may endure in the desert. But when he shall have lifted up himself to God, so as to say to Him out of all his inward parts, "My soul hath thirsted for Thee; how manifoldly for Thee also my flesh!" lest perchance even the things necessary for the flesh of others he ask, and not of God, or else long not for that resurrection of the flesh, which God hath promised to us: when, I say, he shall have lifted up himself, he will have no small consolations.

8. ... But ye have heard but now when the Gospel was being read in what terms He hath notified His Majesty: "I and My Father are One." Behold how great a Majesty and how great an Equality with the Father hath come down to the flesh because of our infirmity. Behold how greatly beloved we have been, before that we loved God, If before that we loved God, so much by Him we were beloved, as that His Son, Equal with Himself, He made a Man for our sake, what doth He reserve for us now loving Him? Therefore many men think it to be a very small thing that the Son of God hath appeared on earth; because they are not in the Holy One, to them hath not appeared the power of the Same and the glory of the Same: that is, not yet have they a heart made holy, whence they may perceive the eminence of that virtue, and may render thanks to God, nor that to which for their own sakes so great an One came, unto what a nativity, unto what a Passion, they are not able to see, His glory and His power.

9. "For better is Thy mercy than lives." Many are the lives of men, but one life God promiseth: and He giveth not this to us as if for our merits but for His mercy. ... For what is so just a thing as that a sinner should be punished? Though a just thing it be that a sinner should be punished, it hath belonged to the mercy of Him not to punish a sinner but to justify him, and of a sinner to make a just man, and of an ungodly man to make a godly man. Therefore "His mercy is better than lives." What lives? Those which for themselves men have chosen. One hath chosen for himself a life of business, another a country life, another a life of usury, another a military life; one this, another that. Divers are the lives, but "better is Thy" life "than" our "lives." ... "My lips shall praise Thee." My lips would not praise Thee, unless before me were to go Thy mercy. By Thy gift Thee I praise, through Thy mercy Thee I praise. For I should not be able to praise God, unless He gave me to be able to praise Him.

10. "So I will speak good of Thee in my life, and in Thy name I will lift up my hands" (ver. 5). Now in my life which to me Thou hast given, not in that which I have chosen after the world with the rest among many lives, but that which Thou hast given to me through Thy mercy, that I should praise Thee. "So I will speak good of Thee in my life." What is "so"? That to Thy mercy I may ascribe my life wherein Thee I praise, not to my merits. "And in Thy name I will lift up my hands." Lift up therefore hands in prayer. Our Lord hath lifted up for us His hands on the Cross, and stretched out were His hands for us, and therefore were His hands stretched out on the Cross, in order that our hands might be stretched out unto good works: because His Cross hath brought us mercy. Behold, He hath lifted up hands, and hath offered for us Himself a Sacrifice to God, and through that Sacrifice have been effaced all our sins. Let us also lift up our hands to God in prayer: and our hands being lifted up to God shall not be confounded, if they be exercised in good works. For what doth he that lifteth up hands? Whence hath it been commanded that with hands lifted up we should pray to God? For the Apostle saith, "Lifting up pure hands without anger and dissension." It is in order that when thou liftest up hands to God, there may come into thy mind thy works. For whereas those hands are lifted up that thou mayest obtain that which thou wilt, those same hands thou thinkest in good works to exercise, that they may not blush to be lifted up to God. "In thy name I will lift up my hands." Those are our prayers in this Idumaea, in this desert, in the land without water and without way, where for us Christ is the Way, but not the way of this earth.

11. ... Already our fathers are dead, but God liveth: here we could not always have fathers, but there we shall alway have one living Father, when we have our father-land. ... What sort of country is that? But thou lovest here riches. God Himself

shall be to thee thy riches. But thou lovest a good fountain. What is more passing clear than that wisdom? What more bright? Whatsoever is an object of love here, in place of all thou shall have Him that hath made all things, "as though with marrow and fatness my soul should be filled: and lips of exultation shall praise Thy name." In this desert, in Thy name I will lift up my hands: let my soul be filled as though with marrow and fatness, "and my lips with exultation shall praise Thy name." For now is prayer, so long as there is thirst: when thirst shall have passed away, there passeth away praying and there succeedeth praising. "And lips of exultation shall praise Thy name."

12. "If I have remembered Thee upon my bed, in the dawnings I did meditate on thee (ver. 7): because Thou hast become my helper" (ver. 8). His "bed" he calleth his rest. When any one is at rest, let him be mindful of God; when any one is at rest, let him not by rest be dissolved, and forget God: if mindful he is of God when he is at rest, in his actions on God he doth meditate. For the dawn he hath called actions, because every man at dawn beginneth to do something. What therefore hath he said? If therefore I was not mindful on my bed, in the dawn also I did not meditate on Thee. Can he that thinketh not of God when he is at leisure, in his actions think of God? But he that is mindful of Him when he is at rest, on the Same doth meditate when he is doing, lest in action he should come short. Therefore he hath added what? "Because Thou has become my helper." For unless God aid our good works, they cannot be accomplished by us. And worthy things we ought to work: that is, as though in the light, since by Christ showing the way we work. Whosoever worketh evil things, in the night he worketh, not in the dawn; according to the Apostle, saying, "They that are drunken, in the night are drunken; and they that sleep, in the night do sleep; let us that are of the day, be sober." He exhorteth us that after the day we should walk honestly: "As in the day, honestly let us walk." And again, "Ye," he saith, "are sons of light, and sons of day; we are not of night nor of darkness." Who are sons of night, and sons of darkness? They that work all evil things. To such a degree they are sons of night, that they fear lest the things which they work should be seen. ... No one therefore in the dawn worketh, except him that in Christ worketh. But he that while at leisure is mindful of Christ, on the Same doth meditate in all his actions, and He is a helper to him in a good work, lest through his weakness he fail. "And in the covering of Thy wings I will exult." I am cheerful in good works, because over me is the covering of Thy wings. If thou protect me not, forasmuch as I am a chicken, the kite will seize me. For our Lord Himself saith in a certain place to that Jerusalem, a certain city, where He was crucified: "Jerusalem," He saith, "Jerusalem, how often I have willed to gather thy sons, as though a hen her chickens, and thou wouldest not." Little ones we are: therefore may God protect us under the shadow of His wings. What when we shall have grown greater? A good

thing it is for us that even then He should protect us, so that under Him the greater, alway we be chickens. For alway He is greater, however much we may have grown. Let no one say, let Him protect me while I am a little one: as if sometime he would attain to such magnitude, as should be self- sufficient. Without the protection of God, nought thou art. Alway by Him let us desire to be protected: then alway in Him we shall have power to be great, if alway under Him little we be. "And in the covering of Thy wings I will exult."

13. "My soul hath been glued on behind Thee" (ver. 9). See ye one longing, see ye one thirsting, see ye how he cleaveth to God. Let there spring up in you this affection. If already it is sprouting, let it be rained upon and grow: let it come to such strength, that ye also may say from the whole heart, "My soul hath been glued on behind Thee." Where is that same glue? The glue itself is love. Have thou love, wherewith as with glue thy soul may be glued on behind God. Not with God, but behind God; that He may go before, thou mayest follow. For he that shall have willed to go before God, by his I own counsel would live, and will not follow the commandments of God. Because of this even Peter was rebuked, when he willed to give counsel to Christ, who was going to suffer for us. ... "Far be it from Thee, O Lord, be Thou merciful to Thyself." And the Lord, "Go back behind Me, Satan: for thou savourest not the things which are of God, but the things which are of men." Wherefore, the things which are of men? Because to go before Me thou desirest, go back behind Me, in order that thou mayest follow me: so that now following Christ lie might say, "My soul hath been glued on behind Thee." With reason he addeth, "Me Thy right hand hath taken up." This Christ hath said in us: that is in the Man which He was bearing for us, which He was offering for us, He hath said this. The Church also said this in Christ, she saith it in her Head: for she too hath suffered here great persecutions, and by her individual members even now she suffereth. ...

14. "But themselves in vain have sought my soul. They shall go unto the lower places of the earth" (ver. 9). Earth they were unwilling to lose, when they crucified Christ: into the lower places of the earth they have gone. What are the lower places of the earth? Earthly lusts. Better it is to walk upon earth, than by lust to go under earth. For every one that in prejudice of his salvation desireth earthly things, is under the earth: because earth he hath put before him, earth upon himself he hath put, and himself beneath he hath laid. They therefore fearing to lose earth, said what of the Lord Jesus Christ, when they saw great multitudes go after Him, forasmuch as He was doing wonderful things? "If we shall have let Him go alive, there will come the Romans, and will take away from us both place and nation." They feared to lose earth, and they went under the earth: there befell them even

what they feared. For they willed to kill Christ, that they might not lose earth; and earth they therefore lost, because Christ they slew. For when Christ had been slain, because the Lord Himself had said to them, "The kingdom shall be taken from you, and shall be given up to a nation doing righteousness:" there followed them great calamities of persecutions: there conquered them Roman emperors, and kings of the nations: they were shut out from that very place where they crucified Christ, and now that place is full of Christian praisers: it hath no Jew, it hath been cleared of the enemies of Christ, it hath been fulfilled with the praisers of Christ. Behold, they have lost at the hands of the Romans the place, because Christ they slew, who to this end slew, that they might not lose the place at the hands of the Romans. Therefore, "They shall enter into the lower places of the earth."

15. "They shall be delivered unto the hands of the sword" (ver. 10). In truth, thus it hath visibly befallen them, they have been taken by storm by enemies breaking in. "Portions of foxes they shall be." Foxes he calleth the kings of the world, that then were when Judaea was conquered. Hear in order that ye may know and perceive, that those he calleth foxes. Herod the king the Lord Himself hath called a fox. "Go ye," He saith, "and tell that fox." See and observe, my brethren: Christ as King they would not have, and portions of foxes they have been made. For when Pilate the deputy governor in Judaea slew Christ at the voices of the Jews, he said to the same Jews, "Your King shall I crucify?" Because He was called King of the Jews, and He was the true King. And they rejecting Christ said, "We have no king but Caesar." They rejected a Lamb, chose a fox: deservedly portions of foxes they were made.

16. "The King in truth," is so written, because they chose a fox, a King in truth they would not have. "The King in truth:" that is, the true King, to whom the title was inscribed, when He suffered. For Pilate set this title inscribed over His Head, "The King of the Jews," in the Hebrew, Greek, and Latin tongues: in order that all they that should pass by might read of the glory of the King, and the infamy of the Jews themselves, who, rejecting the true King, chose the fox Caesar. "The King in truth shall rejoice in God." They have been made portions of foxes. ... "Stopped up is the mouth of men speaking unjust things." No one dareth now openly to speak against Christ, now all men fear Christ. "For stopped up is the mouth of men speaking unjust things." When in weakness the Lamb was, even foxes were bold against the Lamb. There conquered the Lion of the tribe of Judah, and the foxes were silenced.

PSALM LXIV.

1. Though chiefly the Lord's Passion is noticed in this Psalm, neither could the Martyrs have been strong, unless they had beheld Him, that first suffered; nor such things would they have endured in suffering, as He did, unless they had hoped for such things in the Resurrection as He had showed of Himself: but your Holiness knoweth that our Head is our Lord Jesus Christ, and that all that cleave unto Him are the members of Him the Head . ... And let no one say, that now-a-days in tribulation of passions we are not. For alway ye have heard this fact, how in those times the whole Church together as it were was smitten against, but now through individuals she is tried. Bound indeed is the devil, that he may not do as much as he could, that he may not do as much as he would: nevertheless, he is permitted to tempt as much as is expedient to men advancing. It is not expedient for us to be without temptations: nor should we beseech God that we be not tempted, but that we be not "led into temptation."

2. Say we, therefore, ourselves also:" Hearken, O God, to my prayer, while I am troubled; from fear of the enemy deliver my soul" (ver. 1). Enemies have raged against the Martyrs: for what was that voice of Christ's Body praying? For this it was praying, to be delivered from enemies, and that enemies might not have power to slay them. Were they not therefore hearkened to, because they were slain; and hath God forsaken His servants of a contrite heart, and despised men hoping in Him? Far be it. For "who hath called upon God, and hath been forsaken; who hath hoped in Him, and hath been deserted by Him?" They were hearkened to therefore, and they were slain; and yet from enemies they were delivered. Others being afraid gave consent, and lived, and yet the same by enemies were swallowed up. The slain were delivered, the living were swallowed up. Thence is also that voice of thanksgiving, "Perchance alive they would have swallowed us up." Therefore for this prayeth the voice of the Martyrs, "From fear of the enemy deliver Thou my soul:" not so that the enemy may not slay me, but that I may not fear an enemy slaying. For that to be fulfilled in the Psalm the servant prayeth, which but now in the Gospel the Lord was commanding. What but now was the Lord commanding? "Fear not them that kill the body, but the soul are not able to kill; but Him rather fear ye, that hath power to kill both body and soul in the hell of fire." And He repeated, "Yea, I say unto you, fear Him." Who are they that kill the body? Enemies. What was the Lord commanding? That they should not be feared. Be prayer offered, therefore, that He may grant what He hath commanded. "From fear of the enemy deliver my soul." Deliver me from fear of the enemy, and make me submit to the fear of Thee. I would not fear him that killeth the body, but I would fear Him that hath power to kill both body and soul in the hell of fire. For

492

not from fear would I be free: but from fear of the enemy being free, under fear of the Lord a servant.

3. "Thou hast protected me from the gathering together of malignants, and from the multitude of men working iniquity" (ver. 2). Now upon Himself our Head let us look. Like things many Martyrs have suffered: but nothing doth shine out so brightly as the Head of Martyrs; in Him rather let us behold what they have gone through. Protected He was from the multitude of malignants, God protecting Himself, the Son Himself and the Manhood which He was carrying protecting His flesh: because Son of Man He is, and Son of God He is; Son of God because of the form of God, Son of Man because of the form of a servant: having in His power to lay down His life: and to take it again. To Him what could enemies do? They killed body, soul they killed not. Observe. Too little therefore it were for the Lord to exhort the Martyrs with word, unless He had enforced it by example. Ye know what a gathering together there was of malignant Jews, and what a multitude there was of men working iniquity. What iniquity? That wherewith they willed to kill the Lord Jesus Christ. So many good works," He saith, "I have shown to you, for which of these will ye to kill Me?" He endured all their infirm, He healed all their sick, He preached the Kingdom of Heaven, He held not His peace at their vices, so that these same should have been displeasing to them, rather than the Physician by whom they were being made whole: for all these His remedies being ungrateful, like men delirious in high fever raving at the physician, they devised the plan of destroying Him that had come to heal them; as though therein they would prove whether He were indeed a man, that could die, or were somewhat above men, and would not suffer Himself to die. The word of these same men we perceive in the wisdom of Solomon: "with death most vile," say they, "let us condemn Him; let us question Him, for there will be regard in the discourses of Him; for if truly Son of God He is, let Him deliver Him." Let us see therefore what was done.

4. "For they have whet like a sword their tongues" (ver. 3). Which saith another Psalm also, "Sons of men; their teeth are arms and arrows, and their tongue is a sharp sword." Let not the Jews say, we have not killed Christ. For to this end they gave Him to Pilate the judge, in order that they themselves might seem as it were guiltless of His death. ... But if he is guilty because he did it though unwillingly, are they innocent who compelled him to do it? By no means. But he gave sentence against Him, and commanded Him to be crucified: and in a manner himself killed Him; ye also, O ye Jews, killed Him. Whence did ye kill Him? With the sword of the tongue: for ye did whet your tongues. And when did ye smite, except when ye cried out, "Crucify, Crucify"?

5. But on this account we must not pass over that which hath come into mind, lest perchance the reading of the Divine Scriptures should disquiet any one. One Evangelist saith that the Lord was crucified at the sixth hour, and another at the third hour: unless we understand it, we are disquieted. And when the sixth hour was already beginning, Pilate is said to have sat on the judgment-seat: and in reality when the Lord was lifted up upon the tree, it was the sixth hour. But another Evangelist, looking unto the mind of the Jews, how they wished themselves to seem guiltless of the death of the Lord, by his account proveth them guilty, saying, that the Lord was crucified at the third hour. But considering all the circumstance of the history, how many things might have been done, when before Pilate the Lord was being accused, in order that He might be crucified; we find that it might have been the third hour, when they cried out, "Crucify, Crucify." Therefore with more truth they killed at the time when they cried out. The ministers of the magistrate at the sixth hour crucified, the transgressors of the law at the third hour cried out: that which those did with hands at the sixth hour, these did with tongue at the third hour. More guilty are they that with crying out were raging, than they that in obedience were ministering. This is the whole of the Jews' sagacity, this is that which they sought as some great matter. Let us kill and let us not kill: so let us kill, as that we may not ourselves be judged to have killed.

6. "They have bended the bow, a bitter thing, in order that they may shoot in secret One unspotted" (ver. 4). The bow he calleth lyings in wait. For he that with sword fighteth hand to hand, openly fighteth: he that shooteth an arrow deceiveth, in order to strike. For the arrow smiteth, before it is foreseen to come to wound. But whom could the lyings in wait of the human heart escape? Would they escape our Lord Jesus Christ, who had no need that any one should bear witness to Him of man? "For Himself knew what was in man," as the Evangelist testifieth. Nevertheless, let us hear them, and look upon them in their doings as if the Lord knew not what they devise. The expression he used, "They have bended the bow," is the same as, "in secret:" as if they were deceiving by lyings in wait. For ye know by what artifices they did this, how with money they bribed a disciple that clave to Him, in order that He might be betrayed to them, how they procured false witnesses; with what lyings in wait and artifices they wrought, "in order that they might shoot in secret One unspotted." Great iniquity! Behold from a secret place there cometh an arrow, which striketh One unspotted, who had not even so much of spot as could be pierced with an arrow. A Lamb indeed He is unspotted, wholly unspotted, alway unspotted; not one from whom spots have been removed but that hath contracted not any spots. For He hath made many unspotted by forgiving sins, being Himself unspotted by not having sins. "Suddenly they shall shoot Him, and shall not fear. O heart hardened, to wish to kill a Man that did raise the dead! "Suddenly:" that is, insidiously, as if unexpectedly, as if not foreseen. For the Lord

was like to one knowing not, being among men knowing not what He knew not and what He knew: yea, knowing not that there was nothing that He knew not, and that He knew all things, and to this end had come in order that they might do that which they thought they did by their own power.

7. "They have confirmed to themselves malignant discourse" (ver. 5). There were done so great miracles, they were not moved, they persisted in the design of the evil discourse. He was given up to the judge: the judge trembleth, and they tremble not that have given Him up to the judge: trembleth power, and ferocity trembleth not: he would wash his hands, and they stain their tongues. But wherefore this? "They have confirmed to themselves malignant discourse." How many things did Pilate, how many things that they might be restrained! What said he? what did he? But "they have confirmed to themselves malignant discourse: Crucify, crucify." The repetition is the confirmation of the "malignant discourse." Let us see in what manner "they have confirmed to themselves malignant discourse." "Your King shall I crucify?" They said, "We have no king but Caesar alone." He was offering for King the Son of God: to a man they betook themselves: worthy were they to have the one, and not have the Other. "I find not anything in this Man," saith the judge, "wherefore He is worthy of death." And they that "confirmed malignant discourse," said, "His blood be upon us and upon our sons." "They confirmed malignant discourse," not to the Lord, but to" themselves." For how not to themselves when they say, "Upon us and upon our sons"? That which therefore they confirmed, to themselves they confirmed: because the same voice is elsewhere, "They dug before my face a ditch, and fell into it." Death killed not the Lord, but He death: but them iniquity killed, because they would not kill iniquity. ...

8. "They told, in order that they might hide traps: they said, Who shall see them?" (ver. 5). They thought they would escape Him, whom they were killing, that they would escape God. Behold, suppose Christ was a man, like the rest of men, and knew not what was being contrived for Him: doth God also know not? O heart of man! wherefore hast thou said to thyself, Who seeth me? when He seeth that hath made thee? "They said, Who shall see them?" God did see, Christ also was seeing: because Christ is also God. But wherefore did they think that He saw not? Hear the words following.

9. "They have searched out iniquity, they have failed, searching searchings" (ver. 6): that is, deadly and acute designs. Let Him not be betrayed by us, but by His disciple: let Him not be killed by us, but by the judge: let us do all, and let us seem to have done nothing. ...

10. But what befell them? "They failed searching searchings." Whence? Because he saith, "Who shall see them?" that is, that no one saw them. This they were saying, this among themselves they thought, that no one saw them. See what befalleth an evil soul: it departeth from the light of truth, and because itself seeth not God, it thinketh that itself is not seen by God. ...

11. For what followeth? "There shall draw near a man and a deep heart." They said, Who shall see us? They failed in searching searchings, evil counsels. There drew near a man to those same counsels, He suffered Himself to be held as a man. For He would not have been held except He were man, or have been seen except He were man, or have been smitten except He were man, or have been crucified or have died except He were man. There drew near a man therefore to all those sufferings, which in Him would have been of no avail except He were Man. But if He were not Man, there would not have been deliverance for man. There hath drawn near a Man "and a deep heart," that is, a secret "heart:" presenting before human faces Man, keeping within God: concealing the "form of God," wherein He is equal with the Father, and presenting the form of a servant, wherein He is less than the Father. For Himself hath spoken of both: but one thing there is which He saith in the form of God, another thing in the form of a servant. He hath said in the form of God, "I and the Father are one: " He hath said in the form of a servant, "For the Father is greater than I." Whence in the form of God saith He, "I and the Father are one"? ...

12. "Arrows of infants have been made the strokes of them" (ver. 7). Where is that savageness? where is that roar of the lion, of the people roaring and saying, "Crucify, Crucify"? Where are the lyings in wait of men bending the bow? Have not "the strokes of them been made the arrows of infants"? Ye know in what manner infants make to themselves arrows of little canes. What do they strike, or whence do they strike? What is the hand, or what the weapon? what are the arms, or what the limbs?

13. "And the tongues of them have been made weak upon them" (ver. 8). Let them whet now their tongues like a sword, let them confirm to themselves malignant discourse. Deservedly to themselves they have confirmed it, because "the tongues of them have been made weak upon them." Could this be strong against God? "Iniquity," he saith," hath lied to itself;" "their tongues have been made weak upon them." Behold, the Lord hath risen, that was killed. ... What thinkest thou of Him who from the cross came not down, and from the tomb rose again? What therefore did they effect? But even if the Lord had not risen again, what would they have effected, except what the persecutors of the martyrs have also effected? For the

Martyrs have not yet risen again, and nevertheless they have effected nothing; of them not yet rising again we are now celebrating the nativities. Where is the madness of their raging? To what did they bring those their searchings, in which searchings they failed, so that even, when the Lord was dead and buried, they set guards at the tomb? For they said to Pilate, "That deceiver;" by this name the Lord Jesus Christ was called, for the comfort of His servants when they are called deceivers; they say therefore to Pilate, "That deceiver said when yet living, After three days I will rise again:" ... They set for guards soldiers at the sepulchre. At the earth quaking, the Lord rose again: such miracles were done about the sepulchre, that even the very soldiers that had come for guards were made witnesses, if they chose to tell the truth: but the same covetousness which had led captive a disciple, the companion of Christ, led captive also the soldier that was guard of the sepulchre. We give you, they say, money; 7 and say ye, while yourselves were sleeping there came His disciples, and took Him away. ... Sleeping witnesses ye adduce: truly thou thyself hast fallen asleep, that in searching such devices hast failed. If they were sleeping, what could they see? if nothing they saw, how are they witnesses? But "they failed in searching searchings:" failed of the light of God, failed in the very completion of their designs: when that which they willed, nowise they were able to complete, surely they failed. Wherefore this? Because "there drew near a Man and a deep heart, and God was exalted." ...

14. "And every man feared" (ver. 9). They that feared not, were not even men. "Every man feared;" that is, every one using reason to perceive the things which were done. Whence they that feared not, must rather be called cattle, rather beasts savage and cruel. A lion ramping and roaring is that people as yet. But in truth every man feared: that is, they that would believe, that trembled at the judgment to come. "And every man feared: and they declared the works of God." ... "And every man hath feared: and they have declared the works of God, and His doings they have perceived." What is, "His doings they have perceived"? Was it, O Lord Jesu Christ, that Thou wast silent, and like a sheep for a victim wast being led, and didst not open before the shearer Thy mouth, and we thought Thee to be set in smiting and in grief, and knowing how to bear weakness? 10 Was it that Thou wast hiding Thy beauty, O Thou beautiful in form before the sons of men? Was it that Thou didst not seem to have beauty nor grace? Thou didst bear on the Cross men reviling and saying," If Son of God He is, let Him come down from the Cross." ... This thing they, that would have had Him come down from the Cross, perceived not: but when He rose again, and being glorified ascended into Heaven, they perceived the works of God.

15. "The just man shall rejoice in the Lord" (ver. 10). Now the just man is not sad. For sad were the disciples at the Lord's being crucified; overcome with sadness, sorrowing they departed, they thought they had lost hope. He rose again, even when appearing to them He found them sad. He held the eyes of two men that walked in the way, so that by them he was not known, and He found them groaning and sighing, and He held them until He had expounded the Scriptures, and by the same Scriptures had shown that so it ought to have been done as it was done. For He showed in the Scriptures, how after the third day it behoved the Lord to rise again. And how on the third day would He have risen again, if from the Cross He had come down? ... Therefore let us all rejoice in the Lord, let us all after the faith be ONE JUST MAN, and let us all in one Body hold One Head, and let us rejoice in the Lord, not in ourselves: because our Good is not ourselves to ourselves, but He that hath made us. Himself is our good to make us glad. And let no one rejoice in himself, no one rely on himself, no one despair of himself: let no one rely on any man, whom he ought to bring in to be the partner of his own hope, not the giver of the hope.

16. Now because the Lord hath risen again, now because He hath ascended into Heaven, now because He hath showed that there is another life, now because it is evident that His counsels, wherein He lay concealed in deep heart, were not empty, because to this end That Blood was shed to be the price of the redeemed; now because all things are evident, because all things have been preached, because all things have been believed, under the whole of heaven, "the just man shall rejoice in the Lord, and shall hope in Him; and all men shall be praised that are right in heart." ... God is displeasing to thee, and thou art pleasing to thyself, of perverted and crooked heart thou art: and this is the worse, that the heart of God thou wouldest correct by thy heart, to make Him do what thou wilt have whereas thou oughtest to do what He willeth. What then? Thou wouldest make crooked the heart of God which alway is right, according to the depravity of thy own heart? How much better to correct thy heart by the rectitude of God? Hath not thy Lord taught thee this, of Whose Passion but now were we speaking? Was He not bearing thy weakness, when He said, "Sad is My soul even unto death"? Was He not figuring thyself in Himself, when He was saying, "Father, if it be possible, let there pass from Me this cup"?. For the hearts of the Father and of the Son were not two and different: but in the form of a servant He carried thy heart, that He might teach it by His example. Now behold trouble found out as it were another heart of thine, which willed that there should pass away that which was impending: but God would not. God consenteth not to thy heart, do thou consent to the heart of God.

17. What followeth? If "there shall be praised all men right in heart," there shall be condemned the crooked in heart. Two things are set before thee now, choose while there is time. ... If of crooked heart thou hast become, there will come that Judgment, there will appear all the reasons on account of which God doeth all these things: and thou that wouldest not in this life correct thy heart by the rectitude of God, and prepare thyself for the right hand, where "there shall be praised all men right in heart," wilt be on the left, where at that time thou shalt hear, "Go ye into fire everlasting, that hath been prepared for the devil and his angels." And will there be then time to correct the heart? Now therefore correct, brethren, now correct. Who doth hinder? Psalm is chanted, Gospel is read, Reader crieth, Preacher crieth; long-suffering is the Lord; thou sinnest, and He spareth; still thou sinnest, still He spareth, and still thou addest sin to sin. How long is God long-suffering? Thou wilt find God just also. We terrify because we fear; teach us not to fear, and we terrify no more. But better it is that God teach us to fear, than that any man teach us not to fear. ... Thou bringest forth grain, barn expect thou; bringest forth thorns, fire expect thou. But not yet hath come either the time of the barn or the time of the fire: now let there be preparation, and there will not be fear. In the name of Christ both we who speak are living, and ye to whom we speak are living: for amending our plan, and changing evil life into a good life, is there no place, is there no time? Can it not, if thou wilt, be done to-day? Can it not, if thou wilt, be now done? What must thou buy in order to do it, what specifics must thou seek? To what Indies must thou sail? What ship prepare? Lo, while I am speaking, change the heart; and there is done what so often and so long while is cried out for, that it be done, and which bringeth forth everlasting punishment if it be not done.

PSALM LXV.

1. The voice of holy prophecy must be confessed in the very title of this Psalm. It is inscribed, "Unto the end, a Psalm of David, a song of Jeremiah and Ezekiel, on account of the people of transmigration when they were beginning to go forth." How it fired with our fathers in the time of the transmigration to Babylon, is not known to all, but only to those that diligently study the Holy Scriptures, either by hearing or by reading. For the captive people Israel from the city of Jerusalem was led into slavery unto Babylon. But holy Jeremiah prophesied, that after seventy years the people would return out of captivity, and would rebuild the very city Jerusalem, which they had mourned as having been overthrown by enemies. But at that time there were prophets in that captivity of the people dwelling in Babylon, among whom was also the prophet Ezekiel. But that people was waiting until there should be fulfilled the space of seventy years, according to the prophecy of Jeremiah. It came to pass, when the seventy years had been completed, the temple was restored which had been thrown down: and there returned from captivity a great part of that people. But whereas the Apostle saith, "these things in figure happened unto them, but they have been written for our sakes, upon whom the end of the world hath come: "2 we also ought to know first our captivity, then our deliverance: we ought to know the Babylon wherein we are captives, and the Jerusalem for a return to which we are sighing. For these two cities, according to the letter, in reality are two cities. And the former Jerusalem indeed by the Jews is not now inhabited. For after the crucifixion of the Lord vengeance was taken upon them with a great scourge, and being rooted up from that place where, with impious licentiousness being infuriated, they had madly raged against their Physician, they have been dispersed throughout all nations, and that land hath been given to Christians: and there is fulfilled what the Lord had said to them, "Therefore the kingdom shall be taken away from you, and it shall be given to a nation doing justice." But when they saw great multitudes then following the Lord, preaching the kingdom of Heaven, and doing wonderful things, the rulers of that city said," If we shall have let Him go, all men will go after Him, and there shall come the Romans, and shall take from us both place and nation." That they might not lose their place, they killed the Lord; and they lost it, even because they killed. Therefore that city, being one earthly, did bear the figure of a certain city everlasting in the Heavens: but when that which was signified began more evidently to be preached, the shadow, whereby it was being signified, was thrown down: for this reason in that place now the temple is no more, which had been constructed for the image of the future Body of the Lord. We have the light, the shadow hath passed away: nevertheless, still in a kind of captivity we are: "So long as we are," he saith, "in the body, we are sojourning afar from the Lord."

2. And see ye the names of those two cities, Babylon and Jerusalem. Babylon is interpreted confusion, Jerusalem vision of peace. Observe now the city of confusion, in order that ye may perceive the vision of peace; that ye may endure that, sigh for this. Whereby can those two cities be distinguished? Can we anywise now separate them from each other? They are mingled, and from the very beginning of mankind mingled they run on unto the end of the world. Jerusalem received beginning through Abel, Babylon through Cain: for the buildings of the cities were afterwards erected. That Jerusalem in the land of the Jebusites was builded: for at first it used to be called Jebus, from thence the nation of the Jebusites was expelled, when the people of God was delivered from Egypt, and led into the land of promise. But Babylon was built in the most interior regions of Persia, which for a long time raised its head above the rest of nations. These two cities then at particular times were builded, so that there might be shown a figure of two cities begun of old, and to remain even unto the end in this world, but at the end to be severed. Whereby then can we now show them, that are mingled? At that time the Lord shall show, when some He shall set on the right hand, others on the left. Jerusalem on the right hand shall be, Babylon on the left. ... Two loves make up these two cities: love of God maketh Jerusalem, love of the world maketh Babylon. Therefore let each one question himself as to what he loveth: and he shall find of which he is a citizen: and if he shall have found himself to be a citizen of Babylon, let him root out cupidity, implant charity: but if he shall have found himself a citizen of Jerusalem, let him endure captivity, hope for liberty. ... Now therefore let us hear of, brethren, hear of, and sing of, and long for, that city whereof we are citizens. And what are the joys which are sung of to us? In what manner in ourselves is formed again the love of our city, which by long sojourning we had forgotten? But our Father hath sent from thence letters to us, God hath supplied to us the Scriptures, by which letters there should be wrought in us a longing for return: because by loving our sojourning, to enemies we had turned our face, and our back to our fatherland. What then is here sung?

3. "For Thee a hymn is meet, O God, in Sion" (ver. 1). That fatherland is Sion: Jerusalem is the very same as Sion; and of this name the interpretation ye ought to know. As Jerusalem is interpreted vision of peace, so Sion Beholding? that is, vision and contemplation. Some great inexplicable sight to us is promised: and this is God Himself that hath builded the city. Beauteous and graceful the city, how much more beauteous a Builder it hath! "For Thee a hymn is meet, O God," he saith. But where? "In Sion:" in Babylon it is not meet. For when a man beginneth to be renewed, already with heart in Jerusalem he singeth, with the Apostle saying, "Our conversation is in the Heavens." For "in the flesh though walking," he saith, "not after the flesh we war." Already in longing we are there, already hope into that land, as it were an anchor, we have sent before, lest in this sea being tossed we

suffer shipwreck. In like manner therefore as of a ship which is at anchor, we rightly say that already she is come to land, for still she rolleth, but to land in a manner she hath been brought safe in the teeth of winds and in the teeth of storms; so against the temptations of this sojourning, our hope being grounded in that city Jerusalem causeth us not to be carried away upon rocks. He therefore that according to this hope singeth, in that city singeth: let him therefore say, "For Thee a hymn is meet, O God, in Sion." ...

4. "And to Thee shall there be paid a vow in Jerusalem." Here we vow, and a good thing it is that there we should pay. But who are they that here do vow and pay not? They that persevere not even unto the end in that which they have vowed. Whence saith another Psalm "Vow ye, and pay ye unto the Lord your God:" and, "to Thee shall it be paid in Jerusalem." For there shall we be whole, that is, entire in the resurrection of just men: there shall be paid our whole vow, not soul alone, but the very flesh also, no longer corruptible, because no longer in Babylon, but now a body heavenly and changed. What sort of change is promised? "For we all shall rise again," saith the Apostle, "but we shall not all be changed. ... Where is, O death, thy sting?" For now while there begin in use the first-fruits of the mind, from whence is the longing for Jerusalem, many things of corruptible flesh do contend against us, which will not contend, when death shall have been swallowed up in victory. Peace shall conquer, and war shall be ended. But when peace shall conquer, that city shall conquer which is called the vision of peace. On the part of death therefore shall be no contention. Now with how great a death do we contend! For thence are carnal pleasures, which to us even unlawfully do suggest many things: to which we give no consent, but nevertheless in giving no consent we contend. ...

5. "Hearken," he saith, "to my prayer, unto Thee every flesh shall come". (ver. 2). And we have the Lord saying, that there was given to Him "power over every flesh." That King therefore began even now to appear, when there was being said, "Unto Thee every flesh shall come." "To Thee," he saith, "every flesh shall come." Wherefore to Him shall "every" flesh come? Because flesh He hath taken to Him. Whither shall there come every flesh? He took the first-fruits thereof out of the womb of the Virgin; and now that the first-fruits have been taken to Him, the rest shall follow, in order that the holocaust may be completed. Whence then "every flesh"? Every man. And whence every man? Have all been foretold, as going to believe in Christ? Have not many ungodly men been foretold, that shall be condemned also? Do not daily men not believing die in their own unbelief? After what manner therefore do we understand, "Unto Thee every flesh shall come"? By "every flesh" he hath signified, "flesh of every kind:" out of every kind of flesh

they shall come to Thee. What is, out of every kind of flesh? Have there come poor men, and have there not come rich men? Have there come humble men, and not come lofty men? Have there come unlearned men, and not come learned men? Have there come men, and not come women? Have there come masters, and not come servants? Have there come old men, and not come young men; or have there come young men, and not come youths; or have there come youths, and not come boys; or have there come boys, and have there not been brought infants? In a word, have there come Jews (for thence were the Apostles, thence many thousands of men at first betraying, afterwards believing), and have there not come Greeks; or have there come Greeks, and not come Romans; or have there come Romans, and not come Barbarians? And who could number all nations coining to Him, to whom hath been said, "Unto Thee every flesh shall come"?

6. "The discourses of unjust men have prevailed over us, and our iniquities Thou shalt propitiate" (ver. 3). ... Every man, in whatsoever place he is born, of that same land or region or city learneth the language, is habituated to the manners and life of that place. What should a boy do, born among Heathens, to avoid worshipping a stone, inasmuch as his parents have suggested that worship? from them the first words he hath heard, that error with his milk he hath sucked in; and because they that used to speak were elders, and the boy that was learning to speak was an infant, what could the little one do but follow the authority of elders, and deem that to be good which they recommended? Therefore nations that are converted to Christ afterwards, and taking to heart the impieties of their parents, and saying now what the prophet Jeremias himself said, "Truly a lie our fathers have worshipped, vanity which hath not profited them"— when, I say, they now say this, they renounce the opinions and blasphemies of their unjust parents. ... There have led us away men teaching evil things, citizens of Babylon they have made us, we have left the Creator, have adored the creature: have left Him by whom we were made, have adored that which we ourselves have made. For "the discourses of unjust men have prevailed over us:" but nevertheless they have not crushed us. Wherefore? "Our impieties Thou shalt propitiate," is not said except to some priest offering somewhat, whereby impiety may be expiated and propitiated. For impiety is then said to be propitiated, when God is made propitious to the impiety. What is it for God to be made propitious to impiety? It is, His becoming forgiving, and giving pardon. But in order that God's pardon may be obtained, propitiation is made through some sacrifice. There hath come forth therefore, sent from God the Lord, One our Priest; He took upon Him from us that which He might offer to the Lord we are speaking of those same first-fruits of the flesh from the womb of the Virgin. This holocaust He offered to God. He stretched out His hands on the Cross, in order that He might say, "Let My prayer be directed as incense in Thy sight, and the lifting up of My hands an evening sacrifice." As ye

know, the Lord about eventide hung on the Cross: and our impieties were propitiated; otherwise they had swallowed up: the discourses of unjust men had prevailed over us; there had led us astray preachers of Jupiter, and of Saturn, and of Mercury: "the discourses of ungodly men had prevailed over us." But what wilt Thou do? "Our impieties Thou wilt propitiate." Thou art the priest, Thou the victim; Thou the offerer, Thou the offering. ...

7. "Blessed is he whom Thou hast chosen, and hast taken to Thee" (ver. 4). Who is he that is chosen by Him and taken to Him? Was any one chosen by our Saviour Jesus Christ, or was Himself after the flesh, because He is man, chosen and taken to Him? ... Or hath not rather Christ Himself taken to Him some blessed one, and the same whom He hath taken to Him is not spoken of in the plural number but in the singular? For one man He hath taken to Him, because unity He hath taken to Him. Schisms He hath not taken to Him, heresies He hath not taken to Him: a multitude they have made of themselves, there is not one to be taken to Him. But they that abide in the bond of Christ and are the members of Him, make in a manner one man, of whom saith the Apostle, "Until we all arrive at the acknowledging of the Son of God, unto a perfect man, unto the measure of the age of the fulness of Christ." Therefore one man is taken to Him, to which the Head is Christ; because "the Head of the man is Christ." The same is that blessed man that "hath not departed in the counsel of ungodly men," and the like things which there are spoken of: the same is He that is taken to Him. He is not without us, in His own members we are, under one Head we are governed, by one Spirit we all live, one fatherland we all long for. ... And to us He will give what? "He shall inhabit," he saith, "in Thy courts." Jerusalem, that is, to which they sing that begin to go forth from Babylon: "He shall inhabit in Thy courts: we shall be filled with the good things of Thy House." What are the good things of the House of God? Brethren, let us set before ourselves some rich house, with what numerous good things it is crowded, how abundantly it is furnished, how many vessels there are there of gold and also of silver; how great an establishment of servants, how many horses and animals, in a word, how much the house itself delights us with pictures, marble, ceilings, pillars, recesses, chambers:—all such things are indeed objects of desire, but still they are of the confusion of Babylon, Cut off all such longings, O citizen of Jerusalem, cut them off; if thou wilt return, let not captivity delight thee. But hast thou already begun to go forth? Do not look back, do not loiter on the road. Still there are not wanting foes to recommend thee captivity and sojourning: no longer let there prevail against thee the discourses of ungodly men. For the House of God long thou, and for the good things of that House long thou: but do not long for such things as thou art wont to long for either in thy house, or in the house of thy neighbour, or in the house of thy patron. ...

8. "Thy holy Temple is marvellous in righteousness" (ver. 5). These are the good things of that House. He hath not said, Thy holy Temple is marvellous in pillars, marvellous in marbles, marvellous in glided ceilings; but is "marvellous in righteousness." Without thou hast eyes wherewith thou mayest see marbles, and gold: within is an eye wherewith may be seen the beauty of righteousness. If there is no beauty in righteousness, why is a righteous old man loved? What bringeth he in body that may please the eyes? Crooked limbs, brow wrinkled, head blanched with gray hairs, dotage everywhere full of plaints. But perchance because thine eyes this decrepit old man pleaseth not, thine ears he pleaseth: with what words? with what song? Even if perchance when a young man he sang well, all with age hath been lost. Doth perchance the sound of his words please thine ears, that can hardly articulate whole words for loss of teeth? Nevertheless, if righteous he is, if another man's goods he coveteth not, if of his own that he possesseth he distributeth to the needy, if he giveth good advice, and soundly judgeth, if he believeth the entire faith, if for his belief in the faith he is ready to expend even those very shattered limbs, for many Martyrs are even old men; why do we love him? What good thing in him do we see with the eyes of the flesh? Not any. There is therefore a kind of beauty in righteousness, which we see with the eye of the heart, and we love, and we kindle with affection: how much men found to love in those same Martyrs, though beasts tare their limbs! Is it possible but that when blood was staining all parts. when with the teeth of monsters their bowels gushed out, the eyes had nothing but objects to shudder at? What was there to be loved, except that in that hideous spectacle of mangled limbs, entire was the beauty of righteousness? These are the good things of the House of God, with these prepare thyself to be satisfied. ... "Blessed they which hunger and thirst after righteousness, for they shall be filled." "Thy holy Temple is marvellous in righteousness." And that same temple, brethren, do not imagine to be aught but yourselves. Love ye righteousness, and ye are the Temple of God.

9. "Hearken to us, O God, our Saviour" (ver. 5). He hath disclosed now Whom he nameth as God. The "Saviour" specially is the Lord Jesus Christ. It hath appeared now more openly of Whom he had said, "Unto Thee every flesh shall come." That One Man that is taken unto Him into the Temple of God, is both many and is One. In the person of One he hath said, "Hearken, O God, i.e., to my hunger: "3 and because the same One of many is composed, now he saith," Hearken to us, O God, our Saviour." Hear Him now more openly preached: "Hearken to us, O God, our Saviour the Hope of all the ends of the earth and in the sea afar." Behold wherefore hath been said "Unto Thee every flesh shall come." From every quarter they come. "Hope of all the ends of the earth," not hope of one corner, not hope of Judaea alone, not hope of Africa alone, not hope of Pannonia, not hope of East or of West: but "Hope of all the ends of the earth, and in the sea afar:" of the very

ends of the earth. "And in the sea afar:" and because in the sea, therefore afar. For the sea by a figure is spoken of this world, with saltness bitter, with storms troubled; where men of perverse and depraved appetites have become like fishes devouring one another. Observe the evil sea, bitter sea, with waves violent, observe with what sort of men it is filled. Who desireth an inheritance except through the death of another? Who desireth gain except by the loss of another? By the fall of others how many men wish to be exalted? How many, in order that they may buy, desire for other men to sell their goods? How they mutually oppress, and how they that are able do devour! And when one fish hath devoured, the greater the less, itself also is devoured by some greater. ... Because evil fishes that were taken within the nets they said they would not endure; they themselves have become more evil than they whom they said they could not endure. For those nets did take fishes both good and evil. The Lord saith, "The kingdom of Heaven is like to a sein cast into the sea, which gathereth of every kind, which, when it had been filled, drawing out, and sitting on the shore, they gathered the good into vessels, but the evil they cast out: so it shall be," He saith, "in the consummation of the world." He showeth what is the shore, He showeth what is the end of the sea. "The angels shall go forth, and shall sever the evil from the midst of the just, and shall cast them into the furnace of fire: there shall be weeping and gnashing of teeth." Ha! ye citizens of Jerusalem that are within the nets, and are good fishes; endure the evil, the nets break ye not: together with them ye are in a sea, not together with them will ye be in the vessels. For" Hope" He is "of the ends of the earth," Himself is Hope "also in the sea afar." Afar, because also in the sea.

10. "Preparing mountains in His strength" (ver. 6). Not in their strength. For He hath prepared great preachers, and those same He hath called mountains; humble in themselves, exalted in Him. "Preparing mountains in His strength." What saith one of those same mountains? "We ourselves in our own selves have had the answer of death, in order that in ourselves we should not trust, but in God that raiseth the dead." He that in himself doth trust, and in Christ trusteth not, is not of those mountains which He hath prepared in His strength. "Preparing mountains in His strength: girded about in power." "Power," I understand: "girded about," is what? They that put Christ in the midst, "girded about" they make Him, that is on all sides begirt. We all have Him in common, therefore in the midst He is: all we gird Him about that believe in Him: and because our faith is not of our strength, but of His power; therefore girded about He is in His power; not in our own strength.

11. "That troublest the bottom of the sea" (ver. 7). He hath done this: it is seen what He hath done. For He hath prepared mountains in His strength, hath sent

them to preach: girded about He is by believers in power: and moved is the sea, moved is the world, and it beginneth to persecute His saints. "Girded about in power: that troublest the bottom of the sea." He hath not said, that troublest the sea; but "the bottom of the sea." The bottom of the sea is the heart of ungodly men. For just as from the bottom more thoroughly all things are stirred, and the bottom holdeth firm all things: so whatsoever hath gone forth: by tongue, by hands, by divers powers for the persecution of the Church, from the bottom hath gone forth. For if there were not the root of iniquity in the heart, all those things would not have gone forth against Christ. The bottom He troubled, perchance in order that the bottom He might also empty: for in the case of certain evil men He emptied the sea from the bottom, and made the sea a desert place. Another Psalm saith this, "That turneth sea into dry land." All ungodly and heathen men that have believed were sea, have been made land; with salt waves at first barren, afterwards with the fruit of righteousness productive. "That troublest the bottom of the sea: the sound of its waves who shall endure? "Who shall endure," is what? What man shall endure the sound of the waves of the sea, the behests of the high powers of the world? But whence are they endured? Because He prepareth mountains in His strength. In that therefore which he hath said "who shall" endure? he saith thus: We ourselves of our own selves should not be able to endure those persecutions, unless He gave strength.

12. "The nations shall be troubled" (ver. 8). At first they shall be troubled: but those mountains prepared in the strength of Christ, are they troubled? Troubled is the sea, against the mountains it dasheth: the sea breaketh, unshaken the mountains have remained. "The nations shall be troubled, and all men shall fear." Behold now all men fear: they that before have been troubled do now all fear. The Christians feared not, and now the Christians are feared. All that did persecute do now fear. For He hath overcome that is girded about with power, to Him hath come every flesh in such sort, that the rest by their very minority do now fear. And all men shall fear, that inhabit the ends of the earth, because of Thy signs. For miracles the Apostles wrought, and thence all the ends of the earth have feared and have believed. "Outgoings in morning and in evening Thou shall delight :" that is, Thou makest delightful. Already in this life what is there being promised to us? There are outgoings in morning, there are outgoings in the evening. By the morning he signifieth the prosperity of the world, by the evening he signifieth the trouble of the world. ... At first when he was promising gain, it was morning to thee: but now evening draweth on, sad thou hast become. But He that hath given thee an outgoing in the morning, will give one also in the evening. In the same manner as thou hast contemned the morning of the world by the light of the Lord, so contemn the evening also by the sufferings of the Lord, in saying to thy soul, What more will this man do to me, than my Lord hath suffered for me? May I hold

fast justice, not consent to iniquity. Let him vent his rage on the flesh, the trap will be broken, and I will fly to my Lord, that saith to me, "Do not fear them that kill the body, but the soul are not able to kill." And for the body itself He hath given security, saying, "A hair of your head shall not perish." Nobly here he hath set down," "Thou wilt delight outgoings in morning and in evening." For if thou take not delight in the very outgoing, thou wilt not labour to go out thence. Thou runnest thy head into the promised gain, if thou art not delighted with the promise of the Saviour. And again thou yieldest to one tempting and terrifying, if thou find no delight in Him that suffered before thee, in order that He might make an outgoing for thee.

13. "Thou hast visited the earth, and hast inebriated it" (ver. 9). Whence hast inebriated the earth? "Thy cup inebriating how glorious it is!" "Thou hast visited the earth, and hast inebriated it." Thou hast sent Thy clouds, they have rained down the preaching of the truth, inebriated is the earth. "Thou hast multiplied to enrich it." Whence? "The river of God is filled with water." What is the river of God? The people of God. The first people was filled with water, wherewith the rest of the earth might be watered. Hear Him promising water: "If any man thirst, let him come to Me and drink: he that believeth on Me, rivers of living water from his belly shall flow :" if rivers, one river also; for in respect of unity many are one. Many Churches and one Church, many faithful and one Bride of Christ: so many rivers and one river. Many Israelites believed, and were fulfilled with the Holy Spirit; from thence they were scattered abroad through the nations, they began to preach the truth, and from the river of God that was filled with water, was the whole earth watered. "Thou hast prepared food for them: because thus is Thy preparing." Not because they have deserved of Thee, whom Thou hast forgiven sins: the merits of them were evil, but Thou for Thy mercy's sake, "because thus is Thy preparing," thus "Thou hast prepared food for them."

14. "The furrows thereof inebriate Thou" (ver. 10). Let there be made therefore at first furrows to be inebriated: let the hardness of our breast be opened with the share of the word of God, "The furrows thereof inebriate Thou: multiply the generations thereof." We see, they believe, and by them believing other men believe, and because of those others believe; and it is not sufficient for one man, that having become himself a believer, he should gain one. So is multiplied seed too: a few grains are scattered, and fields spring up. "In the drops thereof it shall rejoice, when it shall rise up." That is, before it be perchance enlarged to the bulk of a river, "when it shall rise up, in its drops," that is, in those meet for it, "it shall rejoice." For upon those that are yet babes, and upon the weak, are dropped some portions of the sacraments, because they cannot receive the fulness of the truth.

Hear in what manner he droppeth upon babes, while they are rising up, that is, in their recent rising having small capacities: the Apostle saith, "To you I could not speak as if to spiritual, but as if to carnal, as if to babes in Christ." When he saith, "to babes in Christ," he speaketh of them as already risen up, but not yet meet to receive that plenteous wisdom, whereof he saith, "Wisdom we speak among perfect men." Let it rejoice in its drops, while it is rising up and is growing, when strengthened it shall receive wisdom also: in the same manner as an infant is fed with milk, and becometh fit for meat, and nevertheless at first out of that very meat for which it was not fit, for it milk is made.

15. "Thou shalt bless the crown of the year of Thy goodness" (ver. 11). Seed is now sowing, that which is sown is growing, there will be the harvest too. And now over the seed the enemy hath sown tares; and there have risen up evil ones among the good, false Christians, having like leaf, but not like fruit. For those are properly called tares, which spring up in the manner of wheat, for instance darnel, for instance wild oats, and all such as have the first leaf the same. Therefore of the sowing of the tares thus saith the Lord: "There hath come an enemy, and hath sown over them tares; " but what hath he done to the grain? The wheat is not choked by the tares, nay, through endurance of the tares the fruit of the wheat is increased. For the Lord Himself said to certain workmen desiring to root up the tares, "Suffer ye both to grow unto the harvest." ... Conquer the devil, and thou wilt have a crown. "Thou shalt bless the crown of the year of Thy goodness." Again he maketh reference to the goodness of God, lest any one boast of his own merits. "Thy plains shall be filled with abundance."

16. "The ends of the desert shall grow fat, and the hills shall be encircled with exultation" (ver. 12). Plains, hills, ends of the desert, the same are also men. Plains, because of the equality: because of equality, I say, from thence just peoples have been called plains. Hills, because of lifting up: because God doth lift up in Himself those that humble themselves. Ends of the desert are all nations. Wherefore ends of the desert? Deserted they were, to them no Prophet had been sent they were in like case as is a desert where no man passeth by. No word of God was sent to the nations: to the people Israel alone the Prophets preached. We came to the Lord; the wheat believed among that same people of the Jews. For He said at that time to the disciples, "Ye say, far off is the harvest: look back, and see how white are the lands to harvest." There hath been therefore a first harvest, there will be a second in the last age. The first harvest was of Jews, because there were sent to them Prophets proclaiming a coming Saviour. Therefore the Lord said to His disciples, "See how white are the lands to harvest:" the lands, to wit, of Judaea. "Other men," He saith, "have laboured, and into their labours ye have

entered." The Prophets laboured to sow, and ye with the sickle have entered into their labours. There hath been finished therefore the first harvest, and thence, with that very wheat which then was purged, hath been sown the round world; so that there ariseth an other harvest, which at the end is to be reaped. In the second harvest have been sown tares, now here there is labour. Just as in that first harvest the Prophets laboured until the Lord came: so in that second harvest the Apostles laboured, and all preachers of the truth labour, even until at the end the Lord send unto the harvest His Angels. Aforetime, I say, a desert there was, "but the ends of the desert shall grow fat." Behold where the Prophets had given no sound, the Lord of the Prophets hath been received, "The ends of the desert shall grow fat, and with exultation the hills shall be encircled."

17. "Clothed have been the rams of the sheep" (ver. 13): "with exultation" must be understood. For with what exultation the hills are encircled, with the same are clothed the rams of the sheep. Rams are the very same as hills. For hills they are because of more eminent grace; rams, because they are leaders of the flocks. ... "They shall shout:" thence they shall abound with wheat, because they shall shout. What shall they shout? "For a hymn they shall say." For one thing it is to shout against God, another thing to say a hymn; one thing to shout iniquities, another thing to shout the praises of God. If thou shout in blasphemy, thorns thou hast brought forth: if thou shoutest in a hymn, thou aboundest in wheat.

PSALM LXVI.

1. This Psalm hath on the title the inscription, "For the end, a song of a Psalm of Resurrection." When ye hear "for the end," whenever the Psalms are repeated, understand it "for Christ:" the Apostle saying, "For the end of the law is Christ, for righteousness to every one believing." In what manner therefore here Resurrection is sung, ye wilt hear, and whose Resurrection it is, as far as Himself deigneth to give and disclose. For the Resurrection we Christians know already hath come to pass in our Head, and in the members it is to be. The Head of the Church is Christ? the members of Christ are the Church. That which hath preceded in the Head, will follow in the Body. This is our hope; for this we believe, for this we endure and persevere amid so great perverseness of this world, hope comforting us, before that hope becometh reality. ... The Jews did hold the hope of the resurrection of the dead: and they hoped that themselves alone would rise again to a blessed life because of the work of the Law, and because of the justifications of the Scriptures, which the Jews alone had, and the Gentiles had not. Crucified was Christ, "blindness in part happened unto Israel, in order that the fulness of the Gentiles might enter in:" as the Apostle saith. The resurrection of the dead beginneth to be promised to the Gentiles also that believe in Jesus Christ, that He hath risen again. Thence this Psalm is against the presumption and pride of the Jews, for the comfort of the Gentiles that are to be called to the same hope of resurrection.

2. ... Thence he beginneth, "Be joyful in God." Who? "Every land" (ver. 1). Not therefore Judaea alone. See, brethren, after what sort is set forth the universality of the Church in the whole world spread abroad: and mourn ye not only the Jews, who envied the Gentiles that grace, but still more for heretics wail ye. For if they are to be mourned, that have not been gathered together, how much more they that being gathered together have been divided? "Jubilate in God every land." What is "jubilate"? Into the voice of rejoicings break forth if ye cannot into that of words. For "jubilation" is not of words, but the sound alone of men rejoicing is uttered, as of a heart labouring and bringing forth into voice the pleasure of a thing imagined which cannot be expressed. "Be joyful in God every land:" let no one jubilate in a part: let every land be joyful, let the Catholic Church jubilate. The Catholic Church embraceth the whole: whosoever holdeth a part and from the whole is cut off, should howl, not jubilate.

3. "But play ye to His name" (ver. 2). What hath he said? By you "playing" let His name be blessed. But what it is to "play"? To play is also to take up an instrument which is called a psaltery, and by the striking and action of the hands to accompany voices. If therefore ye jubilate so that God may hear; play also

something that men may both see and hear: but not to your own name. ... For if for the sake of yourselves being glorified ye do good works, we make the same reply as He made to certain of such men, "Verily I say unto you, they have received their reward: " and again, "Otherwise no reward ye will have with your Father that is in Heaven." Thou wilt say, ought I, then, to hide my works, that I do them not before men? No. But what saith He? "Let your works shine before men." In doubt then I shall remain. On one side Thou sayest to me, "Take heed that ye do not your righteousness before men: on the other side Thou sayest to me, "Let your good works shine before men;" what shall I keep? what do? what leave undone? A man can as well serve two masters commanding different things as one commanding different things. I command not, saith the Lord, different things. The end observe, for the end sing: with what end thou doest it, see thou. If for this reason thou doest it, that thou mayest be glorified, I have forbidden it: but if for this reason, that God may be glorified, I have commanded it. Play therefore, not to your own name, but to the name of the Lord your God. Play ye, let Him be lauded: live ye well, let Him be glorified. For whence have ye that same living well? If for everlasting ye had had it, ye would never have lived ill; if from yourselves ye had had it, ye never would have done otherwise than have lived well. "Give glory to His praise." Our whole attention upon the praise of God he directeth, nothing for us he leaveth whence we should be praised. Let us glory thence the more, and rejoice: to Him let us cleave, in Him let us be praised. Ye heard when the Apostle was being read, "See ye your calling, brethren, how not many wise after the flesh, not many mighty, not many noble, but the foolish things of the world God hath chosen to confound the wise." ... But the Lord chose afterwards orators also; but they would have been proud, if He had not first chosen fishermen; He chose rich men; but they would have said that on account of their riches they had been chosen, unless at first He had chosen poor men: He chose Emperors afterwards; but better is it, that when an Emperor hath come to Rome, he should lay aside his crown, and weep at the monument of a fisherman, than that a fisherman should weep at the monument of an Emperor. "For the weak things of the world God hath chosen to confound the strong," etc. ... And what followeth? The Apostle hath concluded, "That there might not glory before God any flesh." See ye how from us He hath taken away, that He might give glory: hath taken away ours, that He might give His own; hath taken away empty, that He might give full; hath taken away insecure, that He might give solid. ...

4. "Say ye to God, How to be feared are Thy works!" (ver. 3). Wherefore to be feared and not to be loved? Hear thou another voice of a Psalm: "Serve ye the Lord in fear, and exult unto Him with trembling." What meaneth this? Hear the voice of the Apostle: "With fear," he saith, "and trembling, your own salvation work ye out." 3 Wherefore with fear and trembling? He hath subjoined the reason:

"for God it is that worketh in you both to will and to work according to good will."
If therefore God worketh in thee, by the Grace of God thou workest well, not by
thy strength. Therefore if thou rejoicest, fear also: lest perchance that which was
given to a humble man be taken away from a proud one. ...Brethren, if against the
Jews of old, cut off from the root of the Patriarchs, we ought not to exalt
ourselves, but rather to fear and say to God, "How to be feared are Thy works:"
how much less ought we not to exalt ourselves against the fresh wounds of the
cutting off! Before there had been cut off Jews, graffed in Gentiles; from the very
graft there have been cut off heretics; but neither against them ought we to exalt
ourselves; lest perchance he deserve to be cut off, that delighteth to revile them
that are cut off. My brethren, a bishop's voice, however unworthy, hath sounded to
you: we pray you to beware, whosoever ye are in the Church, do not revile them
that are not within; but pray ye rather, that they too may be within. For God is able
again to graft them in. Of the very Jews the Apostle said this, and it was done in
their case. The Lord rose again, and many believed: they perceived not when they
crucified, nevertheless afterwards they believed in Him, and there was forgiven
them so great a transgression. The shedding of the Lord's blood was forgiven the
manslayers, not to say, God-slayers: "for if they had known, the Lord of glory they
never would have crucified." Now to the manslayers hath been forgiven the
shedding of the blood of Him innocent: and that same blood which through
madness they shed, through grace they have drunk. ...O fulness of Gentiles, say
thou to God, "How to be feared are Thy works!" and so rejoice thou as that thou
mayest fear, be not exalted above the branches cut off.

5. "In the multitude of thy power Thine enemies shall lie to Thee." For this
purpose he saith, "to Thee thine enemies shall lie," in order that great may be Thy
power. What is this? With more attention hearken. The power of our Lord Jesus
Christ most chiefly appeared in the Resurrection, from whence this Psalm hath
received its title. And rising again, He appeared to His disciples. He appeared not
to His enemies, but to His disciples. Crucified He appeared to all men, rising again
to believers: so that afterwards also he that would might believe, and to him that
should believe, resurrection might be promised. Many holy men wrought many
miracles; no one of them when dead did rise again: because even they that by them
were raised to life, were raised to life to die. ... Because therefore the Jews might
say, when the Lord did miracles, Moses hath done these things, Elias hath done,
Eliseus hath done them: they might for themselves say these words, because those
men also did raise to life dead men, and did many miracles: therefore when from
Him a sign was demanded, of the peculiar sign making mention which in Himself
alone was to be, He saith, "This generation crooked and provoking seeketh a sign,
and a sign shall not be given to it, except the sign of Jonas the Prophet: for as
Jonas was in the belly of the whale three days and three nights, so shall be also the

Son of Man in the heart of the earth three days and three nights." In what way was Jonas in the belly of the whale? Was it not so that afterwards alive he was vomited out? Hell was to the Lord what the whale was to Jonas. This sign peculiar to Himself He mentioned, this is the most mighty sign. It is more mighty to live again after having been dead, than not to have been dead. The greatness of the power of the Lord as He was made Man, in the virtue of the Resurrection doth appear. ...

6. Observe also the very lie of the false witnesses in the Gospel, and see how it is about Resurrection. For when to the Lord had been said, "What sign showest Thou to us, that Thou doest these things?" besides that which He had spoken about Jonah through another similitude of this same thing also He spake, that ye might know this peculiar sign had been especially pointed out: "Destroy this Temple," He saith, "and in three days I will raise it up." And they said, "In forty and six years was builded this temple, and wilt Thou in three days raise it up?" And the evangelist explaining what it was," But this," he saith, "spake Jesus of the Temple of His Body." Behold this His power He said He would show to men in the same thing as that from whence He had given the similitude of a Temple, because of His flesh. which was the Temple of the Divinity hidden within. Whence the Jews outwardly saw the Temple, the Deity dwelling within they saw not. Out of those words of the Lord false witnesses made up a lie to say against Him, out of those very words wherein He mentioned His future Resurrection, in speaking of the Temple. For false witnesses, when they were asked what they had heard Him say, alleged against Him: "We heard Him saying, I will destroy this Temple, and after three days I will raise it up." "After three days I will raise up," they had heard: "I will destroy," they had not heard: but had heard "destroy ye." One word they changed and a few letters, in order to support their false testimony. But for whom changest thou a word, O human vanity, O human weakness? For the Word, the Unchangeable, dost thou change a word? Thou changest thy word, dost thou change God's Word? ... Wherefore said they that Thou hadst said, "I will destroy;" and said not that which Thou saidest, "destroy ye"? It was, as it were, in order that they might defend themselves from the charge of destroying the Temple without cause. For Christ, because He willed it, died: and nevertheless ye killed Him. Behold we grant you, O ye liars, Himself destroyed the Temple. For it hath been said by the Apostle, "That loved me, and gave up Himself for me." It hath been said of the Father, "That His own Son spared not, but gave Him up for us all." ... By all means be it that Himself destroyed the Temple, Himself destroyed that said, "Power I have to lay down My Soul and power I have again to take it: no one taketh it from Me, but I Myself lay it down from Me, and again I take it." Be it that Himself hath destroyed the Temple in His Grace, in your malice. "In the multitude of Thy power thine enemies shall lie to Thee." Behold they lie, behold they are

believed, behold Thou art oppressed, behold Thou art crucified, behold Thou art insulted, behold head is wagged at Thee, "If Son of God He is, let Him come down from the Cross." Behold when Thou wilt, life Thou layest down, and with lance in the side art pierced, and Sacraments from Thy side flow forth; Thou art taken down from the Tree, wound in linens, laid in the sepulchre, there are set guards lest Thy disciples take Thee away; there cometh the hour of Thy Resurrection, earth is shaken, tombs are cloven, Thou risest again in secret, appearest openly. Where then are those liars? Where is the false testimony of evil will? Have not Thine enemies in the multitude of Thy power lied to Thee?

7. Give them also those guards at the Tomb, let them recount what they have seen, let them take money and lie too. ... They too were added to the lie of the enemies: increased was the number of liars, that increased might be the reward of believers. Therefore they lied, "in the multitude of Thy power" they lied: to confound liars Thou hast appeared to men of truth, and Thou hast appeared to those men of truth whom Thou hast made men of truth.

8. Let Jews remain in their lies: to Thee, because in the multitude of Thy power they lied, let there be done that which followeth, "Let every land worship Thee, and play to Thee, play to Thy name, O Most Highest" (ver. 4). A little before, Most Lowly, now Most Highest: Most Lowly in the hands of lying enemies; Most Highest above the head of praising Angels. O ye Gentiles, O most distant nations, leave lying Jews, come confessing. "Come ye, and see the works of the Lord: terrible in counsels above the sons of men" (ver. 5). Son of Man indeed He too hath been called, and verily Son of Man He became: very Son of God in the form of God; very Son of Man in form of a servant: but do not judge of that form by the condition of others alike: "terrible" He is "in counsels above the sons of men." Sons of men took counsel to crucify Christ, being crucified He blinded the crucifiers. What then have ye done, sons of men, by taking keen counsels against your Lord, in whom was hidden Majesty, and to sight shown weakness? Ye were taking counsels to destroy, He to blind and save; to blind proud men, to save humble men: but to blind those same proud men, to the end that, being blinded they might be humbled, being humbled might confess, having confessed might be enlightened. "Terrible in counsels above the sons of men." Terrible indeed. Behold blindness in part to Israel hath happened: behold the Jews, out of whom was born Christ, are without: behold the Gentiles, that were against Judaea, in Christ are within. "Terrible in counsels above the sons of men."

9. Wherefore what hath He done by the terror of His counsel? He hath turned the sea into dry land. For this followeth, "That hath turned the sea into dry land" (ver.

6). A sea was the world, bitter with saltness, troubled with tempest, raging with waves of persecutions, sea it was: truly into dry land the sea hath been turned, now there thirsteth for sweet water the world that with salt water was filled. Who hath done this? He "that hath turned the sea into dry land." Now the soul of all the Gentiles saith what? "My soul is as it were land without water to Thee." "That hath turned the sea into dry land. In the river they shall pass over on foot." Those same persons that have been turned into dry land, though they were before sea, "in the river on foot shall pass over." What is the river? The river is all the mortality of the world. Observe a river: some things come and pass by, other things that are to pass by do succeed. Is it not thus with the water of a river, that from earth springeth and floweth? Every one that is born must needs give place to one going to be born: and all this order of things rolling along is a kind of river. Into this river let not the soul greedily throw herself, let her not throw herself, but let her stand still. And how shall she pass over the pleasures of things doomed to perish? Let her believe in Christ, and she will pass over on foot: she passeth over with Him for Leader, on foot she passeth over.

10. "There we will be joyous in Him." O ye Jews, of your own works boast ye: lay aside the pride of boasting of yourselves, take up the Grace of being joyous in Christ. For therein we will be joyous, but not in ourselves: "there we will be joyous in Him." When shall we joy? When we shall have passed over the river on foot. Life everlasting is promised, resurrection is promised, there our flesh no longer shall be a river: for a river it is now, while it is mortality. Observe whether there standeth still any age. Boys desire to grow up; and they know not how by succeeding years the span of their life is lessened. For years are not added to but taken from them as they grow: just as the water of a river alway draweth near, but from the source it withdraweth. And boys desire to grow up that they may escape the thraldom of elders; behold they grow up, it cometh to pass quickly, they arrive at youth: let them that have emerged from boyhood retain, if they are able, their youth: that too passeth away. Old age succeedeth: let even old age be everlasting; with death it is removed. Therefore a river there is of flesh that is born. This river of mortality, so that it doth not by reason of concupiscence of things mortal undermine and carry him away, he easily passeth over, that humbly, that is on foot, passeth over, He being leader that first hath passed over, that of the flood in the way even unto death hath drunk, and therefore hath lifted up the head. Passing over therefore on foot that river, that is, easily passing over that mortality that glideth along, "there we will be joyous in Him." But now in what save in Him, or in the hope of Him? For even if we are joyous now, in hope we are joyous; but then in Him we shall be joyous. And now in Him, but through hope: "but then face to face." "There we will be joyous in Him."

11. In whom? "In Him that reigneth in His virtue for everlasting" (ver. 7). For what virtue have we? and is it everlasting? If everlasting were our virtue, we should not have slipped, should not have fallen into sin, we should not have deserved penal mortality. He, of His good pleasure, took up that whereunto our desert threw us down. "That reigneth in His virtue for everlasting." Of Him partakers let us be made, in whose virtue we shall be strong, but He in His own. We enlightened, He a light enlightening: we, being turned away from Him, are in darkness; turned away from Himself He cannot be. With the heat of Him we are warmed; from whence withdrawing we had grown cold, to the Same drawing near again we are warmed. Therefore let us speak to Him that He may keep us in His virtue, because "in Him we will be joyous that reigneth in His virtue for everlasting."

12. But this thing is not granted to believing Jews alone. ... "The eyes of Him do look upon the Gentiles." And what do we? The Jews will murmur; the Jews will say, "what He hath given to us, the same to them also; to us Gospel, to them Gospel; to us the Grace of Resurrection, and to them the Grace of Resurrection; doth it profit us nothing that we have received the Law, and that in the justifications of the Law we have lived, and have kept the commandments of the fathers? Nothing will it avail? The same to them as to us." Let them not strive, let them not dispute. "Let not them that are bitter be exalted in their own selves." O flesh miserable and wasting, art thou not sinful? Why crieth out thy tongue? Let the conscience be listened to. "For all men have sinned, and need the glory of God." Know thyself, human weakness. Thou didst receive the Law, in order that a transgressor also of the Law thou mightest be: for thou hast not kept and fulfilled that which thou didst receive. There hath come to thee because of the Law, not the justification which the Law enjoineth, but the transgression which thou hast done. If therefore there hath abounded sin, why enviest thou Grace more abounding. Be not bitter, for "let not them that are bitter be exalted in their own selves." He seemeth in a manner to have uttered a curse in "Let not them that are bitter be exalted;" yea, be they exalted, but not "in themselves." Let them be humbled in themselves, exalted in Christ. For, "he that humbleth himself shall be exalted; and he that exalteth himself shall be humbled." "Let not them that are bitter be exalted in their own selves."

13. "Bless our God, ye nations" (ver. 8). Behold, there have been driven back they that are bitter, reckoning hath been made with them: some have been converted, some have continued proud. Let not them terrify you that grudge the Gentiles Gospel Grace: now hath come the Seed of Abraham, in whom are blessed all nations. Bless ye Him in, whom ye are blessed, "Bless our God, ye nations: and

hear ye the voice of His praise." Praise not yourselves, but praise Him. What is the voice of His praise? That by His Grace we are whatever of good we are. "Who hath set my Soul unto life" (ver. 9) Behold the voice of his praise: "Who hath set my Soul unto life." Therefore in death she was: in death she was, in thyself. Thence it is that ye ought not to have been exalted in yourselves. Therefore in death she was, in thyself: where will it be in life, save in Him that said, "I am the Way, the Truth, and the Life "? Just as to certain believers the Apostle saith, "Ye were sometime darkness, but now light in the Lord." ... "And hath not given unto motion my feet." He hath set my Soul unto life, He guideth the feet that they stumble not, be not moved and given unto motion; He maketh us to live, He maketh us to persevere even unto the end, in order that for everlasting we may live. ...

14. "For thou hast proved us, O God; Thou hast fired us as silver is fired" (ver. 10). Hast not fired us like hay, but like silver: by applying to us fire, Thou hast not turned us into ashes, but Thou hast washed off uncleanness, "Thou hast fired us, as silver is fired." And see in what manner God is wroth against them, whose Soul He hath set unto life. "Thou hast led us into a trap:" not that we might be caught and die, but that we might be tried and delivered from it. "Thou hast laid tribulations upon our back." For having been to ill purpose lifted up, proud we were: having been to ill purpose lifted up, we were bowed down, in order that being bowed down, we should be lifted up for good. "Thou hast laid tribulations on our back:" "Thou hast set men over our heads" (ver. 11). All these things the Church hath suffered in sundry and divers persecutions: She hath suffered this in Her individual members, even now doth suffer it. For there is not one, that in this life could say that he was exempt from these trials. Therefore there are set even men over our heads: we endure those whom we would not, we suffer for our betters those whom we know to be worse. But if sins be wanting, a man is justly superior: but by how much there are more sins, by so much he is inferior. And it is a good thing to consider ourselves to be sinners, and thus endure men set over our heads: in order that we also to God may confess that deservedly we suffer. For why dost thou suffer with indignation that which He doeth who is just? "Thou hast laid tribulations upon our back: Thou hast set men over our heads." God seemeth to be wroth, when He doeth these things: fear not, for a Father He is, He is never so wroth as to destroy. When ill thou livest, if He spareth, He is more angry. In a word, these tribulations are the rods of Him correcting, lest there be a sentence from Him punishing. ...

15. "We have passed through fire and water." Fire and water are both dangerous in this life. Certainly water seemeth to extinguish fire, and fire seemeth to dry up

water. Thus also these are the trials, wherein aboundeth this life. Fire burneth, water corrupteth: both must be feared, both the burning of tribulation and the water of corruption. Whenever there is adversity, and anything which is called unhappiness in this world, there is as it were fire: whenever there is prosperity, and the world's plenty floweth about one, there is as it were water. See that fire burn thee not, nor water corrupt. ... Hasten not to the water: through fire pass over to the water, that thou mayest pass over the water also. Therefore also in the mystic rites and in catechising and in exorcising, there is first used fire. For whence ofttimes do the unclean spirits cry out, "I burn," if that is not fire? But after the fire of Exorcism we come to Baptism: so that from fire to water, from water unto refreshment. But as in the Sacraments, so it is in the temptations of this world: the straitness of fear draweth near first, in place of fire; afterwards fear being removed, we ought to be afraid lest worldly happiness corrupt. But when the fire hath not made thee burst, and when thou hast not sunk in the water, but hast swum out; through discipline thou passest over to rest, and passing over through fire and water, thou art led forth into a place of refreshment. For of those things whereof the signs are in the Sacraments, there are the very realities in that perfection of life everlasting. ... But we are not torpid there, but we rest: nor though it be called heat, shall we be hot there, but we shall be fervent in spirit. Observe that same heat in another Psalm: "nor is there any one that hideth himself from the heat thereof." What saith also the Apostle? "In spirit fervent." Therefore, "we have gone over through fire and water: and Thou hast led us forth into a cool place."

16. Observe how not only concerning a cool place, but neither of that very fire to be desired he hath been silent: "I will enter into Thy House in holocausts" (ver. 13). What is a holocaust? A whole sacrifice burned up, but with fire divine. For a sacrifice is called a holocaust, when the whole is burned. One thing are the parts of sacrifices, another thing a holocaust when the whole is burned and the whole consumed by fire divine, it is called a holocaust: when a part, a sacrifice. Every holocaust indeed is a sacrifice: but not every sacrifice a holocaust. Holocausts therefore he is promising, the Body of Christ is speaking, the Unity of Christ is speaking, "I will enter into Thy House in holocausts." All that is mine let Thy fire consume, let nothing of mine remain to me, let all be Thine. But this shall be in the Resurrection of just men, "when both this corruptible shall be clad in incorruption, and this mortal shall be clad in immortality: then shall come to pass that which hath been written, 'Death is swallowed up in victory.'" Victory is, as it were, fire divine: when it swalloweth up our death also, it is a holocaust. There remaineth not anything mortal in the flesh, there remaineth not anything culpable in the spirit: the whole of mortal life shall be consumed, in order that in life everlasting it may be consummated, that from death we may be preserved in life. These therefore will be the holocausts. And what shall there be "in the holocausts"?

17. "I will render to Thee my vows, which my lips have distinguished" (ver. 14). What is the distinction in vows? This is the distinction, that thyself thou censure, Him thou praise: perceive thyself to be a creature, Him the Creator: thyself darkness, Him the Enlightener, to whom thou shouldest say, "Thou shall light my lamp, O Lord my God, Thou shalt enlighten my darkness." For whenever thou shalt have said, O soul, that from thyself thou hast light, thou wilt not distinguish. If thou wilt not distinguish, thou wilt not render distinct vows. Render distinct vows, confess thyself changeable, Him unchangeable: confess thyself without Him to be nothing, but Himself without thee to be perfect; thyself to need Him, but Him not to need thee. Cry to Him, "I have said to the Lord, My God art Thou, for my good things Thou needest not." Now though God taketh thee to Him for a holocaust, He groweth not, He is not increased, He is not richer, He becometh not better furnished: whatsoever He maketh of thee for thy sake, is the better for thee, not for Him that maketh. If thou distinguishest these things, thou renderest the vows to thy God which thy lips have distinguished.

18. "And my mouth hath spoken in my tribulation." How sweet ofttimes is tribulation, how necessary! In that case what hath the mouth of the same spoken in his tribulation? "Holocausts marrowed I will offer to Thee" (ver. 15). What is "marrowed"? Within may I keep Thy love, it shall not be on the surface, in my marrow it shall be that I love Thee. For there is nothing more inward than our marrow: the bones are more inward than the flesh, the marrow is more inward than those same bones. Whosoever therefore on the surface loveth God, desireth rather to please men, but having some other affection within, he offereth not holocausts of marrow: but into whosesoever marrow He looketh, him He receiveth whole. "With incense and rams." The rams are the rulers of the Church: the whole Body of Christ is speaking: this is the thing which he offereth to God. Incense is what? Prayer. "With incense and rams." For especially the rams do pray for the flocks. "I will offer to Thee oxen with he-goats." Oxen we find treading out corn, and the same are offered to God. The Apostle hath said, that of the preachers of the Gospel must be understood that which hath been written, "Of the ox treading out corn the mouth thou shalt not muzzle. Doth God care for oxen?" Therefore great are those rams, great the oxen. What of the rest, that perchance are conscious of certain sins, that perchance in the very road have slipped, and, having been wounded, by penitence are being healed? Shall they too continue, and to the holocausts shall they not belong? Let them not fear, he hath added he-goats also. "I will offer to Thee oxen with he-goats." By the very yoking are saved the he-goats; of themselves they have no strength, being yoked to bulls they are accepted. For they have made friends of the mammon of iniquity, that the same may receive them into everlasting tabernacles? Therefore those he-goats shall not be on the left, because they have made to themselves friends of the mammon of iniquity. But

what he-goats shall be on the left? They to whom shall be said, "I hungred, and ye gave me not to eat:" not they that have redeemed their sins by almsdeeds.

19. "Come ye, hear, and I will tell, all ye that fear God" (ver. 16). Let us come, let us hear, what he is going to tell, "Come ye, hear, and I will tell." But to whom," Come ye, and hear"? "All ye that fear God." If God ye fear not, I will not tell. It is not possible that it be told to any where the fear of God is not. Let the fear of God open the ears, that there may be something to enter in, and a way whereby may enter in that which I am going to tell. But what is he going to tell? "How great things He hath done to my soul." Behold, he would tell: but what is he going to tell? Is it perchance how widely the earth is spread, how much the sky is extended, and how many are the stars, and what are the changes of sun and of moon? This creation fulfilleth its course: but they have very curiously sought it out, the Creator thereof have not known. This thing hear, this thing receive, "O ye that fear God, how great things He hath done to my soul:" if ye will, to yours also. "How great things He hath done to my soul." "To Him with my mouth I have cried" (ver. 17). "And this very thing, he saith, hath been done to his soul; that to Him with his mouth he should cry, hath been done, he saith, to his soul. Behold, brethren, Gentiles we were, even if not in ourselves, in our parents. And what saith the Apostle? "Ye know, when Gentiles ye were, to idols without speech how ye went up, being led." Let the Church now say, "how great things He hath done to my soul." "To Him with my mouth I have cried." I a man to a stone was crying, to a deaf stock I was crying, to idols deaf and dumb I was speaking: now the image of God hath been turned to the Creator thereof. I that was "saying to a stock, My father thou art; and to a stone, Thou hast begotten me:" now say, "Our Father, which art in Heaven." ... "To Him with my mouth I have cried, and I have exalted Him under my tongue." See how in secret He would be uncorrupt that offereth marrowed holocausts. This do ye, brethren, this imitate, so that ye may say, "Come ye, see how great things He hath done to my soul." For all those things of which he telleth, by His Grace are done in our soul. See the other things of which he speaketh.

20. "If I have beheld iniquity in my heart, may not the Lord hearken" (ver. 18). Consider now, brethren, how easily, how daily men blushing for fear of men do censure iniquities; He hath done ill, He hath done basely, a villain the fellow is: this perchance for man's sake he saith. See whether thou beholdest no iniquity in thy heart, whether perchance that which thou censurest in another, thou art meditating to do, and therefore against him dost exclaim, not because he hath done it, but because he hath been found out. Return to thyself, within be to thyself a judge. Behold in thy hid chamber, in the very inmost recess of the heart, where

thou and He that seeth are alone, there let iniquity be displeasing to thee, in order that thou mayest be pleasing to God. Do not regard it, that is, do not love it, but rather despise it, that is, contemn it, and turn away from it. Whatever pleasing thing it hath promised to allure thee to sin; whatever grievous thing it hath threatened, to drive thee on to evil doing; all is nought, all passeth away: it is worthy to be despised, in order that it may be trampled upon; not to be eyed lest it be accepted. ...

21. "Therefore God hath hearkened to me" (ver. 19). Because I have not beheld iniquity in my heart. "And He hath listened to the voice of my prayer." "Blessed be my God, that hath not thrust away my supplication and His mercy from me" (ver. 20). Gather the sense from that place, where he saith, "Come ye, hear, and I will tell you, all ye that fear God, how great things He hath done to my soul:" he hath both said the words which ye have heard, and at the end thus he hath concluded: "Blessed be my God, that hath not thrust away my supplication and His mercy from me." For thus there arriveth at the Resurrection he that speaketh, where already we also are by hope: yea both it is we ourselves, and this voice is ours. So long therefore as here we are, this let us ask of God, that He thrust not from us our supplication, and His mercy, that is, that we pray continually, and He continually pity. For many become feeble in praying, and in the newness of their own conversion pray fervently, afterwards feebly, afterwards coldly, afterwards negligently: as if they have become secure. The foe watcheth: thou sleepest. The Lord Himself hath given commandment in the Gospel, how "it behoveth men always to pray and not to faint." And he giveth a comparison from that unjust judge, who neither feared God, nor regarded man, whom that widow daily importuned to hear her; and he yielded for weariness, that was not influenced by pity: and the naughty judge saith to himself, "Though neither God I fear, nor men I regard, even because of the weariness which this widow daily putteth upon me, I will hear her cause, and will avenge her." And the Lord saith, "If a naughty judge hath done this, shall not your Father avenge His chosen, that to Him do cry day and night? Yea, I say unto you, He shall make judgment of them speedily." Therefore let us not hint m prayer. Though He putteth off what He is going to grant, He putteth it not away: being secure of His promise, let us not faint in praying, and this is by His goodness. Therefore he hath said, "Blessed is my God, that hath not thrust away my supplication and His mercy from me." When thou hast seen thy supplication "not thrust away from thee," be secure, that His mercy hath not been thrust away from thee.

PSALM LXVII.

1. Your Love remembereth, that in two Psalms, which have been already treated of, we have stirred up our soul to bless the Lord, and with godly chant have said, "Bless thou, O my soul, the Lord." If therefore we have stirred up our soul in those Psalms to bless the Lord, in this Psalm is well said, "May God have pity on us, and bless us" (ver. 1). Let our soul bless the Lord, and let God bless us. When God blesseth us, we grow, and when we bless the Lord, we grow, to us both are profitable. He is not increased by our blessing, nor is He lessened by our cursing. He that curseth the Lord, is himself lessened: he that blesseth the Lord, is himself increased. First, there is in us the blessing of the Lord, and the consequence is that we also bless the Lord. That is the rain, this the fruit. Therefore there is rendered as it were fruit to God the Husbandman, raining upon and tilling us. Let us chant these words with no barren devotion, with no empty voice, but with true heart. For most evidently God the Father hath been called a Husbandman. The Apostle saith, "God's husbandry ye are, God's building ye are." In things visible of this world, the vine is not a building, and a building is not a vineyard: but we are the vineyard of the Lord, because He tilleth us for fruit; the building of God we are, since He who tilleth us, dwelleth in us. And what saith the same Apostle? "I have planted, Apollos hath watered, but the increase God hath given. Therefore neither he that planteth is anything, nor he that watereth, but He that giveth the increase, even God." He it is therefore that giveth the increase. Are those perchance the husbandmen? For a husbandman he is called that planteth, that watereth: but the Apostle hath said, "I have planted, Apollos hath watered." Do we enquire whence himself hath done this? The Apostle maketh answer, "Yet not I, but the Grace of God with me." Therefore whithersoever thou turn thee, whether through Angels, thou wilt find God thy Husbandman; whether through Prophets, the Same is thy Husbandman; whether through Apostles, the very Same acknowledge to be thy Husbandman. What then of us? Perchance we are the labourers of that Husbandman, and this too with powers imparted by Himself, and by Grace granted by Himself. ...

2. "Lighten His countenance upon us." Thou wast perchance going to enquire, what is "bless us"? In many ways men would have themselves to be blessed of God: one would have himself to be blessed, so that he may have a house full of the necessary things of this life; another desireth himself to be blessed, so that he may obtain soundness of body without flaw; another would have himself to be blessed, if perchance he is sick, so that he may acquire soundness; another longing for sons, and perchance being sorrowful because none are born, would have himself to be blessed so that he may have posterity. And who could number the divers wishes

of men desiring themselves to be blessed of the Lord God? But which of us would say, that it was no blessing of God, if either husbandry should bring him fruit, or if any man's house should abound in plenty of things temporal, or if the very bodily health be either so maintained that it be not lost, or, if lost, be regained? ...

3. "Every soul that is blessed is simple," 7 not cleaving to things earthly nor with glued wings grovelling, but beaming with the brightness of virtues, on the twin wings of twin love doth spring into the free air; and seeth how from her is withdrawn that whereon she was treading, not that whereon she was resting, and she saith securely, "The Lord hath given, the Lord hath taken away; as it hath pleased the Lord, so hath been done: be the name of the Lord blessed." ... But let not perchance any weak man say, when shall I be of so great virtue, as was holy Job? The mightiness of the tree thou wonderest at, because but now thou hast been born: this great tree, whereat thou wonderest, under the branches and shade whereof thou coolest thyself, hath been a switch. But dost thou fear lest there be taken away from thee these things, when such thou shalt have become? Observe that they are taken away from evil men also. Why therefore dost thou delay conversion? That which thou fearest when good to lose, perchance if evil thou wilt lose still. If being good thou shalt have lost them, there is by thee the Comforter that hath taken them away: the coffer is emptied of gold; the heart is full of faith: without, poor thou art, but within, rich thou art: thy riches with thee thou carriest, which thou wouldest not lose, even if naked from shipwreck thou shouldest escape. Why doth not the loss, that perchance, if evil, thou wilt lose, find thee good; forasmuch as thou seest evil men also suffer loss? But with greater loss they are stricken: empty is the house, more empty the conscience is. Whatsoever evil man shall have lost these things, hath nothing to hold by without, hath nothing within whereon he may rest. He fleeth when he hath suffered loss from the place where before the eyes of men with the display of riches he used to vaunt himself; now in the eyes of men to vaunt himself he is not able: to himself within he returneth not, because he hath nothing. He hath not imitated the ant, he hath not gathered to himself grains, while it was summer. What have I meant by, while it was summer? While he had quietude of life, while he had this world's prosperity, when he had leisure, when happy he was being called by all men, his summer it was. He should have imitated the ant, he should have heard the Word of God, he should have gathered. together grains, and he should have stored them within. There had come the trial of tribulation, there had come upon him a winter of numbness, tempest of fear, the cold of sorrow, whether it were loss, or any danger to his safety, or any bereavement of his family; or any dishonour and humiliation; it was winter; the ant falleth back upon that which in summer she hath gathered together; and within in her secret store, where no man seeth, she is recruited by her summer toils. When for herself she was gathering together these stores in summer,

all men saw her: when on these she feedeth in winter, no one seeth. What is this? See the ant of God, he riseth day by day, he hasteneth to the Church of God, he prayeth, he heareth lection, he chanteth hymn, he digesteth that which he hath heard, with himself he thinketh thereon, he storeth within grains gathered from the threshing-floor. They that providently hear those very things which even now are being spoken of, do thus, and by all men are seen to go forth to the Church, go back from Church, to hear sermon, to hear lection, to choose a book, open and read it: all these things are seen, when they are done. That ant is treading his path, carrying and storing up in the sight of men seeing him. There cometh winter sometime, for to whom cometh it not? There chanceth loss, there chanceth bereavement: other men pity him perchance as being miserable, who know not what the ant hath within to eat, and they say, miserable he whom this hath befallen, or what spirits, dost thou think, hath he whom this hath befallen? how afflicted is he? He measureth by himself, hath compassion according to his own strength; and thus he is deceived: because the measure wherewith he measureth himself, he would apply to him whom he knoweth not. ... O sluggard, gather in summer while thou art able; winter will not suffer thee to gather, but to eat that which thou shall have gathered. For how many men so suffer tribulation, that there is no opportunity either to read anything, or to hear anything, and they obtain no admittance, perchance, to those that would comfort them. The ant hath remained in her nest, let her see if she hath gathered anything in summer, whereby she may recruit herself in winter.

4. ... There is a double interpretation, both must be given: "lighten," he saith, "Thy face upon us," show to us Thy countenance. For God doth not ever light His countenance, as if ever it had been without light: but He lighteth it upon us, so that what was hidden from us, is opened to us, and that which was, but to us was hidden, is unveiled upon us, that is, is lightened. Or else surely it is, "Thy image lighten upon us:" so that he said this, in "lighten Thy countenance upon us:" Thou hast imprinted Thy countenance upon us; Thou hast made us after Thine image and Thy likeness, Thou hast made us Thy coin; but Thine image ought not in darkness to remain: send a ray of Thy wisdom, let it dispel our darkness, and let there shine in us Thy image; let us know ourselves to be Thine image, let us hear what hath been said in the Song of Songs, "If Thou shalt not have known Thyself, O Thou fair one among women." For there is said to the Church, "If Thou shalt not have known Thyself." What is this? If Thou shalt not have known Thyself to have been made after the image of God. O Soul of the Church, precious, redeemed with the blood of the Lamb immaculate, observe of how great value Thou art, think what hath been given for Thee. Let us say, therefore, and let us long that He "may lighten His face upon us." We wear His face: in like manner as, the faces of emperors are spoken of, truly a kind of sacred face is that of God in His own

image: but unrighteous men know not in themselves the image of, God. In order that the countenance of God may be lightened upon them, they ought to say what? "Thou shalt light my candle, O Lord my God, Thou shalt light my darkness." I am in the darkness of sins, but by the ray of Thy wisdom dispelled be my darkness, may Thy countenance appear; and if perchance through me it appeareth somewhat deformed, by Thee be there reformed that which by Thee hath been formed.

5. "That we may know on earth Thy way" (ver. 2). "On earth," here, in this life, "we may know Thy way." What is, "Thy way"? That which leadeth to Thee. May we acknowledge whither we are going, acknowledge where we are as we go; neither in darkness we can do. Afar Thou art from men sojourning, a way to us Thou hast presented, through which we must return to Thee. "Let us acknowledge on earth Thy way." What is His way wherein we have desired, "That we may know on earth Thy way"? We are going to enquire this ourselves, not of ourselves to learn it. We can learn of it from the Gospel: "I am the Way," the Lord saith: Christ hath said, "I am the Way." But dost thou fear lest thou stray? He hath added, "And the Truth." Who strayeth in the Truth? He strayeth that hath departed from the Truth. The Truth is Christ, the Way is Christ: walk therein. Dost thou fear lest thou die before thou attain unto Him? "I am the Life: I am," He saith, "the Way and the Truth and the Life." As if He were saying, "What fearest thou? Through Me thou walkest, to Me thou walkest, in Me thou restest." What therefore meaneth, "We may know on earth Thy Way," but "we may know on earth Thy Christ"? But let the Psalm itself reply: lest ye think that out of other Scriptures there must be adduced testimony, which perchance is here wanting: by repetition he hath shown what signified, "That we may know on earth Thy Way:" and as if thou wast inquiring, "In what earth, what way?" "In all nations Thy Salvation." In what earth, thou art inquiring? Hear: "In all nations." What way art thou seeking? Hear: "Thy Salvation.' Is not perchance Christ his Salvation? And what is that which the old Symeon hath said, that old man, I say, in the Gospel, preserved full of years even unto the infancy of the Word? For that old man took in his hands the Infant Word of God. Would He that in the womb deigned to be, disdain to be in the hands of an old man? The Same was in the womb of the virgin, as was in the hands of the old man, a weak infant both within the bowels, and in the old man's hand, to give us strength, by whom were made all things; and if all things, even His very mother. He came humble, He came weak, but clothed with a weakness to be changed into strength, because "though He was crucified of weakness, yet He liveth of the virtue of God," the Apostle saith. He was then in the hands of an old man. And what saith that old man? Rejoicing that now he must be loosed from this world, seeing how in his own hand was held He by whom and in whom his Salvation was upheld; he saith what? "Now Thou lettest go," he saith," O Lord, Thy servant in peace, for mine eyes have seen Thy Salvation." Therefore, "May

God bless us, and have pity on us; may He lighten His countenance upon us, that we may know on earth Thy Way!" In what earth? "In all nations?" What Way? "Thy Salvation."

6. What followeth because the Salutation of God is known in all nations? "Let the peoples confess to Thee, O God" (ver. 3); "confess to Thee," he saith, "all peoples." There standeth forth a heretic, and he saith, In Africa I have peoples: and another from another quarter, And I in Galatia have peoples. Thou in Africa, he in Galatia: therefore I require one that hath them everywhere. Ye have indeed dared to exult at that voice, when ye heard, "Let the peoples confess to Thee, O God." Hear the following verse, how he speaketh not of a part: "Let there confess to Thee all peoples." Walk ye in the Way together with all nations; walk ye in the Way together with all peoples, O sons of peace, sons of the One Catholic Church, walk ye in the Way, seeing as ye walk. Wayfarers do this to beguile their toil. Sing ye in this Way; I implore you by that Same Way, sing ye in this Way: a new song sing ye, let no one there sing old ones: sing ye the love-songs of your fatherland, let no one sing old ones. New Way, new wayfarer, new song. Hear thou the Apostle exhorting thee to a new song: "Whatever therefore is in Christ is a new creature; old things have passed away, behold they have been made new." A new song sing ye in the way, which ye have learned "on the earth." In what earth? "In all nations." Therefore even the new song doth not belong to a part. He that in a part singeth, singeth an old song: whatever he please to sing, he singeth an old song, the old man singeth: divided he is, carnal he is. Truly in so far as carnal he is, so far he is old; and in so far as he is spiritual, so far new. See what saith the Apostle: "I could not speak to you as if to spiritual, but as if to carnal." Whence proverb he them carnal? "For while one saith, I am of Paul; but another, I of Apollos: are ye not," he saith, "carnal?" Therefore in the Spirit a new song sing thou in the safe way. Just as wayfarers sing, and ofttimes in the night sing. Awful round about all things do sound, or rather they sound not around, but are still around; and the more still the more awful; nevertheless, even they that fear robbers do sing. How much more safely thou singest in Christ! That way hath no robber, unless thou by forsaking the way fallest in the hands of a robber. ... Why fear ye to confess, and in your confession to sing a new song together with all the earth; in all the earth, in Catholic peace, dost thou fear to confess to God, lest He condemn thee that hast confessed? If having not confessed thou liest concealed, having confessed thou wilt be condemned. Thou fearest to confess, that by not confessing canst not be concealed: thou wilt be condemned if thou hast held thy peace, that mightest have been delivered, by having confessed. "O God, confess to Thee all peoples."

7. And because this confession leadeth not to punishment, he continueth and saith, "Let the nations rejoice and exult" (ver. 4). If robbers after confession made do wail before man, let the faithful after confessing before God rejoice. If a than be judge, the torturer and his fear exact from a robber a confession: yea sometimes fear wringeth out confession, pain extorteth it: and he that waileth in tortures, but feareth to be killed if he confess, supporteth tortures as far as he is able: and if he shall have been overcome by pain, he giveth his voice for death. Nowise therefore is he joyful; nowise exulting: before he confesseth the claw teareth him; when he hath confessed, the executioner leadeth him along a condemned felon: wretched in every case. But" let the nations rejoice and exult." Whence? Through that same confession. Why? Because good He is to whom they confess: He exacteth confession, to the end that He may deliver the humble; He condemneth one not confessing, to the end that He may punish the proud. Therefore be thou sorrowful before thou confessest; after having confessed exult, now thou wilt be made whole. Thy conscience had gathered up evil humours, with boil it had swollen, it was torturing thee, it suffered thee not to rest: the Physician applieth the fomentations of words? and sometimes He lanceth it, He applieth the surgeon's knife by the chastisement of tribulation: do thou acknowledge the Physician's hand, confess thou, let every evil humour go forth and flow away in confession: now exult, now rejoice, that which remaineth will be easy to be made whole. ... "Let the nations rejoice and exult, for Thou judgest the peoples in equity." And that unrighteous men may not fear, he hath added, "and the nations on the earth Thou directest." Depraved were the nations and crooked were the nations, perverse were the nations; for the ill desert of their depravity, and crookedness and perverseness, the Judge's coming they feared: there cometh the hand of the same, it is stretched out mercifully to the peoples, they are guided in order that they may walk the straight way; why should they fear the Judge to come, that have first acknowledged Him for a Corrector? To His hand let them give up themselves, Himself guideth the nations on the earth. But guided nations are walking in the Truth, are exulting in Him, are doing good works; and if perchance there cometh in any water (for on sea they are sailing) through the very small holes, through the crevices into the hold, pumping it out by good works, lest by more and more coming it accumulate, and sink the ship, pumping it out daily, fasting, praying, doing almsdeeds, saying with pure heart, "Forgive us our debts, as also we forgive our debtors"—saying such words walk thou secure, and exult in the way, sing in the way. Do not fear the Judge: before thou wast a believer, thou didst find a Saviour. Thee ungodly He sought out that He might redeem, thee redeemed will He forsake so as to destroy? "And the nations on earth Thou directest."

8. He exulteth, rejoiceth, exhorteth, he repeateth those same verses in exhortation. "The earth hath given her fruit" (ver. 6). What fruit? "Let all peoples confess to

Thee." Earth it was, of thorns it was full; there came the hand of One rooting them up, there came a calling by His majesty and mercy, the earth began to confess; now the earth giveth her fruit. Would she give her fruit unless first she were rained on? Would she give her fruit, unless first the mercy of God had come from above? Let them read to me, thou sayest, how the earth being rained upon gave her fruit. Hear of the Lord raining upon her: "Repent, for the kingdom of heaven is at hand." He raineth, and that same rain is thunder; it terrifieth: fear thou Him thundering, and receive Him raining. Behold, after that voice of a thundering and raining God, after that voice let us see something out of the Gospel itself. Behold that harlot of ill fame in the city burst into a strange house into which she had not been invited by the host, but by One invited she had been called; called not with tongue, but by Grace. The sick woman knew that she had there a place, where she was aware that her Physician was sitting at meat. She has gone in, that was a sinner; she dareth not draw near save to the feet: she weepeth at His feet, she washeth with tears, she wipeth with hair, she anointeth with ointment. Why wonderest thou? The earth hath given her fruit. This thing, I say, came to pass by the Lord raining there through His own mouth; there came to pass the things whereof we read in the Gospel; and by His raining through His clouds, by the sending of the Apostles and by their preaching the truth, the earth more abundantly hath given her fruit, and that crop now hath filled the round world.

9. The fruit of the earth was first in Jerusalem. For from thence began the Church: there came there the Holy Spirit, and filled full the holy men gathered together in one place; miracles were done, with the tongues of all men they spake. They were filled full of the Spirit of God, the people were converted that were in that place, fearing and receiving the divine shower, by confession they brought forth so much fruit, that all their goods they brought together into a common stock, making distribution to the poor, in order that no one might call anything his own, but all things might be to them in common, and they might have one soul and one heart unto God. For there had been forgiven them the blood which they had shed, it had been forgiven them by the Lord pardoning, in order that now they might even learn to drink that which they had shed. Great in that place is the fruit: the earth hath given her fruit, both great fruit, and most excellent fruit. Ought by any means that earth alone to give her fruit? "May there bless us God, our God, may there bless us God" (ver. 7). Still may He bless us: for blessing in multiplication is wont most chiefly and properly to be perceived. Let us prove this in Genesis; see the works of God: God made light, and God made a division between light and darkness: the light He called day, and the darkness He called night. It is not said, He blessed the light. For the same light returneth and changeth by days and nights. He calleth the sky the firmament between waters and waters: it is not said, He blessed the sky: He severed the sea from the dry land, and named both, the dry

land earth, and the gathering together of the waters sea: neither here is it said, God blessed. ...

10. How should we will that to us He come? By living well, by doing well. Let not things past please us; things present not hold us; let us not "close the ear" as it were with tail, let us not press down the ear on the ground; lest by things past we be kept back from hearing, lest by things present we be entangled and prevented from meditating on things future; let us reach forth unto those things which are before, let us forget things past. And that for which now we toil, for which now we groan, for which now we sigh, of which now we speak, which in part, however small soever, we perceive, and to receive are not able, we shall receive, we shall thoroughly enjoy in the resurrection of the just. Our youth shall be renewed as an eagle's, if only our old man we break against the Rock of Christ. Whether those things be true, brethren, which are said of the serpent, or those which are said of the eagle, or whether it be rather a tale of men than truth, truth is nevertheless in the Scriptures, and not without reason the Scriptures have spoken of this: let us do whatever it signifieth, and not toil to discover how far that is true. Be thou such an one, as that thy youth may be able to be renewed as an eagle's. And know thou that it cannot lie renewed, except thine old man on the Rock shall have been broken off: that is, except by the aid of the Rock, except by the aid of Christ, thou wilt not be able to be renewed. Do not thou because of the pleasantness of the past life be deaf to the word of God: do not by things present be so held and entangled, as to say, I have no leisure to read, I have no leisure to hear. This is to press down the ear upon the ground. Do thou therefore not be such an one: but be such an one as on the other side thou findest, that is, so that thou forget things past, unto things before reach thyself out, in order that thine old man on the Rock thou mayest break off. And if any comparisons shall have been made for thee, if thou hast found them in the Scriptures, believe: if thou shalt not have found them spoken of except by report, do not very much believe them. The thing itself perchance is so, perchance is not so. Do thou profit by it, let that comparison avail for thy salvation. Thou art unwilling to profit by this comparison, by some other profit, it mattereth not provided thou do it: and, being secure, wait for the Kingdom of God, lest thy prayer quarrel with thee. For, O Christian man, when thou sayest, Thy Kingdom come, how sayest thou, "Thy kingdom come"? Examine thy heart: see, behold, "Thy kingdom come:" He crieth out to thee, "I come:" dost thou not fear? Often we have told Your Love: both to preach the truth is nothing, if heart from tongue dissent: and to hear the truth is nothing, if fruit follow not hearing. From this place exalted as it were we are speaking to you: but how much we are beneath your feet in fear, God knoweth, who is gracious to the humble; for the voices of men praising do not give us so much pleasure as the devotion of men confessing, and the deeds of men now righteous. And how we have no pleasure but in your

advances, but by those praises how much we are endangered, He knoweth, whom we pray to deliver us from all dangers, and to deign to know and crown us together with you, saved from every trial, in His Kingdom.

PSALM LXVIII.

1. Of this Psalm, the title seemeth not to need operose discussion: for simple and easy it appeareth. For thus it standeth: "For the end, for David himself a Psalm of a Song." But in many Psalms already we have reminded you what is "at the end: for the end of the Law is Christ for righteousness to every man believing:" He is the end which maketh perfect, not that which consumeth or destroyeth. Nevertheless, if any one endeavoureth to inquire, what meaneth, "a Psalm of a Song:" why not either "Psalm" or "Song," but both; or what is the difference between Psalm of Song, and Song of Psalm, because even thus of some Psalms the titles are inscribed: he will find perchance something which we leave for men more acute and more at leisure than ourselves. ...

2. "Let God rise up, and let His enemies be scattered" (ver. 1). Already this hath come to pass, Christ hath risen up, "who is over all things, God blessed for ever," and His enemies have been dispersed through all nations, to wit, the Jews; in that very place, where they practised their enmities, being overthrown in war, and thence through all places dispersed: and now they hate, but fear, and in that very fear they do that which followeth, "And let them that hate Him flee from His face." The flight indeed of the mind is fear. For in carnal flight, whither flee they from the face of Him who everywhere showeth the efficacy of His presence? "Whither shall I depart," saith he, "from Thy Spirit, and from Thy face whither shall I flee?" With mind, therefore, not with body, they flee; to wit, by being afraid, not by being hidden; and not from that face which they see not, but from that which they are compelled to see. For the face of Him hath His presence in His Church been called. ...

3. "As smoke faileth, let them fail" (ver. 2). For they lifted up themselves from the fires of their hatred unto the vapouring of pride, and against Heaven setting their mouth, and shouting," Crucify, Crucify," Him taken captive they derided, Him hanging they mocked: and being soon conquered by that very Person against whom they swelled victorious, they vanished away. "As wax melteth from the face of fire, so let sinners perish from the face of God." Though perchance in this passage he hath referred to those men, whose hard-heartedness in tears of penitence is dissolved: yet this also may be understood, that he threateneth future judgment; because though in this world like smoke, in lifting up themselves, that is, in priding themselves, they have melted away, there will come to them at the last final damnation, so that from His face they will perish for everlasting, when in His own glory He shall have appeared, like fire, for the punishment of the ungodly, and the light of the righteous.

4. "Lastly, there followeth, "And let just men be joyous, and exult in the sight of God, let them delight in gladness" (ver. 3). For then shall they hear," Come, ye blessed of My Father, receive ye the kingdom." "Let them be joyous," therefore, that have toiled, "and exult in the sight of God." For there will not be in this exultation, as though it were before men, any empty boasting; but (it will be) in the sight of Him who unerringly looketh into that which He hath granted. "Let them delight in gladness:" no longer exulting with trembling as in this world, so long as "human life is a trial upon earth." Secondly, he turneth himself to those very persons to whom he hath given so great hope, and to them while here living he speaketh and exhorteth: "Sing ye to God, psalm ye to His name" (ver. 4). Already on this subject in the exposition of the Title we have before spoken that which seemed meet. He singeth to God, that liveth to God: He psalmeth to His name, that worketh unto His Glory. In singing thus, in psalming thus, that is, by so living, by so working, "a way make ye to Him," he saith, "that hath ascended above the setting." A way make ye to Christ: so that through the beautiful feet of men telling good tidings, the hearts of men believing many have a way opened to Him. For the Same is He that hath ascended above the "setting:" either because the new life of one turned to Him receiveth Him not, except the old life shall have set by his renouncing this world, or because He ascended above the setting, when by rising again He conquered the downfall of the body. "For The Lord is His name." Which if they had known, the Lord of glory they never would have crucified.

5. "Exult ye in the sight of Him," O ye to whom hath been said, "Sing ye to God, psalm ye to the name of Him, a way make ye to Him that hath ascended above the setting," also "exult in the sight of Him:" as if "sorrowful, yet alway rejoicing." For while ye make a way to Him, while ye prepare a way whereby He may come and possess the nations, ye are to suffer in the sight of men many sorrowful things. But not only faint not, but even exult, not in the sight of men, but in the sight of God. "In hope rejoicing, in tribulation enduring:" "exult ye in the sight of Him." For they that in the sight of men trouble you, "shall be troubled by the face of Him, the Father of orphans and Judge of widows" (ver. 5). For desolate they suppose them to be, from whom ofttimes by the sword of the Word of God both parents from sons, and husbands from wives, are severed: but persons destitute and widowed have the consolation "of the Father of orphans and Judge of widows:" they have the consolation of Him that say to Him," For my father and my mother have forsaken me, but the Lord hath taken up me:" and they that have hoped in the Lord, continuing in prayers by night and by day: by whose face those men shall be troubled when they shall have seen themselves prevail nothing, for that the whole world hath gone away after Him. For out of those orphans and widows, that is, persons destitute of partnership in this world's hope, the Lord for

Himself doth build a Temple: whereof in continuation he saith, "The Lord is in His holy place."

6. For what is His place he hath disclosed, when he saith, "God that maketh to dwell men of one mood in a house" (ver. 6): men of one mind, of one sentiment: this is the holy place of the Lord. For when he had said, "The Lord is in His holy place:" as though we were inquiring in what place, since He is everywhere wholly, and no place of corporal space containeth Him; forthwith he hath subjoined somewhat, that we should not seek Him apart from ourselves, but rather being of one mood dwelling in a house, we should deserve that He also Himself deign to dwell among us. This is the holy place of the Lord, the thing that most men seek to have, a place where in prayer they may be hearkened unto. ... For as in a great house of a man, the Lord thereof doth not abide in every place whatsoever, but in some place doubtless more private and honourable: so God dwelleth not in all men that are in His house (for He dwelleth not in the vessels of dishonour), but His holy place are they whom "He maketh to dwell of one mood," or "of one manner, in a house." For what are called tro'poi in Greek, by both modi and mores (moods and manners), in Latin may be interpreted. Nor hath the Greek writer, "Who maketh to dwell," but only "maketh to dwell." "The Lord," then, "is in His holy place." ...

7. But to prove that by His Grace He buildeth to Himself this place, not for the sake of the merits preceding of those persons out of whom He buildeth it, see what followeth: "Who leadeth forth men fettered, in strength." For He looseth the heavy bonds of sins, wherewith they were fettered so that they could not walk in the way of the commandments: but He leadeth them forth "in strength," which before His Grace they had not. "Likewise men provoking that dwell in the tombs:" that is, every way dead, taken up with dead works. For these men provoke Him to anger by withstanding justice: for those fettered men perchance would walk, and are not able, and are praying of God that they may be able, and are saying to Him, "From my necessities lead me forth." By whom being heard, they give thanks, saying, "Thou hast broken asunder my bonds." But these provoking men that dwell in the tombs, are of that kind, which in another passage the Scripture pointeth out, saying, "From a dead man, as from one that is not, confession perisheth." Whence there is this saying, "When a sinner shall have come into the depth of evil things, he despiseth." For it is one thing to long for, another thing to fight against righteousness: one thing from evil to desire to be delivered, another thing one's evil doings to defend rather than to confess: both kinds nevertheless the Grace of Christ leadeth forth in strength. With what strength, but that wherewith against sin even unto blood they are to strive? For out of each kind are made meet persons,

whereof to construct His holy place; those being loosened, these being raised to life. For even of the woman, whom Satan had bound for eighteen years, by His command He loosed the bonds; and Lazarus' death by His voice He overcame. He that hath done these things in bodies, is able to do more marvellous things in characters, and to make men of one mood to dwell in a house: "leading forth men fettered in strength, likewise men provoking that dwell in the tombs."

8. "O God, when Thou wentest forth before Thy people" (ver. 7). His going forth is perceived, when He appeareth in His works. But He appeareth not to all men, but to them that know how to spy out His works. For I do not now speak of those works which are conspicuous to all men, Heaven and earth and sea and all things that in them are; but the works whereby He leadeth forth men fettered in strength, likewise men provoking that dwell in the tombs, and maketh them of one manner to dwell in a house. Thus He goeth forth before His people, that is, before those that do perceive this His Grace. Lastly, there followeth, "When Thou wentest by in the desert, the earth was moved" (ver. 8). A desert were the nations, which knew not God: a desert they were, where by God Himself no law had been given, where no Prophet had dwelled, and foretold the Lord to come. "When," then, "Thou wentest by in the desert," when Thou wast preached in the nations; "the earth was moved," to the faith earthly men were stirred up. But whence was it moved? "For the heavens dropped from the face of God." Perchance here some one calleth to mind that time, when in the desert God was going over before His people, before the sons of Israel, by day in the pillar of cloud, by night in the brightness of fire; and determineth that thus it is that "the heavens dropped from the face of God," for manna He rained upon His people: that the same thing also is that which followeth, "Mount Sina from the face of the God of Israel," "with voluntary rain severing God to Thine inheritance" (ver. 9), namely, the God that on Mount Sina spake to Moses, when He gave the Law; so that the manna is the voluntary rain, which God severed for His inheritance, that is, for His people; because them alone He so fed, not the other nations also: so that what next he saith, "and it was weakened," is understood of the inheritance being itself weakened; for they murmuring, fastidiously loathed the manna, longing for victuals of flesh, and those things on which they had been accustomed to live in Egypt. ... Lastly, all those men in the desert were stricken down, nor were any of them except two found worthy to go into the land of promise. Although even if in the sons of them that inheritance be said to have been perfected, we ought more readily to hold to a spiritual sense. For all those things in a figure did happen to them; until the day should break, and the shadows should be removed.

9. May then the Lord open to us that knock; and may the secret things of His mysteries, as far as Himself vouchsafeth, be disclosed. For in order that the earth might be moved to the Truth when into the desert of the Gentiles the Gospel was passing, "the Heavens dropped from the face of God." These are the Heavens, whereof in another Psalm is sung, "The Heavens are telling forth the glory of God." ... So here also, "the Heavens dropped;" but "from the face of God." For even these very persons have been "saved through faith, and this not of themselves, but God's gift it is, not of works, lest perchance any man should be lifted up. For of Himself we are the workmanship," "that maketh men of one mood to dwell in a house."

10. But what is that which followeth," Mount Sina from the face of the God of Israel"? Must there be understood "dropped;" so that what he hath called by the name of Heavens, the same he hath willed to be understood under the name of Mount Sina also; just as we said that those are called. mountains, which were called Heavens? Nor in this sense ought it to move us that He saith "mountain," not mountains, while in that place they were called "Heavens," not Heaven: for in another Psalm also after it had been said, "The Heavens are telling forth the glory of God: " after the manner of Scripture repeating the same sense in different words, subsequently there is said, "And the firmament telleth the works of His hands." First he said "Heavens," not "Heaven:" and yet afterwards not "firmaments," but "firmament." For God called the firmament Heaven, as in Genesis hath been written. Thus then Heavens and Heaven, mountains and mountain, are not a different thing, but the very same thing: just as Churches many, and the One Church, are not a different thing, but the very same thing. Why then "Mount Sina, which gendereth unto bondage "? as saith the Apostle. Is perchance the Law itself to be understood in Mount Sina, as that which "the Heavens dropped from the face of God," in order that the earth might be moved? And is this the very moving of the earth, when men are troubled, because the Law they cannot fulfil? But if so it is, this is the voluntary rain, whereof in confirmation he saith, "Voluntary rain God severing to Thine inheritance:" because "He hath not done so to any nation, and His judgment He hath not manifested to them." God therefore set apart this voluntary rain to His inheritance because He gave the Law. And "there was made weak," either the Law, or the inheritance. The Law may be understood to have been made weak, because it was not fulfilled; not that of itself it is weak, but because it maketh men weak, by threatening punishment, and not aiding through grace. For also the very word the Apostle hath used, where he saith, "For that which was impossible of the Law, wherein it was made weak through the flesh:" willing to intimate that through the Spirit it is fulfilled: nevertheless, itself he hath said is made weak, because by weak men it cannot be fulfilled. But the inheritance, that is, the people, without any doubt is understood to have been made

weak by the giving to them of the Law. For "the Law came in, that transgression might abound." But that which followeth, "But Thou hast made it perfect," to the Law is thus referred, forasmuch as it is made perfect, that is, is fulfilled after that which the Lord saith in the Gospel, "I have not come to annul the Law, but to fulfil." ... There is in these words yet another sense: which seemeth to me more to approve itself. For much more in accordance with the context, grace itself is understood to be the voluntary rain, because with no preceding merits of works it is given gratis. "For if grace, no longer of works: otherwise grace no longer is grace." ... "But to humble men He giveth grace." And it was made weak, but Thou hast made it perfect:" because "virtue in weakness is perfected." Some copies indeed, both Latin and Greek, have not "Mount Sina;" but, "from the face of the God of Sina, from the face of the God of Israel." That is, "The Heavens dropped from the face of God:" and, as if enquiry were made of what God, "from the face of the God," he saith, "of Sina, from the face of the God of Israel," that is, from the face of the God that gave the Law to the people of Israel. Why then "the Heavens dropped from the face of God," from the face of this God, but because thus was fulfilled that which had been foretold, "Blessing He shall give that hath given the Law"? The Law whereby to terrify a man that relieth on human powers; blessing, whereby He delivereth a man that hopeth in God. Thou then, O God, hast made perfect Thine inheritance; because it is made weak in itself, in order that it may be made perfect by Thee.

11. "Thine animals shall dwell therein" (ver. 10). "Thine," not their own; to Thee subject, not for themselves free; for Thee needy, not for themselves sufficient. Lastly, he continueth, "Thou hast prepared in Thine own sweetness for the needy, O God." "In Thine own sweetness," not in his meetness. For the needy he is, for he hath been made weak, in order that he may be made perfect: he hath acknowledged himself indigent, that he may be replenished. This is that sweetness, whereof in another place is said, "The Lord shall give sweetness, and our land shall give her fruit:" in order that a good work may be done not for fear, but for love; not for dread of punishment, but for love of righteousness. For this is true and sound freedom. But the Lord hath prepared this for one wanting, not for one abounding, whose reproach is that poverty: of which sort in another place is said, "Reproach to these men that abound, and contempt to proud men." For those he hath called proud, whom he hath called them that abound.

12. "The Lord shall give the Word" (ver. 11): to wit, food for His animals which shall dwell therein. But what shall these animals work to whom He shall give the word? What but that which followeth? "To them preaching the Gospel in much virtue." With what virtue, but with that strength wherein He leadeth forth men

fettered? Perchance also here he speaketh of that virtue, wherewith in preaching the Gospel they wrought wondrous signs. Who then "shall give the Word to men preaching the Gospel with much virtue"? "The King," he saith, "of the virtues of the Beloved" (ver. 12). The Father therefore is King of the virtues of the Son. For the Beloved, when there is not specified any person that is beloved, by a substitution of name, of the Only Son is understood. Is not the Son Himself King of His virtues, to wit of the virtues serving Himself? Because with much virtue the King of Virtues shall give the Word to men preaching the Gospel, of Whom it hath been said, "The Lord of Virtues, He is the King of Glory? But his not having said King of Virtues, but "King of the Virtues of the beloved," is a most usual expression in the Scriptures, if any one observe: which thing chiefly appeareth in those cases where even the person's own name is already expressed, so that it cannot at all be doubted that it is the same person of whom something is said. Of which sort also is that which in the Pentateuch in many passages is found: "And Moses did it, as the Lord commanded Moses." He said not that which is usual in our expressions, And Moses did, as the Lord commanded him; but, "Moses did as the Lord commanded Moses," as if one person were the Moses whom He commanded, and another person the Moses who did, whereas it is the very same. In the New Testament such expressions are most difficult to find. ... "The King," therefore, "of the virtues of the Beloved," thus may be understood, as if it were to be said, the King of His virtues, because both King of Virtues is Christ, and the Beloved is the very same Christ. However, this sense hath not so great urgency, as that no other can be accepted: because the Father also may be understood as King of the virtues of His Beloved Son, to whom the Beloved Himself saith, "All Mine are Thine, and Thine Mine." But if perchance it is asked, whether God the Father of the Lord Jesus Christ can be called King also, I know not whether any one would dare to withhold this name from Him in the passage where the Apostle saith, "But to the King of ages, immortal, invisible, the only God." Because even if this be said of the Trinity itself, therein is also God the Father. But if we do not carnally understand, "O God, Thy Judgment to the King give Thou, and Thy justice to the Son of the King:" I know not whether anything else hath been said than, "to Thy Son." King therefore is the Father also. Whence that verse of this Psalm, "King of the virtues of the Beloved;" in either way may be understood. When therefore he had said, "The Lord shall give the Word to men preaching the Gospel with much virtue:" because virtue itself by Him is ruled, and serveth Him by whom it is given; the Lord Himself, he saith, who shall give the Word to men preaching the Gospel with much virtue, is the King of the virtues of the Beloved.

13. In the next place there followeth, "Of the Beloved, and of the beauty of the House to divide the spoils." The repetition belongeth to eulogy. ... But whether it be repeated, or whether it be received as spoken once, the word which hath been

set down, namely, "Beloved," I suppose that thus must be understood that which followeth, "and of the beauty of a house to divide the spoils;" as if there were said, "Chosen even to divide the spoils of the beauty of a house," that is, Chosen even for dividing the spoils. For beautiful Christ hath made His House, that is, the Church, by dividing to Her spoils: in the same manner as the Body is beautiful in the distribution of the members. "Spoils" moreover those are called that are stripped off from conquered foes. What this is the Gospel adviseth us in the passage where we read, "No one goeth into the house of a strong man to spoil his vessels, unless first he shall have bound the strong man." Christ therefore hath bound the devil with spiritual bonds, by overcoming death, and by ascending from Hell above the Heavens: He hath bound him by the Sacrament of His Incarnation, because though finding nothing in Him deserving of death, yet he was permitted to kill: and from him so bound He took away his vessels as though they were spoils. For he was working in the sons of disobedience, of whose unbelief he made use to work his own will. These vessels the Lord cleansing by the remission of sins, sanctifying these spoils wrested from the foe laid prostrate and bound, these He hath divided to the beauty of His House; making some apostles, some prophets, some pastors and doctors, for the work of the ministry, for the building up of the Body of Christ. For as the body is one, and hath many members, and though all the members of the body are many, the body is one: so also is Christ. "Are all Apostles? Are all Prophets? Are all Powers? Have all the gifts of healings? Do all speak with tongues? Do all interpret?" "But all these things worketh one and the same Spirit, dividing to each one his own gifts, as He willeth." And such is the beauty of the house, whereto the spoils are divided, that a lover thereof with this fairness being enkindled, crieth out, "O Lord, I have loved the grace of Thy House."

14. Now in that which followeth, he turneth himself to address the members themselves, whereof the beauty of the House is composed, saying, "If ye sleep in the midst of the lots, wings of a dove silvered, and between the shoulders thereof in the freshness of gold" (ver. 13). First, we must here examine the order of the words, in what manner the sentence is ended; which certainly awaiteth, when there is said, "If ye sleep:" secondly, in that which he saith, namely, "wings of dove silvered," whether in the singular number it must be understood as being, "of this wing" thereof, or in the plural as, "these wings." But the singular number the Greek excludeth, where always in the plural we read it written. But still it is uncertain whether it be these wings; or whether, "O ye wings," so as that he may seem to speak to the wings themselves. Whether therefore by the words which have preceded, that sentence be ended, so that the order is, "The Lord shall give the Word to men preaching the Gospel with much virtue, if ye sleep in the midst of the lots, O ye wings of a dove silvered:" or by these which follow, so that the

order is, "If ye sleep in the midst of the lots, the wings of a dove silvered with snow shall be whitened in Selmon:" that is, the wings themselves shall be whitened, if ye sleep in the midst "of the lots:" so that he may be understood to say this to them that are divided to the beauty of the House, as it were spoils; that is, if ye sleep in the "midst of the lots," O ye that are divided to the beauty of the House, "through the manifestation of the Spirit unto profit," so that "to one indeed is given through the Spirit the word of wisdom, to another the word of knowledge," etc., if then ye sleep in the midst of the lots, then the wings of a dove silvered with snow shall be whitened in Selmon. It may also be thus: "If ye being the wings of a dove silvered, sleep in the midst of the lots, with snow they shall be whitened in Selmon," so as that those men be understood who through grace receive remission of sins. Whence also of the Church Herself, is said in the Song of Songs, "Who is She that goeth up whitened?" For this promise of God is held out through the Prophet, saying, "If your sins shall have been like scarlet, like snow I will whiten them." It may also thus be understood, so that in that which hath been said, "wings of a dove silvered," there be understood, ye shall be, so that this is the sense, O ye that like as it were spoils to the beauty of the house are divided, if ye sleep in the "midst of the lots," wings of a dove silvered ye shall be: that is, into higher places ye shall be lifted up, adhering however to the bond of the Church. For I think no other dove silvered can be better perceived here, than that whereof hath been said," One is My dove." But silvered She is because with divine sayings she hath been instructed: for the sayings of the Lord in another place are called "silver with fire refined, purged sevenfold." Some great good thing therefore it is, to sleep in the midst of the lots, which some would have to be the Two Testaments, so that to "sleep in the midst of the lots" is to rest on the authority of those Testaments, that is, to acquiesce in the testimony of either Testament: so that whenever anything out of them is produced and proved, all strife is ended in peaceful acquiescence. ...

15. "Between the shoulders," however. This is indeed a part of the body, it is a part about the region of the heart, at the hinder parts however, that is, at the back: which part of that dove silvered he saith is "in the greenness of gold," that is, in the vigour of wisdom, which vigour I think cannot be better understood than by love. But why on the back, and not on the breast? Although I wonder in what sense this word is put in another Psalm, where there is said, "Between His shoulders He shall overshadow thee, and under His wings thou shalt hope:" forasmuch as under wings there cannot be overshadowed anything but what shall be under the breast. And in Latin, indeed, "between the shoulders," perchance in some degree of both parts may be understood, both before and behind, that we may take shoulders to be the parts which have the head betwixt them; and in Hebrew perchance the word is ambiguous, which may in this manner also be understood: but the word that is in the Greek, meta'phrena, signifieth not anything but at the back, which is "between

the shoulders." Is there for this reason there the greenness of gold, that is, wisdom and love, because in that place there are in a manner the roots of the wings? or because in that place is carried that light burden? For what are even the wings themselves, but the two commandments of love, whereon hangeth the whole Law and the Prophets? what is that same light burden, but that same love which in these two commandments is fulfilled? For whatever thing is difficult in a commandment, is a light thing to a lover. Nor on any other account is rightly understood the saying, "My burden is light," but because He giveth the Holy Spirit, whereby love is shed abroad in our hearts, in order that in love we may do freely that which he that doeth in fear doeth slavishly; nor is he a lover of what is right, when he would prefer, if so be it were possible, that what is right should not be commanded.

16. It may also be required, when it hath not been said, if ye sleep in the lots, but "in the midst of the lots;" what this is, "in the midst of the lots." Which expression indeed, if more exactly it were translated from the Greek, would signify, "in the midst between the lots," which is in no one of the interpreters I have read: therefore I suppose, that what hath been said signifieth much the same, to wit the expression, "in the midst of the lots." Hence therefore what seemeth to me I will explain. Ofttimes this word is wont to be used for uniting and pacifying one thing and another, that they may not mutually disagree: as when God is establishing His covenant s between Himself and His people, this word the Scripture useth; for instead of that expression which is in Latin between Me and you, the Greek hath, in the midst of Me and you. So also of the sign of Circumcision, when God speaketh to Abraham, He saith, "There shall be a testament between Me and thee and all thy seed:" which the Greek hath, in the midst of Me and thee, and the midst of thy seed. Also when He was speaking to Noe of the bow in the clouds to establish a sign, this word very often He repeateth: and that which the Latin copies have, between Me and you, or between Me and every living soul, and whatever suchlike expressions there are used, is found in the Greek to be, in the middle of Me and you, which is ana` me'son. David also and Jonathan establish a sign between them, that they may not disagree with a difference of thought: and that which in Latin is expressed, between both, in the middle of both, the Greek hath expressed in the same word, which is ana` me'son. But it was best that in this passage of the Psalms our translators said not, "among the lots," which expression is more suited to the Latin idiom; but, "in the midst of the lots," as though "in the midst between the lots," which rather is the reading in the Greek, and which is wont to be said in the case of those things which ought to have a mutual consent. ... But why in the "lots" the Testaments should be perceived, though this word is Greek, and the Testament is not so named, the reason is, because through a testament is given inheritance, which in Greek is called klhronomi'a and an heir

klhrono'mos. Now klh^ros in Greek is the term for lot, and lots according to the promise of God are called those parts of the inheritance which were distributed to the people. Whence the tribe of Levi was commanded not to have lot among their brethren, because they were sustained by tithes from them. For, I think, they that have been ordained in the grades of the Ecclesiastical Ministry have been called both Clergy and Clerks, because Matthias by lot was chosen, who we read was the first that was ordained by the Apostles. Henceforth, because of inheritance which is given by testament, as though by that which is made that which maketh, by the name of "lots" the Testaments themselves are signified.

17. Nevertheless, to me here another sense also occurreth, if I mistake not, to be preferred; understanding by cleri the inheritances themselves: so that, whereas the inheritance of the Old Testament, although in a shadow significant of the future, is earthly felicity; but the inheritance of the New Testament is everlasting immortality; to "sleep in the midst of the lots" is not too earnestly now to seek the former, and still patiently to look for the latter. ... And because so well they have slept, on them, as it were on wings now flieth, and with praises is exalted, the Church: to wit, the Dove silvered, in order that by this fame of theirs, posterity having been invited to imitate them, while in like manner the rest also sleep, there may be added wings whereby even unto the end of the world sublimely she may be preached.

18. "While He that is above the heavens distinguisheth kings over Her, with snow they shall be made white in Selmon" (ver. 14). While He "above the heavens," He that ascended over all heavens that He might fulfil all things, "while He distinguisheth kings over Her," that is, over that same "Dove silvered." For the Apostle continueth and saith, and "He hath Himself given some for Apostles, and some Prophets, and some Evangelists, and some Pastors and Teachers." For what other reason is there to distinguish kings over Her, save for the work of the Ministry, for the edification of the Body of Christ: when she is indeed Herself the Body of Christ? But they are called kings from ruling: and what more than the lusts of the flesh, that sin may not reign in their mortal body to obey the desires thereof, that they yield not their members instruments of iniquity unto sin, but yield themselves to God, as though from the dead living, and their members instruments of righteousness to God? For thus shall the kings be distinguished from foreigners, because they draw not the yoke with unbelievers: secondly, in a peaceful manner being distinguished from one another by their proper gifts. For not all are Apostles, or all Prophets, or all Teachers, or all have gifts of healings, or all with tongues do speak, or all interpret. "But all these things worketh one and the same Spirit, dividing proper gifts to each one as He willeth." In giving which

Spirit He that is above the Heavens distinguisheth kings over the Dove silvered. Of which Holy Spirit, when, sent to His Mother full of grace, the Angel was speaking, to her enquiring in what manner it could come to pass that she was announced as going to bear, seeing she knew not a man: ... he saith, "The Holy Spirit shall come over upon thee, and the virtue of the Most Highest shall overshadow thee," that is, shall make a shadow for thee, "wherefore that Holy Thing which shall be born of thee, shall be called the Son of God." That "shadow" again is understood of a defence against the heat of carnal lusts: whence not in carnal concupiscence, but in spiritual belief, the Virgin conceived Christ. But the shadow consisteth of light and body: and further, The "Word" that "was in the beginning," that true Light, in order that a noonday shadow might be made for us; "the Word," I say, "was made Flesh, and dwelled in us."

19. But this mountain he calleth the "mountain of God, a mountain fruitful, a mountain full of curds" (ver. 15), or "a mountain fat." But here what else would he call fat but fruitful? For there is also a mountain called by that name, that is to say, Selmon. But what mountain ought we to understand by "the mountain of God, a mountain fruitful, a mountain full of curds," but the same Lord Christ? Of whom also another Prophet saith, "There shall be manifest in the last times the mountain of the Lord prepared on the top of the mountains"? He is Himself the "Mountain full of curds," because of the babes to be fed with grace as though it were with milk; a mountain rich to strengthen and enrich them by the excellence of the gifts; for even the milk itself whence curd is made, in a wonderful manner signifieth grace; for it floweth out of the overflowing of the mother's Bowels, and of a sweet compassion unto babes freely it is poured forth. But in the Greek the case is doubtful, whether it be the nominative or the accusative: for in that language mountain is of the neuter gender, not of the masculine: therefore some Latin translators have not translated it, "unto the Mountain of God," but, "the Mountain of God." But I think, "unto Selmon the Mountain of God," is better, that is, "unto" the Mountain of God which is called Selmon: according to the interpretation which, as we best could, we have explained above.

20. Secondly, in the expression, "Mountain of God, Mountain full of curds," Mountain" fruitful," let no one dare from this to compare the Lord Jesus Christ with the rest of the Saints, who are themselves also called mountains of God. ... For there were not wanting men to call Him, some John Baptist, some Elias, some Jeremias, or one of the Prophets; He turneth to them and saith, "Why do ye imagine mountains full of curds, a mountain," he saith, "wherein it hath pleased God to dwell therein"? (ver. 16). "Why do ye imagine?" For as they are a light, because to themselves also hath been said, "Ye are the Light of the world," but

something different hath been called "the true Light which enlighteneth every man." so they are mountains; but far different is the Mountain "prepared on the top of the mountains." These mountains therefore in bearing that Mountain are glorious: one of which mountains saith, "but from me far be it to glory, save in the Cross of our Lord Jesus Christ, through whom to me the world hath been crucified, and I to the world:" so that "he that glorieth, not in himself, but in the Lord may glory." "Why" then "do ye imagine mountains full of curds," that" Mountain wherein it hath pleased God to dwell therein"? Not because in other men He dwelleth not, but because in them through Him. "For in Him dwelleth all the fulness of the Godhead," not in a shadow, as in the temple made by king Solomon, but "bodily," that is, solidly and truly. ... "For there is One God, and One Mediator of God and men, the Man Christ Jesus," Mountain of mountains, as Saint of saints. Whence He saith, "I in them and Thou in Me." . ... "Why then do ye imagine mountains full of curds, the mountain wherein it hath pleased God to dwell in Him?" For those mountains full of curds that Mountain the Lord shall inhabit even unto the end, that something they may be to whom He saith, "for without Me nothing ye are able to do."

21. Thus cometh to pass that also which followeth: "The Chariot of God is of ten thousands manifold:" or "of tens of thousands manifold:" or, "ten times thousand times manifold" (ver. 17). For one Greek word, which hath there been used, muriopla'sion, each Latin interpreter hath rendered as best he could, but in Latin it could not be adequately expressed for a thousand with the Greeks is called chi'lia, but muria'des are a number of tens of thousands for one muria`s are ten thousands. Thus a vast number of saints and believers, who by bearing God become in a manner the chariot of God, he hath signified under this name. By abiding in and guiding this, He conducteth it, as though it were His Chariot, unto the end, as if unto some appointed place. For, "the beginning is Christ; secondly, that are of Christ, at the appearing of Him; then the end." This is Holy Church: which is that which followeth, "thousands of men rejoicing." For in hope they are joyful, until they be conducted unto the end, which now they look for through patience. For admirably, when he had said, "Thousands of men rejoicing:" immediately he added, "The Lord is in them." That we may not wonder why they rejoice, "The Lord is in them." For through many tribulations we must needs enter into the kingdom of God? but, "The Lord is in them." Therefore even if they are as it were sorrowful, yet alway rejoicing, though not now in that same end, to which they have not yet come, yet in hope they are rejoicing, and in tribulation patient: for, "The Lord is in them, in Sina in the holy place." In the interpretations of Hebrew names, we find Sina interpreted commandment: and some other interpretations it has, but I think this to be more agreeable to the present passage. For giving a reason why those thousands rejoice, whereof the Chariot of God doth consist, "The

Lord," he saith, "is in them, in Sins in the holy place:" that is, the Lord is in them, in the commandment; which commandment is holy, as saith the Apostle: "Therefore the law indeed is holy, and the commandment is holy, and just, and good." ...

22. In the next place, turning his address to the Lord Himself, "Thou hast gone up," he saith, "on high, Thou hast led captivity captive, Thou hast received gifts in men" (ver. 18). Of this the Apostle thus maketh mention, thus expoundeth in speaking of the Lord Christ.: "But unto each one of us," he saith, "is given grace after the measure of the giving of Christ: for which cause he saith, He hath gone up on high, He hath led captive captivity, He hath given gifts to men." ... And let it not move us that the Apostle making mention of that same testimony saith not, "Thou hast received gifts in men;" but, "He hath given gifts unto men." For he with Apostolic authority hath spoken thus according to the faith that the Son is God with the Father. For in respect of this He hath given gifts to men, sending to them the Holy Spirit, which is the Spirit of the Father and of the Son. But forasmuch as the self-name Christ is understood in His Body which is the Church, wherefore also His members are His saints and believers, whence to them is said, "But ye are the Body of Christ, and the members," doubtless He hath Himself also received gifts in men. Now Christ hath gone up on high, and sitteth at the right hand of the Father: but unless He were here also on the earth, He would not thence have cried, "Saul, Saul, why persecutest thou me?" When the Same saith Himself, "Inasmuch as to one of My least ye have done it, to Me ye have done it:" why do we doubt that He receiveth in His members, the gifts which the members of Him receive?

23. But what is, "Thou hast led captivity captive"? Is it because He hath conquered death, which was holding captive those over whom it reigned? Or hath he called men themselves captivity, who were being held captive under the devil? Which thing's mystery even the title of that Psalm doth contain, to wit, "when the house was being builded after the captivity:" that is, the Church after the coming in of the Gentiles. Calling therefore those very men who were being held captive a captivity, as when "the service" is spoken of there are understood those that serve also, that same captivity he saith by Christ hath been led captive. For why should not captivity be happy, if even for a good purpose men may be caught? Whence to Peter hath been said, "From henceforth thou shall catch men." Led captive therefore they are because caught, and caught because subjugated, being sent under that gentle yoke, being delivered from sin whereof they were servants, and being made servants of righteousness s whereof they were children. Whence also He is Himself in them, that hath given gifts to men, and hath received gifts in men.

And thus in that captivity, in that servitude, in that chariot, under that yoke, there are not thousands of men lamenting, but thousands of men rejoicing. For the Lord is in them, in Sina, in the holy place. ...

24. But what next doth he adjoin? "For they that believe not to dwell" (ver. 18): or, as some copies have, "For not believing to dwell:" for what else are men not believing, but they that believe not? To whom this hath been said, is not easy to perceive. For as though a reason were being given of the above words, when it had been said, "Thou hast led captivity captive, Thou hast received gifts in men:" there hath been added in continuation, "for they that believe not to dwell," that is, not believing that they should dwell. What is this? Of whom saith he this? Did that captivity, before it passed into a good captivity, show whence it was an evil captivity? For through not believing they were possessed by the enemy, "that worketh in the sons of unbelief: among whom ye were sometime, while ye were living among them." By the gifts therefore of His grace, He that hath received gifts in men, hath led captive that captivity. For they believed not that they should dwell. For faith hath thence delivered them, in order that now believing they may dwell in the House of God, even they too becoming the House of God, and the Chariot of God, consisting of thousands of men rejoicing.

25. Whence he that was singing of these things, in the Spirit foreseeing them, even he too being fulfilled with joy hath burst forth s a hymn, saying, "The Lord God is blessed, blessed is the Lord God from day unto day" (ver. 19). Which some copies have, "by day daily," because the Greeks have it thus, hhme'ran kath' hhme'ran: which more exactly would be expressed by, "by day daily." Which expression I think signifieth the same as that which hath been said, to wit, "from day unto day." For daily this He doeth even unto the end, He leadeth captive captivity, receiving gifts in men.

26. And because He leadeth that chariot unto the end, He continueth and saith, "A prosperous journey there shall make for us the God of our healths, our God, the God of making men safe" (ver. 20). Highly is grace here commended. For who would be safe, unless He Himself should make whole? But that it might not occur to the mind, Why then do we die, if through His grace we have been made safe? immediately he added below, "and the Lord's is the outgoing of death:" as though he were saying, Why are thou indignant, O lot of humanity, that thou hast the outgoing of death? Even thy Lord's outgoing was no other than that of death. Rather therefore be comforted than be indignant: for even "the Lord's is the outgoing of death." "For by hope we have been saved: but if that which we see not we hope for, through patience we wait for it." Patiently therefore even death itself

let us suffer, by the example of Him, who though by no sin He was debtor to death, and was the Lord, from whom no one could take away life, but Himself laid it down of Himself, yet had Himself the outgoing of death.

27. "Nevertheless, God shall break in pieces the heads of His enemies, the scalp of hair of men walking on in their transgressions" (ver. 21): that is, too much exalting themselves, being too proud in their transgressions: wherein at least they ought to be humble, saying, "O Lord, be Thou merciful to me a sinner."But He shall break in pieces their heads: for he that exalteth himself shall be humbled. And thus though even of the Lord be the outgoing of death: nevertheless the same Lord, because He was God, and died after the flesh of His own will, not of necessity, "shall break in pieces the heads of His enemies:" not only of those who mocked and crucified Him, and wagged their heads, and said, "If Son of God He is, let Him come down from the Cross;" but also of all men lifting up themselves against His doctrine, and deriding His death as though it were of a man. For that very same One of whom hath been said, "Others He saved, Himself He cannot save," is the "God of our healths," and is the "God of saving men:" but for an example of humility and of patience, and to efface the handwriting of our sins, He even willed that the outgoing of death should be His own, that we: might not fear that death, but rather this from which He hath delivered us through that. Nevertheless, though mocked and dead, "He shall break in pieces the heads of His enemies," of whom He saith, "Raise Thou me up, and I shall render to them:" whether it be good things for evil things, while to Himself He subdueth the heads of them believing, or whether just things for unjust things, while He punisheth the heads of them proud. For in either way are shattered and broken the heads of enemies, when from pride they are thrown down, whether by humility being amended, or whether unto the lowest depths of hell being hurled.

28. "The Lord hath said, Out of Basan I will be turned" (ver. 22): or, as some copies have, "Out of Basan I will turn." For He turneth that we may be safe, of whom above hath been said, "God of our healths, and God of saving men." For to Him elsewhere also is said, "O God of virtues, turn Thou us, and show Thy face, and safe we shall be." Also in another place, "Turn us, O God of our healths." But he hath said, "Out of Basan I will turn." Basan is interpreted confusion. What is then, I will turn out of confusion, but that there is confounded because of his sins, he that is praying of the mercy of God that they may be put away? Thence it is that the Publican dared not even to lift up his eyes to Heaven: so, on considering himself, was he confounded; but he went down justified, because "the Lord hath said, Out of Basan I will turn." Basan is also interpreted drought: and rightly the Lord is understood to turn out of drought, that is, out of scarcity. For they that

think themselves to be in plenty, though they be famished; and full, though they be altogether empty; are not turned. ... "I will turn unto the deep of the sea." If, "I will turn," why, "unto the deep of the sea"? Unto Himself indeed the Lord turneth, when savingly He turneth, and He is not surely Himself the deep of the sea. Doth perchance the Latin expression deceive us, and hath there been put "unto the deep," for a translation of what signifieth "deeply "? For He doth not turn Himself: but He turneth those that in the deep of this world lie sunk down with the weight of sins, in that place where one that is turned saith, "From the depths I have cried to Thee, O Lord." But if it is not, "I will turn," but, "I will be turned unto the deep of the sea;" our Lord is understood to have said, how by His own mercy He was turned even unto the deep of the sea, to deliver even those that were sinners in most desperate case. Though in one Greek copy I have found, not, "unto the deep," but "in the depths," that is, en buthoi^s: which strengtheneth the former sense, because even there God turneth to Himself men crying from the depths. And even if He be understood Himself there to be turned, to deliver such sort also, it is not beside the purpose: and so then He turneth, or else to deliver them is so turned, that His foot is stained in blood. Which to the Lord Himself the Prophet speaketh: "That Thy foot may be stained in blood" (ver. 23): that is, in order that they themselves who are turned to Thee, or to deliver whom Thou art turned, though in the deep of the sea by the burden of iniquity they may have been sunk, may make so great proficiency by Thy Grace (for where there hath abounded sin, there hath superabounded grace), that they may become Thy foot among Thy members, to preach Thy Gospel, and for Thy name's sake drawing out a long martyrdom, even unto blood they may contend. For thus, as I judge, more meetly is perceived His foot stained in blood.

29. Lastly, he addeth, "The tongue of Thy dogs out of enemies by Himself," calling those very same that had been about to strive for the faith of the Gospel, even dogs, as though barking for their Lord. Not those dogs, whereof saith the Apostle, "Beware of dogs:" but those that eat of the crumbs which fall from the table of their masters. For having confessed this, the woman of Canaan merited to hear, "O woman, great is thy faith, be it done to thee as thou wilt." Dogs commendable, not abominable; observing fidelity towards their master, and before his house barking against enemies. Not i only "of dogs" he hath said, but "of Thy dogs:" nor are their teeth praised, but their tongue is: for it was not indeed to no purpose, not without a great mystery, that Gedeon was bidden to lead those alone, who should lap the water of the river like dogs; and of such sort not more than three hundred among so great a multitude were found. In which number is the sign of the Cross because of the letter T, which in the Greek numeral characters signifieth three hundred. Of such dogs in another Psalm also said, "They shall be turned at even, and hunger they shall suffer as dogs." For even some dogs have

been reproved by the Prophet Isaiah, not because they were dogs, but because they knew not how to bark, and loved to sleep. In which place indeed he hath shown, that if they had watched and barked for their Lord, they would have been praiseworthy dogs: just as they are praised, of whom is said, "The tongue of Thy dogs." ...

30. "There have been seen Thy steps, O God" (ver. 24). The steps are those wherewith Thou hast come through the world, as though in that chariot Thou wast going to traverse the round world; which chariot of clouds He intimateth to be His holy and faithful ones in the Gospel, where He saith, "From this time ye shall see the Son of Man coming in the clouds." Leaving out that coming wherein He shall be Judge of quick and dead, "From this time," He saith, "ye shall see the Son of Man coming in clouds." These "Thy steps have been seen," that is, have been manifested, by the revealing the grace of the New Testament. Whence hath been said, "How beautiful are the feet of them that proclaim peace, that proclaim good things!" For this grace and those steps were lying hid in the Old Testament: but when there came the fulness of time, and it pleased God to reveal His Son, that He might be proclaimed among the Gentiles, "there were seen Thy steps, O God: the steps of my God, of the King who is in the holy place." In what holy place, save in His Temple? "For the Temple of God is holy," he saith, "which ye are."

31. But in order that those steps might be seen, "there went before princes conjoined with men psalming, in the midst of damsels players on timbrels" (ver. 25). The princes are the Apostles: for they went before, that the peoples might come in multitudes. "They went before" proclaiming the New Testament: "conjoined with men psalming," by whose good works that were even visible, as it were with instruments of praise, God was glorified. But those same princes are "in the midst of damsels players on timbrels," to wit, in an honourable ministry: for thus in the midst are ministers set over new Churches; for this is "damsels:" with flesh subdued praising God; for this is "players on timbrels," because timbrels are made of skin dried and stretched.

32. Therefore, that no one should take these words in a carnal sense, and by these words should conceive in his mind certain choral bands of wantonness, he continueth and saith, "In the Churches bless ye the Lord" (ver. 26): as though he were saying, wherefore, when ye hear of damsels, players on timbrels, do ye think of wanton pleasures? "In the Churches bless ye the Lord." For the Churches are pointed out to you by this mystic intimation: the Churches are the damsels, with new grace decked: the Churches are the players on the timbrels, with chastened flesh being spiritually tuneful. "In the Churches," then, "bless ye the Lord God

from the wells of Israel." For from thence He first chose those whom He made wells. For from thence were chosen the Apostles; and they first heard, "He that shall have drunk of the water that I shall give him, shall never thirst, but there shall be made in him a well of water springing unto life everlasting."

33. "There is Benjamin the younger in a trance" (ver. 27). There is Paul the last of the Apostles, who saith, "For even I am an Israelite, out of the seed of Abraham, out of the tribe of Benjamin." But evidently "in a trance," all men being amazed at a miracle so great as that of his calling. For a trance is the mind's going out: which thing sometimes chanceth through fear; but sometimes through some revelation, the mind suffering separation from the corporal senses, in order that that which is to be represented may be represented to the spirit. Whence even thus may be understood that which here hath been written, namely, "in a trance;" for when to that persecutor there had been said from Heaven, "Saul, Saul, why persecutest thou me:" there being taken from him the light of the eyes of flesh, he made answer to the Lord, whom in spirit he saw, but they that were with him heard the voice of him replying, though seeing no one to whom he was speaking. Here also the trance may be understood to be that one of his, whereof he himself speaking, saith, that he knew a man caught up even unto the third Heaven; but whether in the body, or whether out of the body, he knew not: but that he being caught up into Paradise, heard ineffable words, which it was not lawful for a man to speak. "Princes of Juda the leaders of them, princes of Zabulon, princes of Nephthalim." Since he is indicating the Apostles as princes, wherein is even "Benjamin the younger in a trance," in which words that Paul is indicated no one doubteth; or when under the name of princes there are indicated in the Churches all men excelling and most worthy of imitation: what mean these names of the tribes of Israel? ... For the names are Hebrew: whereof Juda is said to be interpreted confession, Zabulon habitation of strength, Nephthalim my enlargement. All which words do intimate to us the most proper princes of the Church, worthy of their leadership, worthy of imitation, worthy of honours. For the Martyrs in the Churches hold the highest place, and by the crown of holy worth they do excel. But however in martyrdom the first thing is confession, and for this is next put on strength to endure whatsoever shall have chanced; then after all things have been endured, straits being ended, breadth followeth in reward. It may also thus be understood; that whereas the Apostle chiefly commendeth these three things, faith, hope, love; confession is in faith, strength in hope, breadth in love. For of faith the substance is, that with the heart men believe unto righteousness, but with the mouth confession be made unto salvation. But in sufferings of tribulations the thing itself is sorrowful, but the hope is strong. For, "if that which we see not we hope for, through patience we wait for it." But breadth the shedding abroad of love

in the heart doth give. For "love perfected casteth out fear:" which fear "hath torment," because of the straits of the soul. ...

34. "Command, O God, Thy Virtue" (ver. 28). For one is our Lord Jesus Christ, through whom are all things, and we in Him, of whom we read that He is "the Virtue of God and the Wisdom of God." But how doth God command His Christ, save while He commendeth Him? For "God commendeth His love in us, in that while yet we were sinners, for us Christ died." "How hath He not also with Him given to us all things?" "Command, O God, Thy Virtue: confirm, O God, that which Thou hast wrought in us." Command by teaching, confirm by aiding.

35. "From Thy Temple in Jerusalem, to Thee kings shall offer presents" (ver. 29). Jerusalem, which is our free mother, because the same also is Thy holy Temple: from that Temple then, "to Thee kings shall offer presents." Whatever kings be understood, whether kings of the earth, or whether those whom" He that is above the heavens distinguisheth over the dove silvered; " "to Thee kings shall offer presents." And what presents are so acceptable as the sacrifices of praise? But there is a noise against this praise, from men bearing the name of Christian, and having diverse opinions. Be there done that which followeth, "Rebuke Thou the beasts of the cane" (ver. 30). For both beasts they are, since by not understanding they do hurt: and beasts of the cane they are, since the sense of the Scriptures they wrest according to their own misapprehension. For in the cane the Scriptures are as reasonably perceived, as language in tongue, according to the mode of expression whereby the Hebrew or the Greek or the Latin tongue is spoken of, or the like; that is to say, by the efficient cause the thing which is being effected is implied. Now it is usual in the Latin language for writing to be called style, because with the stilus it is done: so then cane also, because with a cane it is done. The Apostle Peter saith, that "men unlearned and unstable do wrest the Scriptures to their own proper destruction:" these are the beasts of the cane, whereof here is said, "Rebuke Thou the beasts of the cane."

36. Concerning these also is that which followeth, "The congregation of bulls amid the cows of the peoples, in order that there may be excluded they that have been tried with silver." Calling them bulls because of the pride of a stiff and untamed neck: for he is referring to heretics. But by "the cows of the peoples," I think souls easily led astray must be understood, because easily they follow these bulls. For they lead not astray entire peoples, among whom are men grave and stable; whence hath been written, "In a people grave I will praise Thee: " but only the cows which they may have found among those peoples. "For of these are they that steal into houses, and lead captive silly women laden with sins, who are led with

divers lusts, alway learning, and at the knowledge of the truth never arriving." ... For, "may be excluded," hath been said, meaning, may appear, may stand forth: as he saith, "may be made manifest." Whence also, in the art of the silversmith, they are called exclusores, who out of the shapelessness of the lump are skilled to mould the form of a vessel. For many meanings of the holy Scriptures are concealed, and are known only to a few of singular intelligence, and are never vindicated so suitably and acceptably as when our diligence to make answer to heretics constraineth us. For then even they that neglect the pursuits of learning, shaking off their slumber, are stirred up to a diligent hearing, in order that their opponents may be refuted. In a word, how many senses of holy Scriptures concerning Christ as God have been vindicated against Photinus, how many concerning Christ as man against Manichaeus, how many concerning the Trinity against Sabellius, how many concerning the Unity of the Trinity against Arians, Eunomians, Macedonians? How many concerning the Catholic Church in the whole world spread abroad, against Donatists, and Luciferians, and others, whoever they be, that with like error dissent from the truth: how many against the rest of heretics, whom to enumerate or mention were too long a task, and for the present work unnecessary? ... Of whom, as it were bulls, that is, not subject to the peaceful and gentle yoke of discipline, the Apostle maketh mention, in the place where he hath said that such an one must be chosen for the Episcopate as is "able to exhort in sound doctrine and to convince the gainsayers. For there are many unruly;" these are bulls with uplifted neck, impatient of plough and yoke: vain-talkers and leaders astray of minds; which minds this Psalm hath intimated under the name of cows. ...

37. "There shall come ambassadors out of Egypt, Ethiopia shall prevent the hands of Him" (ver. 31). Under the name of Egypt or of Ethiopia, he hath signified the faith of all nations, from a part the whole: calling the preachers of reconciliation ambassadors. "For Christ," he saith, "we have an embassy, God as it were exhorting through us: we beseech you for Christ to be reconciled to God." Not then of the Israelites alone, whence the Apostles were chosen, but also from the rest of the nations that there should be preachers of Christian peace, in this manner hath been mystically prophesied. But by that which he saith, "shall prevent the hands of Him," he saith this, shall prevent the vengeance of Him: to wit, by turning to Him, in order that their sins may be forgiven, lest by continuing sinners they be punished. Which thing also in another Psalm is said," Let us come before the face of Him in confession." As by hands he signifieth vengeance, so by face, revelation and presence, which will be in the Judgment. Because then, by Egypt and Ethiopia he hath signified the nations of the whole world; immediately he hath subjoined, "to God (are) the kingdoms of the earth." Not to Sabellius, not to Arius, not to Donatus, not to the rest of the bulls stiff-necked, but "to God (are) the

kingdoms of the earth." But the greater number of Latin copies, and especially the Greek, have the verses so punctuated, that there is not one verse in these words, "to God the kingdoms of the earth," but, "to God," is at the end of the former verse, and so there is said, "Ethiopia shall come before the hands of her to God," and then there followeth in another verse, "Kingdoms of the earth, sing ye to God, psalm ye to the Lord" (ver. 32). By which punctuation, doubtless to be preferred by the agreement of many copies, and those deserving of credit, there seemeth to me to be implied faith which precedeth works: because without the merits of good works through faith the ungodly is justified, just as the Apostle said, "To one believing in Him that justifieth the ungodly, his faith is counted for righteousness:" in order that afterwards faith itself through love may begin to work. For those alone are to be called good works, which are done through love of God. But these faith must needs go before, so that from thence these may begin, not from these this. ... This is faith, whereof to the Church Herself is said in the Song of Songs, "Thou shalt come and shalt pass hence from the beginning of faith." For She hath come like the chariot of God in thousands of men rejoicing, having a prosperous course, and She hath passed over from this world to the Father: in order that there may come to pass in Her that which the Bridegroom Himself saith, who hath passed hence from this world to the Father? "I will that where I am, these also may be with Me:" but from the beginning of faith. Because then in order that good works may follow, faith doth precede; and there are not any good works, save those which follow faith preceding: nothing else seemeth to have been meant in, "Ethiopia shall come before the hands of her to God," but, Ethiopia shall believe in God. For thus she "shall come before the hands of her," that is, the works of her. Of whom, except of Ethiopia herself? For this in the Greek is not ambiguous: for the word "of her" there in the feminine gender most clearly hath been put down. And thus nothing else hath been said than" Ethiopia shall come before her hands to God," that is, by believing in God she shall come before her works. For, "I judge," saith the Apostle, "that a man is justified through faith without the works of the Law. Is He God of the Jews only? Is He not also of the Gentiles?" So then Ethiopia, which seemeth to be the utmost limit of the Gentiles, is justified through faith, without the works of the Law. ... For the expression in Greek, chei^ra auth^s, which most copies have, both of "hand of her" and "her own hand" may be understood: but that which is uncommon in the Greek copies, cheira`s auth^s, by both "hands of her" and "her own hands," in Latin may be expressed.

38. Henceforward, as if through prophecy all things had been discoursed of which now we see fulfilled, he exhorteth to the praise of Christ, and next He foretelleth His future Advent. "Kingdoms of earth, sing ye to God, psalm ye to the Lord: psalm ye to God, who hath ascended above the Heaven of Heavens to the East" (ver. 33). Or, as some copies have it, "who hath ascended above the Heaven of

Heaven to the East." In these words he preceiveth not Christ, who believeth not His Resurrection and Ascension. But hath not "to the East," which he hath added, expressed the very spot; since in the quarters of the East is where He rose again, and whence He ascended? Therefore above the Heaven of Heaven He sitteth at the right hand of the Father. This is what the Apostle saith, "the Same is He that hath ascended above all Heavens." For what of Heavens doth remain after the Heaven of Heaven? Which also we may call the Heavens of Heavens, just as He hath called the firmanent Heaven: which Heaven, however, even as Heavens we read of, in the place where there is written, "and let the waters which are above the Heavens praise the name of the Lord." And forasmuch as from thence He is to come, to judge quick and dead, observe what followeth: "behold, He shall give His voice, the voice of power." He that like a lamb before the shearer of Him was without voice, "behold shall give His voice," and not the voice of weakness, as though to be judged; but "the voice of power," as though going to judge. For God shall not be hidden, as before, and in the judgment of men not opening His mouth; but "God shall come manifest, our God, and He shall not be silent." Why do ye despair, ye unbelieving men? Why do ye mock? What saith the evil servant? "My Lord delayeth to come." "Behold, He shall give His voice, the voice of power."

39. "Give ye glory to God, above Israel is the magnificence of Him" (ver. 34). Of whom saith the Apostle, "Upon the Israel of God." For "not all that are out of Israel, are Israelites: " for there is also an Israel after the flesh. Whence he saith, "See ye Israel after the flesh." "For not they that are sons of the flesh, are sons of God, but sons of promise are counted for a seed." Therefore at that time when without any intermixture of evil men His people shall be, like a heap purged by the fan, like Israel in whom guile is not, then most pre- eminent "above Israel" shall be "the magnificence" of "Him: and the virtue of Him in the clouds." For not alone He shall come to judgment, but with the elders of His people: to whom He hath promised that they shall sit upon thrones to judge, who even shall judge angels. These be the clouds.

40. Lastly, lest of anything else the clouds be understood, he hath in continuation added, "Wonderful is God in His saints, the God of Israel" (ver. 35). For at that time even most truly and most fully there shall be fulfilled the name Israel itself, which is one "seeing God :" for we shall see Him as He is. "He Himself shall give virtue and strength to His people, blessed be God:" to His people now frail and weak. For "we have this treasure in earthen vessels." But then by a most glorious changing even of our bodies, "He Himself shall give virtue and strength to His people." For this body is sown in weakness, shall rise in virtue. He Himself then shall give the virtue which in His own flesh He hath sent before, whereof the

Apostle saith, "the power of His Resurrection." But strength whereby shall be destroyed the enemy death. Now then of this long and difficultly understood Psalm we have at length by His own aid made an end. "Blessed be God. Amen."

PSALM LXIX.

1. We have been born into this world, and added to the people of God, at that period wherein already the herb from a grain of mustard seed hath spread out its branches; wherein already the leaven, which at first was contemptible, hath leavened three measures, that is, the whole round world repeopled by the three sons of Noe: for from East and West and North and South shall come they that shall sit down with the Patriarchs, while those shall have been driven without, that have been born of their flesh and have not imitated their faith. Unto his glory then of Christ's Church our eyes we have opened; and that barren one, for whom joy was proclaimed and foretold, because she was to have more sons than she that had the husband? her we have found to be such an one as hath forgotten the reproaches and infamy of her widowhood: and so we may perhaps wonder when we chance to read in any prophecy the words of Christ's humiliation, or our own. And it may be, that we are less affected by them; because we have not come at that time when these things were read with zest, in that tribulation abounded. But again if we think of the abundance of tribulations, and observe the way wherein we are walking (if indeed we do walk in it), how narrow it is, and how through straits and tribulations it leadeth unto rest everlasting, and how that very thing which in human affairs is called felicity, is more to be feared than misery; since indeed misery ofttimes doth bring out of tribulation a good fruit, but felicity doth corrupt the soul with a perverse security, and giveth place for the Devil the Tempter— when, I say, we shall have judged prudently and rightly, as the salted victim did, that "human life upon earth is trial," and that no one is at all secure, nor ought to be secure, until he be come to that country, whence no one that is a friend goeth forth, into which no one that is an enemy is admitted, even now in the very glory of the Church we acknowledge the voices of our tribulation: and being members of Christ, subject to our Head in the bond of love, and mutually supporting one another, we will say from the Psalms, that which here we have found the Martyrs said, who were before us; that tribulation is common to all men from the beginning even unto the end. ...

2. The Title of the Psalm is: "Unto the end, in behalf of those that shall be changed, to David himself." Now of the change for the better hear thou; for change either is for the worse or for the better. ... That we have been changed then for the worse, to ourselves let us ascribe: that for the better we are changed, let us praise God. "For those," then," that shall be changed," this Psalm is. But whence hath this change been made but by the Passion of Christ? The very word Pascha in Latin is interpreted passage. For Pascha is not a Greek word but a Hebrew. It soundeth indeed in the Greek language like Passion, because pa'schein signifieth to suffer:

but if the Hebrew expression be examined, it pointeth to something else. Pascha doth intimate passage. Of which even John the Evangelist hath admonished us, who (just before the Passion when the Lord was coming to the supper wherein He set forth the Sacrament of His Body and Blood) thus speaketh: "But when there had come the hour, wherein Jesus was to pass from this world to the Father." He hath expressed then the "passage" of the Pascha. But unless He passed Himself hence to the Father, who came for our sake, how should we have been able to pass hence, who have not come down for the sake of taking up anything, but have fallen? But He Himself fell not; He but came down, in order that He might raise up him that had fallen. The passage therefore both of Him and of us is hence to the Father, from this world to the kingdom of Heaven, from life mortal to life everlasting, froth life earthly to life heavenly, from life corruptible to life incorruptible, from intimacy with tribulations to perpetual security. Accordingly, "In behalf of them that shall be changed," the Psalm's title is. The cause therefore of our change, that is, the very Passion of the Lord and our own voice in tribulations in the text of the Psalm let us observe, let us join in knowing, join in groaning, and in hearing, in joint-knowing, joint-groaning, let us be changed, in order that there may be fulfilled in us the Title of the Psalm, "In behalf of them that shall be changed."

3. "Save me, O God, for the waters have entered in even unto my soul" (ver. 1). That grain is despised now, that seemeth to give forth humble words. In the garden it is buried, though the world will admire the greatness of the herb, of which herb the seed was despised by the Jews. For in very deed observe ye the seed of the mustard, minute, dull coloured, altogether despicable, in order that therein may be fulfilled that which hath been said, We have seen Him, and He had neither form nor comeliness. But He saith, that waters have come in even unto His soul; because those multitudes, which under the name of waters He hath pointed out, were able so far to prevail as to kill Christ. ... Whence then doth He so cry out, as though He were suffering something against His will, except because the Head doth prefigure the Members? For He suffered because He willed: but the Martyrs even though they willed not; for to Peter thus He foretold his passion: "When thou shalt be old," He saith, "another shall gird thee, and lead thee whither thou wilt not." For though we desire to cleave to Christ, yet we are unwilling to die: and therefore willingly or rather patiently we suffer, because no other passage is given us, through which we may cleave to Christ. For if we could in any other way arrive at Christ, that is, at life everlasting, who would be willing to die? For while explaining our nature, that is, a sort of association of soul and body, and in these two parts a kind of intimacy of gluing and fastening together, the Apostle saith, that "we have a House not made with hands, everlasting in the Heavens:" that is, immortality prepared for us, wherewith we are to be clothed at the end, when we

shall have risen from the dead; and he saith, "Wherein we are not willing to be stripped, but to be clothed upon, that the mortal may be swallowed up of life." If it might so be, we should so will, he saith, to become immortal, as that now that same immortality might come, and now as we are it should change us, in order that this our mortal body by life should be swallowed up, and the body should not be laid aside through death, so as at the end again to have to be recovered. Although then from evil to good things we pass, nevertheless the very passage is somewhat bitter, and hath the gall which the Jews gave to the Lord in the Passion, hath something sharp to be endured, whereby they are shown that gave Him vinegar to drink. ... For here both sweet are temporal pleasures, and bitter are temporal tribulations: but who would not drink the cup of tribulation temporal, fearing the fire of hell; and who would not contemn the sweetness of the world, longing for the sweetness of life eternal? From hence that we may be delivered let us cry: lest perchance amidst oppressions we consent to iniquity, and truly irreparably we be swallowed up.

4. Fixed I am in the clay of the deep, and there is no substance" (ver. 2). What called the clay? Is it those very persons that have persecuted? For out of clay man hath been made. But these men by falling from righteousness have become the clay of the deep, and whosoever shall not have consented to them persecuting and desiring to draw him to iniquity, out of his clay doth make gold. For the clay of the same shall merit to be converted into a heavenly form, and to be made associate of those of whom saith the Title of the Psalm, "in behalf of them that shall be changed." But at the time when these were the clay of the deep. I stuck in them: that is, they held Me, prevailed against Me, killed Me. "Fixed" then "I am in the clay of the deep, and there is no substance." What is this, "there is no substance "? Can it be that clay itself is not a substance? What is then, "fixed I am"? Can it be that Christ hath thus stuck? Or hath He stuck, and was not, as hath been said in the book of Job, "the earth delivered into the hands of the ungodly man"? Was He fixed in body, because it could be held, and suffered even crucifixion? For unless with nails He had been fixed, crucified He had not been. Whence then "there is no substance"? Is that clay not a substance? But we shall understand, if it be possible, what is, "and there is no substance," if first we shall have understood what is a substance. For there is substance spoken of even of riches, as we say, he hath substance, and he hath lost substance. ...

5. God is a sort of substance: for that which is no substance, is nothing at all. To be a substance then is to be something. Whence also in the Catholic Faith against the poisons of certain heretics thus we are builded up, so that we say, Father and Son and Holy Spirit are of one substance. What is, of one substance? For example,

if gold is the Father, gold is also the Son, gold also the Holy Spirit. Whatever the Father is because He is God, the same is the Son, the same the Holy Spirit. But when He is the Father, this is not what He is. For Father He is called not in reference to Himself, but in reference to the Son: but in reference to Himself God He is called. Therefore in that He is God, by the same He is a substance. And because of the same substance the Son is, without doubt the Son also is God. But yet in that He is Father, because it is not the name of the substance, but is referred to the Son; we do not say that the Son is Father in the same manner as we say the Son is God. Thou askest what the Father is; we answer, God. Thou askest what is the Father and the Son: we answer, God. If questioned of the Father alone, answer thou God: if questioned of both, not Gods, but God, answer thou. We do not reply as in the case of men, when thou inquirest what is father Abraham, we answer a man; the substance of him serveth for answer: thou inquirest what is his son Isaac, we answer, a man; of the same substance are Abraham and Isaac: thou inquirest what is Abraham and Isaac, we answer not man, but men. Not so in things divine. For so great in this case is the fellowship of substance, that of equality it alloweth, plurality alloweth not. If then it shall have been said to thee, when thou tellest me that the Son is the same as the Father, in fact the Son also is the Father; answer thou, according to the substance I have told thee that the Son is the same as the Father, not according to that term which is used in reference to something else. For in reference to Himself He is called God, in reference to the Father is called Son. And again, the Father in reference to Himself is called God, in reference to the Son He is called Father. The Father as He is called in reference to the Son, is not the Son: the Son as He is called in reference to the Father, is not the Father: what the Father is called in reference to Himself and the Son in reference to Himself, the same is Father and Son, that is, God. What is then, "there is no substance"? After this interpretation of substance, how shall we be able to understand this passage of the Psalm, "Fixed I am in the clay of the deep, and there is no substance"? God made man, He made substance; and O that he had continued in that which God made Him! If man had continued in that which God made him, in him would not have been fixed He whom God begot. But moreover because through iniquity man fell from the substance wherein he was made (for iniquity itself is no substance; for iniquity is not a nature which God formed, but a perverseness which man made); the Son of God came to the clay of the deep, and was fixed; and that was no substance wherein He was fixed, because in the iniquity of them He was fixed. "All things by Him were made, and without Him there was made nothing." All natures by Him were made, iniquity by Him was not made, because iniquity was not made. Those substances by Him were made, which praise Him. The whole creation praising God is commemorated by the, three children in the furnace, and from things earthly to things heavenly, or from things heavenly to things earthly reacheth the hymn of them praising God. Not that all these things have sense to praise; but because all things being well meditated upon, do beget praise, and the heart by considering creation is fulfilled to overflowing with a hymn to the Creator. All things do praise God, but only the things which God hath made. Do ye observe in that hymn that covetousness praiseth God? There even the serpent praiseth God, covetousness praiseth not. For all creeping things are there named in the praise of God: there are named all creeping things; but there are not there named any vices. For vices out of ourselves and out of our own will we have: and vices are not a substance. In these was fixed the Lord, when He suffered persecution: in the vice of the Jews, not in the substance of men which by Him was made.

6. "I have come into the depth of the sea, and the tempest hath made Me to sink down." Thanks to the mercy of Him who came into the depth of the sea, and vouchsafed to be swallowed by the sea whale, but was vomited forth the third day. He came into the depth of the sea, in which depth we were thrust down, in which depth we had suffered shipwreck: He came thither Himself, and the tempest made Him to sink down: for there He suffered waves, those very men; tempests, the voices of men saying, "Crucify, Crucify." Though Pilate said, I find not any cause in this Man why He should be killed: there prevailed the voices of them, saying, "Crucify, Crucify." The tempest increased, until He was made to sink down that had come into the depth of the sea. And the Lord suffered in the hands of the Jews that which He suffered not when upon the waters He was walking: the which not only He had riot suffered Himself, but had not allowed even Peter to suffer it.

7. "I have laboured, crying, hoarse have become my jaws" (ver. 3). Where was this? When was this? Let us question the Gospel. For the Passion of our Lord in this Psalm we perceive. And, indeed, that He suffered we know; that there came in waters even unto His Soul, because peoples prevailed even unto His death, we read, we believe; in the tempest that He was sunk down, because tumult prevailed to His killing, we acknowledge: but that He laboured in crying, and that His jaws were made hoarse, not only we read not, but even on the contrary we read, that He answered not to them a word, in order that there might be fulfilled that which in another Psalm hath been said, "I have become as it were a man not hearing, and having not in his mouth reproofs." And that which in Isaiah hath been prophesied," like a sheep to be sacrificed He was led, and like a lamb before one shearing Him, so He opened not His mouth." If He became like a man not hearing, and having not in His mouth reproofs, how did He labour crying, and how were His jaws made hoarse? Is it that He was even then silent, because He was hoarse with having cried so much in vain? And this indeed we know to have been His voice on the Cross out of a certain Psalm:' "0 God, My God, why hast Thou forsaken Me?" But how great was that voice, or of how long duration, that in it His jaws should

have become hoarse? Long while He cried, "Woe unto you, Scribes and Pharisees:" long while He cried, "Woe unto the world because of offences." And truly hoarse in a manner He cried, and therefore was not understood, when the Jews said, What is this that He saith? "Hard is this saying, who is able to hear it?" We know not what He saith. He said all these words: but hoarse were His jaws to them that understood not His words. "Mine eyes have failed from hoping in My God." Far be it that this should be taken of the person of the Head: far be it that His eyes should have failed from hoping in His God: in whom rather there was God reconciling the world to Himself, and Who was the Word made flesh and dwelled in us, so that not only God was in Him, but also He was Himself God. Not so then: the eyes of Himself, our Head, failed not from hoping in His God: but the eyes of Him have failed in His Body, that is, in His members. This voice is of the members, this voice is of the Body, not of the Head. How then do we find it in His Body and members? ...

8. Thus "there have been multiplied above the hairs of My head they that hate Me gratis" (ver. 4). How multiplied? So as that they might add to themselves even one out of the twelve "There have been multiplied above the hairs of My head they that hate Me for nought." With the hairs of His head He hath compared His enemies. With reason they were shorn when in the place of Calvary He was crucified. Let the members accept this voice, let them learn to be hated gratis. For now, O Christian, if it must needs be that the world hate thee, why dost thou not make it hate thee gratis, in order that in the Body of thy Lord and in this Psalm sent before concerning Him, thou mayest acknowledge thy own voice? How shall it come to pass that the world hate thee gratis? If thou no wise huttest any one, and art still hated: for this is gratis, without cause. ...

9. "O God, Thou hast known mine improvidence" (ver. 5). Again out of the mouth of the Body. For what improvidence is there in Christ? Is He not Himself the Virtue of God, and the Wisdom of God? Doth He call this His improvidence, whereof the Apostle speaketh, "the foolishness of God is wiser than men"? Mine improvidence, that very thing which in Me they derided that seem to themselves to be wise, Thou hast known why it was done. For what was so much like improvidence, as, when He had it in His power with one word to lay low the persecutors, to suffer Himself to be held, scourged, spit upon, buffeted, with thorns to be crowned, to the tree to be nailed? It is like improvidence, it seemeth a foolish thing; but this foolish thing excelleth all wise men. Foolish indeed it is: but even when grain falleth into the earth, if no one knoweth the custom of husbandmen, it seemeth foolish. ... Improvidence it appeareth; but hope maketh it not to be improvidence. He then spared not Himself: because even the Father

spared Him not, but delivered Him up for us all. And of the Same, "Who loved me," saith the Apostle, "and delivered up Himself for me:" for except a grain shall have fallen into the land so that it die, fruit, He saith, it will not yield. This is the improvidence. "And my transgressions from Thee are not concealed." It is plain, clear, open, that this must be perceived to be out of the mouth of the Body. Transgressions none had Christ: He was the bearer of transgressions, but not the committer. "Are not concealed:" that is, I have confessed to Thee, all my transgressions, and before my mouth Thou hast seen them in my thought, hast seen the wounds which Thou wast to heal. But where? Even in the Body, in the members: in those believers out of whom there was now cleaving to Him that member, who was confessing his sins.

10. "Let them not blush in Me, that wait for Thee, O Lord, Lord of virtues" (ver. 6). Again, the voice of the Head, "Let them not blush in Me:" let it not be said to them, Where is He on whom ye were relying? Let it not be said to them, Where is He that was saying to you, Believe yet God, and in Me believe? "Let them not blush in Me, that wait for Thee," O Lord, Lord of virtues. Let them not be confounded concerning Me, that seek Thee, O God of Israel." This also may be understood of the Body, but only if thou consider the Body of Him not one man: for in truth one man is not the Body of Him, but a small member, but the Body is made up of members. Therefore the full Body of Him is the whole Church. With reason then saith the Church, "Let them not blush in Me, that wait for Thee, O Lord, Lord of virtues." ...

11. "For because of Thee I have sustained upbraiding, shamelessness hath covered my face" (ver. 7). No great thing is that which is spoken of in "I have sustained:" but that which is spoken of in "for Thy sake I have sustained," is. For if thou sustainest because thou hast sinned; for thine own sake thou sustainest, not for the sake of God. For to you what glory is there, saith Peter, if sinning ye are punished, and ye bear it? But if thou sustainest because thou hast kept the commandment of God, truly for the sake of God thou sustainest; and thy reward remaineth for everlasting, because for the sake of God thou hast sustained revilings. For to this end He first sustained in order that we might learn to sustain. ..."Shamelessness hath covered my face." Shamelessness is what? Not to be confused. Lastly, it seemeth to be as it were a fault, when we say, the man is shameless. Great is the shamelessness of the man, that he doth not blush. Therefore shamelessness is a kind of folly. A Christian ought to have this shamelessness, when he cometh among men to whom Christ is an offence. If he shall have blushed because of Christ, he will be blotted out from the book of the living. Thou must needs therefore have shamelessness when Thou art reviled because of Christ; when they

say, Worshipper of the Crucified, adorer of Him that died ill, venerator of Him that was slain! here if thou shalt blush thou art a dead man. For see the sentence of Him that deceiveth no one. "He that shall have been ashamed of Me before men, I will also be ashamed of him before the Angels of God." Watch therefore thyself whether there be in thee shamelessness; be thou boldfaced, when thou hearest a reproach concerning Christ; yea be boldfaced. Why fearest thou for thy forehead which thou hast armed with the sign of the Cross? ...

12. "An alien I have become to My brethren, and a stranger to the sons of My mother" (ver. 8). To the sons of the Synagogue He became a stranger. ... Why so? Why did they not acknowledge? Why did they call Him an alien? Why did they dare to say, we know not whence He is? "Because the zeal of Thine House hath eaten Me up:" that is, because I have persecuted in them their own iniquities, because I have not patiently borne those whom I have rebuked, because I have sought Thy glory in Thy House, because I have scourged them that in the Temple dealt unseemly: in which place also there is quoted, "the zeal of Thine House hath eaten Me up." Hence an alien, hence a Stranger; hence, we know not whence He is. They would have acknowledged whence I am, if they had acknowledged that which Thou hast commanded. For if I had found them keeping Thy commandments, the zeal of Thine House would not have eaten Me up. "And the reproaches of men reproaching Thee haven fallen upon Me." Of this testimony Paul the Apostle hath also made use (there hath been read but now the very lesson), and saith, "Whatsoever things aforetime have been written, have been written that we might be instructed." ... Why "Thee"? Is the Father reproached, and not Christ Himself? Why have "the reproaches of men reproaching Thee fallen upon Me"? Because, "he that hath known Me, hath known the Father also:" because no one hath reviled Christ without reviling God: because no one honoureth the Father, except he that honoureth the Son also.

13. "And I have covered in fasting My Soul, and it became to Me for a reviling" (ver. 10). His fasting was, when there fell away all they that had believed in Him; because also it was His hunger, that men should believe in Him: because also it was His thirst, when He said to the woman, I thirst, "give Me to drink:" yea for her faith He was thirsting. And from the Cross when He was saying, "I thirst," He was seeking the faith of them for whom He had said, "Father, forgive them, for they know not what they do." But what did those men give to drink to Him thirsty? Vinegar. Vinegar is also called old. With reason of the old man they gave to drink, because they willed not to be new. Why willed they not to become new? Because to the title of this Psalm whereon is written, "For them that shall be changed," they belonged not. Therefore, "I have covered in fasting My Soul." Lastly, He put from

Him even the gall which they offered: He chose rather to fast than to accept bitterness. For they enter not into His Body that are embittered, whereof in another place a Psalm saith, "They that are embittered shall not be exalted in themselves." Therefore, "I have covered in fasting My Soul: and it became to Me for a reviling." This very thing became to Me for a reviling, that I consented not to them, that is, from them I fasted. For he that consenteth not to men seducing to evil, fasteth from them; and through this fasting earneth reviling, so that he is upbraided because he consenteth not to the evil thing.

14. "And I have set sackcloth my garment" (ver. 11). Already before we have said something of the sackcloth, from whence there is this, "But I, when they were troubling Me, was covering myself with sackcloth, and was humbling My Soul in fasting. I have set sackcloth for My garment:" that is, have set against them My flesh, on which to spend their rage, I have concealed My divinity. "Sackcloth," because mortal the flesh was: in order that by sin He might condemn sin in the flesh. "And I have set sackcloth my garment: and I have been made to them for a parable," that is, for a derision. It is called a parable, whenever a comparison is made concerning some one, when he is evil spoken of. "So may this man perish," for example, "as that man did," is a parable: that is, a comparison and likeness in cursing. "I have been made to them," then, "for a parable."

15. "Against Me were reviling they that were sitting in the gate" (ver. 12). "In the gate" is nothing else but in public. "And against Me they were chanting, they that were drinking wine." Do ye think, brethren, that this hath befallen Christ alone? Daily to Him in His members it happeneth: whenever perchance it is necessary for the servant of God to forbid excess of wine and luxuries in any village or town, where there hath not been heard the Word of God, it is not enough that they sing, nay more even against him they begin to sing, by whom they are forbidden to sing. Compare ye now His fasting and their wine.

16. "But I with My prayer with Thee, O Lord" (ver. 13). But I was with Thee. But how? With Thee by praying. For when thou art evil spoken of, and knowest not what thou mayest do; when at thee are hurled reproaches, and thou findest not any way of rebuking him by whom they are hurled; nothing remaineth for thee but to pray. But remember even for that very man to pray. "But I with my prayer with Thee, O Lord. It is the time of Thy good pleasure, O God." For behold the grain is being buried, there shall spring up fruit. "It is the time of Thy good pleasure, O God." Of this time even the Prophets have spoken, whereof the Apostle maketh mention: "Behold now the time acceptable, behold now the day of salvation." "It is the time of Thy good pleasure, O God. In the multitude of Thy mercy." This is the

time of good pleasure, "in the multitude of Thy mercy." For if there were not a multitude of Thy mercy, what should we do for the multitude of our iniquity? "In the multitude of Thy mercy; Hearken to me in the truth of Thy Salvation." Because He hath said, "of Thy mercy," he hath added truth also: for "mercy and truth" are all the ways of the Lord. Why mercy? In forgiving sins. Why truth? In fulfilling the promises.

17. "Save Thou Me from the mire, that I may not stick" (ver. 14). From that whereof above he had spoken, "Fixed I am in the clay of the deep, and there is no substance." Furthermore, since ye have duly received the exposition of that expression, in this place there is nothing further for you to hear particularly. From hence he saith that he must be delivered, wherein before he said that he was fixed: "Save Thou Me from the mire, that I may not stick." And he explaineth this himself: "Let Me be rescued from them that hate Me." They were themselves therefore the clay wherein he had stuck. But the following perchance suggesteth itself. A little before he had said, Fixed I am; now he saith, Save Thou Me from the mire, that I may not stick:" whereas after the meaning of what was said before he ought to have said, Save Thou Me from the mire where I had stuck, by rescuing Me, not by causing that I stick not. Therefore He had stuck in flesh, but had not stuck in spirit. He saith this, because of the infirmity of His members. Whenever perchance thou art seized by one that urgeth thee to iniquity, thy body indeed is taken, in regard to the body thou art fixed in the clay of the deep: but so long as thou consentest not, thou hast not stuck; but if thou consentest, thou hast stuck. Let then thy prayer be in that place, in order that as thy body is now held, so thy soul may not be held, so thou mayest be free in bonds.

18. "Let not the tempest of waters drown Me" (ver. 15). But already he had been drowned. "I have come into the depth of the sea," thou hast said, and "the tempest hath drowned Me," thou hast said. It hath drowned after the flesh, let it not drown after the Spirit. They to whom was said, If they shall have persecuted you in one city, flee ye into another; had this said to them, that neither in flesh they should stick, nor in spirit. For we must not desire to stick even in flesh; but as far as we are able we ought to avoid it. But if we shall have stuck, and shall have fallen into the hands of sinners: then in body we have stuck, we are fixed in the clay of the deep, it remaineth to entreat for the soul that we stick not, that is, that we consent not, that the tempest of water drown us not, so that we go into the deep of the clay. "Neither let the deep swallow Me, nor the pit close her mouth upon Me." What is this, brethren? What hath he prayed against? Great is the pit of the depth of human iniquity: every one, if he shall have fallen into it, will fall into the deep. But yet if a man being there placed confesseth his sins to his God, the pit will not shut her

mouth upon him: as is written in another Psalm, "From the depths I have cried to Thee, O Lord; Lord, hearken unto my voice." But if there is done in him that which another passage of Scripture saith, "When a sinner shall have come into the depth of evil things, he will despise," upon him the pit hath shut her mouth. Why hath she shut her mouth? Because she hath shut his mouth. He hath lost confession, really dead he is, and there is fulfilled in him that which elsewhere is spoken of," From a dead man, as from one that is not, there perisheth confession."...

19. "Hearken unto me, O Lord, for sweet is Thy mercy" (ver. 16). He hath given this as a reason why He ought to be hearkened unto, because sweet is the mercy of God. ... To a man set in trouble the mercy of God must needs be sweet. Concerning this sweetness of the mercy of God see ye what in another place the Scripture saith: "Like rain in drought, so beautiful is the mercy of God in trouble." That which there he saith to be "beautiful," the same he saith here to be "sweet." Not even bread would be sweet, unless hunger had preceded. Therefore even when the Lord permitteth or causeth us to be in any trouble, even then He is merciful: for He doth not withdraw nourishment, but stirreth up longing. Accordingly what saith he now, "Hearken to me, O Lord, for sweet is Thy mercy"? Now do not Thou defer hearkening, in so great trouble I am, that sweet to me is Thy mercy. For to this end Thou didst defer to succour, in order that to me that wherewith Thou didst succour might be sweet: but now no longer is there cause why Thou must defer; my trouble hath arrived at the appointed measure of distress, let Thy mercy come to do the work of goodness. "After the multitude of Thy pities have regard unto me:" not after the multitude of my sins.

20. "Turn not away Thy face from Thy child" (ver. 17). And this is a commending of humility; "from Thy child," that is, "from Thy little one:" because now I have been rid of pride through the discipline of tribulation, "turn not away Thy face from Thy child." This is that beautiful mercy of God, whereof he spake above. For in the following verse he explaineth that whereof he spake: "For I am troubled, speedily hearken Thou unto me." What is "speedily"? Now there is no cause why Thou must defer it: I am troubled, my affliction hath gone before; let Thy mercy follow.

21. "Give heed to my soul, and redeem her," doth need no exposition: let us see therefore what followeth. "Because of mine enemies deliver me" (ver. 18). This petition is evidently wonderful, neither briefly to be touched upon, nor hastily to be skipped over; truly wonderful: "Because of mine enemies deliver me." What is, "Because of mine enemies deliver me"? ... I see no reason for this petition,

"Because of mine enemies deliver me:" unless we understand it of something else, which when I shall have spoken by the help of the Lord, He shall judge in you, that dwelleth in you. There is a kind of secret deliverance of holy men: this for their own sakes is made. There is one public and evident: this is made because of their enemies, either for their punishment, or for their deliverance. For truly God delivered not the brothers in the book of Maccabees from the fires of the persecutor. ... But again the Three Children openly were delivered from the furnace of fire; because their body also was rescued, their safety was public. The former were in secret crowned, the latter openly delivered: all however saved. ... There is then a secret deliverance, there is an open deliverance. Secret deliverance doth belong to the soul, open deliverance to the body as well. For in secret the soul is delivered, openly the body. Again, if so it be, in this Psalm the voice of the Lord let us acknowledge: to the secret deliverance doth belong that whereof he spake above," Give heed to my soul, and redeem her." There remaineth the body's deliverance: for on His arising and ascending into the Heavens, and sending the Holy Ghost from above, there were converted to His faith they that at His death did rage, and out of enemies they were made friends through His grace, not through their righteousness. Therefore he hath continued, "Because of mine enemies deliver me. Give heed to my soul," but this in secret: but "because of mine enemies deliver" even my body. For mine enemies it will profit nothing if soul alone Thou shalt have delivered; that they have done something, that they have accomplished something, they will believe. "What profit is there in my blood, while I go down into corruption?" Therefore "give heed to my soul, and redeem her," which Thou alone knowest: secondly also, "because of mine enemies deliver me," that my flesh may not see corruption.

22. "Thou knowest my reproach, and my confusion, and my shame" (yet. 19). What is reproach? What is confusion? What shame? Reproach is that which the enemy casteth in the teeth. Confusion is that which gnaweth the conscience. Shame is that which causeth even a noble brow to blush, because of the upbraiding with a pretended crime. There is no crime; or even if there is a crime, it doth not belong to him, against whom it is alleged: but yet the infirmity of the human mind ofttimes is made ashamed even when a pretended crime is alleged; not because it is alleged, but because it is believed. All these things are in the Body of the Lord. For confusion in Him could not be, in whom guilt was not found. There was alleged as a crime against Christians, the very fact that they were Christians. That indeed was glory: the brave gladly received it, and so received it as that they blushed not at all for the Lord's name. For fearlessness had covered the face of them, having the effrontery of Paul, saying, "for I blush not because of the Gospel: for the virtue of God it is for salvation to every one believing." O Paul, art not thou a venerator of the Crucified? Little it is, he saith, for me not to blush for it: nay,

therein alone I glory, wherefore the enemy thinketh me to blush. "But from me far be it to glory, save in the Cross of Jesus Christ, through whom to me the world is crucified, and I to the world." At such a brow as this then reproach alone could be hurled. For neither could there be confusion in a conscience already made whole, nor shame in a brow so free. But when it was being alleged against certain that they had slain Christ, deservedly they were pricked through with evil conscience, and to their health confounded and converted, so that they could say, "Thou hast known my confusion." Thou therefore, O Lord, hast known not only my reproach but also my confusion, in certain shame also: who, though in me they believe, publicly blush to confess me before ungodly men, human tongue having more influence with them than promise divine. Behold ye therefore them: even such are commended to God, not that so He may leave them, but that by aiding them He may make them perfect. For a certain man believing and wavering hath said, "I believe, O Lord, help Thou mine unbelief."

23. "In Thy sight are all they that trouble Me" (ver. 20). Why I have reproach, Thou knowest; why confusion, "Thou knowest; why shame, Thou knowest: therefore deliver Thou me because of mine enemies, because Thou knowest these things of me, they know not; and thus, because they are themselves in Thy sight, not knowing these things, they will not be able to be either confounded or corrected, unless openly Thou shalt have delivered me because of mine enemies. "Reproach my heart hath expected, and misery." What is, "hath expected"? Hath foreseen these things as going to be, hath foretold them as going to be. For He came not for any other purpose. If He had been unwilling to die, neither would He have willed to be born: for the sake of resurrection He did both. For there were two particular things known to us among mankind, but one thing unknown. For we knew that men were born and died: that they rose again and lived for everlasting we knew not. That He might show to us that which we knew not, He took upon Him the two things which we knew. To this end therefore He came. "Reproach my heart hath expected and misery." But the misery of whom? For He expected misery, but rather of the crucifiers, rather of the persecutors, that in them should be misery, in Him mercy. For pitying the misery of them even while hanging on the Cross, He saith, "Father, forgive them, for they know not what they do." What then did it profit, that I expected? That is, what did it profit that I foretold? What did it profit that I said to this end I had come? I came to fulfil that which I said, "I waited for one that together should be made sorrowful, and there was not; and men comforting, and I found not:" that is, there was none. For that which in the former verse He said, "I waited for one that together should be made sorrowful," the same is in the following verse, "and men comforting." But that which in the former verse is, "and there was not;" the same in the following verse is, "and I found not." Therefore another sentence is not added, but the former is repeated. Which

sentence if we reconsider, a question may arise. For were His disciples nowise made sorrowful when He was led to the Passion, when on the tree hanged, when dead? So much were they made sorrowful, that Mary Magdalene, who first saw Him, rejoicing told them as they were mourning what she had seen. The Gospel speaketh of these things: it is not our presumption, not our suspicion: it is evident that the disciples grieved, it is evident that they mourned. Strange women were weeping, when to the Passion He was being led, unto whom turning He saith, "Weep ye, but for yourselves, do not for Me." ... Peter certainly loved very much, and without hesitation threw himself to walk on the waves, and at the voice of the Lord he was delivered: and though following Him when led to the Passion, with the boldness of love, yet being troubled, thrice he denied Him. Whence, except because an evil thing it seemed to him to die? For he was shunning that which he thought an evil thing. This then even in the Lord he was lamenting, which he was himself shunning. On this account even before he had said, "Far be it from Thee, O Lord, merciful be Thou to Thyself: there shall not come to pass this thing:" at which time he merited to hear, "Satan;" after that he had heard, "Blessed art thou, Simon Bar-Jona." Therefore in that sorrowfulness which the Lord felt because of those for whom He prayed, "Father, forgive them, for they know not what they do:" no companion He found. "And I waited for one that together should be made sorrowful, and there was not." There was not at all. "And men comforting, and I found not." Who are men comforting? Men profiting. For they comfort us, they are the comfort of all preachers of the Truth.

24. "And they gave for My food gall, and in My thirst they gave Me vinegar to drink" (ver. 22). This was done indeed to the letter. And the Gospel declareth this to us. But we must understand, brethren, that the very fact that I found not comforters, that the very fact that I found not one that together should be made sorrowful, this was My gall, this to Me was bitter, this was vinegar: bitter because of grief, vinegar because of their old man. For we read, that to Him indeed gall was offered, as the Gospel speaketh; but for drink, not for food. Nevertheless, we must so take and consider that when fulfilled, which here had been before predicted, "They gave for My food gall:" and in that very action, not only in this saying, we ought to seek for a mystery, at secret things to knock, to enter the rent veil of the Temple, to see there a Sacrament, both in what there hath been said and in what there hath been done. "They gave," He saith, "for My food gall:" not the thing itself which they gave was food, for it was drink: but "for food they gave it." Because already the Lord had taken food, and into it there had been thrown gall. But He had taken Himself pleasant food, when He ate the Passover with His disciples: therein He showed the Sacrament of His Body. Unto this food so pleasant, so sweet, of the Unity of Christ, of which the Apostle maketh mention, saying, "For one bread, One Body, being many we are;" unto this pleasant food

who is there that addeth gall, except the gainsayers of the Gospel, like those persecutors of Christ? For less the Jews sinned in crucifying Him walking on earth, than they that despise Him sitting in Heaven. That which then the Jews did, in giving above the food which He had already taken that bitter draught to drink, the same they do that by evil living bring scandal upon the Church: the same do embittered heretics, "But let them not be exalted in their own selves." They give gall after so delectable meat. But what doth the Lord? He admitteth them not to His Body. In this mystery, when they presented gall, the Lord Himself tasted, and would not drink. If we did not suffer them, neither at all should we taste: but because it is necessary to suffer them, we must needs taste. But because in the members of Christ such sort cannot be, they can be tasted, received into the Body they cannot be. "And they gave for My food gall, and in My thirst they gave Me vinegar to drink." I was thirsting, and vinegar I received: that is, for the faith of them I longed, and I found oldness.

25. "Let the table of them be made in their own presence for a trap" (ver. 23). Like the trap which for Me they set, in giving Me such a draught, let such a trap be for them. Why then, "in their own presence"? "Let the table of them be made for a trap," would have been sufficient. They are such as know their iniquity, and in it most obstinately do persevere: in their own presence there is made a trap for them. These are they that, being too destructive, "go down into Hell alive." Lastly, of persecutors what hath been said? Except that the Lord were in us, perchance alive they had swallowed us up. What is alive? Consenting to them, and knowing that we ought not to consent to them. Therefore in their own presence there is made a trap, and they are not amended. Even though in their own presence there is a trap, let them not fall into it. Behold they know the trap, and thrust out foot, and bow their necks to be caught. How much better were it to turn away from the trap, to acknowledge sin, to condemn error, to be rid of bitterness, to pass over into the Body of Christ, to seek the Lord's glory! But so much prevaileth presumption of mind, that even in their own presence the trap is, and they fall into it. "Let the eyes of them be darkened, that they see not," followeth here: that whereas without benefit they have seen, it may chance to them even not to see. "Let the table of them," therefore, "be made in their own presence for a trap." It is not from one wishing, but from one prophesying: not in order that it may come to pass, but because it will come to pass. This we have often remarked, and ye ought to remember it: lest that which the prescient mind saith in the Spirit of God, it should seem with ill will to imprecate. ... Let it then be done to them, "both for a requital and for a stumbling-block." And is this by any means unjust? It is just. Why? For it is "for a requital." For not anything would happen to them, which was not owed. "For a requital" it is done, "and for a stumbling-block:" for they are themselves a stumbling-block to themselves. "Let the eyes of them be darkened, that they see

not, and the back of them alway bow Thou down" (ver. 24). This is a consequence. For they, whose eyes have been darkened that they see not, it followeth, must have their back bowed down. How so? Because when they have ceased to take knowledge of things above, they must needs think of things below. He that well heareth, "lift up the heart," a bowed back hath not. For with stature erect he looketh for the hope laid up for him in Heaven; most especially if he send before him his treasure, whither his heart followeth. But, on the other hand, they perceive not the hope of future life; already being blinded, they think of things below: and this is to have a bowed back: from which disorder the Lord delivered that woman. For Satan hath bound her eighteen years, and her that was bowed down He raised up: and because on the Sabbath He did it, the Jews were scandalized; suitably were they scandalized at her being raised up, themselves being bowed. "Pour forth upon them Thine anger, and let; the indignation of Thine anger overtake them" (ver. 25), are plain words: but nevertheless, in "overtake them" we perceive them as it were fleeing. But whither are they to flee? Into Heaven? Thou art there. Into Hell? Thou art present. Their wings they will not take to fly straight: "Let the indignation of Thine anger overtake them," let it not permit them to escape.

26. "Let the habitation of them become forsaken" (ver. 26). This is now evident. For in the same manner as He hath mentioned not only a secret deliverance of His, saying, "Give heed to My soul, and redeem her;" but also one open after the body, adding, "because of mine enemies deliver me:" so also to these men He foretelleth how there are to be certain secret misfortunes, whereof a little before He was speaking. ... For the blindness of the Jews was secret vengeance: but the open was what? "Let their habitation become forsaken, and in their tabernacles let there not be any one to inhabit." There hath come to pass this thing in the very city Jerusalem, wherein they thought themselves mighty in crying against the Son of God, "Crucify, Crucify;" and in prevailing because they were able to kill Him that raised dead men. How mighty to themselves, how great, they seemed! There followed afterwards the vengeance of the Lord, stormed was the city, utterly conquered the Jews, slain were I know not how many thousands of men. No one of the Jews is permitted to come thither now: where they were able to cry against the Lord, there by the Lord they are not permitted to dwell. They have lost the place of their fury: and O that even now they would know the place of their rest! What profit to them was Caiaphas in saying," "If we shall have let go this man thus, there will come the Romans, and take away from us both place and kingdom"? Behold, both they did not let Him go alive, and He liveth: and there have come the Romans, and have taken from them both place and kingdom. But now we heard, when the Gospel was being read, "Jerusalem, Jerusalem, how often would I have gathered together thy sons, as a hen her chickens under her wings, and thou wouldest not? Behold there is left to you your house forsaken."

27. Why so? "For Him whom Thou hast smitten they have themselves persecuted, and upon the pain of my wounds they have added" (ver. 27). How then have they sinned if they have persecuted one by God smitten? What sin is ascribed to their mind? Malice. For the thing was done in Christ which was to be. To suffer indeed He had come, and He punished him through whom He suffered. For Judas the traitor was punished, and Christ was crucified: but us He redeemed by His blood, and He punished him in the matter of his price. For he threw down the price of silver, for which by him the Lord had been sold; and he knew not the price wherewith he had himself by the Lord been redeemed. This thing was done in the case of Judas. But when we see that there is a sort of measure of requital in all men, and that not any one can be suffered to rage more than he hath received power to do: how have they "added," or what is that smiting of the Lord? Without doubt He is speaking in the person of him from whom He had received a body, from whom He had taken unto Him flesh, that is in the person of mankind, of Adam himself who was smitten with the first death because of his sin. Mortal therefore here are men born, as born with their punishment: to this punishment they add, whosoever do persecute men. For now here man would not have had to die, unless God had smitten him. Why then dost thou, O man, rage more than this? Is it little for a man that some time he is to die? Each one of us therefore beareth his punishment: to this punishment they would add that persecute us. This punishment is the smiting of the Lord. For the Lord smote man with the sentence: "What day ye shall have touched it," He saith, "with death ye shall die." Out of this death He had taken upon Him flesh, and our old man hath been crucified together with Him. By the voice of that man He hath said these words, "Him whom Thou hast smitten they have themselves persecuted, and upon the pain of My wounds they have added." Upon what pain of wounds? Upon the pain of sins they have themselves added. For sins He hath called His wounds. But do not look to the Head, consider the Body; according to the voice whereof hath been said by the Same in that Psalm, wherein He showed there was His voice, because in the first verse thereof He cried from the Cross, "God, My God, look upon Me, why hast Thou forsaken Me?" There in continuation He saith, "Afar from My safety are the words of Mine offences." ...

28. "Lay Thou iniquity upon their iniquity" (ver. 28). What is this? Who would not be afraid? To God is said, "Lay Thou iniquity upon their iniquity." Whence shall God lay iniquity? For hath He iniquity to lay? For we know that to be true which hath been spoken through Paul the Apostle, "What then shall we say? Is there anywise iniquity with God? Far be it." Whence then, "Lay Thou iniquity upon iniquity"? How must we understand this? May the Lord be with us, that we may speak, and because of your weariness may be able to speak briefly. Their iniquity was that they killed a just Man: there was added another, that they crucified the

Son of God. Their raging was as though against a man: but "if they had known, the Lord of Glory they had never crucified." They with their own iniquity willed to kill as it were a man: there was laid iniquity upon their own iniquity, so that the Son of God they should crucify. Who laid this iniquity upon them? He that said, "Perchance they will reverence My Son," Him I will send. For they were wont to kill servants sent to them, to demand rent and profit. He sent the Son Himself, in order that Him also they might kill. He laid iniquity upon their own iniquity. And these things did God do in wrath, or rather in just requital? For, "May it be done to them," He saith, "for a requital and for a stumbling-block." They had deserved to be so blinded as not to know the Son of God. And this God did, laying iniquity upon their iniquity; not in wounding, but in not making whole. For in like manner as thou increasest a fever, increasest a disorder, not by adding disorder, but by not relieving: so because they were of such sort as that they merited not to be healed, in their very naughtiness in a manner they advanced; as it is said, "But evil men and wicked doers advance for the worse:" and iniquity is laid upon their own iniquity. "And let them not enter in Thy righteousness." This is a plain thing.

29. "Let them be blotted out from the book of the living" (ver. 29). For had they been some time written therein? Brethren, we must not so take it, as that God writeth any one in the book of life, and blotteth him out. If a man said, "What I have written I have written," concerning the title where it had been written, "King of the Jews:" doth God write any one, and blot him out? He foreknoweth, He hath predestined all before the foundation of the world that are to reign with His Son in life everlasting. These He hath written down, these same the Book of Life doth contain. Lastly, in the Apocalypse, what saith the Spirit of God, when the same Scripture was speaking of the oppressions that should be from Antichrist? "There shall give consent to him all they that have not been written in the book of life." So then without doubt they will not consent that have been written. How then are these men blotted out from that book wherein they were never written? This hath been said according to their own hope, because they thought of themselves that they were written. What is, "let them be blotted out from the book of life"? Even to themselves let it be evident, that they were not there. By this method of speaking hath been said in another Psalm, "There shall fall from Thy side a thousand, and tens of thousands from on Thy right hand:" that is, many men shall be offended, even out of that number who thought that they would sit with Thee, even out of that number who thought that they would stand at Thy right hand, being severed from the left-hand goats: not that when any one hath there stood, he shall afterwards fall, or when any one with Him hath sat, he shall be cast away; but that many men were to fall into scandal, who already thought themselves to be there, that is, many that thought that they would sit with Thee, many that hoped that they would stand at the right hand, will themselves fall. So then here also they

that hoped as though by the merit of their own righteousness themselves to have been written in the book of God, they to whom is said, "Search the Scriptures, wherein ye think yourselves to have life eternal:" when their condemnation shall have been brought even to their own knowledge, shall be effaced from the book of the living, they shall know themselves not to be there. For the verse which followeth explaineth what hath been said: "And with just men let them not be written." I have said then "Let them be effaced," according to their hope but according to Thy justice I say what?

30. "Poor and sorrowful I am" (ver. 30). Why this? Is it that we may acknowledge that through bitterness of soul this poor One doth speak evil? For He hath spoken of many things to happen to them. And as if we were saying to Him, "Why such things?"—"Nay, not so much!" He answereth, "poor and sorrowful I am." They have brought Me to want, unto this sorrow they have set Me down, therefore I say these words. It is not, however, the indignation of one cursing, but the prediction of one prophesying. For He was intending to recommend to us certain things which hereafter He saith of His poverty and His sorrow, in order that we may learn to be poor and sorrowful. For, "Blessed are the poor, for theirs is the kingdom of Heaven." And," Blessed are they that mourn, for they shall be comforted." This therefore He doth Himself before now show to us: and so, "poor and sorrowful I am." The whole Body of Him saith this. The Body of Christ in this earth is poor and sorrowful. But let Christians be rich. Truly if Christians they are, they are poor; in comparison with the riches celestial for which they hope, all their gold they count for sand. "And the health of Thy countenance, O God, hath taken Me up." Is this poor One anywise forsaken? When dost thou deign to bring near to thy table a poor man in rags? But again, this poor One the health of the countenance of God hath taken up: in His countenance He hath hidden His need. For of Him hath been said, "Thou shalt hide them in the hiding place of Thy countenance." But in that countenance what riches there are would ye know? Riches here give thee this advantage, that thou mayest dine on what thou wilt, whenever thou wilt: but those riches, that thou mayest never hunger. "The health of Thy countenance, O God, hath taken Me up." For what purpose? In order that no longer I may be poor, no longer sorrowful? "I will praise the name of the Lord with a song, I will magnify Him in praise" (ver. 31). Now it hath been said, this poor One praiseth the name of the Lord with a song, he magnifieth Him in praise. When would He have ventured to sing, unless He had been refreshed from hunger? "I will magnify Him with praise." O vast riches! What jewels of God's praise hath he brought out of his inward treasures! These are my riches! "The Lord hath given, the Lord hath taken away." Then miserable he hath remained? Far be it. See the riches: "As it hath pleased the Lord, so hath been done, be the name of the Lord blessed."

31. "And it shall please God:" that I shall praise Him, shall please: "above a new calf, bearing horns and hoofs." More grateful to Him shall be the sacrifice of praise than the sacrifice of a calf. "The sacrifice of praise shall glorify me." "Immolate to God the sacrifice of praise." So then His praise going forth from my mouth shall please God more than a great victim led up to His altar. ... Therefore above this calf my praising shall please Thee, such as hereafter will be, after poverty and sorrow, in the eternal society of Angels, where neither adversary there shall be in battle to be tossed, nor sluggard from earth to be stirred up. "Let the needy see and rejoice" (ver. 32). Let them believe, and in hope be glad. Let them be more needy, in order that they may deserve to be filled: lest while they belch out pride's satiety, there be denied them the bread whereon they may healthily live. "Seek the Lord," ye needy, hunger ye and thirst; for He is Himself the living bread that came down from Heaven. "Seek ye the Lord, and your soul shall live." Ye seek bread, that your flesh may live: the Lord seek ye, that your soul may live.

32. "For the Lord hath hearkened to the poor" (ver. 33). He hath hearkened to the poor, and He would not have hearkened to the poor, unless they were poor. Wilt thou be hearkened to? Poor be thou: let sorrow cry out from thee, and not fastidiousness. "And His fettered ones He hath not despised." Being offended at His servants, He hath put them in fetters: but them crying from the fetters He hath not despised. What are these fetters? Mortality, the corruptibleness of the flesh are the fetters wherewith we have been bound. And would ye know the weight of these fetters? Of them is said, "The body which is corrupted weigheth down the soul." Whenever men in the world will to be rich, for these fetters they are seeking rags. But let the rags of the fetters suffice: seek so much as is necessary for keeping off want, but when thou seekest superfluities, thou longest to load thy fetters. In such a prison then let the fetters abide even alone. "Sufficient for the day be the evil thereof." "Let there praise Him heavens and earth, sea and all things creeping in them" (ver. 34). The true riches of this poor man are these, to consider the creation, and to praise the Creator. "Let there praise Him heavens and earth, sea and all things creeping therein." And doth this creation alone praise God, when by considering of it God is praised?

33. Hear thou another thing also: "for God shall save Sion" (ver. 35). He restoreth His Church, the faithful Gentiles He doth incorporate with His Only-Begotten; He beguileth not them that believe in Him of the reward of His promise. "For God shall save Sion; and there shall be builded the cities of Juda." These same are the Churches. Let no one say, when shall it come to pass that there be builded the cities of Juda? O that thou wouldest acknowledge the Edifice, and be a living stone, that thou mightest enter into Her. Even now the cities of Juda are being

built. For Juda is interpreted confession. By confession of humility there are being builded the cities of Juda: in order that there may remain without the proud, who blush to confess. "For God shall save Sion." What Sion? Hear in the following words: "and the seed of His servants shall possess Her, and they that love His name shall dwell therein" (ver. 36). ...

PSALM LXX.

1. Thanks to the "Corn of wheat," because He willed to die and to be multiplied: thanks to the only Son of God, our Lord and Saviour Jesus Christ, who disdained not to undergo our death, in order that He might make us worthy of His life. Behold Him that was single until He went hence; as He said in another Psalm, "Single I am until I go hence;" for He was a single corn of wheat in such sort as that He had in Himself a great fruitfulness of increase; in how many corns imitating the Passion of Him we exult, when we celebrate the nativities of the Martyrs! Many therefore members of Him, under one Head our Saviour Himself, being bound together in the bond of love and peace (as ye judge it fit that ye know, for ye have often heard), are one man: and of the same, as of one man, the voice is ofttimes heard, in the Psalms, and thus one crieth as though it were all, because all in one are one. ...

2. There is then in this Psalm the voice of men troubled, and so indeed of Martyrs amid sufferings in peril, but relying on their own Head. Let us hear them, and speak with them out of sympathy of heart, though it be not with similarity of suffering. For they are already crowned, we are still in peril: not that such sort of persecutions do vex us as have vexed them, but worse perchance in the midsts of all kinds of so great scandals. For our own times do more abound in that woe, which the Lord cried: "Woe to the world because of scandals." And," Because iniquity hath abounded, the love of man shall wax cold." For not even that holy Lot at Sodom suffered corporal persecution from any one, or had it been told him that he should not dwell there: the persecution of him were the evil doings of the Sodomites. Now then that Christ sitteth in Heaven, now that He is glorified, now that necks of kings are made subject to His yoke, and their brows placed beneath His sign, now that not any one remaineth to dare openly to trample upon Christians, still, however, we groan amid instruments and singers, still those enemies of the Martyrs, because with words and steel they have no power, with their own wantonness do persecute them. And O that we were sorrowing for Heathens alone: it would be some sort of comfort, to wait for those that not yet have been signed with the Cross of Christ; when they should be signed, and when, by His authority attached, they should cease to be mad. We see besides men wearing or their brow the sign of Him, at the same time on that same brow wearing the shamelessness of wantonness, and on the days and celebrations of the Martyrs not exulting but insulting. And amid these things we groan, and this is our persecution, if there is in us the love which saith, "Who is weak, and I am not weak? Who is scandalized, and I burn not?" Not any servant of God, then, is

without persecution: and that is a true saying which the Apostle saith, "But even all men that will to live godly in Christ, shall suffer persecution.".

3. "O God, to my aid make speed" (ver. 1). For need we have for an everlasting aid in this world. But when have we not? Now however being in tribulation, let us especially say, "O God, to my aid make speed." "Let them be confounded and fear that seek my soul." Christ is speaking: whether Head speak or whether Body speak; He is speaking that hath said, "Why persecutest thou Me?" He is speaking that hath said, "Inasmuch as ye have done it to one of the least of Mine, to Me ye have done it." The voice then of this Man is known to be of the whole man, of Head and of Body: that need not often be mentioned, because it is known. "Be they confounded," he saith, "and fear that seek my soul." In another Psalm He saith, "I was looking unto the right and saw, and there was not one that would know Me flight hath perished from Me, and there is not one to seek out My soul." There of persecutors He saith, that there was not one to seek out His soul: but here, "Let them be confounded and fear that seek My soul." ... And where is that which thou hast heard from thy Lord, "Love ye your enemies, do good to them that hate you, and pray for them that persecute you "? Behold thou sufferest persecution, and cursest them from whom thou sufferest: how dost thou imitate the Passions of thy Lord that have gone before, hanging on the cross and saying, "Father, forgive them, for they know not what they do." To persons saying such things the Martyr replieth and saith, thou hast set before me the Lord, saying, "Father, forgive them, for they know not what they do:" understand thou my voice also, in order that it may be thine too: for what have I said concerning mine enemies? "Let them be confounded and fear." Already such vengeance hath been taken on the enemies of the Martyrs. That Saul that persecuted Stephen, he was confounded and feared. He was breathing out slaughters, he was seeking some to drag and slay: a voice having been heard from above, "Saul, Saul, why persecutest thou Me," he was confounded and laid low, and he was raised up to obedience, that had been inflamed unto persecuting. This then the Martyrs desire for their enemies, "Let them be confounded and fear." For so long as they are not confounded and fear, they must needs defend their actions: glorious they think themselves, because they hold, because they bind, because they scourge, because they kill, because they dance, because they insult, and because of all these doings they be some time confounded and fear. For if they be confounded, they will also be converted: because converted they cannot be, unless they shall have been confounded and shall have feared. Let us then wish these things to our enemies, let us wish them without fear. Behold I have said, and let me have said it with you, may all that still dance and sing and insult the Martyrs "be confounded and fear :" at last within these walls confounded may they beat their breasts!

4. "Let them be turned away backward and blush that think evil things to me" (ver. 2). At first there was the assault of them persecuting, now there hath remained the malice of them thinking. In fact, there are in the Church distinct seasons of persecutions following one another. There was made an assault on the Church when kings were persecuting: and because kings had been foretold as to persecute and as to believe, when one had been fulfilled the other was to follow. There came to pass also that which was consequent; kings believed, peace was given to the Church, the Church began to be set in the highest place of dignity, even on this earth, even in this life: but there is not wanting the roar of persecutors, they have turned their assaults into thoughts. In these thoughts, as in a bottomless pit, the devil hath been bound," he roareth and breaketh not forth. For it hath been said concerning these times of the Church, "The sinner shall see, and shall be angry." And shall do what? That which he did at first? Drag, bind, smite? He doeth not this. What then? "With his teeth he shall gnash, and shall pine away." And with these men the Martyr is, as it were, angry, and yet for these men the Martyr prayeth. For in like manner as he hath wished well to those men concerning whom he hath said, "Let them be confounded and fear that seek nay soul:" so also now, "Let them be turned backward, and blush, that think evil things to me." Wherefore? In order that they may not go before, but follow. For he that censureth the Christian religion, and on his own system willeth to live, willeth as it were to go before Christ, as though He indeed had erred and had been weak and infirm, because He either willed to suffer or could suffer in the hands of the Jews; but that he is a clever man for guarding against all these things; in shunning death, even in basely lying to escape death, and slaying his soul that he may live in body, he thinketh himself a man of singular and prudent measures. He goeth before in censuring Christ, in a manner he outstrippeth Christ: let him believe in Christ, and follow Christ. For that which had been desired but now for persecutors thinking evil things, the same the Lord Himself said to Peter. Now in a certain place Peter willed to go before the Lord. ... A little before, "Blessed art thou, Simon Bar-Jona, for flesh and blood hath not revealed it to thee, but My Father which is in Heaven:" now in a moment, "Go back behind Me, Satan." What is, "Go back behind Me"? Follow Me. Thou wiliest to go before Me, thou wiliest to give Me counsel, it is better that thou follow My counsel: this is, "go back," go back behind Me. He is silencing one outstripping, in order that he may go backward; and He is calling him Satan, because he willeth to go before the Lord. A little before, "blessed;" now, "Satan." Whence a little before, "blessed"? Because, "to thee," He saith, "flesh and blood hath not revealed it, but My Father which is in Heaven." Whence now, "Satan"? Because "thou savourest not," He saith, "the things which are of God, but the things which are of men." Let us then that would duly celebrate the nativities of the Martyrs, long for the imitation of the Martyrs; let us not wish to go before the Martyrs, and think ourselves to be of better understanding than they, because we shun sufferings in behalf of righteousness and faith which they

shunned not. Therefore be they that think evil things, and in wantonness feed their hearts, "turned backward and blush." Let them hear from the Apostle afterwards saying, "But what fruit had ye some time in those things at which ye now blush?"

5. What followeth? "Let them be turned away forthwith blushing, that say to me, Well, well" (ver. 3). Two are the kinds of persecutors, revilers and flatterers. The tongue of the flatterer doth more persecute than the hand of the slayer: for this also the Scripture hath called a furnace. Truly when the Scripture was speaking of persecution, it said, "Like gold in a furnace it hath proved them" (speaking of Martyrs being slain), "and as the holocaust's victim it hath received them." Hear how even the tongue of flatterers is of such sort: "The proving," he saith, "of silver and of gold is fire; but a man is proved by the tongue of men praising him." That is fire, this also is fire: out of both thou oughtest to go forth safe. The censurer hath broken thee, thou hast been broken in the furnace like an earthen vessel. The Word hath moulded thee, and there hath come the trial of tribulation: that which hath been formed, must needs be seasoned; if it hath been well moulded, there hath come the fire to strengthen. Whence He said in the Passion, "Dried up like a potsherd hath been My virtue." For Passion and the furnace of tribulation had made Him stronger. ...

6. And what cometh to pass when they are all turned back and blush, whether it be they that seek my soul, or they that think evil things to me, or they that with perverse and feigned benevolence with tongue would soften the stroke which they inflict, when they shall have been themselves turned away and confounded; there shall come to pass what? "Let them exult and be joyous in Thee:" not in me, not in this man or in that man; but in whom they have been made light that were darkness. "Let them exult and be joyous in Thee, all that seek Thee" (ver. 4). One thing it is to seek God, another thing to seek man. "Let them be joyous that seek Thee." They shall not be joyous then that seek themselves, whom Thou hast first sought before they sought Thee. Not yet did that sheep seek the Shepherd, it had strayed from the flock, and He went down to it; He sought it, and carried it back upon His shoulders. Will He despise thee, O sheep, seeking Him, who hath first sought thee despising Him and not seeking Him? Now then begin thou to seek Him that first hath sought thee, and hath carried thee back on His shoulders. Do thou that which He speaketh of, "They that are My sheep hear My voice, and follow Me." If then thou seekest Him that first hath sought thee, and hast become a sheep of His, and thou hearest the voice of thy Shepherd, and followest Him; see what He showeth to thee of Himself, what of His Body, in order that as to Himself thou mayest not err, as to the Church thou mayest not err, that no one may say to thee, that is Christ which is not Christ, or that is the Church which is not the

Church. For many men have said that Christ had no flesh, and that Christ hath not risen in His Body: do not thou follow the voices of them. Hear thou the voice of Himself the Shepherd, that was clothed with flesh, in order that He might seek lost flesh. He hath risen again, and He saith, "Handle ye and see; for a spirit hath not flesh and bones as ye see Me have." He showeth Himself to thee, the voice of Him follow thou. He showeth also the Church, that no one may deceive thee by the name of Church. "It behoved," He saith, "Christ to suffer, and to rise again from the dead the third day, and that there should be preached repentance and remission of sins through all nations, beginning with Jerusalem." Thou hast the voice of Thy Shepherd, do not thou follow the voice of strangers: and a thief thou shalt not fear, if thou shalt have followed the voice of the Shepherd. But how shalt thou follow? If thou shalt neither have said to any man, as if it were by his own merit, Well, well: nor shalt have heard the same with joy, so that thy head be not made fat with the oil of a sinner. "Let all them exult and be joyous in Thee, that seek Thee; and let them say"—let them say what, that exult? "Be the Lord alway magnified!" Let all them say this, that exult and seek Thee. What? "Be the Lord alway magnified; yea, they that love Thy salvation." Not only, "Be the Lord magnified;" but also, "alway." ... A sinner thou art, be He magnified in order that He may call; thou confessest, be He magnified in order that He may forgive: now thou livest justly, be He magnified in order that He may direct: thou perseverest even unto the end, be He magnified in order that He may glorify. "Be the Lord," then, "alway magnified; yea, they love His saving health." For from Him they have salvation, not from themselves. The saving health of the Lord our God, is the Saviour our Lord Jesus Christ: whosoever loveth the Saviour, confesseth himself to have been made whole; whosoever confesseth himself to have been made whole, confesseth himself to have been sick. Not their own saving health, as if they could save themselves of themselves: not as it were the saving health of a man, as though by him they could be saved. "Do not," he saith, "confide in princes, and in the sons of men, in whom there is no safety." Why so? "Of the Lord is safety, and upon Thy people is Thy blessing."

7. Behold, "Be the Lord magnified:" wilt thou never, wilt thou nowhere? In Him was something, in me nothing: but if in Him is whatsoever I am, be He, not I. But thou then what? "But I am needy and poor" (ver. 5). He is rich, He abounding, He needing nothing. Behold my light, behold whence I am illumined; for I cry, "Thou shalt illumine my candle, O Lord." What then of thee? "But I am needy and poor." I am like an orphan, my soul is like a widow destitute and desolate: help I seek, alway mine infirmity I confess. There have been forgiven me my sins, now I have begun to follow the commandments of God: still, however, I am needy and poor. Why still needy and poor? Because "I see another law in my members fighting against the law of my mind." Why needy and poor? Because, "blessed are they

that hunger and thirst after righteousness." Still I hunger, still I thirst: my fulness hath been put off, not taken away. "O God, aid Thou me." Most suitably also Lazarus is said to be interpreted, "one aided:" that needy and poor man, that was transported into the bosom of Abraham; and beareth the type of the Church, which ought alway to confess that she hath need of aid. This is true, this is godly. "I have said to the Lord, My God Thou art." Why? "For my goods Thou needest not." He needeth not us, we need Him: therefore He is truly Lord. For thou art not the very true Lord of thy servant: both are men, both needing God. But if thou supposest thy servant to need thee, in order that thou mayest give him bread; thou also needest thy servant, in order that he may aid thy labours. Each one of you doth need the other. Therefore neither of you is truly lord, and neither of you truly servant. Hear thou the true Lord, of whom thou art the true servant: "I have said to the Lord, My God Thou art." Why art Thou Lord? "Because my goods Thou needest not"? But what of thee? "But I am needy and poor." Behold the needy and poor: may God feed, may God alleviate, may God aid: "O God," he saith, "aid Thou me."

8. "My helper and deliverer art Thou; O Lord, delay not." Thou art the helper and deliverer: I need succour, help Thou; entangled I am, deliver Thou. For no one will deliver from entanglings except Thee. There stand round about us the nooses of divers cares, on this side and on that we are torn as it were with thorns and brambles, we walk a narrow way, perchance we have stuck fast in the brambles: let us say to God, "Thou art my deliverer." He that showed us the narrow way? hath taught us to follow it. ...

9. What is, "delay not"? Because many men say, it is a long time till Christ comes. What then: because we say, "delay not," will He come before He hath determined to come? What meaneth this prayer, "delay not"? May not Thy coming seem to me to be too long delayed. For to thee it seemeth a long time, to God it seemeth not long, to whom a thousand years are one day, or the three hours of a watch. But if thou shalt not have had endurance, late for thee it will be: and when to thee it shall be late, thou wilt be diverted from Him, and wilt be like unto those that were wearied in the desert, and hastened to ask of God the pleasant things which He was reserving for them in the Land; and when there were not given on their journey the pleasant things, whereby perchance they would have been corrupted, they murmured against God, and went back in heart unto Egypt: to that place whence in body they had been severed, in heart they went back. Do not thou, then, so, do not so: fear the word of the Lord, saying, "Remember Lot's wife." She too being on the way, but now delivered from the Sodomites, looked back; in the place where she looked back, there she remained: she became a statue of salt, in order to

season thee. For to thee she hath been given for an example, in order that thou mayest have sense, mayest not stop infatuated on the way. Observe her stopping and pass on: observe her looking back, and do thou be reaching forth unto the things before, as Paul was. What is it, not to look back. "Of the things behind forgetful," he saith. Therefore thou followest, being called to the heavenly reward, whereof hereafter thou wilt glory. For the same Apostle saith, "There remaineth for me a crown of righteousness, which in that day the Lord, the just Judge, shall render to me."

PSALM LXXI.

1. In all the holy Scriptures the grace of God that delivereth us commendeth itself to us, in order that it may have us commended. This is sung of in this Psalm, whereof we have undertaken to speak. ... This grace the Apostle commendeth: by this he got to have the Jews for enemies, boasting of the letter of the law and of their own justice. This then commending in the lesson which hath been read, he saith thus: "For I am the least of the Apostles, that am not worthy to be called an Apostle, because I persecuted the Church of God." "But therefore mercy," he saith, "I obtained, because ignorant I did it in unbelief." Then a little afterwards, "Faithful the saying is, and worthy of all acceptation, that Christ Jesus came into the world to save sinners, of whom I am first." Were there before him not any sinners? What then, was he the first then? Yea, going before all men not in time, but in evil disposition. "But therefore," he saith, "mercy I obtained," in order that in me Christ Jesus might show all long-suffering, for the imitation of those that shall believe in Him unto life eternal: that is, every sinner and unjust man, already despairing of himself, already having the mind of a gladiator, so as to do whatsoever he willeth, because he must needs be condemned, may yet observe the Apostle Paul, to whom so great cruelty and so very evil a disposition was forgiven by God; and by not despairing of himself may he be turned unto God. This grace God doth commend to us in this Psalm also. ...

2. The title then of this Psalm is, as usual, a title intimating on the threshold what is being done in the house: "To David himself for the sons of Jonadab, and for those that were first led captive." Jonadab (he is commended to us in the prophecy of Jeremiah) was a certain man, who had enjoined his sons not to drink wine, and not to dwell in houses, but in tents. But the commandment of the father the sons kept and observed, and by this earned a blessing from the Lord. Now the Lord had not commanded this, but their own father. But they so received it as though it were a commandment from the Lord their God; for even though the Lord bad not commanded that they should drink no wine and should dwell in tents; yet the Lord had commanded that sons should obey their father. In this case alone a son ought not to obey his father, if his father should have commanded anything contrary to the Lord his God. For indeed the father ought not to be angry, when God is preferred before him. But when a father doth command that which is not contrary to God; he must be heard as God is: because to obey one's father God hath enjoined. God then blessed the sons of Jonadab because of their obedience, and thrust them in the teeth of His disobedient people, reproaching them, because while the sons of Jonadab were obedient to their father, they obeyed not their God. But while Jeremiah was treating of these topics, he had this object in regard to the

people of Israel, that they should prepare themselves to be led for captivity into Babylon, and should not hope for any other thing, but that they were to be captives. The title then of this Psalm seemeth from thence to have taken its hue, so that when he had said, "Of the sons of Jonadab;" he added, "and of them that were first led captive:" not that the sons of Jonadab were led captive, but because to them that were to be led captive there were opposed the sons of Jonadab, because they were obedient to their father: in order that they might understand that they had been made captive, because they were not obedient to God. It is added also that Jonadab is interpreted, "the Lord's spontaneous one." What is this, the Lord's spontaneous one? Serving God freely with the will. What is, the Lord's spontaneous one? "In me are, O God, Thy vows, which I will render of praise to Thee." What is, the Lord's spontaneous one? "Voluntarily I will sacrifice to Thee." For if the Apostolic teaching admonisheth a slave to serve a human master, not as though of necessity, but of good will, and by freely serving make himself in heart free; how much more must God be served with whole and full and free will, who seeth thy very will? ... The first man made us captive, the second man hath delivered us from captivity. "For as in Adam all die, so also in Christ all shall be made alive." But in Adam they die through the flesh's nativity, in Christ they are delivered through the heart's faith. It was not in thy power not to be born of Adam: it is in thy power to believe in Christ. Howsoever much then thou shall have willed to belong to the first man, unto captivity thou wilt belong. And what is, shall have willed to belong? or what is, shalt belong? Already thou belongest: cry out, "Who shall deliver me from the body of this death?" Let us hear then this man crying out this.

3. "O God, in Thee I have hoped, O Lord, I shall not be confounded for everlasting" (ver. 1). Already I have been confounded, but not for everlasting. For how is he not confounded, to whom is said, "What fruit had ye in these things wherein ye now blush?" What then shall be done, that we may not be confounded for everlasting? "Draw near unto Him, and be ye enlightened, and your faces shall not blush." Confounded ye are in Adam, withdraw from Adam, draw near unto Christ, and then ye shall not be confounded. "In Thee I have hoped, O Lord, I shall not be confounded for everlasting." If in myself I am now confounded, in Thee I shall not be confounded for everlasting.

4. "In Thine own righteousness deliver me, and save me" (ver. 2). Not in mine own, but in Thine own: for if in mine own, I shall be one of those whereof he saith, "Being ignorant of God's righteousness, and their own righteousness willing to establish, to the righteousness of God they were not made subject." Therefore, "in Thine own righteousness," not in mine. For mine is what? Iniquity hath gone

before. And when I shall be righteous, Thine own righteousness it will be: for by righteousness given to me by Thee I shall be righteous; and it shall be so mine, as that it be Thine, that is, given to me by Thee. For I believe on Him that justifieth an ungodly man, so that my faith is counted for righteousness. Even so then the righteousness shall be mine, not however as though mine own, not as though by mine own self given to myself: as they thought who through the letter made their boast, and rejected grace. ... It is a small thing then that thou acknowledge the good thing which is in thee to be from God, unless also on that account thou exalt not thyself above him that hath not yet, who perchance when he shall have received, will outstrip thee. For when Saul was a stoner of Stephen, how many were the Christians of whom he was persecutor! Nevertheless, when he was converted, all that had gone before he surpassed. Therefore say thou to God that which thou hearest in the Psalm, "In Thee I have hoped, O Lord, I shall not be confounded for everlasting: in Thine own righteousness," not in mine, "deliver me, and save me." "Incline unto me Thine ear." This also is a confession of humility. He that saith, "Incline unto me," is confessing that he is lying like a sick man laid at the feet of the Physician standing. Lastly, observe that it is a sick man that is speaking: "Incline unto me Thine ear, and save me."

5. "Be Thou unto me for a protecting God" (ver. 3). Let not the darts of the enemy reach unto me: for I am not able to protect myself. And a small thing is "protecting:" he hath added, "and for a walled place, that Thou mayest save me." "For a walled place" be Thou to me, be Thou my walled place. ... Behold, God Himself hath become the place of thy fleeing unto, who at first was the fearful object of thy fleeing from. "For a walled place," he saith, be Thou to me, "that Thou mayest save me." I shall not be safe except in Thee: except Thou shalt have been my rest, my sickness shall not be able to be made whole. Lift me from the earth; upon Thee I will lie, in order that I may rise unto a walled place. What can be better walled? When unto that place thou shalt have fled for refuge, tell me what adversaries thou wilt dread? Who will lie in wait, and come at thee? A certain man is Said from the summit of a mountain to have cried out, when an Emperor was passing by, "I speak not of thee:" the other is said to have looked back and to have said, "Nor I of thee." He had despised an Emperor with glittering arms, with mighty army. From whence? From a strong place. If he was secure on a high spot of earth, how secure art thou on Him by whom heaven and earth were made? I, if for myself I shall have chosen another place, shall not be able to be safe. Choose thou indeed, O man, if thou shalt have found one, a place better walled. There is not then a place whither to flee from Him, except we flee to Him. If thou wilt escape Him angry, flee to Him appeased. "For my firmament and my refuge Thou art." "My firmament" is what? Through Thee I am firm, and by Thee I am firm. "For my firmament and my refuge Thou art:" in order that I may be

made firm by Thee, in whatever respects I shall have been made infirm in myself, I will flee for refuge unto Thee. For firm the grace of Christ maketh thee, and immovable against all temptations of the enemy. But there is there too human frailness, there is there still the first captivity, there is there too the law in the members fighting against the law of the mind, and willing to lead captive in the law of sin: still the body which is corrupt presseth down the soul. Howsoever firm thou be by the grace of God, so long as thou still bearest an earthly vessel, wherein the treasure of God is, something must be dreaded even from that same vessel of clay. Therefore" my firmament Thou art," in order that I may be firm in this world against all temptations. But if many they are, and they trouble me: "my refuge Thou art." For I will confess mine infirmity, to the end that I may be timid like a "hare," because I am full of thorns like a "hedgehog." And as in another Psalm is said, "The rock is a refuge for the hedgehogs and the hares:" but the Rock was Christ.

6. "O God, deliver me from the hand of the sinner" (ver. 4). Generally, sinners, among whom is toiling he that is now to be delivered from captivity: he that now crieth, "Unhappy man I, who shall deliver me from the body of this death? The grace of God through Jesus Christ our Lord." Within is a foe, that law in the members; there are without also enemies: unto what cryest thou? Unto Him, to whom hath been cried, "From my secret sins cleanse me, O Lord, anti from strange sins spare Thy servant." ... But these sinners are of two kinds: there are some that have received Law, there are others that have not received: all the heathen have not received Law, all Jews and Christians have received Law. Therefore the general term is sinner; either a transgressor of the Law, if he hath received Law; or only unjust without Law, if he hath not received the Law. Of both kinds speaketh the Apostle, and saith, "They that without Law have sinned, without Law shall perish, and they that in the Law have sinned, by the Law shall be judged." But thou that amid both kinds dost groan, say to God that which thou hearest in the Psalm, "My God, deliver me from the hand of the sinner." Of what sinner? "From the hand of him that transgresseth the Law, and of the unjust man." He that transgresseth the Law is indeed also unjust; for not unjust he is not, that transgresseth the Law: but every one that transgresseth the Law is unjust, not every unjust man doth transgress the Law. For, "Where there is not a Law," saith the Apostle, "neither is there transgression." They then that have not received Law, may be called unjust, transgressors they cannot be called. Both are judged after their deservings. But I that from captivity will to be delivered through Thy grace, cry to Thee, "Deliver me from the hand of the sinner." What is, from the hand of him? From the power of him, that while he is raging, he lead me not unto consenting with him; that while he lieth in wait, he persuade not to iniquity. "From the hand of the sinner and of the unjust man." ...

7. Lastly, there followeth the reason why I say this: "for Thou art my patience" (ver. 5). Now if He is patience rightly, He is that also which followeth, "O Lord, my hope from my youth." My patience, because my hope: or rather my hope, because my patience. "Tribulation," saith the Apostle, "worketh patience, patience probation, but probation hope, but hope confoundeth not." With reason in Thee I have hoped, O Lord, I shall not be confounded for everlasting. "O Lord, my hope from my youth." From thy youth is God thy hope? Is He not also from thy boyhood, and from thine infancy? Certainly, saith he. For see what followeth, that thou mayest not think that I have said this, "my hope from my youth," as if God noways profited mine infancy or my boyhood; hear what followeth: "In Thee I have been strengthened from the womb." Hear yet: "From the belly of my mother Thou art my Protector" (ver. 6). Why then, "from my youth," except it was the period from which I began to hope in Thee? For before in Thee I was not hoping, though Thou wast my Protector, that didst lead me safe unto the time, when I learned to hope in Thee. But from my youth I began in Thee to hope, from the time when Thou didst arm me against the Devil, so that in the girding of Thy host being armed with Thy faith, love, hope, and the rest of Thy gifts, I waged conflict against Thine invisible enemies, and heard from the Apostle, "There is not for us a wrestling against flesh and blood, but against principalities, and powers," etc. There a young man it is that doth fight against these things: but though he be a young man, he falleth, unless He be the hope of Him to whom he crieth, "O Lord, my hope from my youth." "In Thee is my singing alway." Is it only from the time when I began to hope in Thee until now? Nay, but "alway." What is, "alway"? Not only in the time of faith, but also in the time of sight. For now, "So long as we are in the body we are absent from the Lord: for by faith we walk, not by sight: " there will be a time when we shall see that which being not seen we believe: but when that hath been seen which we believe, we shall rejoice: but when that hath been seen which they believed not, ungodly men shall be confounded. Then will come the substance whereof there is now the hope. But, "Hope which is seen is not hope. But if that which we see not we hope for, through patience we wait for it." Now then thou groanest, now unto a place of refuge thou runnest, in order that thou mayest be saved; now being in infirmity thou entreatest the Physician: what, when thou shall have received perfect soundness also, what when thou shall have been made "equal to the Angels of God," wilt thou then perchance forget that grace, whereby thou hast been delivered? Far be it.

8. "As it were a monster I have become unto many" (ver. 7). Here in time of hope, in time of groaning, in time of humiliation, in time of sorrow, in time of infirmity, in time of the voice from the fetters—here then what? "As it were a monster I have become unto many." Why, "As it were a monster"? Why do they insult me that think me a monster? Because I believe that which I see not. For they being happy

in those things which they see, exult in drink, in wantonness, in chamberings, in covetousness, in riches, in robberies, in secular dignities, in the whitening of a mud wall, in these things they exult: but I walk in a different way, contemning those things which are present, and fearing even the prosperous things of the world, and secure in no other thing but the promises of God. And they, "Let us eat and drink, for to-morrow we die." What sayest thou? Repeat it: "let us eat," he saith, "and drink." Come now, what hast thou said afterwards? "for to-morrow we die." Thou hast terrified, not led me astray. Certainly by the very thing which thou hast said afterwards, thou hast stricken me with fear to consent with thee. "For to-morrow we die," thou hast said: and there hath preceded, "Let us eat and drink." For when thou hadst said, "Let us eat and drink;" thou didst add, "for to-morrow we die." Hear the other side from me, "Yea let us fast and pray, 'for to-morrow we die.' " I keeping this way, strait and narrow, "as it were a monster have become unto many: but Thou art a strong helper." Be Thou with me, O Lord Jesus, to say to me, faint not in the narrow way, I first have gone along it, I am the way itself, I lead, in Myself I lead, unto Myself I lead home. Therefore though "a monster I have become unto many;" nevertheless I will not fear, for "Thou art a strong Helper."

9. "Let my mouth be fulfilled with praise, that with hymn I may tell of Thy glory, all the day long Thy magnificence" (ver. 8). What is "all the day long"? Without intermission. In prosperity, because Thou dost comfort: in adversity, because Thou dost correct: before I was in being, because Thou didst make; when I was in being, because Thou didst give health: when I had sinned, because Thou didst forgive; when I was converted, because Thou didst help; when I had persevered, because Thou didst crown.

10. My hope from my youth, "cast me not away in time of old age" (ver. 9). What is this time of old age? "When my strength shall fail, forsake Thou not me." Here God maketh this answer to thee, yea indeed let thy strength fail, in order that in thee mine may abide: in order that thou mayest say with the Apostle, "When I am made weak, then I am mighty." Fear not, that thou be cast away in that weakness, in that old age. But why? Was not thy Lord made weak on the Cross? Did not most mighty men and fat bulls before Him, as though a man of no strength, made captive and oppressed, shake the head and say, "If Son of God He is, let Him come down from the Cross"? Has he deserted because He was made weak, who preferred not to come down from the Cross, lest He should seem not to have displayed power, but to have yielded to them reviling? What did He hanging teach thee, that would not come down, but patience amid men reviling, but that thou shouldest be strong in thy God? Perchance too in His person was said, "As it were

a monster I have become unto many, and Thou art a strong Helper." In His person according to His weakness, not according to His power; according to that whereby He had transformed us into Himself, not according to that wherein He had Himself come down. For He became a monster unto many. And perchance the same was the old age of Him; because on account of its oldness it is not improperly called old age, and the Apostle saith, "Our old man hath been crucified together with Him." If there was there our old man, old age was there; because old, old age. Nevertheless, because a true saying is, "Renewed as an eagle's shall be Thy youth;" He rose Himself the third day, promised a resurrection at the end of the world. Already there hath gone before the Head, the members are to follow. Why dost thou fear lest He should forsake thee, lest He cast thee away for the time of old age, when thy strength shall have failed? Yea at that time in thee will be the strength of Him, when thy strength shall have failed.

11. Why do I say this? "For mine enemies have spoken against me, and they that were keeping watch for My soul, have taken counsel together (ver. 10): saying, God hath forsaken Him, persecute Him, and seize Him, for there is no one to deliver Him" (ver. 11). This hath been said concerning Christ. For He that with the great power of Divinity, wherein He is equal to the Father, had raised to life dead persons, on a sudden in the hands of enemies became weak, and as if having no power, was seized. When would He have been seized, except they had first said in their heart, "God hath forsaken Him?" Whence there was that voice on the Cross, "My God, My God, why hast Thou forsaken Me? So then did God forsake Christ, though "God was in Christ reconciling the world to Himself," though Christ was also God. out of the Jews indeed according to the flesh, "Who is over all things, God blessed for ever,"—did God forsake Him? Far be it. But in our old man our voice it was, because our old man was crucified together with Him: and of that same our old man He had taken a Body, because Mary was of Adam. Therefore the very thing which they thought, from the Cross He said, "Why hast Thou forsaken Me?" Why do these men think Me left alone to their evil? What is, think Me forsaken in their evil? "For if they had known, the Lord of glory they had never crucified. Persecute and seize Him." More familiarly however, brethren, let us take this of the members of Christ, and acknowledge our own voice in these words: because even He used such words in our person, not in His own power and majesty; but in that which He became for our sakes, not according to that which He was, who hath made us.

12. "O Lord, my God, be not far from me" (ver. 12). So it is, and the Lord is not far off at all. For, "The Lord is nigh unto them that have bruised the heart." "My God, unto my help look Thou." "Be they confounded and fail that engage my soul"

(ver. 13). What hath he desired? "Be they confounded and fail." Why hath he desired it? "That engage my soul"? What is, "That engage my soul "? Engaging as it were unto some quarrel. For they are said to be engaged that are challenged to quarrel. If then so it is, let us beware of men that engage our soul. What is, "That engage our soul"? First provoking us to withstand God, in order that in our evil things God may displease us. For when art thou right, so that to thee the God of Israel may be good, good to men fight in heart? When art thou right? Wilt thou hear? When in that good which thou doest, God is pleasing to thee; but in that evil which thou sufferest, God is not displeasing to thee. See ye what I have said, brethren, and be ye on your guard against men that engage your souls. For all men that deal with you in order to make you be wearied in sorrows and tribulations, have this aim, namely, that God may be displeasing to you in that which ye suffer, and there may go forth from your mouth, "What is this? For what have I done?" Now then hast thou done nothing of evil, and art thou just, He unjust? A sinner I am, thou sayest, I confess, just I call not myself. But what, sinner, hast thou by any means done so much evil as he with whom it is well? As much as Gaiuseius?" I know the evil doings of him, I know the iniquities of him, from which I, though a sinner, am very far; and yet I see him abounding in all good things, and I am suffering so great evil things. I do not then say, O God, "what have I done" to Thee, because I have done nothing at all of evil; but because I have not done so much as to deserve to suffer these things. Again, art thou just, He unjust? Wake up, wretched man, thy soul hath been engaged! I have not, he saith, called myself just. What then sayest thou? A sinner I am, but I did not commit so great sins, as to deserve to suffer these things. Thou sayest not then to God, just I am, and Thou art unjust: but thou sayest, unjust I am, but Thou art more unjust. Behold thy soul hath been engaged, behold now thy soul wageth war. What? Against whom? Thy soul, against God; that which hath been made against Him by whom it was made. Even because thou art in being to cry out against Him, thou art ungrateful. Return, then, to the confession of thy sickness, and beg the healing hand of the Physician. Think thou not they are happy who flourish for a time. Thou art being chastised, they are being spared: perchance for thee chastised and amended an inheritance is being kept in reserve. ... Lastly, see what followeth, "Let them put on confusion and shame, that think evil things to me." "Confusion and shame," confusion because of a bad conscience, shame because of modesty. Let this befall them, and they will be good. ...

13. "But I alway in Thee will hope, and will add to all Thy praise" (ver. 14). What is this? "I will add to all Thy praise," ought to move us. More perfect wilt thou make the praise of God? Is there anything to be superadded? If already that is all praise, wilt thou add anything? God was praised in all His good deeds, in every creature of His, in the whole establishment of all things, in the government and

regulation of ages, in the order of seasous, in the height of Heaven, in the fruitfulness of the regions of earth, in the encircling of the sea, in every excellency of the creature everywhere brought forth, in the sons of men themselves, in the giving of the Law, in delivering His people from the captivity of the Egyptians, and all the rest of His wonderful works: not yet He had been praised for having raised up flesh unto life eternal. Be there then this praise added by the Resurrection of our Lord Jesus Christ: in order that here we may perceive His voice above all past praise: thus it is that we rightly understand this also. ...

14. "My mouth shall tell out Thy righteousness" (ver. 15): not mine. From thence I will add to all Thy praise: because even that I am righteous, if righteous I am, is Thy righteousness in me, not mine own: for Thou dost justify the ungodly. "All the day long Thy salvation." What is, "Thy salvation "? Let no one assume to himself, that he saveth himself, "Of the Lord is Salvation." Not any one by himself saveth himself, "Vain is man's salvation." "All the day long Thy Salvation:" at all times. Something of adversity cometh, preach the Salvation of the Lord: something of prosperity cometh, preach the Salvation of the Lord. Do not preach in prosperity, and hold thy peace in adversity: otherwise there will not be that which hath been said, "all the day long." For all the day long is day together with its own night. Do we when we say, for example, thirty days have gone by, mention the nights also; do we not under the very term days include the nights also? In Genesis what was said? "The evening was made, and the morning was made, one day." Therefore a whole day is the day together with its own night: for the night doth serve the day, not the day the night. Whatever thou doest in mortal flesh, ought to serve righteousness: whatever thou doest by the commandment of God, be it not done for the sake of the advantage of the flesh, lest day serve night. Therefore all the day long speak of the praise of God, to wit, in prosperity and in adversity; in prosperity, as though in the day time; in adversity, as though in the night time: all the day long nevertheless speak of the praise of God, so that thou mayest not have sung to no purpose, "I will bless God at every time, alway the praise of Him is in my mouth." ...

15. Therefore, he saith, "For I have not known tradings." What are these tradings? Let traders hear and change their life; and if they have been such, be not such; let them not know what they have been, let them forget; lastly, let them not approve, not praise; let them disapprove, condemn, be changed, if trading is a sin. For on this account, O thou trader, because of a certain eagerness for getting, whenever thou shalt have suffered loss, thou wilt blaspheme; and there will not be in thee that which hath been spoken of, "all the day long Thy praise." But whenever for the price of the goods which thou art selling, thou not only liest, but even falsely

swearest; how in thy mouth all the day long is there the praise of God? While, if thou art a Christian, even out of thy mouth the name of God is being blasphemed, so that men say, see what sort of men are Christians! Therefore if this man for this reason speaketh the praise of God all the day long, because he hath not known tradings; let Christians amend themselves, let them not trade. But a trader saith to me, behold I bring indeed from a distant quarter merchandise unto these places, wherein there are not those things which I have brought, by which means I may gain a living: I ask but as reward for my labour, that I may sell dearer than I have bought: for whence can I live, when it hath been written, "the worker is worthy of his reward"? But he is treating of lying, of false swearing. This is the fault of me, not of trading: for I should not, if I would, be unable to do without this fault. I then, the merchant, do not shift mine own fault to trading: but if I lie, it is I that lie, not the trade. For I might say, for so much I bought, but for so much I will sell; if thou pleasest, buy. For the buyer hearing this truth would not be offended, and not a whit less all men would resort to me: because they would love truth more than gain. Of this then, he saith, admonish me, that I lie not, that I forswear not; not to relinquish business whereby I maintain myself. For to what dost thou put me when thou puttest me away from this? Perchance to some craft? I will be a shoemaker, I will make shoes for men. Are not they too liars? are not they too false-swearers? Do they not, when they have contracted to make shoes for one man, when they have received money from another man, give up that which they were making, and undertake to make for another, and deceive him for whom they have promised to make speedily? Do they not often say, to-day I am about it, to-day I'll get them done? Secondly, in the very sewing do they not commit as many frauds? These are their doings and these are their sayings: but they are themselves evil, not the calling which they profess. All evil artificers, then, not fearing God, either for gain, or for fear of loss or want, do lie, do forswear themselves; there is no continual praise of God in them. How then dost thou withdraw me from trading? Wouldest thou that I be a farmer, and murmur against God thundering, so that, fearing hail, I consult a wizard, in order to learn what to do to protect me against the weather; so that I desire famine for the poor, in order that I may be able to sell what I have kept in store? Unto this dost thou bring me? But good farmers, thou sayest, do not such things. Nor do good traders do those things. But why, even to have sons is an evil thing, for when their head is in pain, evil and unbelieving mothers seek for impious charms and incantations? These are the sins of men, not of things. A trader might thus speak to me—Look then, O Bishop, how thou understand the tradings which thou hast read in the Psalm: lest perchance thou understand not, and yet forbid me trading. Admonish me then how I should live; if well, it shall be well with me: one thing however I know, that if I shall have been evil, it is not trading that maketh me so, but my iniquity. Whenever truth is spoken, there is nothing to be said against it.

16. Let us inquire then what he hath called tradings, which indeed he that hath not known, all the day long doth praise God. Trading even in the Greek language is derived from action, and in the Latin from want of inaction: but whether it be from action or want of inaction, let us examine what it is. For they that are active traders, rely as it were upon their own action, they praise their works, they attain not to the grace of God. Therefore traders are opposed to that grace which this Psalm doth commend. For it doth commend that grace, in order that no one may boast of his own works. Because in a certain place is said, "Physicians shall not raise to life," ought men to abandon medicine? But what is this? Under this name are understood proud men, promising salvation to men, whereas "of the Lord is Salvation." ... With reason the Lord drave from the Temple them to whom He said, "It is written, My House shall be called the House of prayer, but ye have made it a house of trading; " that is, boasting of your works, seeking no inaction, nor hearing the Scripture speaking against your unrest and trading, "be ye still, and see that I am the Lord." ...

17. But there is in some copies, "For I have not known literature." Where some books have "trading," there others "literature:" how they may accord is a hard matter to find out; and yet the discrepancy of interpreters perchance showeth the meaning, introduceth no error. Let us inquire then how to understand literature also, lest we offend grammarians in the same way as we did traders a little before: because a grammarian too may live honourably in his calling, and neither forswear nor lie. Let us examine then the literature which he hath not known, in whose mouth all the day long is the praise of God. There is a sort of literature of the Jews: for to them let us refer this; there we shall find what hath been said: just as when we were inquiring about traders, on the score of actions and works, we found that to be called detestable trading, which the Apostle hath branded, saying, "For being ignorant of God's righteousness, and willing to establish their own, to the righteousness of God they were not made subject." ... Just as then we found out the former charge against traders, that is men boasting of action, exalting themselves because of business which admitteth no inaction, unquiet men rather than good workmen; because good workmen are those in whom God worketh; so also we find a sort of literature among the Jews. ... Moses wrote five books: but in the five porches encircling the pool, sick men were lying, but they could not be healed. See how the letter remained, convicting the guilty, not saving the unrighteous. For in those five porches, a figure of the five books, sick men were given over rather than made whole. What then in that place did make whole a sick man? The moving of the water. When that pool was moved there went down a sick man, and there was made whole one, one because of unity: whatsoever other man went down unto that same moving was not made whole. How then was there commended the unity of the Body crying from the ends of the earth? Another man was not healed, except

again the pool were moved. The moving of the pool then did signify the perturbation of the people of the Jews when the Lord Jesus Christ came. For at the coming of an Angel the water in the pool was perceived to be moved. The water then encircled with five porches was the Jewish nation encircled by the Law. And in the porches the sick lay, and in the water alone when troubled and moved they were healed. The Lord came, troubled was the water; He was crucified, may He come down in order that the sick man may be made whole. What is, may He come down? May He humble Himself. Therefore whosoever ye be that love the letter without grace, in the porches ye will remain, sick ye will be, lying ill, not growing well. ... For the same figure also it is that Eliseus at first sent a staff by his servant to raise up the dead child. There had died the son of a widow his hostess; it was reported to him, to his servant he gave his staff: go thou, he saith, lay it on the dead child. Did the prophet not know what he was doing? The servant went before, he laid the staff upon the dead, the dead arose not. "For if there had been given a law which could have made alive, surely out of the law there had been righteousness." The law sent by the servant made not alive: and yet he sent his staff by the servant, who himself afterwards followed, and made alive. For when that infant arose not, Eliseus came himself, now bearing the type of the Lord, who had sent before his servant with the staff, as though with the Law: he came to the child that was lying dead, he laid his limbs upon it. The one was an infant, the other a grown man: he contracted and shortened in a manner the size of his full growth, in order that he might fit the dead child. The dead then arose, when he being alive adapted himself to the dead: and the Master did that which the staff did not; and grace did that which the letter did not. They then that have remained in the staff, glory in the letter; and therefore are not made alive. But I will to glory concerning Thy grace. ... In that same grace I glorying "literature have not known:" that is, men on the letter relying, and from grace recoiling, with whole heart I have rejected.

18. With reason there followeth, "I will enter into the power of the Lord:" not mine own, but the Lord's. For they gloried in their own power of the letter, therefore grace joined to the letter they knew not. ... But because "the letter killeth, but the Spirit maketh alive:" "I have not known literature, and I will enter into the power of the Lord." Therefore this verse following doth strengthen and perfect the sense, so as to fix it in the hearts of men, and not suffer any other interpretation to steal in from any quarter. "O Lord, I will be mindful of Thy righteousness alone" (ver. 16). ·Ah! "alone." Why hath he added "alone," I ask you? It would suffice to say, "I will be mindful of Thy righteousness." "alone," he saith, entirely: there of mine own I think not. "For what hast thou which thou hast not received? But if also thou hast received, why dost thou glory as if thou hast not received." Thy righteousness alone doth deliver me, what is mine own alone is nought but sins. May I not glory

then of my own strength, may I not remain in the letter; may I reject "literature," that is, men glorying of the letter, and on their own strength perversely, like men frantic, relying: may I reject such men, may I enter into the power of the Lord, so that when I am weak, then I may be mighty; in order that Thou in me mayest be mighty, for, "I will be mindful of Thy righteousness alone."

19. "O God, Thou hast taught me from my youth" (ver. 17). What hast thou taught me? That of Thy righteousness alone I ought to be mindful. For reviewing my past life, I see what was owing to me, and what I have received instead of that which was owing to me. There was owing punishment, there hath been paid grace: there was owing hell, there hath been given life eternal. "O God, Thou hast taught me from my youth." From the very beginning of my faith, wherewith Thou hast renewed me, Thou didst teach me that nothing had preceded in me, whence I might say that there was owing to me what Thou hast given. For who is turned to God save from iniquity? Who is redeemed save from captivity? But who can say that unjust was his captivity, when he forsook his Captain and fell off to the deserter? God is for our Captain, the devil a deserter: the Captain gave a commandment, the deserter suggested guile: where were thine ears between precept and deceit? was the devil better than God? Better he that revolted than He that made thee? Thou didst believe what the devil promised, and didst find what God threatened. Now then out of captivity being delivered, still however in hope, not yet in substance, walking by faith, not yet by sight, "O God," he saith, "Thou hast taught me from my youth." From the time that I have been turned to Thee, renewed by Thee who had been made by Thee, re-created who had been created, re-formed who had been formed: from the time that I have been converted, I have learned that no merits of mine have preceded, but that Thy grace hath come to me gratis, in order that I might be mindful of Thy righteousness alone.

20. What next after youth? For, "Thou hast taught me," he saith, "from my youth:" what after youth? For in that same first conversion of thine thou didst learn, how before conversion thou wast not just, but iniquity preceded, in order that iniquity being banished, there might succeed love: and having been renewed into a new man, only in hope, not yet in substance, thou didst learn how nothing of thy good had preceded, and by the grace of God thou wast converted to God: now perchance since the time that thou hast been converted wilt thou have anything of thine own, and on thy own strength oughtest thou to rely? Just as men are wont to say, now leave me, it was necessary for thee to show me the way; it is sufficient, i will walk in the way. And he that hath shown thee the way, "wilt thou not that I conduct thee to the place?" But thou, if thou art conceited, "let me alone, it is enough, I will walk in the way." Thou art left, and through thy weakness again

thou wilt lose the way. Good were it for thee that He should have conducted thee, who first put thee in the way. But unless He too lead thee, again also thou wilt stray: say to Him then, "Conduct me, O Lord, in Thy way, and I will walk in Thy truth." But thy having entered on the way, is youth, the very renewal and beginning of the faith. For before thou wast walking through thy own ways a vagabond; straying through woody places, through rough places, torn in all thy limbs, thou wast seeking a home, that is, a sort of settlement of thy spirit, where thou mightest say, it is well; and being in security mightest say it, at rest from every uneasiness, from every trial, in a word from every captivity; and thou didst not find. What shall I say? Came there to thee one to show thee the way? There came to thee the Way itself, and thou wast set therein by no merits of thine preceding, for evidently thou wast straying. What, since the time that thou hast set foot therein dost thou now direct thyself? Doth He that hath taught thee the way now leave thee? No, he saith: "Thou hast taught me from my youth; and even until now I will tell forth Thy wonderful works." For a wonderful thing is that which still Thou doest; namely, that Thou dost direct me, who in the way hast put me: and these are Thy wonderful works. What dost thou think to be the wonderful works of God? What is more wonderful among God's wonderful works, than the raising the dead? But am I by any means dead, thou sayest? Unless dead thou hadst been, there would not have been said to thee, "Rise, thou that sleepest, and arise from the dead, and Christ shall enlighten thee." Dead are all unbelievers, all unrighteous men; in body they live, but in heart they are extinct. But he that raiseth a man dead according to the body, doth bring him back to see this light and to breathe this air: but he that raiseth is not himself light and air to him; he beginneth to see, as he saw before. A soul is not so resuscitated. For a soul is resuscitated by God; though even a body is resuscitated by God: but God, when He doth resuscitate a body, to the world doth bring it back: when He doth resuscitate a soul, to Himself He bringeth it back. If the air of this world be withdrawn, there dieth body: if God be withdrawn, there dieth soul. When then God doth resuscitate a soul, unless there be with her He that hath resuscitated, she being resuscitated liveth not. For He doth not resuscitate, and then leave her to live to herself: in the same manner as Lazarus, when he was resuscitated after being four days dead, was resuscitated by the Lord's corporal presence. ... The Lord withdrew from that same city or from that spot, did Lazarus cease to live? Not so is the soul resuscitated: God doth resuscitate her, she dieth if God shall have withdrawn. For I will speak boldly, brethren, but yet the truth. Two lives there are, one of the body, another of the soul: as the life of the body is the soul, so the life of the soul is God: in like manner as, if the soul forsake, the body dieth: so the soul dieth, if God forsake. This then is His grace, namely, that He resuscitate and be with us. Because then He doth resuscitate us from our past death, and doth renew in a manner our life, we say to Him, "O God, Thou hast taught me from my youth." But because He doth not withdraw from those whom He resuscitateth, lest when He shall have withdrawn from them they die, we say to Him, "and even until now I will tell forth Thy wonderful works:" because while Thou art with me I live, and of my soul Thou art the life, which will die if she be left to herself. Therefore while my life is present, that is, my God, "even until now," what next?

21. "And even unto oldness and old age" (ver. 18). These are two terms for old age, and are distinguished by the Greeks. For the gravity succeeding youth hath another name among the Greeks, and after that same gravity the last age coming on hath another name; for presbu'ths signifieth grave, and ge'rwn old. But because in the Latin language the distinction of these two terms holdeth not, both words implying old age are inserted, oldness and old age: but ye know them to be two ages. "Thou hast taught me Thy grace from my youth; and even until now;" after my youth, "I will tell forth Thy wonderful works," because Thou art with me in order that I may not die, who hast come in order that I may rise: "and even unto oldness and old age," that is, even unto my last breath, unless with me Thou shalt have been, there will not be any merit of mine; may Thy grace alway remain with me. Even one man would say this, thou, he, I; but because this voice is that of a certain great Man, that is, of the Unity itself, for it is the voice of the Church; let us investigate the youth of the Church. When Christ came, He was crucified, dead, rose again, called the Gentiles, they began to be converted, became Martyrs strong in Christ, there was shed faithful blood, there arose a harvest for the Church: this is Her youth. But seasons advancing let the Church confess, let Her say, "Even until now I will tell forth Thy wonderful works." Not only in youth, when Paul when Peter, when the first Apostles told: even in advancing age I myself, that is, Thy Unity, Thy members, Thy Body, "will tell forth Thy marvellous works." What then? "And even unto oldness and old age," I will tell forth Thy wonderful works: even until the end of the world here shall be the Church. For if She were not to be here even unto the end of the world; to whom did the Lord say, "Behold, I am with you always, even unto the consummation of the world "? Why was it necessary that these things should be spoken in the Scriptures? Because there were to be enemies of the Christian Faith who would say, "for a short time are the Christians, hereafter they shall perish, and there shall come back idols, there shall come back that which was before. How long shall be the Christians?" " Even unto oldness and old age:" that is, even unto the end of the world When thou, miserable unbeliever, dost expect Christians to pass away, thou art passing away thyself without Christians: and Christians even unto the end of the world shall endure; and as for thee with thine unbelief when thou shalt have ended thy short life, with what face wilt thou come forth to the Judge, whom while thou wast living thou didst blaspheme? Therefore "from my youth, and even until now, and even unto oldness and old age, O Lord, forsake not me." It will not be, as mine enemies say, even for a time. "Forsake not me, until I tell forth Thine arm to every generation that is yet

to come." And the Arm of the Lord hath been revealed to whom? The Arm of the Lord is Christ. Do not Thou then forsake me: let not them rejoice that say, "only for a set time the Christians are." May there be persons to tell forth Thine arm. To whom? "To every generation that is yet to come." If then it be to every generation that is yet to come, it will be even unto the end of the world: for when the world is ended, no longer any generation will come on.

22. "Thy power and Thy righteousness" (ver. 19). That is, that I may tell forth to every generation that is yet to come, Thine arm. And what hath Thine arm effected? This then let me tell forth, that same grace to every generation succeeding: let me say to every man that is to be born, nothing thou art by thyself, on God call thou, thine own are sins, merits are God's: punishment to thee is owing, and when reward shall have come, His own gifts He will crown, not thy merits. Let me say to every generation that is to come, out of captivity thou hast come, unto Adam thou didst belong. Let me say this to every generation that is to come, that there is no strength of mine, no righteousness of mine; but "Thy strength and Thy righteousness, O God, even unto the most high mighty works which Thou hast made." "Thy power and Thy righteousness," as far as what? even unto flesh and blood? Nay, "even unto the most high mighty works which Thou hast made." For the high places are the heavens, in the high places are the Angels, Thrones, Dominions, Principalities, Powers: to Thee they owe it that they are; to Thee they owe it that they live, to Thee they owe it that righteously they live, to Thee they owe it that blessedly they live. "Thy power and Thy righteousness," as far as what? "Even unto the most high mighty works which Thou hast made." Think not that man alone belongeth to the grace of God. What was Angel before he was made? What is Angel, if He forsake him who hath created? Therefore "Thy power and Thy justice even unto the most high mighty works which Thou hast made."

23. And man exalteth himself: and in order that he may belong to the first captivity, he heareth the serpent suggesting, "Taste, and ye shall be as Gods." Men as Gods? "O God, who is like unto Thee?" Not any in the pit, not in Hell, not in earth, not in Heaven, for all things Thou hast made. Why doth the work strive with the Maker? "O God, who is like unto Thee?" But as for me, saith miserable Adam, and Adam is every man, while I perversely will to be like unto Thee, behold what I have become, so that from captivity to Thee I cry out: I with whom it was well under a good king, have been made captive under my seducer; and cry out to Thee, because I have fallen from Thee. And whence have I fallen from Thee? While I perversely seek to be like unto Thee. ...

24. Ill straying, ill presuming, doomed to die by withdrawing from the path of righteousness: behold he breaketh the commandment, he hath shaken off from his neck the yoke of discipline, uplifted with high spirit he hath broken in sunder the reins of guidance: where is he now? Truly captive he crieth, "O Lord, who is like unto Thee?" I perversely willed to be like unto Thee, and I have been made like unto a beast! Under Thy dominion, under Thy commandment, I was indeed like: "But a man in honour set hath not perceived, he hath been compared to beasts without sense, and hath been made like unto them." Now out of the likeness of beasts cry though late and say, "O God, who is like unto Thee?"

25. "How great troubles hast Thou shown to me, many and evil!" (ver. 20). Deservedly, proud servant. For thou hast willed perversely to be like thy God, who hadst been made after the image of thy Lord. Wouldest thou have it to be well with thee, when withdrawing from that good? Truly God saith to thee, if thou withdrawest from Me, and it is well with thee, I am not thy good. Again, if He is good, and in the highest degree good, and of Himself to Himself good, and by no foreign good thing good, and is Himself our chief good; by withdrawing from Him, what wilt thou be but evil? Also if He is Himself our blessedness, what will there be to one withdrawing from Him, except misery? Return thou then after misery, and say, "O Lord, who is like unto Thee? How great troubles hast Thou shown to me, many and evil!"

26. But this was discipline; admonition, not desertion. Lastly, giving thanks, he saith what? "And being turned Thou hast made me alive, and from the bottomless places of the earth again Thou hast brought me back." But when before? What is this "again"? Thou hast fallen from a high place, O man, disobedient slave, O thou proud against thy Lord, thou hast fallen. There hast come to pass in thee," every one that exalteth himself shall be humbled:" may there come to pass in thee, "every one that humbleth himself shall be exalted." Return thou from the deep. I return, he saith, I return, I acknowledge; "0 God, who is like unto Thee? How great troubles hast Thou shown to me, many and evil! and being turned Thou hast made me alive, and from the bottomless places of the earth again Thou hast brought me back." "We perceive," I hear. Thou hast brought us back from the bottomless places of the earth, hast brought us back from the depth and drowning of sin. But why "again"? When had it already been done? Let us go on, if perchance the latter parts of the Psalm itself do not explain to us the thing which here we do not yet perceive, namely, why he hath said "again." Therefore let us hear: "How great troubles Thou hast shown to me, many and evil! And being turned Thou hast made me alive, and from the bottomless places of the earth again Thou hast brought me back." What then? "Thou hast multiplied Thy righteousness,

and being turned Thou hast comforted me, and from the bottomless places of the earth again Thou hast brought roe back" (ver. 21). Behold a second "again"! If we labour to unravel this "again" when written once, who will be able to unravel it when doubled? Now "again" itself is a redoubling, and once more there is written "again." May He be with us from whom is grace, may there be with us the arm also which we are telling forth to every generation that is to come: may He be with us Himself, and as with the key of His Cross open to us the mystery that is locked up. For it was not to no purpose that when He was crucified the veil of the temple was rent in the midst, but to show that through His Passion the secret things of all mysteries were opened. May He then Himself be with men passing over unto Him, be the veil taken away: may our Lord and Saviour Jesus Christ tell us why such a voice of the Prophet hath been sent before, "Thou hast shown to me troubles many and evil: and being turned Thou hast made me alive, and from the bottomless places of the earth again Thou hast brought me back." Behold this is the first "again" which hath been written. Let us see what this is, and we shall see why there is a second "again."

27. ... Therein Christ died, wherein thou art to die: and therein Christ rose again, wherein thou art to rise again. By His example He taught thee what thou shouldest not fear, for what thou shouldest hope. Thou didst fear death, He died: thou didst despair of rising again, He rose again. But thou sayest to me, He rose again, do I by any means rise again? But He rose again in that which for thee He received of thee. Therefore thy nature in Him hath preceded thee; and that which was taken of thee, hath gone up before thee: therein therefore thou also hast ascended. Therefore He ascended first, and we in Him: because that flesh is of the human race. ... Behold one "again." Hear of its being fulfilled from the Apostle: "If then ye have risen with Christ, the things which are above seek ye, where Christ is sitting on the right hand of God; the things which are above mind ye, not the things which are upon the earth." He then hath gone before: already we also have risen again, but still in hope. Hear the Apostle Paul saying this same thing: "Even we ourselves groan in ourselves, looking for the adoption, the redemption of our body." What is it then that Christ hath granted to thee? Hear that which followeth: "For by hope we are saved: but hope which is seen is not hope. For that which a man seeth, why doth he hope for? But if that which we see not we hope for, through patience we wait for it." We have been brought back therefore again from the bottomless places in hope. Why again? Because already Christ had gone before. But because we shall rise again in substance, for now in hope we are living, now after faith we are walking; we have been brought back from the bottomless places of the earth, by believing in Him who before us hath risen again from the bottomless place of the earth ....Thou hast: heard one "again," thou hast heard the other: "again;" one "again" because of Christ going before; and the other,

yet however in hope, and a thing which remaineth to be in substance. "Thou hast multiplied Thy righteousness," already in me believing, already in those that, first have risen again in hope. ... "Thou hast multiplied Thy righteousness, and being turned Thou hast comforted me:" and because of the body to rise again at the end, "even from the bottomless places of the earth again Thou hast brought me back.

28. "For I will confess to Thee in the vessels of a Psalm Thy truth" (ver. 22). The vessels of a Psalm are a Psaltery. But what is a Psaltery? An instrument of wood and strings. What doth it signify? There is some difference between it and a harp: ... there seemeth to be signified by the Psaltery the Spirit, by the harp the flesh. And because he had spoken of two bringings back of ours from the bottomless places of the earth, one after the Spirit in hope, the other after the body in substance; hear thou of these two: "For I will confess to Thee in the vessels of a Psalm Thy truth." This after the Spirit: concerning the body what? "I will psalm to Thee on a harp, Holy One of Israel."

29. Again hear this because of that same "again" and "again." "My lips shall exult when I shall psalm to Thee" (ver. 23). Because lips are wont to be spoken of both belonging to the inner and to the outward man, it is uncertain in what sense lips have been used: there followeth therefore, "And my soul which Thou hast redeemed." Therefore regarding the inward ups having been saved in hope, brought back from the bottomless places of the earth in faith and love, still however waiting for the redemption of our body? we say what? Already he hath said, "And my soul which Thou hast redeemed." But lest thou shouldest think the soul alone redeemed, wherein now thou hast heard one "again," "but still," he saith; why still? "but still my tongue also:" therefore now the tongue of the body: "all day long shall meditate of Thy righteousness" (ver. 24): that is, in eternity without end. But when shall this be? Hereafter at the end of the world, at the resurrection of the body and the changing into the Angelic state. Whence is it proved that this is spoken of the end, "but still my tongue also all day long shall meditate of Thy righteousness"? "When they shall have been confounded and shall have blushed, that seek evil things for me." When shall they be confounded, when shall they blush, save at the end of the world? For in two ways they shall be confounded, either when they shall believe in Christ, or when Christ shall have come. For so long as the Church is here, so long as grain groaneth amid chaff, so long as wheat groaneth amid tares, so long as vessels of mercy groan amid vessels of wrath made for dishonour, so long as lily groaneth amid thorns, there will not be wanting enemies to say," When shall he die, and his name perish?" "Behold there shall come the time when Christians shall be ended and shall be no more: as they began at a set time, so even unto a particular time they shall be." But while

they are saying these things and without end are dying, and while the Church is continuing preaching the Arm of the Lord s to every generation that is to come; there shall come Himself also at last in His glory, there shall rise again all the dead, each with his cause: there shall be severed good men to the right hand, but evil men to the left, and they shall be confounded that did insult, they shall blush that did mock: and so my tongue after resurrection shall meditate of Thy righteousness, all day long of Thy praise, "when they shall have been confounded and shall have blushed, that seek evil things for me."

PSALM LXXII.

1. "For Salomon" indeed this Psalm's title is fore-noted: but things are spoken of therein which could not apply to that Salomon king of Israel after the flesh, according to those things which holy Scripture speaketh concerning him: but they can most pertinently apply to the Lord Christ. Whence it is perceived, that the very word Salomon is used in a figurative sense, so that in him Christ is to be taken. For Salomon is interpreted peace-maker: and on this account such a word to Him most truly and excellently cloth apply, through Whom, the Mediator, having received remission of sins, we that were enemies are reconciled to God. For "when we were enemies we were reconciled to God through the death of His Son." The Same is Himself that Peace-maker .... Since then we have found out the true Salomon, that is, the true Peacemaker: next let us observe what the Psalm cloth teach concerning Him.

2. "O God, Thy judgment to the King give Thou, and Thy justice to the King's Son" (ver. I). The Lord Himself in the Gospel saith, "The Father judgeth not any one, but all judgment He hath given to the Son:" this is then, "O God, Thy judgment to the King give Thou." He that is King is also the Son of the King: because God the Father also is certainly King. Thus it hath been written, that the King made a marriage for His Son. But after the manner of Scripture the same thing is repeated. For that which he hath said in, "Thy judgment;" the same he hath otherwise expressed in, "Thy justice:" and that which he hath said in, "the King," the same he hath otherwise expressed in, "to the King's Son." ... But these repetitions do much commend the divine sayings, whether the same words, or whether in other words the same sense be repeated: and they are mostly found in the Psalms, and in the kind of discourse whereby the mind's affection is to be awakened.

3. Next there followeth, "To judge Thy people in justice, and Thy poor in judgment" (ver. 2). For what purpose the royal Father gave to the royal Son His judgment and His justice is sufficiently shown when he saith," To judge Thy people in justice;" that is, for the purpose of judging Thy people. Such an idiom is found in Salomon: "The Proverbs of Salomon, son of David, to know wisdom and discipline:" that is, the Proverbs of Salomon, for the purpose of knowing wisdom and discipline. So, "Thy judgment give Thou, to judge Thy people:" that is, "Thy judgment" give Thou for the purpose of judging Thy people. But that which he saith before in, "Thy people," the same he saith afterwards in, "Thy poor:" and that which he saith before in, "in justice;" the same afterward in, "in judgment:" according to that manner of repetition. Whereby indeed he showeth, that the

people of God ought to be poor, that is, not proud, but humble. For, "blessed are the poor in spirit, for theirs is the kingdom of Heaven." In which poverty even blessed Job was poor even before he had lost those great earthly riches. Which thing for this reason I thought should be mentioned, because there are certain persons who are more ready to distribute all their goods to the poor, than themselves to become the poor of God. For they are puffed up with boasting wherein they think their living well should be ascribed to themselves, not to the grace of God: and therefore now they do not even live well, however great the good works which they seem to do. ...

4. But seeing that he hath changed the order of the words (though he had first said, "O God, Thy judgment to the King give Thou, and Thy justice to the King's 'Son," putting judgment first, then justice), and hath put justice first, then judgment, saying, "To judge Thy people in justice, and Thy poor in judgment:" he doth more clearly show that he hath called judgment justice, proving that there is no difference made by the order in which the word is placed, because it signifieth the same thing. For it is usual to say "wrong judgment" of that which is unjust: but justice iniquitous or unjust we are not wont to speak of. For if wrong and unjust it be; no longer must it be called justice. Again, by putting clown judgment and repeating it under the name of justice, or by putting down justice and repeating it under the name of judgment, he clearly showeth that he specially nameth that judgment which is wont to be put instead of justice, that is, that which cannot be understood of giving an evil judgment. For in the place where He saith, "Judge not according to persons, but right judgment judge ye;" He showeth that there may be a wrong judgment, when He saith, "right judgment judge ye:" lastly, the one He doth forbid, the other He doth enjoin. But when without any addition He speaketh of judgment, He would at once have just judgment to be understood: as is that which He saith, "Ye forsake the weightier matters of the Law, mercy and judgment." That also which Jeremiah saith is, "making his riches not with judgment." He saith not, making his riches by wrong or unjust judgment, or not with judgment right or just, but not with judgment: calling not anything judgment but what is right and just.

5. "Let the mountains bear peace to the people, and the hills justice" (ver. 3). The mountains are the greater, the hills the less. These are without doubt those which another Psalm hath, "little with great." For those mountains did exult like rams, and those hills like lambs of the sheep, at the departure of Israel out of Egypt, that is, at the deliverance of the people of God from this world's servitude. Those then that are eminent in the Church for passing sanctity, are the mountains, who are meet to teach other men also, by so speaking as that they may be faithfully taught,

by so living as that they may imitate them to their profit: but the hills are they that follow the excellence of the former by their own obedience. Why then "the mountains peace: and the hills justice"? Would there perchance have been no difference, even if it had been said thus, Let the mountains bear justice to the people and the hills peace? For to both justice, and to both peace is necessary: and it may be that under another name justice herself may have been called peace. For this is true peace, not such as unjust men make among them. Or rather with a distinction not to be overlooked must that be understood which he saith, "the mountains peace, and the hills justice"? For men excelling in the Church ought to counsel for peace with watchful care; lest for the sake of their own distinctions by acting proudly they make schisms and dissever the bond of union. But let the hills so follow them by imitation and obedience, that they prefer Christ to them: lest being led astray by the empty authority of evil mountains (for they seem to excel), they tear themselves away from the Unity of Christ. ...

6. Thus also most pertinently may be understood, "let the mountains bear peace to the people," namely, that we understand the peace to consist in the reconciliation whereby we are reconciled to God: for the mountains receive this for His people. ... "Let the mountains, therefore, receive peace for the people, and the hills justice:" so that in this manner, both being at one, there may come to pass that which hath been written, "justice and peace have kissed one another." But that which other copies have, "let the mountains receive peace for the people, and let the hills:" I think must be understood of all sorts of preaching of Gospel peace, whether those that go before, or those that follow after. But in these copies this followeth, "in justice He shall judge the poor of the people." But those copies are more approved of which have that which we have expounded above, "let the mountains bear peace to the people, and the hills justice." But some have, "to Thy people;" some have not to "Thy," but only "to the people."

7. "He shall judge the poor of the people, and shall save the sons of the poor" (ver. 4). The poor and the sons of the poor seem to me to be the very same, as the same city is Sion and the daughter of Sion. But if it is to be understood with a distinction, the poor we take to be the mountains, but the sons of the poor the hills: for instance, Prophets and Apostles, the poor, but the sons of them, that is, those that profit under their authority, the sons of the poor. But that which hath been said above, "shall judge;" and afterwards, "shall save;" is as it were a sort of exposition in what manner He shall judge. For to this end He shall judge, that He may save, that is, may sever from those that are to be destroyed and condemned, those to whom He giveth "salvation ready to be revealed at the" last time. For by such men to Him is said, "Destroy not with ungodly men my soul:" and, "Judge Thou me, O

God, and sever my cause from the nation unholy." We must observe also that he saith not, He shall judge the poor people, but, "the poor of the people." For above when he had said, "to judge Thy people in justice and Thy poor in judgment," the same he called the people of God as His poor, that is, only the good and those that belong to the right hand side. But because in this world those for the right and those for the left feed together, who, like lambs and goats at the last are to be put asunder; the whole, as it is mingled together, he hath called by the name of the People. And because even here he putteth judgment in a good sense, that is, for the purpose of saving: therefore he saith, "He shall judge the poor of the people," that is, shall sever for salvation those that are poor among the people. "And He shall humble the false-accuser." No false-accuser can be more suitably recognised here than the devil. False accusation in his business. "Doth Job worship God gratis?" But the Lord Jesus doth humble him, by His grace aiding His own, in order that they may worship God gratis, that is, may take delight in the Lord. He humbled him also thus; because when in Him the devil, that is, the prince of this world, had found nothing? he slew Him by the false accusations of the Jews, whom the false-accuser made use of as his vessels, working in the sons of unbelief. ...

8. "And He shall endure to the sun," or, "shall endure with the sun" (ver. 5). For thus some of our writers have thought would be more exactly translated that which in the Greek is sumparamenei^. But if in Latin it could have been expressed in one word, it must have been expressed by compermanebit: however, because in Latin the word cannot be expressed, in order that the sense at least might be translated, it hath been expressed by, "He shall endure with the sun." For He shall co-endure to the sun is nothing else but, "He shall endure with the sun." But what great matter is it for Him to endure with the sun, through whom all things were made, and without whom nothing was made, save that this prophecy hath been sent before for the sake of those who think that the religion of the Christian name up to a particular time in this world will live, and afterwards will be no more? "He shall endure" therefore "with the sun," so long as the sun riseth and setteth, that is, so long as these times revolve, there shall not be wanting the Church of God, that is, Christ's body on earth. But that which he addeth, "and before the moon, generations of generations:" he might have expressed by, and before the sun, that is, both with the sun and before the sun: which would have been understood by both with times and before times. That then which goeth before time is eternal: and that is truly to be held eternal which by no time is changed, as, "in the beginning was the Word." But by the moon he hath chosen rather to intimate the waxings and wanings of things mortal. Lastly, when he had said, "before the moon," wishing in a manner to explain for what purpose he inserted the moon, "generations," he saith, "of generations." As though he were saying, before the moon, that is, before the generations of generations which pass away in the

departure and succession of things mortal, like the lunar wanings and waxings. And thus what is better to be understood by His enduring before the moon, than that He taketh precedence of all mortal things by immortality? Which also as followeth may not impertinently be taken, that whereas now, having humbled the false-accuser, He sitteth at the right hand of the Father, this is to endure with the sun. For the brightness of the eternal glory is understood to be the Son: as though the Sun were the Father, and the Brightness of Him His Son. But as these things may be spoken of the invisible Substance of the Creator, not as of that visible creation wherein are bodies celestial, of which bright bodies the sun hath the pre-eminence, from which this similitude hath been drawn: just as they are drawn even from things earthly, to wit, stone, lion, lamb, man having two sons, and the like: therefore having humbled the false-accuser, He endureth with the sun: because having vanquished the devil by the Resurrection, He sitteth at the right hand of the Father, where He dieth no more, and death no longer over Him shall have dominion. This too is before the moon, as though the First-born from the dead were going before the Church, which is passing on in the departure and succession of mortals. These are "the generations of generations." Or perchance it is because generations are those whereby we are begotten mortally; but generations of generations those whereby we are begotten again immortally. And such is the Church which He went before, in order that He might endure before the moon, being the First-born of the dead. To be sure, that which is in the Greek geneas genew^n, some have interpreted, not "generations," but, "of a generation of generations:" because geneas is of ambiguous case in Greek, and whether it be the genitive singular ths genea^s, that is, of the generation, or the accusative plural ta`s genea`s that is, the generations, doth not clearly appear, except that deservedly that sense hath been preferred wherein, as though explaining What he had called "the moon," he added in continuation, "generations of generations,"

9. "And He shall come down like rain into a fleece, and like drops distilling upon the earth" (ver. 6). He hath called to our minds and admonished us, that what was done by Gedeon the Judge, in Christ hath its end. For he asked a sign of the Lord, that a fleece laid on the floor should alone be rained upon, and the floor should be dry; and again, the fleece alone should be dry, and the floor should be rained upon; and so it came to pass. Which thing signified, that, being as it were on a floor in the midst of the whole round world, the dry fleece was the former people Israel. The same Christ therefore Himself came down like rain upon a fleece, when yet the floor was dry: whence also He said, "I am not sent but to the sheep which were lost of the house of Israel." There He chose out a Mother by whom to receive the form of a servant, wherein He was to appear to men: there the disciples, to whom He gave this same injunction, saying, "Into the way of the nations go ye not away, and into the cities of the Samaritans enter ye not: go ye first to the sheep which are

lost of the house of Israel." When He saith, go ye first to them, He showeth also that hereafter, when at length the floor was to be rained upon, they would go to other sheep also, which were not of the old people Israel, concerning whom He saith, "I have other sheep which are not of this fold, it behoveth Me to bring in them also, that there may be one flock and one Shepherd." Hence also the Apostle: "for I say," he saith, "that Christ was a minister of the Circumcision for the truth of God, to confirm the promises of the fathers." Thus rain came down upon the fleece, the floor being yet dry. But inasmuch as he continueth, "but that the nations should glorify God for His mercy:" that when the time came on, that should be fulfilled which by the Prophet He saith, "a people whom I have not known hath served Me, in the hearkening of the ear it hath obeyed Me:" we now see, that of the grace of Christ the nation of the Jews hath remained dry, and the whole round world through all nations is being rained upon by clouds full of Christian grace. For by another word he hath indicated the same rain, saying, "drops distilling:" no longer upon the fleece, but "upon the earth." For what else is rain but drops distilling? But that the above nation under the name of a fleece is signified, I think is either because they were to be stripped of the authority of teaching, just as a sheep is stripped of its skin; or because in a secret place He was hiding that same rain, which He willed not should be preached to uncircumcision, that is, be revealed to uncircumcised nations.

10. "There shall arise in His days justice and abundance of peace, until the moon be taken away" (ver. 7). The expression tollatur some have interpreted by "be taken away," but others by "be exalted," translating one Greek word, which is there used, antanairethh(i)^, just as each of them thought good. But they who have said, "be removed," and they who have said, "be taken away," do not so very much differ. For by the expression, "be removed," custom doth teach us that there should be rather implied, that a thing is taken away and is no more, than that it is raised to a higher place: but "be taken away" can be understood in no other way at all, than that a thing is destroyed: that is, it is no more: but by "be exalted," only that it is raised to a higher place. Which indeed when it is put in a bad sense is wont to signify pride: as is the passage, "In thy wisdom be not exalted." But in a good sense it belongeth to a more exceeding honour, as, for instance, when anything is being raised; as is, "In the nights exalt ye your hands unto holy places, and bless ye the Lord." Here then if we have understood the expression, "be removed," what will be, "until the moon be removed," but that it be so dealt with that it be no more? For perchance he willed this also to be perceived, that mortality is to be no longer, "when the last enemy shall be destroyed, death:" so that abundance of peace may be brought down so far as that nothing may withstand the felicity of the blessed from the infirmity of mortality: which will come to pass in that age, of which we have the faithful promise of God through Jesus Christ our Lord,

concerning which it is said, "There shall arise in His days justice and abundance of peace:" until, death being utterly overcome and destroyed, all mortality be consumed. But if under the term moon, not the mortality of the flesh through which the Church is now passing, but the Church Herself in general hath been signified, which is to endure for everlasting, being delivered from this mortality, thus must be taken the expression, "There shall arise in His days justice and abundance of peace, until the moon be exalted;" as though it were said, There shall arise in His days justice, to conquer the contradiction and rebellion of the flesh, and whereby there may be made a peace so increasing and abundant, until the moon be exalted, that is, until the Church be lifted up, through the glory of the Resurrection to reign with Him, who went before Her in this glory, the first-born of the dead, that He might sit at the right hand of the Father; thus with the sun s enduring before the moon, in the place whereunto hereafter was to be exalted the moon also.

11. "And He shall be Lord from sea even unto sea, and from the river even unto the ends of the round world" (ver. 8): He to wit concerning whom he had said, "There shall arise in His days justice and abundance of peace, until the moon be exalted." If the Church here is properly signified under the term moon, in continuation he showed how widely that same Church He was going to spread abroad, when He added, "and He shall be Lord from sea even unto sea." For the land is encircled by a great sea which is called the Ocean: from which there floweth in some small part in the midst of the lands, and maketh those seas known to us, which are frequented by ships. Again, in "from sea even unto sea" He hath said, that from any one end of the earth even unto any other end, He would be Lord, whose name and power in the whole world were to be preached and to prevail exceedingly. To which, that there might not be understood in any other manner, "from sea even unto sea:" He immediately added, "and from the river even unto the ends of the round world." Therefore that which He saith in "even unto the ends of the round world," the same He had said before in "from sea even unto sea." But in that which now He saith, "from the river," He hath evidently expressed that He willed Christ to publish at length His power from that place from whence also He began to choose His disciples, to wit from the river Jordan, where upon the Lord, on His baptism, when the Holy Ghost descended, there sounded a voice from Heaven, "This is My beloved Son." From this place then His doctrine and the authority of the heavenly ministry setting out, is enlarged even unto the ends of the round world, when there is preached the Gospel of the kingdom in the whole world, for a testimony unto all nations: and then shall come the end.

12. "In His presence shall fall down the Ethiopians, and His enemies shall lick the earth" (ver. 9). By the Ethiopians, as by a part the whole, He hath signified all nations, selecting that nation to mention especially by name, which is at the ends of the earth. By "in His presence shall fall down" hath been signified, shall adore Him. And because there were to be schisms in divers quarters of the world, which would be jealous of the Church Catholic spread abroad in the whole round world, and again those same schisms dividing themselves into the names of men, and by loving the men under whose authority they had been rent, opposing themselves to the glory of Christ which is throughout all lands; so when He had said, "in His presence shall fall down the Ethiopians," He added, "and His enemies shall lick the earth:" that is, shall love men, so that they shall be jealous of the glory of Christ, to whom hath been said, "Be Thou exalted above the Heavens, O God, and above all the earth Thy glory." For man earned to hear, "Earth thou art, and unto earth thou shall go." By licking this earth, that is, being delighted with the vainly talking authority of such men, by loving them, and by counting them for the most pleasing of men, they gainsay the divine sayings, whereby the Catholic Church hath been foretold, not as to be in any particular quarter of the world, as certain schisms are, but in the whole universe by bearing fruit and growing so as to attain even unto the very Ethiopians, to wit, the remotest and foulest of mankind.

13. "The kings of Tharsis and the isles shall offer gifts, the kings of the Arabians and of Saba shall lead presents" (ver. 10). This no longer requireth an expounder but a thinker; yea it doth thrust itself upon the sight not only of rejoicing believers, but also of groaning unbelievers—except perchance we must inquire why there hath been said, "shall lead presents." For there are wont to be led those things which can walk. For could it by any means have been spoken with reference to the sacrifice of victims? Far be it that such "righteousness" should arise in His days. But those gifts which have been foretold as to be led, seem to me to signify men, whom into the fellowship of the Church of Christ the authority of kings doth lead: although even persecuting kings have led gifts, knowing not what they did, in sacrificing the holy Martyrs. "And there shall adore Him all kings of the earth, all nations shall serve Him" (ver. 11).

14. But while he is explaining the reasons why so great honour is paid Him by kings, and He is served of all nations: "because He hath delivered," he saith, "the needy man from the mighty, and the poor man, to whom was no helper"(ver. 12). This needy and poor man is the people of men believing in Him. In this people are also kings adoring Him. For they do not disdain to be needy and poor, that is, humbly confessing sins, and needing the glory of God and the grace of God, in order that this King, Son of the King, may deliver them from the mighty one. For

this same mighty one is he who above was called the Slanderer: whom mighty to subdue men to himself, and to hold them bound in captivity, not his virtue did make, but men's sins. The same is himself also called strong; therefore here mighty also. But He that hath humbled the slanderer and hath entered into the house of the strong man to bind him and to spoil his vessels, He "hath delivered the needy and the poor man." For this neither the virtue of any one could accomplish, nor any just man, nor any Angel. When then there was no helper, by His coming He saved them Himself.

15. But it might occur to one; if because of sins man was held by the devil, have sins pleased Christ, who saved the needy man from the mighty? Far be it. But "He it is that shall spare the helpless and poor man" (ver. 13): that is, shall remit sins to the man, humble and not trusting in his own merits, or hoping for salvation because of his own virtue, but needing the grace of his Saviour. But when he hath added, "and the souls of the poor He shall save:" he hath recommended to our notice both the aids of grace; both that which is for the remission of sins, when he saith, "He shall spare the poor and needy man;" and that which doth consist in the imparting of righteousness, when he hath added, "and the souls of the poor He shall save." For no one is meet of himself for salvation (which salvation is perfect righteousness), unless God's grace aid: because the fulness of the law is nought but love, which doth not exist in us of ourselves, but is shed abroad in our hearts through the Holy Spirit which hath been given unto us.

16. "From usuries and iniquity He shall redeem the souls of them" (ver. 14). What are these usuries but sins, which are also called debts? But I think they have been called usuries, because more of ill is found in the punishments than hath been committed in the sins. For, for example's sake, while a man-slayer killeth only the body of a man, but can no wise hurt the soul; of himself both soul and body is destroyed in hell. Because of such despisers of present commandment and deriders of future punishment hath been said, "I coming would have exacted with usuries," from these usuries are redeemed the souls of the poor by that blood which hath been shed for the remission of sins. He shall redeem, I say, from usuries, by remitting sins which owed larger punishments: but He shall redeem from iniquity, by helping them by grace even to do righteousness. Therefore the same two things have been repeated which were said above. For in that which is above, "He shall spare the helpless and poor man," there is understood "from usuries:" but in that which there he saith, "and the souls of the poor He shall save;" there seemeth to have been implied, "from iniquity:" so that the words "He shall redeem," are understood with both. So when He shall spare the poor and helpless man, and shall save the souls of the poor: thus "from usuries and iniquity He shall redeem the

souls of them. And honourable shall be the name of Him in the presence of them."
For they give honour to His name for so great benefits, and they respond that
"meet and right it is" to render thanks to the Lord their God. Or, as some copies
have it, "and honourable is the name of them in the presence of Him:" for even if
Christians seem despicable to this world, the name of them in the presence of Him
is honourable, who to them hath given it, no longer remembering those names in
His lips, whereby before they used to be called, when they were bound fast by the
superstitions of the Gentiles, or signed with names derived from their own evil
deserts, before they were Christians; which name is honourable in the presence of
Him, even if it seemeth despicable to enemies.

17. "And He shall live, and there shall be given to Him of the gold of Arabia" (ver.
15). There would not have been said, "and He shall live "(for of whom could not
this be said, though living for ever so brief a space of time on this earth?) unless
that life were being recommended to our notice, wherein He "dieth no more, and
death over Him shall have no more dominion." And thus, "and He shall live,': that
was despised in death: for, as another Prophet saith, "there shall be taken away
from the earth the life of Him." But what is, "and there shall be given to Him of
the gold of Arabia"? For the fact that from thence even the former Salomon
received gold, in this Psalm hath been in a figure transferred unto another true
Salomon, that is the true Peace-maker. For the former did not have dominion
"from the river even unto the ends of the round world." Thus then hath been
prophesied, that even the wise men of this world in Christ would believe. But by
Arabia we understand the Gentiles; by gold wisdom which doth as much excel
among all doctrines as gold among metals. Whence hath been written, "Receive ye
prudence as silver, and wisdom as proved gold." " And they shall pray concerning
Himself alway." That which the Greek hath, peri` autou^, some have interpreted
by "concerning Himself," some "for Himself," or "for Him." But what is,
"concerning Himself," except perchance that for which we pray, saying, "Thy
kingdom come"? For Christ's coming shall make present to believers the kingdom
of God. But how to understand "for Him" is difficult; except that when prayer is
made for the Church, for Himself prayer is made, because she is His Body. For
concerning Christ and the Church hath been sent before a great Sacrament, "there
shall be two in one flesh." But now that which followeth, "all the day long," that
is, in all time, "they shall bless Him," is sufficiently evident.

18. "And there shall be a firmament on the earth, on the tops of the mountains"
(ver. 16). For, "all the promises of God in Him are Yea," that is, in Him are
confirmed: because in Him hath been fulfilled whatever hath been prophesied for
our salvation. For the tops ;of the mountains it is meet to understand as the authors

of the divine Scriptures, that is, those persons through whom they were supplied: wherein He is indeed Himself the Firmament: for unto Him all things that have been divinely written are ascribed. But this He willed should be on earth; because for the sake of those that are upon earth, they were written. Whence He came also Himself upon earth, in order that He might confirm all these things, that is, in Himself might show them to have been fulfilled. "For it was necessary," He saith, "for all things to be fulfilled which were written in the Law, and the Prophets, and Psalms, concerning Me:" that is, "in the tops of the mountain." For so there cometh in the last time the evident Mount of the Lord, prepared on the summit of the mountains: of which here he speaketh, "in the tops of the mountains." "Highly superexalted above Libanus shall be His fruit." Libanus we are wont to take as this world's dignity: for Libanus is a mountain bearing tall trees, and the name itself is interpreted whiteness. For what marvel, if above every brilliant state of this world there is superexalted the fruit of Christ, of which fruit the lovers have contemned all secular dignities? But if in a good sense we take Libanus, because of the "cedars of Libanus which He hath planted:" what other fruit must be understood, that is being exalted above this Libanus, except that whereof the Apostle speaketh when he is going to speak concerning that love of his, "yet a pre-eminent way to you I show"? For this is put forward even in the first rank of divine gifts, in the place where he saith, "but the fruit of the Spirit of love:" and with this are conjoined the remaining words as consequent. "And they shall flourish from the city like hay of the earth." Because city is used ambigously, and there is not annexed of Him, or of God, for there hath not been said, "from the city" of Him, or "from the city" of God, but only "from the city:" in a good sense it is understood, in order that from the city of God, that is, from the Church, they may flourish like grass; but grass bearing fruit, as is that of wheat: for even this is called grass in Holy Scripture; as in Genesis there is a command for the earth to bring forth every tree and every grass, and there is not added every wheat: which without doubt would not have been passed over unless under the name of grass this also were understood; and in many other passages of the Scriptures this is found. But if we must take, "and they shall flourish like the grass of the earth," in the same manner as is said, "all flesh is grass, and the glory of a man like the flower of grass :" certainly then that city must be understood which doth intimate this world's society: for it was not to no purpose that Cain was the first to build a city. Thus the fruit of Christ being exalted above Libanus, that is, above enduring trees and undecaying timbers, because He is the everlasting fruit, all the glory of a man according to the temporal exaltation of the world is compared to grass; for by believers and by men already hoping for life eternal temporal felicity is despised, in order that there may be fulfilled that which hath been written, "all flesh is grass, and all the glory of flesh as the flower of grass the grass hath dried, the flower hath fallen off, but the word of the Lord doth endure for ever." There is the fruit of Him exalted above Libanus. For always flesh hath been grass, and the glory of flesh as the flower of grass: but because it was not clearly proved what felicity ought to have been chosen and preferred, the flower of grass was esteemed for a great matter: not only it was by no means despised, but it was even chiefly sought after. As if therefore at that time He shall have begun to be thus, when there is reproved and despised whatever used to flourish in the world, thus hath been said, "superexalted above Libanus shall be the fruit of Him, and they shall flourish from the city like grass of the earth:" that is, glorified above all things shall be that which is promised for everlasting, and compared to the grass of the earth shall be whatever is counted a great matter in the world.

19. "Be," therefore, "the name of Him blessed for ever: before the sun endureth the name of Him" (ver. 17). By the sun times are signified. Therefore for everlasting endureth the name of Him. For eternity doth precede times, and is not bounded by time. "And there shall be blessed in Him all the tribes of the earth." For in Him is fulfilled that which hath been promised to Abraham. "For He saith not, In seeds, as though in many; but as though in one, And to thy Seed, which is Christ." But to Abraham is said, "In thy Seed shall be blessed all the tribes of the earth." And not the sons of the flesh but the sons of promise are counted in the Seed. "All nations shall magnify Him." As if in explanation there is repeated that which above hath been said. For because they shall be blessed in Him, they shall magnify Him; not of themselves making Him to be great, that of Himself is great, but by praising and confessing Him to be great. For thus we magnify God: thus also we say, "Hallowed be Thy name," which is indeed always holy.

20. "Blessed be the Lord God of Israel, who hath done wonderful things alone" (ver. 18). Contemplating all things above spoken of, a hymn bursteth forth; and the Lord God of Israel is blessed. For that is being fulfilled which hath been spoken to that barren woman, "and He that hath delivered Thee, the God of Israel, shall Himself be called of the whole earth." "He doeth" Himself "marvellous things alone:" for whosoever do them, He doth Himself work in them, "who doeth wonderful things alone." "And blessed be the name of His glory for everlasting, and for age of age" (ver. 19). For what else should the Latin interpreters have said, who could not have said for everlasting, and for everlasting of everlasting? For it soundeth as if one thing were meant in the expression "for everlasting," and another thing in the expression "for age:" but the Greek hath eis to`n aiw^na, kai` eis to`n aiw^na tou^ aiw^nos, which perchance more meetly might have been rendered by, "for age, and for age of age:" so that by "for age," might have been understood as long as this age endureth; but "for age of age," that which after the end of this is promised to be. "And there shall be fufilled with the glory of Him every land: so be it, so be it." Thou hast commanded, O Lord, so it is coming to

pass: so it is coming to pass, until that which began with the river, may attain fully even unto the ends of the round world.